Motivation and Work Behavior

Seventh Edition

Motivation and Work Behavior

Seventh Edition

Lyman W. Porter
Graduate School of Management
University of California–Irvine

Gregory A. Bigley
University of Washington

Richard M. Steers
Lundquist College of Business
University of Oregon

Boston   Burr Ridge, IL   Dubuque, IA   Madison, WI   New York   San Francisco   St. Louis
Bangkok   Bogotá   Caracas   Kuala Lumpur   Lisbon   London   Madrid   Mexico City
Milan   Montreal   New Delhi   Santiago   Seoul   Singapore   Sydney   Taipei   Toronto

McGraw-Hill Higher Education

*A Division of The **McGraw-Hill** Companies*

MOTIVATION AND WORK BEHAVIOR
Published by McGraw-Hill/Irwin, a business unit of The McGraw-Hill Companies, Inc.,
1221 Avenue of the Americas, New York, NY, 10020. Copyright © 2003, 1996, 1991,
1987, 1983, 1979, 1975 by The McGraw-Hill Companies, Inc. All rights reserved. No
part of this publication may be reproduced or distributed in any form or by any means, or
stored in a database or retrieval system, without the prior written consent of The
McGraw-Hill Companies, Inc., including, but not limited to, in any network or other
electronic storage or transmission, or broadcast for distance learning.
Some ancillaries, including electronic and print components, may not be available to
customers outside the United States.

This book is printed on acid-free paper.

domestic   1 2 3 4 5 6 7 8 9 0 DOC/DOC 0 9 8 7 6 5 4 3 2
international 1 2 3 4 5 6 7 8 9 0 DOC/DOC 0 9 8 7 6 5 4 3 2

ISBN   0-07-248162-5

Publisher: *John E. Biernat*
Executive editor: *John Weimeister*
Editorial coordinator: *Trina Hauger*
Senior marketing manager: *Ellen Cleary*
Producer, Media technology: *Mark Molsky*
Project manager: *Natalie J. Ruffatto*
Production supervisor: *Gina Hangos*
Designer: *Matthew Baldwin*
Supplement producer: *Betty Hadala*
Senior digital content specialist: *Brian Nacik*
Typeface: *10.5/12 Times Roman*
Compositor: *GAC Indianapolis*
Printer: *R. R. Donnelley*

Library of Congress Cataloging-in-Publication Data

Motivation and work behavior / [compiled by] Lyman W. Porter, Gregory A. Bigley,
Richard M. Steers.-- 7th ed.
        p. cm. -- (McGraw-Hill series in management)
    Rev. ed. of: Motivation and leadership at work / compiled by Richard M. Steers, Lyman
W. Porter, Gregory A. Bigley. 6th ed. c1996.
    Includes bibliographical references and index.
    ISBN 0-07-248162-5 (alk. paper) -- ISBN 0-07-113102-7 (international : alk. paper)
    1. Employee motivation. 2. Leadership. 3. Psychology, Industrial. I. Porter, Lyman W.
II. Bigley, Gregory A. III. Steers, Richard M. IV. Motivation and leadership at work. V.
Series.
HF5549.5.M63 M667 2003
658.3'14--dc21

                                                                    2002023966

INTERNATIONAL EDITION ISBN 0-07-113102-7
Copyright © 2003. Exclusive rights by The McGraw-Hill Companies, Inc. for
manufacture and export. This book cannot be re-exported from the country to which it is
sold by McGraw-Hill.
The International Edition is not available in North America.

www.mhhe.com

About the Authors

Lyman W. Porter is Professor Emeritus of Management in the Graduate School of Management at the University of California, Irvine, where he has been a member of the faculty since 1967. He has served as the president of the Academy of Management and the Society of Industrial-Organizational Psychology and has received Distinguished Scientific Contributions Awards from both organizations. He also received the Distinguished Educator Award from the Academy of Management in 1994. His major fields of interest are management and organizational behavior. He is the author (with Lawrence McKibbin) of *Management Education and Development* (McGraw-Hill, 1988), a major report on the state of business school education and postdegree management development.

Gregory A. Bigley is a Neal and Jan Dempsey Fellow and Assistant Professor of Management at the University of Washington. Prior to joining the University of Washington faculty, he was an Assistant Professor of Management at the University of Cincinnati. His research focuses on the topics of motivation, trust, justice, and the social-psychological foundations of high-reliability/performance organizations. He holds an MBA and a PhD from the University of California–Irvine.

Richard M. Steers is the Kazumitsu Shiomi Professor of Management in the Lundquist College of Business, University of Oregon. His research interests focus on work motivation and cross-cultural influences on management. He is a fellow and past president of the Academy of Management, as well as a fellow of both the American Psychological Society and the Society of Industrial and Organizational Psychology. He is the author of 20 books in the field of management and has served on the editorial boards of *Administrative Science Quarterly, Academy of Management Journal,* and *Academy of Management Review.*

Table of Contents

PART THREE
APPLICATIONS OF MOTIVATIONAL APPROACHES

Preface

In this seventh edition, we have decided to revert to the tradition we established in the first five editions: namely, a focus solely on the topic of motivation in the work setting. In the previous (sixth) edition we had jointly concentrated on both motivation and leadership. However, the recent scholarly literature in these two fields has grown so extensively that we made the decision to return to providing exclusive attention to motivation in the organizational context. We still believe that the two topics of motivation and leadership are closely interrelated and often deserve to be considered together; however, as in real-life work situations, we had to make a choice. That choice was to go back to the roots of this book as exemplified in our title: motivation and work behavior.

As we have done in previous editions, our approach in putting together this edition's readings has been to integrate text material with selections authored by leading academic scholars. As before, the major emphasis in the text and readings is to provide a blend of theoretical formulations, major research findings, and real-world applications relating to our topic of focus. The objective is to help show students how the insights gained from scientific thinking and investigation can inform those who are, or soon will be, engaging in managerial practice. Therefore, the present book, as with earlier editions, is intended for students of general management, organizational behavior, and industrial-organizational psychology who have had some previous exposure to the basic concepts in one or more of these fields and who want to gain a more in-depth level of knowledge and understanding about work motivation.

We have organized the book into three basic sections: Part I opens with an overview of the early work in the field of motivation, together with a reading that summarizes some of the most important recent scholarly advances in the area. The remainder of Part I presents six major contemporary conceptual approaches to the topic: intrinsic motivation, equity theory, organizational justice, reinforcement theory, goal setting, and social cognitive theory/self-efficacy. Part II covers a number of major issues dealing with the book's overall topic, including the roles of: cognitions and attitudes, goals and intentions, affect and mood, social influences, cross-cultural influences, and individual differences. Part III examines applications of motivational approaches in three areas: rewards, punishment, and creativity. Also included at the end of this seventh edition, and a new feature that has been added, is a section that presents a set of brief cases that provide students with the opportunity to apply what they have learned about the topic of the book to dealing with "real-life" on-the-job motivational problems and situations.

The authors want to thank Mary Alice Pike for her helpful administrative assistance on this edition, and John Weimeister, Trina Hauger, and Natalie Ruffatto of McGraw-Hill for their expert guidance and coordination in the editing and production of the book. As in the past, we thank our respective schools—University of California, Irvine; University of Washington; and University of Oregon—for providing stimulating motivational environments in which to work.

Lyman W. Porter
Gregory A. Bigley
Richard M. Steers

Chapter One

Motivation in Organizations

The term "motivation" was originally derived from the Latin word *movere,* which means "to move." However, this one word is obviously an inadequate definition for our purposes here. What is needed is a description that sufficiently covers the various components and processes associated with how human behavior is activated. A brief selection of representative definitions indicates how the term has been used:

> . . . the contemporary (immediate) influence on the direction, vigor, and persistence of action. (Atkinson, 1964)

> . . . how behavior gets started, is energized, is sustained, is directed, is stopped, and what kind of subjective reaction is present in the organism while all this is going on. (Jones, 1955)

> . . . a process governing choice made by persons or lower organisms among alternative forms of voluntary activity. (Vroom, 1964)

> . . . motivation has to do with a set of independent/dependent variable relationships that explain the direction, amplitude, and persistence of an individual's behavior, holding constant the effects of aptitude, skill, and understanding of the task, and the constraints operating in the environment. (Campbell & Pritchard, 1976)

These definitions appear generally to have three common denominators that may be said to characterize the phenomenon of motivation. That is, when we discuss motivation, we are primarily concerned with (1) what energizes human behavior, (2) what directs or channels such behavior, and (3) how this behavior is maintained or sustained. Each of these three components represents an important factor in our understanding of human behavior at work. First, this conceptualization points to energetic forces within individuals that drive them to behave in certain ways and to environmental forces that often trigger these drives. Second, there is the notion of goal orientation on the part of individuals; their behavior is directed *toward* something. Third, this way of viewing motivation contains a *systems orientation;* that is, it considers those forces in individuals and in their surrounding environments that feed back to the individuals either to reinforce the intensity of their drive and the direction of their energy or to dissuade them from their course of action and redirect their efforts. These three components of motivation appear again and again in the theories and research that follow.

The concept of motivation has received considerable attention over the course of this century. Furthermore, the topic of motivation has become increasingly prominent in the efforts of organizational researchers and practicing managers to understand and influence organizational behavior. Despite the intense interest in the area, however, no overall, commonly accepted framework or approach to work motivation currently exists. Nevertheless, a survey of the organization studies literature indicates that the extant theories may be grouped into two general classes: content theories and process theories.

The *content theories* of work motivation assume that factors exist within the individual that energize, direct, and sustain behavior. These approaches to motivation are concerned with the identification of important internal elements and the explanation of how these elements may be prioritized within the individual. In contrast to content theories of motivation, *process theories* of motivation attempt to describe *how* behavior is energized, directed, and sustained. These theories focus on certain psychological processes underlying action. In particular, process theories place heavy emphasis on describing the functioning of the individual's decision system as it relates to behavior.

The remainder of this opening chapter considers an array of motivational theories. We begin with a description of several early psychological approaches to motivation that involved the concepts of instinct, drive, and reinforcement, and which were the precursors of later theories. The next section describes four content models that have been applied to, or have been developed for, work settings: Maslow's hierarchy of needs, Alderfer's existence-relatedness-growth (ERG), Herzberg's motivator-hygiene, and McClelland's learned needs. Following this discussion of content theories, several basic cognitive-type frameworks that are relevant to process theories of work motivation will be briefly summarized. Then two major process conceptualizations are reviewed: Vroom's expectancy theory and the Porter-Lawler model. (Two other important process theories of work motivation—Adams's equity theory and Locke's goal setting theory—will be discussed in two of Chapter 2's readings.) This introductory chapter concludes with an overview of how practicing managers have approached motivational problems at work from the earliest days of this century up to recent times. A reading on current issues in the area of work motivation completes the chapter.

EARLY PSYCHOLOGICAL APPROACHES

Most psychological theories of motivation, both early and contemporary, have their roots—at least to some extent—in the principle of hedonism. This principle, briefly defined, states that individuals tend to seek pleasure and avoid pain. Hedonism assumes a certain degree of conscious behavior on the part of individuals whereby they make intentional decisions or choices concerning future action. In theory, people rationally consider the behavioral alternatives available to them and act to maximize positive results and to minimize negative results. The concept of hedonism dates back to the early Greek philosophers; it later reemerged as a popular explanation of behavior in the 18th and 19th centuries, as seen in the works of philosophers such as Locke, Bentham, Mill, and Helvetius. Bentham even went so far as to coin the term "hedonic calculus" in 1789 to describe the process by which individuals calculate the pros and cons of various acts of behavior.

Toward the end of the 19th century, motivation theory began to move from the realm of philosophy toward the more empirically based science of psychology. As consideration of this important topic grew, it became apparent to those who attempted to use the philosophically based concept of hedonism that several serious problems existed. Vroom explained this dilemma as follows:

> There was in the doctrine no clear-cut specification of the type of events which were pleasurable or painful, or even how these events could be determined for a particular individual; nor did it make clear how persons acquired their conceptions of ways of attaining pleasure and pain, or how the source of pleasure and pain might be modified by experience. In short the hedonistic assumption has no empirical content and was untestable. Any form of behavior could be explained, after the fact, by postulating particular sources of pleasure or pain, but no form of behavior could be predicted in advance. (1964, p. 10)

In an effort to fill this void, several theories of motivation began to evolve that attempted to formulate empirically verifiable relationships among sets of variables which could be used to predict behavior. The earliest such theory centered on the concept of instinct.

Instinct Theories

While not injecting the notion of hedonism, psychologists like James, Freud, and McDougall argued that a more comprehensive explanation of behavior was necessary than simply assuming that a rational person pursues his or her own best interest. In short, they posited two additional variables that were crucial to our understanding of behavior: instinct and unconscious motivation.

Instead of seeing behavior as highly rational, these theorists saw much of it as resulting from instinct. McDougall, writing in 1908, defined an instinct as "an inherited or innate psychophysical disposition which determines its possessor to perceive, or pay attention to, objects of a certain class, to experience an emotional excitement of a particular quality upon perceiving such an object, and to act in regard to it in a particular manner, or at least, to experience an impulse to such an action." However, while McDougall saw instinct as purposive and goal-directed, other instinct theorists, like James, defined the concept more in terms of blind and mechanical action. James (1890) included in his list of instincts the following: locomotion, curiosity, sociability, love, fear, jealousy, and sympathy. James and McDougall believed that every person has such instincts in greater or lesser degree and that these instincts are the prime determinants of behavior. In other words, individuals were seen as possessing automatic predispositions to behave in certain ways, depending on internal and external cues.

The second major concept associated with instinct theories is that of unconscious motivation. While the notion is implicit in the writings of James, it was Freud (1915) who most ardently advocated the existence of such a phenomenon. On the basis of his clinical observations, Freud argued that the most potent behavioral tendencies are not necessarily those that individuals *consciously* determine would be in their best interests. Individuals are not always aware of all their desires and needs. Rather, such unconscious phenomena as dreams, slips of the tongue ("Freudian slips"), and neurotic symptoms were seen by Freud as manifestations of the hedonistic principle on an *unconscious* level. Thus, a major factor in human motivation was seen here as resulting from forces unknown even to the individual.

The instinct theory of motivation was fairly widely accepted during the first quarter of the 20th century. Then, beginning in the early 1920s, it came under increasing attack on several grounds (Hilgard & Atkinson, 1967; Morgan & King, 1966). First, there was the disturbing fact that the list of instincts continued to grow, reaching nearly six thousand in number. The sheer length of such a list seriously jeopardized any attempt at parsimony in the explanation of motivation. Second, the contention that individuals varied greatly in the strengths or intensities of their motivational dispositions was becoming increasingly accepted among psychologists, adding a further complication to the ability of instinct theory to explain behavior fully. Third, some researchers found that at times there may be little relation between the strength of certain motives and subsequent behavior. Fourth, some psychologists came to question whether the unconscious motives as described by Freud were really instinctive or whether they were learned behavior. In fact, this fourth criticism formed the basis of the second "school" of motivation theorists, who later became known as "drive" theorists.

Drive and Reinforcement Theories

Researchers who have been associated with drive theory typically base their work on the influence that learning has on subsequent behavior. Thus, such theories have a historical component, which led Allport (1954) to refer to them as "hedonism of the past"; that is, drive theories generally assumed that decisions concerning present behavior are based in large part on the consequences, or rewards, of past behavior. Where past action led to positive consequences, individuals would tend to repeat such actions; where past actions led to negative consequences or punishment, individuals would tend to avoid repeating them. This position was first elaborated by Thorndike in his "law of effect." Basing his "law" on experimental observations of animal behavior, Thorndike posited:

> Of several responses made to the same situation, those which are accompanied or closely followed by satisfaction to the animal will, other things being equal, be more firmly connected with the situation, so that when it recurs, they will be more likely to occur; those which are accompanied or closely followed by discomfort to the animal will, other things being equal, have their connection with that situation weakened, so that when it recurs, they will be less likely to occur. The greater the satisfaction or discomfort, the greater is the strengthening or weakening of the bond. (1911, p. 244)

While this law of effect did not explain why some actions were pleasurable or satisfying and others were not, it did go a long way toward setting forth an empirically verifiable theory of motivation. Past learning and previous "stimulus-response" connections were viewed as the major causal variables of behavior.

The term "drive" was first introduced by Woodworth (1918) to describe the reservoir of energy that impels an organism to behave in certain ways. While Woodworth intended the term to mean a general supply of energy within an organism, others soon modified this definition to refer to a host of specific energizers (such as hunger, thirst, sex) toward or away from certain goals. With the introduction of the concept of drive, it now became possible for psychologists to predict in advance—at least in theory—not only what goals an individual would strive toward but also the strength of the motivation toward such goals. Thus, it became feasible for researchers to attempt to test the theory in a fairly rigorous fashion, a task that was virtually impossible for the earlier theories of hedonism and instinct.

A major theoretical advance in drive theory came from the work of Cannon in the early 1930s. Cannon (1939) introduced the concept of "homeostasis" to describe a state of disequilibrium within an organism that existed whenever internal conditions deviated from their normal state. When such disequilibrium occurred (as when an organism felt hungry), the organism was motivated by internal drives to reduce the disequilibrium and to return to its normal state. Inherent in Cannon's notion was the idea that organisms exist in a dynamic environment and that the determining motives for behavior constantly change, depending upon where the disequilibrium exists within the system. Thus, certain drives, or motives, may move to the forefront and then, once satisfied, retreat while other drives become paramount. This concept can be seen to a large extent in the later work of Maslow (discussed in a later section).

The first comprehensive—and experimentally specific—elaboration of drive theory was put forth by Hull. In his major work, *Principles of Behavior,* published in 1943, Hull set down a specific equation to explain an organism's "impetus to respond": Effort = Drive × Habit. "Drive" was defined by Hull as an energizing influence that determined the intensity of behavior and that theoretically increased along with the level of deprivation. "Habit" was seen as the strength of relationship between past stimulus and response (S-R). Hull hypothesized that habit strength depended not only upon the closeness of the S-R event to reinforcement but also upon the magnitude and number of such reinforcements. Thus, Hull's concept of habit draws very heavily upon Thorndike's "law of effect." Hull argued that the resulting effort, or motivational force, was a multiplicative function of these two central variables.

If we apply Hull's theory to an organizational setting, we can use the following example to clarify how drive theory would be used to predict behavior. A person who has been out of work for some time (high deprivation level) would generally have a strong need or desire to seek some means to support himself or herself (goal). If, on the basis of *previous* experience, this person draws a close association between the securing of income and the act of taking a job, we would expect him or her to search ardently for employment. Thus, the motivation to seek employment would be seen, according to this theory, as a multiplicative function of the intensity of the need for money (drive) and the strength of the feeling that work has been associated with the receipt of money in the past (habit). Later, in response to empirical evidence that was inconsistent with the theory, Hull (1952) somewhat modified his position. Instead of positing that behavior was wholly a function of antecedent conditions (such as past experience), he added an incentive variable to his equation. His later formulation thus read: Effort = Drive × Habit × Incentive. This incentive factor, added largely in response to the attack by the cognitive theorists (discussed in a later section), was defined in terms of anticipatory reactions to future goals. It was thus hypothesized that one factor in the motivation equation was the size of, or attraction to, future potential rewards, As the size of the reward varied, so too would the motivation to seek such a reward. This major revision by Hull (as amplified by Spence, 1956) brought drive theory into fairly close agreement with the early cognitive theories. However, while cognitive theories have generally been applied to humans, including humans at work, drive theory research has continued, by and large, to study animal behavior in the laboratory.

Just as drive theory draws upon Thorndike's "law of effect," so do modern reinforcement approaches (e.g., Skinner, 1953). The difference is that the former theory emphasizes an internal state (i.e., drive) as a necessary variable to take into account, while reinforcement theory does not. Rather, the reinforcement model places total emphasis on the *consequences* of behavior. Behavior initiated by the individual (for whatever reason) that produces an effect or consequence is called *operant* behavior (i.e., the individual has "operated" on the environment), and the theory deals with the contingent relationships between this operant behavior and the pattern of consequences. It ignores the inner state of the individual and concentrates solely on what happens to a person when he or she takes some action. Thus, strictly speaking, reinforcement theory is not a theory of motivation because it does not concern itself with what energizes or initiates behavior. Nevertheless, since a reinforcement approach provides a powerful means of analysis of what controls behavior (its direction and maintenance), it is typically considered in discussions of motivation.

CONTENT THEORIES OF MOTIVATION

In this section, four of the most prominent content theories of work motivation will be discussed. The first two theories—Maslow's hierarchy of needs and Alderfer's existence-relatedness-growth (ERG)—view needs as sequentially activated. Although not developed explicitly for organizational settings, Maslow's needs hierarchy was the first major theory of motivation to be applied to individuals at work. Alderfer's ERG theory represents an important extension and refinement of the needs hierarchy; ERG theory attempted to deal with some of the deficiencies of Maslow's model. The third theory discussed in this section is Herzberg's motivator-hygiene model. His two-factor theory, as it is often called, was among the very first models of motivation to be developed specifically for work applications. McClelland's learned needs theory is the last framework discussed in the section. His theory represents somewhat of a departure from the other approaches, in that he views needs as socially acquired attributes of the individual, rather than as innate psychological characteristics.

Maslow's Hierarchy of Needs

Maslow's (1954, 1968) needs hierarchy is perhaps the most widely known theory relating individual needs to motivation. The theory attempts to show how the healthy personality grows and develops over time and how that personality comes to manifest itself in motivated behavior.

Maslow (1954) contends that people are wanting beings whose needs guide behavior. According to Maslow, a need influences a person's activities until it has been satisfied. Further, his theory holds that an individual's needs are arranged in a hierarchical fashion, from the very fundamental (e.g., food, shelter) to the most advanced (e.g., self-fulfillment). Individuals, it is hypothesized, attend to needs in a sequential fashion, moving from the bottom of the hierarchy toward the top, as lower-level needs are satisfied. According to Maslow, lower-level needs must be satisfied, in general, before higher-level needs are activated sufficiently to drive behavior. Further, only unsatisfied needs can influence behavior; those that are satisfied do not motivate.

Maslow (1968) distinguishes between two basic categories of needs: deficiency needs and growth needs. He posits that if the individual is to be healthy and secure, deficiency needs must be satisfied. "Needs for safety, the feeling of belonging, love and respect (from others) are all clearly deficits" (Maslow, 1954, p. 10). The individual will fail to develop a healthy personality to the extent that these needs are not met. In contrast, growth needs are those that relate to the development and achievements of one's potential. For Maslow the idea of growth needs is more vague than the concept of deficiency needs: "Growth, individuation, autonomy, self-actualization, self-development, productiveness, self-realization are all crudely synonymous, designating a vaguely perceived area rather than a sharply defined concept" (Maslow, 1968, p. 24).

According to Maslow, individuals are motivated by five general needs that may be classified into either the deficiency or the growth categories.

Deficiency Needs

1 Physiological: The most basic needs in Maslow's hierarchy center around needs related to survival and include the needs for oxygen, food, water, sleep, and so on. In the workplace, such needs are reflected in the individual's concern for basic working conditions (e.g., moderate temperature, clean air).

2 Safety and security: The second level of needs is associated with the safety and security of one's physical and emotional environment. These needs include a desire for stability, order, security, freedom from threats of emotional harm, and protection against accidents. At work, such needs may be represented by a concern for safe working conditions and job security.

3 Belongingness: The third level consists of those needs related to one's desire for acceptance by others, friendship, and love. In organizations, interacting frequently with fellow workers or experiencing employee-centered leadership may help to satisfy these needs.

Growth Needs

4 Esteem and ego: These are the needs for self-respect, self-esteem, and respect and esteem for others. In the workplace, these needs may be reflected in a concern for jobs with higher status and a desire for recognition for the successful accomplishment of a particular task.

5 Self-actualization: The highest need category consists of the need for self-fulfillment. People with dominant self-actualization needs are concerned with developing to their full and unique potential as individuals. In organizations, these needs may be reflected in the desire for work assignments that challenge one's skills and abilities and that allow for creative or innovative approaches.

According to Maslow, individuals move up the needs hierarchy through a dynamic cycle of deprivation, domination, gratification, and activation (Steers and Black, 1994). That is, when the individual experiences deprivation (i.e., an unfulfilled need) at a particular level in the hierarchy, the unsatisfied need will direct the individual's thoughts and actions. For example, a person who is concerned about physical safety will ignore or disregard higher-order needs and devote all of his or her energies to securing a safer environment. However, once this need is met, or gratified, it will cease to dominate the person's consciousness. Instead, needs at the next level in the hierarchy will be activated (in this case, belongingness needs). This cycle is repeated at each level in the hierarchy until the individual reaches the level of self actualization.

Evaluation of Maslow's Hierarchy of Needs Theory

Maslow's work has generated a great deal of research attempting to evaluate the utility of the theory in organizational settings. For example, Porter (1961) found that managers at higher levels of an organization were generally more able than lower-level managers to satisfy their growth needs. These findings follow from the idea that upper-level managers generally have more challenging and autonomous jobs than their lower-level counterparts. As a result, managers in the upper echelons of an organization are in a much better position to pursue their growth needs.

However, although studies have been able to differentiate between jobs that allow for growth need satisfaction and those that hinder it, research has not been able to establish the validity of the need hierarchy itself. In fact, in an extensive review of the research findings associated with Maslow's hierarchy, Wahba and Bridwell (1976) concluded that Maslow's model presents the student of work motivation with a paradox: The theory is widely accepted, but there is little research evidence to support it.

The review evaluated three aspects of Maslow's model. First, no clear evidence was found indicating that human needs can be classified into five distinct categories, or that these categories are structured in a hierarchical way. However, there did seem to be some evidence to support a general classification scheme distinguishing deficiency from growth needs. Second, the review examined the proposition that an unsatisfied need leads an individual to focus exclusively on that need. Some studies supported this proposition while other studies did not. Finally, the review explored the idea that satisfaction of needs at one level activates needs at the next higher level. This proposition was not supported by the research evidence.

Although research findings have failed to support the needs hierarchy model and have questioned its conceptual validity, Maslow's theory continues to be useful in generating ideas about the fundamental nature of human motives. For managers, in particular, the needs hierarchy idea has a commonsense appeal; it is relatively easy to comprehend and has clear implications for management. For example, assuming that many employees have met their deficiency needs, managers can focus on creating a work situation that is aimed at satisfying higher-level growth needs.

In an attempt to overcome some of the problems with Maslow's approach, Alderfer presented his existence-relatedness-growth (ERG) model of motivation. This model will be reviewed next.

Alderfer's Existence-Relatedness-Growth (ERG) Theory

The most popular extension and refinement of Maslow's theory of needs is the one proposed by Alderfer (1972) (Cherrington, 1989). While Maslow's model was not developed specifically for work organizations, Alderfer's theory attempted to establish a conceptualization of human needs that is relevant to organizational settings. In extending Maslow's theory, Alderfer argued that the need categories could be collapsed into three more general classes:

1 Existence. These are needs related to human existence and are comparable to Maslow's physiological needs and certain of his safety needs.

2 Relatedness. These are needs that involve interpersonal relationships in the workplace. Relatedness needs are similar to Maslow's belongingness needs and certain of his safety and esteem/ego needs.

3 Growth. These are needs associated with the development of the human potential. Included in this category are needs corresponding to Maslow's self-esteem and self-actualization needs.

Alderfer's model agrees with Maslow's in positing that individuals tend to move from existence, through relatedness, to growth needs, as needs in each category are satisfied.

However, ERG theory differs from the needs hierarchy model in two important respects. First, Alderfer contends that, in addition to the satisfaction-progression process described by Maslow, a frustration-regression sequence also exists. For example, the ERG model predicts that if an individual is continually frustrated in his or her attempts to satisfy growth needs, then relatedness needs will be reactivated and become the primary drivers of behavior. Second, and especially important, in contrast to the needs hierarchy theory, the ERG model does not hold that one level of needs must be satisfied before needs in the next level can emerge to motivate behavior. Instead, the ERG model proposes that more than one need may be operative in a given individual at any point in time.

Evaluation of Alderfer's ERG Theory

At present, only a few studies have attempted to test ERG theory. Therefore, empirical verification has not been established. However, the studies that have been reported appear to show stronger support for Alderfer's ERG model than for Maslow's hierarchy of needs (e.g., Schneider & Alderfer, 1973). The ERG model appears to be less rigid than the needs hierarchy theory, allowing for more flexibility in describing human behavior.

As with Maslow's theory, ERG theory appears to offer a useful way of thinking about employee motivation. Although there is disagreement between Maslow and Alderfer regarding the exact number of need categories, both theories acknowledge that opportunities for the satisfaction of needs constitute an important element in the motivation of individuals.

Herzberg's Motivator-Hygiene Theory

Herzberg's motivator-hygiene theory is, perhaps, the most controversial theory of work motivation. The original research used in developing the theory was conducted with several hundred accountants and engineers. Herzberg and his colleagues used the critical incident method of obtaining data for their research. That is, the subjects in the study were asked two questions: (1) "Can you describe, in detail, when you felt exceptionally good about your job?" and (2) "Can you describe, in detail, when you felt exceptionally bad about your job?" Herzberg's motivator-hygiene theory, as well as the supporting data, was first published in 1959 (Herzberg, Mausner, & Snyderman) and was subsequently amplified and developed in a later book (Herzberg, 1966).

On the basis of his study, Herzberg reported that employees tended to describe satisfying experiences in terms of factors that were intrinsic to the content of the job itself. These factors were called "motivators" and included such variables as achievement, recognition, the work itself, responsibility, advancement, and growth. Conversely, dissatisfying experiences, called "hygiene" factors, resulted largely from extrinsic, non-job-related factors, such as company policies, salary, coworker relations, and supervisory style. Herzberg argued, on the basis of these results, that eliminating the causes of dissatisfaction (through hygiene factors) would not result in a state of satisfaction. Instead, it would result in a neutral state. Satisfaction (and motivation) would occur only as a result of the use of motivators.

Evaluation of Herzberg's Motivator-Hygiene Theory

Since its inception, Herzberg's theory has been subject to several important criticisms. For example, it has been noted (King, 1970) that the model itself has five different theoretical interpretations and that the available research evidence is not entirely consistent with any of these interpretations. Second, a number of scholars believe the model does not give sufficient attention to individual differences (although Herzberg himself would dispute this) and assumes that job enrichment benefits all employees. Research evidence suggests that individual differences are, in fact, an important moderator of the effects of job enrichment. Finally, research has generally failed to support the existence of two independent factors (motivators and hygiene factors). Even so, the model has enhanced our understanding of motivation at work.

One of the most significant contributions of Herzberg's work was the strong impact it had on stimulating thought, research, and experimentation in the area of motivation at work. This contribution should not be overlooked. Before 1959, little research had been carried out on *work* motivation (with the notable exception of Viteles, 1953, and Maier, 1955), and the research that did exist was largely fragmentary. Maslow's work on needs hierarchy theory and Murray's, McClelland's, and Atkinson's work on achievement motivation theory was concerned largely with laboratory-based findings or clinical observations, and none had seriously addressed the problems of the workplace at that time. Herzberg filled this void by specifically calling attention to the need for increased understanding of the role of motivation in work organizations.

Moreover, he did so in a systematic manner and in language that was easily understood by managers. He advanced a theory that was simple to grasp, was based on some empirical data, and—equally important—offered managers specific recommendations for action to improve employee motivational levels. In doing so, he forced organizations to examine closely a number of possible misconceptions concerning motivation. For example, Herzberg argued that money should not necessarily be viewed as the most potent force on the job. Moreover, he stated that other "context" factors in addition to money which surround an employee's job (such as fringe benefits and supervisory style) should not be expected to affect motivation markedly either. He advanced a strong case that managers must instead give considerable attention to a series of "content" factors (such as opportunities for achievement, recognition, and advancement) that have an important bearing on behavior.

In addition, Herzberg probably deserves a good deal of credit for acting as a stimulus to other researchers who have advocated alternative theories of *work* motivation. A multitude of research articles have been generated as a result of the so-called "Herzberg controversy." Some of these articles (e.g., Bockman, 1971; Whitset & Winslow, 1967) strongly support Herzberg's position, while others (e.g., House & Wigdor, 1967; Vroom, 1964) seriously question the research methodology underlying the theory. Such debate is healthy for any science. The student of motivation should consider Herzberg's theory—or any other such theory—to be one attempt at modeling work behavior. In other words, it appears that a fruitful approach to this "controversial" theory would be to learn from it that which can help us develop better models, rather than to accept or reject the model totally.

It is interesting that, despite the voluminous criticism leveled against the model, Herzberg's motivation-hygiene theory is still popular among managers. Furthermore, Herzberg's theory appears to have an international appeal. Gibson, Ivancevich, and Donnelly (1994) report that in their discussions of motivation applications with numerous managers in Europe, the Pacific Rim, and Latin America, "the Herzberg explanation is referred to more often than any other theory" (p. 156).

McClelland's Learned Needs Theory

Another well-known content theory is the learned needs theory developed by McClelland (1961, 1962, 1965a, 1965b, 1971). He contends that individuals acquire certain needs from the culture of a society by learning from the events that they experience, particularly in early life. Four of the needs that people may learn are the need for achievement (n Ach), the need for power (n Pow), the need for affiliation (n Aff), and the need for autonomy (n Aut). Once learned, these needs may be regarded as personal predispositions that affect the way people perceive work (and other) situations and that influence their pursuit of certain goals.

Need for Achievement (n Ach)

McClelland defined n Ach as "behavior toward competition with a standard of excellence" (McClelland, Atkinson, Clark, & Lowell, 1953). He and his associates conducted their most thorough series of studies on this particular learned need, and identified four characteristics of individuals with a high need for achievement: (1) a strong desire to assume personal responsibility for finding solutions to problems or performing a task, (2) a tendency to set moderately difficult achievement goals and to take calculated risks, (3) a strong desire for concrete performance feedback on tasks, and (4) a single-minded preoccupation with task accomplishment.

The need for achievement is perhaps the most prominent learned need from the standpoint of studying organizational behavior. The challenging nature of a difficult task cues that motive, which, in turn, activates achievement-oriented behavior. Many managerial and entrepreneurial positions are assumed to require such a need in individuals in order for them to be successful. However, when people with a high n Ach are given routine or unchallenging jobs, the achievement motive will probably not be activated. Therefore, there would be little reason to expect individuals with a high n Ach to perform in a superior fashion in such situations (McClelland, 1961).

Need for Power (n Pow)

The n Pow is defined as the need to control the environment, to influence the behavior of others, and to be responsible for them. McClelland contends that individuals with a high n Pow may be characterized by: (1) a desire to direct and control someone else, and (2) a concern for maintaining leader-follower relations. Research evidence suggests that individuals with high n Pow tend to be superior performers, to be in supervisor positions, to have above-average attendance records, and to be rated by others as having good leadership abilities (Steers & Braunstein, 1976).

Need for Affiliation (n Aff)

The need for affiliation is defined as an "attraction to another organism in order to feel reassured from the other that the self is acceptable" (Birch & Veroff, 1966). Individuals with a high n Aff desire to establish and maintain friendly and warm relationships with others. McClelland identified three characteristics of individuals with a high need for affiliation: (1) a strong desire for approval and reassurance from others, (2) a tendency to conform to the wishes and norms of others when pressured by people whose friendship they value, and (3) a sincere interest in the feelings of others.

People who have a high n Aff prefer to work with others rather than to work alone. Therefore, high n Aff individuals tend to take jobs characterized by a high amount of interpersonal contact, such as sales, teaching, public relations, and counseling. There is some evidence to suggest that employees with high n Aff have better attendance records than those with low n Aff (Birch & Veroff, 1966). In addition, some research findings indicate that employees with a high n Aff perform somewhat better in situations where personal support and approval are tied to performance (Chung, 1977; French, 1958).

The organizational implications of the n Aff appear to be fairly clear. McClelland's theory would suggest that n Aff employees will be productive to the extent that supervisors can create a cooperative, supportive work environment where positive feedback is tied to task performance. The explanation for this is that by working hard in such an environment, an individuals with a high n Aff can satisfy his or her affiliation needs.

Need for Autonomy (n Aut)

Need for autonomy is defined as a desire for independence. Individuals with a high n Aut want to work alone, prefer to control their own workplace, and do not want to be hampered by excessive rules or procedures (Birch & Veroff, 1966). Research has found that individuals with a high n Aut tend not to be committed to the goals and objectives of their organizations, not to perform well unless they are allowed to participate in the determination of their tasks, and not to respond to external pressures for conformity to group norms.

Evaluation of McClelland's Learned Needs Theory

Most research evidence offered in support of McClelland's learned needs theory has been provided by McClelland or his associates, with the need for achievement receiving most of the attention from other organizational behavior theorists and researchers. Over the years, there have been a number of serious criticisms of McClelland's work. First, it is argued that the primary research instrument (a projective psychological test called the TAT) used in the studies by McClelland and his colleagues has questionable predictive validity. Second, McClelland's claim that needs, especially n Ach, can be learned by adults conflicts with a large body of literature stating that motives are normally acquired in childhood and that they are difficult to alter in adulthood. McClelland (1962) recognizes this problem but points to evidence from politics and religion that suggests otherwise. Third, McClelland's notion of acquired needs is questioned by some scholars on the grounds that needs may not be acquired *permanently.*

Despite these and other criticisms of McClelland's research and theory, the concept of learned or acquired needs is an important one and has clear applicability to organizational and work settings. It emphasizes, to use psychology terminology, that *nurture*—that is, what kinds of life circumstances people encounter and experience—is as important as *nature*—that is, what people are "born with"—in understanding what motivates human behavior.

PROCESS THEORIES OF MOTIVATION

Content theories of motivation conceptualize behavior as the product of innate psychological characteristics (e.g., needs). In contrast, process theories view behavior as the result, at least in part, of human decision processes. This section begins with a discussion of some of the early cognitive theories that are relevant to motivation and that establish a foundation for the process theories of work motivation. Two of the most important of these process theories will then be examined. The first is Vroom's expectancy theory. The second is the Porter-Lawler model of work motivation, which represents an extension and elaboration of Vroom's theory.

Early Cognitive Theories Relevant to Motivation

The basic tenet of this theoretical framework is that a major determinant of human behavior is the beliefs, expectations, and anticipations individuals have concerning future events. Behavior is thus seen as purposeful, goal-directed, and based on conscious intentions. Two of the most prominent early researchers who developed such cognitive approaches were Tolman and Lewin. While Tolman studied animal behavior and Lewin human behavior, both took the position that organisms make conscious decisions concerning future behavior on the basis of cues from their environment. Such a theory is largely *ahistorical* in nature (as opposed to the historical notion inherent in drive theory, discussed in an earlier section). Tolman (1932) argued, for example, that learning results more from changes in beliefs about the environment than from changes in the strengths of past habits. Cognitive theorists did not entirely reject the concept that past events may be important for present behavior, however. Lewin (1938), whose work is characterized by an ahistorical approach, noted that historical and ahistorical approaches were in some ways complementary. Past occurrences could have an impact on present behavior to the extent that they modified present conditions. For example, the past experience of a child who burned a finger on a hot stove may very likely carry over into the present to influence behavior. In general, however, the cognitive theorists posited that it is the "events of the day" that largely influence behavior; past events are important only to the extent that they affect present and future beliefs and expectations.

In general, cognitive theories of motivation—or expectancy/valence theories (also called "instrumentality" theories), as they later became known—view motivational force as a multiplicative function of two key variables: expectancies and valences. "Expectancies" were seen by Lewin (1938) and Tolman (1959) as beliefs individuals had that particular actions on their part would lead to certain outcomes. "Valence" denoted the amount of positive or negative value placed on *anticipated* outcomes by an individual.

Typically, the early cognitive theories were developed to have general applications. Later, however, cognitive-type models were produced specifically for use in work situations. Two of these process theories will be discussed next.

Vroom's Expectancy Theory

Vroom (1964) presented the first systematic formulation of expectancy theory developed specifically for work situations. His model is based on the assumption that individuals make conscious and rational choices about their work behavior. This perspective contrasts sharply with the idea that people are inherently motivated or unmotivated, as many noncognitive models presume. According to Vroom (1964), employees rationally evaluate various work behaviors (e.g., working overtime versus leaving work early) and then choose those that they believe will lead to the work-related rewards that they value most (e.g., promotions). Put another way, employees will decide to apply effort to those tasks that they find attractive and that they believe they can perform. The attractiveness of a particular task depends upon the extent to which the employee believes that its accomplishment will lead to valued outcomes (John, 1992). A useful way of viewing the model is presented below.

1   Outcomes: These are the anticipated consequences that are relevant to the individual and that are perceived to follow certain of his or her work behaviors, such as a pay raise, a sense of accomplishment, acceptance by peers, fatigue, and so on.

2   Valence: This is the extent to which the *anticipated* outcomes appear attractive or unattractive to the individual. The valence of an outcome can range from -1.0 (a highly undesirable outcome, such as being fired) to $+1.0$ (a very desirable outcome, such as a promotion). Work-related outcomes, such as good pay, a good job, group support, being fired, and so forth, vary in their attractiveness from person to person. Typically, pay raises have high valences for employees. For example, a pay raise may appear very attractive (e.g., the valence is 1.0) to a particular salesperson.

3   E → P Expectancy: This is the *effort-performance* (E → P) *expectancy* (called simply "expectancy" in Vroom's original work) and is defined as an individual's subjective probability that effort will actually lead to performance on some job or task. This degree of belief can vary from 0 (the individual is certain that behavior will *not* lead to performance) to 1.0 (the individual is sure that behavior will lead to performance). For example, a salesperson may feel fairly confident (e.g., an expectancy of 0.8) that working an extra hour per day will result in a 10% increase in his or her product sales for the quarter.

4   P → O Expectancy: This is the *performance-outcome* (P → O) *expectancy* (also called "instrumentality" in Vroom's work) and is defined as an individual's belief that a particular level of performance in a given situation will result in a particular set of outcomes. As with the effort-performance expectancy, the performance outcome expectancy can range from 0 to 1.0, and a person may have any number of outcome expectancies regarding performance. For example, a salesperson may strongly believe (e.g., an expectancy of 0.9) that a 10% increase in his or her product sales for the quarter will result in a pay raise. He or she may believe that there is a slim chance (e.g., an expectancy of 0.1) that this 10% increase in performance will lead to a promotion.

According to the theory, E → P expectancies, P → O expectancies, and the valences of various outcomes (considered by the employee) influence the person's level of motivation. Further, these variables are assumed to operate in a multiplicative fashion. Using the example above, if a pay raise appears very attractive to a salesperson (e.g., valence = 1.0), if the person is fairly confident that an increase in effort will lead to an increase in performance (E → P = 0.8), and if he or she strongly believes that an increase in performance will result in a desired outcome (e.g., a pay raise) (P → O = 0.9), then the individual appears to have a relatively high motivational force ($1.0 \times .8 \times .9 = .72$). However, if the salesperson does not believe that an increase in performance will lead to a pay raise (e.g., P → O = 0.1), then the motivational force will not be nearly so high ($1.0 \times .8 \times .1 = .08$). With this multiplicative model, all three factors must be high for the motivational level of an individual to be high.

Evaluation of Vroom's Expectancy Theory

This theory has generated a considerable body of research, much of which suggests that difficulties are encountered when testing the model (Harrell & Stahl, 1986; Miner, 1980). One problem involves the concept of effort, or motivation, itself. As noted above, the theory attempts to predict the amount of effort that the individual will expend on one or more tasks. However, there is limited agreement about the meaning of effort. Further, expectancy theory, as a process theory, does not specify which outcomes are relevant to a particular individual in a particular situation. Each researcher has tended to address this issue in a unique way. Consequently, no systematic approach has been used across investigations. In addition, and especially important, the expectancy approach contains the implicit assumption that motivation is a conscious rational choice process. That is, individuals are assumed consciously to calculate the pleasure or pain that they expect to attain or avoid when making a choice. However, it is generally accepted that individuals are not always conscious of their motives, expectancies, and perceptual processes. Yet expectancy theory tends to ignore habitual behavior and subconscious motivation.

The Porter-Lawler Model

Porter and Lawler (1968) refined and extended Vroom's (1964) expectancy model. They agree with Vroom that employee effort is jointly determined by the valence that employees place on certain outcomes and the degree to which people believe that their efforts will lead to the attainment of these rewards. However, Porter and Lawler emphasize that effort may not necessarily result in performance. Furthermore, they contend that the relationship between valences and expectancies, on the one hand, and effort or motivation, on the other, is more complicated than Vroom's model suggests. The Porter-Lawler model is presented in Exhibit 1.1.

EXHIBIT 1.1 The Porter-Lawler Model of Work Motivation

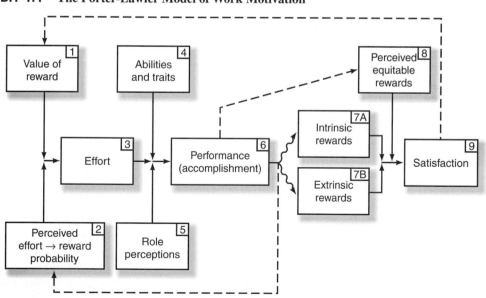

Source: Lyman W. Porter & Edward E. Lawler, *Managerial attitudes and performance.* Homewood, Ill.: Irwin, 1968, p. 165. Reprinted by permission.

The Porter-Lawler model holds that effort may not necessarily result in job performance for two reasons. First, the individual may not have the ability to accomplish the tasks that constitute his or her job. In this case, even if the employee is highly motivated (i.e., expends a lot of effort), performance may not be obtained. Second, the person may not have a good understanding of the task to be performed (i.e., there may be a lack of role clarity). High motivation will not result in job performance if the employee does not have a clear grasp of the ways in which effort may be appropriately directed.

In addition, this model highlights the point that performance and satisfaction may not necessarily be related to each other. Porter and Lawler define satisfaction as "the extent to which rewards actually received meet or exceed the perceived equitable level of rewards" (p. 31). The relationship between performance and satisfaction depends on several factors. For example, in organizations, performance may not always result in expected rewards. Employees are not likely to be satisfied in situations where they are not given the amount of rewards to which they think they are entitled.

Furthermore, the Porter-Lawler model indicates that the nature of the task has implications for the satisfaction-performance linkage. That is, performance on a task may provide the employee with intrinsic rewards, extrinsic rewards, or both. Moreover, the authors suggest that intrinsic rewards can be more closely linked with good performance than extrinsic rewards, because intrinsic rewards can result directly from task performance. In contrast, extrinsic rewards are administered by the organization. In other words, extrinsic rewards depend upon outside sources both for recognition that performance has been attained and for the administration of appropriate compensation.

In addition, the model holds that employees' self-ratings of performance have a major impact on their beliefs about what levels of rewards are equitable. The theory posits that rewards are not evaluated in absolute terms; rather they are assessed subjectively. For example, if employees believe that they have achieved a high level of performance, they will think that they are entitled to greater rewards than would be the case if they thought that their performance was at a low level.

Finally, Porter and Lawler suggest what may happen after an employee performs. Specifically, the rewards that result from a particular level of performance will interact with the employee's perception of them to determine satisfaction. Thus, this model suggests that performance leads to satisfaction, rather than the opposite. This was a significant departure from the traditional thinking.

Evaluation of the Porter-Lawler Model

Some research evidence supports aspects of the model (Roberts & Glick, 1981); however, the model has also been criticized on several grounds (Pinder, 1998). For example, the generalizability of the model may be limited by the fact that the research accompanying the development of the model focused exclusively on pay as it relates to employee motivation. Additional research is needed to test whether other consequences of performance, both positive and negative (e.g., promotion, demotion, fatigue), have the same impact on employees. Also, Porter and Lawler tested their propositions cross-sectionally rather than longitudinally, and this may result in overestimates of the validity of the model (Taylor & Griess, 1976).

On the other hand, this model can provide managers with a useful basis for analyzing and understanding motivational situations in organizational settings. In addition, this model focuses on, and provides guidelines for, how organizations can critically evaluate the effectiveness of their current reward policies and practices.

MANAGERIAL APPROACHES TO MOTIVATION

As we have seen, there has been a gradual evolution in psychological theories of motivation. Similarly, there have been major developments and trends in the way that managers in work organizations approach motivational challenges in the employment situation. Therefore, we now shift our attention directly to the workplace itself and review the changing pattern of managerial approaches to motivating employees. It will be apparent in the following discussion that, although psychological theories and managerial practices relating to motivation developed roughly during the same span of time across the decades of the 20th century, there have been few signs of any sort of cross-fertilization of ideas until relatively recently.

Before the industrial revolution, the major type of "motivation" took the form of fear of punishment—physical, financial, or social. However, as manufacturing processes became more complex, large-scale factories emerged which destroyed many of the social exchange relationships which had existed under the "home industries," or "putting out," system of small manufacturing. These traditional patterns of behavior between workers and their "patrons" were replaced by the more sterile and tenuous relationship between employees and their company. Thus, the industrial revolution was a revolution not only in a production sense, but also in a social sense.

The genesis of this social revolution can be traced to several factors. First, the increased capital investment necessary for factory operation required a high degree of efficiency in order to maintain an adequate return on investment. This meant that an organization had to have an efficient workforce. Second, and somewhat relatedly, the sheer size of these new operations increased the degree of impersonalization in superior-subordinate relationships, necessitating new forms of supervision. Third, and partly as a justification of the new depersonalized factory system, the concept of social Darwinism came into vogue. In brief, this philosophy argued that no person held responsibility for other people and naturally superior people were destined to rise in society, while naturally inferior ones would eventually be selected out of it. In other words, it was "every person for him- or herself" in the workplace.

These new social forcers brought about the need for a fairly well-defined philosophy of management. Many of the more intrinsic motivational factors of the home industry system were replaced by more extrinsic factors. Workers—or, more specifically, "good" workers—were seen as pursuing their own best economic self-interests. The end result of this "new" approach in management was what has been termed the "traditional" model of motivation.

Traditional Model

This model is best represented by the writings of Frederick W. Taylor (1911) and his associates in the scientific management school. Far from being exploitative in intent, scientific management was viewed by these writers as an economic boon to the worker as well as to management. Taylor saw the problem of inefficient production as a problem primarily with management, not workers. It was management's responsibility to find suitable people for a job and then to train them in the most efficient methods for their work. The workers having been thus well trained, management's next responsibility was to install a wage incentive system whereby workers could maximize their income by doing exactly what management told them to do and doing it as rapidly as possible. Thus, in theory, scientific management represented a joint venture of management and workers to the benefit of both. If production problems arose, they could be solved either by altering the technology of the job or by modifying the wage incentive program.

This approach to motivation rested on several very basic assumptions about the nature of human beings. Specifically, workers were viewed as being typically lazy, often dishonest, aimless, dull, and, most of all, mercenary. To get them into the factories and to keep them there, an organization had to pay a "decent" wage, thus outbidding alternative forms of livelihood (e.g., farming). To get workers to produce, tasks were to be simple and repetitive, output controls were to be externally set, and workers were to be paid bonuses for beating their quotas. The manager's major task was thus seen as closely supervising workers to ensure that they met their production quotas and adhered to company rules. In short, the underlying motivational assumption of the traditional model was that, for a price, workers would tolerate the routinized, highly fractionated jobs of the factory. These assumptions and expectations, along with their implied managerial strategies, are summarized in Exhibit 1.2.

As this model became increasingly applied in organizations, several problems began to arise. To begin with, managers, in their quest for profits, began modifying the basic system. While jobs were made more and more routine and specialized (and "efficient" from a mass-production standpoint), management began putting severe constraints on the incentive system, thereby limiting worker income. Workers soon discovered that, although their output was increasing, their wages were not (at least not proportionately). Simultaneously fear of job security arose. As factories became more "efficient," fewer workers were needed to do the job and layoffs and terminations became commonplace. Workers responded to the situation through elaborate and covert methods of restricting output in an attempt to optimize their incomes while protecting their jobs. Unionism began to rise, and the unparalleled growth and efficiency that had occurred under scientific management began to subside.

In an effort to overcome such problems, some organizations began to reexamine the simplicity of their motivational assumptions about employees and to look for new methods to increase production and maintain a steady workforce. It should be pointed out, however, that the primary economic assumption of the traditional model was not eliminated in the newer approaches and that it remains a central concept of many motivational approaches today. Recent studies among both managers and workers indicate that money is a primary motivational force and that many workers will, in fact, select jobs more on the basis of salary prospects than job content. However, newer approaches have tended to view the role of money in more complex terms as it affects motivational force. Moreover, these newer theories argue that additional factors are also important inputs into the decision to produce. One such revisionist approach to motivation at work is the "human relations" model.

Human Relations Model

Beginning in the late 1920s, initial efforts were made to discover why the traditional model was inadequate for motivating people. The earliest such work carried out by Mayo (1933, 1945) and Roethlisberger and Dickson (1939) pointed the way to what was to become the human relations school of management by arguing that it was necessary to consider the "whole person" on the job. These researchers posited that the increased routinization of tasks

EXHIBIT 1.2   General Patterns of Managerial Approaches to Motivation

Traditional Model	Human Relations Model	Human Resources Model
Assumptions		
1 Work is inherently distasteful to most people. 2 What they do is less important than what they earn for doing it. 3 Few want or can handle work which requires creativity, self-direction, or self-control.	1 People want to feel useful and important. 2 People desire to belong and to be recognized as individuals. 3 These needs are more important than money in motivating people to work.	1 Work is not inherently distasteful. People want to contribute to meaningful goals which they have helped establish. 2 Most people can exercise far more creative, responsible self-direction and self-control than their present jobs demand.
Policies		
1 The manager's basic task is to closely supervise and control subordinates. 2 He or she must break tasks down into simple, repetitive, easily learned operations. 3 He or she must establish detailed work routines and procedures, and enforce these firmly but fairly.	1 The manager's basic task is to make each worker feel useful and important. 2 He or she should keep subordinates informed and listen to their objections to his or her plans. 3 The manager should allow subordinates to exercise some self-direction and self-control on routine matters.	1 The manager's basic task is to make use of "untapped" human resources. 2 He or she must create an environment in which all members may contribute to the limits of their ability. 3 He or she must encourage full participation on important matters, continually broadening subordinate self-direction and control.
Expectations		
1 People can tolerate work if the pay is decent and the boss is fair. 2 If tasks are simple enough and people are closely controlled, they will produce up to standard.	1 Sharing information with subordinates and involving them in routine decisions will satisfy their basic needs to belong and to feel important. 2 Satisfying these needs will improve morale and reduce resistance to formal authority—subordinates will "willingly cooperate."	1 Expanding subordinate influence, self-direction, and self-control will lead to direct improvements in operating efficiency. 2 Work satisfaction may improve as a "by-product" of subordinates making full use of their resources.

Source: After Miles, Porter, & Craft, 1966.

brought about by the industrial revolution had served to drastically reduce the possibilities of finding satisfaction in the task itself. They believed that, because of this change, workers would begin seeking satisfaction elsewhere (such as from their coworkers). On the basis of this early research, many of the traditional assumptions were replaced with a new set of propositions concerning the nature of human beings (see Exhibit 1.2). Bendix (1956, p. 294) best summarized this evolution in managerial thinking by noting that the "failure to treat workers as human beings came to be regarded as the cause of low morale, poor craftsmanship, unresponsiveness, and confusion."

The new assumptions concerning the "best" method of motivating workers were characterized by a strong social emphasis. It was argued here that management had a responsibility to make employees *feel* useful and important on the job, to provide recognition, and generally to facilitate the satisfaction of workers' social needs. Attention was shifted away from the study of worker-machine relations and toward a more thorough understanding of interpersonal and group relations at work. Behavioral research into factors affecting motivation began in earnest, and morale surveys came into vogue in an attempt to measure and maintain job satisfaction. The basic ingredient that typically was *not* changed was the nature of the required tasks on the job.

The motivational strategies which emerged from such assumptions were several. First, as noted above, management felt it had a new responsibility to make workers feel important. Second, many organizations attempted to open up vertical communication channels so that employees would know more about the organization and would have greater opportunity to have their opinions heard by management. Company newsletters emerged as one source of downward communication. Employee "gripe sessions" were begun as one source of upward communication. Third, workers were increasingly allowed to make routine decisions concerning their own jobs. Finally, as managers began to realize the existence of informal groups with their own norms and role prescriptions, greater attention was paid to using group incentive systems. Underlying all four of these developments was the presumed necessity of viewing motivation as largely a social process. Supervisory training programs began emphasizing the idea that a supervisor's role was no longer simply that of a taskmaker. Supervisors had also to be understanding and sympathetic to the needs and desires of their subordinates. However, as pointed out by Miles (1965), the basic goal of management under this strategy remained much the same as it had been under the traditional model; that is, both strategies aimed at securing employee compliance with managerial authority.

Human Resources Model

In recent years the assumptions of the human relations model have been widely challenged, not only as an oversimplified and incomplete statement of human behavior at work, but also for being as manipulative as the traditional model. In response to the criticism, a different approach was proposed under various titles, including McGregor's (1960) "Theory Y," Likert's (1967) "System 4," Schein's (1972) "Complex Man," and Miles's (1965) "Human Resources" model. The latter term will be used here as being more descriptive of the underlying philosophy inherent in these new perspectives.

Human resources models generally view humans as being motivated by a complex set of interrelated factors (such as money, need for affiliation, need for achievement, and desire for meaningful work). It is assumed that different employees often seek quite different goals in a job and have a diversity of talents to offer. Under this conceptualization, employees are regarded as reservoirs of potential talent, and management's responsibility is to learn how best to tap such resources.

Inherent in such a philosophy are several fairly basic assumptions about the nature of people. First, it is assumed that people want to contribute on the job. In this sense, employees are viewed as being, to a degree, "premotivated" to perform. In fact, the more people become involved in their work, the more meaningful the job can often become. Second, it is assumed that work does not necessarily have to be distasteful. Many of the current efforts at job enrichment and job redesign are aimed at increasing the potential meaningfulness of work by adding greater task variety, autonomy, responsibility, and so on. Third, it is argued that employees are quite capable of making significant and rational decisions affecting their work and that allowing greater latitude in employee decision making is actually in the best interests of the organization. Finally, it is assumed that increased self-control and direction allowed to employees on the job, plus the completion of more meaningful tasks, can in large measure determine the level of satisfaction on the job. In other words, it is generally assumed that good and meaningful performance leads to job satisfaction and not the reverse, as is assumed in the human relations model.

Certain implied managerial strategies follow naturally from this set of assumptions. In general, this approach would hold that it is management's responsibility first to appreciate the complex nature of motivational patterns. On the basis of such knowledge, management should attempt to determine how best to use the potential resources available to it through its workforce. It should assist employees in meeting some of their own personal goals within the organizational context. Moreover, such a philosophy implies a greater degree of participation by employees in relevant decision-making activities, as well as increased autonomy over task accomplishment. Thus, in contrast to the traditional and human relations models, management's task is seen not so much as one of manipulating employees to accept managerial authority as it is of setting up conditions in which employees can meet their own goals at the same time as meeting the organization's goals.

In conclusion, it should be pointed out that the human resources approach to motivation has only lately begun to receive concentrated attention. Many organizations have attempted to implement one or more aspects of it, but full-scale adoptions of the approach, including the multitude of strategic implications for managers, are still not common. In fact, when one looks across organizations, it becomes readily apparent that aspects of all three models have their advocates. In recent years, in fact, the notion of a multiple strategy—using all three approaches at one time or another depending upon the nature of the organization, its technology, its people, and its goals and priorities—has come to be labeled a "contingency approach" to management. In effect, a contingency perspective allows one to dispense with the unlikely assumption that a single approach will be equally effective under any and all circumstances, and rather substitutes an emphasis on diagnosis of the situation to determine which approach will be more useful and appropriate under the *particular* circumstances.

OVERVIEW OF THE READING

Mitchell and Daniels provide a commentary on the current state of work motivation research and highlight several new directions in which this literature appears to be headed. Of particular interest is the classification system they develop to organize the research for their discussion (see their Figure 1). Essentially, their framework is structured around a series of apparent contrasts (or tensions) in extant theoretical approaches to work motivation.

For instance, they begin by observing that work motivation theories can be classified as either "internal" or "external." The former consists of models identifying psychological factors (e.g., needs, decision-making processes) that energize, direct, and/or maintain people's behavior at work. The latter is comprised of perspectives that highlight aspects of work context (e.g., rewards, culture) that motivate organizational members. The internal category is further subdivided into the two groupings of "thoughtful" (frameworks emphasizing what people think and believe) and "not rational" ("hot" theories pertaining to affect and "cold" theories associated with needs and traits). The category labeled external is subdivided into models focusing on aspects of the job itself (i.e., job design) and those centering on people factors (i.e., social).

It is important to note that, while the Mitchell and Daniel's framework is an interesting and helpful way of organizing the various approaches to work motivation, it is not the only useful means of doing so. For instance, above we employed the more general and traditional categories of "content" versus "process" theories. As discussed, this categorical distinction focuses quite clearly on the critical difference between the *what* and the *how* of work motivation psychology. Other organizing schemes have attempted to show how motivation theories may relate to each other (e.g., Locke, 1997; Whetten & Cameron, 2002). For example, Exhibit 1.3 depicts Locke's (1997) view of how conceptual perspectives may be integrated.

EXHIBIT 1.3 **Integrated Empirical Model of Work Motivation**

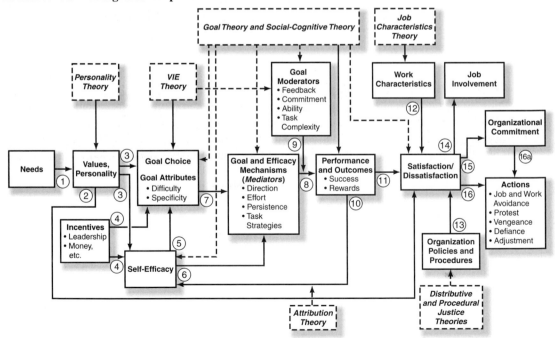

Source: From E. A. Locke, "The motivation to work: What we know," in P. Pintrich and M. Maehr (Eds.), *Advances in motivation and achievement,* vol. 10 (Greenwich CT: JAI Press, in press). Reprinted with permission.

As the authors reiterate and emphasize, there is no universally accepted way of categorizing the various approaches to work motivation. Organizing frameworks, such as the ones mentioned above, represent various "mappings" of the field. However, like different types of geographic maps (e.g., topographical, road), these frameworks highlight distinct and notable aspects of the field's terrain—but they are, of necessity, incomplete. In a general sense, the different organizing schema can be regarded as complementary and can be appreciated for the distinctive insights each offers on the topic.

Mitchell and Daniels conclude their discussion with a set of interesting questions that scholars have yet to answer. For instance, how should the notion of time be incorporated into motivation theories? "What mechanisms are involved with the allocation of effort and time over tasks? How do emotions such as anger and guilt (e.g., over injustice) influence constructs like goal acceptance or self-efficacy? How do distal constructs like personality influence more proximal states like expectancies or goal commitment?"

References

Alderfer, C. P. *Existence, relatedness, and growth.* New York: Free Press, 1972.

Allport, G. W. The historical background of modern psychology. In G. Lindzey (Ed.), *Handbook of social psychology.* Cambridge, Mass.: Addison-Wesley, 1954.

Atkinson, J. W. *An introduction to motivation.* Princeton, N.J.: Van Nostrand, 1964.

Bendix, R. *Work and authority in industry.* New York: Wiley, 1956.

Birch, D., & Veroff, J. *Motivation: A study of action.* Monterey, Calif.: Brooks/Cole, 1966.

Bockman, V. M. The Herzberg controversy. *Personnel Psychology,* 1971, 24, 155–189.

Campbell, J. P., & Pritchard, R. D. Motivation theory in industrial and organizational psychology. In M. D. Dunnette (Ed.), *Handbook of industrial and organizational psychology.* Chicago: Rand McNally, 1976.

Cannon, W. B. *The wisdom of the body.* New York: Norton, 1939.

Cherrington, D. J. *Organizational behavior.* Needham Heights, Mass.: Allyn & Bacon, 1989.

Chung, K. H. *Motivation theories and practices.* Columbus, Ohio: Grid, 1977, pp. 47–48.

French, E. Effects of the interaction of motivation and feedback on task performance. In J. Atkinson (Ed.), *Motives in fantasy, action and society,* Princeton, N.J.: Van Nostrand, 1958, pp. 400–408.

Freud, S. The unconscious. In *Collected papers of Sigmund Freud,* Vol. IV (J. Rivière, Trans.). London: Hogarth, 1949. (First published in 1915.)

Gibson, J. L., Ivancevich, J. M., & Donnelly, J. H., Jr. *Organizations: Behavior, structure, processes.* Boston: Irwin, 1994.

Harrell, A., & Stahl, M. J. Additive information processing and the relationship between expectancy of success and motivational force. *Academy of Management Journal,* 1986, 29, 424–433.

Herzberg, F. *Work and the nature of man.* Cleveland: World Publishing, 1966.

Herzberg, F., Mausner, B., & Snyderman, B. B. *The motivation to work.* New York: Wiley, 1959.

Hilgard, E. R., & Atkinson, R. C. *Introduction to psychology.* New York: Harcourt, Brace & World, 1967.

House, R. J., & Wigdor, L. A. Herzberg's dual-factor theory of job satisfaction and motivation. *Personnel Psychology,* 1967, 20, 369–390.

Hull, C. L. *Principles of behavior.* New York: Appleton-Century-Crofts, 1943.

Hull, C. L. *A behavior system: An introduction to behavior theory concerning the individual organism.* New Haven, Conn.: Yale University Press, 1952.

James, W. *The principles of psychology,* Vols. I and II. New York: Henry Holt, 1890.

John, G. *Organizational behavior: Understanding life at work,* 3rd ed. New York: Harper-Collins, 1992.

Jones, M. R. (Ed.), *Nebraska symposium on motivation.* Lincoln: University of Nebraska Press, 1955.

King, N. Clarification and evaluation of the two-factor theory of job satisfaction. *Psychological Bulletin,* 1970, 74, 18–31.

Lewin, K. *The conceptual representation and the measurement of psychological forces.* Durham, N.C.: Duke University Press, 1938.

Likert, R. *The human organization.* New York: McGraw-Hill, 1967.

Locke, E. A. Toward a theory of task motivation and incentives. *Organizational Behavior and Human Performance,* 1968, 3, 157–189.

Locke, E. A. Goal theory vs. control theory: Contrasting approaches to understanding work motivation. *Motivation and Emotion,* 1991, 15(1), 9–28.

Locke, E. A. 1997. The motivation to work: What we know. *Advances in Motivation and Achievement,* 10, 375-412.

Maier, N. R. F. *Psychology in industry,* 2d ed. Boston: Houghton Mifflin, 1955.

Maslow, A. H. *Motivation and personality.* New York: Harper & Row, 1954.

Maslow, A. H. *Toward a theory of being.* New York: Van Nostrand Reinhold, 1968.

Mayo, E. *The human problems of an industrial civilization.* New York: Macmillan, 1933.

Mayo, E. *The social problems of an industrial civilization.* Cambridge, Mass.: Harvard University Press, 1945.

McClelland, D. C. *The achieving society.* Princeton, N.J.: Van Nostrand, 1961.

McClelland, D. C. Business drive and national achievement. *Harvard Business Review,* 1962.

McClelland, D. C. Achievement motivation can be developed. *Harvard Business Review,* 1965a, 43, 6–24, 178.

McClelland, D. C. Toward a theory of motive acquisition. *American Psychologist,* 1965b, 20, 321–333.

McClelland, D. C. *Assessing human motivation.* New York: General Learning Press, 1971.

McClelland, D. C., Atkinson, J. W., Clark, R. A., & Lowell, E. L. *The achievement motive.* New York: Appleton-Century-Crofts, 1953.

McClelland, D. C. & Burnham, D. H. Power is the great motivator. *Harvard Business Review,* 1976, 54, 100–110.

McDougall, W. *An introduction to social psychology.* London: Methuen, 1908.

McGregor, D. *The human side of enterprise.* New York: McGraw-Hill, 1960.

Miles, R. E. Human relations or human resources? *Harvard Business Review,* 1965, 43(4), 148–163.

Miles, R. E., Porter, L. W., & Craft, J. A. Leadership attitudes among public health officials. *American Journal of Public Health,* 1966, 56, 1990–2005.

Miner, J. *Theories of organizational behavior.* Hinsdale, Ill.: Dryden Press, 1980.

Morgan, C. T., & King, R. A. *Introduction to psychology.* New York: McGraw-Hill, 1966.

Pinder, C. C. *Work motivation in organizational behavior.* Upper Saddle River, N.J.: Prentice Hall.

Porter, L. W. A study of perceived need satisfaction in bottom and middle management jobs. *Journal of Applied Psychology,* 1961, 45, 1–10.

Porter, L. W., & Lawler, E. E. III. *Managerial attitudes and performance.* Homewood, Ill.: Richard D. Irwin, 1968.

Roberts K., & Glick, W. The job characteristics approach to task design: A critical review. *Journal of Applied Psychology,* 1981, 66, 193–217.

Roethlisberger, F., & Dickson, W. J. *Management and the worker.* Cambridge, Mass.: Harvard University Press, 1939.

Schein. E. *Organizational psychology.* Englewood Cliffs, N.J.: Prentice Hall, 1972.

Schneider, B., & Alderfer, C. P. Three studies of measures of need satisfaction in organizations. *Administrative Science Quarterly,* 1973, 18, 489–505.

Skinner, B. F. *Science and human behavior.* New York: Macmillan, 1953.

Spence, K. W. *Behavior theory and conditioning.* New Haven, Conn.: Yale University Press, 1956.

Steers, R. M., & Black, J. S. *Organizational behavior,* 5th ed. New York: HarperCollins, 1994.

Steers, R. M., & Braunstein, D. N. Behaviorally based measure of manifest needs in work settings. *Journal of Vocational Behavior,* 1976, 9, 251–266.

Taylor, E. K., & Griess, T. The missing middle in validation research. *Personnel Psychology,* 1976, 29, 5–11.

Taylor, F. W. *Scientific management.* New York: Harper, 1911.

Thorndike, E. L. *Animal intelligence: Experimental studies.* New York: Macmillan, 1911.

Tolman, E. C. *Purposive behavior in animals and men.* New York: Appleton-Century-Crofts, 1932.

Tolman, E. C. Principles of purposive behavior. In S. Koch (Ed.), *Psychology: A study of science,* Vol. 2, New York: McGraw-Hill, 1959.

Viteles, M. S. *Motivation and morale in industry.* New York: Norton, 1953.

Vroom, V. H. *Work and motivation.* New York: Wiley, 1964.

Wahba, M. A., & Bridwell, L. G. Maslow reconsidered: A review of research on the need hierarchy theory. *Organizational Behavior and Human Performance,* 1976, 15, 212–240.

Whetten, D. A., & Cameron, K. S.. *Developing management skills.* Upper Saddle River, N.J.: Prentice Hall, 2002.

Whitset, D. A., & Winslow, E. K. An analysis of studies critical of the motivation-hygiene theory. *Personnel Psychology,* 1967, 20, 391–416.

Woodworth, R. S. *Dynamic psychology.* New York: Columbia University Press, 1918.

Observations and Commentary on Recent Research in Work Motivation

Terence R. Mitchell
Denise Daniels

In the fifth edition of the *Comprehensive Handbook of Psychology* we review the research on the topic of motivation in Organizational Behavior since 1990 (Mitchell & Daniels, 2002). In that chapter, we set forth an organizing framework for the motivation literature, discuss at length developments in each major subarea (e.g., expectancy, self-efficacy, goal setting) of motivation over the last decade, and identify directions in which the research appears to be currently headed. Here, we do not intend to replicate that review in its detail. We employ the same basic organizing framework (described below), but our discussion of the state of the research on work motivation is more circumscribed and we highlight the new directions this work appears to be taking. In order to avoid duplication in the current volume, we do not emphasize several subjects that are treated in depth elsewhere in the text (especially those covered in individual readings in Chapter 2), such as equity, organizational justice, and reinforcement.

Before proceeding, we would like to explain the genesis for the organizing framework that we employed in the aforementioned review and will use here (Figure 1). There are no universally accepted ways of presenting the various approaches to motivation. Therefore, when reviewing the motivation research, we initially categorized articles according to the major theoretical positions they represented (e.g., expectancy, goal setting, dispositions and traits, etc.). When we examined these categories collectively, we saw contrasts or tensions between perspectives—for instance, some theoretical approaches are internal to the individual (cognitive approaches, dispositional approaches) while others are clearly more external (task design, social influence processes); some are more cognitive in nature (self-regulation, expectancy theory, goal setting, self-efficacy) and others have very little to do with cognitions (genetic disposition, emotion, affect; some are more distal (or distant) to behavior (e.g., needs) whereas others are more proximal to behavior (e.g., goals). It appeared to us that nearly every theoretical approach had an opposing (although not necessarily contradictory) alternative. Therefore, we decided to organize the review around these various polarities or tensions. We discuss internal and external theories, in turn, below.

"INTERNAL" MOTIVATIONAL THEORIES

In this section, we focus on those motivation theories that involve elements, mechanisms, or processes internal to the individual and that explain arousal, intensity and direction of behavior. As Figure 1 indicates, internal theories consist of those that are thoughtful and those that are not rational. We begin with those classified as thoughtful.

Adapted from T. R. Mitchell and D. Daniels, Motivation, in W. C. Borman, D. R. Ilgen, & R. J. Klimoski (Eds.), *Comprehensive Handbook of Psychology*, 5th ed. Vol. 12: *Industrial and Organizational Psychology*. New York: John Wiley & Sons, 2002.

FIGURE 1*

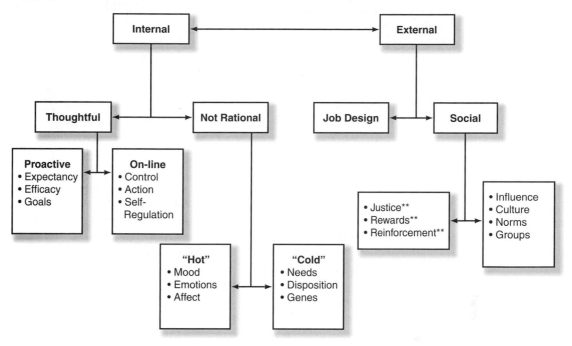

*Adapted from T. R. Mitchell and D. Daniels (2002)
**These topics are discussed in depth elsewhere in this volume. Therefore, we do not emphasize them in this article.

Thoughtful

Theories in the "thoughtful" category are based on a cognitive approach to understanding human behavior. Expectancy, self-efficacy, goal setting, and on-line (control, action, and self-regulation considered collectively) theories are included. The main tenets of expectancy theory are presented in the introduction to the current chapter. Self-efficacy and goal setting are discussed at length in Chapter 2 articles. Here we highlight several new research directions not discussed in other places in this text.

Expectancy Theory

Expectancy theory generated a substantial amount of research and debate in the 20 years immediately following the publication of Vroom's (1964) seminal work. However, it no longer appears to be doing so. In our literature review, we were hard pressed to find current cites relating to expectancy theory at all. Contemporary research that is most directly descended from expectancy approaches relates to occupational or job choice, and realistic job previews. In this arena there is some evidence that information serving to reduce job incumbents' unrealistic expectations for the job leads to lower turnover and higher satisfaction (Buckley, Fedor, Veres, Weise, & Carraher, 1998), as well as higher performance

(Phillips, 1998). Thus, clear and accurate expectations prior to entering a job are important for subsequent adjustment and performance.

While the indirect influence of expectancy theory is being felt in the realistic job preview literature, its lack of direct influence on the motivational field today may be attributed to the rise of other cognitive theories, during what has been referred to as the "cognitive revolution in organizational behavior" (Ilgen, Major, & Tower, 1994). In particular, the current emphasis on goal setting, self-efficacy and self-regulation may have subsumed some of the major concepts within expectancy theory. Locke and Latham (1990, p. 68) pointed out that "[I]n practice, many expectancy measures are probably equivalent to self-efficacy measures, or at least partially so." It is to the theory of self-efficacy that we now turn our attention.

Self-Efficacy

Since the concept of self-efficacy is discussed extensively by Stajkovic and Luthans (this volume), we will highlight only two areas of research that are relatively new in the self-efficacy area. First, there has been quite a bit of effort recently to understand the similarities and differences between self-efficacy and related constructs. Second, there has been some research that has highlighted some of the negative effects of high self-efficacy.

Mitchell (1997) pointed out that self-efficacy is similar to concepts discussed by others, including personal agency beliefs (Ford, 1992), personal efficacy (Gurin & Brim, 1984), capacity beliefs (Skinner, Wellborn, & Connell, 1990), and perceived competence (Deci, 1980, Harter, 1982). Self-efficacy has been differentiated from self-esteem, which tends to be a stable value judgment people make about themselves (Pinder, 1998); and while low self-efficacy on a given task may influence self-esteem, it does not necessarily do so. Brockner (1988) introduced the idea of task-related self-esteem, which appears to be synonymous with the concept of self-efficacy. Confidence is another construct that has much in common with self-efficacy. Trafimow and Sniezek (1994) did studies of performance estimation for items on a general knowledge test. They found that subjects' general confidence (a trait measure) was positively related to their item confidence (similar to self-efficacy). Much confusion has arisen over the difference between self-efficacy and expectancy. While both constructs are subjective estimates of personal capability, the difference is that expectancy relates to a particular performance level of a given task, and self-efficacy is broader in that it can cover multiple performance levels. At a practical level, however, the operational measures for expectancy and self-efficacy are often indistinguishable.

More recently, Eden has forwarded his conceptualization of "means efficacy," which he defines as a person's belief in the tools available to do the job (Eden & Granat-Flomin, 2000). Eden differentiates means-efficacy from self-efficacy in that the former is based on beliefs about factors external to the individual, and the latter is more about internal factors (Eden, 1996). He suggests that self-efficacy together with means-efficacy make up a construct referred to as subjective efficacy, which is a better estimate of future performance than either means- or self-efficacy alone. While self-efficacy has been traditionally understood to include some component of means efficacy (cf. Gist & Mitchell, 1992), this new distinction between internal and external sources of efficacy may be useful.

The last constructs we will address in this section are role-breadth self-efficacy (Parker, 1998) and global, or general, self-efficacy. Role-breadth self-efficacy (RBSE) has appeared recently in the literature as a more global construct than self-efficacy, which is always related to a given task. RBSE relates to people's judgments about their ability to carry out the broader and more proactive roles on the job (beyond the technical requirements). Parker has found that RBSE can be influenced by job enrichment activities. Global or general self-efficacy (GSE) is broader yet, in that it assesses people's beliefs in their capabilities to perform a wide variety of tasks. It is a more traitlike, dispositional variable than is self-efficacy (Eden, 1999). It is unclear at this point exactly how global self-efficacy differs from self-esteem or other more general constructs.

Most of what we have reviewed to this point highlights the positive impact of efficacy on performance. However, there are situations in which high self- or group-efficacy may have a detrimental impact. When initial self-efficacy estimates are too high and performance does not match expectations, people tend to become discouraged and use avoidance strategies (Stone, 1994). Those with high levels of self-efficacy may be more likely to reject negative feedback (Nease, Mudgett, & Quinones, 1999). This may in turn make it more likely for them to fall prey to escalation of commitment and have decreased performance (Goltz, 1999). Whyte (1998) argues that in a group context, overly high group efficacy may be the instigating factor causing groupthink, which may lead to performance decrements.

While there are some potential downsides to high levels of self and group efficacy, in general the research supports the idea that efficacy is an important component of motivation and a strong predictor of performance. Further, research supports the idea that self-efficacy is malleable, and provides several demonstrated ways of improving it. One of the ways in which self-efficacy influences performance is through its influence on self-set goals. It is to the area of goal setting that we now turn our attention.

Goal Setting

The theory of goal setting is the 800-pound gorilla in the work motivation literature; it is quite easily the single most dominant theory in the field, with over a thousand articles and reviews published on the topic in a little over 30 years (Mitchell, Thompson, & George-Falvy, 2000). An article by Locke (1996) included in this volume discusses the foundations of goal-setting theory. Below we highlight several current directions in the area of goal setting, including goal orientation, emotions, and the negative consequences of goals.

Numerous recent studies have focused on the relationship between one's goal orientation (as defined by Dweck, 1986) and performance. Briefly, Dweck described two different goal orientations that people have: learning-goal-oriented individuals are more concerned with mastering the task, and therefore set goals related to learning, while performance-goal-oriented individuals are more interested in performing well on the task, and therefore self-set goals related to task outcome, regardless of mastery level. VandeWalle (1999) reviewed this literature and found that a learning-goal orientation is related to higher self-set goals, seeking training, and feedback-seeking behavior.

While the impact of goal-orientation on self-set goals is clear, their impact on performance is not. Some studies have found that learning-goal orientations lead to higher performance (e.g., Tabernero & Wood, 1999; VandeWalle, 1999; VandeWalle, Brown, Cron, & Slocum, 1999; Brett & VandeWalle, 1999); other studies have found no difference in performance between learning- and performance-goal-oriented individuals (Hoover, et al., 1998a), while still others have found performance-goal-oriented individuals to have higher performance (VandeWalle & Cummings, 1997; Hoover, Johnson, & Schmidt, 1998b; Harackiewicz, et al., in press). Preliminary evidence seems to indicate that these disparate findings might be explained by the type of task: A learning-goal orientation is more likely to lead to increases in performance when the task is complex, whereas a performance-goal orientation is more likely to improve performance if the task is simple (Winters & Latham, 1996; Hoover et al., 1998b). Regardless of what future research will determine on this issue, it is clear that the study of individual differences is making its mark in the goal-setting literature.

Emotions have also been examined recently for their relationship to the goal-setting process (e.g., Brunstein, Dangelmayer, & Schultheiss, 1996; Brunstein, Schultheiss, & Grassmann, 1998; Roney, Higgins, & Shah, 1995). People have emotional reactions to goal attainment as well as the failure to reach goals. An interesting picture of the relationship between affect and goals is emerging, but we have quite a bit of work to do in this area to fully understand the various connections between the goal-setting process and emotion.

Finally, we come to the issue of the negative effects of goals. The overwhelming evidence for goal setting is positive. In other words, the research suggests that goal setting works to improve performance across a variety of contexts, and on numerous tasks. However, while we know quite a bit about the relationship between goals and quantifiable task performance outcomes, we don't necessarily have a clear picture of the effects of goals on affect, extrarole behaviors, performance quality, complex or novel tasks, and interdependent tasks to name a few. For example, we know that goal achievement can lead to feelings of satisfaction (Thomas & Mathieu, 1994), but we know little about the affective consequences of failure to reach a goal (Pinder, 1998). Research by Brunstein (1999; Brunstein & Gollwitzer, 1996) concludes that failure to achieve goals can lead to lowered motivation and performance on future tasks, particularly if the goal is relevant to the person's self-definition, and he or she ruminates on the failure. There is some tantalizing research indicating that specific goals in conjunction with bonuses for goal attainment may have a negative impact on employees' extrarole behaviors (Wright, George, Farnsworth, & McMahon, 1993). Incentives can also decrease performance when they are linked with goals that are viewed as nonattainable (Lee, Locke, & Phan, 1997). We know that quantity and quality goals sometimes interfere with each other (Gilliland & Landis, 1992); however, goals can improve creativity when people work alone and expect their work to be evaluated (Shalley, 1995). We know that goals can decrease performance on complex or novel tasks (Wood et al., 1987; Mitchell et al., 1994), they may increase anxiety (Seta, Seta, & Donaldson, 1992; Wegge, 1999), they may hinder cooperation and decrease performance on interdependent tasks (Mitchell & Silver, 1990), and this effect appears to increase as the group size increases (Seijts & Latham, 2000). Are there other negative impacts of goals? How do we balance the clear positive performance outcomes associated with goal setting with some of these potential downsides? In what situations are these negative outcomes associated with goal setting most likely to be observed? While none of these downsides are likely to call into question the fundamental findings of goal setting, these areas of research are worth pursuing to understand more fully the boundary conditions of the theory. There is still fertile theoretical ground to be explored in the field of goal setting.

On-line Theories

We now turn to the issue of what happens after a person selects a goal and begins working toward it. More than 50 years ago Lewin recognized that there are two stages to the motivational process—what he referred to as "goal setting" and "goal striving" (Lewin, Dembo,

Festinger, & Sears, 1944). What we have discussed until now mostly pertains to the first aspect of this process. Goal setting is by nature forward looking; it anticipates performance levels that are to be achieved in the future. The "goal striving" or in-the-moment aspect of motivation has not been examined in anywhere near the same depth as the more proactive and forward-looking goal setting. That is not to say, however, that it has been ignored. Several researchers have begun to examine this concept, although often under different rubrics, including action theory (Gollwitzer, 1990; Wilpert, 1995), control theory (Lord & Hanges, 1987; Klein, 1989; Carver & Scheier, 1990), and self-regulation theory (Kanfer & Ackerman, 1989). While there is no consensus in the literature on what to call this active-processing component of goal achievement, we will refer to this body of work as "on-line motivation." It is to this area of research that we now turn our attention.

Most of the researchers in the area of on-line motivation focus on the motivational process once a goal has been accepted. Work by Gollwitzer (1990, 1993, 1999) and Bargh (1994, 1999, Bargh & Gollwitzer, 1994) suggests that people move toward their goals by utilizing "implementation intentions," or strategies about when, where, and how goal attainment will be reached. This concept of implementation intentions appears to be very similar to the goal-setting mechanism of "strategy development." Indeed, recent research by Diefendorff and Lord (2000) shows that there are two outcomes associated with planning. The first is intellectual—planning leads to conscious strategy development; the second is volitional—planning leads to increased persistence and confidence and decreased distractibility. Both of these effects are captured in the concept of implementation intentions. What is particularly noteworthy about the Diefendorff and Lord study is that the intellectual effects of planning occur before the task is undertaken, while the volitional effects are "in the moment," frequently in response to changes in the environment.

Further research on implementation intentions indicates that they cause action initiation to become automatic when the appropriate situation arises (Gollwitzer, 1999). That is, implementation intentions effectively create instant habits, or automatic scripts that are called up given the appropriate environmental prime. It is here that the on-line motivation research appears to diverge a bit from the goal-setting research. While goal setting assumes that most human behavior is consciously goal directed, on-line motivational researchers have found evidence that there is much less under volitional control than we may realize. In fact, Bargh and Chartrand (1999) present evidence that most of daily life is driven by nonconscious mental processes, which have the effect of freeing up cognitive capacity for conscious self-regulation. Wegner and Wheatley (1999) demonstrate that we more frequently perceive behavior to be conscious and willful than it actually is. In other words, while we may believe that much of our behavior is conscious and goal directed, it is possible that we are really on autopilot most of the time, behaving in ways that are consistent with cognitive scripts developed long before the situation we are currently encountering.

Action and control theorists have emphasized the feedback loop process through which people compare their current state with the "referent standard" (or goal) (Lord & Hanges, 1987; Klein, 1989). Control theory assumes that when there are discrepancies between one's current state and goal, individuals want to resolve those discrepancies by moving closer to the goal (Carver & Scheier, 1981). Consistent with the concept of implementation intentions, control theories posit the call-up of automatic scripts for frequently encountered situations (Lord & Kernan, 1987; Klein, 1989). When a novel or unexpected situation is encountered, however, more conscious cognitive processing occurs. Work on self-regulation by Kanfer and Ackerman (1989; Kanfer, 1990, 1996) proposes that given a fixed amount of cognitive capacity, performance is likely to decrease when more cognitive processing is required.

Control theory has not been warmly received by goal-setting theorists. One of the major areas of disagreement between the two theories relates to the nature of human beings: Do we seek to reduce feedback loop discrepancies as control theories propose, or are we actively involved in setting goals that require us to "stretch" (create discrepancies) as goal-setting theorists argue? Phillips, Hollenbeck, and Ilgen (1996) found that most people set positive discrepancies for themselves, even after a task is well learned. While this finding does not negate the value that control theory has added to the field, it does raise the question of where one's goals (or referent standard) come from. Control theorists suggest that people have goal hierarchies, and that goals at one level are determined by higher order goals, which are in turn determined by yet higher order goals. Locke (1991) argues that this explanation simply "pushes the tension-reduction problem back a step further" (p. 13). Locke (1991) has also criticized control theory for its deductive approach (rather than the grounded theory, inductive approach used by goal setting).

While there do appear to be a few philosophical and methodological differences between goal-setting and action/control theory, they are remarkably similar in much of their content. Much of the criticism that has been leveled at control theory is somewhat unfortunate, since this approach is much broader than simply motivation. Variations of control theory have been applied to a variety of research fields, including biology, mathematics, public administration, and family and other I/O psychology fields including human error, personality development, work design, and leisure (Wilpert, 1995). A number of European researchers have examined action/control theory applied to goal-oriented work behavior (Frese & Zapf, 1994). Rather than focusing on areas of disagreement between the two approaches, theoretical development might be better served if we viewed goal setting as applicable to the pre-action phase of human behavior, and parts of control theory as more applicable to the on-line active processing phase of human behavior.

Not Rational

Like the "thoughtful" theories of motivation, those approaches that we have labeled "not rational" examine motivation from a perspective that is internal to the individual. Unlike the thoughtful theories, however, this "not-rational" approach focuses on who people are (including traits and dispositions), what they feel and need, rather than what they think and believe. These approaches to motivation are not "irrational" in any sense, but they do not emphasize the cognitive approach to understanding human motivation and behavior that marked the theories of the previous section. Within this "not-rational" grouping, research can be further subdivided into "hot" and "cold" categories. The "hot" theories focus more on transitory mood states and emotions, which have a more direct and proximal impact on motivation and performance. The "cold" theories emphasize dispositions, genetic traits, and needs—more stable, indirect, and distal influences on motivation and performance.

"Hot" Theories: Mood, Emotion, Affect

Before we move into a discussion of what we know about mood, emotion, and affect, it is important that we define what we mean by these terms. We borrow from George and Brief

(1996) the definition of *mood* as a pervasive and generalized affective state, which is influenced by situational factors, but not directed at specific targets. Mood is distinct from emotion, which is directed at someone or something. Affect, on the other hand, is generally agreed to include components of both mood and emotions (Weiss & Brief, in press). So, we can think of *affect* as being a more general term for "feelings," and we can think of *mood* and *emotion* as particular kinds of feelings: The first is a more generalized overall feeling state, while the second is a feeling that is directed at some target.

One issue that has not been well understood relates to the sequence of events surrounding mood, emotion, motivation, and performance. For example, some research has found that affect is influenced by and follows performance (e.g., Fisher & Noble, 2000a; Locke & Latham, 1990). Other research has found affect to influence performance (e.g., Erez et al., 1999). Most likely there is a reciprocal relationship between affect and performance, with some types of emotion and mood more likely to be antecedent to performance-related constructs and other types more likely to be a consequence of it. Some of the discrepancy in findings in this area may be due to the time frame used in measuring affect. As Weiss and Cropanzano (1996) discussed, the impact of affect is immediate—it influences a person when that person is experiencing the affective state. The influence of some kinds of affect is also much stronger than rational analysis at a given moment in time (Loewenstein, 1996). Therefore, research that examines the relationship between affect and other constructs needs to take a more immediate, moment-by-moment perspective rather than a cumulative one. The use of experience sampling and mood diaries (e.g., Weiss et al., 1999; Fisher & Noble, 2000a, 2000b) should be encouraged to tease out some of these relationships.

In general, the research on affect has focused very narrowly on only a few moods and emotions, and most of these moods and emotions have been positive in nature. A couple of intriguing studies have examined the influence of negative affect on work-related outcomes, but these are the exception. For example, George (1990) found that negative affect was a stronger predictor than positive affect of whether or not prosocial behaviors would be exhibited. Raghunathan and Pham (1999) showed that different kinds of negative moods led to different kinds of decision making: Sadness resulted in high-risk/high-reward preferences, while anxiety led to low-risk/low-reward choices. Recent research has also begun to examine the links between anger/frustration and violence on the job. Negative affect is not the only area that needs to be studied. The negative effects of the expression of positive emotions are also worthy of future study. Overall, we still don't know much about the motivational influences of a wide variety of affective states, including envy, fear, guilt, depression, love, compassion, pride, and gratitude, to name a few. Future research needs to help us understand the spectrum of mood and emotion and how these influence both motivation and performance.

"Cold" Theories: Individual Differences

At a broad level, individual differences can be thought of as stable internal characteristics that make each individual unique in behavior and attitude (Ozer & Reise, 1994). In this category are both need theories and dispositional theories. Dispositional theories can be further divided into those that are affective and those that are nonaffective. While affective dispositions are similar to the "hot" theories (which after all include "affect"), they differ in that they are more long-term and stable individual characteristics. In what follows, we discuss new directions of research for need and dispositional theories of individual difference.

Needs are one of the individual differences that received a lot of research years ago, but less has been done recently. Perhaps one of the best examples of new research that draws from need-theory ideas is work by Kanfer and her colleagues (Kanfer, Ackerman, & Heggestad, 1996; Kanfer & Heggestad, 1997; Wanberg, Kanfer, & Rotundo, 1999; Kanfer & Ackerman, in press; Kanfer & Heggestad, in press). Drawing on their research on the self-regulatory process, Kanfer et al. (1996) proposed that differences in self-regulatory ability might be due to individual differences in terms of "motivational skills." Further research indicated that these skills are influenced by motivational traits that fall into two primary "trait clusters": achievement and anxiety (Kanfer & Heggestad, 1997). These two trait clusters are remarkably similar to McClelland's ideas of approach and avoidance orientations. And like the research surrounding McClelland's theory, Kanfer and Heggestad showed support for the idea that "ideally motivated employees" have high achievement and low anxiety traits. Although most current research on individual differences does not directly assess needs as Murray, Maslow, Alderfer, McClelland, and others originally conceptualized them, some new trends, such as the one discussed here, indicate that need-theory concepts are being examined in other theoretical contexts.

As we reviewed the literature on personality and dispositional approaches to motivation, we observed that while this area was not the single biggest under the general topic of motivation (goal setting has that distinction), it is the fastest growing. There is currently quite a bit of attention being paid to individual differences, and there is every indication that this will continue to be the case for the foreseeable future. As Mount and Barrick (1998) state, "Understanding individual differences and their implications for behavior at work is one of the central tenets of our field, and personality characteristics are central to understanding individual differences" (p. 851).

There are at least two topics in the area of dispositions that stand out as needing more attention before we can draw any firm conclusions about their motivational effects. First, there is no clarity about whether the personality-performance findings discussed in the research are consistent across cultures. While Salgado's (1997) European meta-analysis concluded that conscientiousness predicted performance in the European Union, as it does in the United States, there is no evidence demonstrating this link in non-Western cultures. A cross-cultural study examining several personality scales between the United States and India found that while the scales themselves exhibited similar psychometric properties across the two groups, Indian respondents reported lower self-esteem and internal locus of control than their U.S. counterparts (Ghorpade, Hattrup, & Lackritz, 1999). The authors attributed this in part to India's collectivistic culture, where it is viewed as self-aggrandizing to esteem the self. But this also means that assuming similarities of personality traits across cultures may be inappropriate. More comparative studies need to be done before we can say anything with confidence on this topic.

A second topic in this area that is currently generating quite a bit of research is the genetic influence on personality, including the effects of evolutionary psychology (Buss, Haselton, Shackelford, Bleske, & Wakefield, 1998). And the genetic research is also clear that nonaffective dispositions, including work values (Keller, Bouchard, Arvey, Segal, & Dawes, 1992) and traits including extroversion and neuroticism (Viken, Rose, Kaprio, & Koskenvuo, 1994; Loehlen, 1989) also have high heritability coefficients (up to .50). More recent research in psychology has turned toward understanding behavior from an evolutionary perspective. From this perspective, Nicholsen (1997) argued persuasively for a gene-based understanding of personality and behavior, including gender differences, in-group/out-group, and status seeking. Because of the strong genetic influence that has been documented for so many individual differences, it would seem a relatively short step for an evolutionary psychology perspective to be applied in this domain.

"EXTERNAL" MOTIVATIONAL THEORIES

Up until this point, our discussion of new directions in motivation research has centered on subareas that emphasize internal attributes of the individual. Now we shift conceptual gears away from the internal theories of motivation and toward those that focus on external aspects of the task or situation: job design and social context approaches.

Job Design

Job design centers on "the characteristics of jobs and how these affect people's attitudes and behavior" (Wall & Martin, 1994, p. 158). The research during the 1990s tested and refined the Job Characteristics Model (JCM) presented by Hackman and Oldham (1976) that emerged as the major theory in this area. It is clear from this research that job attributes influence motivation and that intrinsic motivation, in particular, can be a powerful prod for effort and persistence. However, two questions have persisted over the years that are setting the direction of new research: (1) What exactly constitutes job design? and (2) What precisely is intrinsic motivation?

A number of authors have attempted to redefine job design as described in the JCM. Wong and Campion (1991), for example, suggested that jobs are really made up of tasks and that we need to examine how these tasks are related to one another to understand their motivational impact. Key dimensions were the value of the separate tasks, their interdependence, and their similarity. Ilgen and Hollenbeck (1992) also attempted to expand our thinking about job design. They included the job characteristics but also included role expectations and, in that manner, incorporated both objective attributes and the social information provided by others. Griffin and McMahan (1994) also suggest a more comprehensive model that includes social comparisons and variables like instrumentalities. However, to date, there is little evidence on the contributions made by these expanded analyses.

Another focus has been the topic of feedback. It is one of the five core attributes of the JCM but also part of goal-setting, reinforcement, expectancy, and efficacy theories as well. As such, it is seen as having broad motivational implications. Of greatest interest to job design researchers has been the type of feedback and how the employee perceives it. Kruger and DeNisi's (1996) meta-analysis shows a positive effect of feedback interventions on performance but lots of variance in that relationship. They suggest that feedback that makes people focus on themselves may be distracting and have negative effects, while task-related feedback could be helpful. Moye, Joseph, and Bartol (1999) provided empirical support for these ideas. Similarly, Harackiewicz, Samsome, and Manderlink (1985) have suggested that feedback that promotes one's sense of personal competency, as opposed to being seen as controlling, can positively influence intrinsic motivation. Thus, the effects of feedback are dependent on how it is given and the focus of the information.

One contextual variable that is being used frequently as a feedback source is monitoring. With advances in technology, video, audio (e.g. phone), and electronic monitoring are increasing in use (Aiello, 1993). While such monitoring may increase performance in some situations (e.g. Eden & Moriah, 1996), there is some indication it increases stress (Aiello & Kolb, 1995), and the more that employees feel they can control it, the less negative its effect on task satisfaction (Stanton & Barnes-Farrell, 1996).

The other main focus has been on such psychological states as intrinsic motivation that are supposedly a result of enriched jobs. A couple of studies tested whether the JCM states of meaningfulness, responsibility, and knowledge of results mediated the job attribute $\rightarrow$ outcome relationship as predicted by Hackman and Oldham (1976). Johns, Xie, and Fang (1992) and Renn and Vandenberg (1995) both found support for this proposition, although the latter study found only partial mediation. Renn and Vandenberg (1995) also suggest that not all three states need to be experienced at the same time for positive attitudes to result.

Some recent research also points out that there are moderators for the task attribute, outcome relationships. For example, Liden, Wayne, and Bradway (1997) demonstrated that the effects of group control of decisions on performance were moderated by task interdependence (people had to interact and coordinate with one another). Similarly, Langfred (1999) found that interdependence moderated the autonomy, group effectiveness relationship. A recent study by Wright and Cordery (1999) demonstrated that more control and autonomy influenced intrinsic motivation and job satisfaction only when there was high production uncertainty. Thus, the effects of these core job dimensions on motivational states and performance outcomes seem to depend on factors like interdependence and uncertainty.

Finally, the construct of empowerment has been studied frequently in the 1990s, and it appears to have some very clear similarities to what is meant by intrinsic motivation. Thomas and Velthouse (1990) suggested that four key dimensions compose the empowerment construct: meaning, competence, choice, and impact. Note that the competence and control aspects of intrinsic motivation suggested by Malone and Lepper (1987) correspond nicely to the competence and choice ideas in empowerment. In addition, meaningfulness is one of the JCM psychological states and is similar to the meaning idea of empowerment, while impact is similar to the JCM attribute of significance. Conger (2000) has reviewed the research on the positive effects of empowerment for individuals, and Kirkman and Rosen (1999) demonstrate similar effects for teams. Thus, empowerment may turn out to be a construct that captures the intrinsic motivation construct but provides more precision as to what is included or omitted.

One thing is very clear. People like interesting, challenging work and they like having some control over what they do. Kovach (1997) reported that employees ranked interesting work as the most important job attribute out of 10. Judge (2000) goes so far as to say that there is "only one clear aspect of the work environment that consistently influences job satisfaction—the intrinsic challenge present in the work itself" (p. 2). It appears that this intrinsic motivation is in many ways a different source of motivation than the outcome-oriented sources suggested by expectancy, goal, reinforcement, and equity approaches. In this sense, it may complement and augment traditional motivational interventions and practices.

Social Theories: Groups and Culture

This last category of motivational theories focuses on those frameworks that emphasize characteristics external to the individual but influenced by other people rather than by aspects of the job itself (like job design). Justice, rewards, and reinforcement are discussed at length elsewhere in this volume. Therefore, new directions in the areas of groups and culture are the last area we will cover. There are two topics in the area of groups and culture that are receiving increased research attention. First is the social identity approach to groups, which says that individuals' self-concept is partly determined by the characteristics of the groups with which they identify. The second area that is receiving increased research attention is that of group-level cognitive constructs, such as group efficacy, group esteem, and group memory. Both of these approaches are discussed briefly below.

Recent research using a social identity theory approach to motivation has its roots in the seminal article by Ashforth and Mael (1989), which emphasized the relationship between organizational membership and the self-concept. Essentially, this theory posits that people define themselves as members of social categories and then attribute characteristics that are typical of these categories to themselves (van Knippenberg, 1999). Once people identify with a group or organization, they tend to act in accordance with that identity, doing things that would be in the best interest of the group or organization in question. Van Knippenberg extends this reasoning to motivation, arguing that since high performance is typically assumed to be in the best interest of the organization, we should find higher levels of motivation among those with a stronger organizational identity. His study assessing the relationship between motivation and organizational identification shows just that (van Knippenberg & van Schie, 1999). The connection between social identity and motivated performance is strengthened by the results from field research conducted by Robinson and O'Leary-Kelly (1998). They found that groups with more antisocial behavior influence individuals to exhibit these behaviors. Apparently social identification can create motivation for both positive and negative performance outcomes.

The second new research direction in the area of group motivation relates to shared cognitions. We have already discussed in this chapter the relationship between group efficacy and performance. Current research on group efficacy is demonstrating that group processes such as coordination lead to higher group efficacy (Seijts, Latham, & Whyte, 2000). Other group-level constructs are also being explored. For example, group esteem has been shown to be related to group decision-making outcomes (Wiesenfeld & Turnheim, 1995), and couples in a close dating relationship have been shown to have a transactive memory (i.e., "a shared system for encoding, storing and retrieving information," p. 923) that is better than either individual's memory (Wegner, Erber, & Raymond, 1991). One of the questions this research has raised is what collective cognitions really mean. Is it possible that groups themselves actually think, remember, or evaluate? Several researchers have written about the complexities involved in doing research on these social cognitions. In general, these reviews argue that the notion of group mind is real and can be demonstrated (Gruenfeld & Hollingshead, 1993), but caution that more conceptual work to understand the notion of shared cognition needs to be done (Klimoski & Mohammed, 1994). Recently, Morgeson and Hofmann (1999) have proposed that group-level cognitions share a similar function to their individual level counterparts but differ in their structure. That is, these individual and group-level constructs may influence individual and group-level behavior in similar ways, but they manifest themselves in different ways depending on the level of analysis. For example, organizations do not "remember" past events, but individual organization members may recall past events through their interactions with one another. So, group-level cognitions occur only in the context of ongoing events and interactions between group members. Overall, the theory and research in this area is provocative, and we would join with others in encouraging more conceptual and empirical work in the area of collective cognitions.

CONCLUSION

The field of motivation is still vibrant and interesting. We have confidence about the meaning of the construct and how it operates. We have a good idea of the mechanisms that create it and sustain it. Recently, the areas of affect, goal setting (especially self-regulation and on-line behavior), individual differences, and justice have captured our attention, while need theories, expectancy theory, and job design have received less attention.

A variety of general principles emerge from our review. First, goals are a major factor on the motivational landscape. Almost every approach to this topic includes goals. Humans are goal setters and goal seekers. People also prefer pleasure to pain and will seek positive outcomes and states and avoid negative ones. Third, we prefer mastery and control to uncertainty and ambiguity. Mastery and control are direct antecedents of our expectations, confidence, and efficacy. We also prefer interesting, stimulating, and satisfying to boring, stressful, and repetitious activities. In addition, we are constantly involved in social interaction and social comparison. We want to have a positive view of ourselves and be liked by others and treated fairly. The social context is a major source of such information. And finally, we are all unique with genetic and personal backgrounds that shape our wants, desires, and reactions to events. These individual differences play a crucial role in understanding motivation and variation in motivation.

Given these different principles and perspectives, it seems unlikely to us that one general theory of motivation is likely to emerge. More likely, orientations will evolve around different perspectives. Ambrose and Kulik (1989), for example, suggest we should focus on classes of behavior such as effort or citizenship behaviors. Mitchell (1997) discussed how different theories could be grouped around the motivational processes of arousal, attention and direction, and intensity and persistence. Others have suggested that we should focus either on the intention/choice activities (prior to action) or the actual on-line behavioral activities (Wilpert, 1995).

The idea of tensions, which we presented in this paper, incorporates some of these orientations. Included are the internal/external, task/social, thoughtful/not rational, hot/cold, and prechoice/on-line distinctions. Presumably, elements of the person and context will help to determine the extent to which one or the other (or both) sides of these dichotomies is operating.

But after doing this review, a number of other "perspectives" occurred to us. Different theories come to mind based on the type of questions we ask. Here are three such questions:

1. What is the underlying dynamic? Some theories seem to focus on things that "pull" us, like social norms (pleasing others) or goals or rewards, while others emphasize a "push" dynamic, like genes, affect, and personality. Are there common motivational principles around which we could group these push or pull orientations?

2. How is time included? Theories like reinforcement and equity require knowledge of the past; the social context, mood, and affect are more "in the moment," while goal setting, efficacy, and expectancy are future oriented. Understanding the contextual and personal factors that trigger our time orientation may help us to predict which theories are operating at a given time for a given person.

3. How malleable are motivational constructs? Some internal (e.g. genes, personality) and external (e.g. job design, norms) motivational variables may be hard to change, while other internal (e.g. mood) or external (e.g. rewards) variables may be easier to change. A better understanding of malleability can help us choose motivational interventions that will have impact.

The above questions are meant to prod our thinking. We believe the field of motivation needs to reorient itself. We know many of the basic principles. But most of the research seems to use the "silo" approach—the researchers test or extend an existing theory and very little integrative or cross-fertilization takes place. Some promising examples are the work of Kanfer and her colleagues (Kanfer & Heggestad, 1997), looking at learning, motivation, and abilities, or the work of Barrick and his colleagues on personality and goal setting (Barrick, Mitchell & Stewart, 2001). More of this type of work is needed.

Finally, specific questions need more research. How do thoughtful processes become more routine? What mechanisms are involved with the allocation of effort and time over tasks? How do emotions such as anger and guilt (e.g. over injustice) influence constructs like goal acceptance or self-efficacy? How do distal constructs like personality influence more proximal states like expectancies or goal commitment? How does the task and social context influence one's mood? These, and many other questions, need more research to be answered.

And, in closing, it is important to point out that we need to keep our eye on practical issues as well. Much more field and longitudinal research is needed to assess the effects of individual motivational interventions and combinations of interventions. We need better diagnostic models and theories evolving from applications. Such research will help us to answer the important questions of when and where particular motivational interventions work as well as why they work.

References

Aiello, J. R. (1993). Computer-based work monitoring: Electronic surveillance and its effects. *Journal of Applied Social Psychology*, 23, 499–507.

Aiello, J. R., & Kolb, K. J. (1995). Electronic performance monitoring and social context: Impact on productivity and stress. *Journal of Applied Psychology*, 80, 339–353.

Ambrose, M. L., & Kulik, C. T. (1999). Old friends, new faces: Motivation research in the 1990s. *Journal of Management*, 25, 231–292.

Ashforth B. E., & Mael, F. (1989). Social identity theory and the organization. *Academy of Management Review*, 14, 20–39.

Bargh, J. A. (1994). The Four Horsemen of automaticity: Awareness, efficiency, intention, and control in social cognition. In R. S. Wyer, Jr., & T. K. Srull (Eds.), *Handbook of Social Cognition* (2nd ed., pp. 1–40). Hillsdale, NJ: Erlbaum.

Bargh, J. A. (1999). The cognitive monster. In S. Chaiken & Y. Trope (Eds.), *Dual Process Theories in Social Psychology* (pp. 361–382). New York: Guilford Press.

Bargh, J. A., & Chartrand, T. L. (1999). The unbearable automaticity of being. *American Psychologist*, 54:7, 462–479.

Bargh, J. A. & Gollwitzer, P. M. (1994). Environmental control of goal-directed action: Automatic and strategic contingencies between situations and behavior. *Nebraska Symposium on Motivation*, 41, 71–124.

Barrick, M. R., Mitchell, T. R., & Stewart, G. L. (2001). Situational and motivational influences on trait-behavior relationships. Paper presented at the annual meetings of the Academy of Management, Washington, D.C. August.

Brett, J. F. & VandeWalle, D. (1999). Goal orientation and goal content as predictors of performance in a training program. *Journal of Applied Psychology*, 84:6, 863–873.

Brockner, J. (1988). *Self-esteem at Work: Research, Theory and Practice.* Lexington, MA: Lexington Books.

Brunstein, J. C. (1999). Motivation and performance following failure: The effortful pursuit of self-defining goals. Paper presented at 3rd conference of work motivation. Sydney, Australia, June.

Brunstein, J. C., Dangelmayer, G., & Schultheiss, O. C. (1996). Personal goals and social support in close relationships: Effects on relationship mood and marital satisfaction. *Journal of Personality and Social Psychology,* 71:5, 1006–1019.

Brunstein, J. C., & Gollwitzer, P. M. (1996). Effects of failure on subsequent performance: The importance of self-defining goals. *Journal of Personality and Social Psychology,* 70, 395–408.

Brunstein, J. C., Schultheiss, O. C., Grassmann, R. (1998). Personal goals and emotional well-being: The moderating role of motive dispositions. *Journal of Personality and Social Psychology,* 75:2, 494–508.

Buckley, M. R., Fedor, D. B., Veres, J. G., Weise, D. S., & Carraher, S. M. (1998). Investigating newcomers' expectations and job-related outcomes. *Journal of Applied Psychology,* 83, 452–461.

Buss, D. M., Haselton, M. G., Shackelford, T. K., Bleske, A. L., & Wakefield, J. C. (1998). Adaptations, expectations, and spandrels. *American Psychologist,* 53(5), 533–548.

Carver, C. S., & Scheier, M. F. (1981). *Attention and Self-regulation: A Control-Theory Approach to Human Behavior.* New York: Springer-Verlag.

Carver, C. S., & Scheier, M. F. (1990). Origins and functions of positive and negative affect: A control-process view. *Psychological Review,* 97, 19–35.

Conger, J. A. (in press). Motivate performance through empowerment. In E. A. Locke (Ed.), *Basic Principles of Organizational Behavior: A Handbook.* Oxford, U.K.: Blackwell.

Deci, E. L. (1980). *The Psychology of Self-determination.* Lexington, MA: Lexington.

Diefendorff, J. M., & Lord, R. G. (2000). The volitional effects of planning on performance and goal commitment. National SIOP meeting, New Orleans, LA.

Dweck, C. S. (1986). Motivational processes affecting learning. *American Psychologist,* 41, 1040–1048.

Eden, D. (1996). From self efficacy to measure efficacy: Internal and external sources of general and specific efficacy. Paper presented at the 1996 Academy of Management Meeting, Cincinnati, OH.

Eden. D. (1999). The impact of self-efficacy on work motivation theory and research. Academy of Management Annual Meeting, August, Chicago, IL.

Eden, D., & Granat-Flomin, R. (2000). Augmenting means efficacy to improve service performance among computer users: A field experiment in the public sector. Presented at the Annual conference of the Society of Industrial and Organizational Psychology, New Orleans, LA.

Eden, D., & Moriah, L. (1996). Impact of internal auditing of branch bank performance: A field experiment. *Organizational Behavior and Human Decision Processes,* 68, 262–271.

Erez, A., Isen, A. M., & Purdy, C. (1999). The influence of positive-affect on expectancy motivation: Integrating affect and cognition into motivation theories. Paper presented at the 1999 Academy of Management Annual Meeting, Chicago, IL.

Fisher, C. D., & Noble, C. S. (2000a). Affect and performance: A within persons analysis. Presented at the Academy of Management Annual Meeting, Toronto, ON.

Fisher, C. D., & Noble, C. S. (2000b). Emotion and the "Illusory Correlation" between job satisfaction and job performance. Presented at the 2nd Conference on Emotions in Organisational Life, Toronto, ON.

Ford, M. E. (1992). *Motivating Humans: Goals, Emotions and Personal Agency Beliefs.* Newbury Park, CA: Sage.

Frese, M., & Zapf, D. (1994). Action as the core of work psychology. In M. D. Dunnette, L. M. Hough, & H. Triandis (Eds.), *Handbook of Industrial and Organizational Psychology* (Vol. 4). Palo Alto, CA: Consulting Psychologist Press.

George, J. M. (1990). Personality, affect and behavior in groups. *Journal of Applied Psychology,* 75, 107–116.

George, J. M., & Brief, A. P. (1996). Motivational agendas in the workplace: The effects of feelings on focus of attention and work motivation. *Research in Organizational Behavior,* 18, 75–109.

Ghorpade, J., Hattrup, K., & Lackritz, J. R. (1999). The use of personality measures in cross-cultural research: A test of three personality scales across two countries. *Journal of Applied Psychology,* 84:5, 670–679.

Gilliland, S. W., & Landis, R. S. (1992). Quality and quantity goals in a complex decision task: Strategies and outcomes. *Journal of Applied Psychology,* 77, 672–681.

Gist, M. E., & Mitchell, T. R. (1992). Self-efficacy: A theoretical analysis of its determinants and malleability. *Academy of Management Review,* 17, 183–211.

Gollwitzer, P. M. (1990). Action phases and mind sets. In E. T. Higgins & R. M. Sorrentino (Eds.), *Handbook of Motivation and Cognition: Foundations of Social Behavior* (Vol. 2, pp. 53–92). New York: Guilford.

Gollwitzer, P. M. (1993). Goal achievement: The role of intentions. In W. Stroebe & M. Hewstone (Eds.), *European Review of Social Psychology* (Vol. 4, pp. 141–185). Chichester, England: Wiley.

Gollwitzer, P. M. (1999). Implementation intentions: Strong effects of simple plans. *American Psychologist,* 54:7, 493–503.

Goltz, S. M. (1999). Self-efficacy's mediating role in success bred recommitment of resources to a failing course of action. Society for Industrial Organizational Psychology Annual Meeting, Atlanta, GA.

Griffin, R. W., & McMahan, G. C. (1994). Motivation through work design. In J. Greenberg (Ed.), *Organizational Behavior: The State of the Science:* 23–43. Hillsdale, NJ: Erlbaum, 40: 287–332.

Gruenfeld, D. H., & Hollingshead, A. B. (1993). Sociocognition in work groups: The evolution of group and integrative complexity and its relation to task performance. *Small Group Research,* 24:3, 383–405.

Gurin, P., & Brim, O. G., Jr. (1984). Change of self in adulthood: The example of sense of control. In P. B. Baltes & O. G. Brim, Jr. (Eds.), *Life-span Development and Behavior* (Vol. 6, pp. 281–334). New York: Academic Press.

Hackman, J. R., & Oldham, G. R. (1976). Motivation through the design of work: Test of a theory. *Organizational Behavior and Human Performance,* 16, 250–279.

Harackiewicz, J. M., Sansone, C., & Manderlink, G. (1985). Competence, achievement orientation, and intrinsic motivation: A process analysis. *Journal of Personality and Social Psychology,* 48, 493–508.

Harackiewicz, J. M., Barron, K. E., Carter, S. M., Lehto, A. T., & Elliot, A. J. (2000, in press). Predictors and consequences of achievement goals in the college classroom: Maintaining interest and making the grade. *Journal of Personality and Social Psychology.*

Harter, S. (1982). The perceived competence scale for children. *Child Development,* 53, 87–97.

Hoover, P., Johnson, D. S., & Schmidt, A. (1998a). Goal orientation effects on motivation: When tasks are dynamically complex. Society for Industrial and Organizational Psychology Annual Conference, Dallas, TX.

Hoover, P., Johnson, D. S., & Schmidt, A. (1998b). Goal orientation and task complexity effects on motivation, affect and performance. Society for Industrial and Organizational Psychology Annual Conference, Dallas, TX.

Ilgen, D. R., & Hollenbeck, J. R. (1992). The structure of work: Job design and roles. In M. Dunnette & L. Hough (Eds.), *Handbook of Industrial and Organizational Psychology* (Vol. 2, pp. 165–207). Palo Alto, CA: Consulting Psychologists Press.

Ilgen, D. R., Major, D. A., & Tower, S. L. (1994). The cognitive revolution in organizational behavior. In J. Greenberg (Ed.), *Organizational Behavior: The State of the Science* (pp. 1–22). Hillsdale, NJ: Erlbaum.

Johns, G., Xie, J. L., & Fang, Y. (1992). Mediating and moderating effects in jobs design. *Journal of Management,* 18, 657–676.

Judge, T. A. (in press). Promote job satisfaction through mental challenge. In E. A. Locke (Ed.), *Basic Principles of Organizational Behavior: A Handbook.* Oxford, U.K.: Blackwell.

Kanfer, R. (1990). Motivation theory and industrial and organizational psychology. In M. D. Dunnette & L. D. Hough (Eds.), *Handbook of Industrial and Organizational Psychology* (pp. 75–170). Palo Alto, CA: Consulting Psychologist Press.

Kanfer, R. (1996). Self-regulatory and other non-ability determinants of skill acquisition. In J. A. Bargh & P. M. Gollwitzer (Eds.), *The Psychology of Action: Linking Cognition and Motivation to Behavior* (pp. 404–423). New York: Guilford.

Kanfer, R., & Ackerman, P. L. (1989). Motivation and cognitive abilities: An integrative/aptitude–treatment interaction approach to skill acquisition. *Journal of Applied Psychology* (monograph), 74, 657–690.

Kanfer, R. & Ackerman, P. L. (in press). Individual differences in work motivation: Further explorations of a trait framework. *Applied Psychology: An International Review.*

Kanfer, R., Ackerman, P. L., & Heggestad, E. D. (1996). Motivational skills and self-regulation for learning: A trait perspective. *Learning and Individual Differences,* 8:3, 185–209.

Kanfer, R., & Heggestad, E. D. (1997). Motivational traits and skills: A person-centered approach in work motivation. *Research in Organizational Behavior* (Vol. 19, pp. 1–56). Greenwich, CT: JAI Press.

Kanfer, R., & Heggestad, E. (in press). Individual differences in trait motivation: Development of the Motivational Trait Questionnaire (MTQ). *International Journal of Educational Research.*

Keller, L. M., & Bouchard, T. J. Jr., Arvey, R. D., Segal, N. L., & Dawes, R. V. (1992). Work values: Genetic and environmental influences. *Journal of Applied Psychology,* 77, 79–88.

Kirkman, B. L., & Rosen, B. (1999). Beyond self-management: Antecedents and consequences of team empowerment. *Academy of Management Journal, 42,* 58–74.

Klein, H. J. (1989). An integrated control theory model of work motivation. *Academy of Management Review, 14,* 150–172.

Klimoski, R., & Mohammed, S. (1994). Team mental model: Construct or metaphor? *Journal of Management, 20:2,* 403–437.

Kovach, D. A. (1997). Do you know your staff? *Industry Trends,* September 26.

Kruger, A. N., & DeNisi, A. (1996). The effects of feedback on performance: A historical review, a meta-analysis and a preliminary feedback intervention theory. *Psychological Bulletin, 119,* 254–284.

Langfred, C. W. (1999). Work group design and autonomy: A field study of the interaction between task interdependence and group autonomy. Paper presented at the National Meeting of the Academy of Management, August, Chicago, IL.

Lee, T. W., Locke, E. A., & Phan, S. H. (1997). Explaining the assigned goal-incentive interaction: The role of self-efficacy and personal goals. *Journal of Management, 23,* 541–559.

Lewin, K., Dembo, T., Festinger, L., & Sears, P. S. (1944). Level of aspiration: In J. McV. Hunt (Ed.), *Personality and the Behavioral Disorders* (Vol. 1, pp. 333–378). New York: Ronald.

Liden, R. C., Wayne, S. J., & Bradway, L. K. (1997). Task interdependence as a moderator of the relation between group control and performance. *Human Relations, 50,* 169–181.

Locke, E. A. (1991). Goal theory versus control theory: Contrasting approaches to understanding work motivation. *Motivation and Emotion, 15,* 9–28.

Locke, E. A. (1996). Motivation through conscious goal setting. *Applied & Preventive Psychology, 5,* 117–124.

Locke, E. A., & Latham, G. P. (1990). *A Theory of Goal Setting and Task Performance.* Englewood Cliffs, NJ: Prentice Hall.

Loehlen, J. C. (1989). Partitioning environmental and genetic contributions to behavioral development. *American Psychologist, 44,* 1285–1292.

Loewenstein, G. (1996). Out of control: Visceral influences on behavior. *Organizational Behavior and Human Decision Processes, 65,* 272–292.

Lord, R. G., & Hanges, P. J. (1987). A control system model of organizational motivation: Theoretical development and applied implications. *Behavioral Science, 32,* 161–178.

Lord, R. G., & Kernan, M. C. (1987). Scripts as determinants of purposeful behavior in organizations. *Academy of Management Review, 12,* 265–277.

Malone, T. W., & Lepper, M. R. (1987). Making learning fun: A taxonomy of intrinsic motivations for learning. In R. E. Snow & M. J. Farr (Eds.), *Aptitude, Learning, and Instruction: Conative and Affective Process Analysis.* (Vol. III, pp. 223–253). Hillsdale, NJ: Erlbaum.

Mitchell, T. R. (1997). Matching motivational strategies with organizational contexts. *Research in Organizational Behavior, 19,* 57–149.

Mitchell, T. R., & Daniels, D. (2002) Motivation. In W. C. Borman, D. R. Ilgen, & R. J. Klimoski (Eds.), *Comprehensive Handbook of Psychology: Industrial and Organizational Psychology,* (5th ed. Vol. 12). New York: John Wiley & Sons.

Mitchell, T. R., Hopper H., Daniels, D., George-Falvy, J., & James, L. R. (1994). Predicting self-efficacy and performance during skill acquisition. *Journal of Applied Psychology, 79:4,* 506–517.

Mitchell, T. R., & Silver, W. S. (1990). Individual and group goals when workers are interdependent: Effects on task strategies and performance. *Journal of Applied Psychology, 75,* 185–193.

Mitchell, T. R., Thompson K., & George-Falvy, J. (2000, in press). Goal setting: Theory and practice. In C. L. Cooper and E. A. Locke (Eds.), *Industrial and Organizational Psychology: Linking Theory with Practice.* Blackwell: Oxford, UK.

Morgeson, F. P., & Hofmann, D. A. (1999). The structure and function of collective constructs: Implications for multilevel research and theory development. *Academy of Management Review, 24:2,* 249–265.

Mount, M. K., & Barrick, M. R. (1998). Five reasons why the "Big Five" article has been frequently cited. *Personnel Psychology, 51:4,* 849–858.

Moye, N. A., Joseph J. E., & Bartol, K. M. (1999). Understanding how feedback cue and sign affect performance, cognition and affective reactions. Paper presented at the Annual Meeting of the Society for Industrial and Organizational Psychology. Atlanta, April.

Nease, A. A., Mudgett, B. O., & Quinones, M. A. (1999). Relationships among feedback sign, self-efficacy, and acceptance of performance feedback. *Journal of Applied Psychology, 84:5,* 806–814.

Nicholson, N. (1997). Hunter-gatherers of the organization: The challenge of evolutionary psychology for management theory and practice. Paper presented at the National Meetings of the Academy of Management. Boston, August.

Ozer, D. J., & Reise, S. P. (1994). Personality assessment. *Annual Review of Psychology, 45,* 357–388.

Parker, S. K. (1998). Enhancing role breadth self-efficacy: The roles of job enrichment and other organizational interventions. *Journal of Applied Psychology,* 83:6, 835–852.

Phillips, J. M. (1998). Effects of realistic job previews on multiple organizational outcomes: A meta-analysis. *Academy of Management Journal, 41,* 673–690.

Phillips, J. M., Hollenbeck, J. R., & Ilgen, D. R. (1996). Prevalence and prediction of positive discrepancy creation: Examining a discrepancy between two self-regulation theories. *Journal of Applied Psychology, 81,* 498–511.

Pinder, C. G. (1998). *Work Motivation in Organizational Behavior.* Upper Saddle River, NJ: Prentice Hall.

Raghunathan, R., & Pham, M. T. (1999). All negative moods are not equal: Motivational influences of anxiety and sadness on decision making. *Organizational Behavior and Human Decision Processes, 79,* 56–77.

Renn, R. W., & Vandenberg, R. J. (1995). The critical psychological states: An underrepresented component in Job Characteristics Model research. *Journal of Management, 21,* 279–303.

Robinson, S. L., & O'Leary-Kelly, A. M. (1998). Monkey see, monkey do: The influence of work groups on the anti-social behavior of employees. *Academy of Management Journal, 41,* 658–672.

Roney, C. R. R., Higgins, E. T., & Shah, J. (1995). Goals and framing: How outcome focus influences motivation and emotion. *Journal of Personality and Social Psychology, 21,* 1151–1160.

Salgado, J. F. (1997). The five factor model of personality and job performance in the European Community. *Journal of Applied Psychology,* 82:1, 30–43.

Seijts, G. H., & Latham, G. P. (2000). The effects of goal setting and group size on performance in a social dilemma. *Canadian Journal of Behavioral Science, 32,* 104–116.

Seits, G. H., Latham, G. P., & Whyte, G. (2000). The effect of self- and group-efficacy on group performance in a mixed motive situation. *Human Performance, 13,* 279–298.

Seta, J. J., Seta, C. E., & Donaldson, S. (1992). The implications of a resource-investment analysis of goal value for performance in audience and solitary settings. *Basic and Applied Social Psychology, 13,* 145–164.

Shalley, C. E. (1995). Effects of coaction, expected evaluation and goal setting on creativity and productivity. *Academy of Management Journal, 38,* 483–503.

Skinner, B. F., Wellborn, J. G., & Connell, J. P. (1990). What it takes to do well in school and whether I've got it: A process model of perceived control and children's engagement and achievement in school. *Journal of Educational Psychology, 82,* 22–32.

Stanton, J. M., & Barnes-Farrell, J. L. (1996). Effects of electronic performance monitoring on personal control, task satisfaction and task performance. *Journal of Applied Psychology, 81,* 738–745.

Stone, D. N. (1994). Overconfidence in initial self-efficacy judgments: Effects on decision processes and performance. *Organizational Behavior and Human Decision Processes, 59,* 452–474.

Tabernero, C., & Wood, R. E. (1998). Role of conceptions of ability in self-regulation and performance on a complex task. Academy of Management Annual Meeting, San Diego.

Thomas, K. M., & Mathieu, J. E. (1994). Role of causal attributions in dynamic self-regulation and goal processes. *Journal of Applied Psychology, 79,* 812–818.

Thomas, K. W., & Velthouse, B. A. (1990). Cognitive elements of empowerment: An "interactive" model of intrinsic task motivation. *Academy of Management Review, 15,* 666–681.

Trafimow, D., & Sniezek, J. A. (1994). Perceived expertise and its effect on confidence. *Organizational Behavior and Human Decision Processes, 57,* 290–302.

VandeWalle, D. (1999). Goal orientation comes of age for adults: A literature review. Academy of Management Annual Meeting, Chicago, IL.

VandeWalle, D., Brown, S. P., Cron, W. L., & Slocum, J. W. Jr. (1999). The influence of goal orientation and self-regulation tactics on sales performance: A longitudinal field test. *Journal of Applied Psychology, 84,* 249–259.

VandeWalle, D., & Cummings, L. L. (1997). A test of the influence of goal orientation on the feedback seeking process. *Journal of Applied Psychology, 82,* 390–400.

Van Knippenberg, D. (1999). Work motivation and performance: A social identity perspective. Presented at the National Academy of Management Meeting. Chicago, IL, August.

Van Knippenberg, D., & Van Schie, E. C. M. (1999). Foci and correlates of organizational identification. *Journal of Occupational and Organizational Psychology, 73,* 137–147.

Viken, R. J., Rose, R. J., Kaprio, J., & Koskenvuo, M. (1994). A developmental genetic analysis of adult personality: Extraversion and neuroticism from 18 to 59 years of age. *Journal of Personality and Social Psychology, 66,* 722–730.

Vroom, V. H. (1964). *Work and Motivation.* New York: Wiley.

Wall, T. D., & Martin, R. (1994). Job and work design. In C. L. Cooper and I. T. Robertson (Eds.), *Key Reviews in Managerial Psychology: Concepts and Research for Practice:* (pp. 158–188). Chichester, U.K.: John Wiley & Sons.

Wanberg, C. R., Kanfer, R., & Rotundo, M. (1999). Unemployed individuals: Motives, job-search competencies, and job-search constraints as predictors of job seeking and reemployment. *Journal of Applied Psychology,* 84:6, 897–910.

Wegge, J. (1999). Participation in group goal setting: Some novel findings and a comprehensive theory as a new ending to an old story. Third International Conference on Work Motivation. Sydney, Australia, June.

Wegner, D. M., Erber, R., & Raymond, P. (1991). Transactive memory in close relationships. *Journal of Personality and Social Psychology,* 61:6, 923–929.

Wegner, D. M. & Wheatley, T. (1999). Apparent mental causation: Sources of the experience of will. *American Psychologist,* 54:7, 480–492.

Weiss, H. M., & Brief, A. P. (2000, in press). Affect at work: An historical perspective. To appear in R. L. Payne & C. L. Cooper (Eds.), *Emotions at Work: Theory, Research, and Applications in Management.* Chichester, U.K.: John Wiley & Sons.

Weiss, H. M., & Cropanzano, R. (1996). Affective Events Theory: A theoretical discussion of the structure, causes and consequences of affective experiences at work. In B. M. Staw & L. L. Cummings (Eds.), *Research in Organizational Behavior, (*Vol. 18, pp. 1–74). Greenwich, CT: JAI Press.

Weiss, H. M., Nicholas, J. P., & Daus, C. S. (1999). An examination of the joint effects of affective experiences and job beliefs on job satisfaction and variations in affective experiences over time. *Organizational Behavior and Human Decision Processes,* 78, 1–24.

Wiesenfeld, B. M., & Turnheim, J. K. (1995). Group esteem: Strategic implications of positive collective evaluations. Presented at the National Academy of Management Annual Meeting. Vancouver, British Columbia, August.

Wilpert, B. (1995). Organizational behavior. *Annual Review of Psychology,* 46, 59–90.

Winters, D., & Latham, G. (1996). The effects of learning versus outcome goals on a simple versus a complex task. *Group and Organizational Management,* 21, 236–250.

Whyte, G. (1998). Recasting Janis's groupthink model: The key role of collective efficacy in decision fiascos. *Organizational Behavior and Human Decision Processes,* 73:2/3, 185–209.

Wong, C., & Campion, M. A. (1991). Development and test of a task level model of motivation job design. *Journal of Applied Psychology,* 76: 825–837.

Wood, R. E., Mento, A. J., & Locke, E. A. (1997). Task complexity as a moderator of goal effects: A meta-analysis. *Journal of Applied Psychology,* 72, 416–425.

Wright, B. M. & Cordery, J. L. (1999). Production uncertainty as a contextual moderator of employee reactions to job design. *Journal of Applied Psychology,* 84, 456–463.

Wright, P. M., George, J. M., Farnsworth, S. R., & McMahan, G. C. (1993). Productivity and extrarole behavior: The effects of goals and incentives on spontaneous helping. *Journal of Applied Psychology,* 78, 374–381.

Chapter Two

Conceptual Approaches to Motivation at Work

As with any topic of scientific inquiry, "motivation" requires theory and conceptual thinking. This is the substance of Chapter 2, where we present a set of articles that provide some of the most advanced analyses of different facets and perspectives on this topic. These kinds of interpretative essays are both useful and necessary before we proceed to the more empirically based research literature in subsequent chapters.

Just as "there are no universally accepted ways of presenting the various approaches to motivation" (per Mitchell and Daniels in Chapter 1), there is no single, accepted theory of work motivation. Instead, there are a number of theoretical and conceptual approaches that, in one way or another, are *relevant to* work motivation. Here, in Chapter 2, we include six of those approaches along with a detailed explication and analysis of each of them. In terms of the road map analogy mentioned in Chapter 1, one might say that each article provides a particular route to "the truth."

If we adopt Mitchell's categorization system (see Figure 1 in his article), one of the approaches covered in this chapter clearly qualifies as "Internal" and "Thoughtful," namely "goal setting" (Locke); one other could be classified as also "Internal" but "Not Rational," namely "intrinsic motivation" (Ryan and Deci). Three others are definitely "External" and "Social" in Mitchell's classification system: "equity theory" (Mowday and Colwell), "organizational justice" (Cropanzano and Rupp), and "reinforcement" (Komaki). However, and continuing with the maxim that there is no universally accepted, nor airtight and unambiguous, classification system of motivational approaches, we can note that the final article in this chapter, by Stajkovic and Luthans, actually combines elements of both "internal" and "external," since it talks about self-efficacy (internal) as part of a larger theoretical framework dealing with "social cognition" (external).

As described in Chapter 1, another potentially useful distinction among some motivational approaches—and a distinction often employed by organizational psychologists—is that between "content" and "process" theories. Thus, the article by Ryan and Deci on intrinsic motivation would fit under the heading of "content" theory because it focuses on *what* it is (the satisfaction of competency, autonomy, and relatedness needs) that provides motivation; four of the other five approaches presented in Chapter 2 could appropriately be placed under the label of "process" theory, since their primary emphasis is on *how* variables combine to influence motivation; and one approach—goal setting—has elements of both content (i.e., type of goal) and process (i.e., how the act of setting a goal helps to determine performance) approaches to motivation. Again, the content-process distinction is a helpful but not a totally satisfactory categorization scheme.

The key point that should be retained from the above discussion is this: Motivation in the work situation is a sufficiently complex phenomenon such that no single theoretical approach or classification system is adequate to fully understand the topic. Each of the different approaches supplies a helpful perspective to think about the topic and, especially, to gain insight into it. Each approach also leaves many unanswered questions, but that is exactly what makes the topic intrinsically interesting and one that can motivate students and researchers alike to learn more about it and develop applications that improve organizational functioning.

OVERVIEW OF THE READINGS

In the first article in this chapter, Ryan and Deci present the case for the importance of intrinsic motivation. The authors describe what they have termed "self-determination theory" (SDT) as an approach to understanding intrinsic motivation. SDT stresses the inherent and innate nature of human growth tendencies and the fundamental psychological needs of competence, autonomy, and relatedness. The theory also underscores the critical necessity for examining the social and organizational contexts that can facilitate or thwart these "positive developmental tendencies."

In the view of Ryan and Deci, "intrinsic motivation [is] the inherent tendency to seek out novelty and challenges, to extend and exercise one's capabilities, to explore and to learn." Such motivation, in SDT theory, can be contrasted directly with "extrinsic motivation," which "refers to the performance of an activity in order to attain some separable outcome." In other words, intrinsic motivation involves "doing an activity for the inherent satisfaction of the activity itself," whereas extrinsic motivation involves doing an activity for some contingent reward supplied as the result of carrying out the activity. (See the subsequent article in this chapter by Komaki on reinforcement theory.) The authors contend that the more that certain aspects or aims of extrinsic motivation can be internalized, or "owned," by the person, the more such motivation can take on the positive features of intrinsic motivation. Their theory suggests that such internalization can be nurtured by environments that support an individual's attainment of feelings of competence, autonomy, and relatedness. Conversely, the absence of organizational or environmental support for developing these feelings fosters conditions that can lead to alienation and disaffection.

The next article, by Mowday and Colwell, examines a theory—equity theory—that was originally developed by psychologist J. Stacy Adams in the 1960s. The article describes the basic formulation of the theory, which is grounded in the concept of social exchange processes, and summarizes a considerable body of related research. As the authors point out, Adams's equity theory focuses on people's reactions to the fairness of outcomes they receive in relation to their perception of the inputs they provide, especially when compared to the perceived outcomes/inputs that others receive. The emphasis of equity theory, therefore, is on the amount of outcome received in relation to input. In terms of the literature on organizational justice, equity theory is concerned with "distributive justice." Equity theory's strong focus on the social comparisons resulting from interactions or "exchanges" among people makes it relevant to many aspects of behavior in organizations, especially those involving the effects of compensation on individuals' levels of motivation for task performance.

While equity theory has made a considerable contribution to our understanding of work motivation and the practice of management over the last several decades, researchers' interest in the theory itself appears to have diminished somewhat in recent years. Nevertheless, however, equity theory has spawned studies in new and related areas that have attracted substantial scholarly attention of late. Cropanzano and Rupp, in the third article in this chapter, explore much of this work on the general topic of organizational justice. Organizational justice researchers distinguish among several different types of justice perceptions—for example, distributive justice, procedural justice, and interactional justice. Distributive justice, as was noted, is at the heart of equity theory and deals with the fairness of rewards (or punishments) "distributed" to employees. Procedural justice focuses on the perceived fairness of the processes through which distribution decisions are made. Finally, interactional justice (which some scholars contend is a subcategory of procedural justice) centers on the fairness of the interpersonal treatment received from others.

In their treatment of the topic of organizational justice, Cropanzano and Rupp discuss the recent research centering on the question of *why* people care about justice in the first place. In addition, the authors review research attempting to answer the question of *how* it is that justice perceptions are established and maintained. A number of models—such as referent cognitions theory, fairness theory, and fairness heuristic theory—have been proposed to explicate the associated psychological processes. Finally, Cropanzano and Rupp make the argument that it is reasonable to treat organizational justice as a motivation topic per se rather than as simply a related subject. Using prominent definitions of motivation, they contend that organizational justice meets criteria for inclusion in the general subject matter area of motivation.

In the fourth article in this chapter, Komaki discusses how reinforcement theory applies to the workplace. The primary emphasis in reinforcement theory is on how the environment can be "constructed" or modified to bring about particular types of effects on a person's behavior. For some time, there has been strong interest in applications of this theory in the everyday work environment. Komaki's article, based on research studies carried out over many years, highlights the issues and problems involved in the implementation of a reinforcement approach, especially those focusing on providing appropriate performance consequences and on obtaining responsive and reliable measures of performance on which to base those consequences. As the article demonstrates, the theory has been used as a basis to improve performance in a wide variety of work situations and on a wide set of target behaviors. Of particular interest, and representing a unique contribution of this article, is a section that explores the issue of how reinforcement theory can help us better understand and explain, from a motivational perspective, why employees do what they do. Komaki concludes her piece with four suggestions for improving our future knowledge of the operation and effects of reinforcement principles and procedures.

The following article by Locke provides an updated review of the findings from over 30 years of research on the effects of conscious goal setting on work performance. It was Locke, following the lead of psychologist T. A. Ryan, who in the mid-1960s introduced the concept of goal setting into the scholarly and research literature relating to performance in work settings. As it turned out, his focus on goal setting was quite consistent with the subsequent widespread adoption of a cognitive approach—the "cognitive revolution"—in the field of psychology. In this article, Locke summarizes some 14 findings that have emerged with reasonable consistency over the years, such as "the more difficult the goal, the greater the achievement," and "goal setting is most effective when there is feedback showing progress in relation to the goal." Toward the end of the article the author examines two issues that have generated considerable controversy over the years: whether assigned goals (vs. goals set by a participative process) will almost always diminish intrinsic motivation, and whether goal setting can ever be harmful. He answers, in effect, "no" to the first question and "yes, under some circumstances" to the second. Overall, the totality of evidence reviewed strongly supports the impact of deliberate intent and purpose on motivation to perform well.

The subject of the final article in this section, by Stajkovic and Luthans, is social cognitive theory (SCT) and its central concept, self-efficacy. SCT was formulated in the 1980s by social psychologist Albert Bandura, and, as its name implies, attempts to explain how individuals think about, or "cognitively process," information coming in from their social environment. Obviously, since work situations are almost always social, to some extent at least, SCT and self-efficacy are clearly relevant to motivated work behavior. The authors provide an overview of SCT, including a summary of five basic human capabilities involved in cognitively processing social information: symbolizing, forethought, vicarious learning, self-regulation, and self-reflection. Self-efficacy—"an individual's belief (confidence) about his or her capabilities to execute a specific task within a given context"—as a component of SCT is related to both self-regulation and self-refection capabilities.

Stajkovic and Luthans explain how self-efficacy affects work motivation and how it relates to other similar concepts prominent in the organizational behavior literature. In addition, they describe how self-efficacy can be measured and outline the types of experiences and information that appear to be critical in the formation of self-efficacy beliefs. Their article concludes with an overall summary of the quantitative evidence from a large number of studies that shows a strong, positive relationship between self-efficacy beliefs and performance of both individuals and groups.

Self-Determination Theory and the Facilitation of Intrinsic Motivation, Social Development, and Well-Being

Richard M. Ryan and Edward L. Deci

The fullest representations of humanity show people to be curious, vital, and self-motivated. At their best, they are agentic and inspired, striving to learn; extend themselves; master new skills; and apply their talents responsibly. That most people show considerable effort, agency, and commitment in their lives appears, in fact, to be more normative than exceptional, suggesting some very positive and persistent features of human nature.

Yet, it is also clear that the human spirit can be diminished or crushed and that individuals sometimes reject growth and responsibility. Regardless of social strata or cultural origin, examples of both children and adults who are apathetic, alienated, and irresponsible are abundant. Such non-optimal human functioning can be observed not only in our psychological clinics but also among the millions who, for hours a day, sit passively before their televisions, stare blankly from the back of their classrooms, or wait listlessly for the weekend as they go about their jobs. The persistent, proactive, and positive tendencies of human nature are clearly not invariantly apparent.

The fact that human nature, phenotypically expressed, can be either active or passive, constructive or indolent, suggests more than mere dispositional differences and is a function of more than just biological endowments. It also bespeaks a wide range of reactions to social environments that is worthy of our most intense scientific investigation. Specifically, social contexts catalyze both within- and between-person differences in motivation and personal growth, resulting in people being more self-motivated, energized, and integrated in some situations, domains, and cultures than in others. Research on the conditions that foster versus undermine positive human potentials has both theoretical import and practical significance because it can contribute not only to formal knowledge of the causes of human behavior but also to the design of social environments that optimize people's development, performance, and well-being. Research guided by self-determination theory (SDT) has had an ongoing concern with precisely these issues (Deci & Ryan, 1985, 1991; Ryan, 1995).

SELF-DETERMINATION THEORY

SDT is an approach to human motivation and personality that uses traditional empirical methods while employing an organismic metatheory that highlights the importance of humans' evolved inner resources for personality development and behavioral self-regulation (Ryan, Kuhl, & Deci, 1997). Thus, its arena is the investigation of people's inherent growth

From *American Psychologist*, 2000, 55(1), 68–78. Reprinted with permission.

tendencies and innate psychological needs that are the basis for their self-motivation and personality integration, as well as for the conditions that foster those positive processes. Inductively, using the empirical process, we have identified three such needs—the needs for competence (Harter, 1978; White, 1963), relatedness (Baumeister & Leary, 1995; Reis, 1994), and autonomy (deCharms, 1968; Deci, 1975)—that appear to be essential for facilitating optimal functioning of the natural propensities for growth and integration, as well as for constructive social development and personal well-being.

Much of the research guided by SDT has also examined environmental factors that hinder or undermine self-motivation, social functioning, and personal well-being. Although many specific deleterious effects have been explored, the research suggests that these detriments can be most parsimoniously described in terms of thwarting the three basic psychological needs. Thus, SDT is concerned not only with the specific nature of positive developmental tendencies, but also examines social environments that are antagonistic toward these tendencies.

The empirical methods used in much of the SDT research have been in the Baconian tradition, in that social contextual variables have been directly manipulated to examine their effects on both internal processes and behavioral manifestations. The use of experimental paradigms has allowed us to specify the conditions under which people's natural activity and constructiveness will flourish, as well as those that promote a lack of self- motivation and social integration. In this way, we have used experimental methods without accepting the mechanistic or efficient causal meta-theories that have typically been associated with those methods.

In this article we review work guided by SDT, addressing its implications for three important outcomes. We begin with an examination of intrinsic motivation, the prototypic manifestation of the human tendency toward learning and creativity, and we consider research specifying conditions that facilitate versus forestall this special type of motivation. Second, we present an analysis of self-regulation, which concerns how people take in social values and extrinsic contingencies and progressively transform them into personal values and self-motivations. In that discussion, we outline different forms of internalized motivation, addressing their behavioral and experiential correlates and the conditions that are likely to promote these different motivations. Third, we focus on studies that have directly examined the impact of psychological need fulfillment on health and well-being.

THE NATURE OF MOTIVATION

Motivation concerns energy, direction, persistence and equifinality—all aspects of activation and intention. Motivation has been a central and perennial issue in the field of psychology, for it is at the core of biological, cognitive, and social regulation. Perhaps more important, in the real world, motivation is highly valued because of its consequences: Motivation produces. It is therefore of preeminent concern to those in roles such as manager, teacher, religious leader, coach, health care provider, and parent that involve mobilizing others to act.

Although motivation is often treated as a singular construct, even superficial reflection suggests that people are moved to act by very different types of factors, with highly varied experiences and consequences. People can be motivated because they value an activity or because there is strong external coercion. They can be urged into action by an abiding interest or by a bribe. They can behave from a sense of personal commitment to excel or from fear of being surveilled. These contrasts between cases of having internal motivation versus being externally pressured are surely familiar to everyone. The issue of whether people stand behind a behavior out of their interests and values, or do it for reasons external to the self, is a matter of significance in every culture (e.g., Johnson, 1993) and represents a basic dimension by which people make sense of their own and others' behavior (deCharms, 1968; Heider, 1958; Ryan & Connell, 1989).

Comparisons between people whose motivation is authentic (literally, self-authored or endorsed) and those who are merely externally controlled for an action typically reveal that the former, relative to the latter, have more interest, excitement, and confidence, which in turn is manifest both as enhanced performance, persistence, and creativity (Deci & Ryan, 1991; Sheldon, Ryan, Rawsthorne, & Hardi, 1997) and as heightened vitality (Nix, Ryan, Manly, & Deci, 1999), self-esteem (Deci & Ryan, 1995), and general well-being (Ryan, Deci, & Grolnick, 1995). This is so even when the people have the same level of perceived competence or self-efficacy for the activity.

Because of the functional and experiential differences between self-motivation and external regulation, a major focus of SDT has been to supply a more differentiated approach to motivation, by asking what kind of motivation is being exhibited at any given time. By considering the perceived forces that move a person to act, SDT has been able to identify several distinct types of motivation, each of which has specifiable consequences for learning, performance, personal experience, and well-being. Also, by articulating a set of principles concerning how each type of motivation is developed and sustained, or forestalled and undermined, SDT at once recognizes a positive thrust to human nature and provides an account of passivity, alienation, and psychopathology.

INTRINSIC MOTIVATION

Perhaps no single phenomenon reflects the positive potential of human nature as much as intrinsic motivation, the inherent tendency to seek out novelty and challenges, to extend and exercise one's capacities, to explore, and to learn. Developmentalists acknowledge that from the time of birth, children, in their healthiest states, are active, inquisitive, curious, and playful, even in the absence of specific rewards (e.g., Harter, 1978). The construct of intrinsic motivation describes this natural inclination toward assimilation, mastery, spontaneous interest, and exploration that is so essential to cognitive and social development and that represents a principal source of enjoyment and vitality throughout life (Csikszentmihalyi & Rathunde, 1993; Ryan, 1995).

Yet, despite the fact that humans are liberally endowed with intrinsic motivational tendencies, the evidence is now clear that the maintenance and enhancement of this inherent propensity requires supportive conditions, as it can be fairly readily disrupted by various nonsupportive conditions. Thus, our theory of intrinsic motivation does not concern what causes intrinsic motivation (which we view as an evolved propensity; Ryan et al., 1997); rather, it examines the conditions that elicit and sustain, versus subdue and diminish, this innate propensity.

Cognitive evaluation theory (CET) was presented by Deci and Ryan (1985) as a subtheory within SDT that had the aim of specifying factors that explain variability in intrinsic motivation. CET is framed in terms of social and environmental factors that facilitate versus undermine intrinsic motivation, using language that reflects the assumption that intrinsic motivation, being inherent, will be catalyzed when individuals are in conditions that conduce toward its expression. In other words, it will flourish if circumstances permit. Put in this way, the study of conditions that facilitate versus undermine intrinsic motivation is an important first step in understanding sources of both alienation and liberation of the positive aspects of human nature.

CET, which focuses on the fundamental needs of competence and autonomy, was formulated to integrate results from initial laboratory experiments on the effects of rewards, feedback, and other external events on intrinsic motivation, and was subsequently tested and extended by field studies in various settings. The theory argues, first, that social–contextual events (e.g., feedback, communication, rewards) that conduce toward feelings of competence during action can enhance intrinsic motivation for that action. Accordingly, optimal challenges, effectance-promoting feedback, and freedom from demeaning evaluations were all found to facilitate intrinsic motivation. For example, early studies showed that positive performance feedback enhanced intrinsic motivation, whereas negative performance feedback diminished it (Deci, 1975), and research by Vallerand and Reid (1984) showed that these effects were mediated by perceived competence.

CET further specifies, and studies have shown (Fisher, 1978; Ryan, 1982), that feelings of competence will not enhance intrinsic motivation unless accompanied by a sense of autonomy or, in attributional terms, by an internal perceived locus of causality (deCharms, 1968). Thus, according to CET, people must not only experience competence or efficacy, they must also experience their behavior as self-determined for intrinsic motivation to be in evidence. This requires either immediate contextual supports for autonomy and competence or abiding inner resources (Reeve, 1996) that are typically the result of prior developmental supports for perceived autonomy and competence.

In fact, most of the research on the effects of environmental events in intrinsic motivation has focused on the issue of autonomy versus control rather than that of competence. Research on this issue has been considerably more controversial. It began with the repeated demonstration that extrinsic rewards can undermine intrinsic motivation. Deci (1975) interpreted these results in terms of rewards facilitating a more external perceived locus of causality (i.e., diminished autonomy). Although the issue of reward effects has been hotly debated, a recent, comprehensive meta-analysis (Deci, Koestner, & Ryan, 1999) confirmed, in spite of claims to the contrary by Eisenberger and Cameron (1996), that all expected tangible rewards made contingent on task performance do reliably undermine intrinsic motivation.

Also, research revealed that not only tangible rewards but also threats, deadlines, directives, pressured evaluations, and imposed goals diminish intrinsic motivation because, like tangible rewards, they conduce toward an external perceived locus of causality. In contrast, choice, acknowledgment of feelings, and opportunities for self-direction were found to enhance intrinsic motivation because they allow people a greater feeling of autonomy (Deci & Ryan, 1985). Field studies have further shown that teachers who are autonomy supportive (in contrast to controlling) catalyze in their students greater intrinsic motivation, curiosity, and desire for challenge (e.g., Deci, Nezlek, & Sheinman, 1981; Flink, Boggiano, & Barrett, 1990; Ryan & Grolnick, 1986). Students taught with a more controlling approach not only lose initiative but learn less effectively, especially when learning requires conceptual, creative processing (Amabile, 1996; Grolnick & Ryan, 1987; Utman, 1997). Similarly, studies showed that autonomy-supportive parents, relative to controlling parents, have children who are more intrinsically motivated (Grolnick, Deci, & Ryan, 1997). Such findings generalized to other domains such as sport and music in which supports for autonomy and competence by parents and mentors incite more intrinsic motivation (e.g., Frederick & Ryan, 1995).

Although autonomy and competence supports are highly salient for producing variability in intrinsic motivation, a third factor, relatedness, also bears on its expression. In infancy, intrinsic motivation is readily observable as exploratory behavior and, as suggested by attachment theorists (e.g., Bowlby, 1979), it is more evident when the infant is securely attached to a parent. Studies of mothers and infants have, indeed, shown that both security and maternal autonomy support predict more exploratory behavior in the infants (e.g., Frodi, Bridges, & Grolnick, 1985). SDT hypothesizes that a similar dynamic occurs in interpersonal settings over the life span, with intrinsic motivation more likely to flourish in contexts characterized by a sense of security and relatedness. For example, Anderson, Manoogian, and Reznick (1976) found that when children worked on an interesting task in the presence of an adult stranger who ignored them and failed to respond to their initiations, a very low level of intrinsic motivation resulted, and Ryan and Grolnick (1986) observed lower intrinsic motivation in students who experienced their teachers as cold and uncaring. Of course, many intrinsically motivated behaviors are happily performed in isolation, suggesting that proximal relational supports may not be necessary for intrinsic motivation, but a secure relational base does seem to be important for the expression of intrinsic motivation to be in evidence.

To summarize, the CET framework suggests that social environments can facilitate or forestall intrinsic motivation by supporting versus thwarting people's innate psychological needs. Strong links between intrinsic motivation and satisfaction of the needs for autonomy and competence have been clearly demonstrated, and some work suggests that satisfaction of the need for relatedness, at least in a distal sense, may also be important for intrinsic motivation. It is critical to remember, however, that people will be intrinsically motivated only for activities that hold intrinsic interest for them, activities that have the appeal of novelty, challenge, or aesthetic value. For activities that do not hold such appeal, the principles of CET do not apply, because the activities will not be experienced as intrinsically motivated to begin with. To understand the motivation for those activities, we need to look more deeply into the nature and dynamics of extrinsic motivation.

SELF-REGULATION OF EXTRINSIC MOTIVATION

Although intrinsic motivation is an important type of motivation, it is not the only type or even the only type of self-determined motivation (Deci & Ryan, 1985). Indeed, much of what people do is not, strictly speaking, intrinsically motivated, especially after early childhood when the freedom to be intrinsically motivated is increasingly curtailed by social pressures to do activities that are not interesting and to assume a variety of new responsibilities (Ryan & LaGuardia, in press).

The real question concerning nonintrinsically motivated practices is how individuals acquire the motivation to carry them out and how this motivation affects ongoing persistence, behavioral quality, and well-being. Whenever a person (be it a parent, teacher, boss, coach, or therapist) attempts to foster certain behaviors in others, the others' motivation for the behavior can range from amotivation or unwillingness, to passive compliance, to active personal commitment. According to SDT, these different motivations reflect differing degrees to which the value and regulation of the requested behavior have been internalized and integrated. Internalization refers to people's "taking in" a value or regulation, and integration refers to the further transformation of that regulation into their own so that, subsequently, it will emanate from their sense of self.

Internalization and integration are clearly central issues in childhood socialization, but they are also continually relevant for the regulation of behavior across the life span. In nearly every setting people enter, certain behaviors and values are prescribed, behaviors that are not interesting and values that are not spontaneously adopted. Accordingly, SDT has addressed the issues of (a) the processes through which such nonintrinsically motivated behaviors can become truly self-determined, and (b) the ways in which the social environment influences those processes.

The term *extrinsic motivation* refers to the performance of an activity in order to attain some separable outcome and, thus, contrasts with *intrinsic motivation,* which refers to doing an activity for the inherent satisfaction of the activity itself. Unlike some perspectives that view extrinsically motivated behavior as invariantly nonautonomous, SDT proposes that extrinsic motivation can vary greatly in its relative autonomy (Ryan & Connell, 1989; Vallerand, 1997). For example, students who do their homework because they personally grasp its value for their chosen career are extrinsically motivated, as are those who do the work only because they are adhering to their parents' control. Both examples involve instrumentalities rather than enjoyment of the work itself, yet the former case of extrinsic motivation entails personal endorsement and a feeling of choice, whereas the latter involves compliance with an external regulation. Both represent intentional behavior (Heider, 1958), but they vary in their relative autonomy. The former, of course, is the type of extrinsic motivation that is sought by astute socializing agents regardless of the applied domain.

Within SDT, Deci and Ryan (1985) introduced a second subtheory, called organismic integration theory (OIT), to detail the different forms of extrinsic motivation and the contextual factors that either promote or hinder internalization and integration of the regulation for these behaviors. Figure 1 illustrates the OIT taxonomy of motivational types, arranged from left to right in terms of the degree to which the motivations emanate from the self (i.e., are self-determined).

At the far left of the self-determination continuum is amotivation, the state of lacking the intention to act. When amotivated, people either do not act at all or act without intent—they just go through the motions. Amotivation results from not valuing an activity (Ryan, 1995), not feeling competent to do it (Bandura, 1986), or not expecting it to yield a desired outcome (Seligman, 1975). To the right of amotivation in Figure 1 are five classifications of motivated behavior. Although many theorists have treated motivation as a unitary concept, each of the categories identified within OIT describes theoretically, experientially, and functionally distinct types of motivation. At the far right of the continuum is the classic state of intrinsic motivation, the doing of an activity for its inherent satisfactions. It is highly

FIGURE 1

The Self-Determination Continuum Showing Types of Motivation with Their Regulatory Styles, Loci of Causality, and Corresponding Processes

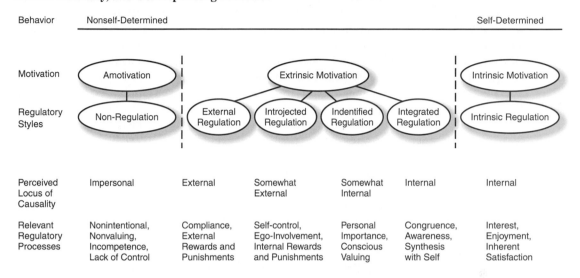

autonomous and represents the prototypic instance of self-determination. Extrinsically motivated behaviors, by contrast, cover the continuum between amotivation and intrinsic motivation, varying in the extent to which their regulation is autonomous.

The extrinsically motivated behaviors that are least autonomous are referred to as *externally regulated.* Such behaviors are performed to satisfy an external demand or reward contingency. Individuals typically experience externally regulated behavior as controlled or alienated, and their actions have an external perceived locus of causality (deCharms, 1968). External regulation is the type of motivation focused on by operant theorists (e.g., Skinner, 1953), and it is external regulation that was typically contrasted with intrinsic motivation in early laboratory and field studies.

A second type of extrinsic motivation is labeled *introjected regulation.* Introjection involves taking in a regulation but not fully accepting it as one's own. It is a relatively controlled form of regulation in which behaviors are performed to avoid guilt or anxiety or to attain ego enhancements such as pride. Put differently, introjection represents regulation by contingent self-esteem (Deci & Ryan, 1995). A classic form of introjection is ego involvement (deCharms, 1968; Nicholls, 1984; Ryan, 1982), in which people are motivated to demonstrate ability (or avoid failure) in order to maintain feelings of worth. Although internally driven, introjected behaviors still have an external perceived locus of causality and are not really experienced as part of the self. Thus, in some studies, external regulation (being interpersonally controlled) and introjected regulation (being intrapersonally controlled) have been combined to form a controlled motivation composite (e.g., Williams, Grow, Freedman, Ryan, & Deci, 1996).

A more autonomous, or self-determined, form of extrinsic motivation is *regulation through identification.* Identification reflects a conscious valuing of a behavioral goal or regulation, such that the action is accepted or owned as personally important. Finally, the most autonomous form of extrinsic motivation is *integrated regulation.* Integration occurs when identified regulations are fully assimilated to the self, which means they have been evaluated and brought into congruence with one's other values and needs. Actions characterized by integrated motivation share many qualities with intrinsic motivation, although they are still considered extrinsic because they are done to attain separable outcomes rather than for their inherent enjoyment. In some studies, identified, integrated, and intrinsic forms of regulation have been combined to form an autonomous motivation composite.

As people internalize regulations and assimilate them to the self, they experience greater autonomy in action. This process may occur in stages, over time, but we are not suggesting that it is a developmental continuum in the sense that people must progress through each stage of internalization with respect to a particular regulation. Rather, they can relatively readily internalize a new behavioral regulation at any point along this continuum depending on both prior experiences and current situational factors (Ryan, 1995). Nonetheless, the range of behaviors that can be assimilated to the self increases over time with increased cognitive capacities and ego development (Loevinger & Blasi, 1991), and there is evidence that children's general regulatory style does tend to become more internalized or self-regulated over time (e.g., Chandler & Connell, 1987).

Ryan and Connell (1989) tested the formulation that these different types of motivation, with their distinct properties, lie along a continuum of relative autonomy. They investigated achievement behaviors among school children and found that external, introjected, identified, and intrinsic regulatory styles were intercorrelated according to a quasi-simplex pattern, thus providing evidence for an underlying continuum. Furthermore, differences in the type of extrinsic motivation were associated with different experiences and outcomes. For example, the more students were externally regulated the less they showed interest, value, and effort toward achievement and the more they tended to disown responsibility for negative outcomes, blaming others such as the teacher. Introjected regulation was positively related to expending more effort, but it was also related to feeling more anxiety and coping more poorly with failures. In contrast, identified regulation was associated with more interest and enjoyment of school and with more positive coping styles, as well as with expending more effort.

Other studies in education extended these findings, showing that more autonomous extrinsic motivation was associated with more engagement (Connell & Wellborn, 1991), better performance (Miserandino, 1996), lower dropout (Vallerand & Bissonnette, 1992), higher quality learning (Grolnick & Ryan, 1987), and better teacher ratings (Hayamizu, 1997), among other outcomes.

In the realm of health care, greater internalization has been associated with greater adherence to medications among people with chronic illnesses (Williams, Rodin, Ryan, Grolnick, & Deci, 1998), better long-term maintenance of weight loss among morbidly obese patients (Williams et al., 1996), improved glucose control among diabetics (Williams, Freedman, & Deci, 1998), and greater attendance and involvement in an addiction-treatment program (Ryan, Plant, & O'Malley, 1995).

Demonstrations of positive outcomes being associated with more internalized motivation have also emerged in other diverse domains, including religion (Ryan, Rigby, & King, 1993), physical exercise (Chatzisarantis, Biddle, & Meek, 1997), political activity (Koestner, Losier, Vallerand, & Carducci, 1996), environmental activism (Green-Demers, Pelletier,

& Menard, 1997), and intimate relationships (Blais, Sabourin, Boucher, & Vallerand, 1990), among others.

The advantages of greater internalization appear, then, to be manifold (Ryan et al., 1997), including more behavioral effectiveness, greater volitional persistence, enhanced subjective well-being, and better assimilation of the individual within his or her social group.

Facilitating Integration of Extrinsic Motivation

Given the significance of internalization for personal experience and behavioral outcomes, the critical issue becomes how to promote autonomous regulation for extrinsically motivated behaviors. That is, what are the social conditions that nurture versus inhibit internalization and integration?

Because extrinsically motivated behaviors are not typically interesting, the primary reason people initially perform such actions is because the behaviors are prompted, modeled, or valued by significant others to whom they feel (or want to feel) attached or related. This suggests that relatedness, the need to feel belongingness and connectedness with others, is centrally important for internalization. Thus, OIT proposes that internalization is more likely to be in evidence when there are ambient supports for feelings of relatedness. For example, Ryan, Stiller, and Lynch (1994) showed that the children who had more fully internalized the regulation for positive school-related behaviors were those who felt securely connected to, and cared for by, their parents and teachers.

The relative internalization of extrinsically motivated activities is also a function of perceived competence. People are more likely to adopt activities that relevant social groups value when they feel efficacious with respect to those activities. As is the case with all intentional action, OIT suggests that supports for competence should facilitate internalization (Vallerand, 1997). Thus, for example, children who are directed to perform behaviors before they are developmentally ready to master them or understand their rationale would be predicted, at best, only to partially internalize the regulations, remaining either externally regulated or introjected.

Finally, the experience of autonomy facilitates internalization and, in particular, is a critical element for a regulation to be integrated. Contexts can yield external regulation if there are salient rewards or threats and the person feels competent enough to comply; contexts can yield introjected regulation if a relevant reference group endorses the activity and the person feels competent and related; but contexts can yield autonomous regulation only if they are autonomy supportive, thus allowing the person to feel competent, related, and autonomous. To integrate a regulation, people must grasp its meaning and synthesize that meaning with respect to their other goals and values. Such deep, holistic processing (Kuhl & Fuhrmann, 1998) is facilitated by a sense of choice, volition, and freedom from excessive external pressure toward behaving or thinking a certain way. In this sense, support for autonomy allows individuals to actively transform values into their own.

Again, research results have supported this reasoning. For example, Deci, Eghrari, Patrick, and Leone (1994) demonstrated in a laboratory experiment that providing a meaningful rationale for an uninteresting behavior, along with supports for autonomy and relatedness, promoted its internalization and integration. Controlling contexts yielded less overall internalization, and the internalization that did occur in those contexts tended to be only introjected. Using parent interviews, Grolnick and Ryan (1989) found greater internalization of school-related values among children whose parents were more supportive of autonomy and relatedness. Strahan (1995) found that parents who were more autonomy-supportive promoted greater religious identification, as opposed to introjection, in their offspring. Williams and Deci (1996), using a longitudinal design, demonstrated greater internalization of biopsychosocial values and practices among medical students whose instructors were more autonomy-supportive. These are but a few of the many findings suggesting that supports for relatedness and competence facilitate internalization and that supports for autonomy also facilitate integration of behavioral regulations. When that occurs, people feel not only competent and related but also autonomous as they carry out culturally valued activities.

One further point needs to be made regarding the controversial issue of human autonomy. The concept of autonomy has often been portrayed as being antagonistic to relatedness or community. In fact, some theories equate autonomy with concepts such as individualism and independence (e.g., Steinberg & Silverberg, 1986), which do indeed imply low relatedness. But, within SDT, autonomy refers not to being independent, detached, or selfish but rather to the feeling of volition that can accompany any act, whether dependent or independent, collectivist or individualist. In fact, recent research in Korean and U.S. samples has found a more positive relation between autonomy and collectivistic attitudes than between autonomy and individualistic attitudes (Kim, Butzel, & Ryan, 1998). Furthermore, research has shown positive, rather than negative, links between relatedness to parents and autonomy in teenagers (Ryan & Lynch, 1989; Ryan et al., 1994). Clearly, then, we do not equate autonomy with independence or individualism.

Alienation and Its Prevention

SDT aims to specify factors that nurture the innate human potentials entailed in growth, integration, and well-being, and to explore the processes and conditions that foster the healthy development and effective functioning of individuals, groups, and communities. But a positive approach cannot ignore pathology or close its eyes to the alienation and inauthenticity that are prevalent in our society and in others. Accordingly, we investigate nonoptimal (as well as optimal) developmental trajectories, much as is done in the field of developmental psychopathology (e.g., Cicchetti, 1991). We now turn to a brief consideration of that issue.

By definition, intrinsically motivated behaviors, the prototype of self-determined actions, stem from the self. They are unalienated and authentic in the fullest sense of those terms. But, as already noted, SDT recognizes that extrinsically motivated actions can also become self-determined as individuals identify with and fully assimilate their regulation. Thus, it is through internalization and integration that individuals can be extrinsically motivated and still be committed and authentic. Accumulated research now suggests that the commitment and authenticity reflected in intrinsic motivation and integrated extrinsic motivation are most likely to be evident when individuals experience supports for competence, autonomy, and relatedness.

It is the flip side of this coin, however, that speaks directly to the issues of alienation and inauthenticity and is relevant to such questions as why employees show no initiative, why teenagers reject their schools' values, and why patients adhere so poorly to treatment. SDT understands such occurrences in terms of the undermining of intrinsic motivation and, perhaps even more typically, the failure of internalization. To explain the causes of such diminished functioning, SDT suggests turning first to individuals' immediate social contexts and then to their developmental environments to examine the degree to which their needs for competence, autonomy, and relatedness are being or have been thwarted. We maintain that by failing to provide supports for competence, autonomy, and relatedness, not only of children but also of students, employees, patients, and athletes, socializing agents and organizations contribute to alienation and ill-being. The fact that psychological-need deprivation appears to be a principal source of human distress suggests that assessments and interventions would do well to target these primary foundations of mental health.

PSYCHOLOGICAL NEEDS AND MENTAL HEALTH

As we have seen, both the cognitive evaluation and organismic integration components of SDT have led us to posit a parsimonious list of three basic psychological needs as a means of organizing and interpreting a wide array of empirical results, results that seemed not to be readily and satisfactorily interpretable without the concept of needs. Much of our more recent work has used the concept of three basic psychological needs to address new phenomena and, more particularly, to evaluate the postulate that these three needs are innate, essential, and universal.

By our definition, a basic need, whether it be a physiological need (Hull, 1943) or a psychological need, is an energizing state that, if satisfied, conduces toward health and well-being but, if not satisfied, contributes to pathology and ill-being. We have thus proposed that the basic needs for competence, autonomy, and relatedness must be satisfied across the life span for an individual to experience an ongoing sense of integrity and well-being or "eudaimonia" (Ryan & Frederick, 1997; Waterman, 1993). Accordingly, much of our research now focuses on the link between satisfaction of the basic psychological needs and the experience of well-being.

Specifying psychological needs as essential nutriments implies that individuals cannot thrive without satisfying all of them, any more than people can thrive with water but not food. Thus, for example, a social environment that affords competence but fails to nurture relatedness is expected to result in some impoverishment of well-being. Worse yet, social contexts that engender conflicts between basic needs set up the conditions for alienation and psychopathology (Ryan et al., 1995), as when a child is required by parents to give up autonomy in order to feel loved.

To suggest that the three needs are universal and developmentally persistent does not imply that their relative salience and their avenues for satisfaction are unchanging across the life span or that their modes of expression are the same in all cultures. The very fact that need satisfaction is facilitated by the internalization and integration of culturally endorsed values and behaviors suggests that individuals are likely to express their competence, autonomy, and relatedness differently within cultures that hold different values. Indeed, the mode and degree of people's psychological-need satisfaction is theorized to be influenced not only by their own competencies but, even more important, by the ambient demands, obstacles, and affordances in their sociocultural contexts. Thus, to posit universal psychological needs does not diminish the importance of variability in goals and orientations at different developmental epochs or in different cultures, but it does suggest similarities in underlying processes that lead to the development and expression of those differences.

Our recent investigations of the importance of basic psychological needs have addressed three questions: Are the pursuit and attainment of all culturally congruent aspirations and life values associated with well-being? Do need-related processes operate similarly within different cultural circumstances? Is within-person variability in basic need satisfaction related to variability in well-being indicators? We briefly consider some of this work.

First, we discuss the relation of personal goals to well-being. We have hypothesized that the pursuit and attainment of some life goals will provide relatively direct satisfaction of the basic needs, thus enhancing well-being (Ryan, Sheldon, Kasser, & Deci, 1996), whereas the pursuit and attainment of other goals does not contribute to and may even detract from basic need satisfactions, leading to ill-being. In accord with this reasoning, T. Kasser and Ryan (1993, 1996) examined individual differences in the emphasis people place on intrinsic aspirations (goals such as affiliation, personal growth, and community that directly satisfy basic needs) compared with extrinsic aspirations (goals such as wealth, fame, and image that at best indirectly satisfy the needs). They found, first, that placing strong relative importance on intrinsic aspirations was positively associated with well-being indicators such as self-esteem, self-actualization, and the inverse of depression and anxiety, whereas placing strong relative importance on extrinsic aspirations was negatively related to these well-being indicators. Ryan, Chirkov, Little, Sheldon, Timoshina, and Deci (1999) replicated these findings in a Russian sample, attesting to the potential generalizability of the findings across cultures.

These findings go beyond goal importance per se. Both Ryan, Chirkov, et al. and T. Kasser and Ryan (in press) have found that whereas self-reported attainment of intrinsic aspirations was positively associated with well-being, attainment of extrinsic aspirations was not. Further, Sheldon and Kasser (1998) found in a longitudinal study that well-being was enhanced by attainment of intrinsic goals, whereas success at extrinsic goals provided little benefit. Together, these results suggest that even highly efficacious people may experience less than optimal well-being if they pursue and successfully attain goals that do not fulfill basic psychological needs. We hasten to add, however, that the meaning of specific goals is culturally influenced, so that how specific goals relate to well-being can vary across cultures, although the relation between underlying need satisfaction and well-being is theorized to be invariant.

Clearly, there are many factors that lead people to emphasize certain life goals that may not be need fulfilling. For example, exposure to the commercial media can prompt a focus on materialism (Richins, 1987), which provides only fleeting satisfactions and could actually detract from basic need fulfillment and, thus, well-being. Prior deficits in need fulfillment (e.g., from poor caregiving) might also lead individuals to yearn for more extrinsic goals as a substitute or compensatory mechanism. In fact, T. Kasser, Ryan, Zax, and Sameroff (1995) found that teens who had been exposed to cold, controlling maternal care (as assessed with ratings by the teens, mothers, and observers) were more likely to develop materialistic orientations, compared with better nurtured teens who more strongly valued the intrinsic goals of personal growth, relationships, and community. In short, cultural and developmental influences produce variations in the importance of goals, the pursuit of which, in turn, yields different satisfaction of basic needs and different levels of well-being.

In other research, we have examined the relations of people's reports of need satisfaction to indicators of well-being in various settings. For example, V. Kasser and Ryan (in press) found that supports for autonomy and relatedness predicted greater well-being among nursing home residents. Baard, Deci, and Ryan (1998) showed that employees' experiences of satisfaction of the needs for autonomy, competence, and relatedness in the workplace predicted their performance and well-being at work. Such research shows that within specific domains, especially those central to the lives of individuals, need satisfaction is correlated with improved well-being.

A more compelling way of demonstrating the essential relations between need fulfillments and mental health has been the examination of role-to-role and day-to-day fluctuations in basic need satisfaction and their direct effects on variability in well-being, while controlling for individual differences and various confounding variables. For example, Sheldon et al. (1997) demonstrated that satisfaction in each of several life roles (e.g., student, employee, friend), relative to the individual's own mean satisfaction, was attributable to the degree to which that role supports authenticity and autonomous functioning. Similarly, in a study that examined daily variations in well-being, Sheldon, Reis, and Ryan (1996) used hierarchical linear modeling to show that within-person daily fluctuations in the satisfaction of autonomy and competence needs predicted within-person fluctuations in outcomes such as mood, vitality, physical symptoms, and self-esteem. In a more recent study, Reis, Sheldon, Gable, Roscoe, and Ryan (in press) found that variations in the fulfillment of each of the three needs (i.e., competence, autonomy, and relatedness) independently predicted variability in daily well-being. These studies support the view that basic psychological needs are determinative with regard to optimal experience and well-being in daily life.

CONCLUSIONS

Debates concerning the activity or passivity, responsibility or indolence, of human beings have been perennial (Kohn, 1990). As psychology has become more advanced, both in terms of our understanding of evolution and neurobiology and of social behavior and its causation, ample support for both perspectives could be garnered. SDT addresses this issue by attempting to account for both the activity and the passivity, the responsibility and the indolence. To do this, we have assumed that humans have an inclination toward activity and integration, but also have a vulnerability to passivity. Our focus, accordingly, has been to specify the conditions that tend to support people's natural activity versus elicit or exploit their vulnerability.

Our early investigations focused on the social conditions that enhance versus diminish a very positive feature of human nature, namely, the natural activity and curiosity referred to as intrinsic motivation. We found that conditions supportive of autonomy and competence reliably facilitated this vital expression of the human growth tendency, whereas conditions that controlled behavior and hindered perceived effectance undermined its expression. Subsequently, we investigated the acquisition and regulation of nonintrinsically motivated behaviors and, here too, we found evidence of the dramatic power of social contexts to enhance or hinder the organismic tendency to integrate ambient social values and responsibilities. Contexts supportive of autonomy, competence, and relatedness were found to foster greater internalization and integration than contexts that thwart satisfaction of these needs. This latter finding, we argue, is of great significance for individuals who wish to motivate others in a way that engenders commitment, effort, and high-quality performance.

Yet, our primary concern throughout this program of research has been the well-being of individuals, whether they are students in classrooms, patients in clinics, athletes on the playing field, or employees in the workplace. As formulated by SDT, if the social contexts in which such individuals are embedded are responsive to basic psychological needs, they provide the appropriate developmental lattice upon which an active, assimilative, and integrated nature can ascend. Excessive control, nonoptimal challenges, and lack of connectedness, on the other hand, disrupt the inherent actualizing and organizational tendencies endowed by nature, and thus such factors result not only in the lack of initiative and responsibility but also in distress and psychopathology.

Knowledge concerning the nutriments essential for positive motivation and experience and, in turn, for enhanced performance and well-being has broad significance. It is relevant to parents and educators concerned with cognitive and personality development because it speaks to the conditions that promote the assimilation of both information and behavioral regulations. It is also relevant to managers who want to facilitate motivation and commitment on the job, and it is relevant to psychotherapists and health professionals because motivation is perhaps the critical variable in producing maintained change. Thus, by attending to the relative presence or deprivation of supports for basic psychological needs, practitioners are better able to diagnose sources of alienation versus engagement, and facilitate both enhanced human achievements and well-being.

References

Amabile, T. M. (1996). *Creativity in context.* New York: Westview Press.

Anderson, R., Manoogian, S. T., & Reznick, J. S. (1976). The undermining and enhancing of intrinsic motivation in preschool children. *Journal of Personality and Social Psychology, 34,* 915–922.

Baard, P. P., Deci, E. L., & Ryan, R. M. (1998). *Intrinsic need satisfaction: A motivational basis of performance and well-being in work settings.* Unpublished manuscript, Fordham University.

Bandura, A. (1986). *Social foundations of thought and action: A social cognitive theory.* Englewood Cliffs, NJ: Prentice Hall.

Baumeister, R., & Leary, M. R. (1995). The need to belong: Desire for interpersonal attachments as a fundamental human motivation. *Psychological Bulletin, 117,* 497–529.

Blais, M. R., Sabourin, S., Boucher, C., & Vallerand, R. J. (1990). Toward a motivational model of couple happiness. *Journal of Personality and Social Psychology, 59,* 1021–1031.

Bowlby, J. (1979). *The making and breaking of affectional bonds.* London: Tavistock.

Chandler, C. L., & Connell, J. P. (1987). Children's intrinsic, extrinsic and internalized motivation: A developmental study of children's reasons for liked and disliked behaviours. *British Journal of Developmental Psychology, 5,* 357–365.

Chatzisarantis, N. L. D., Biddle, S. J. H., & Meek, G. A. (1997). A self-determination theory approach to the study of intentions and the intention–behaviour relationship in children's physical activity. *British Journal of Health Psychology, 2,* 343–360.

Cicchetti, D. (1991). Fractures in the crystal: Developmental psychopathology and the emergence of self. *Developmental Review, 11,* 271–287.

Connell, J. P., & Wellborn, J. G. (1991). Competence, autonomy and relatedness: A motivational analysis of self-system processes. In M. R. Gunnar & L. A. Sroufe (Eds.), *Minnesota Symposium on Child Psychology* (Vol. 22, pp. 43–77). Hillsdale, NJ: Erlbaum.

Csikszentmihalyi, M., & Rathunde, K. (1993). The measurement of flow in everyday life: Toward a theory of emergent motivation. In J. E. Jacobs (Ed.), *Developmental perspectives on motivation* (pp. 57–97). Lincoln: University of Nebraska Press.

deCharms, R. (1968). *Personal causation.* New York: Academic Press.

Deci, E. L., (1975). *Intrinsic motivation.* New York: Plenum.

Deci, E. L. Eghrari, H., Patrick, B. C., & Leone, D. R. (1994). Facilitating internalization: The self-determination theory perspective. *Journal of Personality, 62,* 119–142.

Deci, E. L., Koestner, R., & Ryan, R. M. (1999). A meta-analytic review of experiments examining the effects of extrinsic rewards on intrinsic motivation. *Psychological Bulletin, 125,* 627–668.

Deci, E. L., Nezlek, J., & Sheinman, L. (1981). Characteristics of the rewarder and intrinsic motivation of the rewardee. *Journal of Personality and Social Psychology, 40,* 1–10.

Deci, E. L., & Ryan, R. M. (1985). *Intrinsic motivation and self-determination in human behavior.* New York: Plenum.

Deci, E. L., & Ryan, R. M. (1991). A motivational approach to self: Integration in personality. In R. Dienstbier (Ed.), *Nebraska Symposium on Motivation: Vol. 38. Perspectives on motivation* (pp. 237–288). Lincoln: University of Nebraska Press.

Deci, E. L., & Ryan, R. M. (1995). Human autonomy: The basis for true self-esteem. In M. Kernis (Ed.), *Efficacy, agency, and self-esteem* (pp. 31–49). New York: Plenum.

Eisenberger, R., & Cameron, J. (1996). Detrimental effects of reward: Reality or myth? *American Psychologist, 51,* 1153–1166.

Fisher, C. D. (1978). The effects of personal control, competence, and extrinsic reward systems on intrinsic motivation. *Organizational Behavior and Human Performance, 21,* 273–288.

Flink, C., Boggiano, A. K., & Barrett, M. (1990). Controlling teaching strategies: Undermining children's self-determination and performance. *Journal of Personality and Social Psychology, 59,* 916–924.

Frederick, C. M., & Ryan, R. M. (1995). Self-determination in sport: A review using cognitive evaluation theory. *International Journal of Sport Psychology, 26,* 5–23.

Frodi, A., Bridges, L., & Grolnick, W. S. (1985). Correlates of mastery-related behavior: A short-term longitudinal study of infants in their second year. *Child Development, 56,* 1291–1298.

Green-Demers, I., Pelletier, L. G., & Menard, S. (1997). The impact of behavioural difficulty on the saliency of the association between self-determined motivation and environmental behaviours. *Canadian Journal of Behavioural Science, 29,* 157–166.

Grolnick, W. S., Deci, E. L., & Ryan, R. M. (1997). Internalization within the family. In J. E. Grusec & L. Kuczynski (Eds.), *Parenting and children's internalization of values: A handbook of contemporary theory* (pp. 135–161). New York: Wiley.

Grolnick, W. S., & Ryan, R. M. (1987). Autonomy in children's learning: An experimental and individual difference investigation. *Journal of Personality and Social Psychology, 52,* 890–898.

Grolnick, W. S., & Ryan, R. M. (1989). Parent styles associated with children's self-regulation and competence in school. *Journal of Educational Psychology, 81,* 143–154.

Harter, S. (1978). Effectance motivation reconsidered: Toward a developmental model. *Human Development, 1,* 661–669.

Hayamizu, T. (1997). Between intrinsic and extrinsic motivation. *Japanese Psychological Research, 39,* 98–108.

Heider, F. (1958). *The psychology of interpersonal relations.* New York: Wiley.

Hull, C. L. (1943). *Principles of behavior: An introduction to behavior theory.* New York: Appleton-Century-Crofts.

Johnson, F. A. (1993). *Dependency and Japanese socialization.* New York: NYU Press.

Kasser, T., & Ryan, R. M. (1993). A dark side of the American dream: Correlates of financial success as a life aspiration. *Journal of Personality and Social Psychology, 65,* 410–422.

Kasser, T., & Ryan, R. M. (1996). Further examining the American dream: Differential correlates of intrinsic and extrinsic goals. *Personality and Social Psychology Bulletin, 22,* 80–87.

Kasser, T., & Ryan, R. M. (in press). Be careful what you wish for: Optimal functioning and the relative attainment of intrinsic and extrinsic goals. In P. Schmuck & K. M. Sheldon (Eds.), *Life goals and well-being.* Lengerich, German: Pabst Science.

Kasser, T., Ryan, R. M., Zax, M., & Sameroff, A. J. (1995). The relations of maternal and social environments to late adolescents' materialistic and prosocial values. *Developmental Psychology, 31,* 907–914.

Kasser, V., & Ryan, R. M. (in press). The relation of psychological needs for autonomy and relatedness to vitality, well-being, and mortality in a nursing home. *Journal of Applied Social Psychology.*

Kim, Y., Butzel, J. S., & Ryan, R. M. (1998). *Interdependence and well-being: A function of culture and relatedness needs.* Paper presented at The International Society for the Study of Personal Relationships. Saratoga Spring, NY., June.

Koestner, R., Losier, G. F., Vallerand, R. J., & Carducci, D. (1996). Identified and introjected forms of political internalization: Extending self-determination theory. *Journal of Personality and Social psychology, 70,* 1025–1036.

Kohn, A. (1990). *The brighter side of human nature*. New York: Basic Books.

Kuhl, J., & Fuhrmann, A. (1998). Decomposing self-regulation and self-control. In J. Heckhausen & C. Dweck (Eds.), *Motivation and self-regulation across the life-span* (pp. 15–49). New York: Cambridge University Press.

Loevinger, J., & Blasi, A. (1991). Development of the self as subject. In J. Strauss & G. Goethals (Eds.), *The self: Interdisciplinary approaches* (pp. 150–167). New York: Springer-Verlag.

Miserandino, M. (1996). Children who do well in school: Individual differences in perceived competence and autonomy in above-average children. *Journal of Educational Psychology, 88,* 203–214.

Nicholls, J. G. (1984). Achievement motivation: Conceptions of ability, subjective experience, task choice, and performance. *Psychological Review, 91,* 328–346.

Nix, G., Ryan, R. M., Manly, J. B., & Deci, E. L. (1999). Revitalization through self-regulation: The effects of autonomous and controlled motivation on happiness and vitality. *Journal of Experimental Social Psychology, 35,* 266–284.

Reeve, J. (1996). *Motivating others*. Needham Heights, MA: Allyn & Bacon.

Reis, H. T. (1994). Domains of experience: Investigating relationship processes from three perspectives. In R. Erber & R. Gilmour (Eds.), *Theoretical frameworks for personal relationships* (pp. 87–110). Hillsdale, NJ: Erlbaum.

Reis, H. T., Sheldon, K. M., Gable, S. L., Roscoe, J., & Ryan, R. M. (in press). Daily well-being: The role of autonomy, competence, and relatedness. *Personality and Social Psychology Bulletin.*

Richins, M. (1987). Media, materialism and human happiness. *Advances in Consumer Research, 14,* 352–356.

Ryan, R. M. (1982). Control and information in the intra-personal sphere: An extension of cognitive evaluation theory. *Journal of Personality and Social Psychology, 43,* 450–461.

Ryan, R. M., (1995). Psychological needs and the facilitation of integrative processes. *Journal of Personality, 63,* 397–427.

Ryan, R. M., Chirkov, V. I., Little, T. D., Sheldon, K. M., Timoshina, E., & Deci, E. L. (1999). The American dream in Russia: Extrinsic aspirations and well-being in two cultures. *Personality and Social Psychology Bulletin, 25,* 1509–1524.

Ryan, R. M. & Connell, J. P. (1989). Perceived locus of causality and internalization. *Journal of Personality and Social Psychology, 57,* 749–761.

Ryan, R. M., Deci, E. L., & Grolnick, W. S. (1995). Autonomy, relatedness, and the self: Their relation to development and psychopathology. In D. Cicchetti & D. J. Cohen (Eds.), *Developmental psychopathology: Theory and methods* (pp. 618–655). New York: Wiley.

Ryan, R. M., & Frederick C. M. (1997). On energy, personality, and health: Subjective vitality as a dynamic reflection of well-being. *Journal of Personality, 65,* 529–565.

Ryan, R. M., & Grolnick, W. S. (1986). Origins and pawns in the classroom: Self-report and projective assessments of individual differences in children's perceptions. *Journal of Personality and Social Psychology, 50,* 550–558.

Ryan, R. M., Kuhl, J., & Deci, E. L. (1997). Nature and autonomy: Organizational view of social and neurobiological aspects of self-regulation in behavior and development. *Development and Psychopathology, 9,* 701–728.

Ryan, R. M., & La Guardia, J. G. (in press). What is being optimized over development? A self-determination theory perspective on basic psychological needs across the life span. In S. Qualls & R. Abeles (Eds.), *Dialogues on psychology and aging.* Washington, DC: American Psychological Association.

Ryan, R. M., & Lynch J. (1989). Emotional autonomy versus detachment: Revisiting the vicissitudes of adolescence and young adulthood. *Child Development, 60,* 340–356.

Ryan, R. M., Plant, R. W., & O'Malley, S. (1995). Initial motivations for alcohol treatment: Relations with patient characteristics, treatment involvement and dropout. *Addictive Behaviors, 20,* 279–297.

Ryan, R. M., Rigby, S., & King, K. (1993). Two types of religious internalization and their relations to religious orientations and mental health. *Journal of Personality and Social Psychology, 65,* 586–596.

Ryan, R. M., Sheldon, K. M., Kasser, T., & Deci, E. L. (1996). All goals are not created equal: An organismic perspective on the nature of goals and their regulation. In P. M. Gollwitzer & J. A. Bargh (Eds.), *The psychology of action: Linking cognition and motivation to behavior* (pp. 7–26). New York: Guilford Press.

Ryan, R. M., Stiller, J., & Lynch, J. H. (1994). Representations of relationships to teachers, parents, and friends as predictors of academic motivation and self-esteem. *Journal of Early Adolescence, 14,* 226–249.

Seligman, M. E. P. (1975). *Helplessness*. San Francisco: Freeman.

Sheldon, K. M., & Kasser, T. (1998). Pursuing personal goals: Skills enable progress, but not all progress is beneficial. *Personality and Social Psychology Bulletin, 24,* 1319–1331.

Sheldon, K. M., Reis, H. T., & Ryan, R. (1996). What makes for a good day? Competence and autonomy in the day and in the person. *Personality and Social Psychology Bulletin, 22,* 1270–1279.

Sheldon, K. M., Ryan, R. M., Rawsthorne, L., & Hardi, B. (1997). Trait self and true self: Cross-role variation in the Big Five traits and its relations with authenticity and subjective well-being. *Journal of Personality and Social Psychology, 73,* 1380–1393.

Skinner, B. F. (1953). *Science and human behavior.* New York: Macmillan.

Steinberg, L., & Silverberg, S. (1986). The vicissitudes of autonomy in adolescence. *Child Development, 57,* 841–851.

Strahan, B. J. (1995). *Marriage, family and religion.* Sydney, Australia: Adventist Institute.

Utman, C. H. (1997). Performance effects of motivational state: A meta-analysis. *Personality and Social Psychology Review, 1,* 170–182.

Vallerand, R. J. (1997). Toward a hierarchical model of intrinsic and extrinsic motivation. In M. P. Zanna (Ed.), *Advances in experimental social psychology* (Vol. 29, pp. 271–360). San Diego, CA: Academic Press.

Vallerand, R. J., & Bissonnette, R. (1992). Intrinsic, extrinsic, and amotivational styles as predictors of behavior: A prospective study. *Journal of Personality, 60,* 599–620.

Vallerand, R. J., & Reid, G. (1984). On the causal effects of perceived competence on intrinsic motivation: A test of cognitive evaluation theory. *Journal of Sport Psychology, 6,* 94–102.

Waterman, A. S. (1993). Two conceptions of happiness: Contrasts of personal expressiveness and hedonic enjoyment. *Journal of Personality and Social Psychology, 64,* 678–691.

White, R. W. (1963). *Ego and reality in psychoanalytic theory.* New York: International Universities Press.

Williams, G. C., & Deci, E. L. (1996). Internalization of biopsychosocial values by medical students. *Journal of Personality and Social Psychology, 70,* 767–779.

Williams, G. C., Freedman, Z. R., & Deci, E. L. (1998). Supporting autonomy to motivate glucose control in patients with diabetes. *Diabetes Care, 21,* 1644–1651.

Williams, G. C., Grow, V. M., Freedman, Z., Ryan, R. M., & Deci, E. L. (1996). Motivational predictors of weight loss and weight-loss maintenance. *Journal of Personality and Social Psychology, 70,* 115–126.

Williams, G. C., Rodin, G. C., Ryan, R. M., Grolnick, W. S., & Deci, E. L. (1998). Autonomous regulation and long-term medication adherence in adult outpatients. *Health Psychology, 17,* 269–276.

Employee Reactions to Unfair Outcomes in the Workplace: The Contributions of Adams's Equity Theory to Understanding Work Motivation

Richard T. Mowday and Kenneth A. Colwell

> President of Urban League Calls for Review of Equity
> Employers Maintaining Vigilance in the Face of Layoff Rage
> A Survey of Wall St. Finds Women Disheartened

The three newspaper headlines reprinted above, all taken from the *New York Times* at the time this was being written, suggest that issues about fairness and the implications of treating people unfairly are ongoing and important societal concerns. The president of the Urban League was concerned about unfair treatment of blacks in the criminal justice system (Toner, 2001), while "layoff rage" refers to retaliation against employers by employees who feel they have been unfairly laid off (Tahmincioglu, 2001). For example, one laid-off employee reportedly sabotaged his employer's computer system by deleting critical files, causing $20 million in damage and delaying a public stock offering. On Wall Street, a survey found that women employed by the major securities firms were dissatisfied with the progress that had been made to help women advance in their careers relative to males (Abelson, 2001).

Few would deny that fairness—being treated fairly and treating others fairly—is desirable. Although few would dispute the importance of fairness, it is more difficult to know what it means to be fair or how people make judgments about whether or not they have been treated fairly. One answer to this question was provided almost 40 years ago by J. Stacy Adams, a behavioral science researcher working at the time for the General Electric Company. His influential publications introducing equity theory (Adams 1963, 1965) generated considerable research interest in the motivational implications of unfair treatment in the workplace and can be considered as one of the foundations of contemporary interest in the broader field of organizational justice (see the following reading by Cropanzano and Rupp).

The purpose of this reading is to present Adams's equity theory and to examine the research that has tested the theory and that has been motivated by the theory. Based on a large number of research studies, we will identify a number of contextual and individual difference factors that may need to be incorporated into the theory. Finally, several areas of contemporary concern to researchers and business managers will be examined through the lens of equity theory.

EQUITY THEORY

Before presenting equity theory, it is useful to place it within the broader context of research on organizational justice. Greenberg (1987) provided a taxonomy of the field of organizational justice that distinguished theories according to whether they are concerned with content versus process and reflect reactive versus proactive actions. The taxonomy is reproduced in Figure 1. Adams's equity theory is distinguished from other justice theories in that it focuses on how people *react* to the *content* of allocation decisions, frequently referred to as *distributive justice*. The theory is not concerned with how allocation decisions are made.

FIGURE 1
Taxonomy of Organizational Justice Theories

	Content-Process Dimension	
Reactive-Proactive Dimension	**Content**	**Process**
Reactive	*Reactive content* Equity theory (Adams, 1965)	*Reactive process* Procedural justice theory (Thibaut & Walker, 1975)
Proactive	*Proactive content* Justice judgment theory (Leventhal, 1976)	*Proactive process* Allocation preference theory (Leventhal et al., 1980)

Source: Greenberg (1987).

Instead, equity theory makes predictions about how people judge whether the allocations they receive in organizations (e.g., pay) are fair and how people react when they think they have been treated unfairly.

Building on earlier work by Homans (1961) on exchange relationships and by Festinger (1957) on cognitive dissonance, Adams's equity theory is notable for its simplicity in describing how people make judgments in deciding whether they have been treated fairly in an allocation decision and its apparent precision in predicting how people will react to unfair treatment. The basic process underlying equity theory is depicted in Figure 2.

Antecedents of Inequity

Adams described the employment relationship as an exchange relationship in which employees contributed inputs and received outcomes in return. Inputs or investments are things that employees contribute to the employment relationship, including education, previous work experience, effort on the job, and training. Outcomes are what the employee receives in exchange for his or her inputs. The most important outcome in research on equity theory has been pay, although outcomes can include a broad range of things (e.g., recognition, praise by supervisors, promotions, status). To be considered as inputs or outcomes, they must be recognized by one or both parties to the exchange and be considered relevant to the exchange (i.e., have some marginal utility).

Adams also suggested that individuals weight their inputs and outcomes by their importance to the individual. For example, someone with a degree from an Ivy League school may place greater weight on education as an input than another individual who was educated at a state college. Similarly, for some people pay may be the most important outcome at work, while for others it might be a challenging new work assignment. Adams proposed that people separately summed the weighted inputs and outcomes to develop summary measures.

To make judgments about whether an exchange is equitable or inequitable, Adams said that people compare the ratio of their (called "person") outcomes to inputs with the ratio of outcome to inputs of another individual or group (called "other"). Other can be the person with whom you are engaged in an exchange, another individual engaged in an exchange with the same third party (e.g., coworker), or the person in a previous job or anticipated work situation. The process through which individuals select referent others has been the subject of considerable discussion (Goodman, 1974; Kulik & Ambrose, 1992). Adams predicted that the referent other would most often be a different individual. However, in a study of restaurant managers, Summers and DeNisi (1990) found that 34.5% of their sample used themselves as a referent, 20% reported relying on referents inside the organization, 5.5% used referents outside the organization, and 37.8% used a generalized referent. Although the

FIGURE 2

A Representation of Equity Theory as Originally Discussed by Adams (1963)

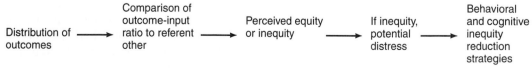

selection of a referent other introduces a degree of ambiguity into the theory, the important point is that people arrive at judgments about fairness through a social comparison process.

Equity is said to exist whenever the ratio of person's outcomes to inputs equals the ratio of other's outcomes and inputs.

$$\frac{O_p}{I_p} = \frac{O_o}{I_o}$$

Inequity exists whenever the two ratios are unequal.

$$\frac{O_p}{I_p} < \frac{O_o}{I_o} \text{ or } \frac{O_p}{I_p} > \frac{O_o}{I_o}$$

Several important aspects of how Adams defined inequity should be noted. First, the conditions necessary to produce feelings of equity or inequity are based on the individual's perceptions of input and outcomes, not necessarily the objective characteristics of the situation. Although Adams felt that people would be heavily influenced by reality, not all research evidence bears this out. For instance, Summers and DeNisi (1990) found that among a sample of the restaurant managers they studied, 65% reported feeling unfairly paid even though an objective salary survey reported that these managers generally received higher levels of compensation than comparable managers in other restaurants. Second, inequity does not necessarily exist if a person has high inputs and low outcomes as long as the referent other also has high inputs and low outcomes. Finally, inequity exists both when someone is underpaid and overpaid relative to the referent comparison. Adams anticipated that an individual's threshold for overpayment would be greater than their threshold for underpayment. As might be expected, individuals are somewhat more willing to accept good fortune (overpayment) than being treated unfairly (underpayment).

Consequences of Inequity

The relevance of Adams's theory to motivation is derived from the predicted consequences of inequity. The major predictions of the theory are: (1) perceived inequity creates tension or distress in the individual; (2) the amount of tension is proportional to the magnitude of the inequity; (3) the tension created in the individual will motivate him or her to reduce it; and (4) the strength of the motivation to reduce inequity is proportional to the perceived inequity. In other words, inequitable treatment causes tension or distress, and people are motivated to do something about it.

The ways individuals go about trying to reduce inequity are referred to as inequity reduction strategies. Adams described six alternative methods of restoring equity: (1) altering inputs, (2) altering outcomes, (3) cognitively distorting inputs or outcomes, (4) leaving the field, (5) taking actions designed to change the inputs or outcomes of the referent other, or (6) changing the comparison other.

By way of illustrating how this might work, pity the plight of Roger Clemens of the New York Yankees (cf. Verducci, 2000). On August 11, 2000, he signed a two-year contract with the Yankees for $30.9 million dollars, or $15.45 million per year. Three months later, Clemens learned that Alex Rodriguez signed a contract with the Texas Rangers worth $252 million over 10 years, or $25.2 million per year. Although Rodriguez is one of the top shortstops in the league, Clemens is recognized as one of baseball's top pitchers. If Clemens compared his ratio of outcomes to inputs with Rodriguez's ratio, he might feel inequitably treated (i.e., underpaid). What could he do to resolve the inequity? One prediction made by Adams's theory is that Clemens could reduce his inputs (i.e., not pitch as hard). Alternatively, he could cognitively readjust his outcomes (e.g., Clemens could place greater weight on the championship rings he has earned by playing on a team that is a perennial contender for the World Series). Another way to resolve the inequity is for Clemens to stop comparing himself with Rodriguez and pick a comparison other who provides a more equitable comparison (e.g., Kevin Brown of the Dodgers who earns $15 million a year). Finally, Clemens can leave the Yankees at the end of his two-year contract and attempt to strike a better deal with another team (leave the field).

This example may seem a little extreme given the amounts of money involved, although a study discussed below suggests that even highly paid athletes are not immune to feelings of inequity. However, it does help illustrate the alternative ways of reducing perceived inequity. One of the areas of theoretical ambiguity in equity theory concerns predicting which method of inequity reduction a person will take. Adams felt that people would select a method of reducing inequity that maximized positively valent outcomes and/or minimized increasing effortful inputs. However, the inability of the theory to predict precisely which method of inequity reduction a person will select has been a major source of criticism. Moreover, theoretical ambiguity exists because multiple outcomes are consistent with the theory. For example, if Roger Clemens stopped pitching as hard we could assume he was decreasing his inputs, as predicted by the theory. On the other hand, if Roger Clemens continues pitching as hard as he ever did, this may also be consistent with the theory (e.g., he cognitively readjusted his outcomes or changed his referent other).

Extensions of Equity Theory

Although the mathematical formulation of equity theory is elegant in its simplicity, it does not accurately model all possible situations. Walster, Bercheid, and Walster (1976) noted that a problem occurs when inputs and/or outcomes are negative. Consider a situation in which a person's inputs have a value of 5 and outcomes are -10 compared to a referent other who has inputs and outcomes of -5 and 10, respectively. Using Adams's formula, these two ratios are equal and a condition of equity exists.

$$\frac{O_p}{I_p} = \frac{-10}{5} = -2 \text{ and } \frac{O_o}{I_o} = \frac{10}{-5} = -2$$

Obviously, a situation in which a person makes positive inputs but receives negative outcomes is inequitable when compared to a person making negative inputs but receiving positive outcomes. Walster et al. (1976) proposed an alternative formulation that overcomes this problem. Equity and inequity are defined by the following relationship, where k_p and k_o are exponents that take on the value of $+1$ or -1 depending on the sign of person and other's inputs and person and other's outcomes.

$$\frac{Outcomes_p - Inputs_p}{(|Inputs_p|)^k_p} \text{ compared with } \frac{Outcomes_o - Inputs_o}{(|Inputs_o|)^k_o}$$

Others have also offered mathematical reformulations of equity theory in attempts to better capture the complexity of reactions to inequity found in research. For example, Coser and

Dalton (1983) incorporated time as a variable in the mathematical formula to account for a finding from a study by Lawler, Koplin, Young, and Fadem (1968), which is reviewed in greater depth later in this reading.

RESEARCH ON EQUITY THEORY

Equity theory has been extensively studied over the years, although the focus of this body of research has evolved over time. Initial research focused on testing predictions of the theory with respect to pay and was largely confined to experimental laboratory studies or experimental studies in simulated organizations. More recently, research on equity theory has moved from the laboratory into the field and has focused on a variety of attitudinal and behavioral outcomes. A number of reviews of research on equity theory have been published over the years (Lawler, 1968; Adams & Freedman, 1976; Mowday, 1979; Greenberg, 1982, 1990a; Ambrose & Kulik, 1999; Colquitt, Conlon, Wesson, Porter, & Ng, 2001). These reviews have generally concluded that the major predictions of the theory have been supported, although support for underpayment inequity has been stronger than the support for overpayment. Although a number of studies have supported the overpayment predictions, questions have been raised about the methods used to manipulate perceptions of overpayment in the laboratory (e.g., Schwab, 1980). Also, there are questions whether perceptions of overpayment exist, at least for long, in the absence of experimental manipulations to create them.

Because research on equity theory has been comprehensively reviewed frequently and quite recently, there is little point in reviewing the research evidence again here. Instead, an appreciation for the research evidence on equity theory can be gained by examining several studies that are illustrative of this research. We will begin by examining one of the early studies of overpayment inequity. We then review three additional studies conducted more recently. These studies were not selected randomly. Instead, each was chosen because it illustrates a particular research methodology and/or presents findings that help extend our understanding of inequity.

Traditional Laboratory Research on Equity Theory

Lawler et al. (1968) conducted one of the early tests of Adams's predictions about overpayment inequity when individuals are paid on a piece-rate basis. This is a particularly interesting prediction because of the complexity of resolving the inequity. When individuals are paid by the hour, Adams predicted they would work harder, increasing their contributions, to reduce overpayment inequity. However, this strategy won't work in the case of piece-rate payment when you are paid for each part produced or interview conducted because working harder simply increases your outcomes and increases the inequity. When paid by the piece rate, Adams predicted that people would produce fewer, higher quality outputs. This strategy combines increasing inputs with lower outcomes.

Lawler et al. (1968) hired 40 high school and college students to conduct interviews. Students were hired to work six hours divided into three two-hour sessions. The established pay rate was $.30 per interview conducted. Perceived equity was manipulated when students reported for work. They were randomly assigned to either an equitable or overpayment condition. Equitably paid students were told that they were well qualified to conduct public opinion interviews. To induce perceptions of overpayment inequity, the other group was told that there has been a mistake in hiring because they didn't have the necessary experience to conduct interviews. Because they had already reported to work, however, they would be hired and paid the same amount as other interviewers with much more experience.

As predicted by Adams, in the first two-hour interviewing session inequitably overpaid students conducted fewer interviews of higher quality than equitably paid students. Interestingly, the dramatic differences found in the first session dissipated in the second and third sessions. A measure of self-perceptions of qualifications for doing the job of interviewing suggests what might have happened. Although overpaid subjects reacted as predicted in the first session, they may have resolved the inequity in subsequent sessions by simply increasing their perceived qualifications as an interviewer (i.e., increasing their inputs relative to outcomes). The highest perceived qualifications were found among the overpaid students after the third session. Thus, in the long-term students acted in ways to reduce the perceived overpayment inequity but in ways less costly to themselves.

Although convincing students that they may not be qualified for a job was a standard way of inducing overpayment inequity in early studies, it was subsequently criticized because it could have also threatened job security and/or self-esteem (Schwab, 1980). Students might have worked harder to conduct high-quality interviews simply because they were afraid of losing their jobs and/or wanted to prove to themselves they were qualified. Subsequent studies using different manipulations to induce feelings of overpayment did not always support Adams's predictions (e.g., Lawler 1968).

Survey Research on Distributive and Procedural Justice

Although Adams's theory generated considerable interest in the process through which people evaluate the outcomes they receive in the workplace (distributive justice), recent interest in organizational justice has focused on the perceptions of the process through which outcomes are allocated, or procedural justice. There is considerable evidence that people look at both the outcomes they receive and the process through which those outcomes were determined. People may not react as negatively to receiving inequitable outcomes if they understand the reason for the decision and/or feel that the process through which the decision was made was fair (cf. Brocker & Wiesenfeld, 1996).

A study conducted by Sweeney and McFairlin (1993) illustrates the use of questionnaires to study the relationship of distributive and procedural justice perceptions. They compared four possible models of this relationship among engineers working for a public utility company in the Midwest. One model predicted that distributive and procedural justice perceptions predict different outcomes. This model builds on research by Folger and Konovsky (1989) that found that distributive justice perceptions predict individual-level outcomes such as pay satisfaction, while procedural justice predicts more global system evaluations such as organizational commitment. The second model suggested that perceptions of procedural justice affect perceptions of distributive justice. The third model predicted that perceptions of distributive and procedural justice have additive effects in predicting attitudes in the workplace. The final model is the reverse of the second: Perceptions of distributive justice influence perceptions of procedural justice.

Sweeney and McFarlin (1991) measured behavioral and procedural justice by means of a questionnaire distributed by mail to engineers. The criterion measures they examined included pay-level satisfaction and organizational commitment. They analyzed the relationship of distributive and procedural justice using sophisticated causal modeling and found the greatest support for what was called the "two factor" model. This model, the first one discussed above, suggests that distributive and procedural justice are both important but each predict different outcomes. Distributive justice was more highly related to pay-level satisfaction, while procedural justice was more predictive of organizational commitment.

Although moving research on equity out of the experimental laboratory and into the field using alternative methodologies has been an important step in more comprehensively testing the theory, it may have come at the cost of theoretical precision. The most common measure of distributive justice developed by Price and Mueller (1986) asks people if they believe they have been treated fairly with respect to job responsibilities, experience, stress, effort, and good performance. Recall that Adams suggested that perceptions of inequity occur both when an individual is underpaid and overpaid. Unfortunately, Price and Mueller's (1986) measure only looks at overall perceptions of being fairly rewarded and does not distinguish different reasons why perceived unfairness occurs. As research has increasingly focused more on the concept of distributive justice and less on perceptions of inequity, our understanding of the reasons people feel unfairly treated may have diminished and the results have become harder to compare with the predictions of equity theory.

Archival Studies of Equity Theory in Professional Sports

One of the strengths of early research on equity theory was that it focused on behaviors by examining the performance implications of being underpaid or overpaid. As research on equity theory has moved from the laboratory into the field, the emphasis on behaviors relative to attitudes has diminished because performance data are often more difficult to come by (Ambrose & Kulik, 1999). One area in which this is not the case is professional sports. In Major League Baseball, for example, extensive performance data are available on each player in the league. Some of the most interesting applications of equity theory have been conducted in studies of Major League Baseball and professional basketball. Because this literature is extensive (Lord & Hohenfeld, 1979; Duchon & Jago, 1981; Hauenstein & Lord, 1989; Harder, 1991, 1992), we review only Harder's work here. It is briefly reviewed here to illustrate the extension of equity theory into the field using archival performance data and because it provides a strong test of equity theory predictions.

Harder (1991) studied the performance of 106 nonpitchers who participated in the free-agent reentry draft during the period 1977–80. It was reasoned that players seeking to become free agents were dissatisfied with the pay being offered by their teams and thus could be considered to be in an underreward inequity condition. The standard prediction in equity theory is that individuals who perceive they are underrewarded will decrease their inputs. However, if baseball players decrease their performance, this may hurt their chances of signing a more lucrative contract later on. Because rewards in baseball are performance based, this becomes very similar to the piece-rate underpayment condition.

Based on extensive research on the salary and performance of baseball players, Harder (1991) found that the strongest predictor of salary for nonpitchers was slugging percentage (total sum of bases attained with base hits divided by total times at bat). Simple batting average, although important, is less strongly related to salary. Harder (1991) predicted that players who felt underpaid could not afford to reduce their slugging percentage because this would decrease future salary. However, they might decrease their batting average to reduce the inequity.

Harder (1991) found that free agency significantly decreased a player's batting average in the option year. Although expectancy theory might have predicted an increase in slugging percentage because this performance variable is linked to pay, this was not found.

In a follow-up study examining both professional baseball players and basketball players, Harder (1992) found additional support for equity theory predictions. Using more sophisticated wage determination models, Harder (1992) was able to develop a measure of both underreward and overreward. Among baseball players who were overrewarded, runs created increased in three of the four years studied. Underrewarded baseball players were more likely to lower batting averages, although this effect was weaker and only found in two of the four years. In contrast, professional basketball players who were underrewarded tended to take more shots but score fewer points, while overrewarded basketball players increased their performance in areas unrelated to scoring (e.g., assists, rebounds, blocked shots). This was interpreted as suggesting the underrewarded basketball players acted more selfishly (focused on individual scoring) while overrewarded players were more team-oriented and cooperative.

A Field Experiment on Perceived Inequity and Employee Theft

In one of the cleverest investigations of equity in organizations, Greenberg (1990b) used the occasion of a temporary 15% reduction in pay in two manufacturing plants to study how employees reacted. Both plants were owned by same parent company but operated in different geographic locations. Because the company lost two major contracts, management decided on a temporary reduction in pay in lieu of layoffs. The way this decision was announced was manipulated across the two plants.

In Plant A, called the adequate explanation condition, management held a 90-minute meeting with employees explaining the reasons for the temporary reduction, answering questions and offering apologies and expressions of remorse for the decision. In Plant B, called the inadequate explanation condition, the meeting was 15 minutes long. The decision was announced and briefly explained, but without apologies or expressions of remorse by managers. A third plant in which no pay reductions were necessary was included in the study as a control group.

Greenberg (1990b) monitored changes in employee theft rates and turnover as a consequence of the pay reduction. Equity theory would predict that employees who had their pay reduced would feel underrewarded and could resolve the inequity by either decreasing their inputs (working less hard), increasing outcomes (theft), or leaving the company (turnover). As predicted by equity theory, employee theft increased significantly in both the adequate and inadequate explanation plants (no change was found in the control plant). However, the increase was much greater in the inadequate explanation plant. Employee turnover also increased among employees receiving an inadequate explanation. When the temporary pay reduction ended, employee theft rates returned to their previous levels in both plants.

It is important to note that Greenberg's (1990b) study was primarily designed to manipulate procedural justice by providing different explanations for the pay reduction. However, a clear effect on employee theft was also found in the plant receiving an adequate explanation. This is consistent with equity theory predictions. The fact that the increase in employee theft was so much greater in the plant given an inadequate explanation suggests that Adams's theory may be incomplete without including procedural justice as a major variable.

CONTEXTUAL AND INDIVIDUAL DIFFERENCE VARIABLES AND EQUITY THEORY

One of the most attractive features of Adams's original statements of equity theory was its simplicity and apparent precision. After almost 40 years of empirical research, it should not come as a surprise to learn that things are not as simple as Adams may have thought. Based on a number of research studies, we know that a variety of contextual and individual difference factors may influence how people react to perceived inequities. These factors are depicted as moderator variables in Figure 3 and are discussed briefly below. In interpreting Figure 3, the reader is cautioned that the research evidence on contextual and individual difference moderators is not precise enough to determine exactly where in the process the moderating effect occurs. One reason is that studies of equity theory rarely, if ever, comprehensively measure all five steps in the process specified by Adams. For example, the prototypical test of equity theory creates conditions of perceived inequity by manipulating outcomes and then examines behavioral reactions. Comparisons of outcome-input ratios and distress are often unmeasured variables. Thus, although we have suggestive evidence of contextual and individual difference moderators, we lack a precise understanding of how they operate.

Contextual Factors

Although the theory as originally proposed by Adams was a general model, a number of research studies have demonstrated that the process outlined in the theory can be influenced by a number of contextual factors. For example, Greenberg's (1990b) research on employee theft demonstrated that perceptions of procedural justice can influence how employees react to a temporary reduction in pay. Brockner and Wiesenfeld (1996) reviewed over 40 studies that have found an interaction between perceived fairness of outcomes and perceived procedural fairness, causing them to conclude that "the effects of what you do depend on how you do it" (p. 206).

Griffeth, Vecchio and Logan (1989) hired 66 students to work on a proofreading task in which perceptions of underpayment inequity, equitable payment, and overpayment inequity were manipulated. Students were led to believe that they would be working with another student who was either interpersonally attractive or unattractive based on attitude similarity. In addition to confirming the predictions of equity theory, this study also found an interaction between reactions to inequity and the attractiveness of a coworker. For example, in the high-attraction condition it was found that overpaid students produced higher quality work than comparably overpaid students in the low-attraction condition. Presumably, people are more motivated to rectify overpayment inequities when they are attracted to the other person who is being underpaid.

Another important contextual factor anticipated by Adams is the nature of the relationship between pay and performance. As noted in reviewing Harder's (1991) study of Major League Baseball players, inequity reduction strategies are sensitive to whether pay is strongly or weakly related to performance. When the relationship is strong, inequitably paid

FIGURE 3
Contextual and Individual Difference Influences on Equity Theory*

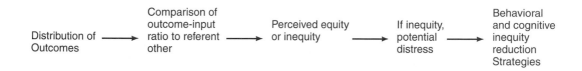

Contextual Factors
• Procedural justice
• Relationship to
  referent other
• Compensation
  system
• Time
• Presentation of outcomes
• Culture

Distribution of ⟶ Comparison of outcome-input ratio to referent other ⟶ Perceived equity or inequity ⟶ If inequity, potential distress ⟶ Behavioral and cognitive inequity reduction Strategies

Individual Differences
• Gender
• Exchange orientation
• Organizational
  Commitment

*Contextual factors and individual differences are portrayed as general moderators because although the research literature clearly supports these variables as moderating the equity theory process, the research evidence is not precise enough to identify at which steps in the equity theory process the moderation takes place.

players could not reduce performance without also decreasing future rewards. Not surprisingly, the baseball players Harder studied chose alternative forms of inequity reduction that were less costly.

The study conducted by Lawler et al. (1968) found that inequity reduction strategies are sensitive to effects of time. Although the students hired in this study behaved as predicted by the theory in the short term, this effect did not persist. In the longer term, students adopted an alternative inequity reduction strategy that was less costly to them personally.

In an interesting study of the effects of information processing on perceived inequities, Bazerman, Loewenstein, and White (1992) manipulated how people evaluated allocation decisions by presenting different allocation outcomes separately or as multiple options. For example, subjects in the rating condition were asked to separately state their preference between an allocation that maintained equality ($500 for self/$500 for other) and an allocation in which their outcomes increased but were inequitable ($600 for self/$800 for other). The other condition asked for preferences among multiple allocations presented at the same time. They found that alternative ways of presenting information about outcomes influences how people weigh interpersonal comparisons. Subjects in two studies paid greater attention to the equity of their payoffs when they evaluated a single outcome than when multiple outcomes were evaluated. In the single outcome condition, subjects tended to prefer an equitable outcome ($500 self/$500 other) to the alternative ($600 self/$800 other) even though it lowered their outcomes. In the latter case, subjects acted in ways that increased their own absolute payoffs.

Finally, although equity may be a preferred norm in North America, it may not be preferred in other cultures. In other cultures, it may be more appropriate to distribute outcomes based on an equality norm or based on need than based on contributions (Leventhal, 1976). Early studies comparing reactions to inequity and preferences for outcomes relative to inputs found differences in how individuals in the United States respond compared to individuals from other countries (e.g., Weick, Bougon, & Maruyama, 1976). For example, Levine (1993) found that social comparison processes were important in Japanese manufacturing plants and that overpayment inequity within a plant was associated with lower morale and commitment, a finding consistent with the more egalitarian culture in Japan.

Individual Factors

Although Adams did not incorporate individual differences into this theory, the importance of considering them was recognized by others. Tornow (1971) observed that the classification of a variable as either an input or an outcome was ambiguous and that people may have a tendency to be input or outcome oriented. Reanalyzing data from a previous study, it was found that people who were outcome oriented were more sensitive to overpayment inequity than individuals who were input oriented.

Building on this idea, Huseman, Hatfield, and Miles (1987) introduced an individual difference variable they labeled equity sensitivity. They reasoned that some people may actually prefer inequitable outcomes. They identified three types of people: "benevolents," who prefer being underpaid; "equity sensitives," who prefer equity and thus behave in inequitable situations as the theory would predict; and "entitleds," who prefer overpayment. Subsequently, the equity sensitivity construct was refined to suggest that benevolents may not actually prefer being underpaid but have a greater tolerance for this form of inequity (King, Miles & Day, 1993). Similarly, entitleds were predicted to have a greater tolerance for overpayment. Although they found some support for their reconceptualization of construct, their research has been criticized on both conceptual (Greenberg, 1990a) and measurement grounds (Sauley & Bedeian, 2000).

In a comprehensive review of individual differences in justice behavior, Major and Deaux (1982) found evidence supporting gender differences in response to inequitable treatment. In general, females may be more tolerant of underpayment inequity than males. Writing more broadly on the topic of comparable worth, Greenberg (1990c) reviewed research that suggests that females may simply experience less perceived inequity because they prefer comparing themselves to other females in similar jobs than to males. As the article from the *New York Times* referred to at the start of this chapter suggests, however, inequitable treatment of females in the workplace is certainly not always tolerated.

Finally, in a provocative study of reactions to employee layoffs in organizations, Brockner, Tyler and Cooper-Schneider (1992) found individual attitudes toward the organization can moderate reactions to unfair treatment. They studied full-time employees in a financial services firm that had undergone layoffs. Employees who reported having the highest commitment to the organization responded to perceived unfair treatment in the layoff process more negatively than individuals with lower levels of commitment.

EMERGING SOURCES OF INEQUITY IN THE WORKPLACE

As long as exchange relationships take place, there will be the possibility, if not strong probability, of perceived inequitable treatment. Although most managers strive to treat their employees fairly, it is hard to imagine that perceived inequity won't exist, if only because we know that people often have wildly inflated estimates of their performance contributions. In addition, there are some emerging sources of inequity that are interesting to consider.

Frank and Cook (1995) have noted a contemporary trend toward what they have called "winner-take-all" markets. Although standard economic theory suggests that people should be paid in proportion to the value of their productive contributions, Frank and Cook (1995) provide a number of examples where the difference in performance between two individuals may be 10% but the difference in their pay is much higher (e.g., 1,000% or more).

A good illustration of a winner-take-all market was provided by Friedman's (1999) analysis of the wage structure of the National Basketball Association. Professional basketball teams have 12 players, all of whom must be highly skilled just to make it into the NBA. On the 1997 Chicago Bulls, Michael Jordan's salary was $31.3 million, and he had additional income from endorsements of $47 million. On the same team as Jordan was a player named Joe Kleine, who made the league minimum salary of $272,250. Clearly, Jordan was the star player on the Bulls, but the disparity in pay between Jordan and Kleine is difficult to justify given the far smaller difference in their basketball skills. As the level of pay going to the superstars like Jordan continues to rise, the existence of a salary cap means that more and more players in the league, including some starters, will earn the league minimum. In fact, that's exactly what is happening. Friedman (1999) reports that the proportion of players making the league minimum has steadily increased over the years. He notes that low team morale, which would be predicted by equity theory, was a particular problem on the Houston Rockets, which had three highly paid superstars and a majority of players making the league minimum wage.

Admittedly, it is difficult to feel too sorry for professional athletes making $272,250 a year. However, Frank and Cook (1995) argue that the societal distribution of income is increasingly characterized by a huge gap between the top and the bottom. Friedman (1999, p. 309) reports that "the incomes of the poorest fifth of working families in America dropped by 21% between 1979 and 1995, adjusted for inflation, while the income of the richest fifth jumped by 30% during the same period." The gap between the richest and poorest Americans is growing and at the same time the middle class is shrinking.

Nowhere is the gap between the top and the bottom more evident than in executive compensation. *Fortune* magazine estimates that compensation for the average New York schoolteacher increased 20% from 1990 to 2000, while the compensation of the CEO of the largest conglomerate (Jack Welch of General Electric) increased 2,496% during the same time period (Loomis, 2001). A number of popular business periodicals have been critical of increases in executive compensation, both because the increases are growing so fast and the absolute levels of compensation have grown so large. In 2001, *Fortune* reported that the highest paid executive in the United States was Steven Jobs of Apple Computer. His total compensation in 2000 was estimated by *Fortune* to be $872 million, including $1 in salary he is paid as CEO, the $92 million Gulfstream jet he was given by the board of directors of Apple, and stock options (Colvin, 2001). In the previous year, his total compensation was estimated to be $381 million.

One of the reasons that executive compensation may have grown out of control is a direct application of the principles of equity theory. Colvin (2001, p. 70) described how the process works. Assume a poorly performing company fires their CEO and hires a new one to turn things around. The new CEO demands a signing bonus because of the stock options she or he forgoes by leaving their old job (for Gary Wendt, who left General Electric Capital for Conseco, the signing bonus was $45 million). It would make little sense to pay the new CEO less than the poorly performing CEO who was fired, so there is often a hefty increase in the pay package. As a result, the median pay in that industry increases. Compensation consultants who are most often hired by management will note the increase and use it to justify higher compensation for other executives at other companies in the industry. Colvin (2001) reports that most boards of directors believe their CEO ranks in the 75th percentile or above, thus driving median compensation even higher. Thus, the desire to maintain equity in executive compensation when no CEOs are perceived to be average or below average performers may be one of the causes of the relentless increases that have taken place.

One might predict that CEOs would experience overpayment inequity, although one suspects this doesn't happen because they compare themselves with other CEOs who are also richly rewarded. However, the view from the bottom of the organization may be quite different. Cowherd and Levine (1992) examined interclass pay equity in 102 corporate business units. After controlling for inputs and other variables that may influence differences in pay, they calculated the pay differential between lower level employees and top managers. They predicted that large pay differentials would result in lower employee motivation and that this could negatively influence the overall effectiveness of the business unit. Using a measure of perceived product quality, Cowherd and Levine (1992) found that the smaller the difference between pay at the bottom and top of the business units, the greater the perceived product quality. It appears that lower level employees pay attention to rewards received by top executives and that the increasing levels of rewards received by top managers may come at the expense of decreased performance.

Another source of emerging inequity in work organizations is the increasing use of contingent, part-time, or permanent-temporary employees. Baron and Kreps (1999) report that the use of temporary workers increased 175% and part-time workers increased by 21% from 1980 to 1988. Often these workers perform the same jobs as regular employees, although at lower wages and with no or reduced benefits. These employment practices are similar to the two-tier wage structures adopted by many airlines in the 1980s in which newly hired employees were paid much less and would never be paid as much as regular employees who did the same work. Research based on equity theory predicts that individuals in the bottom tier would perceive this situation to be inequitable, and there is evidence in support of this prediction (Martin & Peterson, 1987). Interestingly, Capelli and Sherer (1990) found higher satisfaction among employees on the lower paying tier of an airline, a finding that was explained by the different referent comparisons used by each group.

Baron and Kreps (1999) suggest that managers are sensitive to perceived inequities in the workplace and try to minimize perceived inequity by how work is organized and where jobs are located. For example, Baron and Kreps (1999) report that contingent and temporary workers are often placed on different shifts or in different physical locations than regular employees for precisely this reason. Additional evidence that perceived inequity is managed in the workplace has been provided by Zenger (1992). He analyzed the common practice in organizations of only rewarding performance at the extremes (i.e., to limit performance distinctions and rewards to a relatively few high and low performers and disregard performance distinctions for the majority of moderate performers). His analysis demonstrates that only rewarding extreme high performers limits the number of inequity pay comparisons that can be made by the large number of employees in the middle. He argued that at the extremes of performance the benefits of rewarding performance are high and the likelihood of comparison costs low. In contrast, when finer distinctions in performance are made among employees, the costs of inequitable comparisons far outweigh the benefits of increased performance. While Zenger (1992) felt this was an efficient practice overall, the practice of "reward the extremes" was not without costs. In a study conducted among engineers in two high-technology firms, he found that employees who indicated they were most likely to leave the organization were extreme low performers and above-average (but below the extreme high) performers. Turnover intentions were lowest for extreme high and below-average performers. Thus, after removing the extremes of high and low performance from consideration, the companies Zenger (1992) studied were losing their above-average performers (who were being underpaid relative to their performance contributions) and retaining their below-average performers (who were being overpaid).

THE MOTIVATIONAL IMPLICATIONS OF EQUITY THEORY

Adams's equity theory has made an important contribution to our understanding of motivation and to the practice of management by highlighting the importance of social comparison processes and the consequences of perceived inequity. In and of itself, equity theory is not a comprehensive theory of motivation. Instead, it focuses more narrowly on the process through which individuals evaluate and react to the outcomes they receive. Given the central importance of the linkage between performance and rewards in most theories of motivation (e.g., expectancy theory and reinforcement theory), however, the concept of equity is critical to our understanding of motivation. For example, expectancy theory focuses more attention in understanding motivation on the relationship between performance and rewards, suggesting that higher levels of performance should be followed by higher levels of rewards that lower levels of performance. Although this relationship is important, Adams's theory suggests that the process through which employees evaluate their rewards is more complicated because it involves social comparison processes. In other words, the motivational implications of rewards depend both on what we receive and what we receive relative to others. For this reason, several motivation theorists have suggested that the concept of equity be incorporated into more comprehensive motivation theories such as expectancy theory (e.g., Lawler, 1968).

Although Adams's equity theory generated considerable research interest after it was first introduced, in more recent years interest among researchers in the theory, although still apparent, has waned. There are several reasons for this. First, it would be unrealistic to think that the high level of interest that equity theory generated could be maintained in the long run. Researchers tested the basic predictions of the theory and found that they were generally supported. With additional tests of the theory likely to produce diminishing returns to knowledge, researchers simply turned their attention to other things. Second, as research progressed it became apparent that the theory was not without limitations. For example, the lack of precision in predicting how individuals will respond to perceived inequity limits the utility of the theory. As the example of Roger Clemens discussed earlier illustrates, it is difficult to design unequivocal tests of the theory because very different behavioral responses to inequity are equally plausible. Another limitation that has been noted is that equity theory may only account for one of several important dimensions of justice or fairness in the workplace. In recent years, researchers have focused more attention on procedural justice than on distributive justice.

Even though research interest in equity theory may have diminished, its importance to understanding motivation and to the practice of management has not. For managers, equity theory alerts them to situations in which perceived inequity could have adverse implications for employee motivation For example, Rousseau (2001) has written of the increasingly common practice of "idiosyncratic deals" in which valued employees are given special privileges that may not be available to all employees (e.g., time away from work to care for a parent). Although job requirements that are sensitive to the differing needs of individual employees are important to retaining talent, managers must recognize that other employees may view such arrangements as inequitable and take steps to minimize the potential negative consequences.

In addition to the continuing practical significance of equity theory, it is also evident that the theory continues to provide valuable theoretical contributions to understanding behavior in a variety of organizational contexts. This is evident in the recent studies reviewed earlier of professional athletes (Harder, 1991) and the effects of wage differentials in the workplace (Cowherd & Levin, 1992). It is also evident in the fact that equity has become an important explanatory variable in fields beyond organizational behavior, including economics (Akerlof, 1984; Fehr & Schmidt, 1999), consumer behavior (Hoffman & Kelley, 2000), and marital relationships (Buunk & Van Yperen, 1991). Equity theory may have been introduced into the literature almost 40 years ago, but its value in helping to understand employee motivation has withstood the test of time.

References

Abelson, R. 2001. A survey of Wall St. finds women disheartened. *New York Times,* July 26.

Adams, J. S. 1963. Toward an understanding of inequity. *Journal of Abnormal and Social Psychology,* 67: 422–436.

Adams, J. S. 1965. Inequity in social exchange. In L. Berkowitz (Ed.), *Advances in Experimental Social Psychology.* 267–299. New York: Academic Press.

Adams, J. S., & Freedman, S. 1976. Equity theory revisited: Comments and annotated bibliography. In L. Berkowitz and E. Walster (Eds.), *Advances in Experimental Social Psychology.* 43–90. New York: Academic Press.

Akerlof, G. A. 1984. Gift exchange and efficiency-wage theory: Four views. *American Economic Review,* 74: 79–83.

Ambrose, M. L., & Kulik, C. T. 1999. Old friends, new faces: Motivation research in the 1990s. *Journal of Management,* 25: 231–292.

Baron, J. N., & Kreps, D. M. 1999. *Strategic Human Resource Management.* New York: John Wiley & Sons.

Bazerman, M. H., Loewenstein, G. F., & White, S. B. 1992. Reversals of preference in allocation decisions: Judging an alternative versus choosing among alternatives. *Administrative Science Quarterly,* 37: 220–240.

Brockner, J., Tyler, T. R., & Cooper-Schneider, R. 1992. The influence of prior commitment to an institution on reactions to perceived unfairness: The higher they are, the harder they fall. *Administrative Science Quarterly,* 37: 241–261.

Brockner, J., & Wiesenfeld, B. M. 1996. An integrative framework for explaining reactions to decisions: Interactive effects of outcomes and procedures. *Psychological Bulletin,* 120: 189–208.

Buunk, B. P., & Van Yperen, N. W. 1991. Referential comparisons, relational comparisons, and exchange orientation: Their relation to marital satisfaction. *Personality and Social Psychology Bulletin,* 17: 709–717.

Capelli, P., & Sherer, P. D. 1990. Assessing worker attitudes under a two-tier wage plan. *Industrial and Labor Relations Review,* 43: 225–244.

Colquitt, J. A., Conlon, D. E., Wesson, M. J., Porter O. L. H., & Ng, K. Y. 2001. Justice at the millennium: A meta-analytic review of 25 years of organizational justice research. *Journal of Applied Psychology,* 86: 425–445.

Colvin, G. 2001. The great CEO pay heist. *Fortune,* June 25.

Coser, R., & Dalton, D. 1983. Equity theory and time: A reformulation. *Academy of Management Review,* 8: 311–319.

Cowherd, D. M., & Levine, D. I. 1992. Product quality and pay equity between lower-level employees and top management: An investigation of distributive justice. *Administrative Science Quarterly,* 37: 302–320.

Duchon, D., & Jago, A. G. 1981. Equity and the performance of major league baseball players: An extension of Lord and Hohenfeld. *Journal of Applied Psychology,* 66: 728–732.

Fehr, E., & Schmidt, K. M. 1999. A theory of fairness, competition, and cooperation. *Quarterly Journal of Economics,* 114: 817–869.

Festinger, L. 1957. *A Theory of Cognitive Dissonance.* Stanford: Stanford University Press.

Folger, R., & Konovsky, M. A. 1989. Effects of procedural and distributive justice on reactions to pay raise decisions. *Academy of Management Journal,* 32: 115–130.

Frank, R. H., & Cook, P. J. 1995. *The Winner-Take-All Society.* New York: Martin Kessler Books.

Friedman, T. L. 1999. *The Lexus and the Olive Tree.* New York: Anchor Books.

Goodman, P. S. 1974. An examination of referents used in the evaluation of pay. *Organizational Behavior and Human Performance,* 12: 170–195.

Greenberg, J. 1982. Approaching equity and avoiding inequity in organizations. In J. Greenberg and R. L. Cohen (Eds.), *Equity and Justice in Social Behavior.* 389–435. New York: Academic Press.

Greenberg, J. 1987. A taxonomy of organizational justice theories. *Academy of Management Review,* 12: 9–22.

Greenberg, J. 1990a. Organizational justice: Yesterday, today, and tomorrow. *Journal of Management,* 16: 399–432.

Greenberg, J. 1990b. Employee theft as a reaction to underpayment inequity: The hidden costs of pay cuts. *Journal of Applied Psychology,* 75: 561–568.

Greenberg, J. 1990c. Comparable worth: A matter of justice. In G. R. Ferris and K. M. Rowland (Eds.). *Research in Personnel and Human Resources Management.* 265–301. Greenwich, CT L:JAI Press.

Griffeth, R. W., Vecchio, R. P., & Logan, J. W. Jr. 1989. Equity theory and interpersonal attraction. *Journal of Applied Psychology,* 74: 394–401.

Harder, J. W. 1991. Equity theory versus expectancy theory: The case of major league baseball free agents. *Journal of Applied Psychology,* 76: 458–464.

Harder, J. W. 1992. Play for pay: Effects of inequity in a pay-for-performance context. *Administrative Science Quarterly,* 37: 321–333.

Hauenstein, N. M. A., & Lord, R. G. 1989. The effects of final-offer arbitration on the performance of major league baseball players: A test of equity theory. *Human Performance,* 2: 147–165.

Hoffman, K. D., & Kelley, S. W. 2000. Perceived justice needs and recovery evaluation: A contingency approach. *European Journal of Marketing,* 34: 418–423.

Homans, G. C. 1961. *Social Behavior: Its Elementary Forms.* New York: Harcourt, Brace & World.

Huseman, R. C., Hatfield, J. D., & Miles, E. W. 1987. A new perspective on equity theory: The equity sensitivity construct. *Academy of Management Review,* 12: 222–234.

King, W. C. Jr., Miles, E. W., & Day, D. D. 1993. A test and refinement of the equity sensitivity construct. *Journal of Organizational Behavior,* 14: 301–317.

Kulik, C. T., & Ambrose, M. L. 1992. Personal and situational determinants of referent choice. *Academy of Management Review,* 17: 212–237.

Lawler, E. E. 1968. Equity theory as a predictor of productivity and work quality. *Psychological Bulletin,* 70: 596–610.

Lawler, E. E., Koplin, C. A., Young, T. F., & Fadem, J. A. 1968. Inequity reduction over time and an induced overpayment situation. *Organizational Behavior and Human Performance,* 51: 403–410.

Leventhal, G. S. 1976. Fairness in social relationships. In J. Thibaut, J. Spence, and R. Carson (Eds.), *Contemporary Topics in Social Psychology.* 211–239. Morristown, NJ.: General Learning Press.

Leventhal, G. S. 1980. What should be done with equity theory? In K. Gergen, M. S. Greenberg, & R. H. Willis (Eds.), *Social Exchange: Advances in Theory and Research.* 27–55. New York: Plenum.

Levine, D. I. 1993. What do wages buy? *Administrative Science Quarterly,* 38: 462–483.

Lord, R. G., & Hohenfeld, J. A. 1979. Longitudinal field assessment of equity effects on the performance of major league baseball players. *Journal of Applied Psychology,* 64: 19–26.

Loomis, C. J. 2001. This stuff is wrong. *Fortune,* June 25.

Martin, J. E., & Petersen, M. M. 1987. Two-tier wages structures: Implications for equity theory. *Academy of Management Journal,* 30: 297–315.

Major, B., & Deaux, K. 1982. Individual differences in justice behavior. In J. Greenberg and R. L. Cohen (Eds.), *Equity and Justice in Social Behavior.* 43–76. New York: Academic Press.

Mowday, R. T. 1979. Equity theory predictions of behavior in organizations. In R. M. Steers and L. W. Porter (Eds.), *Motivation & Work Behavior.* 53–71. New York: Academic Press.

Price, J. L., & Mueller, C. W. 1986. *Handbook of Organizational Measurement.* Marshfield, MA.: Pitman Publishing.

Rousseau, D. M. 2001. The idiosyncratic deal: Flexibility versus fairness? *Organizational Dynamics,* 29: 260–273.

Sauley, K. S., & Bedeian, A. G. 2000. Equity sensitivity: Construction of a measure and examination of its psychometric properties. *Journal of Management,* 26: 885–910.

Schwab, D. P. 1980. Construct validity in organizational behavior. In B. M. Staw and L. L. Cummings (Eds.), *Research in Organizational Behavior.* 3–43. Greenwich, CT: JAI Press.

Summers, T. P., & DeNisi, A. S. 1990. In search of Adams' other: Reexamination of referents used in the evaluation of pay. *Human Relations,* 43: 497–511.

Sweeney, P. D., & McFarlin, D. B. 1993. Workers' evaluations of the "ends" and the "means": An examination of four models of distributive and procedural justice. *Organizational Behavior and Human Decision Processes,* 53: 23–40.

Tahmincioglu, E. 2001. Employers maintaining vigilance in the face of layoff rage. *New York Times,* August 1.

Thibaut, J., & Walker, L. 1975. *Procedural Justice: A Psychological Analysis.* Hillsdale, NJ: Lawrence Erlbaum.

Toner, R. 2001. President of Urban League calls for review of inequity. *New York Times,* July 30.

Tornow, W. W. 1971. The development and application of an input-outcome moderator test on the perception and reduction of inequity. *Organizational Behavior and Human Performance,* 6: 614–638.

Verducci, T. 2000. Powerball. *Sports Illustrated,* December 18: 102.

Walster, E., Bercheid, E., & Walster, G. 1976. New directions in equity research. In L. Berkowitz (Ed.), *Advances in Experimental Social Psychology.* 1–42. New York: Academic Press.

Weick, K. E., Bougon, M. G., & Maruyama, G. 1976. The equity context. *Organizational Behavior and Human Performance,* 15: 32–65.

Zenger, T. R. 1992. Why do employers only reward extreme performance? Examining the relationships among performance, pay, and turnover. *Administrative Science Quarterly,* 37: 198–219.

An Overview of Organizational Justice: Implications for Work Motivation

Russell Cropanzano
Deborah E. Rupp

In recent years, organizational justice has emerged as a critical variable for understanding work behavior. When individuals believe they are being treated fairly, they tend to exhibit higher levels of job performance and more organizational citizenship behavior (Colquitt, Conlon, Wesson, Porter, & Ng, 2001), while engaging in fewer conflicts and less counter-productive activity (Cohen-Charash & Spector, 2001). Given the ubiquity of these findings, justice has become relevant to motivation, at least because it predicts the direction and energy of important work behaviors. Given these observations, this chapter will review organizational justice from the perspective of work motivation. In the opening section, we discuss some lingering issues of structure. This will provide a framework for organizing the rest of our discussion. Subsequent to the opening, we divide the justice literature into two parts. In keeping with research on work motivation (e.g., Campbell & Prichard, 1976; Kanfer, 1991), we observe that inquiry into justice has followed two related traditions: content and process. The content tradition, outlined in our second section, discusses why justice matters to individuals. The process tradition, which we take up in the third section, emphasizes the cognitive and affective processes by which individuals formulate and act upon their feelings of (in)justice. Finally, with this review behind us, we conclude this chapter with a short discourse on the relationship between justice and work motivation.

SOME THOUGHTS ON THE STRUCTURE OF JUSTICE

Generally speaking, most if not all justice researchers would divide justice perceptions into at least two types—distributive and procedural. Distributive justice refers to the fairness of outcome allocations. Procedural justice refers to the perceived fairness of the allocation process. Bies (1987) and Bies and Moag (1986) suggest that individuals also consider the fairness of the interpersonal treatment they receive from others. They term this "interactional justice" (Sitkin & Bies, 1993). Bies (2001) recommends that interactional justice be considered a third type of fairness, while others (e.g., Tyler & Blader, 2000) prefer to view interpersonal treatment as a social aspect of procedural justice (for a discussion of these issues see Bobocel & Holmvall, 2001). Finally, some scholars have gone a step further and subdivided interactional justice into two parts—informational justice, which refers to the presence of explanations and social accounts, and interpersonal justice, which refers to the dignity and respect that one receives (Greenberg, 1993). Recent evidence suggests that this four-part model is generally valid (Colquitt, 2001; Colquitt et al., 2001), though research exploring informational and interpersonal justice is limited. As a result, our review will refer mostly to research involving distributive, procedural, and interactional justice, with the caveat that a four-type model could eventually prove to be the more useful structure.

THREE MOTIVES UNDERLYING WORKPLACE JUSTICE

Intuitively, it makes good sense to postulate that employees care about their economic outcomes. Money, for example, can buy social status, health care, educational opportunities, enjoyable vacations, and a comfortable retirement. We would be stunned if people didn't care about these things! Concern over justice, on the other hand, is somewhat more enigmatic. It is not readily obvious why individuals should be concerned with things as ephemeral as ethical standards and interpersonal treatment. As we have observed elsewhere (Cropanzano, Rupp, Mohler, & Schminke, 2001), researchers in this area have proposed three basic motives underlying the concern for organizational justice: instrumental self-interest, interpersonal relationships, and moral principles. In this section, we will briefly consider each.

Instrumental Self-Interest and Organizational Justice

Loosely speaking (and see Cropanzano, Rupp, et al., 2001, for exceptions), the instrumental model suggests that justice is motivated, at least in part, by self-interest. Justice is instrumental because in the long run people are more likely to profit from a fair system than from an unfair one (Shapiro, 1993). Hence, employees are willing to trade off a short-term cost for the long-term gains that come from organizational justice.

From this instrumental perspective, organizational justice shares much with theories of motivation that emphasize the pursuit of personally desirable objectives, such as valance-instrumentality-expectancy (VIE) theory (for a meta-analytic review see Van Eerde & Thierry, 1996). There is, however, a difference in emphasis. Justice research focuses on (at least) two important elements (cf. Cropanzano & Ambrose, 2001). First, instrumental justice highlights the long-term. Accordingly, employees care about justice because they are enlightened enough to consider their future benefits, while not becoming too absorbed in short-term losses. Second, organizational justice stresses the use of allocation processes, as well as interpersonal treatment, for divining one's future benefits. Hence, individuals use the allocation process as a forecasting device for long-term profits.

Evidence for the instrumental model can be gleaned from the fact that individuals are likely to judge a process or outcome as fair when it is favorable to them (e.g., Conlon, 1993; Wade-Benzoni, Tenbrunsel, & Bazerman, 1996). Yet it is critical that we not overstate this point. One of the most important contributions of organizational justice research is the demonstration that economic outcomes are only *partial* determinants of fairness perceptions. Even when outcomes are unfavorable, individuals are likely to report just treatment so long as procedural and/or interactional fairness are maintained (Cropanzano, Byrne, Bobocel, & Rupp, 2001; Tyler & Blader, 2000; Tyler & Smith, 1998). Outcome favorability is one determinant of justice perceptions, but only part—and perhaps not the most important part—of the story. To better understand the consequences of aversive outcomes, let's consider two conditions under which they tend to be emphasized.

The Two-Factor Model

Both unfavorable and unfair outcomes tend to be better predictors of criteria that pertain directly to the outcome in question, while process and interactional factors seem to better predict reactions to the decision maker or to the organization as a whole (Cropanzano & Schminke, 2001; Tyler & Blader, 2000). Sweeney and McFarlin (1993) have dubbed this the *two-factor model*. For example, in a classic study, Folger and Konovsky (1989) studied reactions to pay raises. When participants felt the size of their pay raise was inappropriately low they were especially likely to be dissatisfied with it. On the other hand, the fairness of the pay raise process was a better predictor of supervisory trust and organizational commitment.

Interaction with Process

It is often the case that outcomes, be they unfair or unfavorable, interact with process and interpersonal treatment to predict worker reactions. Brockner and Wiesenfeld (1996) and Cropanzano and Schminke (2001) provide reviews of this interaction effect. Process and interpersonal treatment seem to matter most when the outcomes are less beneficial than they could have been. In other words, when outcomes are advantageous, procedural justice and interactional justice tend not to predict as well as they do when outcomes are disadvantageous. Most of the research to date has examined the two-way interaction either between outcome and process or between outcome and interpersonal treatment. In an extension, Skarlicki and Folger (1997) tested the three-way interaction between distributive, procedural, and interactional justice. They found that this three-way effect contributed significantly to the prediction of workplace deviance.

Interpersonal Relationships and Organizational Justice

Interpersonal models of organizational justice tend to emphasize the relationships among group members. In understanding the rule of organizational justice in work behavior, scholars have analyzed fairness in view of two models of motivation: social exchange theory (Blau, 1964) and the social identity theory (Tyler & Smith, 1998).

Application of Social Exchange Theory to Organizational Justice

There are many social exchange theories (Cropanzano, Rupp, et al., 2001). Generally speaking, contemporary versions of these frameworks tend to describe two types of interpersonal relationships (cf. Blau, 1964; Organ, 1988; Masterson, Lewis, Goldman, & Taylor, 2000). Economic exchange relationships involve relatively concrete, often monetary benefits that are exchanged in a one-to-one fashion. At the other end of the continuum are social exchange relationships. These may involve relatively abstract benefits, emotional attachments, and open-ended commitments without the necessity of immediate payback.

Organizational justice, especially procedural and interactional justice, is expected to create social exchange relationships. These relationships have been operationalized by such constructs as organizational support (Moorman, Blakely, & Niehoff, 1998), leader–member exchange (Cropanzano, Prehar, & Chen, in press), and trust (Konovsky & Pugh, 1994). Regardless of their operationalization, these social exchange relationships, in turn, are anticipated to engender citizenship behaviors and high job performance. Evidence of this relationship is generally supportive (Cropanzano, Rupp, et al., 2001; Rupp & Cropanzano, in press). Contemporary social exchange research has identified three mechanisms by which fairness and social exchange relationships promote more effective work behavior.

First, contemporary social exchange approaches often emphasize the *obligations* engendered by different sorts of relationships (Organ, 1988). Most generally, one needs to keep whatever obligations he or she has agreed to, whether they are concrete and *quid pro quo* (for economic exchanges) or abstract and open-ended (for social exchanges). Thus, when we violate those obligations we are likely to be seen as unfair. Within contemporary social exchange theory, the most commonly discussed obligation is *reciprocity* (for a recent discussion, see Fehr & Gächter, 2000). For example, Masterson et al. (2000, p. 738) suggests that "exchanges . . . yield a pattern of reciprocal obligation in each party." Not repaying someone for his or her favorable treatment of us would be considered unfair.

A second causal mechanism that has been suggested by some contemporary social exchange theorists is that of *trust.* Konovsky and Pugh (1994, p. 659) have argued that trust (which they view as one manifestation of a social exchange relationship) requires "evidence of self-sacrifice and responsiveness to another person's needs." More generally, those who are involved in close relationships are likely to "behave in ways that are . . . directed toward serving the collectivity" (p. 659). In other words, when one identifies with a group, he or she is more likely to put the group's needs above narrow self-interest. Such behavior is seen as just and further engenders trustworthiness.

A third important factor is the internalization of principles. According to Cropanzano, Rupp et al. (2001), when one is committed to a group, he or she may come to internalize the moral principles and values of that collective. In other words, he or she may be socialized into genuinely accepting certain moral standards (Cropanzano, Byrne, et al., 2001). Hence, people behave fairly because they have come to believe that this is the right or ethical thing to do. The fact that people can internalize different standards brings us to the issue of moral principles, which we shall address momentarily.

Application of Social Identity Theory to Organizational Justice: The Group-Value/Relational Model

Tyler and Lind (1992) have proposed a second interpersonal model of justice, which is based on social identity theory (Tyler & Smith, 1998). This framework has been termed the group-value (Lind & Tyler, 1988) or relational (Lind, 1995) model. According to the group-value/relational model, individuals wish to be included in important social groups. Hence, they are very sensitive to messages that pertain to their standing (Tyler & Blader, 2000, p. 90, use the term "status") within desirable collectives. Justice (especially procedural justice) is valued "because experiencing those procedures leads them to feel valued as people and as group members" (Tyler & Blader, p. 90). Injustice, on the other hand, implies low standing. There is a good deal of evidence supporting the group-value/relational model (Cropanzano, Rupp, et al., 2001).

Moral Principles and Organizational Justice

The self-interested and interpersonal approaches are each interpretable in terms of well-known theories of motivation. For instance, the instrumental perspective could be explicated in VIE terms, whereas the interpersonal perspective has drawn closely from both social exchange and social identity theories. In the last several years a more unique approach to organizational justice has emerged. Bies (1993, 2001) and Folger (1994, 1998, 2001) have argued that individuals are often concerned with ethical standards. Thus, it is possible that employees often behave fairly and react to unfairness because they are committed to moral principles. According to this perspective, justice matters for its own sake, apart from whether it impacts one's economic "bottom line" or maintains one's standing within a valued group. Tests of this model have generally been supportive (see Cropanzano, Rupp, et al., 2001; Henrich, Boyd, Bowles, Camerer, Fehr, Gintis, & McElreath, 2001).

Within this framework, empirical tests have generally proceeded by ruling out self-interested and interpersonal considerations (Kahneman, Knetsch, & Thaler, 1986; Turillo, Folger, Lavelle, Umphress, & Gee, in press). All of the studies described in these two papers use resource allocation tasks to determine if participants will allocate less resources to teammates who have acted unfairly in the past, even if such an action would mean that they themselves would have to make a sacrifice. These studies provide participants information about the extent to which their teammates' past resource allocation decisions were fair. The results show that individuals are willing to make monetary sacrifices to punish unfairness, even when they have no information regarding their teammates' identities, when their teammate will not be made aware of their decision, and when they are guaranteed not to have any future contact with their teammates. Several variations of the experimental task have been used, incorporating various independent variables and experimental controls, and the results across all studies seem to suggest that people react to unfairness for reasons other than self-interest and interpersonal/relational concerns. It seems that under these conditions, participants internalize justice as an end in itself rather than a means toward a self-serving or interpersonal end (see Turillo et al., in press, for more detail).

PROCESS MODELS OF ORGANIZATIONAL JUSTICE

Thus far, we have reviewed three classifications of justice motives: the instrumental, relational, and moral principles. What these three families have in common is that they are *content theories* of justice in that they seek to explain *why* justice is important to individuals. However, as motivation researchers have pointed out (cf. Campbell & Prichard, 1976; Kanfer, 1991), it is also important to build *process* theories. In the present context, process theories seek to explain *how* such justice judgments are formed (Cropanzano et al., 2001; Gilliland, Benson, & Schepers, 1998). These theories explicate sundry assortments of cognitive steps and necessary environmental conditions that influence justice perceptions, affective reactions, and motivated behavior stemming from such perceptions. Due to space limitations, we will discuss only a few illustrative theories here.

Referent Cognitions Theory

Folger has proposed *Referent Cognitions Theory* (RCT) (Folger, 1986a, 1986b, 1987; Cropanzano & Folger, 1989). RCT predicts that individuals determine the fairness of an event by evaluating the procedures that lead to the outcomes they receive. Moreover, injustice is most likely to be perceived when unjustified procedures yield unfavorable outcomes. Using RCT language, judgments of unfairness result when an individual believes an alternative procedure *should* have been used, and such a procedure *would* have lead to a more favorable outcome. Thus, rather than using other people as referents to make justice judgments, RCT maintains that individuals instead make comparisons using imagined procedural alternatives to make comparisons.

According to this model, *high-referent* individuals are aware that alternative procedures would lead to a better outcome, where *low-referent* individuals are not aware of such alternatives. Because of the ability to generate possible procedural alternatives, high referents are more likely to perceive injustice than low referents. Research in this area has found that referent level is less unimportant when individuals have the freedom to decide what processes will be used to make decisions (i.e., have choice). This is because, when given this freedom, they will choose a process they feel will lead to a favorable outcome and will be unable to fault authority on procedural grounds in the event they receive an unfavorable outcome. Other factors found to interact with referent level are procedural justification (Folger, Rosenfield, Robinson, 1983), and believing that a favorable outcome will be received sometime in the future (Folger, Rosenfield, Rheaume, & Martin, 1983).

RCT takes into account both outcomes and processes in explaining how justice judgments are formed. Second, the model shows that referents can be both real (e.g., equity theory's referent other) as well as imagined (e.g., RCT's referent cognitions). Despite these extensions, questions remain unanswered in our quest to understand the justice process. Specifically, how exactly are these judgments formed (Folger & Cropanzano, 2001)? Does the process differ when socioemotional outcomes are on the line? How do moral principles related to justice impact the formation of justice judgments (Folger & Cropanzano, 1998)? Such questions led Folger to extend RCT to include such factors. This expanded theory has been termed *Fairness Theory* (Folger & Cropanzano 1998, 2001).

Fairness Theory

Building on RCT, Fairness Theory seeks to identify conditions that must be met in order for an injustice to be perceived. According to this theory, something first must occur that threatens an individual's well-being, followed by a judgment determining who is accountable for the event. Once such a situation has been established, three conditions must be met in order for the event to be perceived as unfair.

First, the individual must be able to imagine alternative situations that could have arisen that would have resulted in less adversity than the one at hand. Comparing the event to these cognitions involves a comparison similar to the one laid out in RCT. However, the generation of alternatives and the comparison process can involve both relational and economic considerations. As in RCT, this first condition is the *would* component because it asks the question of whether alternative actions on the part of the accountable party would have resulted in less adversity.

Second, the perceiver determines if it was in the accountable party's power to act differently. This is termed the *could* component because it asks whether the responsible party could have acted differently. Research in this area has shown that the social account provided to the perceiver for the action taken often mitigates this condition (Bies, 1987, 2001; Bobocel, McCline, & Folger, 1997; Tyler & Bies, 1990). That is, when it is explained to employees why a particular action had to be taken, perceivers are less likely to imagine scenarios where those responsible for the situation could have acted any differently.

The third condition that is necessary for injustice to be perceived involves morality-based justice. In addition to believing that an alternative situation *would* have led to better outcomes and that those in power *could* have acted differently, the individual making the fairness judgment must also believe that the responsible party *should* have acted differently because their action violated some moral standard of interpersonal conduct. This condition, therefore, has been termed the *should* component.

Thus Fairness Theory states that if an individual's well-being is threatened and those in power would, could, and should have acted differently, the situation will be considered unfair. As Fairness Theory was formulated only recently, empirical tests of the model are only now beginning to appear. Generally speaking, they seem to be supportive (Collie, Bradley, & Sparks, 2001; Collie, Sparks, & Bradley, 2001), though more research is needed. In addition, studies exploring the power of morality-based justice provide some additional evidence supporting the should component (Kahneman et al., 1986; Turillo et al., in press).

Fairness Heuristic Theory

A third process theory has been proposed by Lind and his colleagues (Lind, 2001; van den Bos, Lind, & Wilke, 2001). Termed *Fairness Heuristic Theory* (FHT), this model provides a framework outlining why justice evaluations are used to regulate behavior, how such evaluations are formed, and how such judgments impact future actions and justice judgments, all within a group value/relational framework. This theory differs from the other process theories described in this chapter in that it focuses on the cognitive limitations involved in processing relational information and explains how fairness information serves as an aid in making sense of the plethora of interpersonal stimuli we must face in our daily lives.

FHT proposes that employees use fairness information to simplify these large processing demands. In other words, individuals use fairness information as a cognitive heuristic in determining their group status and whether authority figures can be trusted. The theory includes three stages by which such justice judgments are formed. In the *preformation phase,* information is gathered regarding whether or not an individual or social entity can be trusted. If explicit trustworthiness evidence is unavailable, the employee will use fairness information to make this determination. In the second phase, the *formation phase,* the actual justice judgment is formed. The goal of this phase is to collect information regarding the individual's inclusion within the social group of interest. Many of the factors revealed by justice research such as voice, access, value, and respect come into play here. Also, studies have found that the information collected early in this process has a strong influence on how subsequent information is interpreted (van den Bos, Vermunt, & Wilke, 1997). Because information about procedures is usually the first piece of information available to individuals, procedural justice is especially important in this phase, especially if the authority figure is a member of the in-group (van den Bos et al., 2001). This finding has been used to explain the "fair process effect" found in many studies on organizational justice.

The third phase is the *postinformation phase.* This phase attempts to outline the process by which the fairness evaluations made in the formation phase guide behavior as well as subsequent fairness judgments. Although FHT has yet to outline exactly how this process is carried out, the empirical evidence available seems to suggest that fairness evaluations do serve as a heuristic framework in interpreting and making decisions about future events.

In summary, FHT provides a useful model for understanding how fairness information is used to make sense of the complex patterns of information received by employees in their working lives. Various studies have provided empirical support for fairness heuristic theory. For example, van den Bos and colleagues showed that information received first has a much stronger effect on fairness judgments than what comes next (van den Bos et al., 1997). These findings have several important implications (Lind, 2001). First, initial fairness judgments perpetuate themselves. That is, once the initial fairness evaluation is made, it is very difficult to alter this evaluation in that one is typically "stuck" at the level of the initial fairness judgment. Second, organizations should pay special attention to the fairness of procedures employees are first exposed to when they enter the organization. These findings suggest that providing fair procedures at the onset, perhaps in interviewing and training stages, may have a strong effect on employees' subsequent reactions to organizational outcomes. A third implication has been termed the "substitutability implication" (Lind, 2001). This refers to the fact that if one type of fairness information is missing (i.e., information about procedures or outcomes), individuals will simply substitute procedural fairness for distributive fairness judgments or vice versa. The fair process effect would be one example of this phenomenon, but it is important to realize that the opposite can occur as well.

Another important finding shows that it is sometimes difficult to assess the fairness of outcomes. This occurs because many situations lack information about the outcomes of referent others (van den Bos et al., 1997). For example, it is often difficult to determine if you are being compensated fairly if you are unaware of the salaries made by your coworkers or those in similar positions. Van den Bos et al. showed that the fair process effect that occurs when referent information is absent is much less pronounced in the presence of this type of information.

Another empirical test of FHT showed that individuals use fairness judgments as a heuristic for evaluating situations when information such as trustworthiness is unavailable (van den Bos, Wilke, & Lind, 1998). These researchers found that individuals have much less need to use procedural fairness as a heuristic substitute when direct evidence regarding the trustworthiness of the authority is available. This finding, which has been replicated in an applied setting (van den Bos & van Schie, 1998), provides yet another situation in which the fair process effect might not occur.

Dual-Level Cognitive Processing Taxonomies

FHT theory explicitly incorporates notions of controlled versus automatic processing into its model. However, justice researchers have taken a closer look at all of the justice process theories (those included in this chapter and others) and have found this processing continuum useful in understanding situations where the different theories are appropriate. The dual-level processing literature is complex and has been approached in different ways within the subfields of decision making, attitude formation, and persuasion (Chaiken & Trope, 1999; Petty & Cacioppo, 1986; Schneider & Shiffrin, 1977; for more thorough review of this literature, see Bargh, 1996; Carlson & Smith, 1996, and Kunda, 1999). Defined broadly, the model states that one's judgment about a particular event may arise via two processes. First, one might engage in controlled, conscious, systematic, or effortful processing. Such processing requires active attention and a good deal of cognitive effort. In contrast, such judgments can also be made "off line." This more automatic, unconscious, or mindless process often occurs when individuals do not possess the cognitive resources to engage in effortful systematic processing. In such situations where specific details cannot be attended to, people often rely on cognitive heuristics or shortcuts to allow them to make the most accurate judgment possible given the resources they do have available.

To date, there have been a few recent justice studies that have incorporated a dual-processing framework. Bobocel et al (1997) present a model that shows how the type of cognitive processing affects how manager explanations for unfavorable events are perceived. This model shows how employee motivation and ability to process information determine whether the explanations are processed in a systematic or heuristic manner, as well as how these levels of processing affect the perceived adequacy of explanations and attitudes toward the policy being explained.

Other researchers have applied a dual-level processing framework to their conceptualizations of justice as well. For example, Goldman and Thatcher (in press) propose a social information processing model of organizational justice. Similarly, Ellard and Skarlicki (in press) present an insightful cognitive processing model explaining third party reactions to injustice and their attributions of deservingness. Their work attempts to show how the theory of just world beliefs (Lerner, 1980) is a model of automatic processing, whereas Feather's (1999) model of deservingness applies to systematic processing.

SOME CONCLUDING THOUGHTS: WHEREFORE ORGANIZATIONAL JUSTICE AMIDST THEORIES OF WORK MOTIVATION?

Our goal in this review was to provide the reader with a general introduction to an exciting research topic. We have discussed the structure of justice, three motives that underlie justice, and four processing models that seek to articulate how justice perceptions are constructed. We hope our brief overview has piqued the reader's interest. Before parting, it is worthwhile to take one look back at organizational justice from the perspective of work motivation. Throughout this chapter, we have observed a good deal of conceptual interplay. For instance, the self-interested approach to justice is quite consistent with similar models of motivation. Of course, the borrowing of ideas does not, in and of itself, ensure that fairness should be classified as a motivational topic per se.

To make this case it is helpful to take a closer look at two definitions of work motivation and assess the extent to which research on justice conforms to each. We shall review two examples here. In the first edition of the *Handbook of Industrial and Organizational Psychology,* Campbell and Prichard (1976, p. 65) define motivation as "a set of independent/ dependent variable relationships that explain the direction, amplitude, and persistence of an individual's behavior, and holding constant the effects of aptitude, skill, and understanding of the task, and the constraints operating in the situation." Similarly, in the second edition of that same *Handbook,* Kanfer (1990, p. 78) observes that "*motivation* may be defined as intra- and interindividual variability in behavior *not due solely* to individual differences in ability or to overwhelming environmental demands that coerce or force behavior" (italics in original).

As we have seen, organizational justice meets the criteria outlined by these definitions in at least three ways. Most obviously, justice theories have had a good deal of success in explaining effective and ineffective work behaviors (e.g., Cohen-Charash & Spector, 2001; Colquitt et al., 2001). Moreover, while theories of justice emphasize important elements of the situation (most notably, outcomes, processes, and their like), these stimuli are not viewed as inexorably powerful. Instead, theories of justice tend to focus on the individual's personal understanding or construal of these elements (cf. van den Bos & Lind, 2001), as well as on the very human concerns of standing (Tyler & Smith, 1998), moral principles (Folger, 1994, 1998, 2001), and so on. Put differently, theories of justice, as is true for most theories of motivation, emphasize the active sense-making and assignment of meanings that go on in work (and other) settings. Individual behavior results not from the stimuli themselves but from the meanings (in this case, just or unjust) that have been assigned. Finally, research on human ability and task skills is conspicuously (and perhaps a bit unfortunately) absent from most organizational justice studies. Within the confines of their conceptual frameworks, justice theories view individuals as acting more upon their fairness appraisals and less upon their idiosyncratic abilities.

From the perspective of these definitions, it is reasonable to treat organizational justice as a motivational topic. Justice is clearly something that matters to workers, and as such it serves to influence their behavior and attitudes. In this vein, it should not surprise us that investigations of workplace fairness have drawn some important insights from the motivation literature, as well as from other sources. No less important are the implications of justice research for work motivation. Organizational fairness underscores the moral considerations that lie behind a good deal of motivated work behavior. Hopefully, this valuable cross-fertilization will continue.

References

Bargh, J. A. (1996). Automaticity in social psychology. In E. T. Higgins & A. W. Kruglanski (Eds.), *Social psychology: Handbook of basic principles* (pp. 196–183). New York: Guilford Press.

Bies, R. J. (1987). The predicament of injustice: The management of moral outrage. In L. L. Cummings & B. M. Staw (Eds.), *Research in organizational behavior* (Vol. 9, pp. 289–319). Greenwich, CT: JAI Press.

Bies, R. J. (1993). Privacy and procedural justice in organizations. *Social Justice Research, 6,* 69–86.

Bies, R. J. (2001). Interactional (in)justice: The sacred and the profane. In J. Greenberg & R. Cropanzano (Eds.), *Advances in organizational justice* (pp. 89–118). Stanford, CA: Stanford University Press.

Bies, R. J., & Moag, J. S. (1986). Interactional justice: Communication criteria for fairness. In B. Sheppard (Ed.), *Research on negotiation in organizations* (Vol. 1, pp. 43–55). Greenwich, CT: JAI Press.

Blau, P. M. (1964). *Exchange and power in social life.* New York: John Wiley & Sons.

Bobocel, D. R., & Holmvall, C. (2001). Are interactional justice and procedural justice different? Framing the debate. In S. Gilliland, D. Steiner, & D. Skarlicki (Eds.), *Research in social issues in management: Theoretical and cultural perspectives on organizational justice* (pp. 85–110). Greenwich, CT: Information Age Publishing.

Bobocel, D. R., McCline, R. L., & Folger, R. (1997). Letting them down gently: Conceptual advances in explaining controversial organizational policies. In C. L. Cooper & D. M. Rousseau (Eds.), *Trends in organizational behavior* (Vol. 4, pp. 73–88). New York: John Wiley & Sons.

Brockner, J., & Wiesenfeld, B. M. (1996). An integrative framework for explaining reactions to decisions: Interactive effects of outcomes and procedures. *Psychological Bulletin, 20,* 189–208.

Carlston, D. E., & Smith, E. R. (1996). Principles of mental representation. In E. T. Higgins & A. W. Kruglanski (Eds.), *Social psychology: Handbook of basic principles* (pp. 184–210). New York: The Guilford Press.

Campbell, J. P., & Prichard, R. D. (1976). Motivation theory in industrial and organizational psychology. In M. D. Dunnette (Ed.), *Handbook of industrial and organizational psychology* (pp. 131–146). Chicago, IL: Rand McNally.

Chaiken, S., & Trope, Y. (1999). *Dual-process theories in social psychology.* New York: Guilford.

Cohen-Charash, Y., & Spector, P. E. (2001). The role of justice in organizations: A meta-analysis. *Organizational Behavior and Human Decision Processes, 86,* 278–321.

Collie, T., Bradley, G., & Sparks, B. A. (2001). Fairness process revisited: Differential effects of interactional and procedural justice in the presence of social comparison equity information. Unpublished manuscript.

Collie, T., Sparks, B. A., & Bradley, G. (2001). Understanding the role of interactional justice in service recovery: A test of fairness theory. Paper presented at the meeting of the American Marketing Association's Service Interest Group. Sydney, Australia.

Colquitt, J. A. (2001). On the dimensionality of organizational justice: A construct validation of a measure. *Journal of Applied Psychology, 86,* 425–446.

Colquitt, J. A., Conlon, D. E., Wesson, M. J., Porter, C. O. L. H., & Ng, K. Y. (2001). Justice at the millennium: A meta-analytic review of 25 years of organizational justice research. *Journal of Applied Psychology, 86,* 425–445.

Conlon D. E. (1993). Some tests of the self-interest and group-value models of procedural justice: Evidence from an organizational appeal procedure. *Academy of Management Journal, 36,* 1109–1124.

Cropanzano, R., & Ambrose, M. L. (2001). Procedural and distributive justice are more similar than you think: A monistic perspective and a research agenda. In J. Greenberg & R. Cropanzano (Eds.), *Advances in organizational justice* (pp. 119–151). Stanford, CA: Stanford University Press.

Cropanzano, R., Byrne, Z. S., Bobocel, D. R., & Rupp, D. R. (2001). Moral virtues, fairness heuristics, social entities, and other denizens of organizational justice. *Journal of Vocational Behavior, 58,* 164–2001.

Cropanzano, R., & Folger, R. (1989). Referent cognitions and task decision autonomy: Beyond equity theory. *Journal of Applied Psychology, 74,* 293–299.

Cropanzano, R., Prehar, C., & Chen, P. Y. (in press). Using social exchange theory to distinguish procedural and interactional justice. *Group and Organization Management.*

Cropanzano, R., Rupp, D. E., Mohler, C. J., & Schminke, M. (2001). Three roads to organizational justice. In J. Ferris (Ed.), *Research in personnel and human resources management* (Vol. 20, pp. 1–113). Greenwich, CT: JAI Press.

Cropanzano, R., & Schminke, M. (2001). Using social justice to build effective work groups. In M. Turner (Ed.), *Groups at work: Advances in theory and research* (pp. 143–171). Hillsdale, NJ: Erlbaum.

Ellard, J. H., & Skarlicki, D. P. (in press). A deservingness analysis of third-party observers' responses to employee mistreatment. In Gilliland, Steiner, & D. P. Skarlicki (Eds.), *Organizational justice beyond the organization.* Greenwich, CT: Information Age Publishers.

Feather, N. T. (1999). Judgments of deservingness: Studies in the psychology of justice and achievement. *Personality and Social Psychology Review, 3,* 86–107.

Fehr, E., & Gächter, S. (2000). Fairness and retaliation: The economics of reciprocity. *Journal of Economic Perspectives, 14,* 159–181.

Folger, R. (1986a). Rethinking equity theory: A referent cognitions model. In H. W. Beirhoff, R. L. Cohen, & J. Greenberg (Eds.), *Justice in social relations* (pp. 145–162). New York: Plenum Press.

Folger, R. (1986b). A referent cognitions theory of relative deprivation. In J. M. Olson, C. P. Herman, & M. P. Zanna (Eds.), *Relative deprivation and social comparison: The Ontario symposium* (Vol. 4, pp. 33–55). Hillsdale, NJ: Erlbaum.

Folger, R. (1987). Reformulating the preconditions of resentment: A referent cognitions model. In J. C. Masters & W. P. Smith (Eds.), *Social comparison, social justice, and relative deprivation* (pp. 183–215). Hillsdale, NJ: Lawrence Erlbaum Associates.

Folger, R. (1994). Workplace justice and employee worth. *Social Justice Research, 7,* 225–241.

Folger, R. (1998). Fairness as a moral virtue. In M. Schminke (Ed.), *Managerial ethics: Moral management of people and processes* (pp. 13–34). Mahwah, NJ: Erlbaum.

Folger, R. (2001). Fairness as deonance. In S. W. Gilliland, D. D. Steiner, & D. P. Skarlicki (Eds.), *Research in social issues in management* (Vol. 1, pp. 3–33). New York: Information Age Publishers.

Folger, R., & Cropanzano, R. (1998). *Organizational justice and human resource management.* Beverly Hills, CA: Sage.

Folger, R., & Cropanzano, R. (2001). Fairness theory: Justice as accountability. In J. Greenberg & R., Folger (Eds.), *Advances in organizational justice* (pp. 1–55). Lexington, MA: New Lexington Press.

Folger, R., & Konovsky, M. A. (1989). Effects of procedural and distributive justice on reactions to pay raise decisions. *Academy of Management Journal, 32,* 115–130.

Folger, R., & Martin, C. (1986). Relative deprivation and referent cognitions: Distributive and procedural justice effects. *Journal of Experimental Social Psychology, 22,* 531–546.

Folger, R., Rosenfield, D., Rheaume, K., & Martin, C. (1983). Relative deprivation and referent cognitions. *Journal of Experimental Social Psychology, 19,* 172–184.

Folger, R., Rosenfield, D., & Robinson, T. (1983). Relative deprivation and procedural justification. *Journal of Personality and Social Psychology, 45,* 268–273.

Gilliland, S. W., Benson, L., III, & Schepers, D. H. (1998). A rejection threshold in justice evaluations: Effects on judgment and decision-making. *Organizational Behavior and Human Decision Processes, 76,* 113–131.

Goldman, B. M., & S. M. B. Thatcher (in press). A social information processing view of organizational justice. In Gilliland, Steiner, & D. P. Skarlicki (Eds.), *Organizational justice beyond the organization.* Greenwich, CT: Information Age Publishers.

Greenberg, J. (1993). The social side of fairness: Interpersonal and informational classes of organizational justice. In R. Cropanzano (Ed.), *Justice in the workplace: Approaching fairness in human resource management* (pp. 79–103). Hillsdale, NJ: Lawrence Erlbaum Associates.

Henrich, J., Boyd, R., Bowles, S., Camerer, C., Fehr, E., Gintis, H., & McElreath, R. (2001). In search of *homo economics:* Behavioral experiments in 15 small-scale societies. *The American Economic Review, 91,* 73–78.

Kahneman, D., Knetsch, J. L., & Thaler, R. H. (1986). Fairness and the assumptions of economics. *Journal of Business, 59,* 285–300.

Kanfer, R. (1991). Motivation theory and industrial and organizational psychology. In M. D. Dunnette (Ed.), *Handbook of industrial and organizational psychology* (2nd ed., Vol. 1, pp. 76–170). Palo Alto, CA: Consulting Psychologists Press.

Konovsky, M. A., & Pugh, S. D. (1994). Citizenship behavior and social exchange. *Academy of Management Journal, 37,* 656–669.

Kunda, Z. (1999). *Social cognition: Making sense of people.* Cambridge, MA: MIT Press.

Lerner, M. J. (1980). *The belief in a just world: A fundamental delusion.* New York: Plenum Press.

Lind, E. A. (1995). Justice and authority relations in organizations. In R. Cropanzano & M. K. Kacmar (Eds.), *Organizational politics, justice, and support: Managing the social climate of the workplace* (pp. 83–96). Westport, CT: Quorum Books.

Lind, E. A. (2001). Fairness heuristic theory: Justice judgments as pivotal cognitions in organizational relations. In J. Greenberg & R. Cropanzano (Eds.), *Advances in organizational justice.* Stanford, CA: Stanford University Press.

Lind, E. A., & Tyler, T. R. (1988). *The social psychology of procedural justice.* New York: Plenum.

Masterson, S. S., Lewis, K., Goldman, B. M., & Taylor, M. S. (2000). Integrating justice and social exchange: The differing effects of fair procedures and treatment on work relationships. *Academy of Management Journal, 43,* 738–748.

Moorman, R. H., Blakely, G. L., & Niehoff, B. P. (1998). Does perceived organizational support mediate the relationship between procedural justice and organizational citizenship behavior? *Academy of Management Journal, 41,* 351–357.

Organ, D. W. (1988). *Organizational citizenship behavior: The good soldier syndrome.* Lexington, MA: Lexington Books.

Petty, R. E., & Cacioppo, J. T. (1986). *Communication and persuasion: Central and peripheral routes to attitude change.* New York: Springer-Verlag.

Rupp, D. E., & Cropanzano, R. (in press). The Mediating Effects of Social Exchange Relationships in Predicting Workplace Outcomes from Multifoci Organizational Justice. *Organization Behavior and Human Decision Processes.*

Schneider, W., & Shiffrin, R. M. (1977). Controlled and information processing: Detection, search, and attention. *Psychological Review, 84,* 1–66.

Shapiro, D. L. (1993). Reconciling theoretical differences among procedural justice researchers by re-evaluating what it means to have one's view "considered": Implications for third-party managers. In R. Cropanzano (Ed.), *Justice in the workplace: Approaching fairness in human resources management* (pp. 51–78). Hillsdale, NJ: Erlbaum.

Sitkin, S. B., & Bies, R. J. (1993). Social accounts in conflict settings. *Human Relations, 46,* 349–370.

Skarlicki, D. P., & Folger, R. (1997). Retaliation in the workplace: The role of distributive, procedural, and interactional justice. *Journal of Applied Psychology, 82,* 434–443.

Sweeney, P. D., & McFarlin, D. B. (1993). Workers' evaluations of the "ends" and the "means": An examination of four models of distributive justice and procedural justice. *Organizational Behavior and Human Decision Processes, 55,* 23–40.

Turillo, C. J., Folger, R., Lavelle, J. J., Umphress, E., & Gee, J. (in press). Is virtue its own reward? Self-sacrificial decisions for the sake of fairness. *Organizational Behavior and Human Decision Processes.*

Tyler, T. R. (1997). The psychology of legitimacy: A relational perspective on voluntary deference to authorities. *Personality and Social Psychology Review, 1,* 323–345.

Tyler, T. R., & Bies, R. J. (1990). Beyond formal procedures: The interpersonal context of procedural justice. In J. Carroll (Ed.), *Advances in applied social psychology: Business settings* (pp. 77–98). Hillsdale, NJ: Erlbaum.

Tyler, T. R., & Blader, S. L. (2000). *Cooperation in groups: Procedural justice, social identity, and behavioral engagement.* Philadelphia, PA: Psychology Press.

Tyler, T. R., & Lind, E. A. (1992). A relational model of authority in groups. In M. P. Zanna (Ed.), *Advances in experimental social psychology* (Vol. 25, pp. 115–191). San Diego, CA: Academic Press.

Tyler, T. R., & Smith, H. J. (1998). Social justice and social movements. In D. Gilbert, S. T. Fiske, & G. Lindzey (Eds.), *Handbook of social psychology* (Vol. 4, pp. 595–629). Boston, MA: McGraw-Hill.

Van den Bos, K., Bruins, J., Wilke, H. A. M., & Dronkeert, E. (1999). Sometimes unfair procedures have nice aspects: On the psychology of the fair process effect. *Journal of Personality and Social Psychology, 77,* 324–366.

Van den Bos, K., Lind, E. A., Vermunt, R., & Wilke, H. A. M. (1997). How do I judge my outcome when I do not know the outcome of others? The psychology of the fair process effect. *Journal of Personality and Social Psychology, 72,* 1034–1046.

Van den Bos, K., Lind, E. A., & Wilke, H. A. M. (2001). The psychology of procedural and distributive justice viewed from the perspective of fairness heuristic theory. In R. Cropanzano (Ed.), *Justice in the workplace,* Vol. 2: *From theory to practice.* Mahwah, NJ: Erlbaum.

Van den Bos, K., & Van Schie, E. C. M. (1998). Procedural and distributive justice in child day care centers. Unpublished manuscript, Department of Social and Organizational Psychology, Leiden University, the Netherlands.

Van den Bos, K., Vermunt, R., & Wilke, H. A. M. (1997). Procedural and distributive justice: What is fair depends more on what comes first than on what comes next. *Journal of Personality and Social Psychology, 77,* 95–104.

Van den Bos, K., Wilke, H. A. M., & Lind, E. A. (1998). When do we need procedural fairness? The role of trust in authority. *Journal of Personality and Social Psychology, 75,* 1449–1458.

Van den Bos, K., Wilke, H. A. M., Lind, E. A., & Vermunt, R. (1998). Evaluating outcomes by means of the fair process effect: Evidence for different processes in fairness and satisfaction judgments. *Journal of Personality and Social Psychology, 74,* 1493–1503.

Van Eerde, W., & Thierry, H. (1996). Vroom's expectancy models and work-related criteria: A meta-analysis. *Journal of Applied Psychology, 81,* 575–586.

Wade-Benzoni, K. A., Tenbrunsel, A. E., & Bazerman, M. H. (1996). Egocentric interpretations of fairness in asymmetric, environmental social dilemmas: Explaining harvesting behavior and the role of communication. *Organizational Behavior and Human Decision Processes, 67,* 111–126.

Reinforcement Theory at Work: Enhancing and Explaining What Employees Do

Judith L. Komaki[1]

How do you motivate workers to do things the right way—day in and day out, season after season? Whether in the public or private sector, urban or rural, this is the question that I often get asked.

In this chapter we will examine psychologist B. F. Skinner's (1974) operant conditioning, or reinforcement theory. With its emphasis on the consequences of performance and its insistence on responsive and reliable measures of performance, the theory has been applied in situations such as that described by the Danish writer Isak Dinesen (1938). On her coffee farm in the Nygong Hills in Kenya, she talks of her never-ending need to ensure that workers are diligent in pruning the plants, picking the coffee beans, carting the beans to the factory, drying them in the big rotating wheel of the coffee dryer, as well as the hulling, grading, and sorting of the coffee and packing it into carefully sewn sacks. Then, with the coffee safely on its way to market, it all begins again with the planting and the pruning of a new crop. Done season after season, it was work that her personnel knew well because they had done it all so often before.

Motivating workers to change and maintain their performance over extended periods remains a formidable challenge as attested to by practitioners and scholars alike (Campbell & Pritchard, 1976; Drucker, 1999). To this day, Herzberg's 1986 *Harvard Business Review* article, "One More Time: How Do You Motivate Employees?" remains among the most requested writings on the subject.

[1]With a special note of thanks to Warren Steinman, Sid Bijou, and Milton Blood, who introduced me in the late 60s and early 70s to reinforcement theory and industrial/ organizational psychology; to Tim Coombs, Tom Redding, and Steve Schepman, who in the mid-80s and late 90s scrutinized hundreds of articles for a review of the literature spanning 30 years (2000); and finally to Martin Luther King (1963) and Don Baer, Mont Wolf, and Todd Risley (1968), who spurred me on with their dreams to make this world a better place. This chapter is dedicated to all those who continue to dream.

As a learning theory, reinforcement theory naturally assumes that we can learn, we are not indelibly marked, and, as a result, we can change. My fellow grad students and I witnessed dramatic changes—civil rights legislation, the ending of a war—brought about by freedom riders and Vietnam war protesters. We too brimmed with optimism. Our hopes were fueled in the late 1960s by reports showing the first applications of reinforcement theory. Children who were labeled "autistic" and destined to spend the remainder of their lives within these walls began to communicate and to help themselves when they were reinforced for successive approximations to desired behaviors (Lovaas, 1966). First-graders in a disadvantaged neighborhood learned skills critical to their further achievement (Becker, Madsen, Arnold, & Thomas, 1967). We even saw on the evening news that the Army was successfully using a token economy program with Army recruits who were meeting the rigorous standards of their superiors during boot camp (Datel & Legters, 1971). Pioneers using reinforcement principles in applied settings—Don Baer, Mont Wolf, and Todd Risley (1968)—urged us on. They predicted that doing research on "socially important behaviors, such as mental retardation, crime, mental illness, or education . . . will lead to a better state of society" (p. 91).

So when my colleagues and I went to work sites, we set up positive reinforcement programs. Some concerned traditional areas, increasing productivity and reducing absenteeism. But we also made sure that staff provided quality services and employees performed safely. In promoting safety, for instance, we did not dwell on accident-prone workers or probe for personality or demographic characteristics, none of which can be changed. Instead, we focused on the organization and what it can do to rearrange the work environment. We maneuvered within the constraints of the situation with the existing personnel and facilities. We specified what workers needed to do. We did not just measure the easy stuff. We went beyond counting accidents and actually developed new ways of measuring safety. But I'm getting ahead of myself. Perhaps it is enough to say that this proactive, idealistic stance influenced the measurement and motivational strategies reinforcement theorists used.

This chapter discusses how reinforcement theory can be used to improve performance and to maintain it over extended periods. The features and steps in setting up a positive reinforcement program are described, as well as the results of over 100 experiments, all meticulously controlled. The chapter's second part shows how reinforcement theory can be used to explain as well as improve behavior. The principles of positive and negative reinforcement, punishment by application and removal, and extinction are described. I discuss why well-meaning people sometimes do perplexing things; why managers who believe in merit promote on seniority; and why professors who genuinely believe in the importance of education neglect their teaching. I end with a wish list for the next millennium.

USING REINFORCEMENT THEORY TO ENHANCE PERFORMANCE

Two Major Features

Focus on Performance Consequences

A major tenet of reinforcement theory is that behavior is a function of its consequences, which can be the feedback we receive and the comments we hear. When a packaging supervisor grins, thrusts out his hand for a quick congratulatory shake, and says to workers, "Good running last night, 537 cases," his action and his statements are considered to be consequences (Gellerman, 1976).

In virtually all positive reinforcement programs, consequences or reinforcers are delivered. At least five types have been provided:

1. *Organizational consequences:* These include promotions, special training opportunities, and benefits, all indigenous to a particular organization. In a regional transportation authority, benefits—such as free gasoline and free monthly passes—were offered to workers by researchers Haynes, Pine, and Fitch (1982) as an incentive for reducing accidents in a bus system.

2. *Activity:* Another class of consequences, derived from the Premack (1965) principle, is referred to as an activity consequence. Any behavior engaged in more frequently than another can be used as a consequence. If getting mail occurs more often than answering mail, the former can be used to reinforce the latter. A novel application of the Premack principle took place in a sales organization. When investigators Gupton and LeBow (1971) found making new sales to be much lower in frequency than getting renewal sales, they made the former contingent on the latter. When the callers could do the higher frequency activity only after doing the lower frequency activity, they substantially increased new service sales.

3. *Social:* Typically expressed by individuals, social consequences include commendations, compliments, criticism, reviews, and recognition of a job well done. For example, a manager in a city agency wrote down comments about the clerk-typists' performance: "Your typing percentage is up 15% over last week. Keep it up!" Or, "Your score was 100% this week. I knew you could do it. Fantastic!" (Nordstrom, Hall, Lorenzi, & Delquadri, 1988, p. 100).

4. *Informational:* These consequences, as the label suggests, are ones in which information is provided about a person's performance. The information can be conveyed as feedback notes passed on to supervisors (Fox & Sulzer-Azaroff, 1987) or as graphs depicting baseline and intervention levels of workers' performance (Nasanen & Saari, 1987). The information itself can also vary. In the area of safety, the information ranged from the percentage of correct housekeeping practices (Nasanen & Saari, 1987) to audiograms showing temporary hearing losses that occurred when ear plugs were not worn (Zohar, Cohen, & Azar, 1980).

5. *Generalized:* These reinforcers gain their potency from their ability to be exchanged for backup reinforcers. Examples include cash, frequent flyer awards, and trading stamps. Coupons were earned by trainees in a job-training center (Deluga & Andrews, 1985–1986). These coupons could be exchanged for the chance to select where, how and with whom they did clerical jobs, which served as backup reinforcers.

As we can see, many kinds of consequences have been used as positive reinforcers. Sometimes, only one type was introduced. A prevalent pairing was social and informational consequences. Besides praise, managers often provided feedback. A manager in the Nordstrom et al. (1988) study not only wrote down comments such as "fantastic" but would also describe how "the percent of pages typed correctly was determined" when telling typists about their performance (p. 102).

A host of consequences was used to lessen the frequent procrastination associated with long-range, relatively unstructured projects such as completing master's theses (Dillon et al., 1980). Realizing how easy it is to let more immediately pressing activities disrupt progress, the authors devised a system of weekly deadlines and monitoring, and at least three types of consequences: (a) organizational, in that the advisor would send out letters of recommendation based only on a student's satisfactory progress; (b) generalized, in that a point system earned students positive (and negative) points toward recommendation letters; and (c) informational, with students receiving information about points earned the previous week and cumulatively.

When consequences like these were arranged to follow desired performance, substantial and meaningful changes, as detailed in the findings section, took place.

Insistence on Responsive and Reliable Measures of Performance

Another critical feature of reinforcement theory is its requirement to obtain direct, frequent, and reliable assessments that reflect worker performance. Without a proper measurement system, consequences related to performance cannot be provided. To reinforce students for their progress on master's theses, one must have a measure that sensitively reflects their progress.

Both reinforcement theorists (Foster & Cone, 1986; Goldfried & Kent, 1972) and industrial/organizational psychologists (Campbell, 1990; James, 1973) stress the importance of defining and measuring target behaviors. Steers, Porter, and Bigley (1996) emphasize that even in "the best-designed reward systems . . . , the evaluation or appraisal of performance [is] perhaps the most basic concern" (p. 500).

In response to this, five criteria are recommended (Komaki, 1998a). These, given as the mnemonic, are SURF&C. They stand for:

S: The target or dependent variable should be sampled (S) directly rather than using a filtered or secondary source. This means workers or the products of their work are observed firsthand instead of relying on their own or on coworkers' reports.

U: The target should be primarily under (U) the workers' control, responsive to their efforts, and minimally affected by extraneous factors.

R: Independent observers or raters should obtain interrater reliability (R) scores of 80% to, ideally, 90% or better during the formal data collection period. This means that raters go independently to sample workers' performance using the same scoring system and then they check to see if they agree on their observations. They do not stop practicing and, in some cases, revamping the scoring system until they can agree on at least 80% of their observations.

F: The target should be assessed frequently (F)—often and regularly—at least 20 and ideally 30 times during the intervention period. And,

C: Evidence should be obtained indicating that the target is "critical" (C) for the desired result. To do this, one collects data on the target and the desired result (e.g., one would collect data on the target—a checklist for selling behaviors—and the desired result—sales). If the target is considered critical, there would be a positive correlation between the checklist scores and sales.

The criteria of U and C are concerned with *what* is measured, the criteria of S, R, and F with *how* the information is collected.

Many traditional measures do not meet the SURF&C criteria. Injury frequency rates and productivity indices are not under (U) workers' control. Little if any evidence exists that customers like sales personnel to use their names, so indicating such usage may not be critical (C) to making a sale. Problems also often exist over how information is collected. Customer service is not sampled directly (S), but sales or traffic patterns are relied upon instead. Little effort is made to show that supervisory ratings are reliable (R). Performance appraisals typically occur infrequently (F).

So, in seeking to reduce accidents, reinforcement theorists do not look exclusively at accidents because they are not always under the control of workers. Instead, investigators focus on safety practices. They look at whether workers lift properly and how they handle sharp tools, practices that are for the most part under (U) their control. To ensure that the measure meets the criterion of criticality (C), tallies are made of the counts of safety practices and accidents and a correlational analysis is done to see if the two are related to one another. One study by Reber and Wallin (1983) looked at counts of safety practices and found the higher the practices, the lower the injuries per department, and hence critical (C) to the goal of injury reduction.

Data are typically collected so that the S, R, and F criteria are met. Trained observers visit work sites and sample (S) work practices. They collect information frequently (F), at least weekly. Lastly, interrater reliability (R) checks are done in which two observers independently record, identify agreements between raters, and then calculate a percentage agreement score (number of agreements/number of agreements and disagreements). Checklist revisions continue until agreement is reached on the scoring of checklist items almost all the time. When this criterion is achieved, then and only then are the terms considered to be acceptably defined. Reliability checks are also used in training observers who are not considered trained until they can pass the interrater reliability test. During formal data collection, raters are regularly checked to see if they have become stricter or more lenient since training completion.

Four-Step Process

To see how this works, let us examine a program I carried out with two students at Georgia Tech (Komaki, Barwick, & Scott, 1978).

Example: Injuries had risen sharply at a wholesale bakery and management was alarmed. To encourage employees to maintain safe practices, we introduced a positive reinforcement program that differed from the usual approach of posting signs and admonishing workers to be careful.

Step 1: Specify desired behavior. First, we defined desired work practices. To establish what workers should do to avoid having similar accidents in the future, we listed definitions, for example, walk around a conveyer belt, look toward knife being sharpened, and used verbs such as "turn off" and "release" rather than adjectives such as "careful" and "conscientious." To ensure these definitions were clearly understood, each had to meet the test of interrater reliability, in which two raters independently collected data and then checked for agreements. When the criterion of 90% or better was achieved, only then were the terms considered acceptably defined.

Step 2: Measure desired performance. Observers, trained until they passed interrater reliability tests, went to the work site and recorded whether workers were performing safely or unsafely. Observations were made often, an average of four times weekly. Interrater reliability checks were conducted regularly.

Step 3: Provide frequent, contingent, positive consequences. The consequence for safe practices was feedback. We posted safety scores on a graph so workers could see quickly how the score compared with their previous record. We displayed graphs prominently, enabling a healthy rivalry between departments; when workers asked, we told them what they had done correctly and incorrectly.

Step 4: Evaluate effectiveness on the job. To evaluate the program's effectiveness, we used a within-group research design—the multiple-baseline design across groups. The two groups were the wrapping and make-up departments and we collected data on both. The program was staggered: after 5½ weeks in wrapping and after 13½ weeks in make-up.

The results: From performing safely 70 percent and 78 percent of the time, employees in the two departments went to 96 percent and 99 percent, respectively. Within a year, the total of lost-time injuries fell from 53 to 10. Although this is only one of a series of examples, it shows the four steps used in executing a positive reinforcement program.

So if Isak Dinesen had wanted to bolster her planting, I would have recommended she use the same steps to create a positive reinforcement program. She would specify soil condition, location and size of the holes, and placement and tapping of the roots. She would then measure how carefully workers dug the holes and placed the plants. Lastly, she would provide workers with a variety of consequences, interjecting casual comments throughout, giving raises, bonuses, and promotions contingent on work quality, perhaps even offering butter cake with freshly brewed coffee as the sun set on the Nygong Mountains.

Findings over the Past 30 Years

In the late 1960s, industrial/organizational (I/O) psychologists identified reinforcement theory as an innovative approach to motivation (Nord, 1969; Porter, 1973). Since then, hundreds of studies have been published and reviewed (e.g., Balcazar, Shupert, Daniels, Mawhinney, & Hopkins, 1989; Johnson, Redmon, & Mawhinney, 2001; O'Hara, Johnson, & Beehr, 1985; Stajkovic & Luthans, 1997). A recent review reports on 126 studies (Komaki, Coombs, Redding, & Schepman, 2000). It differs from previous reviews: in breadth—30 years of studies are reviewed that range from the earliest studies done in the late 1960s to the latest in 1998; in richness—the studies are presented question-by-question, and for each one information is presented about the subjects and setting and the dependent variable; and in rigor—only studies meeting strict content and methodological standards are included. To be included in the review, the dependent variable had to assess performance at work, the subjects had to function normally in a setting enabling continuity over time, and the design used (typically a within-group reversal or multiple-baseline) had to allow for causal conclusions to be drawn confidently.

Of the 72 studies looking at positive reinforcement for which conclusions could be drawn, 58 studies were in support, 10 showed mixed support, and only 4 did not show any support. The success rate: 93%.

Experiments Have Been Conducted with a Wide Range of Subjects and Settings over Extended Periods of Time

Although many of the earliest were conducted in the public sector, at least half the 126 studies were done in the private sector. Forty-six percent took place in the public sector: in mental health facilities (Parsons & Reid, 1995), social service agencies such as group homes (Harchik, Sherman, Sheldon, & Strouse, 1992), and educational settings (Wilk & Redmon, 1998). Fifty-four percent were in the private sector: in department stores (Luthans, Paul, & Taylor, 1985) and factories (Wittkopp, Rowan, & Poling, 1990). Locations included the United States as well as the Middle East (Elizur, 1987) and Europe (Nasanen & Saari, 1987; Welsh, Luthans, & Sommer, 1993).

Subjects include baseball players (Heward, 1978), real estate agents (Anderson, Crowell, Sucec, Gilligan, & Wikoff, 1982), and psychiatrists (Jones, Morris, & Barnard, 1985/1986). Nonsupervisory personnel predominated, with 87% of the studies including hourly and/or salaried employees. But 5% of the studies included both supervisory and nonsupervisory personnel and another 6% included only supervisory personnel.

Sample sizes in the studies included as many as 1,000 miners (Fox et al., 1987). Two-fifths had 10 or fewer subjects, whereas almost two-fifths had 20 or more subjects, with one-sixth of the studies with over 100 subjects.

The results were not short-lived. Studies averaged 6.8 months and data were collected during the intervention which averaged 3.3 months. These figures were calculated from studies occurring during the most recent 10 years, indicating the extended time periods were not limited to the oldest studies.

Target Behaviors Focus on Task Execution and Vary Widely

The execution of psychomotor tasks was the topic of 96% of the studies. Such tasks, says McGrath (1984), "are very heavily represented in the workaday world and, against the base rate, are quite underrepresented in research on groups" (p. 65).

The most popular target area, accounting for almost one-fifth of the studies, was production/production-related. Improving the quality of sorting and loading of packages in a package delivery company was considered a production-related task (Kortick & O'Brien, 1996). The second highest dependent variable was attendance and punctuality, a critical factor in organizations, which rely on having a certain number of qualified workers present before running equipment or assembly lines (Kempen & Hall, 1977). Another area of concern to both management and workers—safety and health—has been the topic of 13% of the studies. Working together, employees in a fiberglass-reinforced plastics plant were also able to reduce their exposure to likely carcinogenic substances such as styrene and to improve chances of remaining healthy (Hopkins, Conard, & Smith, 1986). Quality of service has been a regular subject of interest in both the public and private sectors, accounting for 11 and 9%, respectively, of the studies. In the public sector, the focus is on ensuring that programs developed for patients, clients, and students are delivered as planned. Johnson and Fawcett (1994) improved the performance of receptionists at a human service organization. In the private sector, tellers in banks (Elizur, 1987) improved their interactions with customers.

Evidence Indicates that Antecedents Are Not as Powerful as They Are Often Assumed to Be

Another finding concerned a prevalent management strategy, that of giving antecedents such as instructing or beseeching people. Reinforcement theorist Aubrey Daniels (1994) describes how common antecedents are. When confronted with workforce problems: "We send memos, have meetings, write policies, hold classes. . . . Interestingly, when these methods don't get the desired response. . . , we tell the same people again, usually in the same ways. . . . We send new memos (with bolder type, capital letters, and even exclamation marks) about old memos that were ignored" (pp. 17–18). These tactics—memos, policies, training—are referred to as antecedents because they typically precede workers' performance. Antecedents have a special place in reinforcement theory, serving an educational or cueing role—clarifying expectations for performance, specifying the relationship between behavior and its consequences, and/or signaling occasions in which consequences are likely to be provided. But they do not serve as the primary motivational force. Only consequences do that.

Results of the experiments confirm the roles of both antecedents and consequences. A total of 13 of 14 studies in the review found that consequences improved performance above and beyond that of antecedents alone. In the experiment by researchers Chhokar and Wallin (1984), the antecedents, training and goal setting, were first implemented, followed by a consequence, feedback. Only when once or twice weekly feedback was introduced did performance significantly improve from 80.9% to 94.6% and 96.8%. Based on the results, Chhokar and Wallin conclude that "the results that performance reached the set goal level only after feedback was provided, . . . declined when feedback was withdrawn, and improved again when feedback was reintroduced, highlight the importance of feedback for improving performance over and above the level achieved with only goal setting" (p. 529). These data are particularly important because instructions and exhortations often look deceptively effective. They sometimes work for a day, perhaps even a month. But they do not necessarily result in sustained improvements.

Studies Confirm the Importance of Contingent Reinforcement

Another timely issue concerns contingent reinforcement over and above that of noncontingent or full pay. Let us look at a study by researchers Pierce and Risley (1974). Despite the study being almost 30 years ago, it still uses management strategies present today. Confronted with what they considered inadequate performance, Pierce and Risley attempted to shore up workers' performance by implementing two classic management remedies: (a) using job descriptions that made it clear what workers were supposed to do, and (b) threatening to fire the workers if they did not improve., The job descriptions had a minimal impact, with workers completing only 50% to 75% of their assigned tasks. The threats had an initial effect with improvements the first day, but after three days performance declined to its former levels. Only when a contingent pay system was instituted did performance improve so that workers were completing nearly 100% of their work. The director of the urban recreation program made it clear that "instead of pay being based on the amount of time they spend in the community center, pay would instead be based on the proportion of their job they completed each day. They would now be paid for their work time instead of clock time" (p. 211). Five of the six studies in the review examining contingent pay show that paying workers by clock time rather than work time will not necessarily translate into sustained improvements in performance, and that contingent pay can improve performance above and beyond that of full pay.

The next section takes a different perspective and describes how reinforcement theory not only can be used to change, but also to explain, workers' actions.

USING REINFORCEMENT THEORY TO UNDERSTAND WHY PEOPLE DO WHAT THEY DO

Reinforcement theory can also be used to explain why people sometimes do things not immediately apparent. Why do workers perform unsafely even though aware of the dangers? Why do managers give appraisals they know to be less than accurate? Why do they promote based on seniority rather than merit? Instead of invoking demographic characteristics or personality traits—none of which can be readily altered—one can look to the consequences that occur, many of which the organization can rearrange. In reinforcement theory, the principles of negative reinforcement, punishment by application, punishment by removal, and extinction, as well as positive reinforcement, all involve the consequences of behavior. Positive and negative reinforcement strengthen, and punishment and extinction weaken behaviors. Together, they provide a basis for better understanding and ultimately for making better-informed positive changes.

How Undesired Behaviors Are Sometimes Mistakenly Reinforced

Positive Reinforcement Inappropriately Applied

As seen, positive reinforcement can be used in a constructive, planned-out way. It is also possible to use it inadvertently to reward the very things we abhor.

The case of the procrastinating staff, identified by Terry Coombs, is an example. The head of a public relations firm could not understand why her staff kept postponing things. Yet an analysis of what happened with a 10th-year anniversary celebration shows how her staff may have been reinforced—albeit unintentionally. The staff knew they needed to produce a report describing the company's history and current activities, but they believed that the project would not take long. Two months before the celebration, they began to gather information and found that the report was far more complicated than originally expected. Because of the deadline, the head of the firm permitted the hiring of temporary staff at company expense and set all other work aside. When the report was finally completed in a frenzy of activity, she gave the staff a bonus for working so hard to meet the deadline. Although the agency head did not intend to encourage the very thing she despised, it is easy to see in Table 1 how her staff might have been positively reinforced and why they might still procrastinate on future projects.

The principle of positive reinforcement helps to explain why professors may spend more time and effort on their research than on their teaching. Among the questions to be asked are:

TABLE 1   **Chart Illustrating Positive and Negative Reinforcement at Work**

Behavior	Consequence	Principle
Staff procrastinates until two months before deadline.	Followed by positive reinforcers—extra personnel hired, workload lightened, bonus paid for effort extended.	Positive reinforcement
Boss recommends individual for promotion with adequate record, who is highest in seniority.	Avoids complaints of favoritism and a grievance being filed with union.	Negative reinforcement

What are the consequences for the desired behavior of teaching? and what are the consequences for publishing? In most universities, it is absolutely essential that professors publish. Given the consequences, professors may neglect preparations for lectures and examinations because they are promoted primarily for publications.

Seeing Negative Reinforcement at Work

The principle of negative reinforcement can also help elucidate why people do what they do. Negative reinforcement involves escaping from or avoiding negative or aversive consequences such as nagging, censure, or litigation. A classic example is the boss who espouses merit but promotes based on seniority. Why might a manager promote someone with only an adequate record rather than an exemplary employee? Because of the consequences the boss avoids (Table 1). If the promoted employee is higher in seniority, the manager can point to that and hence avoid complaints of favoritism or bias.

The same principle helps us to understand why some die-hard Wordstar fans (with the initials LWP and JLK) refused to learn WordPerfect (to avoid the hassles connected with changing to a new system). It also illuminates why people often remain quiet in the face of corruption (hence avoiding censure from coworkers). Negative reinforcement can explain why some lieutenants in the New York Police Department choose to stay lieutenants rather than strive for promotion to captain (to avoid increased scrutiny that comes with the extra responsibility and restrictions on movements and hours).

How Desired Behaviors Are Inadvertently Discouraged

In contrast to the reinforcement principles, three principles—punishment by application, punishment by removal, and extinction—explain why behaviors are weakened. The principles may be applied deliberately or unintentionally.

Unintentionally Punishing Workers for Performing as Desired

One reason workers fail to do as they are asked is because they are sometimes punished for so doing.

An example: Mager and Pipe (1984), in a book on analyzing performance problems, describe how one was called in to solve an "attitude problem" on the part of physicians who were resisting the use of computers to place prescriptions. An analysis revealed many negative consequences attached to using the computer. The area of the terminals was crowded, noisy, and busy, with no room to work. Moreover, the terminals were placed so that people looking

TABLE 2   **Chart Illustrating Punishment by Application and by Removal**

Behavior	Consequence	Principle
Emery Air Freight employees fill out damage forms.	Followed by aversive consequences —heavier workload, complaints from airline representatives.	Punishment by application
Administrator comes in under budget.	Gets positive reinforcer withdrawn, i.e., budget slashed for next fiscal year.	Punishment by removal

through bifocals became uncomfortable. When these negative consequences were changed, the "attitude problem" disappeared and the physicians began using the computers regularly.

Another example of punishment by application, this one was obtained from a seatmate on an airplane: As project head of a major research laboratory, he was bemoaning the lack of creativity of the engineers in his group. When asked what were the consequences of the engineers pioneering new areas, it became apparent that they had to deal with a bevy of negative consequences: time-consuming, seemingly fruitless literature searches; difficulties communicating concepts, which were, as yet, incomprehensible to their peers; and spending inordinate amounts of time before having anything to show for their efforts. As a result of all of these negative consequences being applied (hence the term punishment by application), it is no wonder that some engineers shunned such endeavors and returned to more tried-and-true research topics.

The principle of punishment by application also explains why employees at Emery Air Freight often neglected to fill out damage forms about packages damaged during shipment ("At Emery Air Freight," 1973). The paperwork was time-consuming, it took time away from company priorities, and airline representatives were likely to complain (Table 2). As a "reward" for this, the following year's budget is cut. It is hardly surprising that next year, the administrator's efficiency tends to lapse.

Another example of punishment by removal: Tom Wolfe, in his book *The Right Stuff* (1979), refers to the reluctance of young fighter pilots to acknowledge when they had maneuvered themselves into a bad corner and could not get out. Such an admission triggered a complex and very public chain of events: All other incoming flights were held up, fire trucks trundled out to the runway, and the bureaucracy geared up to investigate (punishment by application). Perhaps most importantly, the pilot's peers began to ask whether the pilot had "the right stuff." The desired behavior (that of responsibly admitting to a problem) is followed by the loss of the most important conviction on the part of the pilot's peers.

Reinforcement theorists do not recommend punishment procedures as a way of changing behavior. Instead, these principles can be best used to better understand why people do not always do what they are urged to do. Based on this awareness, ways can then be devised to take into account the consequences, eliminating where possible the punishing ones, and ensuring positive, frequent and contingent consequences for what is desired.

Extinction in Action

The principle of extinction, stopping or not ever delivering positive reinforcers, also explains why workers do not always do what they apparently should. Management cannot understand why workers ignore safety, take dangerous shortcuts, and lift improperly. To understand why,

TABLE 3   **Chart Illustrating Extinction at Work**

Behavior	Consequence	Principle
Workers perform safely.	Few positive reinforcers, e.g., little management or committee recognition, few coworker comments.	Extinction

we must examine the consequences to workers when they perform safely, using their knees rather than their back to lift, for instance (Table 3). Nothing much happens. Coworkers rarely comment. Management recognition is rare.

Using All the Principles to Analyze a Situation

To see how the principles, as a group, can be used, let us review a final example. In an article entitled "The Politics of Employee Appraisal," Longenecker, Sims, and Gioia (1987) describe what happens when managers do and do not appraise performance as accurately as they might. Table 4 shows what happens. When managers act as desired—using measures of performance that are responsive and critical and directly, frequently, and reliably sampling performance, there are few positive consequences. Raises and promotions are not necessarily forthcoming. Coworkers rarely comment. Upper-level management recognition is rare. Even when a manager does a thorough evaluation, a disgruntled employee may complain or file a grievance, setting in motion time-consuming and distasteful consequences. The few positive consequences—that of building a credible case for promotion or termination—are typically delayed. In contrast, when managers neglect to do accurate appraisals, there are few sanctions. Furthermore, when managers inflate their evaluations, they can avoid such distasteful consequences as being the bad guy, confronting pissed-off employees, and hanging their "dirty laundry" in public. Similarly, when managers deflate their appraisals, they can sometimes shock a poor performer into doing better or they can teach a rebellious worker who's the boss. With few positive consequences for performing as desired and almost no negative consequences for failing to appraise accurately, one can understand why managers might fail at properly evaluating candidates, despite cogent reasons to do otherwise.

Together, the principles of positive and negative reinforcement help to explain why well-intentioned people sometimes do baffling things, and the principles of punishment by application, withdrawal and extinction demonstrate why employees sometimes fail to do what seems in their best interests.

FUTURE

At the start of the 21st century, I propose four new directions.

Do More Experiments Organizationwide

My first suggestion is to expand the scope of the studies, going beyond single individuals or departments to encompass the organization as a whole. Perhaps the study that comes the closest to this ideal is Kortick and O'Brien's (1996) experiment in an internationally renowned

TABLE 4   **Chart Illustrating How the Principles of Behavior Can Be Used in Tandem to Explain Why Managers May not Evaluate Employees as Accurately as They Could**

Behavior	Consequence	Principle
Managers give accurate appraisal based on employee's performance by seeking out measures that are responsive, critical, and where needed exculpatory, and by directly, frequently, and reliably sampling performance.	Pay, raises, promotions not contingent on what or how performance is appraised. Little management recognition. Few peer comments.	Extinction
	Occasional complaint or grievance filed by disgruntled employee.	Punishment by application
	Build documentation that can speed up promotion or termination for deserving employee.	Positive reinforcement
Manager gives inaccurate appraisal:	Infrequent reprimands. Pay and raises still forthcoming.	Lack of punishment by application and removal
a. by inflating it, or	Earns gratitude for not creating permanent record of poor performance.	Positive reinforcement
	Promotes poor-performing employee "up and out" of department.	Negative reinforcement
b. by deflating it.	Shocks employee into performing better. Teaches rebellious employee who's boss.	Positive reinforcement
	Gets poor-performing employee to leave.	Negative reinforcement

package delivery company. The great majority of the 100-plus employees were involved. After dividing them into leagues and divisions, the authors introduced an internal competition, dubbed the "world series of quality control," which led to playoffs and finals. Winning teams received a combination of informational, generalized, and social consequences. After the consequences, the speed and accuracy of package delivery soared. Company officials were so pleased, they expanded the competition between facilities in the entire Northeast.

Look Upwards to Supervisory Personnel

The second suggestion is to seek out bosses. Because the principles of reinforcement theory are not restricted to online personnel, I would like to see more supervisors being studied, as researchers have done with managers of an insurance company (Nemeroff & Consentino, 1979), an owner and operator of a small business (Gaetani, Johnson, & Austin, 1983), school principals (Gillat & Sulzer-Azaroff, 1994), and supervisors, the supervisors of the supervisors, and on up to the vice presidents and the CEO (Methot, Williams, Cummings, & Bradshaw, 1996).

A related recommendation is to develop a model concerned with the upper echelons of organizations. Leaders typically make their contribution through their followers rather than by producing a tangible result themselves. So it is often difficult to carry out the first step in any reinforcement program and specify what managers should do. A start has been made. Based on the theory of operant conditioning, I have developed an operant model of effective supervision (Komaki, 1998b). Studies testing the model show that effective leaders monitor more often—they examine the work and observe workers in action—and provide more consequences—they let workers know when they do well and coach them about how to improve. Furthermore, research shows that the top-notch leaders use a particular sequence, with monitors routinely preceding consequences in what we refer to as an AMC sequence, where "A" stands for an Antecedent (an order or instruction), "M" for a Monitor, and "C" for a Consequence. And the exemplary leaders do these AMCs quickly.

Document the Impact of Using Performance Measures Differing in Quality

Another suggestion is to look at how indices of performance that range in quality affect performance and morale. Experiences in two organizations suggests that bettering the quality of the measures can result in considerable improvements, at least in performance. At an air freight company, Doyle and Shapiro (1980) found that numerous errors and delays occurred in tracking shipment counts: "it took from three to five months for feedback on sales to reach" sales representatives, and "it was often impossible to determine whether they or the salespeople on the other end should get credit for the sale" (p. 139). This lack of consistency in pinpointing who was responsible for closing the sale was the cause of problems in motivating sales personnel. In this case, the appraisal system was redesigned to ensure accurate and timely sales information. After this change, the three test offices "moved to among the top producers in their respective regions, increasing shipments an average of 34.7%" (p. 140).

In the U.S. Marines, revisions to a measure of preventive maintenance (PM) resulted in substantial improvements in performance (Komaki, 1998a). During Year 1, I developed a measure indicating the time Marines spent doing PM and introduced a program, the PM Liberty Call, that included prompt dismissal, a highly regarded consequence at the end of the work week. Data were collected for a year. Surprisingly, no changes were forthcoming. The failure forced me to see how I had fallen prey to expediency. Among the reasons for the failure was the measure. Time spent doing PM could be easily and reliably defined in four words—"manipulating tools or equipment." It entailed no specialized knowledge. Interrater reliability was obtained quickly. Unfortunately, it did not meet the criterion of being under workers' control. The marines complained that they could not spend time doing PM if they were sent elsewhere to get inoculation shots or to paint toolboxes. In Year 2, I redesigned the measure to that it was primarily under the Marines' control, thus meeting all of the SURF&C criteria. Even though the consequence was less potent, utilizing only feedback, significant improvements were found. Supervisory personnel rated the intervention as "very" to "extremely" effective. All parties agreed that they had a better idea of the maintenance effort.

One unit supervisor remarked that the targets were "probably as objective as any evaluation could be" (p. 271).

While these studies illustrate what can happen when measures are changed to meet SURF&C criteria, it would be instructive to document what happens when using more traditional measures that do not meet them. A negative effect on both the performance and morale of otherwise diligent employees is predicted. Results from such a study might help convince organizations to expend the additional resources needed to improve what is measured—ensuring it is under control and critical—and how it is measured, ensuring performance is directly, frequently, and reliably sampled.

Use What We Already Know about Reinforcement Theory to Address Social Justice Issues

Bringing everything together, I recommend applying reinforcement theory to prevent employment discrimination, "unquestionably the major civil rights battleground of the 21st century" (Roberts & White, 1998, back cover). Despite the dreams of Martin Luther King (1963), an elusive but persistent problem exists—the uneven application of subjective standards to minority and majority employees. Sometimes the minority are African-Americans at Texaco (*Roberts v. Texaco*, 1994). Sometimes the minority are women at the Voice of America (Kilborn, 2000). But regardless of who files suit, plaintiffs contend they were unable to get a job, had limited job opportunities, or were paid less than others, not because of their ability, effort, or performance, but because of appraisers' expectations of their race, national origin, age, religion, or gender. In the Texaco case, the lead plaintiff, Bari-Ellen Roberts, charged that there was "a statistically significant pattern of discrimination" pointing to African-Americans, who earned less than Caucasians in all 10 salary groups.

Because the performance appraisal (PA) system forms the foundation for virtually every personnel decision made (Smither, 1998), the PA system is often singled out. The Texaco case was no exception. As evidence, Roberts (1994) pointed out that in Texaco's own survey, employees throughout the company saw "criteria other than performance as being barriers to promotions, with most employees feeling that: promotions are based on who you know, rather than performance." Unfortunately, constructive alternatives are rarely offered. The typical prescription—awareness or diversity training—does not directly address problems with the PA system. After an extensive review of the literature on the impacts of diversity initiatives, Lobel (1999) concludes: "Research on behavior changes in individuals as a result of diversity management activities is unfortunately absent" (p. 468).

To mitigate these problems, we propose redesigning the PA system so that it reflects the employee's performance and not the rater's idiosyncrasies or biases. To do this, we recommend ensuring that appraisals meet SURF&C criteria. Of particular relevance is the test of interrater reliability (IRR) in which two raters independently sample the work, using the same standards, and then check to see each time they agree or disagree. It is enticing to speculate what might occur if the managers at Texaco would use the IRR test during the development of a new appraisal system. Doing this would no doubt generate discussion about what it means to "communicate well" and "problem solve," two qualities listed on Texaco's appraisal form. Doing the IRR test would no doubt raise questions about what constitutes performance worthy for promotion. To ensure that managers can make the necessary nuanced and judicious judgments about performance, the IRR test should be a criterion in training raters. Lastly, at the time of the formal appraisal, the IRR test should be used to provide evidence that standards are not shifting over time and that the evaluation is not simply a function of a particular appraiser.

But we must not stop there. To ensure that these changes are implemented, we must go beyond the usual exhortations and secure motivation at all levels of the organization. For this, we recommend setting up a positive reinforcement program: (a) specifying what is desired—ensuring the performance measure is critical and under the control of workers and making sure that managers directly, frequently, and reliably sample performance; (b) monitoring whether the managers are implementing the PA system as outlined and then basing their decisions on the PA system; and (c) providing a host of consequences, ensuring that they are positive, frequent, and contingent on the PA system. Social and informational consequences should be used in which casual comments are interjected weekly and feedback received monthly. Of utmost importance, however, are organization consequences. Such valued reinforcers as promotions, pay increases, and bonuses should be made contingent on implementing the PA system and basing decisions on these evaluations.

Has anything like this been done? Texaco, in what is an unprecedented "experiment" mandated by a court-ordered settlement, has implemented an incentive program for upper-level managers using a combination of consequences: organizational (in the form of bonuses contingent on employees' responses to a Vision and Values Survey and the hiring and promotion of minority and women employees and making promotions contingent on their superiors' assessment of their interest in meeting diversity goals) (Texaco Equality and Fairness Task Force, 1998, 1999, 2000, 2001). Texaco's attempts, while laudable, do not go far enough. It is not clear how the standards supervisors use to evaluate are indeed "specific, measurable, achievable, relevant, time bound and documented." So far, none of the consequences are contingent on the PA system. Instead, Texaco has relied on antecedents—printing up brochures, clarifying how the appraisal system should work. The results have been mixed. Employees remain skeptical. In 2000 on a survey, employees were asked whether the "employee evaluation process supports a fair and unbiased environment." Only 37% of respondents agreed. And in 2001, employees were still complaining that some managers are not "devot[ing] enough time or they do not feel comfortable conducting meetings with employees to set objectives and evaluate performance. As a result, the process is done in a hurried or superficial manner."

Currently, my colleagues and I are conducting a year-long experiment in the New York City Police Department (Komaki, Traficante, & Stein, in progress). The purpose is to see whether supervisors can be motivated, using a positive reinforcement program, to obtain more frequent, direct, and reliable samples of performance and whether officers will then see their supervisors as being more fair. If experiments like this one are successful, it will indicate that reinforcement theory can be used to address one of the most pressing social justice issues of our times.

In closing, if Isak Dinesen were to ask for recommendations in 2003, I would suggest that she concentrate not just on her plantation workers but on herself as the boss. I would also advocate that she scrutinize her PA systems, looking at how she collects information about individual employees, groups such as her planting, roasting, and transport crews, as well as her organization as a whole. Lastly, I would encourage her to ensure that all her employees are rewarded not by the color of their skin but on the quality of their performance. In this way, we can build upon what we have discovered reinforcement theory can do and move toward a better social state, whether in a police station in Forest Hills or on a farm in Nygong Hills.

References

Anderson, D. C., Crowell, C. R., Sucec, J., Gilligan, K. D., & Wikoff, M. (1982). Behavior management of client contacts in a real estate brokerage: Getting agents to sell more. *Journal of Organizational Behavior Management, 4*(1–2), 67–95.

"At Emery Air Freight: Positive reinforcement boosts performance." (1973). *Organizational Dynamics, 1*(3), 41–50.

Baer, D. M., Wolf, M. M., & Risley, T. R. (1968). Some current dimensions of applied behavior analysis. *Journal of Applied Behavior Analysis, 1*, 91–97.

Balcazar, F. E., Shupert, M. K., Daniels, A. C., Mawhinney, T. C., & Hopkins, B. L. (1989). An objective review and analysis of ten years of publication in the *Journal of Organizational Behavior Management. Journal of Organizational Behavior Management, 10*(1), 7–37.

Becker, W. C., Madsen, C. H. Jr., Arnold, C. R., & Thomas D. R. (1967). The contingent use of teacher attention and praise in reducing classroom behavior problems. *The Journal of Special Education, 1*(3), 287–307.

Blackmon, D. (1997, March 11). Consultant's advice on diversity was anything but diverse. *New York Times,* pp. 1, 4.

Campbell, J. P. (1990). Modeling the performance prediction problem in industrial and organizational psychology. In M. D. Dunnette & L. M. Hough, (Eds.), *Handbook of industrial and organizational psychology* (pp. 687–732). Palo Alto, CA: Consulting Psychologists Press.

Campbell J. P., & Pritchard, R. D. (1976). Motivation theory in industrial organizational psychology. In M. D. Dunnette (Ed.), *Handbook of industrial and organizational psychology* (pp. 63–130). New York: Wiley.

Daniels, A. C. (1994). *Bringing out the best in people.* New York: McGraw-Hill.

Datel, W. E., & Legters, L. J. (1971). The psychology of the army recruit. *Journal of Biological Psychology, 12* (2), 34–40.

Deluga, R. J., & Andrews, H. M. (1985/1986). A case study investigating the effects of a low-cost intervention to reduce three attendance behavior problems in a clerical training program. *Journal of Organizational Behavior Management, 7* (3/4), 115–124.

Deutsch, C. H. (1996, December 1). Diversity training: just shut up and hire. *New York Times,* p. D4.

Dillon, M. J., Kent, H. M., & Malott, R. W. (1980). A supervisory system for accomplishing long-range projects: An application to master's thesis research. *Journal of Organizational Behavior Management, 2* (3), 213–228.

Dinesen, I. (1938). *Out of Africa.* New York: Vintage.

Doyle, S. X., & Shapiro, B. P. (1980, May–June). What counts most in motivating your sales force. *Harvard Business Review,* 133–140.

Drucker, P. F. (1999). *Management challenges for the 21st century.* New York: HarperBusiness.

Elizur, D. (1987). Effect of feedback on verbal and non-verbal courtesy in a bank setting. *Applied Psychology: An International Review, 36* (2), 147–156.

Farren, C., & Nelson, B. (1999). Retaining diversity. *Executive Excellence, 16,* 7.

Foster, S. L., & Cone, J. D. (1986). Design and use of direct observation procedures. In A. R. Ciminero, K. S. Calhoun, & H. E. Adams (Eds.), *Handbook of behavioral assessment* (2nd ed., pp. 253–324). New York: Wiley-Interscience.

Fox, C. J., & Sulzer-Azaroff, B. (1987). Increasing completion of accident reports. *Journal of Safety Research, 18* (2), 65–71.

Fox, D. K., Hopkins, B. L., & Anger, W. K. (1987). The long-term effects of a token economy on safety performance in open-pit mining. *Journal of Applied Behavior Analysis, 20* (3), 215–224.

Gaetani, J. J., Johnson, C. M., & Austin, J. T. (1983). Self-management by an owner of a small business: Reduction of tardiness. *Journal of Organizational Behavior Management, 5* (1), 31–39.

Gellerman, S. W. (1976, March–April). Supervision: Substance and style. *Harvard Business Review,* 89–99.

Gillat, A., & Sulzer-Azaroff, B. (1994). Promoting principles: Managerial involvement in instructional improvement. *Journal of Applied Behavior Analysis, 27* (1), 115–129.

Goldfried, M. R., & Kent, R. N. (1972). Traditional versus behavioral personality assessment: A comparison of methodological and theoretical assumptions. *Psychological Bulletin, 77,* 409–420.

Gupton, T., & LeBow, M. D. (1971). Behavior management in a large industrial firm. *Behavior Therapy, 2,* 78–82.

Harchik, A. E., Sherman, J. A., Sheldon, J. B., & Strouse, M. C. (1992). Ongoing consultation as a method of improving performance of staff members in a group home. *Journal of Applied Behavior Analysis, 25* (3), 599–610.

Haynes, R. S., Pine, R. C., & Fitch, H. G. (1982). Reducing accident rates with organizational behavior modification. *Academy of Management Journal, 25,* 407–416.

Herzberg, F. (1968). One more time: How do you motivate employees? *Harvard Business Review, 46,* 53–62.

Heward, W. L. (1978). Operant conditioning of a .300 hitter? The effects of reinforcement on the offensive efficiency of a barnstorming baseball team. *Behavior Modification, 2,* 25–40.

Hopkins, B. L., Conrad, R. J., & Smith, M. J. (1986). Effective and reliable behavioral control technology. *American Industrial Hygiene Association Journal, 47* (12), 785–791.

James, L. R. (1973). Criterion models and construct validity for criteria. *Psychological Bulletin, 80,* 75–83.

Johnson, C. M., Redmon, W. K., & Mawhinney, T. C. (Eds.). (2001). *Handbook of organizational performance: Behavior analysis and management.* New York: Haworth.

Johnson, M. D., & Fawcett, S. B. (1994). Courteous service: Its assessment and modification in a human service organization. *Journal of Applied Behavior Analysis, 27,* 145–152.

Jones H. H., Morris, E. K., & Barnard, J. D. (1985/1986). Increasing staff completion of civil commitment forms through instructions and graphed group performance feedback. *Journal of Organizational Behavior Management, 7* (3/4), 29–43.

Kempen, R. W., & Hall, R. V. (1977). Reduction of industrial absenteeism: Results of a behavioral approach. *Journal of Organizational Behavior Management, 1* (1), 1–21.

Kilborn, P. T. (2000, March 24). For women in bias case, the wounds remain. *New York Times,* p. A14.

Komaki, J. L. (1998a). When performance improvement is the goal: A new set of criteria for criteria. *Journal of Applied Behavior Analysis, 31,* 263–280.

Komaki, J. L. (1998b). *Leadership from an operant perspective.* London: Routledge.

Komaki, J. L., Barwick, K. D., & Scott, L. R. (1978). A behavioral approach to occupational safety: Pinpointing and reinforcing safety performance in a food manufacturing plant. *Journal of Applied Psychology, 63,* 434–445.

Komaki, J. L., Coombs, T., Redding, Jr., T. P., & Schepman, S. (2000). A rich and rigorous examination of applied behavior analysis research in the world of work. In C. L. Cooper & I. T. Robertson (Eds.), *International Review of Industrial and Organizational Psychology 2000* (pp. 265–367). Sussex, England: John Wiley.

Komaki, J. L., Traficante, T., & Stein, A. (in progress). Treating officers with respect: A two-way street. Experiment being conducted in The New York City Police Department.

Kortick, S. A., & O'Brien, R. M. (1996). The world series of quality control: A case study in the package delivery industry. *Journal of Organizational Behavior Management, 16,* (2), 77–93.

Lobel, S. A. (1999). Impacts of diversity and work-life initiatives in organizations. In G. N. Powell (Ed.), *Handbook of gender and work* (pp. 453–474). Thousand Oaks, CA: Sage.

Longenecker, C. O., Sims, H. P., Jr., & Gioia, D. A. (1987). Behind the mask: The politics of employee appraisal. *The Academy of Management Executive, 1,* 183–193.

Lovaas, O. I. (1966). A program for the establishment of speech in psychotic children. In J. K. Wing (Ed.), *Early childhood autism.* London: Pergamon.

Luthans, F., Paul, R., & Taylor, L. (1985). The impact of contingent reinforcement on retail salespersons' performance behaviors: A replicated field experiment. *Journal of Organizational Behavior Management, 7* (1/2), 25–35.

Mager, R. F., & Pipe, P. (1984). *Analyzing performance problems: You really oughta wanna* (2nd ed). Belmont, CA: Lake.

McGrath, J. E. (1984). *Groups: Interaction and performance.* Englewood Cliffs, NJ: Prentice Hall.

Methot, L. L., Williams, W. L., Cummings, A., & Bradshaw, B. (1996). Measuring the effects of a manager-supervisor training program through the generalized performance of managers, supervisors, front-line staff and clients in a human service setting. *Journal of Organizational Behavior Management, 16* (2), 3–34.

Nasanen, M., & Saari, J. (1987). The effects of positive feedback on housekeeping and accidents at a shipyard. *Journal of Occupational Accidents, 8,* 237–250.

Nemeroff, W. F., & Cosentino, J. (1979). Utilizing feedback and goal setting to increase performance appraisal interviewer skills of managers. *Academy of Management Journal, 22* (3), 566–575.

Nord, W. R. (1969). Beyond the teaching machine: The neglected area of operant conditioning in the theory and practice of management. *Organizational Behavior and Human Performance, 4,* 375–401.

Nordstrom, R., Hall, R. V., Lorenzi, P., & Delquadri, J. (1988). Organizational behavior modification in the public sector: Three field experiments. *Journal of Organizational Behavior Management, 9* (2), 91–112.

O'Hara, K., Johnson, C. M., & Beehr, T. A. (1985). Organizational behavior management in the private sector: A review of empirical research and recommendations for further investigation. *Academy of Management Review, 10,* 848–864.

Parsons, M. B., & Reid, D. H. (1995). Training residential supervisors to provide feedback for maintaining staff teaching skills with people who have severe disabilities. *Journal of Applied Behavior Analysis, 28* (3), 317–322.

Pierce, C. H., & Risley, T. R. (1974). Improving job performance of neighborhood youth corps aides in an urban recreation program. *Journal of Applied Behavior Analysis, 7* (2), 207–215.

Porter, L. W. (1973). Turning work into nonwork: The rewarding environment. In M. D. Dunnette (Ed.), *Work and nonwork in the year 2001* (pp. 113–133). Belmont, CA: Wadsworth.

Premack, D. (1965). Reinforcement theory. In D. Levine (Ed.), *Nebraska symposium on motivation.* Lincoln: University of Nebraska Press.

Roberts v. Texaco Inc., 94 Civ. 2015 CLB (1994).

Roberts, B., with White, J. E. (1998). *Roberts vs. Texaco: A true story of race and corporate America.* New York: Avon.

Skinner, B. F. (1974). *About behaviorism.* New York: Vintage.

Smither, J. W. (Ed.). (1998). *Performance appraisal.* San Francisco: Jossey-Bass.

Stajkovic, A. D., & Luthans, F. (1997). A meta-analysis of the effects of organizational behavior modification on task performance, 1975–95. *Academy of Management Journal, 40* (5), 1122–1149.

Steers, R. M., Porter, L. W., & Bigley, G. A. (1996). *Motivation and leadership at work.* New York: McGraw-Hill.

Task Force (1998, 1999, 2000). First, Second, and Third Annual Report of the Equality and Fairness Task Force. (http://www.texaco.com)

Welsh, D. H., Luthans, F., & Sommer, S. M. (1993). Organizational behavior modification goes to Russia: Replicating an experimental analysis across cultures and tasks. *Journal of Organizational Behavior Management, 13* (2), 15–35.

Wilk, L. A., & Redmon, W. K. (1998). The effects of feedback and goal setting on the productivity and satisfaction of university admissions staff. *Journal of Organizational Behavior Management, 18* (1), 45–68.

Wittkopp, C. J., Rowan, J. F., & Poling, A. (1990). Use of a feedback package to reduce machine set-up time in a manufacturing plant, *Journal of Organizational Behavior Management, 11* (2), 7–22.

Zohar, D., Cohen, A., & Azar, N. (1980). Promoting increased use of car protectors in noise through information feedback. *Human Factors, 22* (1), 69–79.

Motivation through Conscious Goal Setting

Edwin A. Locke

The study of human motivation has always been considered by psychologists to be a very difficult undertaking, especially because motivation is something inside the organism. But the fundamental difficulty has actually been self-imposed or, more specifically, imposed by false philosophical assumptions. Two key assumptions were that: (a) only material events could be causal, and (b) only entities that were directly, externally, perceivable could be admitted into the realm of science. Accepting these positivist premises meant that: (a) consciousness could

From *Applied and Preventive Psychology,* 1996, 5, 117–124. Reprinted with permission.

not be considered a cause of action; and (b) making valid inferences about internal events, especially if they were mental events in other people, was logically impermissible.

Historically, motivational psychologists have tried to conform to these strictures by *externalizing* or *materializing* their key concepts. Skinnerian behaviorism, for example, externalized motivation by attributing it to reinforcers (consequences of action) and treating the human mind as an epiphenomenon. Drive-reduction theorists like Hull kept motivation inside the organism but attributed it to strictly physiological mechanisms. Both approaches assumed the validity of psychological determinism—the doctrine that man has no choice with respect to his beliefs, choices, thinking or actions. Both also barred introspection as a scientific method on the grounds that it could not be publicly verified and that, even if it were, the data obtained thereby were causally insignificant (due to determinism or materialism).

Beginning in the late 1960s the positivist paradigm in psychology began to fall apart for a number of reasons. First, it had lost support in philosophy (e.g., Blanshard, 1962). Second, the materialist approaches did not work. Human action cannot, in fact, be understood by looking at man only from the outside or only at his internal physiology. The recognition of these facts ushered in the "cognitive revolution" in psychology; it became the dominant paradigm by the end of the 1970s or early 1980s.

The cognitive revolution gradually gained philosophical support. Of crucial (though long unrecognized) relevance was the work of philosopher Ayn Rand (1990) who demonstrated that consciousness (along with existence and identity) was an axiom, that is, a perceptually self-evident primary that forms the base of all knowledge and cannot be denied without self-contradiction (Locke, 1995). She showed also that volition (free will) is an axiom, thus philosophically justifying the study of consciousness (Binswanger, 1991; Peikoff, 1992).

As to the issue of introspection, one's mental contents and processes can be directly observed only in oneself, but each person can observe the same, basic, cognitive processes in themselves as everyone else (e.g., belief, imagination, desire, purpose, memory, emotion, etc.). People can make errors when they introspect, but they can also make errors when they perform addition and subtraction—which does not refute the validity of mathematics. The validity of introspective reports must be judged the same way as the validity of any other inference—by determining whether the totality of the evidence justifies the conclusion. For example, if a person claimed not to be afraid of heights yet began to sweat and shake when approaching high places, consistently did everything in his power to avoid going near such places, and evaded discussing the issue, we would justifiably conclude that the person's report was erroneous. It is a scientific question to determine under what conditions one can elicit the most accurate introspective reports from another person (e.g., see Crutcher, 1994). The approach of goal setting theory is consistent with, although its beginnings somewhat antedated, the cognitive revolution. The theory is based on what Aristotle called *final causality,* that is, action caused by a purpose. It accepts the axiomatic status of consciousness and volition. It also assumes that introspective reports provide (in principle) useful and valid data for formulating psychological concepts and measuring psychological phenomena (e.g., purpose, goal commitment, self-efficacy, etc.).

I began to consider goal setting as an approach to human motivation in the mid-1960s. At that time, in addition to the behaviorist and physiological approaches, David McClelland's approach via subconscious motives was much in vogue. While McClelland acknowledged the existence and importance of human consciousness, he did not think much could be gained from studying conscious motives. However, the results he obtained from studying subconscious motives were often unpredictable and undependable. There were frequent post hoc explanations of anomalous findings, switches of measures and of dependent variables, and negative results (e.g., McClelland, 1961). About this time, T. A. Ryan (a professor at Cornell where I was doing my graduate work) suggested that a fruitful approach to human motivation might be to simply ask people what they were trying to accomplish when they took an action. (This view is fully developed in Ryan, 1970.) He proposed approaching human motivation starting with the individual's immediate intentions, then building from there to explain the sources of the intentions and so on. (Ryan typically did not use the term goal despite the similarity in meaning to intent.) This is the approach that I chose to follow.

There were three reasons for choosing it: (a) It was philosophically sound. (b) It was consistent with introspective evidence revealing that human action as such is *normally* purposeful. Underlying such action is a fundamental biological principle: that all living organisms engage in goal-directed action as a necessity of survival (Binswanger, 1990). In the higher organisms internal, goal-directed actions are automatic (e.g., digestion, cell repair), but molar actions are guided normally by consciously held goals, that is, purposes. In the lower animals these consist of momentary desires. In man, goals are (or at least can be) set volitionally by a process of reasoning and may cover the range of a lifetime. (Of course, since man can make errors in choosing goals, all goal-directed action does not facilitate survival and may even undermine it.) (c) The third reason was practical—the approach worked, as we shall see below.

As an industrial–organizational psychologist, my interest was in explaining why some people (ability and knowledge aside) perform better on work tasks than others. My starting point was to look at what they were consciously trying to accomplish when they performed tasks, that is, what goals they were aiming for. As a doctoral student I began a program of research that has continued for some 30 years. Much of the work has been collaborative, especially with Gary Latham, who has conducted numerous field studies on goal setting. These have been an important complement to my studies, which have been performed predominantly in laboratory settings. To date there have been more than 500 studies of goal setting conducted by myself, Latham, and many others. The most complete statements of goal-setting theory is found in Locke and Latham (1990). The findings referred to below can be found in this book, unless otherwise referenced.

The typical experimental paradigm in goal setting studies is as follows: Subjects are given a task to perform (e.g., brainstorming, simple addition, a management simulation; in field settings, natural work tasks are used) and are assigned various performance goals to attain within a specified time limit [e.g., "do your best"; "attain a score of 25(20, 15)"]. They are given feedback showing progress in relation to the goals, where relevant. Subjects may also be asked to fill out questionnaires asking them to describe: their personal goals (irrespective of assigned goals); their degree of self-efficacy; their degree of goal commitment; etc. There are many variants on this basic model. For example, goals may be self-set rather than assigned; subjects may participate in setting goals; goal conflict may be induced; strategies for reaching goals may have to be discovered, etc. (Locke & Latham, 1990).

Good attributes—A goal as the object or aim of an action. Goals have both an internal and an external aspect. Internally, they are ideas (desired ends); externally, they refer to the object or condition sought (e.g., a job, a sale, a certain performance level). The idea guides action to attain the object. Two broad attributes of goals are *content* (the actual object sought) and *intensity* (the scope, focus, complexity etc. of the choice process). Qualitatively, the content of a goal is whatever the person is seeking. Quantitatively, two attributes of content, *difficulty* and *specificity,* have been studied.

Finding #1. The more difficult the goal, the greater the achievement.

This finding may seem surprising in view of the more intuitively appealing inverse-U function, predicted by Atkinson (1958) and others. However, we have found it almost impossible to replicate Atkinson's original finding (Locke & Latham, 1990). Our linear function assumes, however, that the individual is committed to the goal and possesses the requisite ability and knowledge to achieve it. Without these, performance does drop at high goal levels.

Finding #2. The more specific or explicit the goal, the more precisely performance is regulated.

High goal specificity is achieved mainly through quantification (increase sales by 10%) or enumeration (here is a list of tasks to be accomplished). Thus it reduces *variance* in performance, providing the individual can control performance. This is not to say that specificity is always desirable (it may not be in some creative innovation situations), but only that it has certain effects.

Finding #3. Goals that are both specific and difficult lead to the highest performance.

Especially relevant here are the many studies that have compared the effect of specific, hard goals with goals such as "do your best." People do not actually do their best when trying to do their best because, as a vague goal, it is compatible with many different outcomes, including those lower than one's best.

The aspect of intensity that has been most studied in goal setting research is that of goal *commitment,* the degree to which the person is genuinely attached to and determined to reach the goals.

Finding #4. Commitment to goals is most critical when goals are specific and difficult.

When goals are easy or vague, it is not hard to get commitment, because it does not require much dedication to reach easy goals, and vague goals can be easily redefined to accommodate low performance. When goals are specific and hard, the higher the commitment the better the performance. The next question to address is: what influences goal commitment?

Finding #5. High commitment to goals is attained when (a) the individual is convinced that the goal is important; and (b) the individual is convinced that the goal is attainable (or that, at least, progress can be made toward it). (These are the same factors that influence goal choice)

There are many ways to convince a person that a goal is important. Due to the demand characteristics inherent in most laboratory settings, it is quite sufficient to simply *ask for compliance* after providing a plausible rationale for the study. In work situations, the supervisor or leader can use *legitimate authority* to get initial commitment. Continued commitment might require additional incentives such as *supportiveness, recognition, and rewards.* Financial incentives may facilitate commitment and performance, except when rewards are offered for attaining impossible goals; here, performance actually drops (Lee, Locke, & Phan, 1994). *Participation* by subordinates in setting goals (that is, joint goal setting by supervisor and subordinate) leads to higher commitment than curtly telling people what to do with no explanation, but it does not lead to (practically significant) higher commitment than providing a convincing rationale for an assigned goal (Latham, Erez, & Locke, 1968). We have found subordinate participation to be most beneficial for formulating strategies for reaching goals (Latham, Winters, & Locke, 1994) providing they possess relevant knowledge (Scully, Kirkpatrick, & Locke, 1995). *Self-set goals* can be highly effective in gaining commitment, although they may not always be set as high as another person would assign (Locke, 1966).

Commitment can be enhanced by effective *leadership* (Locke & associates, 1991). Relevant leadership techniques include:

- providing and communicating an inspiring vision for the company or organization

- acting as role model for the employees

- expecting outstanding performance

- promoting employees who embrace the vision and dismissing those who reject it

- delegating responsibility ("ownership") for key tasks; goal setting itself can be delegated for capable, responsible employees

- expressing (genuine) confidence in employee capabilities

- enhancing capabilities through training

- asking for commitment in public

Although the above discussion focused on external factors that promote goal commitment, it should be stressed that people have the capacity to *commit themselves* to goals, although the methods by which they do it have not been studied extensively. Presumably these methods would include: choosing values or long-range purposes that they want to attain, identifying why those values are important to them (including linking their goals and values to their self-concept), identifying how specific goals would help achieve their values, identifying the benefits of those goals, specifying plans (including training and knowledge seeking) that would make goal attainment possible, volitionally keeping their knowledge in mind when confronted by setbacks and obstacles, and rewarding themselves internally for goal progress. These are, in fact, some of the ingredients of *self-management training* (which will be discussed at more length below), which has been widely used in a number of fields including therapy, dieting, smoking-cessation, and management (Bandura, 1986; Frayne & Latham, 1987). It has also been found that people who engage in more *intensive cognitive processing* regarding their goals and their plans to attain them are more likely to actually carry out the relevant actions than those who engage in less intensive processing (Gollwitzer, Heckhausen, & Ratajczak, 1990).

The issue of becoming convinced that the goal is attainable was implicit in some of the above findings (e.g., training, modeling). People are most likely to believe they can attain a goal when they believe that it is within their capacity. This implies three paths to commitment: *adjust the goal* to the person's present capacity; raise the person's capacity through providing *training and experience;* or change the person's perspective on their capacity through *expressions of confidence and role modeling* (Bandura, 1986). The person does not have to believe that total success is possible (an important issue when goals are difficult) as long as they believe that partial success or progress toward the goal (e.g., in the form of subgoal achievement) is meaningful. This brings us to another important concept in goal setting theory, that of self-efficacy.

Self-efficacy. The term self-efficacy refers to task-specific confidence and is a key component of Bandura's (1986) social–cognitive theory. Bandura has shown that self-efficacy can be raised by: enactive mastery, persuasion, and role modeling—all referred to above. In organizational settings enactive mastery can be assured by providing people with needed experience and training and also by selecting people based on their skills and abilities. Persuasion may include not only verbal expressions of confidence but also giving people information regarding what task strategies to use. The effectiveness of role modeling depends on the attributes of the model and on the person observing the model (Bandura, (1986). Several points of connection between social–cognitive theory and goal setting theory have been studied:

Finding #6. In addition to having a direct effect on performance, self-efficacy influences: (a) the difficulty level of the goal chosen or accepted, (b) commitment to goals, (c) the response to negative feedback or failure, and (d) the choice of task strategies.

People with high self-efficacy are more likely to set high goals or to accept difficult, assigned goals, to commit themselves to difficult goals, to respond with renewed efforts to setbacks, and to discover successful task strategies. Thus the effects of self-efficacy on performance are both direct and indirect (through various goal processes). Additionally, goal choice and commitment can be influenced through role modeling.

Feedback. For people to pursue goals effectively, they need some means of checking or tracking their progress toward their goal. Sometimes this is self-evident to perception, as when a person walks down a road towards a distant but visible town or cuts the grass on a large lawn. In such cases, deviations from the path to the goal are easily seen and corrected. Contrast this, however, with a sales goal whose attainment requires scores of sales over a period of many months. Here some formal means of keeping score is needed so that people can get a clear indication if they are moving fast enough and in the right direction.

Finding #7. Goal setting is most effective when there is feedback showing progress in relation to the goal. (Technically speaking, feedback is a moderator of the goal-performance relationship.)

Goal-setting theory disputes the notion that feedback exerts an automatic, "reinforcing" effect on performance. When provided with feedback on their own performance or that of others, people often spontaneously set goals to improve over their previous best or beat the performance of others simply as a way of challenging themselves, but this is not inevitable. The goal set may be higher or lower than the performance level previously achieved. The effect of performance feedback (knowledge of score) depends on the goals set in response to it.

Finding #8. Goal setting (along with self-efficacy) mediates the effect of knowledge of past performance on subsequent performance.

When people receive negative performance feedback, they are typically unhappy and may also experience doubts about their ability. Those who can sustain their self-efficacy under such pressure tend to maintain or even raise their subsequent goals, retain their commitment, intensify their search for better strategies, and thereby improve their subsequent performance. Those who lose confidence will tend to lower their goals, decrease their efforts, and lessen the intensity and effectiveness of their strategy search. Self-efficacy changes following failure may be affected by the types of causal attributions people make (Bandura, 1986).

Mechanisms. How, specifically, do goals regulate performance? Primarily by affecting the three aspects of motivated action: direction, intensity, and duration.

Finding #9. Goals affect performance by affecting the direction of action, the degree of effort exerted, and the persistence of action over time.

The directive aspect is fairly obvious. A person who has a goal to maximize quality of performance will focus more attention and action on quality than on, for example, quantity or speed. When there is conflict between two or more goals, performance with respect to each goal may be undermined (Locke, Smith, Erez, Chah, & Shaffer, 1994).

Effort is roughly proportional to the judged difficulty of the goal—which is why difficult goals ordinarily lead to higher performance than easy goals. Persistence refers to directed effort extended over time. Harder goals typically lead to more persistence than easy goals, because, given commitment, they take longer to reach and may require overcoming more obstacles. These mechanisms operate almost automatically or, at least routinely, once a goal is committed to, because most people have learned, by about the age of 6, that if they want to achieve something they have to: pay attention to it to the exclusion of other things, exert the needed effort, and persist until it is achieved.

There is another, more indirect goal mechanism—that of task strategies or plans. Most goals require the application of task-specific procedures in addition to attention and effort if they are to be attained. For example, a student who wants to get an A in a psychology course needs to know how to study in general, how to study psychology in particular, how to identify what is needed for an A in this course, and how to implement this knowledge. There are several things we have learned about the relationship of goals and plans.

Finding #10. (a) Goals stimulate planning in general. Often the planning quality is higher than that which occurs without goals. (b) When people possess task or goal-relevant plans as a result of experience or training, they activate them virtually automatically when confronted with a performance goal. (c) Newly learned plans or strategies are most likely to be utilized under the stimulus of a specific, difficult goal.

People recognize that goals require plans and seek either to use what they already know or to make new plans when they want to reach goals. Sometimes such plans are quite pedestrian. For example, to attain difficult, quantity goals people may simply sacrifice quality—a common trade-off with which everyone is familiar. When people are given training in a new strategy, they do not always use it consistently unless they must attain goals that cannot otherwise be attained.

When tasks are complex, a number of new issues arise. The direct goal mechanisms are less adequate than in the case of simple tasks for attaining the goal. (Compare, for example, the efficacy of effort alone in leading to high performance when doing push-ups vs. playing chess.) The path to the goal is less clear, and there may be no relevant prior experience or training which they can fall back on. In such cases people are forced to discover new strategies; sometimes they do this poorly especially if the goals are specific and difficult. The reason appears to be that under this type of pressure, tunnel vision inhibits effective search procedures. The evidence so far indicates that:

Finding #11. When people strive for goals on complex tasks, they are least effective in discovering suitable task strategies if: (a) they have no prior experience or training on the task; (b) there is high pressure to perform well; and (c) there is high time pressure (to perform well immediately).

Goals as mediators. More than 25 years ago I speculated that goals might mediate the effects of other motivators such as feedback, participation, and money incentives have on performance (Locke, 1968). More recently, I suggested that goals, along with self-efficacy, might mediate the effects of values and personality on performance (Locke, 1991b). There is firm support for goals and self-efficacy as mediators of feedback (Locke & Latham, 1990). Feedback is most effective in motivating improved performance when it is used to set goals. Feedback alone is just information. To act on the basis of information, people need to know or decide what it means—that is, what significance it has. In a goal-setting context, this means knowing what a good or desirable score is and what a bad or undesirable score is. If no such judgment is made, the feedback will probably be ignored, Similarly, participation seems to motivate performance to the extent that it leads to higher goals, higher self-efficacy or higher commitment (Latham et al., 1994; Locke & Latham, 1990). The same has recently been found with respect to monetary incentives (Lee, Locke, & Phan, 1994), although all studies do not show consistent findings (see Locke & Latham, 1990, ch. 6).

More recent studies have shown evidence for goals or goals plus self-efficacy as a mediator of personality (Barrick, Mount, & Strauss, 1993; Lerner & Locke, 1995; see also Taylor, Locke, Lee, & Gist, 1984) and charismatic leadership (Kirkpatrick & Locke, in press). In other words, these variables affect performance through their effects on goals and self-efficacy. This is not to claim that goals fully mediate the effect of all personality and incentives on performance, but there is evidence to suggest:

Finding #12. Goals (including goal commitment), in combination with self-efficacy, mediate or partially mediate the effects of several personality traits and incentives on performance.

The logic behind this model is that goals and self-efficacy are the immediate regulators of much human action, and that they, therefore, reflect the individual's assessment of the value of incentives and of the applicability of values and traits to specific situations (Locke, 1991b).

Self-management. I noted earlier that goal-directed actions and choices are not necessarily "imposed" or even encouraged by environments (e.g., organizational demands). People have the choice to manage their own lives by setting their own purposes and working to achieve them (Binswanger, 1991). With the help of training programs, people can be helped to manage their own actions more effectively. Frayne and Latham (1987) and Latham and Frayne (1989), for example, trained employees to reduce their own absenteeism rate through training in self goal setting, self-administered feedback, problem solving (strategy formation), self-commitment through rewards and punishments, and self-motivation after setbacks. The training produced significant reductions in absences in both 6- and 9-month follow-ups. Two studies by Gist and her colleagues (Gist, Bavetta, & Stevens, 1990; Gist, Stevens, & Bavetta, 1991) used self-management training to develop and foster the retention and generalization of salary negotiation skills. But training is not always required for self-motivation to occur. In a longitudinal study of AT&T male managers, Howard and Bray (1988) found that ambition, measured basically by the manager's own goal for the number of levels he wanted to be promoted in the future, was a significant predictor (and the best motivational predictor) of number of promotions received across a span of 25 years! Thus we can say that:

Finding #13. Goal-setting and goal-related mechanisms can be trained and/or adopted in the absence of training for the purpose of self-regulation.

Affect. Emotion is a type of automatic, partly subconscious, psychological estimate—an estimate of the relationship of things to oneself. More precisely, emotions are the form in which one experiences automatized value judgments, that is, judgments of objects, events, and situations (as consciously and/or subconsciously perceived and understood) according to the standard of one's values (Locke, 1976). Events and situations seen as threatening to one's values give rise to negative emotions (e.g., fear, anxiety, dissatisfaction), whereas events and situations seen as furthering one's values produce positive emotions (e.g., happiness, satisfaction, love). In goal-setting contexts, the immediate value standard is one's goal, that is, the level of performance desired or sought. Thus goal achievement leads to satisfaction and goal failure to dissatisfaction. (There are deeper value judgments that underlie and color situationally specific judgments, e.g., the value of achievement, one's self-concept, but I will not address that issue here).

There is an interesting and, at first glance, nonintuitive finding pertaining to the relation of goals to satisfaction. High goals lead to *less* performance satisfaction, on the average, than easy goals (Mento, Locke, & Klein, 1992). This seems paradoxical in that higher goals are *more* motivating than lower goals in terms of effort and performance. The explanation is that high goals require higher standards of attainment than low goals, so that self-satisfaction is harder to achieve. This is why, if people could set their own goals without penalty, they would set them lower rather than higher. However, in the real world, more rewards accrue to people who set high goals for themselves than those who set low goals (e.g., personal pride, better jobs, higher income, more options), thus inducing people not to set their goals too low. At the same time, higher goals require more effort, ability, and risk than lower goals, thus limiting the number of people who set their goals high. As noted earlier, people choose goals based both on what is important to them and what they think they are capable of. Thus to summarize:

Finding #14. Goals serve as standards of self-satisfaction, with harder goals demanding higher accomplishment in order to attain self-satisfaction than easy goals.

Goals can also be used to enhance task interest, reduce boredom, and promote goal clarity. When used to punish or intimidate people, however, goals increase stress and anxiety.

Goal-setting dilemmas. If hard or difficult goals lead to higher performance and lower satisfaction than easy goals, there is obviously a problem of how to get people (or oneself) to be both happy and productive. There are obvious benefits and penalties of trying for too little in life as well as for trying for too much. Obviously, the key principle here is *personal context.* Life goals must be based on what one really wants out of life (not on what other people want one to want) and on one's true capabilities. If one wants to pursue challenging goals, these goals do not have to be attained all at once but can be pursued over an extended time period. Lower subgoals can be set as steps to a longer term and higher goal. Partial success can be credited by others and oneself. Failure can be treated or framed as a learning experience, not as proof of incompetence. New skills can be acquired as needed, and jobs can be chosen, when possible, to match one's aspirations and abilities.

Another dilemma is how to structure reward systems in organizations. I noted earlier that if incentives were offered for goals that could not be reached, lower motivation and performance resulted as compared to hourly payment or piece-rate pay (Lee, Phan, & Locke, 1994). This might suggest that moderate goals would be ideal; however, moderate goals in work situations do not stay moderate for long, because people improve their strategies and skills over time. Thus a difficult juggling act would be required to maintain an effective system. Another possibility would be to set goals to motivate people but pay for performance, regardless of goal level. This would be similar to a piece-rate system. Or multiple goal levels could be set, from moderately easy to almost impossible, and pay could be proportional to the highest level attained. This would guarantee some reward even for moderate attainments but would stimulate higher attainments as well. Incentives can be dangerous if they encourage tunnel vision and thereby the neglect of important nongoal activities. Clearly many interesting studies could be done to explore this issue in more detail.

APPLIED EXAMPLE

Since this is an applied and preventive psychology journal, I thought it might be of interest to readers to show how goal-setting theory could be used to help deal with a real-world problem. (I will not use weight-loss or exercise programs as examples, because they have already been described in published studies, e.g., Bandura & Simon, 1977). Let us say that you are the chairman of an academic department and you want to help a new assistant professor to get tenure. Let us further assume that it is a publish-or-perish university and that the professor is in the summer of her fourth year with a below average, but not hopeless, record for scholarship. You sit down with her and go over her vita. So far she has two published articles in good journals, one in a mediocre journal, and four papers under review. She also has six more projects in the works, which can be submitted in the next year. The first task is to figure out what will be needed to make tenure. Let's say she will need about 10 papers, 8 in good journals. Since tenure review will occur in 2 years, and since all projects do not work out, you would suggest that she have *all six* of the "in the works" projects submitted by January of her last year (that is, in the next 18 months). This is to allow time to revise and resubmit before the September deadline. Furthermore, you advise that all "revise and resubmit" revisions on these and the "under review" manuscripts be done within 30 to 60 days. These are the goals. How do you get commitment? If the professor decides that she does not really want to be an academic in this institution, suggest that she look for work elsewhere. But if she does want to succeed, then the main issue is confidence building. Express confidence based on the work to date. Suggest role models. Be supportive: ask her what you can do to help (e.g., some extra assistants for data analysis; time off in the summer; reduced committee work). If previous rejections of papers have been demoralizing, suggest some alternative strategies (e.g., reframe and submit to a different journal, combine two papers into one, etc.).

To ensure careful tracking (feedback regarding progress), have her make a schedule indicating when each in process manuscript will be submitted. Go over time-utilization issues (goal priorities) and strategies (e.g., has she delegated as much of the busy work as possible? Is she going overboard on teaching? Is she working enough hours? Is she going to too many professional meetings? Is she spending too much time writing conference papers?)

To further help develop effective plans, have her consult with other junior and senior faculty to see if they have any tips for her. Persuade her to let colleagues (expeditiously) review her papers before submission and also help to interpret letters from editors. Finally, tell her you *want* her to make it (if you do) and the reasons why.

It is true that faculty are supposed to be self-managing and usually they are, but they still may need a little help (i.e., mentoring, role modeling) along the way. As someone who has been the chairman of a faculty area for 12 years, I can report that I and my senior faculty have used the above procedures with very good success. I hope the readers of this journal will find these ideas useful also.

GENERALITY OF GOAL-SETTING THEORY

Thus far goal setting has been studied using: more than 40,000 subjects (ranging from children to research scientists) in eight countries, both laboratory and field settings, more than 88 different tasks, time spans of 1 min to several years, goals set by several different methods, dependent variables of many types, and levels of analysis ranging from the individual to the group to the organizational. Goal-setting effects are quite robust, typically yielding a success rate of 90%, even including studies that made methodological and/or theoretical errors. The evidence indicates that goal-setting theory involves a motivational principle of fundamental importance, even though there are many motivational issues it does not deal with (e.g., the subconscious). Furthermore, there are many interesting theoretical issues still to be explored (e.g., goal setting in dynamic environments, self-commitment techniques, goals and problem solving, short- vs. long-term goals).

RELATION TO OTHER THEORIES

Although space does not permit a detailed exposition here, goal-setting theory has been connected to several other motivation theories. Its many ties to *social–cognitive theory* (Bandura, 1986) were noted earlier. It has also been linked to *expectancy theory* in that expectancies and valences affect goal choice and commitment. Like self-efficacy, effort-performance expectancy also has a direct effect on performance. Also, as noted, we have not found support for *Atkinson's* (1958) *theory* of an inverse-U relationship between probability of success and level of performance. There are potential links to *attribution theory* and *mood theory,* but these have rarely been studied. Thus far, we have found no relationship between *McClelland's projective need for achievement* measure and goal choice in specific situations.

Deci and Ryan's (1985) concept of *intrinsic motivation* has garnered considerable attention, especially among social psychologists; several studies have examined its relationship to goal setting. Deci and Ryan argued that people have innate needs for self-determination (autonomy) and competence, and that these regulate action most strongly when people are challenged and yet free from external constraints or pressures and from "controlling" situations such as incentive pay—that is, when they have the most freedom of choice. (For a critique of Deci's theory, see Bandura, 1986.) One would expect that assigned goals would be especially prone to undermine intrinsic motivation (defined as free time spent on a focal task), especially as compared to participatively set goals. However, the research to date shows no consistent pattern of findings; participative goal setting does not consistently lead to higher intrinsic motivation than assigned goals (see Locke &Latham, 1990, ch. 2). Part of the problem may be that there are too many ambiguities in intrinsic motivation theory to allow unequivocal predictions to be made. For example, how do we know when challenge ends and threat begins? What is the relation of competence to self-efficacy? If people, in fact, possess volition or free will (Binswanger, 1991), how can incentives that one consents to pursue undermine it?

Control theory is a popular model of motivation that has tried to incorporate goal theory and many other theories into an overarching framework focused around the negative feedback loop (see Locke & Latham, 1990, ch. 1). There are several reasons for rejecting this model: (a) it is based on a machine metaphor that is not applicable to conscious, rational beings, (b) the model is not databased, and (c) its attempts to revise the model to incorporate discoveries made by other theories rob the model of any unique identity (Locke, 1991a; see also Locke & Latham, 1990, ch. 1).

DYSFUNCTIONS OF GOALS

Is goal setting ever harmful? Certainly, if goals are set for the wrong outcome or if there is goal conflict (Locke et al., 1994). Goals that do not change when relevant circumstances change may promote undue rigidity. We have noted that specific, challenging goals given in the absence of relevant expertise may undermine the discovery of useful task strategies. Goals that are set too high can be demoralizing; there is a fine line between stretching people and discouraging them. A great deal depends on sustaining self-efficacy in the face of setbacks. Goals can be used as a defensive maneuver by people who try to take pride in their aspirations without actually doing anything to achieve them. Obviously these (and many other) issues are ripe for further study.

References

Atkinson, J. W. (1958). Towards experimental analysis of human motivation in terms of motives, expectancies and incentives. In J. W. Atkinson (Ed.), *Motives in fantasy, action & society*. Princeton, NJ: Van Nostrand.

Bandura, A. (1986). *Social foundations of thought and action: A social–cognitive view*. Englewood Cliffs, NJ: Prentice Hall.

Bandura, A., & Simon, K. M. (1977). The role of proximal intentions in self-regulation of refractory behavior. *Cognitive Theory & Research, 1,* 177–193.

Barrick, M. R., Mount, M. K., & Strauss, J. P. (1993). Conscientiousness and performance of sales representatives: Test of the mediating effects of goal setting. *Journal of Applied Psychology, 78,* 715–722.

Binswanger, H. (1990). *The biological basis of teleological concepts*. Los Angeles: Ayn Rand Institute Press.

Binswanger, H. (1991). Volition as cognitive self-regulation. *Organizational Behavior and Human Decision Processes, 50,* 154–178.

Blanshard, B. (1962). *Reason and analysis*. La Salle, IL: Open Court.

Crutcher, R. J. (1994). Telling us what we know: The use of verbal report methodologies in psychology research. *Psychological Science, 5,* 241–244.

Deci, E. L., & Ryan, R. M. (1985). *Intrinsic motivation and self-determination in human behavior*. New York: Plenum.

Frayne, C. A., & Latham, G. P. (1987). Application of social learning theory to employee self-management of attendance. *Journal of Applied Psychology, 72,* 387–392.

Gist, M. E., Bavetta, A. G., & Stevens, C. K. (1990). Transfer training method: Its influence on skill generalization, skill repetition, and performance level. *Personnel Psychology, 43,* 501–523.

Gist, M. E., Stevens, C. K., & Bavetta, A. G. (1991). Effects of self-efficacy and post-training intervention on the acquisition and maintenance of complex interpersonal skills. *Personnel Psychology, 44,* 837–861.

Gollwitzer, P. M., Heckhausen, H., & Ratajczak, K. (1990). From weighing to willing: Approaching a change decision through pre- or postdecisional mentation. *Organizational Behavior and Human Decision Processes, 45,* 41–65.

Howard, A., & Bray, D. W. (1988). *Managerial lives in transition.* New York: Guilford Press.

Kirkpatrick, S., & Locke, E. A. (in press). Direct and indirect effects of three core charismatic leadership components on performance and job attitudes. *Journal of Applied Psychology.*

Latham, G. P., Erez, M., & Locke, E. A. (1988). Resolving scientific disputes by the joint design of crucial experiments by the antagonists: Application to the Erez–Latham dispute regarding participation in goal setting. *Journal of Applied Psychology* (Monograph), *73,* 753–772.

Latham, G. P., & Frayne, C. A. (1989). Self-management training for increasing job attendance: A follow-up and replication. *Journal of Applied Psychology 74,* 411–416.

Latham, G. P., Winters, D. C., & Locke, E. A. (1994). Cognitive and motivational effects of participation: A mediator study. *Journal of Organizational Behavior, 15,* 49–63.

Lee, T., Locke, E. A., & Phan, S. H. (1994). Explaining the assigned goal-incentive interaction: The role of self-efficacy and personal goals. Unpublished manuscript, College of Business & Management, University of Washington, Seattle.

Lerner, B., & Locke, E. A. (1995). The effects of goal setting, self-efficacy, competition, and personal traits on the performance of an endurance task. *Journal of Sport & Exercise Psychology, 17,* 138–152,

Locke, E. A. (1966). The relationship of intentions to level of performance. *Journal of Applied Psychology 50,* 60–66.

Locke, E. A. (1968). Toward a theory of task motivation and incentives. *Organizational Behavior and Human Performance, 3,* 157–189.

Locke, E. A. (1976). The nature and causes of job satisfaction. In M. D. Dunnette (Ed.), *Handbook of industrial and organizational psychology.* Chicago: Rand-McNally.

Locke, E. A. (1991a). Goal theory vs. control theory: Contrasting approaches to understanding work motivation. *Motivation & Emotion, 15,* 9–28.

Locke, E. A. (1991b). The motivation sequence, the motivation hub and the motivation core. *Organizational Behavior & Human Decision Processes, 50,* 288–299.

Locke, E. A. (1995). Beyond determinism and materialism, or isn't it time we took consciousness seriously? *Journal of Behavior Therapy & Experimental Psychiatry, 26,* 265–273.

Locke, E. A., & Latham, G. P. (1990). *A theory of goal setting & task performance.* Englewood Cliffs, NJ: Prentice Hall.

Locke, E. A., Smith, K. G., Erez, M. E., Chah, D-Ok, & Shaffer, A. (1994). The effects of intra-individual goal conflict on performance. *Journal of Management, 20,* 67–91.

Locke, E. A., & associates (1991). *The essence of leadership.* New York: Lexington (Macmillan).

McClelland, D. (1961). *The achieving society.* Princeton, NJ: Van Nostrand.

Mento, A. J., Locke, E. A., & Klein, H. J. (1992). Relationship of goal level to valence and instrumentality. *Journal of Applied Psychology, 77,* 395–405.

Peikoff, L. (1992). *Objectivism: The philosophy of Ayn Rand.* New York: Dutton.

Rand, A. (1990). *Introduction to Objectivist epistemology.* New York: NAL Books.

Ryan, T. A. (1970). *Intentional behavior.* New York: Ronald Press.

Scully, J., Kirkpatrick, S., & Locke, E. A. (1995). Knowledge as a determinant of the effects of participation on performance and attitudes. *Organizational Behavior & Human Decision Processes, 61,* 276–288.

Taylor, M. S., Locke, E. A., Lee, C., & Gist, M. E. (1984). Type A behavior and faculty research productivity: What are the mechanisms? *Organizational Behavior & Human Performance, 34,* 402–418.

Social Cognitive Theory and Self-efficacy: Implications for Motivation Theory and Practice

Alexander D. Stajkovic
Fred Luthans

The purpose of this article is to show how social cognitive theory (SCT) and its main construct of self-efficacy can contribute to the better understanding and practice of work motivation. We first summarize and relate the five basic human capabilities identified by Stanford psychologist Albert Bandura that are generally recognized as the core of SCT: (1) symbolizing, (2) forethought, (3) vicarious learning, (4) self-regulation, and (5) self-reflection. The balance of the article is concerned with self-efficacy. Closely related to self-regulation and reflection, self-efficacy is defined as an individual's belief (or confidence) about his or her abilities to mobilize motivation, cognitive resources, and courses of action needed to successfully execute a specific task within a given context (Bandura, 1997; Stajkovic & Luthans, 1998a, 1998b). We suggest that self-efficacy makes an important contribution to work motivation.

THE CURRENT MOTIVATIONAL PARADOX AT WORK

Now in the uncertain economy of the 21st century, more than ever, organizations face the dilemma of becoming more effective by improving performance, but without increasing costs. Since this is the era of artificial intelligence—computer-aided designs, computer-aided manufacturing, and e-business—the typical response in recent years has been downsizing, e-engineering and the extensive use of product, process, and information technology. However, largely overlooked and even degraded by downsizing, e-engineering, and the spur for the use of information technology have been human resources and the role they can play in meeting competitive demands. There is a strange paradox in these recent developments. As Pfeffer (1995) points out, if intelligence is so helpful to organizational success in its artificial form, then why do the potential benefits of real, human intelligence continue to be so neglected.

One possible answer to this paradox is that we have tended to take a negative rather than a proactive positive approach to both the academic and practice sides of managing work performance (Luthans, 2002, in press). We have concentrated too much on what is wrong with employees and managers, their dysfunctions and weaknesses (e.g., how to motivate inept employees, overcome resistance to change, cope with stress) rather than emphasize and build on their strengths. We would argue that self-efficacy (or self-confidence), drawn from social cognitive theory, is the pervading psychological mechanism for positively motivating human resources. As Bandura (1986) suggests, "unless people believe that they can produce desired effects and forestall undesired ones by their actions, they have little incentive to act. Whatever other factors may operate as motivators, they are rooted in the core belief that one has the power to produce the desired results" (p. 228). Thus, we offer social cognitive theory and its main construct of self-efficacy (Bandura, 1986, 1997) as a needed positive approach to motivation theory and practice.

A SOCIAL COGNITIVE THEORY FOUNDATION

Social cognitive theory is based upon but more comprehensive than social learning and/or the behavioral approach to human action. For example, SCT includes motivational and self-regulatory mechanisms, which extend beyond learning and/or modifying behavior through reinforcing consequences. Moreover, in SCT, learning is viewed as knowledge acquisition through cognitive processes of information. In other words, in SCT, the "social" part acknowledges the environmental origins of much of human thought and action, whereas the "cognitive" portion recognizes the influential contribution of cognitive processes to human motivation and action. For example, on the one hand, much of employees' knowledge and behaviors are generated from the organizational environment in which they operate. On the other hand, organizational participants still process and act upon available information differently depending on their unique personal characteristics.

Drawing from a considerable stream of basic research and SCT, Bandura and others have advanced the concept of self-efficacy. This increasingly recognized psychological construct deals specifically with the control of human action through people's beliefs in their capabilities to affect the environment and produce desired outcomes by their actions. For instance, unless employees believe that they can gather up the necessary behavioral, cognitive, and motivational resources to successfully execute the task in question (whether working on a product/service or developing a strategic plan), they will most likely dwell on the formidable aspects of the required performance, exert insufficient effort, and, as a result, not do well or even fail on the task. This personal confidence, or more precisely self-efficacy, plays a pivotal role in SCT. In his recent, comprehensive book on self-efficacy and personal control, Bandura (1997) provides an in-depth conceptual analysis and empirical support of how self-efficacy operates in concert with sociocognitive determinants represented by SCT in determining human motivation, adaptation, and change. We believe that the conceptual richness of SCT and the implications that self-efficacy seems to have for human performance in organizations can make a value-added contribution to work motivation theory and practice.

The Explanatory Power of SCT

The widely recognized cognitively based work motivation theories closely associated with needs, equity, or expectancies concentrate on a process-oriented analysis of the factors influencing the relationship between human action and environmental outcomes. However, they generally do not specify the underlying mechanisms that mediate or can affect the strength of the proposed relationships. SCT, on the other hand, specifies factors by which human action is determined, and defines several basic human capabilities through which the cognitive motivational processes operate to initiate, execute, and maintain work behavior.

In particular, according to SCT, people are neither spontaneous personal self-agents nor, as reinforcement theory would suggest, automatic transmitters of environmental influences. SCT explains behavior in organizations in terms of the reciprocal causation among the person (unique personal characteristics such as ability), the environment (consequences from the organizational environment such as pay for performance), and the behavior itself (previous successful or unsuccessful performances). As shown in Figure 1, because of these combined, reciprocal influences, under SCT organizational participants would at the same

FIGURE 1 Triadic Influence in Social Cognitive Theory

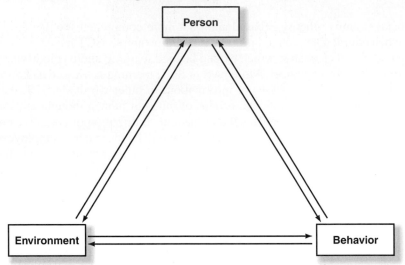

time be both products and producers of their motivation, their respective environments, and their behaviors.

In SCT, the triangular influences among the person, environment, and behavior do not necessarily imply symmetry in the strength of the bidirectional influences. For example, although all three factors may be present at a particular time in a particular organizational environment, that does not mean that they all exert equal and simultaneous influence on the employee. This implies that the strength of mutual influences between any of the two factors is not fixed in reciprocal causation. Thus, it is critically important to recognize that the relative influences exerted by one, two, or three interacting factors on motivated behavior will vary depending on different activities, different individuals, and different circumstances. Bandura (1986) provides the following simple, yet illustrative example:

> If people are dropped into deep water, they will all promptly swim however uniquely varied they might be in their cognitive or behavioral repertoires. . . . On the other hand, if a person plays piano for his/her own enjoyment, such behavior is self-regulated over a long period of time by its sensory effects, and cognitive and environmental influences are involved in this process by a lesser extent. . . . Finally, in deciding what book to check from the library, personal preferences hold the sway. (p. 24)

The Basic Human Capabilities According to SCT

SCT explains the nature of bidirectional reciprocal influences through five basic human capabilities: (1) symbolizing, (2) forethought, (3) vicarious learning, (4) self-regulation, and (5) self-reflection. Employees use these basic capabilities to self-influence themselves in order to initiate, regulate, and sustain their own behavior. Figure 2 provides a descriptive summary. These five capabilities have strong explanatory powers particularly in helping us understand why employees may be motivated differently in the same organizational circumstances.

FIGURE 2 Basic Human Capabilities According to Social Cognitive Theory

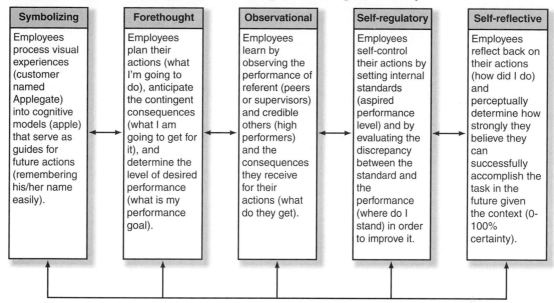

Symbolizing Capability

SCT posits that humans have an extraordinary symbolizing capability that allows them to adapt successfully to their respective environments. By using symbols (e.g., a flag), people process and transform visual experiences into internal cognitive models that in turn serve as guides for future actions (e.g., patriotic behaviors). Through the symbolizing activity, people also ascribe meaning, form, and duration to their past experiences.

Forethought Capability

Bandura argues that people not only react to their environments but also self-regulate their behaviors by forethought. In particular, people plan courses of action for the near future, anticipate the likely consequences of their future actions, and set goals for themselves. Thus, through forethought, employees initiate and guide their actions in an anticipatory fashion. In other words, the future acquires causal properties by being represented cognitively by forethought exercised in the present.

Vicarious Learning Capability

According to SCT, almost all forms of learning can occur vicariously by observing the behavior of others and the subsequent consequences of their behaviors. Employees' capacity to learn by observation enables them to obtain and accumulate rules for initiating and controlling different behavioral patterns without having to acquire them gradually by risky trial and error. The acquisition of knowledge vicariously is critical for both learning and human performance. Since behavioral trials and errors can (and often do) result in costly consequences, chances for effective performance would be seriously diminished if employees were able to learn only from the consequences of their actions. The more complex the action, and the more costly and hazardous (in both the safety and political sense) the possible mistakes, the stronger must be the reliance on vicarious learning from competent models.

Self-regulatory Capability

Human self-regulatory capability plays the central role in SCT, as it does in other prominent theories of self-regulation and motivation (Hollenbeck, 1989; Locke & Latham, 1990). According to the principle of self-regulation, people do not behave to suit the preferences or demands of others. Much of work behavior is initiated and regulated by internal self-set standards and self-evaluative reactions to exerted behaviors. After personal standards have been set, incongruity between a behavior and the standard against which it is measured activates self-evaluative reactions, which, in turn, serve to further influence subsequent action. Even if there is no incongruity between self-standards and present performance, according to SCT, people may set higher standards for themselves and activate future behaviors to satisfy the new standards (Bandura, 1997). For example, the success of empowerment programs depends on such self-regulation capabilities.

Self-reflective Capability

The self-reflective capability in SCT can be defined as human self-reflective consciousness. Self-reflective consciousness enables people to think and analyze their experiences and thought processes. By reflecting on their different personal experiences, managers and employees can generate specific knowledge about their environment and about themselves. Among the types of knowledge that people can derive from self-reflection, according to SCT, *none is more central* to human agency than people's judgment of their capabilities to deal effectively with specific environmental realities. These types of perceptions are referred to as self-efficacy beliefs. We would argue that self-efficacy has formidable predictive powers and thus carries a number of important implications for motivating human performance in today's organizations.

THE SELF-EFFICACY COMPONENT OF SCT

Self-efficacy refers to an individual's belief (confidence) about his or her capabilities to execute a specific task within a given context. As a work motivation process, self-efficacy operates as follows. Before organizational participants select their choices and initiate their effort, they tend to evaluate and integrate information about their perceived capabilities. Self-efficacy determines whether an employee's work behavior will be initiated, how much effort will be expended, and how long that effort will be sustained, especially in light of disconfirming evidence. Critical to work performance is that employees with high self-efficacy will activate sufficient effort that, if well executed, produces successful outcomes. On the other hand, employees with low self-efficacy are likely to cease their efforts prematurely and fail on the task.

Self-efficacy and Work Performance

Self-efficacy has a relatively established body of research showing its positive impact on work-related performance. For example, our 1998 meta-analysis included 114 studies and

21,616 subjects. The results indicated a significant .38 weighted average correlation between self-efficacy and work-related performance. This average correlation explains 14.44% of the variance, but when converted to the commonly used effect size statistic used in meta-analysis, the transformed value represents a 28% average increase in performance due to self-efficacy. Put into Grissom's (1994) index of practical utility, there is 72% probability that employees with high self-efficacy for a specific task will have better performance than those with low self-efficacy. By comparison, these results for self-efficacy represent a greater average gain in performance than the results from meta-analyses of popular work motivation techniques such as goal setting (13.6%, see Wood, Mento, & Locke, 1987), feedback (13.6%, see Kluger & DeNisi, 1996), or our own O.B. Mod. approach (17%, see Stajkovic & Luthans, 1997). Based on meta-analytic research to date, self-efficacy also appears to be a better predictor of work performance than either job satisfaction (e.g., Judge, Thoresen, Bono, & Patton, 2001), or Big Five personality traits (e.g., Barrick & Mount, 1991).

Self-efficacy and Work Motivation

Besides its positive impact on work performance, self-efficacy also makes a contribution to work motivation. SCT acknowledges that employees base their actions on both intrinsic (desires) and extrinsic (contingent consequences from the environment) motivation. However, in addition, SCT posits that employees also act on their self-efficacy beliefs of how well they can perform the behaviors necessary to succeed. Thus, under SCT, employee behavior cannot be fully predicted without considering his/her self-efficacy. For example, employees with low self-efficacy doubt that they can do what is necessary to succeed. By the same token, a sense of high personal efficacy may help sustain motivated efforts, even in light of adverse conditions and uncertain outcomes. At the same time, it is unlikely that employees would act based on high self-efficacy beliefs if they didn't expect certain incentive motivators, such as recognition or extra pay, from those behaviors. In other words, employee self-efficacy can be predictive, but it does not negate the importance of motivation to pursue the initial course of action.

Self-efficacy Dimensions

As shown in Figure 3, three dimensions of self-efficacy seem to have particular importance for human performance in organizations. First is the magnitude of self-efficacy beliefs. This

FIGURE 3 **Dimensions of Self-efficacy**

Magnitude	Strength	Generality
What level of task difficulty and complexity (e.g., low, moderate, high) an employee believes he or she can accomplish. Levels of task difficulty and complexity represent different degrees of challenge for successful task performance.	How certain an employee is about performing at the level of task difficulty and complexity indicated by magnitude of self-efficacy. The higher the strength of self-efficacy, the greater the likelihood of successful performance.	Self-efficacy is generalized across similar activity domains. They can vary on modalities on which ability is expressed (behavioral, cognitive), characteristics of the situations, or people receiving the behaviors.

refers to the level of task difficulty that a person believes he or she is capable of executing. Second is the strength of self-efficacy. This refers to whether the judgment about magnitude is strong (perseverance in coping efforts despite disconfirming experiences), or weak (easily questioned in the face of difficulty). Third, self-efficacy may vary in generality. Some experiences create efficacy beliefs specific to a particular task (e.g., computer programming). Other experiences may influence more generalizable self-efficacy beliefs potentially spanning across domain-related tasks and/or situations (e.g., in-house and external sales; being able to get things organized). Although the generality dimension was introduced by Bandura at the same time as self-efficacy strength and magnitude, to date this self-efficacy dimension has not generated much theory development and/or empirical research.

HOW SELF-EFFICACY IS DISTINCTIVE FROM OTHER ORGANIZATIONAL BEHAVIOR CONCEPTS

At first glance, self-efficacy appears similar to self-esteem, expectancy, and locus of control concepts of personality and motivation. However, to understand conceptual independence and apply self-efficacy effectively, we need to understand the sometimes subtle, but important, differences.

Self-esteem

One of the traditional constructs most commonly equated with self-efficacy is self-esteem. Although conceptually similar, self-esteem and self-efficacy are quite different. The first difference is the domain that self-esteem and self-efficacy cover. Self-esteem is conceptually portrayed as a global construct that represents a person's self-evaluations across a wide variety of different situations. In contrast, self-efficacy is the individual's belief about a task-and-context-specific capability. Second, self-esteem tends to be more stable, almost traitlike, whereas self-efficacy is statelike, a dynamic construct which changes over time as new information and task experiences are obtained. Finally, self-esteem is based on an introspective reflective evaluation of self (e.g., feelings of self-worth) that is usually derived from perceptions about several personal characteristics (intelligence, integrity, etc.). By contrast, some people might have high self-efficacy for some tasks (e.g., technically based problem solving) and, at the same time, very low self-efficacy about other tasks (e.g., writing technical reports). However, neither of these self-efficacy beliefs is necessarily likely to produce any changes in one's overall self-esteem.

Motivational Expectancies

Self-efficacy may also appear similar to both effort-performance expectancy (called E1 in the motivational literature) and the performance-outcome expectancy (E2). Both E1 and self-efficacy concepts would posit that successful performance depends on employee effort. Self-efficacy beliefs are similar to the employee E1 perceptions of the relationship between the degree of effort put forth and the level of performance. However, there are also several differences. First, compared to E1, self-efficacy beliefs are based on a broader domain of perceptions such as personal ability, skills, knowledge, previous task experience, and complexity of the task to be performed, as well as on the states of psychomotor reactions (e.g., positive/

negative emotions, stress, fatigue). Second, self-efficacy includes generative capability (e.g., a salesperson may generalize self-efficacy for selling to a closely related activity such as training new staff in effective sales techniques). Third, self-efficacy distinguishes between several construct and measurement dimensions (e.g., strength, magnitude, generality, composite).

There is also a difference between self-efficacy and E2. Specifically, self-efficacy and E2 (performance-outcome expectancy) refer to different parts and sequencing of the motivational continuum. For example, Bandura distinguished self-efficacy and E2 by arguing that an efficacy pertains to a belief of one's ability to execute a certain behavior pattern (e.g., I believe I can do this task), whereas an outcome expectation (E2) tends to be a judgment of the likely consequences such behavior will produce (e.g., I believe what I do will produce desired outcomes). Thus, the employee's assessment of self-efficacy usually comes first before any behavior-outcome expectations (E2) are made.

Locus of Control

Locus of control, as a widely recognized variable in the theory of personality and motivation, is also similar, but importantly different from self-efficacy. The locus of control framework is traditionally used to explain whether outcomes of an individual's behaviors are controlled internally or externally. According to this conceptual framework, people learn generalized expectancies to view events either as being directly determined by their own behavior (e.g., ability or effort) or as being beyond their control (e.g., luck or task difficulty). In other words, individuals develop expectancies about the locus of control.

People with an internal locus of control believe they are in control of their own fate, feel that their actions have an impact on the environment, and assign personal responsibilities for the consequences of their own behavior. In contrast, individuals with an external locus of control take the consequences of their lives as the result of destiny, luck, chance, or any other random factor. According to externals, little can be done to affect their own surroundings. Bandura has argued that LOC is primarily concerned with causal beliefs about action-outcome contingencies. Self-efficacy, on the other hand, refers to an individual's beliefs about his or her abilities to successfully execute a specific task.

Self-efficacy vs. General Self-efficacy

Self-efficacy viewed as a traitlike, dispositional personal characteristic is labeled general self-efficacy. This generalized conception has recently been used as another form of self-efficacy in empirical research on work motivation (e.g., Eden & Zuk, 1995). At first glance, the two views of efficacy may appear similar and equivalent. However, according to Bandura's theory building and considerable empirical research, self-efficacy and general self-efficacy represent very different constructs, both conceptually and psychometrically (e.g., measurement).

In particular, Bandura portrays self-efficacy as a task- and situation- (domain) specific cognition (specific self-efficacy). In contrast, general self-efficacy is defined as a generalized trait representing one's overall estimate of his/her ability to perform a wide variety of jobs under different conditions. Thus, whereas self-efficacy represents a dynamic motivational belief system that may vary depending on unique properties of each task and work situation, general self-efficacy represents an "enduring" personal trait that (supposedly) generalizes and successfully applies to a wide range of different situations.

Differences in the measurement of the two variables include questionable relevance of general self-efficacy scales to a specific task or job typically explored by specific self-efficacy. For example, whereas measures of self-efficacy relate to specific task demands (see detailed description in the next section and Figure 4), a typical general self-efficacy item is exemplified by a global statement such as "I do not seem capable of dealing with most problems that come up in life." Obviously, these types of general self-efficacy items/measures fall short in terms of specifying what exactly they relate to, which brings up the question of their construct validity. However, research on developing general efficacy scales continues (e.g., Chen, Gully, & Eden, 2001), and in the future may make a relatively stronger contribution to work motivation.

SELF-EFFICACY MEASUREMENT

Like any psychological construct, self-efficacy must be validly and reliably measured to make a meaningful contribution to work motivation theory and research. In this regard, Bandura's conceptualization of the magnitude and strength of perceived self-efficacy provides a psychometrically sound measure. Magnitude of self-efficacy measures the level of task difficulty that a person believes he or she is capable of executing. Strength of self-efficacy indicates whether the individual's belief about magnitude is strong and likely to produce perseverance in coping efforts, or weak and easily questioned in the face of difficulty. As shown in Figure 4, the design of the self-efficacy scale usually consists of two columns. Column A measures the magnitude of self-efficacy; the total number of Yes's, each corresponding to the particular level of task difficulty. Column B measures self-efficacy strength; the total summary of certainty ratings for each magnitude level indicated by a Yes. This definition of self-efficacy

FIGURE 4   **Self-efficacy Scale**

Please use the scale below to indicate:

(a) *Whether you believe that you are capable or not* (yes, no) of performing this task at each of the levels outlined in this scale. Please use column A for these responses.

(b) *How certain you are* (0–100%) about each yes/no response. For example, 0% would indicate no chance, whereas 100% would indicate absolute certainty. Please use column B for these responses.

Number of tasks in a given amount of time For example:	Column A CAN DO (Y = yes) (N = no)	Column B CERTAINTY (0–100%)
I believe I can do 2 . . . in, say, 1 minute		
I believe I can do 4 . . . in 1 minute		
I believe I can do 6 . . . in 1 minute		
I believe I can do 8 . . . in 1 minute		
I believe I can do 10 . . . in 1 minute		
I believe I can do 12 . . . in 1 minute		
I believe I can do 14 . . . in 1 minute		
I believe I can do 16 . . . in 1 minute		
I believe I can do 18 . . . in 1 minute		
I believe I can do 20 . . . in 1 minute		

strength coincides with what is labeled as the Composite 1 measure of self-efficacy (i.e., the strength percentages for each "Yes" are summed to get the self-efficacy score). Empirical research has generally validated this measure of self-efficacy and demonstrated it to be more reliable than other measurement approaches (e.g., Lee & Bobko, 1994).

DETERMINANTS OF SELF-EFFICACY

Besides the theoretical underpinnings and measurement of self-efficacy, Bandura has identified (see Figure 5) the four major categories of experiences and sources of information that determine self-efficacy beliefs. Although all of these determinants may influence efficacy expectations, it is critically important to recognize that the actual impact of any relevant information on self-efficacy beliefs will depend on how it is cognitively processed. Thus, self-efficacy expectations are, in fact, formed on the basis of subjective perceptions of personal and situational factors, rather than on the direct impact of "objective" reality.

Enactive Mastery Experience

Research has indicated that succeeding on a challenging task (e.g., successful enactive mastery experience) provides the strongest information for the development of self-efficacy beliefs. This is because enactive mastery is the only antecedent of self-efficacy that provides direct performance information for the formation of stable and accurate efficacy beliefs. This does not mean, however, that changes in self-efficacy will occur as a direct result of performance accomplishment. Rather, self-efficacy formation will depend on *how employees psychologically process* the information that the previous performance generated. In other words, it is not performance per se that causes changes in self-efficacy but rather what the individual personally makes of diagnostic information resulting from that performance (including weighing of both ability and nonability factors relative to performance success). As a result, the same performance attainment can produce varying changes in the level of subsequent self-efficacy.

FIGURE 5   **Determinants of Self-efficacy**

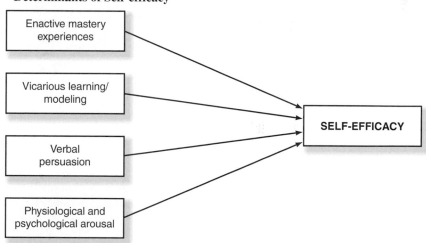

For example, even a small performance improvement in a difficult organizational context (high task complexity, limited resources, short time span, etc.) can produce a large increase in an employee's self-efficacy if the individual evaluates personal and situational factors in a way that confirms the belief: "I have what it takes to succeed on this task." In contrast, consider an employee working in a nondemanding environment characterized by, say, low task complexity, low skill utilization requirements, and low memory-processing demands. In this case, the individual may weigh even a substantial increase in performance as "what was expected" and the level of self-efficacy may be unaffected. Moreover, if employees find out that their improved performance was below average standards for that particular task, the experience may even lower their self-efficacy. Clearly, the level of performance does not equate with the level of self-efficacy, since estimation of personal efficacy is a cognitive process that involves more factors than just executed action. These other factors fall into two categories, the first related to the situation, and the second to perceptions of one's ability.

Situational Factors

A number of environmental factors can produce disparities in the assessment of personal efficacy due to different demands they may impose. They are: (a) the amount of available resources (e.g., time, staff) necessary to complete the task successfully, (b) interdependence of the particular task with other functions in the organization, (c) physical distractions (e.g., noise, interruptions), (d) the amount of physiological and/or psychological danger present in the environment, (e) amount of help received, and (f) type of supervision. All of these factors may negatively influence estimates of self-efficacy by increasing personal anxiety, thoughts of failure, and amount of stress, and by reducing the coping mechanism.

Conception of Ability

In addition to considering situational variables, the extent to which employees will change their self-efficacy as a result of previous performance is also determined by their conceptions of their ability. Ability could be perceived as a given entity (e.g., a talent) or as an acquirable skill. Each of these conceptions of ability can influence the way performance information is processed. For example, studies (e.g., Wood & Bandura, 1989) have shown that if employees conceive of ability as an incremental skill, they tend to be more task diagnostic, less prone to negative impact of failures (e.g., stress, anxiety), and ultimately maintain higher self-efficacy. However, if an employee perceives ability as a given entity, he/she is likely to perceive performance mistakes as indicative of intellectual (in)capacity, which may imply lack of personal control. The perceived lack of control leads to anxiety, which, in turn, diminishes learning. The final result is a lowering of an employee's estimate of self-efficacy, a tendency to set lower goals, development of ineffective task strategies, and ultimately lower performance. Accordingly, managers should consider helping their employees to establish a conception of ability as an incremental skill.

Vicarious Learning and/or Modeling

Since much of employees' knowledge about their capabilities is generated from the social environment in which they work, to rely solely on enactive experiences would limit the sources of accurate efficacy appraisals. Given the amount of diagnostic information available in an organizational context, self-efficacy assessments are also influenced by vicarious learning, or more commonly called modeling, which occurs by observing competent and relevant others perform a similar task and be reinforced for it. The greater the perceived similarity between the model and the observer in terms of personal characteristics relevant to the task performance, the greater the model's influence on the observer's learning and subsequent self-efficacy. Employees may turn to competent colleagues or mentors for knowledge of the task, needed skills, or effective strategies for successful task performance. Learning from modeled accomplishments is especially important when employees have little prior enactive experiences (e.g., undertaking a novel task) on which to base their assessments of self-efficacy.

Modeling can also be practically used as a training approach to enhance employees' self-efficacy. In this mode of influence, managers can develop effective strategies for coping with cognitive and behavioral intricacies of a particular job, then convey these strategies to employees and, ultimately, use them in an efficacy-enhancing training program (see also Bandura, 2000). This modeling program for developing employee self-efficacy would include clear specification of the following components:

1. The task product (what is expected as a result of this task).

2. Number and nature of behavioral acts (what activities are involved, and how many activities are needed).

3. Sources of information cues (where necessary information for the performance of the task could be found, e.g., price list for selling products).

4. Optimal sequencing requirements among behavioral activities (in what sequence the acts need to be performed for optimal performance, e.g., greeting the customer first and then asking what they need).

5. Nature and frequency of temporal changes in the sequencing requirements among behavioral activities (determining whether sequencing among behavioral acts changes, and if it does, how it changes for different circumstances, e.g., changes in performance acts of an air-traffic controller for different weather conditions).

6. Necessary performance means (e.g., what technology is needed for successful performance).

7. Applicable utility of the available performance means (determining whether available means are appropriate for successful performance).

8. Developing and evaluating alternative courses of action and information processing.

Each of these steps is first explained and enacted by the model (trainer, coach, colleague, or mentor), whose performance is then replicated by the trainees in a gradual fashion step by step. The model follows the performance of the trainees and provides positive feedback. Mastering a modeled performance in terms of skills and task strategies enhances employees' beliefs about their capabilities to successfully execute the job in the future. In essence, the training provides an enacted mastery experience, which positively influences subsequent self-efficacy.

Verbal Persuasion

Verbal persuasion by someone the employee trusts and views as competent (as it relates to the job to be performed) serves as another means of strengthening self-efficacy. The purpose of self-efficacy enhancement by verbal persuasion does not necessarily involve increasing the level of skill and ability, but rather focusing on the cognitive appraisal of an individual's self-efficacy in terms of enhancing the beliefs as to what employees can do with what they already have. However, for this mode of increasing self-efficacy to work, employees should already have some reason to believe that they have (or can develop) the ability to accomplish the task. Expressing a faith in one's ability is particularly relevant in times when employees have performance difficulties and may question their personal efficaciousness.

Physiological and Psychological Arousal

The fourth major source of self-efficacy is the state of physiological and/or psychological/ emotional arousal. This source of efficacy information is important because people tend to perceive physiological and/or psychological/ emotional activations as signs of vulnerability and dysfunction. Since, for example, high levels of stress at work are likely to impair performance, employees may be more inclined to feel efficacious for the successful performance when not preoccupied by fatigue and/or emotional agitation. However, employees differ in their proneness to get inhibited by physical or emotional distractions. For example, the more employees are involved in a certain activity, the less they focus on and notice aversive stressful distractions. In contrast, self-directed rather than task-directed attention brings to the fore physical and/or psychological agitation. Finally, employees with already high efficacy beliefs may view psychological arousal as an energizing factor whereas low-efficacy people tend to view it as a performance debilitator. Moreover, while being physically fit and healthy may not contribute much to one's self-efficacy, being exhausted or ill can be devastating to self-efficacy.

FROM SELF-EFFICACY TO COLLECTIVE EFFICACY

To reflect the increasing importance of work teams in today's organizations, attention has recently been given to determining how to effectively motivate employees working in groups. As a part of this trend, Bandura has extended social cognitive theory from the focus on individual level of analysis and self-efficacy to the group level of analysis and corresponding construct of collective efficacy. Collective efficacy is defined as a group's shared belief in its joint capabilities to perform courses of action required to successfully achieve a certain level of performance (Bandura, 1997; Stajkovic & Lee, 2001).

Conceptual Nature of Collective Efficacy

According to SCT, collective efficacy has the same antecedents as self-efficacy, operates through similar processes, and has basically the same correlates and consequences. In fact, collective efficacy is rooted in self-efficacy since, as Bandura (1982) puts it, "inveterate self-doubters are not easily forged into a collectively efficacious force" (p. 143). This is because efficacy beliefs of individuals are not detached from the group in which they function, nor is the group's efficacy independent of the efficacy of the individuals comprising the group. In other words, it is as hard to individually estimate collective efficacy without considering relevant group processes (e.g., how well do we get along) as it is to provide an assessment of collective efficacy without considering how well each member can execute his/her roles.

SCT proposes collective efficacy as a critical factor in determining group motivation and performance. This is because, on the one hand, group successful performance is largely the product of the cooperative and coordinative dynamics of group members, as well as of their shared knowledge, skills, and abilities. On the other hand, according to SCT, collective efficacy determines what groups choose to do, how much effort they put into it, and how long they sustain their effort in the face of adverse circumstances. Thus, regardless of how skilled group members may be as individuals, if they do not believe that they can work well together as a unit, they are likely to expend insufficient effort, give up easily in the face of obstacles, and ultimately, perform poorly in a collective endeavor.

Motivational Power of Collective Efficacy

Research over the years has sent mixed signals regarding the effectiveness of groups and teams. While group-level research has largely supported the positive relationship between groups and employee affect, only mixed results have been found for the impact of groups on work performance. In contrast, research on collective efficacy has importantly shown its strong relationship to work performance. In particular, a just completed meta-analysis (2,687 groups) by Stajkovic and Lee (2001) found an average correlation of .45 between collective efficacy and group performance. This average correlations accounts for 20% of the variance, but when transformed to the effect size statistic, it represents a 34% improvement in performance. Using the same probability of success as we showed for self-efficacy, this practically suggests there is a 76% probability that a high collective efficacy group will outperform a low collective efficacy group. These findings, in addition to previous empirical evidence (e.g., Gibson, 1999), suggest that collective efficacy may indeed be a critically important motivational construct in predicting group performance.

CONCLUSION

We have offered social cognitive theory and primarily self-efficacy, but also collective efficacy, as a value-added contribution to understanding work motivation and its effective application. Specifically, SCT and both self-efficacy and collective efficacy were shown to have both explanatory and predictive powers and to be quite different from related psychological constructs such as self-esteem, expectancies (both E1 and E2), and locus of control. Most importantly, not only can SCT provide comprehensive understanding of work motivation, but self-efficacy and collective efficacy, with their clearly demonstrated strong relationships (at different levels of analysis) with work-related task performance, seem to have considerable implications for improving human performance in organizations.

In particular, the average correlations between self-efficacy and performance of .38 and the relationship of .45 between collective efficacy and performance are based on considerable evidence. In particular, over two decades, 32,236 (21,616 + 10,620) participants, 2,687 groups, and two meta-analyses, we have cumulative evidence indicating that efficacy beliefs are an effective predictor of performance at both the individual and group levels. These findings for both self and collective efficacy—what could be called "the efficacy force"—add empirical support for the important implications that social cognitive theory and efficacy have for the theory and practice of work motivation.

References

Bandura, A. (1986). *Social foundations of thought and action: A social cognitive theory.* Englewood Cliffs, NJ: Prentice Hall.

Bandura, A. (1997). *Self-efficacy: The exercise of control.* New York: Freeman & Company.

Bandura, A. (2000). Cultivate self-efficacy for personal and organizational effectiveness. In Locke, E. A. (Ed.), *The Blackwell handbook of principles of organizational behavior,* pp. 120–136. Oxford, U.K.: Blackwell.

Barrick, M. R., & Mount, M. K. (1991). The big five personality dimensions and job performance: A meta-analysis. *Personnel Psychology, 44,* 1–26.

Chen, G., Gully, S. M., & Eden, D. (2001). Validation of a New General Self-efficacy Scale. *Organizational Research Methodology, 4,* 62–83.

Eden, D., & Zuk, Y. (1995). Seasickness as a self-fulfilling prophecy: Raising self-efficacy to boost performance at sea. *Journal of Applied Psychology, 80,* 628–635.

Gibson, C. B. (1999). Do they do what they believe they can? Group efficacy and group effectiveness across tasks and cultures. *Academy of Management Journal, 42,* 138–152.

Grissom, R. J. (1994). Probability of the superior outcome of one treatment over another. *Journal of Applied Psychology, 79,* 314–316.

Judge, T. A., Thoresen, C. J., Bono, J. E., & Patton, G. K. (2001). The job satisfaction–job performance relationship: A qualitative and quantitative review. *Psychological Bulletin, 127,* 376–407.

Kluger, A. N., & DeNisi, A. (1996). The effects of feedback interventions on performance: A historical review, a meta-analysis, and a preliminary feedback intervention theory. *Psychological Bulletin, 119,* 254–284.

Lee, C., & Bobko, F. (1994). Self-efficacy beliefs: Comparison of five measures. *Journal of Applied Psychology, 79,* 364–369.

Luthans, F. (2002, in press). Positive organizational behavior (POB), *Academy of Management Executive.*

Pfeffer, J. (1995). *Competitive advantage through people: Unleashing the power of the workforce.* Boston: Harvard Business School Press.

Stajkovic, A. D., & Luthans, F. (1998a). Self-efficacy and work-related performance: A meta-analysis. *Psychological Bulletin, 124,* 240–261.

Stajkovic, A. D., & Luthans, F. (1998b). Social cognitive theory and self-efficacy: Going beyond traditional motivational and behavioral approaches. *Organizational Dynamics, 26*(4), 62–74.

Wood, R. E., Mento, A. J., & Locke, E. A. (1987). Task complexity as a moderator of goal effects: A meta-analysis. *Journal of Applied Psychology, 72,* 416–425.

Wood, R. E., & Bandura, A. (1989). Impact of conceptions of ability on self-regulatory mechanisms and complex decision making. *Journal of Personality and Social Psychology, 56,* 407–415.

Chapter **Three**

The Role of Cognitions, Beliefs and Attitudes in Motivation

People's thoughts—their cognitions—influence their motivation. Such cognitions include beliefs, in other words a person's understandings about the nature or characteristics of objects in the environment. They also include attitudes, a person's favorable or unfavorable reactions to, or feelings about, those objects. Common sense and considerable research evidence attest to the fact that the mental element plays a very large role in the process we call motivation. The three readings in this chapter will illustrate different aspects of that role in determining the motivation of individuals working in organizations.

For many years, one of the most controversial issues in the field of motivation has been the relationship between job attitudes and employee performance. The origins of the controversy stem from disagreements not only about the causal relationships between the two sets of variables but also about their meanings and measurements. For example: How should we measure an attitude? What constitutes good job performance? Should we measure job performance at the individual or at the group level? Should we focus on short-term or long-term results? And, especially, do positive attitudes lead to good performance or does good performance lead to positive attitudes, or is the process reciprocal? Alternatively, are there intervening variables that moderate or in some way affect the relationship between the two? The resolution of this controversy can have a major impact both on theory development and on managerial practice.

Traditionally, job attitudes have been viewed as following from beliefs about the job and then leading to job behaviors through intentions (see Exhibit 3.1). For example, particular beliefs about the job (e.g., this is a dull, dirty job) lead to negative job attitudes (e.g., job dissatisfaction), which in turn can lead to behavioral intentions (e.g., intent to leave). These behavioral intentions are then often translated into actual behavior (e.g., leaving the organization), assuming the person is able to carry out the intention. Or, the person who is dissatisfied may decide to put forth less effort on the job as a way of expressing his or her

EXHIBIT 3.1   **Beliefs, Attitudes, Intentions, and Behavior**

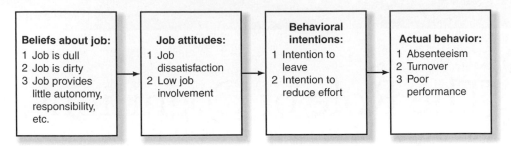

Source: Fishbein, 1967

frustrations with the job. In both cases, the traditional model suggests that behaviors (including job performance) are largely influenced by attitudes.

The problem with this traditional model is that real-life experiences tell us that this relationship often is more complicated than the one we just described. For example, negative job attitudes do not always lead to poor performance, high levels of turnover, or frequent absenteeism. Clearly, there must be other factors that influence the relationship between attitudes and behavior. For instance, an unhappy employee may wish to leave his or her job but have no alternative employment readily available and thus continues to remain on the job for the time being. Moreover, some unhappy employees may be driven by a strong work ethic to continue to produce on the job, regardless of their degree of frustration and dissatisfaction. To put this another way, there can be considerable slippage between job beliefs and attitudes, on the one hand, and behavior on the other. Beliefs and attitudes can be strongly influential, but they are not always 100% determinative of what people actually do.

OVERVIEW OF THE READINGS

The first reading in this section, by Staw, analyzes the "happy worker is a productive worker" hypothesis. First, he argues that attitudes such as job satisfaction may be as much "dispositional," that is, a function of a person's relatively stable characteristics, as they are "situational," or a function of reaction to specific circumstances. Thus, he contends that such attitudes as job satisfaction may not be easy to change. Likewise, he emphasizes that workers' job performance also is not always easy to modify, since it is often strongly affected by many other factors, including technological and operational processes, in addition to workers' attitudes. Thus, in his view, it is a potentially difficult task for organizations to bring about a happy-productive worker combination. However, he offers some basis for optimism that this can happen if one or more "motivational systems" are considered and implemented effectively. The three approaches involve individually-oriented, group-oriented and organizationally oriented sets of action steps. He concludes that, using one or more of these approaches, "it is at least possible to create changes that can overwhelm the forces for stability in both job attitudes and performance."

The second reading, by Rousseau and Tijoriwala, describes an interesting field study of employees' cognitive interpretations—that is, their "motivated reasoning"—of a major organizational change program and the associated explanations of management regarding the need for the change. Specifically, the researchers were interested in examining two types of beliefs of the employees who were subjected to the change program: the reasons they attributed (to management) for why the change was made, and the acceptability of those reasons from their point of view. The results indicated that in this case, the organization's stated purposes for the change did have an impact on how workers interpreted the changes, but those effects were not always as managers intended. Such variables as trust in management also impacted the employees' search for an understanding of the aims to be achieved by the changes. The issues discussed in this article have a number of implications for how the interpretation of the reasons for major organizational changes can affect the subsequent work motivation of those who must adapt to the changes.

The last reading in this chapter provides an overview of recent thinking and research by psychologists regarding what has come to be called "positive psychology" and how that general approach can be applied to behavior in the work situation (i.e., "positive organizational behavior"). Essentially, this article reviews how five "human resource strengths and psychological capacities" of individuals can be measured, further developed, and used effectively to motivate improvement in their performance in work contexts. These five potential strengths are confidence or self-efficacy, hope, optimism, happiness or subjective well-being, and emotional intelligence. They all involve a strong cognitive component and, as the author, Luthans, points out, have both dispositional (traitlike) and situational (statelike) characteristics. The challenge for organizations and managers, as emphasized in Staw's opening article, will be to implement programs and actions that will in fact result in increased positive capacities of the type discussed in this article. If that can be achieved, it would open up major opportunities for motivating superior work performance. However, it won't be easy!

Reference

Fishbein, M. (Ed.). (1967) *Readings in attitude theory and measurement.* New York: Wiley.

Organizational Psychology and the Pursuit of the Happy/Productive Worker

Barry M. Staw

What I am going to talk about in this article is an old and overworked topic, but one that remains very much a source of confusion and controversy. It is also a topic that continues to attract the attention of managers and academic researchers alike, frequently being the focus of both popular books and scholarly articles. This issue is how to manage an organization so that employees can be both happy and productive—a situation where workers and managers are both satisfied with the outcomes.

The pursuit of the happy/productive worker could be viewed as an impossible dream from the Marxist perspective of inevitable worker-management conflict. Such a goal could also be seen as too simple or naive from the traditional industrial relations view of outcomes being a product of necessary bargaining and compromise. Yet, from the psychological perspective, the pursuit of the happy/productive worker has seemed a worthwhile though difficult endeavor, one that might be achieved if we greatly increase our knowledge of work attitudes and behavior. In this article, I will examine this psychological perspective and try to provide a realistic appraisal of where we now stand in the search for satisfaction and productivity in work settings.

APPROACHES TO THE HAPPY/PRODUCTIVE WORKER

One of the earliest pursuits of the happy/productive worker involved the search for a relationship between satisfaction and productivity. The idea was that the world might be neatly divided into situations where workers are either happy and productive or unhappy and unproductive. If this were true, then it would be a simple matter to specify the differences between management styles present in the two sets of organizations and to come up with a list of prescriptions for improvement. Unfortunately, research has never supported such a clear relationship between individual satisfaction and productivity. For over thirty years, starting with Brayfield and Crockett's classic review of the job satisfaction-job performance literature,[1] and again with Vroom's discussion of satisfaction-job performance research,[2] organizational psychologists have had to contend with the fact that happiness and productivity may not necessarily go together. As a result, most organizational psychologists have come to accept the argument that satisfaction and performance may relate to two entirely different individual decisions—decisions to participate and to produce.[3]

Though psychologists have acknowledged the fact that satisfaction and performance are not tightly linked, this has not stopped them from pursuing the happy/productive worker. In fact, over the last thirty years, an enormous variety of theories have attempted to show how managers can reach the promised land of high satisfaction and productivity. The theories shown in Table 1 constitute only an abbreviated list of recent attempts to reach this positive state.

TABLE 1   **Paths to the Happy/Productive Worker**

Worker Participation	The Pursuit of Excellence
Supportive Leadership	Socio-Technical Systems
9–9 Systems	Organizational Commitment
Job Enrichment	High Performing Systems
Behavior Modification	Theory Z
Goal Setting	Strong Culture

None of the theories in Table 1 has inherited the happy/productive worker hypothesis in the simple sense of believing that job satisfaction and performance generally co-vary in the world *as it now exists.* But these models all make either indirect or direct assumptions that *it is possible* to achieve a world where both satisfaction and performance will be present. Some of the theories focus on ways to increase job satisfaction, with the implicit assumption that performance will necessarily follow; some strive to directly increase performance, with the assumption that satisfaction will result; and some note that satisfaction and performance will be a joint product of implementing certain changes in the organization.

Without going into the specifics of each of these routes to the happy/productive worker, I think it is fair to say that most of the theories in Table 1 have been oversold. Historically, they each burst on the scene with glowing and almost messianic predictions, with proponents tending to simplify the process of change, making it seem like a few easy tricks will guarantee benefits to workers and management alike. The problem, of course, is that as results have come in from both academic research and from wider practical application, the benefits no longer have appeared so strong nor widespread. Typically, the broader the application and the more well-documented the study (with experimental controls and measures of expected costs and benefits), the weaker have been the empirical results. Thus, in the end, both managers and researchers have often been left disillusioned, skeptical that any part of these theories are worth a damn and that behavioral science will ever make a contribution to management.

My goal with this article is to *lower our expectations*—to show why it is so difficult to make changes in both satisfaction and performance. My intention is not to paint such a pessimistic picture as to justify not making any changes at all, but to inoculate us against the frustrations of slow progress. My hope is to move us toward a reasoned but sustainable pursuit of the happy/productive worker—away from the alternating practice of fanfare and despair.

CHANGING JOB ATTITUDES

Although organizational psychologists have accepted the notion that job satisfaction and performance do not necessarily co-vary, they have still considered job attitudes as something quite permeable or subject to change. This "blank state" approach to job attitudes comes from prevailing psychological views of the individual, where the person is seen as a creature who constantly appraises the work situation, evaluates the merits of the context, and formulates an attitude based on these conditions. As the work situation changes, individuals are thought to be sensitive to the shifts, adjusting their attitudes in a positive or negative direction. With such an approach to attitudes, it is easy to see why job satisfaction has been a common target of organizational change, and why attempts to redesign work have evolved as a principal mechanism for improving job satisfaction.

Currently, the major debate in the job design area concerns whether individuals are more sensitive to objective job conditions or social cues. In one camp are proponents of job re-design who propose that individuals are highly receptive to concrete efforts to improve working conditions. Hackman and Oldham, for example, argue that satisfaction can be in-creased by improving a job in terms of its variety (doing a wider number of things), identity (seeing how one's various tasks make a meaningful whole), responsibility (being in charge of one's own work and its quality), feedback (knowing when one has done a good job), and significance (the meaning or relative importance of one's contribution to the organization or society in general).[4] In the opposing camp are advocates of social information processing. These researchers argue that jobs are often ambiguous entities subject to multiple interpre-tations and perceptions.[5] Advocates of social information processing have noted that the pos-itive or negative labeling of a task can greatly determine one's attitude toward the job, and that important determinants of this labeling are the opinions of co-workers who voice posi-tive or negative views of the work. These researchers have shown that it may be as easy to persuade workers that their jobs are interesting by influencing the *perception* of a job as it is to make objective changes in the work role.

The debate between job design and social information processing has produced two re-cent shifts in the way we think about job attitudes. First, organizational psychology now places greater emphasis on the role of cognition and subjective evaluation in the way people respond to jobs. This is probably helpful, because even though we have generally measured job conditions with perceptual scales, we have tended to confuse these perceptions with ob-jective job conditions. We need to be reminded that perceptions of job characteristics do not necessarily reflect reality, yet they can determine how we respond to that reality.

The second shift in thinking about job attitudes is a movement toward situationalism, stressing how even slight alterations in job context can influence one's perception of a job. It is now believed that people's job attitudes may be influenced not only by the objective properties of the work, but also by subtle cues given off by co-workers or supervisors that the job is dull or interesting. I think this new view is a mistake since it overstates the role of external influence in the determination of job attitudes. The reality may be that individuals are quite resistant to change efforts, with their attitudes coming more as a function of per-sonal disposition than situational influence.

THE CONSISTENCY OF JOB ATTITUDES

Robert Kahn recently observed that, although our standard of living and working conditions have improved dramatically since World War II, reports of satisfaction on national surveys have not changed dramatically.[6] This implies that job satisfaction might be something of a "sticky variable," one that is not so easily changed by outside influence. Some research on the consistency of job attitudes leads to the same conclusion. Schneider and Dachler, for example, found very strong consistency in satisfaction scores over a 16-month longitudinal study (averaging .56 for managers and .58 for non-managers).[7] Pulakos and Schmitt also found that high school students' pre-employment expectations of satisfaction correlated sig-nificantly with ratings of their jobs several years later.[8] These findings, along with the fact that job satisfaction is generally intertwined with both life satisfaction and mental health, imply that there is some ongoing consistency in job attitudes, and that job satisfaction may be determined as much by dispositional properties of the individual as any changes in the situation.

A Berkeley colleague, Joseph Garbarino, has long captured this notion of a dispositional source of job attitudes with a humorous remark, "I always told my children at a young age that their most important decision in life would be whether they wanted to be happy or not; everything else is malleable enough to fit the answer to this question." What Garbarino implies is that job attitudes are fairly constant, and when reality changes for either the better or worse, we can easily distort that reality to fit our underlying disposition. Thus, individuals may think a great deal about the nature of their jobs, but satisfaction can result as much from the unique way a person views the world around him as from any social influence or objective job characteristics. That is, individuals predisposed to be happy may interpret their jobs in a much different way than those with more negative predispositions.

The Attitudinal Consistency Study

Recently, I have been involved with two studies attempting to test for dispositional sources of job attitudes. In the first study, Jerry Ross and I reanalyzed data from the National Longitudinal Survey, a study conducted by labor economists at Ohio State.[9] We used this survey to look at the stability of job attitudes over time and job situations. The survey's measures of attitudes were not very extensive but did provide one of the few available sources of data on objective job changes.

The National Longitudinal Survey data revealed an interesting pattern of results. We found that job satisfaction was fairly consistent over time, with significant relationships among job attitudes over three- and five-year time intervals. We also found that job satisfaction showed consistency *even when people changed jobs.* This later finding is especially important, since it directly contradicts the prevailing assumptions of job attitude research.

Most job design experiments and organizational interventions that strive to improve job attitudes change a small aspect of work, but look for major changes in job satisfaction. However, the National Longitudinal Survey data showed that when people changed their place of work (which would naturally include one's supervisor, working conditions, and procedures), there was still significant consistency in attitudes. One could, of course, argue that people leave one terrible job for another, and this is why such consistency in job attitudes arises. Therefore, we checked for consistency across occupational changes. The National Longitudinal Survey showed consistency not only across occupational changes, but also when people changed *both* their employers and their occupations. This evidence of consistency tells us that people may not be as malleable as we would like to think they are, and that there may be some underlying tendency toward equilibrium in job attitudes. If you are dissatisfied in one job context, you are also likely to be dissatisfied in another (perhaps better) environment.

The Dispositional Study

The consistency data from the National Longitudinal Survey, while interesting, do not tell us what it is that may underlie a tendency to be satisfied or dissatisfied on the job. Therefore, Nancy Bell (a doctoral student at the Berkeley Business School), John Clausen (a developmental sociologist at Berkeley), and I undertook a study to find some of the dispositional sources of job satisfaction.[10] We sought to relate early personality characteristics to job attitudes later in life, using a very unusual longitudinal data source.

There are three longitudinal personality projects that have been running for over fifty years at Berkeley (the Berkeley Growth Study, the Oakland Growth Study, and the Guidance Study), and they have since been combined into what is now called the Intergenerational Study. Usually when psychologists speak of longitudinal studies, they mean data collected from one- or two-year intervals. These data span over 50 years. Usually, when psychologists refer to personality ratings, they mean self-reports derived from the administration of various questionnaires. Much of the Intergenerational Study data are clinical ratings derived from questionnaires, observation, and interview materials evaluated by a different set of raters for each period of the individual's life. Thus, these data are of unusual quality for psychological research.

Basically what we did with data from the Intergenerational Study was to construct an affective disposition scale that measured a very general positive-negative orientation of people. We then related this scale to measures of job attitudes at different periods in people's lives. The ratings used for our affective disposition scale included items such as "cheerful," "satisfied with self," and "irritable" (reverse coded), and we correlated this scale with measures of job and career satisfaction. The results were very provocative. We found that affective dispositions, from as early as the junior-high-school years, significantly predicted job attitudes during middle and late adulthood (ages 40–60). The magnitude of correlations was not enormous (in the .3 to .4 range). But these results are about as strong as we usually see between two attitudes measured on the same questionnaire by the same person at the same time—yet, these data cut across different raters and over fifty years in time.

What are we to conclude from this personality research as well as our reanalyses of the National Longitudinal Survey? I think we can safely conclude that there is a fair amount of consistency in job attitudes and that there may be dispositional as well as situational sources of job satisfaction. Thus, it is possible that social information processing theorists have been on the right track in viewing jobs as ambiguous entities that necessitate interpretation by individuals. But it is also likely that the interpretation of jobs (whether they are perceived as positive or negative) can come as much from internal, dispositional causes (e.g., happiness or depression) as external sources. Consequently, efforts to improve job satisfaction via changes in job conditions will need to contend with stable personal dispositions toward work—forces that may favor consistency of equilibrium in the way people view the world around them.

THE INTRANSIGENCE OF JOB PERFORMANCE

Although we have not conducted research on the consistency of performance or its resistance to change, I think there are some parallels between the problems of changing attitudes and performance. Just as job attitudes may be constrained by individual dispositions, there are many elements of both the individual and work situation that can make improvements in job performance difficult.[11]

Most of the prevailing theories of work performance are concerned with individual motivation. They prescribe various techniques intended to stimulate, reinforce, or lure people into working harder. Most of these theories have little to say about the individual's limits of task ability, predisposition for working hard, or the general energy or activity level of the person. Somewhat naively, our theories have maintained that performance is under the complete control of the individual. Even though there are major individual differences affecting the quantity or quality of work produced, we have assumed that *if the employee really wants to perform better, his or her performance will naturally go up.*

There already exist some rather strong data that refute these implicit assumptions about performance. A number of studies[12] have shown that mental and physical abilities can be reliable predictors of job performance, and it is likely that other dispositions (e.g., personality characteristics) will eventually be found to be associated with effective performance of certain work roles. Thus, influencing work effort may not be enough to cause wide swings in performance, unless job performance is somewhat independent of ability (e.g., in a low skill job). Many work roles may be so dependent on ability (such as those of a professional athlete, musician, inventor) that increases in effort may simply not cause large changes in the end product.

In addition to ability, there may also be other individual factors that contribute to the consistency of performance. People who work hard in one situation are likely to be the ones who exert high effort in a second situation. If, for example, the person's energy level (including need for sleep) is relatively constant over time, we should not expect wide changes in available effort. And, if personality dimensions such as dependability and self-confidence can predict one's achievement level over the lifecourse,[13] then a similar set of personal attributes may well constitute limitations to possible improvements in performance. Already, assessment centers have capitalized on this notion by using personality measures to predict performance in many corporate settings.

Performance may not be restricted just because of the individual's level of ability and effort, however. Jobs may *themselves* be designed so that performance is not under the control of the individual, regardless of ability or effort. Certainly we are aware of the fact that an assembly line worker's output is more a product of the speed of the line than any personal preference. In administrative jobs too, what one does may be constrained by the work cycle or technical procedures. There may be many people with interlocking tasks so that an increase in the performance of one employee doesn't mean much if several tasks must be completed sequentially or simultaneously in order to improve productivity. Problems also arise in situations where doing one's job better may not be predicated upon a burst of energy or desire, but upon increases in materials, financial support, power, and resources. As noted by Kanter, the administrator must often negotiate, hoard, and form coalitions to get anything done on the job, since there are lots of actors vying for the attention and resources of the organization.[14] Thus, the nature of the organization, combined with the abilities and efforts of individuals to maneuver the organization, may serve to constrain changes in individual performance.

ASSESSING THE DAMAGE

So far I have taken a somewhat dark or pessimistic view of the search for the happy/productive worker. I have noted that in terms of satisfaction and performance, it may not be easy to create perfect systems because both happiness and performance are constrained variables, affected by forces not easily altered by our most popular interventions and prescriptions for change. Should organizational psychologists therefore close up shop and go home? Should we move to a more descriptive study of behavior as opposed to searching for improvements in work attitudes and performance?

I think such conclusions are overly pessimistic. We need to interpret the stickiness of job attitudes and performance not as an invitation to complacency or defeat, but as a realistic assessment that it will take very strong treatments to move these entrenched variables. Guzzo, Jackson, and Katzell have recently made a similar point after a statistical examination (called meta-analysis) of organizational interventions designed to improve productivity.[15] They noted that the most effective changes are often *multiple treatments*, where several things are changed at once in a given organization. Thus, instead of idealistic and optimistic promises, we may literally need to throw the kitchen sink at the problem.

The problem of course is that we have more than one kitchen sink! As noted earlier, nearly every theory of organizational behavior has been devoted to predicting and potentially improving job attitudes and performance. And, simply aggregating these treatments is not likely to have the desired result, since many of these recommendations consist of conflicting prescriptions for change. Therefore, it would be wiser to look for compatible *systems* of variables that can possibly be manipulated in concert. Let us briefly consider three systems commonly used in organizational change efforts and then draw some conclusions about their alternative uses.

THREE SYSTEMS OF ORGANIZATIONAL CHANGE

The Individually Oriented System

The first alternative is to build a strong individually-oriented system, based on the kind of traditional good management that organizational psychologists have been advocating for years. This system would emphasize a number of venerable features of Western business organizations such as:

- Tying extrinsic rewards (such as pay) to performance.

- Setting realistic and challenging goals.

- Evaluating employee performance accurately and providing feedback on performance.

- Promoting on the basis of skill and performance rather than personal characteristics, power, or connections.

- Building the skill level of the workforce through training and development.

- Enlarging and enriching jobs through increases in responsibility, variety, and significance.

All of the above techniques associated with the individually-oriented system are designed to promote both satisfaction and productivity. The major principle underlying each of these features is to structure the work and/or reward system so that high performance is either intrinsically or extrinsically rewarding to the individual, thus creating a situation where high performance contributes to job satisfaction.

In practice, there can be numerous bugs in using an individually-oriented system to achieve satisfaction and performance. For example, just saying that rewards should be based on performance is easier than knowing what the proper relationship should be or whether there should be discontinuities at the high or low end of that relationship. Should we, for instance, lavish rewards on the few highest performers, deprive the lowest performers, or establish a constant linkage between pay and performance? In terms of goal-setting, should goals be set by management, workers, or joint decision making, and what should the proper baseline be for measuring improvements? In terms of job design, what is the proper combination of positive social cues and actual job enrichment that will improve motivation and satisfaction?

These questions are important and need to be answered in order to "fine-tune" or fully understand an individually-oriented system. Yet, even without answers to these questions, we already know that a well-run organization using an individually-oriented system *can* be effective. The problem is we usually don't implement such a system, either completely or very well, in most organizations. Instead, we often compare poorly managed corporations using individually-oriented systems (e.g., those with rigid bureaucratic structures) with more effectively run firms using another motivational system (e.g., Japanese organizations), concluding that the individual model is wrong. The truth may be that the individual model may be just as correct as other approaches, but we simply don't implement it as well.

The Group-Oriented System

individually-oriented systems are obviously not the only way to go. We can also have a group-oriented system, where satisfaction and performance are derived from group participation. In fact, much of organizational life could be designed around groups, if we wanted to capitalize fully on the power of groups to influence work attitudes and behavior.[16] The basic idea would be to make group participation so important that groups would be capable of controlling both satisfaction and performance. Some of the most common techniques would be:

- Organizing work around intact groups.

- Having groups charged with selection, training, and rewarding of members.

- Using groups to enforce strong norms for behavior, with group involvement in off-the-job as well as on-the-job behavior.

- Distributing resources on a group rather than individual basis.

- Allowing and perhaps even promoting intergroup rivalry so as to build within-group solidarity.

Group-oriented systems may be difficult for people at the top to control, but they can be very powerful and involving. We know from military research that soldiers can fight long and hard, not out of special patriotism, but from devotion and loyalty to their units. We know that participation in various high-tech project groups can be immensely involving, both in terms of one's attitudes and performance. We also know that people will serve long and hard hours to help build or preserve organizational divisions or departments, perhaps more out of loyalty and altruism than self-interest. Thus, because individuals will work to achieve group praise and adoration, a group-oriented system, effectively managed, can potentially contribute to high job performance and satisfaction.

The Organizationally-Oriented System

A third way of organizing work might be an organizationally-oriented system, using the principles of Ouchi's Theory Z and Lawler's recommendations for developing high-performing systems.[17] The basic goal would be to arrange working conditions so that individuals gain satisfaction from contributing to the entire organization's welfare. If individuals were to identify closely with the organization as a whole, then organizational performance would be intrinsically rewarding to the individual. On a less altruistic basis, individuals might also gain extrinsic rewards from association with a high-performing organization, since successful organizations may provide greater personal opportunities in terms of salary and promotion. Common features of an organizationally-oriented system would be:

- Socialization into the organization as a whole to foster identification with the entire business and not just a particular subunit.

- Job rotation around the company so that loyalty is not limited to one subunit.

- Long training period with the development of skills that are specific to the company and not transferable to other firms in the industry or profession, thus committing people to the employing organization.

- Long-term or protected employment to gain organizational loyalty, with concern for survival and welfare of the firm.

- Decentralized operations, with few departments or subunits to compete for the allegiance of members.

- Few status distinctions between employees so that dissension and separatism are not fostered.

- Economic education and sharing of organizational information about products, financial condition, and strategies of the firm.

- Tying individual rewards (at all levels in the firm) to organizational performance through various forms of profit sharing, stock options, and bonuses.

The Japanese have obviously been the major proponents of organizationally-oriented systems, although some of the features listed here (such as profit sharing) are very American in origin. The odd thing is that Americans have consistently followed an organizationally-oriented system for middle and upper management and for members of professional organizations such as law and accounting firms. For these high-level employees, loyalty may be as valued as immediate performance, with the firm expecting the individual to defend the organization, even if there does not seem to be any obvious self-interest involved. Such loyalty is rarely demanded or expected from the lower levels of traditional Western organizations.

EVALUATING THE THREE SYSTEMS

I started this article by noting that it may be very difficult to change job performance and satisfaction. Then I noted that recognition of this difficulty should not resign us to the present situation, but spur us to stronger and more systemic actions—in a sense, throwing more variables at the problem. As a result, I have tried to characterize three syndromes of actions that might be effective routes toward the happy/productive worker.

One could build a logical case for the use of any of the three motivational systems. Each has the potential for arousing individuals, steering their behavior in desired ways, and building satisfaction as a consequence of high performance. Individually-oriented systems work by tapping the desires and goals of individuals and by taking advantage of our cultural affinity for independence. Group-oriented systems work by taking advantage of our more social selves, using group pressures and loyalty as the means of enforcing desired behavior and dispensing praise for accomplishments. Finally, organizationally-oriented systems function by building intense attraction to the goals of an institution, where individual pleasure is derived from serving the collective welfare.

If we have three logical and defensible routes toward achieving the happy/productive worker, which is the best path? The answer to this question will obviously depend on how the question is phrased. If "best" means appropriate from a cultural point of view, we will get one answer. As Americans, although we respect organizational loyalty, we often become suspicious of near total institutions where behavior is closely monitored and strongly policed—places like the company town and religious cult. If we define "best" as meaning the highest level of current performance, we might get a different answer, since many of the Japanese-run plants are now outperforming the American variety. Still, if we phrase the question in terms of *potential* effectiveness, we may get a third answer. Cross-cultural comparisons, as I mentioned, often pit poorly managed individually-oriented systems (especially those with non-contingent rewards and a bureaucratic promotion system) against more smoothly running group or organizationally-oriented systems. Thus, we really do not know which system, managed to its potential, will lead to the greatest performance.

Mixing the Systems

If we accept the fact that individual, group, and organizationally oriented systems may each do *something* right, would it be possible to take advantage of all three? That is, can we either combine all three systems into some suprasystem or attempt to build a hybrid system by using the best features of each?

I have trepidations about combining the three approaches. Instead of a stronger treatment, we may end up with either a conflicted or confused environment. Because the individually-oriented system tends to foster competition among individual employees, it would not, for example, be easily merged with group-oriented systems that promote intragroup solidarity. Likewise, organizationally-oriented systems that emphasize how people can serve a common goal may not blend well with group-oriented systems that foster intergroup rivalry. Finally, the use of either a group- or organizationally-oriented reward system may diminish individual motivation, since it becomes more difficult for the person to associate his behavior with collective accomplishments and outcomes. Thus, by mixing the motivational approaches, we may end up with a watered-down treatment that does not fulfill the potential of *any* of the three systems.

In deciding which system to use, we need to face squarely the costs as well as benefits of the three approaches. For example, firms considering an individually-oriented system should assess not only the gains associated with increases in individual motivation, but also potential losses in collaboration that might result from interpersonal competition. Similarly, companies thinking of using a group-oriented system need to study the trade-offs of intergroup competition that can be a byproduct of increased intragroup solidarity. And, before thinking that an organizationally-oriented system will solve all the firm's problems, one needs to know whether motivation to achieve collective goals can be heightened to the point where it outweighs potential losses in motivation toward personal and group interests. These trade-offs are not trivial. They trigger considerations of human resource policy as well as more general philosophical issues of what the organization wants to be. They also involve technical problems for which current organizational research has few solutions, since scholars have tended to study treatments in isolation rather than the effect of larger systems of variables.

So far, all we can be sure of is that task structure plays a key role in formulating the proper motivational strategy. As an example, consider the following cases: a sales organization can be divided into discrete territories (where total performance is largely the sum of individual efforts), a research organization where several product groups are charged with making new developments (where aggregate performance is close to the sum of group efforts), and a high-technology company where success and failure are due to total collaboration and collective effort. In each of these three cases, the choice of the proper motivational system will be determined by whether one views individual, group, or collective efforts as the most important element. Such a choice is also determined by the degree to which one is willing to sacrifice (or trade-off) a degree of performance from other elements of the system, be they the behavior of individuals, groups, or the collective whole. Thus, the major point is that each motivational system has its relative strengths and weaknesses—that despite the claims of many of our theories of management, there is no simple or conflict-free road to the happy/productive worker.

CONCLUSION

Although this article started by noting that the search for the happy/productive worker has been a rather quixotic venture, I have tried to end the discussion with some guarded optimism. By using individual, group, and organizational systems, I have shown how it is *at least possible* to create changes that can overwhelm the forces for stability in both job attitudes and performance. None of these three approaches is a panacea that will solve all of an organization's problems, and no doubt some very hard choices must be made between them. Yet, caution need not preclude action. Therefore, rather than the usual academic's plea for further research or the consultant's claim for bountiful results, we need actions that are flexible enough to allow for mistakes and adjustments along the way.

References

1. A. H. Brayfield and W. H. Crockett, "Employee Attitudes and Employee Performance," *Psychological Bulletin*, 51 (1955):396–424.
2. Victor H. Vroom, *Work and Motivation* (New York, NY: Wiley, 1969).
3. James G. March and Herbert A. Simon, *Organizations* (New York, NY: Wiley, 1958).
4. Richard J. Hackman and Greg R. Oldham, *Work Redesign* (Reading, MA: Addison-Wesley, 1980).
5. E.g., Gerald R. Salancik and Jeffrey Pfeffer, "A Social Information Processing Approach to Job Attitudes and Task Design," *Administrative Science Quarterly*, 23 (1978): 224–253.
6. Robert Kahn (1985).
7. Benjamin Schneider and Peter Dachler, "A Note on the Stability of the Job Description Index," *Journal of Applied Psychology*, 63 (1978):650–653.

8. Elaine D. Pulakos and Neal Schmitt, "A Longitudinal Study of a Valence Model Approach for the Prediction of Job Satisfaction of New Employees," *Journal of Applied Psychology*, 68 (1983):307–312.

9. Barry M. Staw and Jerry Ross, "Stability in the Midst of Change: A Dispositional Approach to Job Attitudes," *Journal of Applied Psychology*, 70 (1985):469–480.

10. Barry M. Staw, Nancy E. Bell, and John A. Clausen, "The Dispositional Approach to Job Attitudes: A Lifetime Longitudinal Test," *Administrative Science Quarterly* (March 1986).

11. See Lawrence H. Peters, Edward J. O'Connor, and Joe R. Eulberg, "Situational Constraints: Sources, Consequences, and Future Considerations," in Kendreth M. Rowland and Gerald R. Ferris, eds., *Research in Personnel and Human Resources Management*, Vol. 3 (Greenwich, CT: JAI Press, 1985).

12. For a review, see Marvin D. Dunnette, "Aptitudes, Abilities, and Skills," in Marvin D. Dunnette, ed., *Handbook of Industrial and Organizational Psychology* (Chicago, IL: Rand McNally, 1976).

13. As found by John Clausen, personal communications, 1986.

14. Rosabeth M. Kanter, *The Change Masters* (New York, NY: Simon & Schuster, 1983).

15. Richard A. Guzzo, Susan E. Jackson, and Raymond A. Katzell, "Meta-analysis Analysis," in Barry M. Staw and Larry L. Cummings, eds., *Research in Organizational Behavior*, Vol. 9 (Greenwich, CT: JAI Press, 1987).

16. See Harold J. Leavitt, "Suppose We Took Groups Seriously," in E. L. Cass and F. G. Zimmer, eds., *Man and Work in Society* (New York, NY: Van Nostrand, 1975).

17. William Ouchi, *Theory Z: How American Business Can Meet the Japanese Challenge* (Reading, MA: Addison-Wesley, 1981); Edward E. Lawler, III, "Increasing Worker Involvement to Enhance Organizational Effectiveness," in Paul Goodman, ed., *Change in Organizations* (San Francisco,: Jossey-Bass, 1982).

What's a Good Reason to Change? Motivated Reasoning and Social Accounts in Promoting Organizational Change

Denise M. Rousseau and Snehal A. Tijoriwala

> "We want to care for patients not paper."
> "Nurses are able to share in their own future."
> "Added responsibility without monetary reimbursement."
>   —Three contrasting views of the same restructuring

Downsizing and restructuring have brought about radical changes in employment relationships worldwide (Kanter, 1989). These events are blamed for increased employee stress and dissatisfaction (Mirvis & Hall, 1994) and, when poorly implemented, for reduced performance and commitment and increased perceptions of injustice (Novelli, Kirkman, & Shapiro, 1995; Schneider & Bowen, 1995). Global competition, cost pressures, innovations in information technology, and rising customer expectations are seen to necessitate organizational changes and put pressure on employers to effectively manage these changes (Handy, 1989; Kanter, 1989).

The causal frameworks employees use to understand change are not well understood, despite the general finding that the way employees interpret the reasons for change influences their reactions to it (Shapiro, Buttner, & Barry, 1994). How organizations frame change affects

From *Journal of Applied Psychology*, 84(4), 514–528. Reprinted with permission.

employee responses (Fairhurst & Sarr, 1996; Pondy, 1978). However, we know that not all reasons used to explain change are credible or acceptable to employees (Bies & Moag, 1986; Bies & Shapiro, 1993). The present study investigates the role of reasons in motivating complex organizational change from the perspective of social accounts and motivated reasoning.

By joining these two perspectives to study complex organizational change, the present study is distinct from previous research on reasons and change. Typically, such studies are conducted in the laboratory (Bies & Shapiro, 1993; Shapiro, 1991) or involve field studies of a discrete event (e.g., introduction of a no-smoking policy; Greenberg, 1994). The present study, in contrast, investigates a major change intervention, where several competing reasons for change can exist simultaneously. (Indeed, the opening quotes are anecdotal evidence that recipients of the same change can have different interpretations.) Extending previous studies that limited their focus largely to managerial communication (Bies & Shapiro, 1993; Bies, Shapiro, & Cummings, 1988; Greenberg, 1994), this study also examines the roles played by individual, relational, and social information-processing factors in shaping interpretations of change. By considering factors at both the individual and work-group levels, we investigated the possible origins of the competing and diverse views employees can have regarding change.

HOW REASONS FOR CHANGE ARE UNDERSTOOD

We review two major theories regarding causal explanations to understand how employees interpret the reasons for change (social accounts and motivated reasoning): Although social accounts theory focuses on reasons as a managerial intervention, motivated reasoning theory focuses on how individuals generate their own causal explanations.

Social Accounts

Social accounts have been defined as managerial justifications and excuses (Sitkin & Bies, 1993, p. 350) that are used to explain actions undertaken by persons or firms, such as citing economic conditions as a motivation for change. Sitkin and Bies describe three categories of social accounts studied by researchers: *mitigating responsibility*, which are used to alter perceptions of causality for an incident or action; *exonerating motives*, which attempt to legitimate the action by appealing to higher-level values; and *reframing outcomes* which alter perceptions regarding the consequences of the action. Mitigating accounts have been found to lessen apparent responsibility for unfavorable outcomes and reduce feelings of unfairness and disapproval ("No one could have anticipated the decline in demand"). Exonerating accounts attempt to clarify basic premises underlying the actions, such as appealing to a shared goal (e.g., "competitive superiority," Sitkin & Bies, 1993, p. 356). Reframing accounts alters perceptions regarding consequences ("Downsizing today will create a more competitive organization and stable employment in the future"). Reasons that refocus attention externally (e.g., claiming economic justification for the change) can be a mix of all three forms of account; they are thought to unite manager and subordinate (Coser, 1956) and reduce the conflict between them in times of change (Sitkin & Bies, 1993).

The social accounts managers offer influence employee reactions as a function of the adequacy or credibility of the reason and the sincerity of the account giver (Bies, 1987). Outcome negativity—the degree of adversity the change recipient associates with the change—has been also examined as a factor in social accounts research, but the results have been mixed: Shapiro et al. (1994) found that perceived adequacy of accounts is greater under conditions of low outcome severity, whereas Shapiro (1991) found the opposite. We note that in both studies, the expected outcomes of change were negative, without any potential benefits to employees, and the effectiveness measure of the account was its adequacy in lessening the outcome's perceived severity.

In general, social accounts research focuses on changes that are adverse or negative in character (e.g., job losses, budget cuts, wage freezes, or failure to receive promised benefits or rewards). Accounts play the role of excuses or justifications used to influence a person's perceptions of responsibility for an action, the motives behind it, and its unfavorability. Typical accounts examined include external factors (e.g., economic downturns) or lack of managerial control (e.g., changes instituted by new owners many levels removed from the supervisor who offers the account; Bies & Moag, 1986). The most typical outcome focused on in this research is the perceived legitimacy of the explanation given. The purpose of social accounts is to create beliefs on the part of recipients that change is justified. In the context of organizational change, we are interested in two beliefs: the reasons employees perceive to motivate the change (why change occurs) and the legitimacy they attribute to those reasons (acceptability of a reason to the recipient). The present study distinguishes between perceived reasons and the perceived legitimacy of those reasons in investigating how change recipients understand the processes associated with managerially driven change. Consistent with social accounts theory, we made the following hypothesis.

> *Hypothesis 1*: Belief in the social account that management has expressed will be positively related to the perceived legitimacy of that explanation.

Note that given the absence of a theoretical basis, we make no specific prediction regarding the relationship between perceived legitimacy and other reasons employees interpreted for the change, aside from the managerial account. However, we recognize that in complex organizational change, recipients may believe that a variety of reasons motivated it.

Bies (1987) argues that employees who trust management are more likely to accept the managerial account as justifying the change. Trust can influence both the credibility of the actual reason (whether it is believed to be true) as well as belief in its legitimacy (whether it is justified). Where employees trust management, the managerial account will be more credible. In the context of a high trust manager–employee relationship, the account's credibility should promote its legitimacy by reducing suspicion and the search for disconforming information.

> *Hypothesis 2*: Trust moderates the relationship between belief in the managerial account and the account's perceived legitimacy. High trust levels will be associated with a stronger relationship between beliefs in the managerial account and its perceived legitimacy.

Limitations of Social Accounts Theory

By focusing on reasons offered by managers, social accounts theory gives a framework for understanding the perceived legitimacy of reasons formally articulated during the change process. However, employees are not passive recipients of change; they can draw their own interpretations and act on their own understandings of it (Shapiro, Lewicki, & Devine, 1995). In complex organizational change, multiple competing (as well as complementary) reasons for change may exist simultaneously. In these situations, explanations managers offer for change may not be believed, heard, understood, or recalled.

The same change intervention can give rise to very different causal explanations from the perspective of employees. Restructurings may be viewed as motivated by the desire for better market position (Porter, 1990), improved customer service (Schneider & Bowen, 1995), cost containment (Harrison, 1994), or a more motivating environment for the workforce (Reichheld, 1996). The latter, in effect, can be viewed as an end in itself or as a means of achieving sustainable competitive advantage through improved worker motivation (Pfeffer, 1994). Given the potential for several reasons to be attributed simultaneously, two employees may have very different views of why their organization has instituted change, as in the words of two nurses in the same hospital implementing a flatter organizational hierarchy:

1. "We are becoming more professional and better able to improve our own practice through the change."

2. "(The change was introduced) so some bigwig with an MBA gets to look good."

To understand the origin of such divergent interpretations of the reasons for change and how they affect implementation, we examined the factors that affect causal reasoning generally.

Motivated Reasoning

People seek causal explanations for unusual or unexpected events (Weiner, 1985). Motivated reasoning addresses how a particular reason is adopted to explain such an event. From this perspective, employees are not passive recipients of change messages but active information processors who engage in causal selection (Einhorn & Hogarth, 1986; McGill, 1995). Moreover, the causal backgrounds people possess (e.g., facts, perspectives, emphases) are an amalgam of past experience, available information, and individual cognitive processes that can lead employees of the same organization to generate different explanations for the same event (McGill, 1995). Although managers may offer a social account for their actions, a variety of other factors can shape employees' information processing regarding change, including coworker opinions and past experiences with management.

The informal network or grapevine frequently is an important source of information during change (Krackhardt & Hanson, 1993). Social information processing shapes the causal explanations people adopt, particularly where there is consensus among coworkers (Einhorn & Hogarth, 1986; Salancik & Pfeffer, 1978). Thus, the beliefs of one's work group can be expected to impact the beliefs adopted by a given individual as to why change has occurred:

Hypothesis 3: Work-group beliefs will be positively related to individual perceptions of the reasons for change.

Ample evidence exists that an employee's relationship with the organization shapes his or her interpretation of its actions, particularly because this relationship is a product of the employee's history with the organization (Rousseau, 1995). Employee reasoning may be shaped by perceptions of the organization's trustworthiness and other factors related to the employment relationship (e.g., high affective commitment or attachment to the firm). During planned change, the quality of the employment relationship plays an important role in promoting employee acceptance and involvement (Pfeffer, 1994; Rousseau, 1996). Mishra (1996) notes that a key aspect of trust is one's perception of frankness and honesty on the part of the other: Undistorted communication reinforces trust, whereas lies and distortions decrease it. Moreover, McAllister (1995) maintains that a perception of reliability and dependability may be a precursor to developing beliefs that the relationship entails reciprocated care and concern.

Using social accounts theory as a basis, we argued previously that employees are more likely to believe the social accounts offered by credible managers. High trust increases the likelihood that reasons for change will be viewed as functional—that is to say, well-intentioned and constructive. However, social accounts theory does not indicate the kind of causal reasoning low trust might generate. Motivated reasoning theory suggests that employees seek explanations for change whether or not a managerial account is offered. Moreover, this theory predicts that under conditions of low trust, attributions consistent with dysfunctional experiences (i.e., nonconstructive or at odds with the broader interests of the firm and its members) are likely. To understand the effects of motivated reasoning, we differentiate the legitimacy attributed to a reason for change (i.e., whether or not an explanation is considered adequate or appropriate in a specific situation) from its functionality. Although legitimacy is situation-specific, functionality is a generic aspect of reasons, reflecting the extent to which a reason generally can be construed to support constructive goals of the larger firm such as progress or development (e.g., quality, continuous improvement, organizational survival) or nonconstructive goals, such as self-serving interests of particular persons or groups (e.g., self-aggrandizing senior managers). We postulate that low trust can itself generate explanations in the minds of employees that differ from those offered by managers and reflect negative evaluations of managers' intent (e.g., the real reasons may be seen as political or self-serving).

Hypothesis 4: Trust will be negatively related to beliefs in dysfunctional reasons for change.

Conversely, we made the following hypothesis:

Hypothesis 5: Trust will be positively related to beliefs in functional reasons for change.

According to social accounts research, high trust should generate greater acceptance of managerially offered explanations. Moreover, motivated reasoning suggests that high-trust individuals would be more likely to consider reasons for change legitimate (i.e., acceptable and appropriate), whether or not managers offer those reasons.

Hypothesis 6: Trust will be positively related to perceived legitimacy of reasons for change.

Note, however, that the premise behind this main effect of trust on perceived legitimacy differs from that of the interaction effect in H2. Because motivated reasoning describes how individuals generate explanations, reasons need not be directly communicated by a trusted source to be viewed as credible. However, where managers are trusted, that trust should promote acceptance of change generally and therefore enhance legitimacy of any reasons associated with it.

Another relational factor that can shape interpretations of the reasons for change is the psychological contract, a fundamental aspect of the employment relationship. Psychological contracts refer to beliefs that the employee and employer hold regarding their mutual obligations. Changes can be interpreted in the context of these beliefs (Levinson, 1962; Rousseau, 1995), and the nature of employees' psychological contracts can affect their reasoning regarding change. Relational contracts entail mutual obligations between employee and employer to support each other's interests, typically through commitments regarding job security and loyalty, and involve an open-ended, long-term exchange with a high degree of flexibility. These contracts are believed to have a broader zone of acceptance (Rousseau, 1995), suggesting that parties to such contractual arrangements are more likely to be accepting of change and the reasons offered for it. In contrast, transactional contracts are characterized by monetary obligations on the part of the employer and performance of specific, often narrow, job duties on the part of the employee (Macneil, 1985; Rousseau, 1989). With their limited, largely economic involvement and lower levels of emotional attachment, transactional contracts have narrower flexibility; changes would require a renegotiation of the contract and possibly changes in the parties involved (e.g., replacing one person with another). Thus, transactional contacts are likely to be associated with lower acceptance of change and the reasons offered by managers.

> *Hypothesis 7*: The extent to which an employee is party to a relational contract will be positively related to his or her perceptions of the legitimacy of the reasons for change.

> *Hypothesis 8*: The extent to which an employee is party to a transactional contract will be negatively related to his or her perceptions of the legitimacy of the reasons for change.

Managerially driven changes are not necessarily composed of a single event or unified message. Rather, change recipients must interpret a complex array of facts regarding the change, their relations to the firm, and their coworkers' perceptions in understanding the underlying motivations for changes management has introduced. The reliance of previous social accounts research on laboratory settings might have limited its ability to assess the effects of these contextual features. However, we note that proponents of social accounts have addressed aspects of motivated reasoning by addressing why some people are more likely to believe an account in the first place (e.g., trust; Bies, 1987). Further, we suggest that these two perspectives are not necessarily incompatible. Because motivated reasoning theory articulates more specifically the role that organizational context can play in shaping how employees interpret significant events, joining motivated reasoning with social accounts theory can be especially fruitful in understanding complex organizational change.

Implementation of Change

The reasons motivating organizational change, both real and perceived, have received relatively little attention in research on the implementation of complex organizational interventions. We postulate that reasons, particularly their adequacy or legitimacy, play an important role in shaping the success of the implementation process. When organizational actions are interpreted in a broader normative framework that legitimates their motives, individual acceptance and commitment can be enhanced (Fairhurst & Sarr, 1996). Research on transformational leadership stresses the importance of appealing to normative values (Bass, 1985). Moreover, research on social accounts suggests that accounts are more likely to be perceived as adequate where managers use normative appeals and consequently do not appear to have self-serving motives (Bies, 1987; Shapiro, 1991). In consequence, we postulate that legitimacy of reasons is directly related to employee implementation of change:

> *Hypothesis 9*: Perceived legitimacy of reasons will be positively related to change implementation.

Another major factor that motivates change is the perception that benefits (as opposed to losses) can be accessed through implementation. We note that social accounts research has not addressed changes that introduce benefits (e.g., new skills, development opportunities, greater challenge). Indeed, to date, it has focused on negative experiences (e.g., job loss). Social accounts theory also typically focuses on discrete events, such as smoking policies and layoffs, rather than more complex events, such as culture change or restructuring, where some benefits may be expected in the long term. In complex organizational change, individuals may experience both losses (e.g., uncertainty, deskilling, job insecurity) and gains (e.g., greater autonomy, development opportunities). However, losses are likely to occur relatively early in the process (particularly psychological stresses associated with change and uncertainty; Rousseau, 1995, 1996). The more fully a change is implemented, the more likely it is that employees will access its benefits.

Hypothesis 10: The degree of implementation will be positively related to employee experiences of beneficial consequences of change.

METHOD

Participants

Registered nurses (RNs) in 34 inpatient units at a large northeastern U.S. hospital were the participants of this study ($n = 501$). The average age at the time of the survey was 33 years, 92% were women, and 85% worked full time. On average, the nurses had been employed with the hospital for 7 years and had been with their current unit for 5 years. The sample included nurses with a wide range of educational qualifications: 23% had RN diplomas, 25% had associate degrees, 46% had bachelor's degrees, 4% had master's degrees, and 2% had other qualifications. All nurses surveyed had been with the hospital throughout the entire period of the change.

The hospital, part of an integrated academic health care system, had 746 licensed beds and more than 5,000 full-time employees. At this site, we investigated the implementation of self-managing work groups among nurses. At the time of the survey, the hospital had implemented a program to promote the empowerment of nurses by giving them responsibility and accountability for decision making about clinical practice (referred to here as *the change*). Although the change began 2 years before the survey, our interviews with nursing leadership suggested that nursing units, and the nurses within these units, experienced varying degrees of implementation. This variation in implementation provided an opportunity to investigate cross-sectionally the factors contributing to effective change management in a single organization. Nursing units were grouped into sets of two to five, to form a cluster headed by a nurse manager/clinical director. The average number of nurses in a single unit was 30. Each clinical director oversaw 60 to 150 nurses.

The Change

The organizational intervention consisted of a complex restructuring of the nursing division of the hospital following a program referred to as Shared Governance (SG; Porter-O'Grady, 1984). SG replaces the traditional hierarchy—charge nurses on each shift, head nurses on each unit, nurse managers over clusters of units, and higher-level nursing admin-istrators—with a streamlined, decentralized decision-making system. Under SG, charge nurses and head nurses were eliminated, and nurse managers coordinated the efforts of sev-eral units (typically four). An array of decisions formerly made by nursing leadership were pushed down to the nurses who provide direct patient care. Proponents of SG maintain that autonomy, authority, and control should be vested in the person who provides services so he or she can decide what to do, execute the action, and enforce those decisions (Porter-O'Grady, 1984).[1]

In SG, a council, or subset of nurses in each unit, makes decisions formerly made by nurs-ing managers. The SG model includes four councils within each unit: quality (focusing on continuous improvement), practice (focusing on patient care procedures), education (identi-fying training and development needs), and research (supporting development of nursing re-search programs intended to ultimately yield publications by unit nurses). To integrate activities throughout the hospital, representatives from different units sit on hospital-wide councils in each of these areas. A management council composed of nurse managers, which reports directly to the vice president of nursing, is intended to be the primary link between the units and hospital administration. Porter-O'Grady (1984, p. 84) acknowledges

> While investing power and accountability in the professional staff may arouse some concern
> from the traditional nursing administrator, this leader will be relieved to know the exercise of
> individual power in a shared framework is limited at best.

We note that cost cutting by eliminating expensive layers of management also is reported as a purpose of SG (Porter-O'Grady, 1984).

The Implementation

At the outset, all nurses in the hospital received training in the SG model and were asked to volunteer to serve on councils within their units. When more than the requisite number volun-teered, coworkers voted for their council representatives. Most of the head and charge nurses who were removed from their positions returned to the role of staff nurse. Nurse managers nominated nurses from within their clusters to participate on the four hospital-wide councils.

---

[1] To understand Shared Governance in the context of the nursing profession, it is helpful to consider current trends in that profession. Goodrick and Meindl (1995), in their investigation of ideological transformation in the nursing profession, characterize the trend toward expanding the managerial responsibilities of nurses and giving them greater autonomy over their own clinical practice in terms of a century-long evolution of nursing. The traditional ideology of nursing was that of a feminine vocation, consistent with maternal devotion, focusing on the womanly duty of service to others and submission to authority, including that of physicians. The renewal of the women's movement in the 20th century helped loosen the constraints of nursing as womanly duty by helping to legitimate a professional agenda (Bullough & Bullough, 1984; Goodrick & Meindl, 1995). Fundamental shifts in health care have occurred in conjunction with a spillover of the managerial ideology from the corporate sector, with its goals of maximizing efficiency, into contemporary hospitals (e.g., "Ex-manager describes the profit-driven life inside Columbia/HCA," 1997). However, in nursing the humanistic emphasis on patient care has often been experienced as inconsistent with increased standardization and fewer personal relationships implied by professionalization (Gadow, 1980) as well as greater emphasis on health care as a business. Shared Governance and the appeal to concern for patient care quality expressed in its implementation melds the humanistic and managerial ideologies, consistent with recent trends in nursing to find a middle ground between humanism and managerialism (Goodrick & Meindl, 1995).

At the time SG was introduced into the hospital, nursing leadership gave speeches, sent internal memoranda, and walked the halls to send a message that SG would promote nursing professionalism, improve care quality by empowering caregivers to make appropriate decisions without oversight, and enhance the skills and competence of nurses. As emphasized by the hospital's vice president of nursing,

> Continuous improvement of patient care is the point of Shared Governance. For this to happen, nurses need to think of themselves as professionals and let go of traditional ways of thinking about nursing. To make Shared Governance work, increased nursing professionalism is required.

Note that the formal reason stated by nursing leadership for SG implementation was to improve the quality of patient care by enhancing nursing professionalism. Thus, improvement in care quality was the social account managers offered to justify the change. This conforms to what Sitkin and Bies referred to as an *exonerating account*—legitimating the motives for the change by placing management's actions within a broader normative framework. Thus, even negative consequences from the change (e.g., increased stress during the transition to SG, more work for the same pay) might be seen as derived from legitimate motives. In this context, according to Sitkin and Bies (1993), "anger and disapproval engendered . . . may be suppressed, in part because such feelings are not deemed appropriate given the legitimate purposes that ostensibly motivated the acts" (p. 356).

SG had been initiated in this hospital 2 years prior to the survey conducted in this research. At this point in time, implementation across units within the nursing department varied widely, with some units having fully developed SG council decision systems and others having virtually no SG-related practices in place. The time lag between the implementation of the change and survey administration raises the issue of whether there was a mortality bias due to the attrition of employees dissatisfied with the change. However, during this period, voluntary attrition was under 2%, the latter due substantially to retirement. Thus, a mortality bias is unlikely.

Measurement

Questionnaires were sent to RNs in the inpatient units who were listed in the Human Resource Department's database. Respondents filled out the questionnaire voluntarily, typically on the job. The unit of analysis in this study is the individual nurse. The total number of nurses participating reflects a response rate of 48.5%. Using a structured questionnaire, respondents were asked to give their perceptions of the change and to estimate its impact on their work life and the work practices in their units. Scales developed for this study were subject to principal-axis factor analysis with varimax rotation. All scales were based on factors with eigenvalues greater than 1 and included those items meeting the requirements of simple structure (Comrey, 1973). The specific items used can be found in the Appendix.

Reasons.   The reasons respondents attributed to the change were measured using a 1 (*not at all*) to 5 (*very great*) scale. Respondents were asked to rate the extent to which they believed the managerial account (quality), economic factors, and self-serving managerial motives were the reason for the change. Reasons were derived from pilot interviews with staff nurses and managers prior to the development of the survey. Eleven items were used that yielded three factors. Alpha reliabilities were .81 (Quality), .71 (Economic), and .76 (Self-Serving). On the basis of information obtained from our pilot interviews and a content analysis of the reasons, Quality and Economic are treated as functional reasons for the purposes of hypothesis testing, and Self-Serving is treated as a dysfunctional reason for change.

Legitimacy of reasons. Legitimacy was measured using the same items but with a different frame of reference (see Appendix) as described for Reasons above. Respondents were asked whether the reason was "legitimate, acceptable, and appropriate to you." The eleven items yielded the same factor structure for Legitimacy as for Reasons. Alpha reliabilities were .82 (Quality Legitimacy), .82 (Economic Legitimacy), and .75 (Self-Serving Legitimacy).

Work-group level reasons. For each nurse, we computed the mean score of his or her coworkers' ratings for each of the three measures of reasons for change by summing the unit's total score, subtracting the nurse's own score, and taking the average. This coworker average was used as a measure of the social construction of the reasons within each unit. To determine whether aggregation was appropriate, we ran a Within and Between Analysis (WABA; Dansereau, Alutto, & Yammarino, 1984). Results indicated that the effects each Reasons measure had on other variables included in the study were both between as well as within the nursing units. That finding was consistent with the dual-role perceived reasons plays in this study, both as an individual perception as well as a work-group level variable.

Psychological contracts. We examined nurses' beliefs about their obligations to their employer by asking them the extent to which they had committed to engage in specific behaviors as part of their employment with the hospital, using a 1 (*not at all*) to 5 (*to a very great extent*) scale. The obligations surveyed were derived from the literature on nursing roles (e.g., Gadow, 1980) and field interviews with staff nurses and nurse managers in this hospital. Principal axes factor analyses revealed two factors with eigenvalues greater than 1. The patterns observed here were consistent with previous research in a non-nursing population (Robinson & Rousseau, 1994). Scales are based on items with factor loadings exceeding .4.

Relational contract (α = .82). Consistent with previous research on relational contracts reporting open-ended conditions of employment without clear performance specifications (Rousseau, 1989), this factor reflects obligations focusing on attachment to the employer, including loyalty, continuity, and willingness to accept new assignments.

Transactional contract (α = .83). Reflects obligations to provide a basic level of performance with limited involvement with the organization (Rousseau, 1995). Because nurses are professionals, educated in nursing skills and codes of conduct, a transactional contract consists of adherence to basic professional standards that would apply to any organization in which the nurse might work.

Trust. We measured the extent to which respondents experienced nursing leadership as trustworthy and credible regarding this particular change by using two items assessing the credibility of nursing administration and the nurse managers within each unit, using a 1 (*not at all*) to 5 (*very highly*) scale. The alpha reliability was .80.

Implementation. The goals that hospital leadership established for this change included improvements in professional and leadership development, nursing decision making, and clinical practice quality. Nurses were asked to compare the outcomes before and after implementation of the change. Six items measuring implementation yielded a single factor (α = .87). Individual assessments of implementation are appropriate in this context because the change was intended to alter the day-to-day experience of the staff nurses within their unit.

To evaluate the convergent validity of the implementation measures, three raters who were blind to the nursing units' questionnaire results scored each unit on its degree of implementation, using a scale from 1 to 10. The raters discussed their scores to reconcile any differences and generated a global implementation score for each unit (ranging from 1 to 8, with a median of 4). This global score was compared with the mean perceived implementation score for the nurses in each unit, producing a zero-order correlation between the global and individual implementation measures of .46 ($p < .001$). This validity coefficient suggests good convergence between individual nurse perceptions and the level of implementation within each unit. As an additional validity check, individual participation on hospital-wide councils (obtained from archival records) was dummy-coded. Council participation correlated significantly ($r = .16$, $p < .001$) with individual nurses' assessments of change implementation.

Consequences.   To examine the perceived benefits or losses nurses reported as a result of the change, we used two indicators: quality of care ($\alpha = .71$) and employability ($\alpha = .67$).

Analysis

We used interaction effects by using hierarchical moderated multiple regression with significance tests based on difference in R^2 with and without the interaction term. We tested hypotheses regarding direct effects by using a path analytic approach based on maximum likelihood estimation (MLE). Three separate path models were estimated, one for each of the three reasons (quality, economics, self-serving) studied here. Because of the complex set of factors postulated to affect the judgment processes of change recipients, the path model tested the effects of reasons on legitimacy, controlling for contextual factors. Effects of contextual factors on legitimacy were examined controlling for actual reasons. Effects of legitimacy on implementation were examined controlling for contextual factors and perceived reasons. Lastly, effects of implementation on consequences were examined controlling for all other variables in the model. This approach, consistent with Baron and Kenny (1986), makes possible a robust test of the hypotheses. We used MLE in the path analysis because of the likelihood that correlated errors existed in our questionnaire-based independent variables (Breen, 1996).

RESULTS

Table 1 presents means, standard deviations, and zero-order correlations among measures used in this study. Note that matched *t* tests contrasting the perceived reasons for the change demonstrate significant differences ($p < .001$) among all three. Economic factors, on average, are seen as the strongest actual reasons for the change, whereas quality reasons are the lowest rated, despite the fact that management offered quality improvement as its social account for the change. However, quality and economic factors were rated similarly in terms of legitimacy with each receiving a moderate rating (2.75 and 2.76, respectively). As expected, self-serving reasons were rated significantly lower ($p < .001$, $M = 2.09$) on legitimacy than either quality or economic reasons.

Hypothesis 1 predicted that quality reasons—the social account offered for the change— would be positively related to the perceived legitimacy of quality as a reason for the

TABLE 1 Descriptive Statistics

Variable	M	SD	1	2	3	4	5	6	7	8	9	10	11	12	13	14
Antecedents																
1. Transactional	4.76	0.39														
2. Relational	2.60	1.01	.17**													
3. Trust	2.65	1.01	.10*	.16**												
4. Group quality	2.56	0.38	.02	.17**	.07											
5. Group economic	3.71	0.23	.06	.01	.01	−.04										
6. Group self-serving	3.50	0.32	.02	−.05	−.01	−.49**	.43**									
Reasons																
7. Quality	2.56	1.13	.02	.19**	.36**	.15**	−.03	−.09*								
8. Economic	3.71	0.81	.12**	.08	.13**	.01	.03	.01	−.01							
9. Self-serving	3.50	1.11	.03	−.02	−.20**	−.06	.00	.07	−.40**	.46**						
Legitimacy of reasons																
10. Quality	2.75	1.27	.08	.05	.25**	.12**	−.05	−.06	.50**	.05	−.24**					
11. Economic	2.76	0.97	.10*	.25**	.34**	.11*	.04	−.02	.37**	.28**	−.10*	.34**				
12. Self-serving	2.09	1.07	−.06	.21**	.12**	.05	.11*	.04	.14**	.10*	.16**	−.18**	.46**			
Change																
13. Implementation	2.97	0.62	.07	.13**	.42**	.06	.01	−.00	.43**	−.02	−.27**	.34**	.23**	.07		
14. Quality of care	2.68	0.67	.08	.07	.28**	.10*	.00	−.05	.38**	−.14**	−.28**	.30**	.16*	.08	.64**	
15. Employability	2.44	0.84	.04	.09	.28**	.07	.06	.01	.23**	−.04	−.17**	.19**	.09	.05	.40**	.32**

Note. N = 501.
* p < .05.   ** p < .01.

166

TABLE 2   **Maximum Likelihood Estimates for Different Types of Reasons**

Independent variable	Reason	Legitimacy	Implementation	Quality of care	Employability
Quality reasons					
Transactional	−.04	.07*			
Relational	.11**	−.08			
Trust	.35**	.08*			
Group quality reason	.11**				
Quality reason		.49**	.35**	.10**	.07
Legitimacy			.18**	.05	.04
Implementation				.58**	.36**
Function of log likelihood = 1,621.59					
Economic reasons					
Transactional	.10*	.01			
Relational	.04	.18**			
Trust	.11**	.29**			
Group economic reason	.03				
Economic reason		.23**	−.09*	−.15**	−.04
Legitimacy			.27**	.05	.01
Implementation				.63**	.40**
Function of log likelihood = 749.15					
Self-serving reasons					
Transactional	.05	−.12**			
Relational	.02	.21**			
Trust	−.22**	.15**			
Group self-serving reason	.07*				
Self-serving reason		.20**	.29**	−.13**	_.08*
Legitimacy			.12**	.06*	.03
Implementation				.61**	.37**
Function of log likelihood = 1,531.68					

* $p < .05$.   ** $p < .01$ (one-tailed).

change. This hypothesis is supported with both a significant zero-order correlation ($r = .50$, $p < .01$) and a path coefficient of .49 ($p < .01$; Table 2). Note that the correlations between economic reasons and self-serving reasons and their respective legitimacy measures are positive but significantly lower. This suggests that managerial accounts accepted as true by change recipients are more likely to be seen as legitimate than other interpretations of the change.

Hypothesis 2 tested the moderating role of trust in the relationship between reasons and legitimacy, as predicted by social accounts theory (Table 3). High trust levels are associated with a stronger relationship between reasons and legitimacy, but only for the managerial account. A moderating effect was found for quality reasons—$\beta = .40$, $p < .05$, where the difference between R^{2b} and R^{2a} was significant, $F(3, 431) = 4.62$, $p < .01$—but not for economic ($\beta = .15$, ns) or self-serving reasons ($\beta = .25$, ns).

TABLE 3 Summary of Hierarchical Regression Analysis for Legitimacy of Different Types of Reasons

Independent variable	β	R^2	ΔR^2
Legitimacy of quality reasons			
Quality reason	.25*		
Trust	−.15		
Step 1		.28**	
Interaction	.40*		
Step 2		.29**	.01**
Legitimacy of economic reasons			
Economic reason	.18		
Trust	.18		
Step 1		.182	
Interaction	.15		
Step 2		.183	.001
Legitimacy of self-serving reasons			
Dysfunctional reason	.01		
Trust	−.03		
Step 1		.05	
Interaction	.25		
Step 2		.06	.01

Note. ΔR^2 indicates the difference between hierarchical regression R^2 values when the interaction term is included (Step 2) and when it is excluded (Step 1).
* $p < .05$.   ** $p < .01$.

We now turn to the hypotheses derived from the motivated reasoning framework (Figures 1–3). Hypothesis 3 predicted that work-group beliefs regarding reasons would be positively related to individual beliefs. A significant relationship is found for quality reasons ($\beta = .11$, $p < .05$), and for self-serving reasons ($\beta = .07, p < .05$), but there is no relationship for economic reasons ($\beta = -.01, ns$).

Trust was postulated to play a role in explaining perceived reasons for change. Hypothesis 4 postulated that trust would be negatively related to beliefs in dysfunctional (i.e., self-serving) reasons for change, which is supported ($\beta = -.22, p < .01$). Hypothesis 5 predicted that trust would be positively related to both economic and quality reasons, which also is supported: (quality: $\beta = .35, p < .01$; economic: $\beta = .11, p < .01$). Hypothesis 6 postulated that trust would have a positive relationship with perceived legitimacy of reasons for change. This prediction was supported for all three reasons: economic ($\beta = .29, p < .01$), self-serving ($\beta = .15, p < .01$), and quality reasons ($\beta = .08, p < .05$).

Hypothesis 7 predicted that relational contracts would be positively related to perceptions of legitimacy, a finding supported for both self-serving ($\beta = .21, p < .01$) and economic reasons ($\beta = .18, p < .01$) but not for quality, $\beta = -.08, ns$). Thus, relational contracts appear to make employees more accepting of the legitimacy of change, at least for those reasons that do not directly originate from formal managerial communication. In contrast, transactional contracts were predicted in Hypothesis 8 to have a negative relationship with perceived legitimacy of change, a finding supported for self-serving reasons ($\beta = -.12, p < .05$) only. This finding suggests that transactional contracts are linked to low levels of

FIGURE 1   **Maximum likelihood estimation for quality reasons. Double-headed arrows are correlations. * *p* < .05.   ** *p* < .01   *** *p* < .001 (one-tailed).**

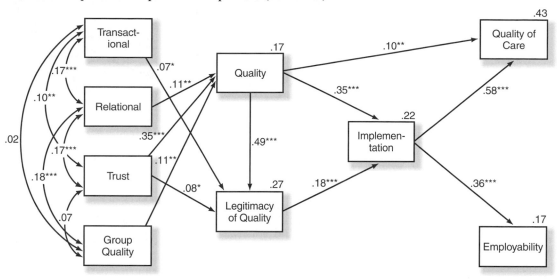

FIGURE 2   **Maximum likelihood estimation for economic reasons. Double-headed arrows are correlations. * *p* < .05.   ** *p* < .01   *** *p* < .001 (one-tailed).**

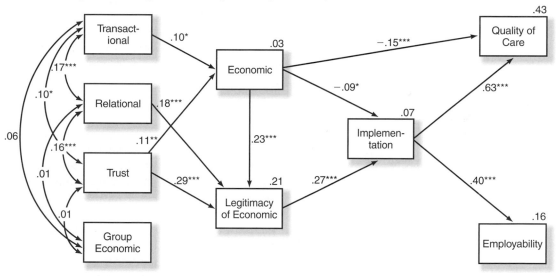

tolerance for poorly justified change, perhaps because of the lower trust and flexibility associated with these contracts (Rousseau, 1995).

Surprisingly, transactional contracts are positively related to legitimacy of quality reasons ($\beta = .07, p < .05$). The basis for this positive relationship is unclear. However, given that the

FIGURE 3 **Maximum likelihood estimation for dysfunctional reasons. Double-headed arrows are correlations. * *p* < .05.   ** *p* < .01   *** *p* < .001 (one-tailed).**

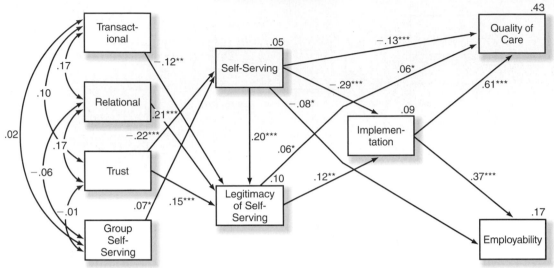

transactional contract characterizing nurses in this study reflects meeting basic professional standards, without specific obligations to the particular employer, it is likely that transactional contract's relationship with the legitimacy of quality reasons derives from adherence to standards of nursing professionalism (Goodrick & Meindl, 1995).

Hypothesis 9 predicted that the perceived legitimacy of reasons would be positively related to implementation, which is supported for all three types of reasons (*p* < .01). Finally, consistent with Hypothesis 10, implementation was positively related to improvements in quality of care and employability (*p* < .01) in all three models.

DISCUSSION

This study adopted a multifaceted view of the process whereby individual, relational, and social factors influence how recipients interpret complex change and the social accounts that are offered regarding it. To a great extent, motivated reasoning and social accounts seek to explain different phenomena. Although motivated reasoning seeks to explain how an individual arrives at a particular causal interpretation, social accounts research focuses on how a particular source of information regarding reasons, typically the managers involved in implementing change, shapes perceptions of adequacy or legitimacy of reasons. However, in the quest to understand the contextual factors shaping beliefs regarding social accounts, researchers have moved in the direction of motivated reasoning by examining such factors as employee trust in management (e.g., Bies, 1987). We suggest that these perspectives can be effectively combined to better understand reactions to planned organizational change.

By extending social accounts theory to better understand how managerial accounts function in complex organizational change, this study demonstrates that the context in which managerial accounts are offered can have powerful effects not only on the account's legitimacy (the traditional dependent variable in social accounts research) but also on the successful implementation of change. Moreover, it demonstrates that managerial accounts do not provide the whole picture in terms of the employee's understanding of the reasons for change. Consistent with motivated reasoning theory (Ajzen, 1985; McGill, 1989), change recipients do in fact form alternative explanations for change as a function of their trust in management, the psychological contract characterizing their relationship to the firm, and the beliefs held by their coworkers.

Our results suggest that the managerial account was more effective at justifying change than the two other causal interpretations employees deduced, a finding consistent with the theory of social accounts (Bies & Moag, 1987; Sitkin & Bies, 1993). However, this study also demonstrates that managerial accounts are not always received or remembered as managers intend. As one nurse relates her experience, "Maybe the administration could have had a meeting with staff to discuss/explain the hospital's rationale for going for Shared Governance. (But) one and a half years ago, it was sprung upon us suddenly (and) no one was prepared." Because complex change involves a variety of events, a social account of change is not necessarily a one-time thing. Analysis of data regarding hospital-wide council participation (not presented here) indicated that nurses involved in the councils were much more likely to believe that the change was associated with the managerial account, the need to improve care quality, than were nonparticipating peers because that topic was the repeated focus of council discussions. As one nurse who served on the quality council reported: "After being on quality council, I felt differently about myself, knew more about what was happening in the hospital, and was better able to persuade . . . why we should make a change in our unit. I felt people listened to me better. It changed the way I thought about myself as a nurse."

To a great extent, research on change has focused on management's perspective. Blau (1996) has cogently argued for the existence of distinct frames of reference for evaluating organizational actions and accountabilities—and a managerial perspective is only one of many. In a sense, the present study reframes the focus of research on social accounts to address the individual employee's role as an active participant in change. As the change studied here demonstrates, the causal accounts managers offer are not always accepted and may not even be received in the way they are intended. Moreover, reasons for complex organizational change can be difficult for managers to explain and for change recipients to understand. (One nurse said she believed that the change toward self-managing work groups was a form of "communism.")[2] In a sense, all organizational transformations risk a crisis of legitimacy. Change can alter core features of the organization and its relations with employees (Trice & Beyer, 1986), creating a sense of both confusion and loss (Bridges, 1991) even when management intends for employees to benefit from the change.

---

[2]Goodrick and Meindl (1995) maintain that despite resistance there has been a melding of managerial and humanistic ideologies in nursing to bridge two otherwise contradictory belief systems (humanistic concern and economic values). This evolution reflects a larger trend in the United States, with the increased popularity of business-management concepts extending the assumptions of private business firms into other organizations, including governments and nonprofits such as churches. However, such evolutionary processes are marked by resistance against revising the existing ideological order. In nursing, there has been resistance to the shifting emphasis on economic factors in clinical decision making (Bullough & Bullough, 1984), making it more likely that processes of social construction and resulting group-level effects on individual nurses would focus on the ideologically consistent message of quality improvement.

It is noteworthy that, in the organization we studied, economic motives were the most frequently attributed reason for change. However, despite the fact that economic reasons were rated to be as legitimate as quality improvement, economic reasons had comparatively weaker effects on implementation. This finding raises the question of whether economic factors alone are sufficient motivators of change for non-managerial employees. It is also possible that economic reasons had a weaker effect on implementation because they were not the social account offered by management. It is plausible that reasons for change outside the managerial account might lack sufficient supporting information to effectively promote change. However, economic reasons might also be less motivating than quality reasons because economic factors, though perceived to be relevant and legitimate, carry with them the connotation of adverse consequences such as loss of job security. (We are unable to test for the connotations of losses and gains associated with the reasons for change in the present study because we measure actual consequences rather than anticipated ones.)

Unless organizations implementing change in response to economic factors make an effort to address the benefits workers can expect to receive, employees might be more anxious about such changes, particularly in settings such as hospitals where economic factors were not traditionally evoked to motivate change.[3] In the case of this study's nurse population, quality improvement was consistent with the humanitarian core values of the nursing profession (Goodrick & Meindl, 1995)—and perhaps was an easier, more culturally compatible account for managers to offer.

This study raises the question of how best to provide information about the reasons for change. Given the central role played by trust, consistent information from credible sources over time appears to be key. Motivated reasoning is particularly pertinent to complex organizational change because complex interventions are more likely to engender active employee information seeking than are simpler interventions such as discrete policy changes (e.g., introducing nonsmoking policies; Babocel, McCline, & Folger, 1997). During complex change, the individuals' need for information typically increases, whereas both the quantity and quality of available information often decline (Bridges, 1991; Rousseau, 1996). This information gap evokes active employee sensemaking (Weick, 1995); that is, greater efforts to gather information and interpret events, typically through reliance on informal sources, observation, and recall. Thus, change recipients are likely to rely on a variety of information sources to make sense of what is happening, leading to more complex understandings of any managerial accounts provided as well as personally generated alternative explanations. The role of work-group beliefs in shaping individual attributions suggests that group-level interventions (e.g., meetings within each unit to discuss the reasons behind the change and its implementation) may be important to reinforce organization-wide change efforts.

---

[3]Using scenarios based on the facts of the organizational setting studied here, a follow-up study using masters-level students in business and health care management contrasted the impact of economic versus quality reasons on perceptions of losses and gains (Rousseau & Tijoriwala, 1997). Results indicate that economic reasons are associated with greater anticipated losses from change and quality reasons are associated with greater anticipated gains. Thus, we infer that at the time changes are introduced, economic reasons might tend to signal to change recipients that they stand to lose something (e.g., job security) as a result of the change, whereas quality reasons signal potential improvements and benefits (e.g., improved customer satisfaction or patient care).

Interestingly, the nature of the employment relationship plays a role in shaping whether the managerially offered account is received and believed, as well as in legitimating that account. Trust can operate here in two ways: first, by promoting a willingness to pay attention to managerial communications so the message is received, and second, increasing the believability of explanations that otherwise might appear to be imprecise, unclear, or confusing.

Management credibility, on the basis of a history of good-faith relations with employees, is likely to engender a positive response to change and the perception that reasons offered are legitimate (Kramer, 1996). Although distrust tends to promote monitoring, the informal seeking of information to discredit managerial accounts (Clark & Reis, 1988), high trust is likely to be associated with acceptance of information provided by management and a reduction of information-gathering efforts. Our findings support the argument that high trust creates a broad zone of acceptance of the exigencies of complex organizational change, whereas low trust necessitates greater care in the implementation process (Rousseau, 1996).

Psychological contracts play a particularly important role in influencing legitimacy in the eyes of employees. During change, transactional contracts can lead to a greater focus on the monetary nature of the exchange and less willingness to accept new responsibilities without increased compensation. In the words of one nurse with a transactional contract, "The hospital takes advantage of staff—we take on more responsibility and workload with no compensation or reward for all the hard work." In contrast, a relational contract reflects other-oriented and needs-based thinking, where a broad array of inducements and contributions form the exchange. As one nurse with a highly relational contract indicated, "The individual employee (has) more opportunity to develop his or her professional goals, which leads to growth in organization and client satisfaction." Employee psychological contracts with a strong relational quality have been theorized to create a greater zone of acceptance, that is, a willingness to accommodate to needs and requests expressed by the employer (Rousseau, 1995; Shapiro et al., 1995). Promoting such a broad zone of acceptance is likely to be affected by organizational conditions that strengthen the employment relationship, such as perceived organizational support (Eisenberger, Huntington. Hutchinson, & Sowa, 1986) and a history of good faith and fair dealing (Rousseau, 1996).

Lastly, reasons for change are likely to play a greater role in motivating change in its early phases. Once implementation is under way, the extent to which the change takes hold influences whether people experience its intended benefits. Although several of the work units studied here were still in the earliest stages of implementation after 2 years, our results demonstrate that the extent of implementation is positively related to perceived gains from change, specifically improvements in patient care quality and in nursing employability. Because implementation is a matter of degree, studies of planned organizational change might do well to consider the extent to which change recipients have accessed gains (or losses) from the change as one factor affecting responses to the change's later phases.

There are several methodological concerns with regard to this study. First, a one-time questionnaire was used to gather most of the data. Although path analytic methods were used to analyze the data, longitudinal data would have provided a more robust test of causation. Second, the alpha reliability of one measure of benefits, employability, was .67, below the conventional standard of .70. We included this measure in our analyses because research on this important variable is absent, despite the widespread concern that employees and the public have regarding the impact of organizational changes on job security or loss. We note that this variable enters into only one of the ten hypotheses, and its results are significant. Third, the reasons employees attributed to the change, although plausible in a variety of organizational settings, do not fully represent the domain of potential reasons that change recipients in other organizations might attribute. The three reasons used here were identified by extensive interviews with nurses prior to the construction and administration of the questionnaire. Thus, the reasons are applicable in this setting, and the scales developed to assess them may be idiosyncratic to this organization. However, grounded in the context of this organization, the reasons measured here do yield results largely consistent with motivated reasoning and social accounts theory.

A final concern we raise is the use of questionnaire data for all major variables studied. Although our results do show fairly high discriminant validity across different measures, relational factors, in particular trust, play a central role in most observed relationships. For this reason, we have used statistical tests that reduce some of the biases associated with multicollinearity (e.g., use of differences in our R^2s to test for moderator effects).

CONCLUSION

The causal interpretations employees rely on to understand change reflect a system of beliefs regarding their relationship with the organization and its management. The social influence of coworkers also plays a role in shaping how change is interpreted. For highly committed employees who trust management and are party to strong relational contracts, managerial accounts may be enough to legitimate change and begin the process of motivating employee participation. However, in complex organizational change, managerial accounts are not necessarily always heard, let alone understood. Our findings suggest that employees hear different messages from management depending on the nature of their relationship with the organization. Although managerial accounts are often needed to motivate change, such accounts may not be sufficient to directly alter behavior for workers low on trust or in settings where their coworkers do not believe management. In such circumstances, it may be critical to provide sufficient justification for change in the form of demonstrable benefits and valued consequences over time. Although a strong employment relationship is a predictor of implementation success, it can also be an outcome of effectively implemented change.

References

Ajzen, I. (1985). From intentions to actions: A theory of planned behavior. In J. Kuhn & J. Bechmann (Eds.), *Action control: From cognition to behavior* (pp. 11–39). Berlin, Germany: Springer-Verlag.

Babocel, D. R., McCline, R. L., & Folger, R. (1997). Letting them down gently: Conceptual advances in explaining controversial organizational policies. In C. L. Cooper & D. M. Rousseau (Eds.), *Trends in organizational behavior* (Vol. 4, pp. 73–87). London: Wiley.

Baron, R., & Kenny, D. (1986). The moderator–mediator variable distinction in social psychological research: Conceptual strategies and statistical considerations. *Journal of Personality and Social Psychology, 51,* 1173–1182.

Bass, B. M. (1985). *Leadership and performance beyond expectations.* New York: Free Press.

Bies, R. J. (1987). The predicament of injustice: The management of moral outrage. In L. L. Cummings & B. M. Staw (Eds.), *Research in organizational behavior* (Vol. 9, pp. 289–319). Greenwich, CT: JAI Press.

Bies, R. J., & Moag, J. S. (1986). Interactional justice: Communication criteria of fairness. In M. H. Bazerman,

R. Lewicki, & B. Sheppard (Eds.), *Research on negotiations in organizations* (Vol. 1, pp. 43–55). Greenwich, CT: JAI Press.

Bies, R. J., & Shapiro, D. L. (1993). Interactional fairness judgements: The influence of causal accounts. *Social Justice Research, 1,* 199–218.

Bies, R. J., Shapiro, D. L., & Cummings, L. L. (1988). Causal accounts and managing organizational conflict: Is it enough to say it's not my fault. *Communication Research, 15,* 381–399.

Blau, J. R. (1996). Organizations as overlapping jurisdictions: Restoring reason in organization accounts. *Administrative Science Quarterly, 41,* 172–179.

Breen, R. (1996). *Regression models: Censored, sample selected or truncated data.* [Quantitative Applications in the Social Sciences Series No. 07–111]. Thousand Oaks, CA: Sage.

Bridges, W. (1991). *Managing transitions: Making the most of change.* Reading, MA: Addison-Wesley.

Bullough, V. L., & Bullough, B. (1984). *The politics of nursing.* East Norwalk, CT: Appleton-Century-Crofts.

Clark, M. S., & Reis, H. T. (1988). Interpersonal processes in close relationships. *Annual Review of Psychology, 39,* 609–672.

Comrey, A. L. (1973). *An introduction to factor analysis.* New York: Academic Press.

Coser, L. A. (1956). *The function of social conflict.* New York: Free Press.

Dansereau, F., Alutto, J. A., & Yammarino, F. J. (1984). *Theory testing in organizational behavior: The variant approach.* Englewood Cliffs, NJ: Prentice Hall.

Einhorn, H. J., & Hogarth, R. M. (1986). Judging probable cause. *Psychological Bulletin, 99,* 3–19.

Eisenberger, R., Huntington, R., Hutchinson, S., & Sowa, D. (1986). Perceived organizational support. *Journal of Applied Psychology, 71,* 500–507.

Ex-manager describes the profit-driven life inside Columbia/HCA. (1997, May 30). *Wall Street Journal,* pp. Al, A6.

Fairhurst, G. T., & San, R. A. (1996). *The art of framing: Managing the language of leadership.* San Francisco: Jossey-Bass.

Gadow, S. (1980). Existential advocacy: Philosophical foundation of nursing. In S. F. Spicker & S. Gadow (Eds.), *Nursing: Images and ideals* (pp. 79–101). New York: Springer.

Goodrick, E., & Meindl, J. R. (1995, August). *Evolutionary bridging: The ideological transformation of the nursing profession.* Paper presented at the meeting of the Academy of Management, Vancouver, British Columbia, Canada.

Greenberg, J. (1994). Using social fair treatment to promote acceptance of a work site smoking ban. *Journal of Applied Psychology, 79,* 288–301.

Handy, C. (1989). *The age of unreason.* Cambridge, MA: Harvard Business School Press.

Harrison, B. (1994). *Lean and mean: The changing landscape of corporate power in the age of flexibility.* New York: Basic Books.

Kanter, R. M. (1989). *When giants learn to dance.* New York: Simon & Schuster.

Krackhardt, D., & Hanson, J. R. (1993, July–August). Informal networks: The company behind the chart. *Harvard Business Review, 71,* 104–111.

Kramer, R. M. (1996). Divergent realities and convergent disappointments in the hierarchic relation: Trust and the intuitive auditor at work. In R. M. Kramer & T. R. Tyler (Eds.), *Trust in organizations: Frontiers of theory and research* (pp. 216–245). Thousand Oaks, CA: Sage.

Levinson, H. (1962). *Organizational diagnosis.* Cambridge, MA: Harvard University Press.

Macneil, I. R. (1985). Relational contract: What we do and do not know. *Wisconsin Law Review,* 483–525.

McAllister, D. J. (1995). Affect- and cognition-based trust as foundations for interpersonal cooperation in organizations. *Academy of Management Journal, 38,* 24–59.

McGill, A. L. (1989). Context effects in judgments of causation. *Journal of Personality and Social Psychology, 57,* 189–200.

McGill, A. L. (1995). American and Thai managers' explanations for poor company performance: Role of perspective and culture in causal selection. *Organizational Behavior and Human Decision Processes, 61,* 16–27.

Mirvis, P. H., & Hall, D. T. (1994). Psychological success and the boundaryless career. *Journal of Organizational Behavior, 15,* 365–380.

Mishra, A. K. (1996). Organizational responses to crisis: The centrality of trust. In R. M. Kramer & T. R. Tyler (Eds.), *Trust in organizations: Frontiers of theory and research* (pp. 261–287). Thousand Oaks, CA: Sage.

Novelli, L., Kirkman, B. L., & Shapiro, D. L. (1995). Effective implementation of organizational change: An organizational justice perspective. In C. L. Cooper & D. M. Rousseau (Eds.), *Trends in organizational behavior* (Vol. 2, pp. 15–36). Chichester, England: Wiley.

Pfeffer, J. (1994). *Competitive advantage through people: Unleashing the power of the workforce.* Boston: Harvard Business School Press.

Pondy, L. R. (1978). Leadership is a language game. In M. W. McCall & M. M. Lombardo (Eds.), *Leadership: Where else can we go?* Durham, NC: Duke University Press.

Porter, M. E. (1990). *The competitive advantage of nations.* New York: Free Press.

Porter-O'Grady, T. (1984). *Shared governance for nursing: A creative approach to professional accountability.* Rockville, MD: Aspen Systems.

Porter-O'Grady, T. (1992). *Implementing shared governance: Creating professional organizations.* St. Louis, MO: Mosby.

Reichheld, F. F. (1996). *The loyalty effect: The hidden force behind growth, profits, and lasting value.* Boston: Harvard Business School Press.

Robinson, S. L., & Rousseau, D. M. (1994). Violating the psychological contract: Not the exception but the norm. *Journal of Organizational Behavior, 15,* 245–259.

Rousseau, D. M. (1989). Psychological and implied contracts in organizations. *Employee Rights and Responsibilities Journal, 2,* 121–139.

Rousseau, D. M. (1995). *Psychological contracts in organizations: Understanding written and unwritten agreements.* Newbury Park, CA: Sage.

Rousseau, D. M. (1996). Changing the deal while keeping the people. *Academy of Management Executive, 10,* 50–61.

Rousseau, D. M., & Tijoriwala, S. A. (1997). *Reasons for change and the attribution of loss.* Pittsburgh, PA: Carnegie Mellon University, Heinz School of Public Policy.

Salancik, G. R., & Pfeffer, J. (1978). A social information processing approach to job attitudes and task design. *Administrative Science Quarterly, 23,* 224–253.

Schneider, B., & Bowen, D. E. (1995). *Winning the service game.* Cambridge, MA: Harvard Business School Press.

Shapiro, D. L. (1991). The effects of explanations on negative reactions to deceit. *Administrative Science Quarterly, 36,* 614–630.

Shapiro, D. L., Buttner, E. H., & Barry, B. (1994). Explanations: What factors enhance their perceived adequacy? *Organizational and Human Decision Processes, 58,* 346–368.

Shapiro, D. L., Lewicki, R., & Devine, P. (1995). When do employees choose deceptive tactics to stop unwanted organizational change? A relational perspective. In R. J. Bies, R. J. Lewicki, & B. Sheppard (Eds.), *Research on negotiations in organizations* (Vol. 5, pp. 155–183). Greenwich, CT: JAI Press.

Shortell, S. M., Morrison, E. M., & Friedman, B. (1990). *Strategic choices for America's hospitals: Managing change in turbulent times.* San Francisco: Jossey-Bass.

Sitkin, S. B., & Bies, R. J. (1993). Social accounts in conflict situations: Using explanations to manage conflict. *Human Relations, 46,* 349–370.

Trice, H. M., & Beyer, J. M. (1986). Charisma and its routinization in two social movement organizations. In B. M. Staw & L. L. Cummings (Eds.), *Research in organizational behavior* (Vol. 8, pp. 113–164). Greenwich, CT: JAI Press.

Weick, K. E. (1995). *Sensemaking in organizations.* Thousand Oaks, CA: Sage.

Weiner, B. (1985). "Spontaneous" causal thinking. *Psychological Bulletin, 97,* 74–84.

Appendix 1

Questionnaire Scales

Reasons and Legitimacy Measures

"We would like to ask you two question regarding the reasons for change at _____. First, *in your opinion*, what are the *reasons* why _____ is implementing Shared Governance? Second to what extent to you think these reasons are *legitimate*, that is, appropriate and acceptable to you? Please go down the list twice. First answer the question in terms of whether each item is a reason for the change to Shared Governance at _____. Then, go down the list again and answer the question in terms of whether the reason is legitimate, acceptable, and appropriate to you."

Quality
>   Improve quality of work life
>   Improve quality of care
>   Increase nursing professionalism

Economic
>   Respond to changes in government regulation
>   Increase organizational profitability
>   Cut costs
>   Adjust to greater competition
>   Keep the hospital from losing money

Self-Serving
>   Get more work out of nurses for the same pay
>   For political reasons
>   Following current management fads

Psychological Contract Measures
>   "Let's consider the promises *you* have made to _____. In exchange for its commitments to you, you have made certain promises. *To what extent have you promised, implicitly or explicitly, to provide each of the following?* (Indicate your answer using the 1–5 scale.) Keep in mind we are *not* asking what you should provide _____ or what you believe _____ prefers. Instead, we are interested in what you *actually* promised to provide."

Relational Contract
>   Stay with hospital a minimum of two years after accepting job
>   Not look for a job elsewhere
>   Not support hospital's competitors
>   Accept a job change within your unit
>   Accept an internal transfer if necessary
>   Travel if necessary
>   Accept a transfer to another geographic location

Transactional Contract
>   Meet minimal acceptable standards for performance
>   Perform your job in a reliable manner
>   Behave in a professional manner
>   Protect confidential information
>   Dress in a professional manner
>   Follow hospital's norms and policies

Trust
>   "How credible or believable is the information each of the following *provides* to you regarding the change toward Shared Governance?"
>   Nursing administration
>   Clinical directors

Actual Changes
"What is the impact, that is, the gains and losses of Shared Governance, to you personally? Compare your present situation to what it was *before* Shared Governance was introduced."

Quality of Care
Performance quality
Ability to provide quality care

Employability
Job security
Employability throughout one's career

Implementation
Skills used in the job
Professional status
Personal development
Leadership development
Control over important aspects of my work
Understanding my role as a nurse

Positive Organizational Behavior (POB)

Implications for Leadership and HR Development and Motivation

Fred Luthans

Since the generally recognized very beginning of the organizational behavior (OB) field at the Hawthorne Works of the Western Electric Company, a clear relationship between workers' positive feelings and their performance has been documented. Over the years, OB researchers have demonstrated the importance of directly related constructs such as positive reinforcement and positive affect, positively oriented employee attitudes, incentive motivators, and even humor. All have been found to have a significant impact on performance. However, in spite of a positive perspective to OB having such an auspicious beginning, a fair amount of research support, and considerable face validity (i.e., it makes sense that confident, happy, optimistic employees at all levels are more productive), the OB field has arguably given relatively more attention to human dysfunctions and fixing weaknesses. Representative examples would include the search for how to better motivate marginal, inert, and problem employees; how to improve dysfunctional employee attitudes and behaviors such as resistance to change; and how to more effectively manage conflict and cope with stress and burnout.

Adapted from Luthans's POB article in *Academy of Management Executive* (2002, in press). For related articles, also see Luthans (2001, 2002; Luthans & Jensen, 2001; Luthans, Luthans, Hodgetts, & Luthans, 2001).

In the meantime, the "real world" popular best-sellers tend to be very positively oriented. Starting many years ago with Norman Vincent Peale's message of the "power of positive thinking" to Steven Covey's "seven habits" of highly effective people to today's runaway best seller by Spencer Johnson searching for "Who Moved My Cheese?", all have struck a very positive chord with professional managers. These positive, feel-good books cannot and should not be ignored. If the assumed goal is organizational, work-related performance improvement (instead of normative self-development), then both the OB academics and the "airport book" authors need to recognize and respect each other's purpose and role. However, with but a few exceptions, such as Gallup's recent best-selling books *First, Break All the Rules* (Buckingham & Coffman, 2001) and *Now, Discover Your Strengths* (Buckingham & Clifton, 1999), which are based on considerable empirical data analyzed by OB methodologies, and journals such as *Academy of Management Executive, Sloan Management Review* and *Organizational Dynamics*, which have the mission of translating academic-based theory and research into practice, the chasm seems to be widening.

The time has come to begin to build bridges between the OB field and the popular bestsellers. There seems little question that if the OB field proactively takes a positive approach, this would be a great first step. The popular authors recognize the importance of a positive approach to managing self and others but generally fail to inform or guide managers what and how to do it. This is where POB theories, research findings, and applications can make a needed, important contribution. My contention is not that the current OB field is all wrong and should be abandoned. After all, this would be a negative approach in itself. Rather, I argue that the time has come for a proactive positive approach as outlined in this article.

Obviously, there is much more to effective management of self and others than simply taking a positive approach. I propose that taking a positive perspective emphasizing managers' and employees' strengths rather than their weaknesses and the introduction of some new positively oriented OB concepts can help to contribute to more effective development and motivation of both managers/leaders themselves and their human resources. However, instead of borrowing from the platitudes and following "just do it" admonitions of the popular authors, to provide sustainable understanding and how to take a positive approach and build on people's strengths, POB must draw from the strengths of traditional OB by taking a theory-based and research-driven approach that can then be translated to effective application and practice.

DEFINING POSITIVE ORGANIZATIONAL BEHAVIOR (POB)

Using the positive psychology movement (e.g., see special issues in the January 2000 and March 2001 *American Psychologist* and Winter 2001 *Journal of Humanistic Psychology*) and traditional OB as the foundation and point of departure, I will specifically define *positive organizational behavior (POB)* as the study and application of positively oriented human resource strengths and psychological capacities that can be measured, developed, and effectively managed for performance improvement in today's workplace. Such a definition of POB would seem to incorporate many existing OB concepts in the domains of attitudes, personality, motivation, or leadership. However, to get around the criticism that nothing new is really being contributed (i.e., old wine in a new POB bottle), the criterion of relative uniqueness is added.

Also, the definitional criteria of being measurable and making a demonstrated contribution to performance improvement requires sound theory and research and thus clearly differentiates POB from the positively oriented, normative, personal-development best-sellers.

The definitional criterion of being developmental requires the POB constructs to be more statelike and rules out many of the more fixed, traitlike personality, attitudinal, and motivational variables traditionally associated with OB. Although there is a fine and somewhat controversial and arbitrary line between psychological states and traits (e.g., see Allen & Potkay, 1981, 1983; Zuckerman, 1983), being able to train and develop a positive approach to OB for managers themselves and with their people is critical to POB. Importantly, this developmental, resilience capability helps differentiate POB from positive psychology per se, much of traditional OB, and even the most recent "hard-wired" perspective being suggested by the evolutionary and neuropsychological approaches to OB (e.g., see Nicholsen, 1998; Pierce & White, 1999).

As to the relationship with motivation, POB is not intended to be a motivation theory per se. Rather, like OB in general, POB and its concepts that meet the definitional inclusion criteria have indirect, and in some cases direct, impact on self-motivation and motivating today's human resources for performance improvement. In one sense, motivation as a psychological construct and process is very closely related with positivity. In particular, widely recognized and used motivational concepts such as effort, striving, perseverance, incentive, aspiration, equity, achievement, and goal attainment have a very positive connotation. On the other hand, classical motivational wants, needs, deprivation, inequity, frustration, and deficiencies do not. POB and its attendant unique concepts are not intended to be equated with motivation or motivated effort. Instead, the POB approach in general and the various POB concepts that meet the criteria can perhaps best be portrayed as both motivated and motivating. For example, a positive outcome expectancy may motivate POB concepts or processes, while in terms of motivating self and others, the POB concepts and processes may regulate effort, striving, perseverance, level of aspiration, achievement, and goal attainment. Thus, this article is concerned with both HR development *and* motivation for performance improvement.

To best meet the operationally defined inclusion criteria for POB, I have CHOSEn the organizational leader and human resource strengths and psychological capacities of *c*onfidence (self-efficacy), *h*ope, *o*ptimism, *s*ubjective well-being (happiness), and *e*motional intelligence (or the acronym CHOSE). The following sections summarize the background and POB criteria fit of each of these five constructs, relevant applications to date, and potential practical implications for self and HR development and motivation.

CONFIDENCE OR SELF-EFFICACY: THE POB CONCEPT WITH THE MOST BACKUP

Although perhaps not as central to POB as, say, hope or optimism, most would agree that confidence—or more broadly and precisely used in psychology, the term self-efficacy—is a human resource strength and has the psychological capacity for developing and motivating improved performance. This POB concept has extensive theory building and research over the years. Self-efficacy may not measure up for fit as well as the other proposed concepts of

POB in terms of positivity and uniqueness. However, except for a small core group of academic researchers/advocates, efficacy is generally ignored or given very little attention in OB; see, for example, any OB textbook or HRM program. On the other hand, it could be argued that self-efficacy may best meet the remaining three POB criteria of valid measurement, ease of development, and potential motivation for performance improvement. In particular, the leading self-efficacy theorist and researcher, Albert Bandura (1986, 1997), strongly emphasizes that self-efficacy is the most pervading and important of the psychological mechanisms for positivity. He declares, "Unless people believe that they can produce desired effects and forestall undesired ones by their actions, they have little incentive to act. Whatever other factors may operate as motivators, they are rooted in the core belief that one has the power to produce desired results" (2000, p. 120). This proactive, positive efficacy belief is right in line with the POB approach.

The formal definition of self-efficacy that is usually used is Bandura's early statement of personal judgment or belief of "how well one can execute courses of action required to deal with prospective situations" (1982, p. 122). A somewhat broader, more workable definition for POB would be provided by Stajkovic and Luthans: "Self-efficacy refers to an individual's conviction (or confidence) about his or her abilities to mobilize the motivation, cognitive resources, and courses of action needed to successfully execute a specific task within a given context" (1998b, p. 66). It is important to note that these accepted definitions deal with efficacy for a specific task. An example of this statelike efficacy would be a systems analyst who may have high self-efficacy on solving a particular programming problem but low self-efficacy on writing up a report for the CIO on how the problem was solved. General self-efficacy, on the other hand, is conceptually the opposite; it is traitlike. That is, general efficacy is stable over time and across situations; in this regard it is like a personality trait and therefore does not meet the POB definitional criterion of being open to development. Bandura contends with his years of theory building and basic research that "an efficacy belief is not a decontextualized trait" (1997, p. 42). In POB, positive efficacy is treated as a state that can be developed and effectively managed.

The Process and Impact of Self-efficacy in POB

The self-efficacy process can positively affect human functioning before choices are selected and motivated effort is initiated. First, people tend to cognitively weigh, evaluate, and integrate information about their perceived capabilities. Importantly, this initial stage of the efficacy process has little to do with individuals' abilities or resources per se, but rather with how they perceive or believe they can use these abilities and resources to accomplish the given task in this context. A positive evaluation/perception leads to the expectations of personal efficacy, which, in turn, leads to positive choices, motivational effort, and perseverance. In addition, there is research evidence (see Mager, 1992) that positive efficacy and confidence can also directly affect positive thought patterns and resistance to stress.

The above examples of the direct impact of confidence or positive efficacy on employee motivation is illustrative of the potential power of understanding and applying POB. Importantly, perhaps the best profile of a high performer on a given task would be the highly confident employee who really gets into the task; gives whatever motivated effort it takes to successfully accomplish the task; perseveres when meeting obstacles, frustrations, or setbacks; has very positive self-thoughts; and is resistant to stress and burnout.

As if this high-performance profile is not enough, positive efficacy can also play a vital role in other important self and employee motivation dimensions such as goal aspirations and the perceived opportunities of a given project. The level of goal selected, amount of motivated effort expended to reach the selected goal, and the reaction and perseverance when problems are encountered in progressing toward the goal can all be greatly affected by positive efficacy (Bandura, 2000; Locke & Latham, 1990). So do the motivational incentives employees anticipate. Those with positive efficacy expect to succeed and gain favorable incentive motivators, while those with negative efficacy expect to fail and conjure up disincentives (i.e., "I won't get anything out of this anyway"). These motivational dimensions of confidence or positive efficacy are relevant not only to human resource performance on a task but also to a manager's strategy formulation, entrepreneurial start-ups, and even managing very difficult situations in transitional economies in post-communist countries (e.g., see Luthans, Stajkovic & Ibrayeva, 2000).

Specific Guidelines for Applying Self-efficacy to Develop and Motivate

In addition to meeting the POB criteria of positivity, uniqueness, and valid measurement (see Lee & Bobko, 1994), self-efficacy has a relatively established body of knowledge as to its applicability and significant impact on human resource performance. Specifically, in the Stajkovic and Luthans (1998a) meta-analysis of 114 studies and 21,616 subjects, a highly significant .38 weighted-average correlation between self-efficacy and work-related performance was found.

Because self-efficacy is a state, and there is such strong research support for the relationship between efficacy and work-related performance, efficacy training and development can have a positive impact on employee performance. Training can be set up around each (and in combination) of the four recognized sources of efficacy: (1) successful experiences; (2) vicarious learning or modeling; (3) positively oriented persuasion and feedback; and (4) physiological and psychological arousal (Bandura, 1997, 2000; Stajkovic & Luthans, (1998a, 1998b). For example, allowing trainees (both managers themselves and human resources in general) to experience success, practice frequently, observe relevant models, and receive positive feedback could all enhance their positive efficacy and resulting motivation to perform.

Unlike the popular self-development books, Bandura (2000) suggests techniques for how to develop self-regulatory competencies (i.e., self-motivation). Specifically, he suggests a variety of interlinked self-referent processes such as self-monitoring, self-efficacy appraisal, personal goal setting, and use of self-motivating incentives. Whether using the more pragmatic training aimed directly at enhancing the four sources or this self-motivational approach, there is proven effectiveness of this training and development of efficacy of organizational participants that can result in motivated performance improvement (Combs & Luthans, 2001; Gist, 1989; Gist, Bavett, & Stevens, 1990).

Besides training/development, positive efficacy also has implications for self-managed teams, job design, goal setting, and leadership. Some examples would be to enhance positive efficacy to better motivate productive teamwork and collective efficacy of self-managed teams. Other approaches would be to use job designs that provide more responsibility, challenge, and empowered personal control over the work in order to enhance the job holder's positive efficacy and resulting motivated performance. In setting goals, the goal difficulty and commitment will be affected by positive efficacy. By the same token, goal progress and attainment will in turn affect positive efficacy and subsequent performance.

Perhaps at least potentially the most significant, but still largely overlooked, implication for POB application lies in leadership efficacy. Although the importance of a leader's confidence has been recognized in the leadership literature over the years, to date there has been very little attempt to measure, research, and apply the proposition that a leader's efficacy will have a strong positive impact on followers. That is, the leader can serve as a positive model to enhance followers' efficacy and motivation. In total, there seems little question that a positive efficacy state has considerable implications for organizational leader and human resource development and motivation.

HOPE: A NEW CONCEPT FOR POB

Most people think of hope in terms of the feeling that "things will turn out for the best." Throughout history, the value of hope in human functioning has run the whole gamut. For example, Benjamin Franklin warned that "He who lives upon hope will die fasting," but philosopher Thomas Hobbes noted, "Appetite, with an opinion of attaining is called hope; the same, without such opinion, despair." As a positive psychology and now POB concept, however, hope has taken on a specific meaning. The operational definition, theory building, and research by clinical psychologist C. Rick Snyder (2000) is the most widely recognized. He believes that hope reflects not only the individual's motivational effort to achieve goals but also the person's belief that successful plans can be formulated and pathways identified in order to attain the goals. Snyder (2000) defines "being hopeful" as believing you can set goals, figure out how to achieve them, and motivate yourself to accomplish them; or simply hope involves both "willpower" and "waypower."

Considerable research so far by Snyder and his colleagues indicates that this defined hope has a very positive impact on academic achievement, athletic accomplishment, emotional health, and the ability to cope with illness and other hardships. The high-hope individual tends to be more certain of her or his goals and challenged by them; values progress towards goals as well as the goals themselves; enjoys interacting with people and readily adapts to new and collaborative relationships; is less anxious, especially in evaluative, stressful situations; and is more adaptive to environmental change (Snyder, 1997, 2000; Snyder, Tran, Schroeder, Pulvers, Adam, & Laub, 2000). This profile would seem to be ideal for today's managers and employees, yet, to date, such defined hope has received virtually no attention in the organizational behavior and HRM literature nor been researched in the workplace. However, hope definitely meets the inclusion criteria for POB. Besides being positive and unique to the OB field, it can be measured, developed and seemingly easily managed for motivated performance improvement.

How Hope Differs from Other POB Constructs

On the surface hope appears very similar to the other POB constructs, especially self-efficacy and optimism. Snyder (2000) and others (e.g., Magaletta & Oliver, 1999) do recognize similarities, but also give considerable attention to the conceptual independence of hope and the discriminant validity of the hope measures. For example, the willpower component of hope is similar to efficacy expectancies, and the hope pathways are close to efficacy outcome expectancies. However, Bandura (1997) would argue that the efficacy expectancies are all important, while Snyder's hope treats willpower (efficacy) and pathways (outcomes) as equally important. They operate in a combined, iterative manner.

As to optimism, Snyder (2000) points out that optimism expectancies are formed through others and forces outside self (i.e., Seligman's external attributional explanatory style, explained next), while hope pathways are initiated and determined through self. Snyder emphasizes that optimism does not imply pathways at all, but this is the vital part of hope. This pathways notion of hope also conceptually differentiates this POB construct from traditionally recognized OB constructs such as goal setting. The intent of this article is not to make such conceptual analyses, but like hope, each of the other selected POB constructs does have considerable evidence of theoretical independence and discriminant validity measures.

Hope Can Be Treated as Statelike

Along with the question of conceptual similarities and differences is whether hope (as well as the other PUB constructs) is a state or a trait. As was noted in the introductory comments, there is a fine, somewhat arbitrary, distinction between a state and a trait. As was just discussed in the case of self-efficacy, most conceptualizations of all the POB constructs, including hope, recognize them as being both traitlike and statelike. The key for POB is that hope (and the others) can be developed and lead to motivated performance. Importantly, hope (and the other POB constructs) has been theoretically proposed as being a traitlike disposition, but (like the others) is also proposed as being statelike, open to development and change. For example, Snyder and his colleagues have developed valid measures of hope as both a disposition and a state (Snyder et al., 1991, 1996). The psychometric analysis also indicates these hope scales are relatively uninfluenced by social desirability (Magaletta & Oliver, 1999).

The Potential for Hope in Developing and Motivating Human Resources

Although not yet directly tested in workplace applications, related research has found a significant relationship between hope measures and work-related goal expectancies, perceived control, self-esteem, positive emotions, coping, and achievement (e.g., see Curry, Snyder, Cook, Ruby, & Rehm, 1997). This growing research effort has found hope strongly related to academic and athletic success and mental and physical health. The carryover implications for human resource management seem clear. For example, there is already evidence that those with hope in stressful professions such as human services perform better and survive with the most satisfaction, are less emotionally exhausted, and are most likely to stay (Kirk & Koeske, 1995). However, research is still needed on the role of hope in other types of work. Like self-efficacy, hope may play an especially important role in certain types of jobs, such as in product development or sales, as well as having relevant applications to entrepreneurship and international human resource management in struggling economies. Our own initial research studies are finding that managers' level of hope is significantly related to their units' profitability and the satisfaction and retention of their employees (Peterson & Luthans, 2001). Finally, since hope is also statelike, it can be enhanced by training and development.

Some specific HR practice guidelines drawn from Snyder's work on developing hope would include: (1) obtain goal acceptance and commitment through participation and building self-efficacy; (2) determine specific stretch goals; (3) clarify goals and use a "stepping" method to break down complex, long-term strategies into substeps; (4) develop specific alternate and contingency pathways to goals; (5) develop the skill of "regoaling," which is to recognize the utility of persistence in the face of absolute goal blockage (i.e., avoid false hope); and (6) conduct mental rehearsals of important upcoming events. In total, the POB concept of hope seems to have considerable untapped potential for the development and effective management of self and human resources.

OPTIMISM: THE HEART OF POB

In defining optimism, positive psychologists go way beyond the old adage of the "power of positive thinking." Instead, optimism is treated as a cognitive characteristic in terms of motivational concepts such as positive outcome expectancy and/or a positive causal attribution. However, as the opening comments relating the POB concepts to motivation theory pointed out and positive psychologist Chris Peterson recently observed, "Optimism is not simply cold cognition, and if we forget the emotional flavor that pervades optimism, we can make little sense of the fact that optimism is both motivated and motivating" (2000, p. 45).

An attributional approach to optimism is most closely associated with the work of Seligman (1998). He uses the term "explanatory style" to depict how an individual attributes the causes of failure, misfortune or bad events as follows: (1) *Pessimists* make internal (their own fault), stable (will last a long time), and global (will undermine everything they do) attributions; and (2) *Optimists* make external (not their fault), unstable (temporary setback), and specific (problem only in this situation) attributions.

Similar to the other POB constructs, optimism can and sometimes is depicted as dispositional, traitlike. However, the temporariness and specificity of attributions (e.g., the attribution style used to explain events depends on the situation) also lend themselves to treating optimism as statelike, and thus are subject to learning and development. Seligman (1998) spells out this statelike notion of optimism in his well-received popular book, *Learned Optimism*. Everyday observation and empirical evidence finds that neutrals or even pessimists can be turned into optimists and vice-versa. Importantly for the POB approach, optimism has been shown to be significantly linked with desirable managerial/leadership and human resources characteristics such as happiness, perseverance, achievement, and health (Peterson, 2000; Seligman, 1998).

Role of Optimism in Developing and Motivating Human Resources

As discussed above, there is no question that optimism meets the POB criteria of being positive, relatively unique to the OB field, measurable, and able to be developed and managed for human resource performance improvement. It is both motivated and motivating and is related to desirable manager and employee characteristics. Obviously, by extrapolating this profile, at least realistic optimism can be a very positive motivational force in the workplace. For example, optimists are easily motivated to work harder; are more satisfied and have high morale; have high levels of motivational aspiration and set stretch goals; persevere in the face of obstacles and difficulties; analyze personal failures and setbacks as temporary, not a personal inadequacy, and view them as one-time, unique circumstances; and tend to make one feel upbeat and invigorated both physically and mentally. There are some jobs where such optimism would be obviously very valuable (e.g., sales, advertising, public relations, product design, customer service, and in the health and social services fields). However, there are also certain jobs that at least mild pessimism would be beneficial (e.g., some technical jobs such as safety engineering or jobs in financial control and accounting). It is for these reasons that realistic (Schneider, 2001) and/or flexible optimism is called for in POB.

For direct application of optimism in the workplace, Seligman again leads the way with his pioneering work at Metropolitan Life Insurance. After conferring with the president of this huge company, he was able to test the obvious hypothesis that optimism and its attendant motivation and perseverance was the key to sales success. A shortened version of his theory-based Attributional Style Questionnaire (ASQ) was administered to determine the explanatory styles of 200 experienced Met Life sales agents. Results were that sales agents who scored in the top optimistic half of the ASQ had sold 37% more insurance on average in their first 2 years than agents who scored in the pessimistic half. Agents whose ASQ optimism scores were in the top 10% sold 88 percent more than the most pessimistic tenth (Seligman, 1998). He also found that optimistic agents were much less likely to quit (a big problem in the insurance industry where about half turn over the first year).

He next launched a full-blown study involving 15,000 applicants to Met Life, who took both the standard industry selection test and the ASQ. One thousand were hired and, in addition, 129 more were hired (called the "Special Force") that had scored in the top half for optimism of those taking the ASQ, but had failed the industry test. The optimists (those who scored in the top half of the ASQ) outsold the pessimists by only 8% in the first year but 31% in the second year. The "Special Force" outsold the pessimists in the regular force by 21% the first year and 57% the second. This Special Force sold about the same as the optimists in the regular force. Met Life, on the basis of Seligman's studies, then adopted the ASQ as an important part of their selection process of new agents.

In addition to the comprehensive Met Life study, there have been other studies that test the impact of optimism in the workplace. For instance, a study by Boyatzis (1982) examined competent managers and found that they attribute their failures to a correctable mistake and then they persevere (i.e., an optimistic explanatory style). Other work on optimism has been applied to leadership. For instance, there has been wide recognition given in leadership theory to the importance of optimism. Recent studies have found the measured optimism of military cadets had a significant relationship with an expert's rating of their leadership potential (Chemers, Watson, & May, 2000). Another study found that a sample of business leaders were on average more optimistic than a normative sample; those most effective in initiating change were less pessimistic; and the more optimistic the leader, the more optimistic the followers (Wunderley, Reddy, & Dember, 1998). This latter finding implies that leaders can diffuse optimism into their workforce. There also have been publicized applications of deliberate attempts to use optimism in HRM such as in the selection process. One example is the highly successful Men's Wearhouse discount retailer, where an HRM executive recently declared:

> We don't look for people with specific levels of education and experience. We look for one criterion for hiring: optimism. We look for passion, excitement, energy. We want people who enjoy life. (Ransdell, 1998, p. 66)

Southwest Airlines is widely known for doing the same thing in its selection process.

Besides selection, another example is American Express Financial Advisors that uses optimism training with their associates. Such optimism training can follow specific guidelines such as: (1) identify self-defeating beliefs when faced with a challenge; (2) evaluate the accuracy of the beliefs (the trainees are encouraged to dispute their beliefs by proving them incorrect, select the least damaging cause thereby placing less blame on self, be realistic about implications, and/or assess the usefulness of holding the beliefs); and (3) once beliefs are discounted or improved, replace them with more constructive and accurate beliefs (Schulman, 1999). Overall, the past, present, and future of optimism as a POB construct seems very "optimistic."

HAPPINESS OR SUBJECTIVE WELL-BEING (SWB)

In addition to confidence/self-efficacy, hope, and optimism, the case can be made that happiness also meets the criteria of POB. In line with making the case for POB in general, the increasing popularity and importance of happiness reflects societal trends valuing the good life. Almost everyone now rates happiness over money (e.g., in a recent survey of 7,204 college students in 42 countries, only 6% rated money more important than happiness; see Diener, 2000; Suh, Diener, Oishi, & Triandis, 1998).

Similar to the departure from the common usage of other POB concepts such as self-efficacy for confidence, psychological theory and research prefers to use the broader term subjective well-being, or simply SWB, instead of happiness. Sometimes the terms are used interchangeably, but SWB is usually considered more comprehensive than happiness and involves people's affective (moods and emotions) and cognitive evaluations of their lives—their life satisfaction. Under this meaning, it is not necessarily what in reality happens to people that determines their state of happiness or subjective well-being, but instead how they emotionally interpret and cognitively process what happens to them that is the key.

Positive psychologist Ed Diener's (2000; Diener, Suh, Lucas, & Smith, 1999) work over the past three decades is most closely associated with SWB. In a theoretical analysis, Diener (2000) and his research group (Diener et al., 1999) make a break from simple feelings of happiness and just the demographic characteristics that correlate with it. Over 30 years ago, the derived profile of the happy person was dominated by descriptive demographics such as being young, well-educated, either sex, married, and well paid. Instead, interest has now shifted to the processes that underlie life satisfaction. Specifically, there has been a movement away from *who* is happy (i.e., the demographics) to *when* and *why* people are happy and on *what* the processes are that influence SWB (Diener, 2000). To recognize the comprehensive nature of SWB, Diener (2000) and colleagues have identified the positive components such as: (1) *life satisfaction* (the global judgments of one's life); (2) *satisfaction with important domains* (examples would include one's work); and (3) *positive affect* (the experience of many pleasant emotions and moods).

Diener and others have developed a number of valid measures of SWB components and their combinations over the years. Although questionnaires are mostly used, there are a few studies that use naturalistic experience sampling and even physiological measures, informants, and memory and reaction time. The research in recent years has mainly been concerned with SWB's underlying processes of personality, goals, adaptation, and coping (Diener, 2000; Diener et al., 1999)

The Potential for Applying SWB in the Workplace

Although not included in the mainstream organizational behavior or work motivation literature, SWB discussions in psychology do specifically mention work and the workplace as one of its domains, and there are some relevant research studies. In particular, SWB has a direct interest in and relationship with job satisfaction. A meta-analysis of 34 studies found an average correlation of .44 between job satisfaction and life satisfaction (Tait, Padgett, & Baldwin, 1989). To determine whether job satisfaction leads to SWB or vice-versa, Judge and his colleagues, using causal statistical designs, found that SWB was a significant predictor of job satisfaction 5 years later, but not vice-versa (Judge & Hulin, 1993; Judge & Watanabe, 1993). Thus, it appears that people who are satisfied with their lives tend to find more satisfaction in their work.

Even though there is a good start, the potential contribution that SWB can make to a POB approach seems to be just scratching the surface. Specifically, SWB will affect and be affected by life-impacting recent events such as the 9/11 terrorist attack on America and its economic and psychological aftermath, but also dramatic workplace changes such as telecommuting, virtual offices and teams, the digital divide, the 24/7 global competitive environment, and work-family practices. For example, ways to effectively develop and manage self and human resources' SWB in these "hot" but challenging dimensions of today's workplace would include making sure telecommuters and virtual team members have regularly scheduled face-to-face social opportunities with fellow employees (Fordyce, 1983; Okun, Stock, Haring, & Witter, 1984). Also, job assignments and career counseling need to maintain an optimal "flow" so that the manager's/employee's technical and family challenges are aligned with his/her time and skill. (Csikszentmihali, 1990, 1997). Both social relations and flow have been demonstrated to enhance individuals' SWB. In these turbulent times, there seems little question that SWB as a POB concept will take on added importance in future research and application in the workplace.

CURRENTLY POPULAR EMOTIONAL INTELLIGENCE OR EI

The important role that positive emotions have played in psychology over the years and Gardner's (1983) recognition of multiple intelligences can be used as a point of departure for the inclusion of emotional intelligence in POB. Although EI's theoretical roots are usually considered to go back many years to what was called social intelligence, Salovey and Mayer (1990) are usually given credit for providing the first definition about a decade ago, and their continuing work on EI provides the most comprehensive theory.

Initially, they defined emotional intelligence as "the subset of social intelligence that involves the ability to monitor one's own and others' feelings and emotions, to discriminate among them and to use this information to guide one's thinking and actions" (Salovey & Mayer, 1990, p. 189). More recently, they have noted that EI lies at the intersection of emotion and cognition and have identified the major components of EI as including the ability to: (1) perceive and express emotion; (2) assimilate emotion in thought; (3) understand and reason with emotion; and (4) regulate emotion in self and others (Mayer, Salovey, & Caruso, 2000). However, it was psychologist/journalist Goleman's (1995) best-selling book *Emotional Intelligence* that greatly popularized the construct. He simply defined emotional intelligence or EI as the capacity for recognizing one's own emotions and those of others.

EI as a POB Concept

Goleman, like Gardner (1983) before him, makes a clear distinction between IQ and EI (or sometimes called EQ as a take-off from IQ). The EI literature carefully points out that IQ and EQ are certainly not the same (i.e., IQ reflects mathematical/logical and verbal/linguistic dimensions and EQ the capacity for recognizing one's own and others emotions), but also do not necessarily have an inverse relationship. Initially, Goleman gave considerable attention to the role of genetic endowment, the brain, and even personality traits, but later emphasized that learning and emotional maturity play an important role in EI development. In his second book, *Working with Emotional Intelligence*, he states:

> Our level of emotional intelligence is not fixed genetically, nor does it develop only in early childhood. Unlike IQ, which changes little after our teen years, emotional intelligence seems to be largely learned, and it continues to develop as we go through life and learn from our experiences—our competence in it can keep growing. . . . There is an old-fashioned word for this growth in emotional intelligence: maturity. (1998b, p. 17)

These seeming contradictions between the roles of genetic endowment, the brain, personality traits, and learning/development have drawn criticism (e.g., Mayer et al., 2000). However, there is recent evidence that college students (full-time, part-time, and adult executive education students) have significantly improved (a range of 50–300%) their measured (behavioral scoring and paper-and-pencil assessments) EI from the time they enter an MBA program/curriculum designed to enhance their EI until they leave (Cameron, 1999). Goleman also cites "studies that have tracked people's level of emotional intelligence through the years show that people get better and better in these capabilities as they grow more adept at handling their empathy and social adroitness" (1998b, p. 7).

Even though Mayer and Solovey continue to build theory and measures (e.g., their Multifactor Emotional Intelligence Scale, or MEIS, is demonstrating predictive validity; see, for example, Ciarrochi, Chan, & Caputi, 2000), there is still some controversy surrounding EI. However, the time has come to recognize the impact that EI can have as a POB concept. EI is positive and relatively unique for OB, and there is enough supporting evidence that it can be measured and developed and can motivate performance improvement in today's workplace.

The Impact EI May Have in the Workplace

Goleman's publications and speaking/consulting on EI has considerable appeal with practicing managers. When he published *Emotional Intelligence* in 1995, Goleman had primarily aimed his book at the educational community, where it did receive a good response. However, he also received an unexpected overwhelming response from the business world. He recalls, "responding to a tidal wave of letters and faxes, e-mails and phone calls, requests to speak and consult, I found myself on a global odyssey, talking to thousands of people, from CEOs to secretaries, about what it means to bring emotional intelligence to work" (1998b, pp. 4–5). The appeal mostly came from the realization on the part of organizational participants at all levels that both success and effectiveness has more to do with what Goleman described as EI (i.e., self-awareness, self-regulation, self-motivation, empathy and social skills) than with raw intelligence (IQ), technical expertise, or even experience.

Initial Applied and Research Support for EI

Beyond the relevance of the work done on emotion and multiple intelligences, Mayer and Salovey's continuing work, Goleman's professional writing, and a few others, to date not much has been done directly on EI in the workplace. Examples of exceptions include a recent academic theoretical analysis indicating that EI may help facilitate individual employee adaptation and change (Huy, 1999) and academic propositions relating EI to teamwork, team performance, self and supervisor ratings, organizational commitment, organizational citizenship behaviors, and stress reduction (Abraham, 1999; Ashkanasy & Haertel, 2000; Bar-On, Brown, Kirkcaldy, & Thome, 2000).

In terms of empirical research, there is some longitudinal evidence indicating that EI is a better predictor of life success (economic well-being, satisfaction with life, friendship, family life), including occupational attainments, than IQ (Cameron, 1999; Stenberg, 1996). This type of evidence has been extrapolated to the catchy phrase: "IQ gets you hired, but EQ gets you promoted." Recent surveys do indicate that the majority of human resource managers believe this statement to be true and that it may even hold for highly technical jobs such as scientists and engineers. When the 10–15% of scientists/engineers judged to be "stars" at AT&T's Bell Labs were compared to everyone else, it was found that neither academic talent nor IQ was a good predictor of on-the-job productivity. Rather, the difference was that the stars were observed (not quantitatively measured) to use EI dimensions such as social skills to build a network of relationships that they could call on and would get right back to them to help solve a problem or handle a crisis (Kelley & Caplan, 1993). Also, the Center for Creative Leadership found that "derailed executives" (rising stars who flamed out) failed because of EI-type problems (poor working relations, too authoritarian, too ambitious, conflict with upper management) rather than a lack of technical ability (Gibbs, 1995; Goleman, 1998).

Application of EI to Executive Leadership

Most recently, Goleman has moved EI into the broader-based domain of leadership. He drew upon a large random sample ($N=3,871$) from a consulting firm database of 20,000 executives to find six distinct leadership styles that relate to the different components of EI (Goleman, 1998a, 2000). Well-known social psychologist David McClelland had earlier found that leaders with EI competencies were more effective than counterparts without them. For example, in one study of division heads of a global food and beverage company, McClelland had found that of those leaders with EI competencies, 87% placed in the top third for bonuses based on performance and their divisions on average outperformed yearly revenue targets by 15–20% (Goleman, 2000). Thus, based on these types of findings, Goleman went on to identify specific EI competencies (e.g., initiative, empathy, self-awareness) associated with each style of leadership.

Besides Goleman's work on leadership, OB research, such as a study finding that levels of self-awareness significantly related to measures of EI and transformational leadership behaviors, is starting to emerge (Sosik & Megeriam, 1999). Well-known leadership researchers such as Bass (2002) and George (2000) are beginning to directly explore the role of EI.

Other EI Applications

Based on the popularity of Goleman's writings/programs and the slowly emerging theoretical and empirical base, today's organizations are starting to implement various EI approaches (Cooper, 1997; Stuller, 1997). For example, the U.S. Air Force uses EI tests to select applicants after finding that their recruiters who had high EI scores were 2.6 times more successful. Big corporations such as American Express, Bank of America, Ford, GE, CIGNA, Blue Cross Blue Shield, and McNeil/Johnson and Johnson are known for developing in-house EI strategies, which mainly consist of self-awareness and empathy training using exercises and modeling. For example, Ford built collective emotional intelligence into their Lincoln Continental team (about 1,000 people and a $1 billion budget) that resulted in one of the automaker's first programs to meet or exceed all objectives. In the service sector, Blue Cross/Blue Shield uses an EI counseling/training approach to help their employees in developing self-awareness and empathy to deal with change, emotionally charged work situations, and professional goals.

There are also applications of EI being made internationally. For example, EI training is conducted at both Hong Kong Telecom and for Hong Kong government employees to manage their own and others' emotions in order to better cope with and effectively resolve emotional issues and complaints. Overall, there seems little doubt of the importance and relevancy of EI as a POB concept, but even relatively more than the others, there is need for additional theory development, valid measures, and especially research in future effective application.

SUMMARY AND CONCLUSIONS

This article proposes positive organizational behavior (POB) and the attendant concepts of confidence/self-efficacy, hope, optimism, subjective well-being/happiness, and emotional intelligence. Briefly summarized in Figure 1, I CHOSE these five concepts because they best meet the definition of POB and fit the specific criteria of being: (1) positive, (2) unique, (3) measurable, (4) capable of being learned and developed, and (5) adaptable to motivating human resources for performance improvement. Relatively most attention was given to confidence because of the considerable theory, research, and application given to self-efficacy over the years. Some may argue against giving such weight to self-efficacy because it is given only indirect attention in positive psychology and it is not unique enough. I would argue that self-efficacy, the belief or confidence that one can successfully accomplish a given task, is extremely positive and, even though it is in the mainstream of psychology (if not positive psychology), it has been largely overlooked by the OB field, and therefore meets the relative uniqueness criterion for POB. As for the other three criteria of being validly measured, open to statelike development, and having implications for workplace performance improvement, the discussion indicated positive efficacy may make the best fit.

The remaining four POB concepts of hope, optimism, subjective well-being, and emotional intelligence certainly meet the positivity and uniqueness standards for POB but have a degree of variability in meeting the remaining criteria. For example, to date, EI has some problems with measurement, and all four can be conceptualized as having some traitlike dispositional characteristics. Importantly, however, as was pointed out in the discussion of each, all four most assuredly also have statelike capabilities adaptable to self and human resource development. The traitlike characteristics would suggest application to the HR selection process, but unless they are statelike, POB would not be able to significantly contribute to HR development and the most important fifth criterion of being adaptable to HRM for motivating performance improvement. This performance improvement criterion is yet to be fully demonstrated by research and practice in the workplace. However, for the future, the application to both organizational leaders' and their human resources' development and motivation is what

FIGURE 1 Representative POB Concepts (CHOSE)

The following concepts meet the criteria for being included in POB by being positive, relatively unique to OB, measurable, and capable of developing and motivating organizational leaders and human resources.

1. **CONFIDENCE/SELF-EFFICACY:** One's belief (confidence) in being able to successfully execute a specific task in a given context.
   - Specific not general
   - Performance process: involvement, effort, perseverance
   - Sources: mastery experiences, vicarious learning/modeling, social persuasion, physiological/psychological arousal

2. **HOPE:** One who sets goals, figures out how to achieve them (identify pathways) and is self-motivated to accomplish them, that is, willpower and "waypower."
   - Beyond feelings of things will work out for the best
   - Brand new concept for OB with considerable performance potential
   - Valid measures show positive link with goal expectancies, perceived control, self-esteem, positive emotions, coping, and achievement

3. **OPTIMISM:** Positive outcome expectancy and/or a positive causal attribution, but is still emotional and linked with happiness, perseverance, and success.
   - Beyond "Power of Positive Thinking"
   - Both motivated and motivating
   - Seligman's optimistic Explanatory Style of bad event: external, unstable, specific

4. **SUBJECTIVE WELL-BEING:** Beyond happiness emotion, how people cognitively process and evaluate their lives, the satisfaction with their lives.
   - Beyond demographics to *when* and *why* people are happy
   - Components of SWB: life satisfaction, satisfaction with important domains such as the workplace, and positive affect
   - SWB leads to job satisfaction, but not necessarily the reverse

5. **EMOTIONAL INTELLIGENCE:** Capacity for recognizing and managing one's own and others emotions—self awareness, self-motivation, being empathetic, and having social skills.
   - Currently very popular
   - One of the multiple intelligences
   - "IQ gets you the job, EQ gets you promoted."

will be the real value of POB. This development and performance orientation is what separates POB from the broader-based, more end-in-itself positive psychology movement and the normative self-development popular books. This article will hopefully generate the needed research and effective practice on the CHOSE concepts and others that need to be added to make POB a reality for developing and motivating organizational leaders and their human resources in the challenging years ahead.

References

Abraham, R. 1999. Emotional intelligence in organizations: A conceptualization. *Genetic, Social, and General Psychology Monographs*, 125(2): 209–224.

Allen, B. P., & Potkay, C. R. 1981. On the arbitrary distinction between states and traits. *Journal of Personality and Social Psychology*, 41: 916–928.

Allen, B. P., & Potkay, C. R. 1983. Just as arbitrary as ever. *Journal of Personality and Social Psychology*, 44: 1087–1089.

Ashkanasy, N. M., & Haertel, C. E. (Eds.). 2000. *Emotions in the workplace: Research, theory and practice*. Westport, CT: Quorum Books/Greenwood Publishing.

Bandura, A. 1982. Self-efficacy mechanism in human agency. *American Psychologist*, 37: 122–147.

Bandura, A. 1986. *Social foundations of thought and action*. Englewood Cliffs, NJ: Prentice Hall.

Bandura, A. 1997. *Self-efficacy: The exercise of control*. New York: Freeman.

Bandura, A. 2000. Cultivate self-efficacy for personal and organizational effectiveness. In Locke, E.A. (Ed.), *The Blackwell handbook of principles of organizational behavior*: 120–136. Oxford, U.K.: Blackwell.

Bar-On, R. 1997. *Bar-On Emotional Quotient Inventory: Technical Manual*. New York, NY: Multi-Health Systems.

Bar-On, R., Brown, J. M., Kirkcaldy, B. D., & Thome, E. P. 2000. Emotional expression and implications for occupational stress: An application of the Emotional Quotient Inventory (EQ-i). *Personality and Individual Differences*, 28: 1107–1118.

Bass, B. M. 2000. Cognitive, social, and emotional intelligence of transformational leaders. In Riggio, R. E., Murphy, S., & Pirozzolo, F. J. (Eds.), *Multiple intelligences and leadership*: 105–118. Mahwah, NJ: Lawrence Erlbaum.

Boyatzis, R. 1982. *The competent manager: A model for effective performance*. New York: Wiley.

Buckingham, M., & Clifton, D. 2001. *Now, discover your strengths*. New York: The Free Press.

Buckingham, M., & Coffman, C. 1999. *First, break all the rules*. New York: Simon & Schuster.

Cameron, K. 1999. Developing emotional intelligence at the Weatherhead School of Management. *Strategy: The Magazine of Weatherhead School of Management*, Winter: 2–3.

Chemers, M. M., Watson, C. B., & May, S. T. 2000. Dispositional affect and leadership effectiveness: A comparison of self-esteem, optimism, and efficacy. *Personality and Social Psychology Bulletin*, 26: 267–277.

Ciarrochi, J. V., Chan., A. V. C., & Caputi, P. 2000. A critical evaluation of the emotional intelligence construct. *Personality and Individual Differences*, 28: 539–561.

Combs, G. M., & Luthans, F. 2001. The impact of self-efficacy on diversity training effectiveness: A field experimental analysis. Paper presented at Academy of Management, OB Division, Washington, DC.

Cooper, R. K. 1997. Applying emotional intelligence in the workplace. *Training and Development*, December: 31–38.

Csikszentmihalyi, M. 1990. *Flow: The psychology of optimal experience*. New York: Harper & Row.

Csikszentmihalyi, M. 1997. *Activity, experience, and personal growth*. Champaign, IL: Human Kinetics.

Curry, L. A., Snyder, C. R., Cook, D. L., Ruby, B. C., & Rehm, M. 1997. Role of hope in academic and sport achievement. *Journal of Personality and Social Psychology*, 73: 1257–1267.

Diener, E. 2000. Subjective well-being: The science of happiness and a proposal for a national index. *American Psychologist*, 55: 34.

Diener, E., Suh, E. M., Lucas, R. E., & Smith, H. L. 1999. Subjective well-being: Three decades of progress. *Psychological Bulletin*, 125: 276–302.

Fordyce, M. 1983. A program to increase happiness. *Journal of Counseling Psychology*, 30: 483-498.

Gardner, H. 1983. *Frames of mind: The theory of multiple intelligences*. New York: Basic Books.

George, J. M. 2000. Emotions and leadership: The role of emotional intelligence. *Human Relations*, 53: 1027–1055.

Gibbs, N. 1995. The EQ factor. *Time*, October 2: 61.

Gist, M. E. 1989. The influence of training method on self-efficacy and idea generation among managers. *Personnel Psychology*, 42: 787–805.

Gist, M. E., Bavetta, A. G., & Stevens, C. K. 1990. Transfer training method. *Personnel Psychology*, 43: 501–523.

Goleman, D. 1995. *Emotional intelligence*. New York: Bantam Books.

Goleman, D. 1998a. What makes a leader? *Harvard Business Review*, November–December: 94–102.

Goleman, D. 1998b. *Working with emotional intelligence*. New York: Bantam Books.

Goleman, D. 2000. Leadership that gets results. *Harvard Business Review*, March–April: 79–90.

Huy, Q. N. 1999. Emotional capability, emotional intelligence, and radical change. *Academy of Management Review*, 14:325–345.

Judge, T. A., & Hulin, C. L. 1993. Job satisfaction as a reflection of disposition: A multiple source causal analysis. *Organizational Behavior and Human Decision Processes*, 56: 388–421.

Judge, T. A., & Watanabe, S. 1993. Another look at the job satisfaction–life satisfaction relationship. *Journal of Applied Psychology*, 78: 939–948.

Kelley, R., & Caplan, J. 1993. How Bell Labs creates star performers. *Harvard Business Review*, July–August: 128–139.

Kirk, S., & Koeske, G. 1995. The fate of optimism: A longitudinal study of case managers' hopefulness and subsequent morale. *Research in Social Work Practice*, 5(1): 47–61.

Lee, C., & Bobko, P. 1994. Self-efficacy beliefs: Comparison of five measures. *Journal of Applied Psychology*, 79: 364–369.

Locke, E. A., & Latham, G. P. 1990. *A theory of goal setting and task performance*. Englewood Cliffs, NJ: Prentice Hall.

Luthans, F. 2001. The case for positive organizational behavior (POB). *Current Issues in Management*, 1(1): 10–21.

Luthans, F. 2002. Positive psychology approach to OB. In Luthans, F., *Organizational behavior*, 9th ed., 286–322. New York: McGraw-Hill/Irwin.

Luthans, F., & Jensen, S. M. 2001. Positive organizational behavior: A new approach to global management. *Nanyang (Singapore) Business Review*, 1(1): 14–25.

Luthans, F., Luthans, K. W., Hodgetts, R. M., & Luthans, B. C. 2001. Positive approach to leadership (PAL): Implications for today's organizations. *The Journal of Leadership Studies* 8(2), in press.

Luthans, F., Stajkovic, A. D., & Ibrayeva, E. 2000. Environmental and psychological challenges facing entrepreneurial development in transitional economies. *Journal of World Business* 35: 95–110.

Magaletta, P. R., & Oliver, J. M. 1999. The hope construct, will and ways: Their relations with self-efficacy, optimism, and general well-being. *Journal of Clinical Psychology*, 55: 539–551.

Mager, R. F. 1992. No self-efficacy, no performance. *Training*, 32: 34–36.

Mayer, J. D., Salovey, P., & Caruso, D. 2000. Models of emotional intelligence. In Sternberg, R. J. (Ed.), *Handbook of intelligence*. Cambridge, UK: Cambridge University Press.

Nicholsen, N. 1998. How hardwired is human behavior? *Harvard Business Review*, July–August: 135–147.

Okun, M., Stock, W., Haring, M., & Witter, R. 1984. Health and subjective well-being: A meta-analysis. *International Journal of Aging and Human* Development 19: 111–132.

Peterson, C. 2000. The future of optimism. *American Psychologist*, 55: 44–55.

Peterson, S. J., & Luthans, F. 2001. Does the manager's level of hope matter? Preliminary research evidence of a positive impact. Unpublished manuscript.

Pierce, B. D., & White, R. 1999. The evolution of social structure: Why biology matters. *Academy of Management Review*, 24: 843–853.

Ransdell, E. 1998. They sell suits with soul. *Fast Company*, October: 66–68.

Salovey, P., & Mayer, J. D. 1990. Emotional intelligence. *Imagination, Cognition and* Personality, 9(3): 185–211.

Scheier, M. F., & Carver, C. S. 1992. Effects of optimism on psychological and physical well being. *Cognitive Therapy and Research*, 16: 201–228.

Schneider, S. L. 2001. In search of realistic optimism: Meaning, knowledge, and warm fuzziness. *American Psychologist*, 56: 250–263.

Schulman, P. 1999. Applying learned optimism to increase sales productivity. *Journal of Personal Selling & Sales Management*, 19: 31–37.

Seligman, M. E. P. 1998. *Learned optimism*. New York: Pocket Books.

Seligman, M. E. P., & Csikszentmihalyi, M. 2000. Positive psychology: An introduction. *American Psychologist*, 55: 5–14.

Snyder, C. R. 1997. Hope: An individual motive for social commerce. *Group Dynamics*, 1: 107–118.

Snyder, C. R. 2000. *Handbook of Hope*. San Diego, CA: Academic Press.

Snyder, C. R., Tran, T., Schroeder, L., Pulvers, K., Adams, J., & Laub, L. 2000. Teaching the hope recipe: Setting goals, finding pathways to those goals, and getting motivated. *National Education Service*: 46–50.

Snyder, C. R., Harris, C., Anderson, J. R., Holleran, S. A., Irving, L. M., Sigmon, S. T., Yoshinobu, L., Gibb, J., Langelle, C., Harney, P. 1991. The will and the ways: Development and validation of an individual-differences measure of hope. *Journal of Personality and Social Psychology,* 60: 570–585.

Snyder, C. R., Sympson, S. C., Ybasco, F. C., Borders, T. F., Babyak, M. A., Higgins, R. L. 1996. Development and validation of the State Hope Scale. *Journal of Personality and Social Psychology,* 70: 321–335.

Sosik, J. J., & Megerian, L. E. 1999. Understanding leader emotional intelligence and performance. The role of self-other agreement on transformational leadership perceptions. *Group and Organization Management*, 24: 367–390.

Stajkovic, A. D., & Luthans, F. 1998a. Self-efficacy and work-related performance: A meta-analysis. *Psychological Bulletin*, 124: 240–261.

Stajkovic, A. D., & Luthans, F. 1998b. Social cognitive theory and self-efficacy: Going beyond traditional motivational and behavioral approaches. *Organizational Dynamics*, 26(4): 62–74.

Stenberg, R. 1996. *Successful intelligence*. New York: Simon & Schuster.

Stuller, J. 1997. EQ: Edging toward respectability. *Training*, June: 43–48.

Suh, E., Diener, E., Oishi, S., & Triandis, H. 1998. The shifting basis of life satisfaction judgments across cultures: Emotions versus norms. *Journal of Personality and Social Psychology*, 74: 482–493.

Tait, M., Padgett, M. Y., & Baldwin, T. T. 1989. Job satisfaction and life satisfaction: A reexamination of the strength of the relationship and gender effects as a function of the date of the study. *Journal of Applied Psychology,* 74: 502–507.

Wanberg, C. R. 1997. Antecedents and outcomes of coping behaviors among unemployed and reemployed individuals. *Journal of Applied Psychology*, 82: 731–744.

Wunderley, L. J., Reddy, W. B., & Dember, W. N. 1998. Optimism and pessimism in business leaders. *Journal of Applied Social Psychology*, 28: 751–760.

Zuckerman, M. 1983. The distinction between trait and state scales is *not* arbitrary. *Journal of Personality and Social Psychology*, 44: 1083–1086.

Chapter **Four**

The Role of Goals and Intentions in Motivation

Goals and intentions are obviously a subset of cognitions. Because the topic has received so much attention in the work motivation literature in recent years ("the 800-pound gorilla in the work motivation literature," as Mitchell put it in his article in Chapter 1), we devote a separate chapter to this subject rather than including it as part of the preceding chapter (Chapter 3) on "The Role of Cognitions . . ." The dominant theory of goal setting, by Locke, was previously covered in his article on the subject in Chapter 2. In the present chapter, we include several articles that deal with research findings relating to specific aspects of the goal-setting process and to some of the effects of goals on performance and behavior.

As Locke stressed in his article, goals involve certain kinds of ideas, namely those that are addressed to "the object or aim of an action." Thus, as Locke also noted, an emphasis on goals and goal setting in the work motivation literature is also consistent with the "cognitive revolution" in psychology that began in the late 1970s and is still a highly prominent at the beginning of the 21st century. It is, therefore, no accident that scholars in the field of motivation in organizational settings have made the study of the effects of goals a significant and often-researched topic. Much of the early work was focused on determining whether goal setting has a positive effect on work performance. That issue, as Locke's article summarizes, has been settled in the affirmative in terms of a general finding: "Goals affect performance by affecting the direction of action, the degree of effort exerted, and the persistence of action over time" ("Finding #9"). Furthermore, research has also shown that certain types of goals, those that are specific and difficult, tend to produce the most consistent positive effects on performance.

What has not been settled yet in any comprehensive way is how well a goal-setting approach works on a day-to-day basis within the larger organizational context. Although a fair amount of field research has been carried out demonstrating the positive effects of goal setting on performance enhancement for specific individuals or groups in actual work situations, we still know relatively little about how well it works as a widespread motivational approach on a long-term basis when implemented on a broad scale within complexly structured organizations. To illustrate this point, one only has to consider the fate of many Management

By Objectives (MBO) programs that were highly popular in the corporate sector in the 1970s and 1980s. Although such MBO programs involve more than just goal setting, especially issues relating to the measurement of performance and any follow-up efforts to deal with lack of goal attainment, they probably have constituted the most widely implemented type of organizational goal-setting-based initiatives in the "real world" of work. Many of these former MBO programs have been discontinued, and their popularity today is greatly decreased compared to several decades ago. The reasons: difficulties of sustaining the programs on a systematic basis across time in organizationally complex circumstances and the frequent problems in maintaining employee and managerial interest. (For an excellent discussion of MBO programs in relation to goal setting, see Pinder [1998, pp. 393–406].) The lesson to be learned from organizations' experiences with MBO programs is not that the basic principles of goal setting do not work; rather, it is that there are major obstacles in translating those principles into formal organizationwide systems of motivation intended to be effective on a more or less "permanent" or at least long-term basis. Therefore, evidence from the forays of many companies into the MBO realm suggests that trying to turn the high potential of goal setting approaches into effective, consistent, and persistent organizational practices remains a major managerial challenge.

OVERVIEW OF THE READINGS

As we noted at the outset of this chapter, the articles that follow address several specific issues related to goals and goal setting and their effect on motivation and performance. The first article, by Klein et al., involves a systematic, quantitative review (a "meta-analysis") of the findings from 80-plus studies on the impact of goal commitment—the "determination to reach goals." The authors' synthesis of the results of these studies looked at both the antecedents and the consequences of goal commitment. What was found was that the expectancy and attractiveness of goal attainment contributed to goal commitment, and goal commitment in turn had a "strong positive effect" on performance. Their findings help shed light on what factors are necessary conditions for the process of goal setting to achieve its potentially positive effects on performance.

Much of the goal setting literature to date has focused on the effects of goal setting on the performance of individuals. The next article in this chapter, however, shifts the focus to an assessment of the influence of group goals on group performance. Here again, as with the preceding article by Klein et al., the authors (O'Leary-Kelly, Martocchio, and Frink) utilized meta-analytic quantitative techniques to review the findings from 10 studies of group goals. In addition, however, they also conducted a qualitative analysis of the findings from 29 studies (including the 10 studies in the meta-analysis) that investigated the phenomenon of group goals. This qualitative analysis centered on a set of eight variables that potentially could moderate the relationship between group goals and group performance. These include such moderator variables as goal specificity, goal difficulty, goal source, and the like. The overall findings showed that goal setting had a main effect: that is, groups that set goals had higher performance than groups that did not. However, in those studies where this result did not occur (and consistent issues raised in our earlier discussion), it was in "field settings and when organization members were working in intact teams toward assigned goals over time."

In the third article in this chapter, Crown and Rosse address a different aspect of the issue of the effect of group goals on performance: namely, the combination of individual *and* group goals in influencing performance. The primary issue they examined was the focus or nature of individual goals and how that variable might impact the performance of groups of which individuals were a part. Their study involved 60 intact groups and an experimental task. The results indicated that for interdependent tasks it was especially important for individuals to have goals for how their individual contributions could contribute to group goals, as well as also having goals for the group. This combination was better than a focus only on purely individual goals or only on group goals. More broadly, this study emphasizes the complexity of combining individual and group goals in a group performance work situation.

Reference

Pinder, C. C. (1998). *Work motivation in organizational behavior.* Upper Saddle River, NJ: Prentice Hall.

Goal Commitment and the Goal-Setting Process: Conceptual Clarification and Empirical Synthesis

Howard J. Klein
Michael J. Wesson
John R. Hollenbeck
Bradley J. Alge

Motivation continues to be a compelling topic for managers and researchers. In this vast literature, goals have emerged as a central, pervasive construct (Austin & Vancouver, 1996). Goals are particularly integral among current theories of motivation that emphasize self-regulation. These perspectives include task goal theory (e.g., Locke & Latham, 1990), social–cognitive theory (e.g., Bandura, 1986), resource allocation theory (e.g., Kanfer & Ackerman, 1989), and control theory (Klein, 1989). These theories differ in several respects, but all feature goals as a central determinant of motivation (Phillips, Hollenbeck, & Ilgen, 1996). The bulk of the work examining goals as predictors of performance has been done within task goal theory. The basic finding from this theory is that under certain conditions, specific, difficult goals can lead to higher levels of performance relative to vague or easy goals (see Locke & Latham, 1990). One of the most often cited assumptions or conditions necessary for this relationship to hold is that there is *commitment* to that specific, difficult goal. Goal commitment, one's determination to reach a goal (Locke & Latham, 1990), has been a central concept in goal-setting theory since its inception.

In his 1968 article that launched the theory, as well as in two subsequent reviews of the goal-setting literature (Locke, Shaw, Saari, & Latham, 1981; Locke & Latham, 1990), Locke and his colleagues recognized that if there is no commitment, a goal can have no motivational effect. Although goal commitment has played a central conceptual role in the development of task goal theory, the empirical examination of goal commitment was largely absent from early goal-setting research. Two separate reviews published in the late 1980s (Hollenbeck & Klein, 1987; Locke, Latham, & Erez, 1988) noted that the body of empirical evidence on goal commitment's consequences and antecedents was insufficient given the variable's central role in the goal-setting process. In fact, Hollenbeck and Klein concluded that the most frequent treatment of goal commitment in the goal-setting literature was to not measure the variable at all but then to offer it up as an unvalidated, post hoc explanation whenever the goal difficulty effect was negligible, weak, or conditional on other variables.

Those reviews reiterated the important role of goal commitment, documented the absence of systematic research investigating this crucial construct, and provided frameworks for guiding its investigation. Research in the area of goal setting has paid more attention to the construct of goal commitment in the wake of those reviews. The purpose of this article is to report the results of a meta-analysis that examined the consequences and antecedents of goal commitment. This meta-analysis updates the goal commitment literature roughly 10 years after the Locke et al. (1988) and Hollenbeck and Klein (1987) reviews and, using that

From *Journal of Applied Psychology*, 1999, 84(6), 885–896. Reprinted with permission.

aggregate empirical evidence, seeks to clarify the role of goal commitment in the goal-setting process and identify key areas for future research.

CONSEQUENCES OF GOAL COMMITMENT

The primary consequence of goal commitment is to moderate the relationship between goal difficulty and performance. There is considerable confusion in the literature about this relationship despite the fact that this assertion is consistent with both early (Locke, 1968) and more recent (Locke & Latham, 1990) formulations of task goal theory. The confusion stems in part from the specific form of this moderated relationship, technically referred to as an *uncrossed interaction* (Stone & Hollenbeck, 1984). As illustrated in Figure 1, high performance comes about only when goal difficulty and goal commitment are both high. Difficult goals do not lead to high performance when commitment is low and high levels of commitment to easy goals also fail to generate high performance. Stated differently, a strong linear relationship should be evident between goal difficulty and performance when commitment is high and goal difficulty should be unrelated to performance when commitment is low. Because of the uncrossed nature of this interaction, main effects rather than the interaction can be expected under certain operational conditions. In such situations, the failure to observe a significant interaction does not mitigate or refute the critical role of goal commitment.

For example, the moderation hypothesis assumes that there is sufficient variance in both goal commitment and goal difficulty. This is often not the case in goal setting research or practice. Goal commitment cannot moderate the relationship between goal difficulty and performance if there is little variance in commitment. To function as a moderator, some

FIGURE 1   Conceptual Interactive Relationship between Goal Difficulty and Goal Commitment

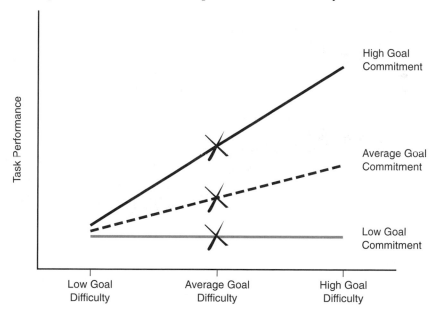

202 Part Two *Central Issues in Motivation at Work*

individuals must have high commitment, some moderate commitment, and some low commitment. In situations in which goals are self-set, goal commitment is generally high and invariant (Hollenbeck & Brief, 1987). Even when goals are assigned, situational demands (e.g., incentives, competition, experimenter demand, legitimate power) often result in uniformly high levels of commitment (Locke & Latham, 1990). Under such circumstances a main effect of goal difficulty on performance should be evident and goal commitment should have negligible effects, main or interactive (e.g., Klein, 1991; Matsui, Kakuyama, & Onglatco, 1987; Wright & Kacmar, 1995). Even when there is variance in commitment, either within or across studies, there should be a main effect for goal difficulty on performance, averaged across all levels of commitment. The dashed line in Figure 1 shows this average effect. This main effect for goal difficulty on task performance across studies has been documented elsewhere (e.g., Mento, Steel, & Karren, 1987), and establishing this parameter was not a purpose of the present study.

Goal commitment also cannot moderate the relationship between goal difficulty and performance if there is insufficient variance in goal difficulty levels. That is, some individuals must have easy goals, some moderate goals, and others difficult goals. Although this is the case in some situations, all employees or participants are often assigned the same challenging goal that violates this assumption. In situations in which only challenging goals are present, commitment can be expected to have a main effect on performance (e.g., Harrison & Liska, 1994; Johnson & Perlow, 1992; Klein & Kim, 1998). When everyone has the same difficult goal, individuals with higher commitment to that goal should outperform those with lower commitment. Even when there is variance in goal difficulty, either within or across studies, this main effect for goal commitment on performance should be evident, averaged across all levels of goal difficulty. The average effect for goal commitment is illustrated by the Xs corresponding to "average goal difficulty" in Figure 1. When goal difficulty levels are averaged, higher levels of commitment are associated with higher levels of performance. Unlike the main effect of goal difficulty, this overall main effect for goal commitment has not been established meta-analytically and thus serves as the first purpose of this meta-analysis.

Hypothesis 1: There will be a positive relationship between goal commitment and performance averaged across studies.

Although range restriction in either goal difficulty or commitment is a common problem within studies, there have been studies with sufficient variance in both goal difficulty and goal commitment that have supported the interactive effect (e.g., Erez & Zidon, 1984; Tubbs, 1993). Across the research that has been conducted, the interactive nature of the relationship depicted in Figure 1 should also be evident. Figure 1 suggests that low standings on either variable will negate the generally positive relationship between performance and the other variable. Thus, the relationship between commitment and performance will be stronger with difficult goals relative to easy goals. That is, goal difficulty moderates the relationship between commitment and performance. This moderating effect of goal difficulty on the commitment–performance relationship has not been fully examined meta-analytically and thus serves as the second purpose of this meta-analysis.

Hypothesis 2: There will be a significant amount of variability in the goal commitment–performance relationship that cannot be explained by sampling error or artifacts.

Hypothesis 3: Goal difficulty will moderate the relationship between goal commitment and performance, such that the relationship between commitment and performance will be stronger for difficult goals relative to easy ones.

In the goal setting literature, this interaction is typically stated in terms of commitment moderating the goal difficulty–performance relationship. Hypothesis 3 has goal difficulty moderating the goal commitment–performance relationship because goal difficulty levels can be categorized more objectively for conducting a meta-analytic moderator analysis than levels of goal commitment. Because interactive relationships are symmetrical in nature (Cohen & Cohen, 1983), the conclusion that goal difficulty moderates the goal commitment–performance relationship necessarily substantiates the idea that goal commitment moderates the goal difficulty–performance relationships. Thus, the way we used meta-analysis to test for moderation was indirect, but the overall conclusion remained the same: High levels of both commitment and goal difficulty are necessary to achieve high levels of performance.

An alternative approach to meta-analytically test the interaction hypothesis would be to directly aggregate the effect sizes for this interaction reported in the literature (e.g., Donovan & Radosevich, 1998). Such an approach is problematic because of serious limitations in the data available in the literature. First, only a handful of published studies have reported directly testing the interaction hypothesis using multiple regression. Second, for some of those studies, an interaction would not be expected because of the problem of restricted variance discussed earlier. For example, Donovan and Rodosevich (1998) included Harrison and Liska (1994) in their analysis even though goals were held constant in that study. Third, some studies presenting strong evidence of the interaction effect (e.g., Erez & Zidon, 1984) did not use a multiple regression approach and could not be included. Also excluded from such an approach are the dozens of published studies that examined goals, commitment, and performance but did not report any moderator analyses. As a result, Donovan and Radosevich's analyses were limited to data from only 6 published articles, whereas the current meta-analytic test for moderation was based on data from more than 60 published articles. To directly test the interaction hypothesis based on a representative sample of all studies measuring goals, commitment, and performance, one would need to have the study intercorrelations between the main effect variables and their cross-products. Such statistics do not exist in the literature.

ANTECEDENTS OF GOAL COMMITMENT

If goal commitment has important performance consequences, as predicted, then attention must also be directed at factors that affect goal commitment. The final purpose of this meta-analysis is to examine antecedents of goal commitment. Hollenbeck and Klein (1987), consistent with Locke et al. (1981), used an expectancy theory framework in delineating the determinants of goal commitment. The attractiveness of goal attainment and the expectancy of goal attainment are thus thought to be the most proximal antecedents of goal commitment. Across the accumulated literature, those two variables along with motivational force, the multiplicative combination of expectancy and attractiveness, should be strongly related to goal commitment. Although previous meta-analyses (e.g., Klein, 1991; Wofford, Goodwin,

& Premack, 1992) have provided support for these relationships, in the current study we used a substantially larger sample of studies than earlier efforts.

> *Hypothesis* 4: There will be positive relationships between goal commitment and expectancy, attractiveness, and motivational force averaged across studies.

Although expectancy and attractiveness were the most proximal antecedents of goal commitment in Hollenbeck and Klein's (1987) model, several other variables were identified as likely to affect goal commitment through their effects on the expectancy and attractiveness of goal attainment. Empirical evidence exists for some of these relationships but not for others. Furthermore, the variables included in Hollenbeck and Klein's model were provided to be illustrative rather than a comprehensive or exhaustive set of antecedents. Although the additional antecedents of goal commitment suggested in that model and other past reviews should also relate to goal commitment, we offer no formal hypotheses with respect to all of these variables. We summarize the findings in the literature for all other correlates of goal commitment, whether explicitly identified in a previous review or not.

METHOD

Literature Search

Although there has been a recent surge in research on goal commitment, we did not limit this meta-analysis to those latest findings. Studies included in prior reviews were also incorporated here to provide a comprehensive analysis. We conducted a search for studies reporting empirical findings involving goal commitment. Both computer and manual methods were used in identifying relevant studies to obtain the largest sample possible. First, computerized searches were conducted through both the PsycLIT and ABI/Inform databases using the key words *goal commitment, goal acceptance,* and *goal difficulty.* Second, previous reviews of the goal commitment literature (Hollenbeck & Klein, 1987; Locke & Latham, 1990; Locke et al., 1988; Wofford et al., 1992) were examined. Next, we manually searched the *Academy of Management Journal, Human Performance, Journal of Applied Psychology, Journal of Applied Social Psychology, Journal of Management, Organizational Behavior and Human Decision Processes,* and *Personnel Psychology* from January 1987 through May 1998. We chose these journals because they were most likely to contain goal-setting studies given the distribution of articles identified through the previous steps. Studies published before 1987 should have been included in the previous reviews of goal commitment. Finally, the reference lists of studies identified using these procedures were examined for any additional studies.

This search of the literature identified 174 published articles, dissertations, book chapters, and conference papers. From these, the following criteria for inclusion were used for the current meta-analyses: (a) Goal commitment or goal acceptance had to be measured in the study and (b) suitable statistics had to be present to calculate an effect size between goal commitment and at least one other construct. The application of these inclusion criteria resulted in the identification of 74 studies. Nine of these studies included more than one sample or study, bringing the total to 83 independent samples. Sample sizes ranged from 20 to 406 ($M = 105.06$, $SD = 72.11$). The studies included in the meta-analyses are indicated by an asterisk in the reference list. Note that more than half ($n = 48$) of these studies were published after the reviews by Hollenbeck and Klein (1987) and Locke et al. (1988).

Coding of Studies and Constructs

Each study was coded for sample size, effects between the constructs of interest, and measurement reliability. Two of the authors each coded half of the studies, with 10 studies coded by both authors. The agreement between the raters was 95% on those studies. All disagreements were resolved through discussion with the first author. In addition, information was collected on each study regarding several potential moderators: (a) task complexity (using the categories provided by Wood, Mento, & Locke, 1987); (b) incentives (yes vs. no); and (c) goal origin (self-set vs. participative vs. assigned). These variables were identified as potential moderators based on previous goal-setting meta-analyses (Mento et al., 1987; Wofford et al., 1992; Wood et al., 1987). Given the small number of studies identified using participatively set goals, we focused the goal origin analyses only on self-set versus assigned goals.

Goal difficulty was also coded as a moderator to test Hypothesis 3. In doing so, studies (or conditions within studies) were categorized as using easy, moderate, or difficult goals. That categorization was based on the objective probability of goal attainment when possible. Goals reported or judged as having an objective probability of attainment of less than 15% were coded as difficult;[1] goals between 16% and 50% were coded as moderate; and goals reported or judged as having an objective probability of attainment greater than 50% were coded as easy. The coding of the other constructs examined was relatively straightforward. In several cases, similar constructs were combined in the interest of parsimony. We further explain those variables.

Goal commitment. Although conceptual distinctions can be made between the constructs of goal acceptance and goal commitment, studies that examined one or the other are included here under the term *goal commitment.* This is consistent with previous reviews (e.g., Hollenbeck & Klein, 1987; Locke & Latham, 1990) and the emerging consensus that commitment is the more inclusive construct. All self-report measures of goal commitment were included in this analysis, even those using single-item measures. Excluded were studies using only discrepancy measures of goal commitment (see Wright, O'Leary-Kelly, Cortina, Klein, & Hollenbeck, 1994) or studies in which participants evaluated the commitment of others.

Performance. For the majority of studies, objective performance indexes were available to use as the measure of task performance. When both objective and subjective measures were available, we used the objective measure. In instances in which multiple dimensions of performance were evaluated, we chose the measure closest to the goal of interest as the performance measure (in most cases, this was the quantity of work).

Expectancy. Studies examining a variety of expectancy constructs (e.g., outcome expectancies, effort–performance expectancies) were included in this category as were self-efficacy expectations. Although conceptually distinct, nearly identical measures have been used to assess self-efficacy and expectancy in the goal-setting literature (Klein, 1991).

---

[1] In experimental studies assigning goals of varying difficulty levels, a "difficult" goal has often been defined as having an objective probability of attainment of 10%. For the purposes of this review, using a cutoff of 10% in categorizing goal difficulty was viewed as overly restrictive. Our use of 15% in this review should not be viewed as a recommended operationalization of difficult goals in future experimental manipulations.

Attractiveness. Direct measures of the attractiveness of goal attainment were grouped with measures of valance or instrumentality.

Goal level. The performance level specified in the goal for which commitment was assessed was used as the measure of goal difficulty level. If, for example, a study assigned goals and assessed commitment to those assigned goals but later also assessed personal goals, the assigned goal level was used in the meta-analysis. In studies in which commitment was assessed relative to personal goals, the difficulty of those self-set goals was used.

Ability. Measures of ability were combined with the commonly used surrogates for ability, namely previous or practice performance. When measures of both ability and past performance were available, we used the ability measure.

Feedback. Two groupings of measures were created concerning feedback or knowledge of results. The first, provision of feedback, included studies comparing feedback with no-feedback conditions as well as those measuring or manipulating the amount of feedback provided. The second set of studies, type of feedback, included studies that measured or manipulated the nature or some other dimension of the feedback received by study participants.

Meta-Analytic Procedures

Meta-analyses were conducted using the procedures outlined by Hunter and Schmidt (1990). Their procedures examined the degree to which correlation differences across studies could be accounted for by statistical artifacts (e.g., sampling error and unreliability) and allowed for the correction of these correlations to obtain the true population correlation. Population correlations were estimated for each of the relationships using the observed correlations weighted for sample size and the calculated variance of correlations across samples. Each sample-weighted correlation was corrected for measurement error in goal commitment. Reliability information was presented for more than 75% of the goal commitment measurements. The average reliability for goal commitment was .81. When unreported, this mean was used for correction purposes. We did not correct for measurement error in goal difficulty, performance, or the coded antecedents because most of these measures were objective in nature, were experimentally manipulated, or the reliabilities were unreported in the literature. The moderating effects discussed in this study were analyzed using the guidelines set by Hunter and Schmidt (1990) and Whitener (1990). We examined the percentage of variance explained by artifacts according to Hunter and Schmidt's 75% rule and homogeneity significance tests; we also examined the credibility intervals for the degree of spread and the inclusion of zero.

RESULTS AND DISCUSSION

Consequences of Goal Commitment

Hypotheses 1–3 concerned the relationship between goal commitment and performance. The meta-analytic results for this relationship are provided in Table 1. The mean corrected effect size (r_c) between goal commitment and performance was .23. The 95% confidence interval (CI) for this weighted mean correlation did not include zero, supporting Hypothesis 1, which predicted a positive relationship between goal commitment and performance across studies. Hypothesis 2 predicted a significant amount of variability in this relationship that would not be explained by sampling error or artifacts. As indicated in Table 1, only 27% of the variance in results across studies was attributable to sampling error. The homogeneity chi-square was significant at the .01 level, indicating support for Hypothesis 2 and a high probability that moderators of this relationship were present.

Hypothesis 3 predicted that goal difficulty would moderate this relationship. The results of the moderation analysis, also presented in Table 1, reflect the predicted pattern illustrated in Figure 1. The relationship between commitment and performance was stronger for difficult goals relative to easy goals, supporting Hypothesis 3. The corrected average correlation for difficult goals ($r_c = .35$) was significantly higher ($p < .05$) than the average correlation for moderate ($r_c = .20$) or low ($r_c = .18$) goals, as evidenced by the fact that the 95% CI for difficult goals did not overlap with the CIs for moderate or low goals. Further support for the moderating effect was evident in the increased variance accounted for by sampling error for the subsets relative to the overall effect. The homogeneity chi-square was nonsignificant for the low goal-difficulty category but significant for the high and moderate subsets, suggesting the presence of additional moderators.

Other potential moderators (e.g., goal origin, task complexity, incentives) of the goal commitment–performance relationship were examined but not supported. Secondary moderators within levels of goal difficulty were not examined because of the diminished number of studies in each subset. Although all of the sampling variance was not accounted for, strong support was found for Hypotheses 1–3. There was a strong cross-situational positive relationship between goal commitment and performance. In addition, moderator analyses showed that the effect of goal commitment on performance was considerably stronger in situations in which difficult goals were used. Given the previously established robust relationship between goal difficulty and task performance (Locke & Latham, 1990; Mento et al., 1987), these findings highlight the importance of facilitating commitment to difficult goals.

Antecedents of Goal Commitment

Hypothesis 4 predicted positive relationships between goal commitment and expectancy, attractiveness, and motivational force. The meta-analytic results for these relationships are provided in Table 2. All three weighted mean correlations had CIs that placed them significantly different from zero, supporting the hypothesis. For expectancy, the mean effect size,

TABLE 1 **Meta-Analysis Results of the Goal Commitment–Task Performance Relationship**

Goal Difficulty Level	k	N	r	Lower 95% CI	Upper 95% CI	% Due to Sampling Error	χ^2	r_c
High	17	1,293	.31	.25	.38	52.88	32.15*	.35
Moderate	22	3,093	.18	.12	.24	29.77	73.90**	.20
Low	16	1,531	.16	.10	.22	71.94	22.24	.18
Overall	66	7,952	.20	.16	.25	26.77	246.53**	.23

Note. Significant correlations are those whose confidence intervals do not include zero. k = number of correlations; N = total number of individuals across the k samples; r = mean sample weighted correlation; 95% CI = 95% confidence interval of the weighted mean correlation; % due to sampling error = percentage of variance explained by sampling error alone; χ^2 = homogeneity of effect sizes within each class; r_c = mean weighted correlation corrected for goal commitment unreliability.
* $p < .05$. ** $p < .01$.

TABLE 2 **Meta-Analysis Results of the Proximal Antecedents of Goal Commitment**

Variable	k	N	r	Lower 95% CI	Upper 95% CI	% Due to Sampling Error	χ^2	r_c
Expectancy	24	2,995	.32	.26	.39	24.90	95.89**	.36
Attractiveness	13	2,075	.26	.18	.34	19.41	54.34**	.29
Motivational force	4	593	.30	.06	.54	9.16	43.71**	.33

Note. Significant correlations are those whose confidence intervals do not include zero. k = number of correlations; N = total number of individuals across the k samples; r = mean sample weighted correlation; 95% CI = 95% confidence interval of the weighted mean correlation; % due to sampling error = percentage of variance explained by sampling error alone; χ^2 = homogeneity of effect sizes within each class; r_c = mean weighted correlation corrected for goal commitment unreliability.
** $p < .01$.

corrected for measurement error (r_c) was .36. The weighted mean effects were .29 for attractiveness and .33 for motivational force. For all three relationships, substantial variance in results across studies remained after accounting for sampling error and the homogeneity chi-squares were significant at the .01 level. Although not a focus of the current study, different operationalizations of these variables (e.g., summated vs. single value expectancies) have been shown to moderate these relationships (Klein, 1991). Although there may be additional moderators, Hypothesis 4 was supported in that there were strong positive overall relationships between goal commitment and attractiveness of goal attainment, expectancy of goal attainment, and motivational force.

We did not formulate any specific hypotheses about the numerous distal antecedents of goal commitment. The meta-analytic results for these other correlates of commitment are provided in Table 3, organized by the amount of evidence available for each antecedent. There are relatively few additional variables that have been extensively studied. Of these, significant positive relationships were found for ability $(r_c = .18)$, volition $(r_c = .40)$, affect $(r_c = .22)$, goal specificity $(r_c = .19)$, task experience $(r_c = .24)$, and both the provision $(r_c = .13)$ and type $(r_c = .30)$ of feedback. Higher levels of commitment resulted from having high ability, a voice in the determination of the goal, task or job satisfaction, specific goals, task experience, receiving feedback on one's performance, and the form of that feedback. Except for the provision of feedback, substantial variance across studies remained after accounting for sampling error, and the homogeneity chi-squares were significant. A significant relationship could not be inferred for age, which was not surprising because there is no conceptual basis for such a relationship.

Goal difficulty was the most frequently examined correlate of goal commitment. Conceptually, the literature has focused on the interaction between goal difficulty and commitment in determining performance rather than on the relationship between goal difficulty level and goal commitment.

In fact, neither Hollenbeck and Klein (1987) nor Locke et al. (1988) included goal difficulty in their discussions of the antecedents of goal commitment. At a simple level, one might expect goal commitment to decline as goals become objectively more difficult. This relationship is more complex than that, however, and the corrected average correlation reported in Table 3 is close to zero $(r_c = .03)$. The low correlation and the wide variance observed across studies indicates a strong possibility for moderators. Goal origin was examined

TABLE 3 **Meta-Analysis Results for the Distal Antecedents of Goal Commitment**

Variable	k	N	r	Lower 95% CI	Upper 95% CI	% Due to Sampling Error	χ^2	r_c
Goal level	40	4,892	.03	−.05	.11	12.70	314.91**	.04
Ability/past performance	19	2,431	.16	.08	.24	22.85	83.12**	.18
Volition (participation)	17	2,007	.37	.28	.46	16.57	102.22**	.40
Affect	7	750	.20	.11	.29	53.42	13.12*	.22
Explicitness (goal specificity)	7	968	.17	.04	.31	21.12	33.03**	.19
Task information/experience	6	565	.22	.06	.38	25.84	23.21**	.24
Provision of feedback	6	772	.12	.04	.21	70.78	8.47	.13
Type of feedback	5	404	.27	.12	.42	36.82	13.61**	.30
Age	5	519	.08	−.02	.18	78.03	6.40	.09
Task complexity	3	186	−.50	−.64	−.35	53.90	5.57	
Strategy development	3	320	.21	.11	.32	100.00	1.11	
Incentives	3	340	.20	.10	.31	100.00	2.66	
Need for achievement	3	324	.17	.01	.34	40.73	7.37*	
Leadership	3	243	.12	.00	.25	100.00	0.36	
Education	3	343	.04	−.07	.14	100.00	1.64	
Social influence	2	208	.45	.32	.58	70.14	2.85	
Supervisor supportiveness	2	93	.38	.20	.55	100.00	0.79	
Publicness	2	248	.19	.07	.31	100.00	0.93	
Type A personality	2	499	.12	.03	.20	100.00	0.36	
Stress	2	252	−.10	−.36	.17	21.75	9.19**	
Goal stability	1	39	.42					
Endurance (persistence)	1	184	.30					
Procedural justice	1	186	.29					
Performance constraints	1	45	−.27					
Goal conflict	1	132	.24					
Organizational commitment	1	75	.20					
Locus of control	1	190	−.18					
Perfectionism	1	261	.07					
Self-esteem	1	88	−.03					
Authority	0							
Competition	0							
Job involvement	0							

Note. Significant correlations are those whose confidence intervals do not include zero. Variables in italics are those identified in previous reviews by Hollenbeck and Klein (1987) and Locke, Latham, and Erez (1988). k = number of correlations; N = total number of individuals across the k samples; r = mean sample weighted correlation. 95% CI = 95% confidence interval of the weighted mean correlation; % due to sampling error = percentage of variance explained by sampling error alone; χ^2 = homogeneity of effect sizes within each class; r_c = mean weighted correlation corrected for goal commitment unreliability.
* $p < .05$. ** $p < .01$.

as a potential moderator based on the findings by Wofford et al. (1992), who examined personal and assigned goals separately. In the current analysis, the average weighted effect (r_c) was −.09 for assigned goals (95% CI = −.19 to .03; 12.06% of variance due to sample error), $\chi^2(18, N = 2,424) = 157.61, p < .01$. For self-set goals there was an overall positive relationship $(r_c = .16)$ that was significantly different from zero based on the CI (.06 to .25;

25.16% of variance due to sample error), $\chi^2(14, N = 1,630) = 59.63, p < .01$. For both subsets, the significant homogeneity statistics indicated that goal origin alone did not explain the variability in sample effects.

Consideration of the more proximal antecedents of commitment may help explain the relationship between goal difficulty level and goal commitment and the moderating role of goal origin. Although the objective probability of attainment becomes lower as goals become more difficult, this is not necessarily reflected in individual expectations of goal attainment (i.e., self-efficacy can remain high). In addition, although objectively difficult goals may have lower probabilities of attainment, they also often have higher instrumentalities (Matsui et al., 1981; Mento, Locke, & Klein, 1992). Perhaps there tends to be high commitment to difficult personal goals because those self-chosen goals tend to have high instrumentalities and expectancies higher than warranted by their objective difficulty. For assigned goals, there is likely to be much more variability in both the expectancy and attractiveness of goal attainment because of other individual and situational factors. Future researchers need to directly examine this suggested role of goal origin, expectancies, and attractiveness in understanding the goal difficulty–goal commitment relationship.

Other antecedents, although not studied extensively, have at least been replicated, allowing for the calculation of an average correlation. Because these effects were based on a small number of independent samples, these results must be evaluated with caution. Several other variables have been examined only once. The effects for these variables should not be interpreted as estimates of population correlations. They are included in Table 3 only to provide a comprehensive summary of the variables that have been examined as potential antecedents of goal commitment and to identify relationships in need of replication. Also listed in Table 3 are authority, competition, and job involvement. These variables were identified in previous reviews as potential antecedents of goal commitment but have not been examined empirically.

Study Limitations

By their very nature, meta-analyses call for many subjective decisions (Wanous, Sullivan, & Malinak, 1989). For example, decisions were made here regarding study inclusion, significance thresholds, and classification rules. These decisions were made as objectively as possible, but the potential for bias needs to be recognized. A second limitation is the heterogeneity in many overall effect sizes, suggesting that the simple weighted mean correlations do not adequately describe all sampling variance. Although we conducted a few moderator analyses, some of which helped to reduce this heterogeneity, the requirements for complete homogeneity were often not achieved. For some antecedent variables, this heterogeneity is likely attributable to the variety of constructs or operationalizations that were combined into a single category (e.g., feedback type).

Another limitation was the inability to conduct a hierarchical breakdown of moderators because of the limited number of studies in each subset. Problems with statistical power and meta-analysis have been discussed elsewhere (Hunter & Schmidt, 1990; Sackett, Harris, & Orr, 1986). It would also have been useful to conduct a meta-analytic path analysis (e.g., Hom, Caranikas-Walker, Prussia, & Griffeth, 1992). Unfortunately, we could not find sufficient data in the literature to generate a complete meta-analytic correlation matrix among the variables of interest. Another limitation is the lack of consistency with which the goal commitment construct has been operationalized, which makes it difficult to argue that all included studies were measuring the exact same thing (see Tubbs & Dahi, 1991, and Wright et al., 1994). Although we limited the operationalizations, we included a variety of measures. Finally, as mentioned earlier, the data available in the literature and the fact that variation in goal commitment is often limited, as is the variation in goal level, made it inappropriate to use meta-analysis to directly examine goal commitment as a moderator in the goal difficulty–performance relationship.

Future Research Needs

Hollenbeck and Klein (1987) noted that goal commitment was not measured or mentioned in the majority of goal-setting studies they reviewed. They and Locke and Latham (1990) recommended that goal commitment be measured in all goal-setting studies, even if goal commitment is not a variable of interest. By doing so, goal commitment serves as a manipulation check and can be used to test the most likely explanation if hypothesized goal effects are not observed. It appears that recent researchers have largely followed this advice, although we did not attempt to identify goal-setting studies not assessing goal commitment. This is evidenced by the large number of studies identified in our literature search and not included in this meta-analysis because the only statistics reported concerning goal commitment were to convey that all participants were committed to the goals being investigated.

A disadvantage of this practice is that goal commitment is often a secondary variable. That is, commitment is measured without specific hypotheses aimed at exploring its nature and role, and statistical relationships are not reported between goal commitment and the other variables being studied. Furthermore, when goal commitment is used as a manipulation check, steps are often taken to ensure high and invariant levels of commitment instead of taking steps to maximize variability in order to observe relationships with goal commitment. As a result, although goal commitment has been included in a greater percentage of goal setting studies, what researchers have learned about goal commitment is not fully reflected by that attention. This lack of attention to goal commitment as a primary variable of interest is best exemplified by the relatively few studies that have specifically and appropriately examined the interactive effect of goal commitment and goal difficulty on performance. Thus, a first need is for additional research to verify directly what this meta-analysis has shown indirectly: that with sufficient variance in both goal commitment and goal difficulty levels, goal commitment moderates the relationship between goal difficulty and task performance.

The current meta-analysis, consistent with Hollenbeck and Klein's (1987) model, showed that the expectancy and attractiveness of goal attainment were highly related to goal commitment. Although several other variables were also found to relate to goal commitment, in this meta-analysis we could not test the mediating role of expectancy and attractiveness implicit in Hollenbeck and Klein's model. In addition, relatively few researchers have directly examined that relationship (e.g., Klein & Wright, 1994; Wright & Kacmar, 1995). Further examination of this linkage is a second area for future research. A third area for future research concerns the examination of previously identified antecedents that have been infrequently examined (e.g., goal conflict, performance constraints) or not examined at all (e.g., authority, competition). In addition, there may be other variables (e.g., conscientiousness, goal orientation) that, although not previously identified, are worthy of investigation as antecedents of goal commitment.

A strength of the recent goal commitment literature is the definition and measurement of the construct. In particular, the use of a variety of single-item measures has given way to the use of multi-item, standardized, reliable instruments. Hollenbeck, Williams, and Klein's (1989) scale and its derivatives are the most commonly used measures of goal commitment. There has also been greater convergence between the use of the terms *goal acceptance* and *goal commitment*. Whereas previously the two terms were the source of much confusion and were used interchangeably, *goal commitment* has emerged as the more inclusive of the two constructs and has received the bulk of attention in recent years. Despite this convergence on the meaning and measurement of goal commitment, there is still some debate over both of these issues (DeShon & Landis, 1997; Tubbs, 1993). Empirical studies clarifying these remaining points of contention represent another future research need.

Much of the goal commitment literature has assumed that high commitment is desirable. The escalation of commitment literature (e.g., Staw, 1982) clearly suggests, however, that there are situations in which high commitment is dysfunctional. It is also conceivable that there are situations in which excessively high commitment is detrimental to individual well-being because of the stress, anxiety, or other health risks caused by relentless goal striving (e.g., workaholism). Research examining potential negative implications of goal commitment is thus warranted. A final important area for future research is the examination of commitment to multiple goals. An individual's commitment to a particular goal is most meaningful relative to that same person's commitment to other goals. One may be highly committed to a work-related goal, but if that person is even more committed to a conflicting family-related goal, high commitment to the work goal will not be predictive of performance. Few researchers have examined commitment to multiple goals (e.g., Crown & Rosse, 1995; Locke, Smith, Erez, Chah, & Schaffer, 1994).

Conclusion

On the basis of a small sample of studies, Donovan and Radosevich (1998) concluded that the evidence in the literature did not support the importance or hypothesized role of goal commitment in the goal-setting process. Results of the current study, using a larger and more representative sample of studies, refute those assertions. The main findings of this review are as follows: (a) Goal commitment had a strong positive effect on performance across studies; (b) goal difficulty moderated this relationship (and hence goal commitment moderated the goal difficulty–performance relationship); (c) expectancy and attractiveness of goal attainment, the antecedents thought to be most proximal, were strongly and positively related to goal commitment; and (d) only a handful of relationships were shown to have been well documented in the literature between goal commitment and more distal antecedents (e.g., ability, volition).

Goals are central to current treatments of work motivation, and goal commitment is a necessary condition for difficult goals to result in higher task performance. A decade ago, the call was made for more systematic research investigating this crucial construct. The number of recent studies identified in this meta-analysis suggests that goal commitment has received increased attention. However, the limited number of studies directly and appropriately examining the interaction between goal commitment and performance, the conceptual confusion that remains about this relationship, and the sparse attention given to several previously identified antecedent variables suggest that this research has not been sufficiently systematic. We hope that this conceptual clarification and empirical synthesis will facilitate more systematic research in the next decade.

References

References marked with an asterisk indicate studies included in the meta-analysis.

*Allscheid, S. P., & Cellar, D. F. (1996). An interactive approach to work motivation: The effects of competition, rewards, and goal difficulty on task performance. *Journal of Business and Psychology, 11,* 219–237.

*Anderson, J. C., & O'Reilly, C. A. (1981). Effects of an organizational control system on managerial satisfaction and performance. *Human Relations, 34,* 491–501.

*Austin, J. T. (1989). Effects of shifts in goal origin on goal acceptance and attainment. *Organizational Behavior and Human Decision Processes, 44,* 415–435.

Austin, J. T., & Vancouver, J. B. (1996). Goal constructs in psychology: Process and content. *Psychological Bulletin, 120,* 338–375.

Bandura, A. (1986). *Social foundations of thought and action: A social—cognitive view.* Englewood Cliffs, NJ: Prentice Hall.

*Brunstein J. C. (1993). Personal goals and subjective well-being: A longitudinal study. *Journal of Personality and Social Psychology, 65,* 1061–1070.

Cohen, J., & Cohen, P. (1983). *Applied multiple regression/correlation analysis for the behavioral sciences* (2nd ed). Hillsdale, NJ: Erlbaum.

Crown, D. F., & Rosse, J. G. (1995). Yours, mine, and ours: Facilitating group productivity through the integration of individual and group goals. *Organization Behavior and Human Decision Processes, 64,* 138–150.

*DeShon R., & Alexander, R. (1996). Goal setting effects on implicit and explicit learning of complex tasks. *Organizational Behavior and Human Decision Processes, 65,* 18–36.

DeShon, R. & Landis, R. S. (1997). The dimensionality of the Hollenbeck, Williams, and Klein (1989) measure of goal commitment on complex tasks. *Organizational Behavior and Human Decision Processes, 70,* 105–116.

*De Souza, G., & Klein, H. J. (1995). Emergent leadership in the group goal-setting process. *Small Group Research, 26,* 475–496.

*Dodd, N. G., & Anderson, K. S. (1996). A test of goal commitment as a moderator of the relationship between goal level and performance. *Journal of Social Behavior and Personality, 11,* 329–336.

Donovan, J. J., & Radosevich, D. J. (1998). The moderating role of goal commitment on the goal difficulty–performance relationship: A meta-analytic review and critical reanalysis. *Journal of Applied Psychology, 83,* 308–315.

*Durham, C. C., Knight, D., & Locke, E. A. (1997). Effects of leader role, team-set goal difficulty, efficacy, and tactics on team effectiveness. *Organizational Behavior and Human Decision Processes, 72,* 203–231.

*Earley, P. C. (1985a). Influence of information, choice and task complexity upon goal acceptance, performance, and personal goals. *Journal of Applied Psychology, 70,* 481–491.

*Earley, P. C. (l985b, August). *The influence of goal setting methods on performance, goal acceptance, self-efficacy expectations, and expectancies across levels of goal difficulty.* Paper presented at the 93rd Annual Convention of the American Psychological Association, Los Angeles.

*Earley, P. C., & Kanfer, R. (1985). The influence of component participation and role models on goal acceptance, goal satisfaction, and performance. *Organizational Behavior and Human Decision Processes, 36,* 378–390.

*Early, P. C., Shalley, C. E., & Northcraft, G. B. (1992). I think I can, I think I can: Processing time and strategy effects of goal acceptance/rejection decisions. *Organizational Behavior and Human Decision Processes, 53,* l–13.

*Erez, M., & Arad, R. (1986). Participative goal setting: Social, motivational, and cognitive factors. *Journal of Applied Psychology, 71,* 591–597.

*Erez, M., Earley, C. P., & Hulin, C. L. (1985). The impact of participation on goal acceptance and performance: A two-step model. *Academy of Management Journal, 28,* 50–66.

*Erez, M., & Somech, A. (1996). Is group productivity loss the rule or the exception? Effects of culture and group-based motivation. *Academy of Management Journal, 39,* 1513–1537.

Erez, M., & Zidon, I. (1984). Effect of goal acceptance on the relationship of goal difficulty to performance. *Journal of Applied Psychology, 69,* 69–78.

*Flett, G. L., Sawatzky, D. L., & Hewitt, P. L. (1995). Dimensions of perfectionism and goal commitment: A further comparison of two perfectionism measures. *Journal of Psychopathology and Behavioral Assessment, 17,* 111–124.

*French, J. P. R., Kay, E., & Meyer, H. H. (1966). Participation and the appraisal system. *Human Relations, 19,* 3–19.

*Guhde, L. M. (1991). *The influence of task complexity, strategy and group goals on performance and goal acceptance.* Unpublished doctoral dissertation, Kent State University, Kent, OH.

*Hanges, P. J. (1986). *A catastrophe model of control theory's decision mechanism: The effects of goal difficulty, task difficulty, goal direction and task direction on goal commitment.* Unpublished doctoral dissertation, University of Akron, Akron, OH.

*Hanges, P. J., Alexander, R. A., & Herbert, G. R. (1987, April). *Using regression analysis to empirically verify catastrophe models.* Paper presented at the annual Society of Industrial and Organizational Psychology meeting, Atlanta, GA.

*Harrison D. A., & Liska, L. Z. (1994). Promoting regular exercise in organizational fitness programs: Health related differences in motivational building blocks. *Personnel Psychology, 47,* 47–71.

*Hinsz, V. B., Kalnbach, L. R., & Lorentz, N. R. (1997). Using judgmental anchors to establish challenging self-set goals without jeopardizing commitment. *Organizational Behavior and Human Decision Processes, 71,* 287–308.

Hollenbeck, J. R., & Brief, A. P. (1987). The effects of individual differences and goal origin on the goal setting process. *Organizational Behavior and Human Decision Processes, 40,* 392–414.

Hollenbeck, J. R., & Klein, H. J. (1987). Goal commitment and the goal-setting process: Problems, prospects, and proposals for future research. *Journal of Applied Psychology, 72,* 212–220.

*Hollenbeck, J. R., Williams, C. L., & Klein, H. J. (1989). An empirical examination of the antecedents of commitment to difficult goals. *Journal of Applied Psychology, 74,* 18–23.

Hom, P. W., Caranikas-Walker, F., Prussia, G. E., & Griffeth, R. W. (1992). A meta-analytical structural equations analysis of a model of employee turnover. *Journal of Applied Psychology, 77,* 890–909.

*Huber, V. L., & Neale, M. A. (1986). Effects of cognitive heuristics and goals on negotiator performance and subsequent goal setting. *Organizational Behavior and Human Decision Processes, 38,* 342–365.

Hunter, J. E., & Schmidt, G. L. (1990). *Methods of meta-analysis. Correcting error and bias in research findings.* Newbury Park, CA: Sage.

*Ivancevich, J. M., & McMahon, J. T. (1977a). Education as a moderator of goal setting effectiveness. *Journal of Vocational Behavior, 11,* 3–94.

*Ivancevich, J. M., & McMahon, J. T. (1977b). Black-white differences in a goal-setting program. *Organizational Behavior and Human Performance, 20,* 287–300.

*Ivanceyich, J. M., & McMahon, J. T. (1977c). A study of task goal attributes, higher order need strength, and performance. *Academy of Management Journal, 20,* 552–563.

*Johnson, D. S., & Perlow, R. (1992). The impact of need for achievement components on goal commitment and performance. *Journal of Applied Social Psychology, 22,* 1711–1720.

Kanfer, R., & Ackerman, P. L. (1989). Motivation and cognitive abilities: An integrative/aptitude-treatment approach to skill acquisition. *Journal of Applied Psychology, 74,* 657–690.

*Kernan, M. C., & Lord, R. G. (1988). Effects of participative vs. assigned goals and feedback in a multi-trial task. *Motivation & Emotion, 12,* 75–86.

Klein, H. J. (1989). An integrated control theory model of work motivation. *Academy of Management Review, 14,* 150–172.

*Klein, H. J. (1991). Further evidence on the relationship between goal setting and expectancy theories. *Organizational Behavior and Human Decision Processes, 49,* 230–257.

*Klein, H. J., & Kim, J. S. (1998). A field study of the influence of situational constraints, leader-member exchange, and goal commitment on performance. *Academy of Management Journal, 41,* 88–95.

*Klein, H. J., & Mulvey, P. W. (1995). Two investigations of the relationships among group goals, goal commitment, cohesion, and performance. *Organizational Behavior and Human Decision Processes, 61,* 44–53.

*Klein, H. J., & Wright, P. M. (1994). Antecedents of goal commitment: An empirical examination of personal and situational factors. *Journal of Applied Social Psychology, 24,* 95–114.

*Kolb, D. A., Winter, S. K., & Berlew, D. E. (1968). Self-directed change: Two studies. *Journal of Applied Behavioral Science, 4,* 453–471.

*Latham, G. P., & Steele, T. P. (1983). The motivational effects of participation versus goal setting on performance. *Academy of Management Journal, 26,* 406–417.

*Lee, T. W., Locke, E. A., & Phan, S. H. (1997). Explaining the assigned goal-incentive interaction: The role of self-efficacy and personal goals. *Journal of Management, 23,* 541–559.

*Lese K. P., & Robbins, S. B. (1994). Relationship between goal attributes and the academic achievement of Southeast Asian adolescent refugees. *Journal of Counseling Psychology, 41,* 45–52.

Locke, E. A. (1968). Toward a theory of task motivation and incentives. *Organizational Behavior and Human Performance, 3,* 157–189.

*Locke, E. A., Fredrick, E., Buckner, E., & Bobko, P. (1984). Effect of previously assigned goals on self-set goals and performance. *Journal of Applied Psychology, 69,* 694–699.

*Locke E. A., Fredrick, E., Lee, C., & Bobko, P. (1984). Effect of self-efficacy, goals, and task strategies on task performance. *Journal of Applied Psychology, 69,* 241–251.

Locke, E. A., & Latham, G. P. (1990). *A theory of goal setting and task performance.* Englewood Cliffs, NJ: Prentice Hall.

*Locke, E. A., Latham, G. P., & Erez, M. (1988). The determinants of goal acceptance and commitment. *Academy of Management Review, 13,* 23–39.

Locke, E. A., Shaw, K. N., Saari, L. M., & Latham, G. P. (1981). Goal setting and task performance: 1969–1980. *Psychological Bulletin, 90,* 125–152.

*Locke E. A., Smith, K. G., Erez, M., Chah, D., & Schaffer, A. (1994). The effects of intra-individual goal conflict on performance. *Journal of Management, 20,* 67–91.

*Martocchio, J. J., & Dulebohn, J. (1994). Performance feedback in training: The role of perceived controllability. *Personnel Psychology, 47,* 357–373.

*Mathieu J. E. (1992). The influence of commitment to assigned goals and performance on subsequent self-set goals and performance. *Journal of Applied Social Psychology, 22,* 1012–1029.

*Matsui, T., Kakuyama, T., & Onglatco, M. U. (1987). Effects of goals and feedback on performance in groups. *Journal of Applied Psychology, 72,* 407–415.

*McCaul K. D., Hinsz, V. B., & McCaul, H. S. (1987). The effects of commitment to performance goals on effort. *Journal of Applied Social Psychology, 17,* 437–452.

*Mento, A. J., Cartledge, N. D., & Locke, E. A. (1980). Maryland vs. Michigan vs. Minnesota: Another look at the relationship of expectancy and goal difficulty to task performance. *Organizational Behavior and Human Performance, 25,* 419–440.

Mento, A. J., Locke, E. A., & Klein, H. J. (1992). The relationship of goal level to valence and instrumentality. *Journal of Applied Psychology, 77,* 395–405.

Mento, A. J., Steel, R. P., & Karren, R. J. (1987). A meta-analytic study of the effects of goal setting on task performance: 1966–1984. *Organizational Behavior and Human Decision Processes, 39,* 52–83.

*Mone, M. A., & Baker, D. D. (1989). Stage of task learning as a moderator of the goal-performance relationship. *Human Performance, 2,* 85–99.

*Oldham, G. R. (1975). The impact of supervisory characteristics on goal acceptance. *Academy of Management Journal, 18,* 461–475.

*Oliver, R. L., & Brief, A. P. (1983). Sales managers goal commitment correlates. *Journal of Personal Selling and Sales Management, 3,* 11–17.

*Orbach, I., Iluz, A., & Rosenheim, E. (1987). Value systems and commitment to goals as a function of age, integration of personality, and fear of death. *International Journal of Behavioral Development, 10,* 225–239.

*Organ, D. W. (1977). Intentional vs. arousal effects of goal setting. *Organizational Behavior and Human Performance, 18,* 378–389.

Phillips, J. M., Hollenbeck, J. R., & Ilgen, D. R. (1996). Prevalence and prediction of positive discrepancy creation: Examining a discrepancy between two self-regulation theories. *Journal of Applied Psychology, 81,* 498–511.

*Podsakoff, P. M., MacKenzie, S. B., & Ahearne, M. (1997). Moderating effects of goal acceptance on the relationship between group cohesiveness and productivity. *Journal of Applied Psychology, 82,* 974–983.

*Racicot, B. M., Day, D. V., & Lord, R. G. (1991). Type A behavior pattern and goal setting under different conditions of choice. *Motivation & Emotion, 15,* 67–79.

*Renn, R. W. (1998). Participation's effect on task performance: Mediating roles of goal acceptance and procedural justice. *Journal of Business Research, 41,* 115–125.

*Riedel, J. A.. Nebeker, D. M., & Cooper, B. L. (1988). The influence of monetary incentives on goal choice, goal commitment, and task performance. *Organizational Behavior and Human Decision Processes, 42,* 155–180.

*Roberson, L. (1989). Assessing personal work goals in the organizational setting: Development and evaluation of the work concerns inventory. *Organizational Behavior and Human Decision Processes, 44,* 345–367.

*Roberson, L. (1990). Prediction of job satisfaction from characteristics of personal work goats. *Journal of Organizational Behavior, 11,* 29–41.

*Sabol, B. A. (1979). *The relationship of goal acceptance, goal orientation and participation in goal setting to employee performance.* Unpublished doctoral dissertation, Case Western Reserve University, Cleveland, OH.

Sackett, P. R., Harris, M. M., & Orr, J. M. (1986). On seeking moderator variables in the meta-analysis of correlational data: A Monte-Carlo investigation of statistical power and resistance to Type-1 error. *Journal of Applied Psychology, 71,* 302–310.

*Sagie, A. (1996). Effects of leader's communication style and participative goal setting on performance and attitudes. *Human Performance, 9,* 51–64.

*Shalley, C. E., & Oldham, G. R. (1985). The effects of goal difficulty and expected external evaluation on intrinsic motivation: A laboratory study. *Academy of Management Journal, 28,* 628–640.

*Shutz, P. A. (1993). Additional influences on response certitude and feedback requests. *Contemporary Educational Psychology, 18,* 427–44l.

*Smith, J. A., Hauenstein, N. M. A., & Buchanan, L. B. (1996). Goal setting and exercise performance. *Human Performance, 9,* 141–154.

Staw, B. M. (1982). Counterforces to change. In P. S. Goodman & Associates (Eds.), *Change in organizations* (pp. 87–121). San Francisco: Jossey-Bass.

Stone, E. F., & Hollenbeck, J. R. (1984). Some issues associated with moderated regression. *Organizational Behavior and Human Performance, 34,* 195–213.

*Theodorakis, Y. (1996). The influence of goals, commitment, self-efficacy and self-satisfaction on motor performance. *Journal of Applied Sport Psychology, 8,* 171–182.

*Tubbs, M. E. (1993). Commitment as a moderator of the goal-performance relation: A case for clearer construct definition. *Journal of Applied Psychology, 78,* 86–97.

*Tubbs, M. E., & Dahl, J. G. (1991). An empirical comparison of self-report and discrepancy measures of goal commitment. *Journal of Applied Psychology, 76,* 708–716.

*Tziner, A., & Kopelman, R. (1988). Effects of rating format on goal-setting dimensions: A field experiment. *Journal of Applied Psychology, 73,* 323–326.

*Vance, R. J., & Collela, A. (1990). Effects of two types of feedback on goal acceptance and personal goals. *Journal of Applied Psychology, 75,* 68–76.

*Vancouver, J. B. (1997). The application of HLM to the analysis of the dynamic interaction of environment, person and behavior. *Journal of Management, 23,* 795–818.

Wanous, J. P., Sullivan, S. E., & Malinak, J. (1989). The role of judgment calls in meta-analysis. *Journal of Applied Psychology, 74,* 259–264.

*Weingart, L. R., & Weldon, E. (1991). Processes that mediate the relationship between a group goal and group member performance. *Human Performance, 4,* 33–54.

Whitener, E. M. (1990). Confusion of confidence intervals and credibility intervals in meta-analysis. *Journal of Applied Psychology, 75,* 315–321.

*Whitney K. (1994). Improving group task performance: The role of group goals and group efficacy. *Human Performance 7,* 55–78.

Wofford, J. C., Goodwin, V. L., & Premack, S. (1992). Meta-analysis of the antecedents of personal goal level and of the antecedents and consequences of goal commitment. *Journal of Management, 18,* 595–615.

*Wofford, J. C., & Srinivason, T. N. (1983). Experimental tests of the leader-environment-follower interaction theory of leadership. *Organizational Behavior and Human Decision Processes 32,* 35–54.

Wood, R. E., Mento, A. J., & Locke, E. A. (1987). Task complexity as a moderator of goal effects: A meta-analysis. *Journal of Applied Psychology, 72,* 416–425.

*Wright, P. M. (1989). Test of the mediating role of goals in the incentive-performance relationship. *Journal of Applied Psychology, 74,* 699–705.

*Wright, P. M., Hollenbeck, J. R., Wolf, S., & McMahan, G. C. (1995). The effects of varying goal difficulty operationalizations on goal setting outcomes and processes. *Organizational Behavior and Human Decision Processes, 61,* 28–43.

*Wright, P. M., & Kacmar, K. M. (1994). Goal specificity as a determinant of goal commitment and goal change. *Organizational Behavior and Human Decision Processes, 59,* 242–260.

*Wright, P. M., & Kacmar, K. M. (1995). Mediating roles of self-set goals, goal commitment, self-efficacy, and attractiveness in the incentive-performance relation. *Human Performance, 8,* 263–296.

*Wright, P. M., O'Leary-Kelly, A. M., Cortina, J. M., Klein, H. J., & Hollenbeck, J. R. (1994). On the meaning and measurement of goal commitment. *Journal of Applied Psychology, 79,* 795–803.

*Yukl, G. A., & Latham, G. P. (1978). Interrelationships among employee participation, individual differences, goal difficulty, goal acceptance, goal instrumentality, and performance. *Personnel Psychology, 31,* 305–323.

A Review of the Influence of Group Goals on Group Performance

Anne M. O'Leary-Kelly
Joseph J. Martocchio
Dwight D. Frink

Research findings regarding goal setting in groups are beginning to accumulate, likely as a result of the recognition that much of the work in organizations is performed in groups (Austin & Bobko, 1985). Many researchers and practitioners now view groups as the basic building blocks of organizations (Goodman, 1986; Goodman, Ravlin, & Schminke, 1987; Guzzo & Shea, 1992; Hackman & Morris, 1975). Group-based activities, such as autonomous work groups, quality circles, project teams, focus groups, multifunction work teams, labor-management participation programs, and team chief executive officers, are becoming commonplace in organizations today (Goodman, 1986; Goodman et al., 1987; Guzzo & Shea, 1992). In addition, it is generally expected that organizations will continue to rely on group-based activities in the future (Guzzo & Shea, 1992; Reich, 1983). Given the prominence of groups, information related to group goal setting is increasingly valuable.

Goal-setting theory suggests that goals are associated with enhanced performance because they mobilize effort, direct attention, and encourage persistence and strategy development (Locke & Latham, 1990). Although research on the effects of group goals is not as extensive as that on individual goal setting (Locke & Latham, 1990), several studies have addressed the issue; Locke and Latham noted 41 studies to date that "appeared to have used group goals insofar as this could be inferred from the reports" (1990: 44). In a qualitative review, they found that 93 percent of these studies indicated that group goals had positive or contingently positive results on group performance. Although this information is useful, it is not complete. The purpose of the present study was to expand on these findings in three ways: to (1) review the studies from a second, quantitative perspective, (2) provide information on effect size, and (3) consider the generalizability of the group goal effect across settings, subjects, and tasks.

Qualitatively reviewing research, as Locke and Latham (1990) did, is one method for summarizing research results. A second method is to conduct a meta-analytic review, which statistically, or quantitatively, cumulates research findings. Although it is important to recognize that meta-analytic results are not free from subjectivity (Guzzo, Jackson, & Katzell, 1987), this technique does provide a second perspective on existing research. Guzzo and colleagues (1987) suggested that different types of literature reviews could be arranged along a "continuum of quantification," with traditional narrative reviews (qualitative) anchoring one end and meta-analytic reviews (quantitative) anchoring the other. Both types of literature review are useful, and each is subject to different weaknesses; qualitative reviews are more susceptible to Type I errors, or inference of relationships that do not exist, and meta-analytic reviews are more prone to Type II errors, or failure to detect actual relationships because of

From *Academy of Management Journal*, 1994, 37(5), 1285–1301. Reprinted with permission.

low statistical power. Jick (1979) encouraged the use of both qualitative and quantitative methods to increase the accuracy of conclusions because the weaknesses of one method are offset by the strengths of the other.

Locke and Latham's (1990) qualitative review clearly concluded the existence of a positive group goal effect on group performance, but not all the studies they reviewed showed evidence of such an effect. Although we consider it likely that group goal setting is positively related to group performance, it is useful to examine this question from a second, quantitative perspective. On the basis of Locke and Latham's qualitative review, we tested the following proposition:

> Proposition 1: *The mean effect size of group goal setting on group performance will be greater than zero.*

Meta-analytic review was expected to be useful not only for providing a second perspective on the group goal–group performance relationship, but also for providing information on the size of the group goal effect. Given that Locke and Latham's (1990) review of the research on group goal setting was a qualitative one, they were unable to determine the group goal effect size. No research to date has reviewed group goal studies to estimate the average effect size.

Previous research has also not addressed the generalizability of the group goal effect. In assessing external validity, it is important to consider both the types of goals that have been investigated to date and the types of research designs that have been used in these investigations. Specifically, we explored the influence of eight variables on the group goal effect: goal specificity, goal difficulty, goal source, task type, subject type, experimental setting, group type, and time.

According to individual goal-setting theory, goals are effective because they indicate the level of performance that is acceptable (Locke & Latham, 1990). Specific goals are critical to the individual goal effect because they establish one minimum acceptable performance level, but ambiguous goals either do not make clear the appropriate performance level or indicate to individuals that a range of performance levels is acceptable (Locke & Latham, 1990). In groups, the ambiguity surrounding the definition of acceptable performance may be compounded because several goals operate simultaneously. Zander (1980) suggested that at least four types of goals exist in group contexts: (1) each member's goal for the group, (2) each member's goal for himself or herself, (3) the group's goal for each member, and (4) the group's goal for itself. In view of the existence of these numerous and potentially inconsistent goals, it is likely that goal specificity will also be critically important to the group goal effect.

Individual-level goal-setting theory also suggests that goal difficulty is a critical issue. Difficult goals, if accepted, lead to greater individual effort and persistence (Locke & Latham, 1990; Locke, Shaw, Saari, & Latham, 1981; Tubbs, 1986). Although it is likely that difficult group goals are associated with increased group member effort and persistence (Locke & Latham, 1990), it is important to recognize that the group context provides other stimuli to effort and persistence. For example, previous research suggests that the cohesion of a group may influence group performance, with members of cohesive groups more likely to participate in coordinated patterns of behavior (Levine & Moreland, 1990). Members of a cohesive group working toward an easy goal might, therefore, exert effort beyond their expected individual contributions in order to maintain goodwill within the group. If several group members do so, even easy goals may be associated with high group performance. On the other hand, research on social loafing (e.g., Price, 1987) has demonstrated that group members who feel their contributions are unidentifiable may exert little effort on behalf of a group. If several members engage in this behavior, even difficult goals may be associated with low group performance. The group context therefore adds complications to the goal difficulty issue that are not evident at the individual level, making its relationship to group performance particularly worthy of consideration.

At the individual level, an issue that has generated a great deal of controversy is the influence of the source of goals—whether they are participatively set or assigned—on performance (Latharn, Erez, & Locke, 1988; Locke & Latham, 1990). Although the motivational effects of participation have been largely disproved (Locke & Latham, 1990; Wagner & Gooding, 1987), little research has explored its cognitive effects, or the extent to which participation may clarify expectations and thereby enhance performance (Locke & Latham, 1990). These cognitive effects seem particularly important in group settings. Steiner (1972) suggested that groups are often less than maximally effective because of such process losses as poor coordination and differing group member perspectives concerning the correct pattern of collective action. If participation has positive cognitive effects (e.g., expectations are clarified), process loss may be diminished and group performance enhanced.

The type of task in which a group is engaged may influence the existence or strength of the group goal effect. At the individual level, researchers have employed numerous task types (Locke & Latham, 1990). Although researchers have generated a variety of group task typologies, a central distinction in one early typology concerns the degree of interaction required among group members (McGrath & Altman, 1966). Some tasks require members to work relatively independently, and others necessitate interdependent action. It is not clear whether group goal studies have adequately considered both task types.

The types of subjects and the experimental settings used in the studies conducted to date are also informative regarding the external validity of the group goal effect. At the individual level, goal-setting studies have involved numerous subject types in both laboratory and field settings (Locke & Latham, 1990). However, to date, the types of subjects and settings employed across group goal studies have not been summarized. Such a summary would provide insight into the question of how generalizable the group goal effect actually is. Clearly, if most research has involved students in laboratory settings, the existence of a group goal effect in organizational settings should not be assumed because of low ecological validity (Locke, 1986). It is important to establish that the group goal effect exists outside of controlled, experimental settings.

The type of group and the time period over which the goal effect is studied are also important in assessing the generalizability of the group goal effect. Most definitions of the term "group" suggest a collection of individuals with a shared past and an anticipated future (McGrath, 1984). McGrath distinguished between natural groups, which exist independent of research activities, and concocted groups, which are created for the purpose of research. To date, no research has examined the types of groups that have been used across group goal studies. It is, therefore, unclear whether the group goal effect can be generalized to both group types. In addition, because groups develop and evolve, the time period over which goal setting is examined is important. The extent to which the group goal effect has been examined over varied time spans is unclear, limiting the confidence with which researchers can generalize the group goal effect to organizational settings.

In summary, in this study we cumulated empirical research in order to draw preliminary conclusions about the existence and strength of the group goal effect and to determine how certain goal characteristics (specificity, difficulty, and source) influence it. In addition, we gathered information on the types of studies that have been conducted to date in order to establish the generalizability of the effect and pinpoint the types of future studies that should be conducted.

METHODS

Two strategies were used to identify studies that have investigated the group goal effect. First, we conducted computer searches of *Psyclit,* a database available from the American Psychological Association, and the *American Business Index*. Second, all studies identified in Locke and Latham's (1990) qualitative review were examined. This search resulted in 29 studies that investigated the effect of group goal setting (versus no group goal setting) on group performance. The number of studies reviewed here differs from the number Locke and Latham mentioned for two reasons: (1) some studies lacked a measure of the effect of group goals on performance and (2) some studies examined either the goal or the performance variables at different levels of analysis (e.g., individual level or organizational level).

Next, the 29 studies were examined to determine their value for a meta-analytic review. We excluded 17 of these studies from further analysis because they lacked the information required by meta-analysis for estimating the effect of group goals on group performance; 2 others were excluded because the goal-setting effect was confounded by some other manipulation. An analysis of these excluded studies indicated that they did not differ significantly from the included studies along any of the variables considered here; for example, 83 percent of the included and 88 percent of the excluded studies involved interdependent tasks. A list of excluded studies is available upon request.

This process resulted in 26 usable effect size values; these were derived from 10 studies because there were multiple trials in several studies. Although a data set of 26 is not large, meta-analytic results employing smaller samples have provided meaningful information; Martocchio and O'Leary (1989) studied 19 effect sizes, and Premack and Wanous (1985), 4–19. Over the 26 effect sizes included in the meta-analysis, data for a total of 163 groups and 1,684 individuals were reviewed. Table 1 [deleted] lists the studies included in the meta-analysis.

We operationally measured the goal-setting effect by comparing groups that were involved in goal setting to groups with no goals or low goals. For each study, we converted the actual result (a t, F, r, or a mean and standard deviation) into the effect size statistic d, which measures the standardized mean difference between the two groups. Transformations to d were based on formulas presented in Rosenthal and Rosnow (1984).

The Hunter and Schmidt (Hunter & Schmidt, 1990; Hunter, Schmidt, & Jackson, 1982) meta-analytic method was used to cumulate the effect sizes found in the studies. For each study, d was calculated as the ratio of the difference between means to the standard deviation. Hunter and colleagues recommended using the pooled, within-group standard deviation, rather than the standard deviation for the comparison group, because the sampling error is smaller. Estimates of variance due to sampling error (σ_e^2) and the population variance for effect sizes (σ_δ^2) were calculated using procedures explained in Hunter and colleagues

(1982). It was not possible to make statistical corrections for artifacts other than sampling error because of lack of information in the primary studies.

One assumption underlying the calculation of d is that samples are independent; however, this assumption was not met here. In each of two studies, three effect sizes were based on the same group of subjects. Hunter and colleagues (1982) termed this problem *conceptual replication* and suggested that one solution is to allow the effect sizes to be contributed as separate values. Although doing so violates the assumption of independence, it will not result in significant error if the number of values contributed by each sample is small in comparison to the total number of samples.

RESULTS

Table 2 reports the results of the meta-analysis. As shown in this table, $\bar{d}$ was equal to .92, suggesting that the mean performance level of groups that had goals was almost one standard deviation higher than the performance groups that did not have goals. This effect size is considered large (Cohen, 1977) and also compares favorably with the individual goal effect, which has been estimated as ranging from .52 to .82 (Locke & Latham, 1990).

In order to determine whether conceptual replication biased the obtained results, we conducted a second meta-analysis that excluded the two studies (six effect sizes) with effects based on dependent samples. The results were similar to those reported in Table 2 ($\bar{d} = 1.04$, $\sigma_d^2 = .74$, $\sigma_e^2 = .64$, $\sigma_g^2 = .10$).

Credibility intervals (Schmidt & Hunter, 1977; Whitener, 1990) are use in meta-analysis to test for the operation of moderator variables. For example, task type would be a moderator if a stronger relationship between goals and performance existed for interdependent than for independent tasks. Consideration of moderators is important because it provides additional information about when and how a goal effect operates.

Credibility intervals are calculated by using the corrected standard deviation around the mean corrected effect size. A large credibility interval or one including zero suggests there are several subpopulations, or one or more moderator variables in operation (Whitener, 1990). Table 2, footnote b, shows the credibility interval for the group goal effect found in this meta-analysis; it includes zero, suggesting the existence of one or more moderator variables.

Although the credibility interval indicates moderator variables, and goal theory identifies possible moderators, including the eight variables discussed earlier, we did not test these meta-analytically because of the current state of the group goal literature. An examination of

TABLE 2 Summary of Meta-Analytic Results for Group Goal-Setting Effect[a,b]

$\bar{d}$	σ_d	σ_d^2	σ_e^2	σ_δ^2	k	Number of Groups	Number of Subjects
.92	.86	.74	.71	.04	26	163	1,684

[a] The abbreviations are as follows: $\bar{d}$ is the difference in effects between studies with and without goal setting weighted for sample size; σ_d is the estimated standard deviation of the standardized group goal-setting effect; σ_e^2 is the estimated variance due to sampling error; σ_δ^2 is the estimated population subgroup difference; and k is the number of effect sizes.
[b] The 95 percent credibility interval includes $-.77 < \bar{d} < 2.61$.

the eight variables shows little variance within each. For example, in regard to task type, over 80 percent of the studies to date have considered groups performing an interdependent task, and fewer than 20 percent have examined groups working on independent tasks. Given this lack of variance, meta-analytic consideration of the influence of task type on the group goal effect would not be conclusive.

The low variance on moderator variables across studies greatly limits our knowledge of the generalizability of the group goal effect. Although the meta-analytic review and previous qualitative reviews suggest a strong effect, more interesting information would be provided by moderators that identify the boundaries of or variations in the size of the effect.

Given the importance of these potential moderators to defining the generalizability of the group goal effect, we summarize the types of group goal studies that have been conducted to date and their representativeness in terms of these variables. This information is useful both for drawing tentative conclusions about the influence of the variables and for determining which variables require future research attention. Locke and Latham (1990) provided a similar analysis of the individual goal literature; however, neither those authors nor others have considered the current state of the group goal literature in regard to these potentially important variables. In this review, we consider all 29 group goal studies . . .

A QUALITATIVE REVIEW OF POTENTIAL MODERATING VARIABLES

Differences in research design and setting across the studies were coded in the following manner: (1) for goal specificity, each study was classified as having a specific goal or an unclear level of specificity; (2) for goal difficulty, a difficult goal or an unclear level of difficulty; (3) for goal source, an assigned or a participatively set goal; (4) task type was independent or interdependent; (5) subject type was student or organization; (6) experimental setting was laboratory or field; and (7) group type was intact or newly formed. (8) For the eighth variable, time, the choices were (*a*) one manipulation of group goal setting followed by one performance measure or (*b*) multiple instances of goal setting and performance measurement or performance measurement at multiple points following a group goal intervention. Two of us independently coded each study on the relevant variables and discussed the few instances of disagreement to achieve a final rating. Subsequently, we compared the ratings of a subset (25%) of the studies to determine interrater agreement. The raters were in complete agreement in the rating of goal difficulty, goal specificity, subject type, experimental setting, group type, and time. In rating goal source and task type, raters disagreed in one instance each, leading to a percentage agreement of 86 percent and a kappa of .69.

Table 3 classifies the studies according to ratings on these variables and type of findings for group goal setting. This analysis shows that 83 percent of the studies reported a positive effect, 10 percent showed mixed results,[1] and only 7 percent noted negative results. These findings are in line with those of Locke and Latham (1990), who noted that 93 percent of group goal studies showed positive or contingently positive results. We discuss results regarding each variable below.

---

[1]A study was classified as mixed when different performance measures yielded different (positive and negative) results.

TABLE 3   Classification of Studies According to Moderators[a]

	Research Results					
	Positive		Negative		Mixed	
Moderator	Number	Percentage	Number	Percentage	Number	Percentage
Goal specificity						
Specific goal	20	69			1	3
Specificity unclear	4	14	2	7	2	7
Goal difficulty						
Difficult goal	13	45	1	3	2	7
Difficulty unclear	11	38	1	3	1	3
Goal source						
Assigned	14	52	2	7.5	2	7.5
Participatively set	9	33				
Task type						
Independent	4	17				
Interdependent	16	70	1	4	2	9
Subject type						
Students	6	24				
Organization members	15	60	2	8	2	8
Setting						
Laboratory	5	17			1	3
Field	19	66	2	7	2	7
Group type						
Intact group	18	62	2	7	2	7
Newly formed group	6	21			1	3
Time						
One time period	3	10				
Over time	21	73	2	7	3	10

[a] Studies do not sum to 29 for all moderator categories because of either insufficient information in the primary studies or additional but unique categories.

Goal Specificity

Most of the studies (72%) utilized goals that were clearly specific; in the remainder of cases the extent of goal specificity could not be determined. As Table 3 shows, goal specificity appeared to be related to finding a group goal effect; 95 percent of the studies that clearly used specific goals yielded positive results, but only 50 percent of those that did not clarify goal specificity did so.

Using 1980 as a cutoff, we divided the studies into subgroups representing early and recent goal-setting research. We chose 1980 because it is the approximate mean and median year of the studies examined and close to the year in which Locke and colleagues (1981) published their influential review, which stimulated interest in goal setting. Prior to 1980, only 58 percent of the studies used specific goals, and after this date, 82 percent did so.

Goal Difficulty

Approximately half (55%) the studies used goals that were difficult; in the remainder the degree of goal difficulty could not be assessed, given the information reported. In the studies with difficult goals, 81 percent of the results were positive (a group goal effect was found). When the difficulty level was unclear, a group goal effect was found in 85 percent of the studies. Prior to 1980; only 33 percent of the studies demonstrated that the group's goals were difficult; after 1980, this percentage increased to 71 percent.

Goal Source

The majority (67%) of the studies involved assigned group goals. All the negative and mixed results occurred when goals were assigned Specifically, a positive goal effect was found in 78 percent of the studies that employed an assigned goal and in 100 percent of the studies that employed a participatively set goal. Prior to 1980, 82 percent of the studies used assigned goals, and only 18 percent had participatively set goals. Since 1980, the number of studies in these two categories has begun to converge, with 56 percent using assigned and 44 percent using participative goals.

Task Type

For the 23 studies that could be classified (there was insufficient information regarding the task for 6 studies), 83 percent involved an interdependent task and 17 percent asked group members to work independently. All the negative and mixed results occurred for groups working on tasks requiring interaction; however, it should be noted that there were few studies that employed independent tasks. All the studies that employed independent tasks were published after 1980.

Subject Type

The majority of studies (76%) examined organization members rather than students (24%); four studies were not included because they involved other, unique subject types. All the negative and mixed results occurred in studies of organization members. There appeared to be a trend toward increased use of student subjects: prior to 1980, only 10 percent of studies used students, and 90 percent used organization members; after 1980, 33 percent of the studies involved students and 67 percent, organization members.

Setting

Closely related to the type of subjects employed is the type of research setting used. Most of the 29 studies (80%) were conducted in a work setting, with only 20 percent in a laboratory setting. Further examination showed that a group goal effect was reported in 83 percent of the laboratory studies and in 83 percent of the field studies. The trend regarding research setting mimics that discussed for subject type: there appears to be a movement away from field research (17% lab and 83% field research prior to 1980) toward laboratory research (24% lab and 76% field research after 1980).

Group Type

Most of the studies (76%) employed intact groups rather than newly formed groups (24%). A group goal effect was reported in 86 percent of the studies using newly formed groups and 82 percent of the studies using intact groups. In addition, it appears that researchers are moving from a reliance upon intact groups (83% intact, 17% new prior to 1980) to greater use of newly formed groups (71% intact, 29% new since 1980).

Time

In the vast majority (90%) of the 29 studies, either group goal setting was repeated or the goal effect was measured at multiple points in time. Only three studies measured the goal effect after one performance trial. Although all the negative and mixed results occurred in studies that measured goal effects over time, it is important to recognize that the number of one-trial studies was small. A breakdown of studies by publication date indicated that all studies assessing the goal effect over only one performance trial had been published since 1980.

DISCUSSION

A meta-analytic (quantitative) review supported an earlier qualitative review (Locke & Latham, 1990) suggesting positive results related to the group goal effect. More specifically, the meta-analytic results suggested that the mean performance level of groups that set goals is almost one standard deviation higher than that of groups that do not set goals.

A qualitative review was also conducted to determine the external validity of the group goal effect. Our findings suggest that researchers have largely concentrated on exploring the group goal effect for organization members, in field settings, over time. Clearly, these trends reflect well on the generalizability of the group goal effect to organizational settings. In addition, these results compare favorably with goal research at the individual level. Locke and Latham (1990) reported that 39 percent of individual goal studies were conducted in the field and that most research subjects were college students, whereas we found that at the group level, 79 percent were field studies and 76 percent employed organization members.

Although most studies indicated the existence of a group goal effect, it is useful to examine the studies that did not. The majority of the negative and mixed results occurred in field settings and when organization members were working in intact teams toward assigned goals over time. This pattern is noteworthy but not surprising, given that such a scenario maximizes the number of extraneous variables that might influence the goal-performance relationship.

For example, the performance of an intact, compared to a newly formed, team is likely to be influenced by many factors other than the group's goal. In such complex environments, it becomes less likely that equivalent research results will be consistently obtained.

It is also interesting to note that negative results were never obtained when group goal setting was examined using students as subjects. Although it should be recognized that fewer studies used students than organization members, this result does suggest that generalizations from student to organizational populations should be made with care.

It is important to note that since 1980, group goal researchers have increasingly used student subjects and laboratory settings. However, this trend toward increased experimental control appears to reflect attempts to understand more about how group goal processes operate, as opposed to simply establishing the existence of a group goal effect. All the laboratory studies and all the studies using students have investigated processes that mediate the group goal–group performance effect (e.g., Klein & Mulvey, 1988; Smith, Locke, & Barry, 1990; Weingart, 1992; Weingart & Weldon, 1991; Weldon, Jehn, & Pradhan, 1991). Of course, these processes must be examined for different types of subjects and settings before their validity can be assumed.

At the individual level, the importance of specificity and difficulty to the goal effect is well documented (Locke & Latham, 1990). At the group level, we found that most studies employed specific group goals and that groups that had specific goals showed higher instances of positive results than did groups for which specificity levels were unclear. As mentioned earlier, specificity may be a particularly critical issue in groups, where numerous and competing goals can lead to increased ambiguity.

Many of the studies, particularly those published prior to 1980, were unclear as to the difficulty of the goal the groups were working toward; they examined the goal-performance relationship, not the relationship between clearly difficult goals and performance. However, the percentage of studies reporting a goal effect was similar whether or not difficulty was examined in the study. These similar results can be explained in two ways. First, although the authors of the ambiguous studies did not measure goal difficulty, it may be that the goals involved were in fact difficult. If this is the case, it is not surprising that the results of the studies that did manipulate goal difficulty are similar to those of the studies that did not do so. It is encouraging to note that most recent studies have been very clear as to the difficulty level of the goals used.

A second explanation is that the ambiguous studies did not employ goals that subjects found difficult. This explanation for the similarity of the findings of the difficult-goal and ambiguous studies suggests that the use of difficult goals is less important to achieving a performance effect in groups than it is for individuals. Although this explanation is not intuitively appealing, given the strong influence of goal difficulty at the individual level, it should be considered. As indicated earlier, group contexts include other potential influences on individual effort and persistence such as group cohesion and social loafing. The extent to which such factors interact with goal difficulty to encourage group member effort is a question worthy of future research attention.

Despite the strong group goal effect found in the meta-analytic review, the qualitative review emphasized several problems in the current set of group goal studies that may limit the external validity of this finding. First, most group goal studies to date have used assigned goals. Given the increased participation of workers in organizational work groups (Lawler,

1986), research on participatively set goals seems especially important. The extent to which group goals operate differently or are more or less effective when set participatively than when assigned is uncertain. There was some preliminary evidence in our review to suggest that a positive group goal effect is more likely to occur when goals are participatively set. Although this evidence should not be overinterpreted, given the small number of studies using participative goals, it does suggest that future research in this area is warranted.

A second potential problem in the current set of group goal studies is the type of task employed. Group members were asked to work on an interdependent task in most of the studies, and our results suggest that group goals can be effective with these tasks. However, we know little about whether group goals are effective with independent tasks. Because many individuals in organizations work independently on group tasks (Weldon & Mustari, 1988), future research should address the group goal effect using this type of task. Because an independent group task may closely approximate an individual task, it seems likely that research will establish a group goal effect for this task type. The interesting question, however, is whether the size of the group goal effect depends on the type of task employed. Do groups that require group members to work alone show stronger group goal effects, or are groups that work interdependently benefited more by group goal setting?

Most of the studies we reviewed used intact rather than newly formed groups. In one sense, this imbalance is encouraging because it suggests that researchers are using real groups; that is, intact social systems with boundaries and differentiated member roles (Alderfer, 1977; Hackman, 1990). On the other hand, this imbalance makes it difficult to generalize the group goal effect to situations in which newly formed groups are working toward a group goal. Future research might consider the extent to which the effects of goal setting change as the life cycle of a group progresses.

In conclusion, we examined existing research addressing the relationship between group goals and group performance. An understanding of this relationship is increasingly important because organizations are clearly becoming more group-based (Goodman, 1986; Goodman et al., 1987; Guzzo & Shea, 1992; Hackman & Morris, 1975). Although there are innumerable types of groups operating in organizations today, including autonomous work groups, project groups, and multifunction work teams, these groups share one common characteristic: they exist for the purpose of pursuing some objective or goal. A clear understanding of group goal setting and its ability to influence groups as they work toward their goals is, therefore, critically important. This study contributes to this effort by outlining the current state of the group goal literature so that future research efforts can be most productively channeled.

References

Alderfer, C. P. 1977. Group and intergroup relations. In J. R. Hackman & J. L. Suttle (Eds.), *Improving the quality of work life:* 227–296. Pallisades, CA: Goodyear.

Anderson, D. C., Crowell, C. R., Doman, M., & Howard, G. S. 1988. Performance posting, goal setting, and activity-contingent praise as applied to a university hockey team. *Journal of Applied Psychology,* 73: 87–95.

Austin, J. T., & Bobko, P. 1985. Goal-setting theory: Unexplored areas and future research needs. *Journal of Occupational Psychology,* 58: 289–308.

Baumler, J. V. 1971. Defined criteria of performance in organizational control. A*dministrative Science Quarterly,* 16: 340–350.

Becker, L. J. 1978. Joint effect of feedback and goal setting on performance: A field study of residential energy conservation. *Journal of Applied Psychology,* 63: 428–433.

Buller, B. F. 1988. Long-term performance effects of goal setting and team-building interventions in an underground silver mine. *Organizational Development Journal,* 6: 82–93.

Buller, B. F., & Bell, C. H. 1986. Effects of team building and goal setting on productivity: A field experiment. *Academy of Management Journal,* 29: 305–328.

Cohen, J. 1977. *Statistical power analysis for the behavioral sciences.* New York: Academic Press.

Emmert, G. D. 1978. Measuring the impact of group performance feedback versus individual performance feedback. *Journal of Organizational Behavior Management,* 1: 134–141.

Fellner, D. J., & Sulzer-Azaroff, B. 1985. Occupational safety: Assessing the impact of adding assigned or participative goal setting. *Journal of Organizational Behavior Management,* 7(1/2): 3–24.

French, J. R. P. 1950. Field experiments: Changing group productivity. In J. G. Miller (Ed.), *Experiments in social process: A symposium on social psychology:* 81–96. New York: McGraw-Hill.

Goodman, P. S. 1986. Impact of task and technology on group performance. In P. S. Goodman & Associates (Eds.), *Designing effective work groups:* 120–167. San Francisco: Jossey-Bass.

Goodman, P. S., Ravlin, E., & Schminke, M. 1987. Understanding groups in organizations. In L. L. Cummings & B. M. Staw (Eds.), *Research in organizational behavior,* vol. 9: 121–173. Greenwich, CT: JAI Press.

Guzzo, R. A., Jackson, S. E., & Katzell, R. A. 1987. Meta-analysis analysis. In L. L. Cummings & B. M. Staw (Eds.), *Research in organizational behavior,* vol. 9: 407–442. Greenwich, CT: JAI Press.

Guzzo, R. A., & Shea, G. P. 1992. Group performance and intergroup relations in organizations. In M. D. Dunnette (Ed.), *Handbook of industrial and organizational psychology:* 269–313. Chicago: Rand McNally.

Hackman, J. R. 1990. *Groups that work and those that don't.* San Francisco: Jossey-Bass.

Hackman. J. R., & Morris, C. G. 1975. Group tasks, group interaction process, and group performance effectiveness: A review and proposed integration. In L. Berkowitz (Ed.), *Advances in experimental social psychology,* vol. 9: 45–99. New York: Academic Press.

Hunter, J. E., & Schmidt, F. L. 1990. *Methods of meta-analysis: Correcting error and bias in research findings.* Newbury Park, CA: Sage.

Hunter, J. E., Schmidt. F. L., & Jackson, G. B. 1982. *Meta-analysis: Cumulating research findings across studies.* Beverly Hills, CA: Sage.

Jick, T. D. 1979. Mixing qualitative and quantitative methods: Triangulation in action. *Administrative Science Quarterly,* 24: 602–611.

Klein, H. J., & Mulvey, P. W. 1988. *The setting of goals in group settings: An investigation of group and goal processes.* Working paper no. 88–65, Ohio State University, Columbus.

Koch, J. L. 1979. Effects of goal specificity and performance feedback to work groups on peer leadership, performance, and attitudes. *Human Relations,* 32: 819–840.

Komaki, J., Barwick, K. D., & Scott, L. R. 1978. A behavioral approach to occupational safety: Pinpointing and reinforcing safe performance in a food manufacturing plant. *Journal of Applied Psychology,* 63: 434–445.

Latham, G. P., Erez, M., & Locke, E. A. 1988. Resolving scientific disputes by the joint design of crucial experiments by the antagonists. *Journal of Applied Psychology,* 73: 753–772.

Latham, G. P., & Locke, E. A. 1975. Increasing productivity with decreasing time limits: A field replication of Parkinson's law. *Journal of Applied Psychology,* 60: 524–526.

Latham, G. P., & Yukl, G. A. 1975. Assigned versus participative goal setting with educated and uneducated woods workers. *Journal of Applied Psychology,* 60: 299–302.

Lawler, E. E. III. 1986; *High involvement management.* San Francisco: Jossey-Bass.

Lawrence, L. C., & Smith, P. C. 1955. Group decision and employee participation. *Journal of Applied Psychology,* 39: 334–337.

Lee, C. 1988. The relationship between goal setting, self-efficacy, and female field hockey team performance. *International Journal of Sport Psychology,* 20(2): 147–161.

Levine, J. M., & Moreland, R. L. 1990. Progress in small group research. In M. R. Rosenzweig & L. W. Porter (Eds.), *Annual review of psychology,* vol. 41: 585–634. Palo Alto, CA: Annual Reviews.

Locke, E. A. 1986. *Generalizing from laboratory to field settings.* Lexington, MA: Lexington Books.

Locke, E. A., & Latham, G. P. 1990. *A theory of goal setting and task performance.* Englewood Cliffs, NJ: Prentice Hall.

Locke, E. A., Shaw, K. M., Saari, L. M., & Latham, G. P. 1981. Goal setting and task performance: 1969–1980. *Psychological Bulletin*, 90: 125–152.

Martocchio, J. J., & O'Leary, A. M. 1989. Sex differences in occupational stress: A meta-analytic review. *Journal of Applied Psychology*, 74: 495–501.

McCarthy, M. 1978. Decreasing the incidence of "high bobbins" in a textile spinning department through a group feedback procedure. *Journal of Organizational Behavior Management*, 1: 150–154.

McGrath, J. E. 1984. *Groups: Interaction and performance.* Englewood Cliffs, NJ: Prentice Hall.

McGrath, J. E., & Altman, I. 1966. *Small group research: A synthesis and critique of the field.* New York: Holt, Rinehart & Winston.

Pearson, C. A. L. 1987. Participative goal setting as a strategy for improving performance and job satisfaction: A longitudinal evaluation with railway track maintenance gangs. *Human Relations*, 40: 473–488.

Premack, S. L., & Wanous, J. P. 1985. A meta-analysis of realistic job preview experiments. *Journal of Applied Psychology*, 70: 706–719.

Price, K. H. 1987. Decision responsibility, task responsibility, identifiability, and social loafing. *Organizational Behavior and Human Decision Processes*, 40: 330–345.

Pritchard, R. D., Jones, S. D., Roth, P. L., Stuebing, K. K., & Ekeberg, S. E. 1988. Effects of group feedback, goal setting, and incentives on organizational productivity. *Journal of Applied Psychology*, 73: 337–358.

Reber, R. A., & Wallin, J. A. 1984. The effects of training, goal setting, and knowledge of results on safe behavior: A component analysis. *Academy of Management Journal*, 27: 544–560.

Reich, R. B. 1983. *The next American frontier.* New York: Times Books.

Ronan, W. W., & Latham, G. P. 1973. Effects of goal setting and supervision on worker behavior in an industrial situation. *Journal of Applied Psychology*, 58: 302–307.

Rosenthal, R., & Rosnow, R. L. 1984. *Essentials of behavioral research.* New York: McGraw-Hill.

Rowe, B. J. 1981. Use of feedback and reinforcement to increase the telephone reporting of independant automobile appraisers. *Journal of Organizational Behavior Management*, 3(2): 35–40.

Runnion, A., Johnson, T., & McWhorter, J. 1978. The effects of feedback and reinforcement on truck turnaround time in materials transportation. *Journal of Organizational Behavior Management*, 1: 110–117.

Schmidt, F. L., & Hunter, J. E. 1977. Development of a general solution to the problem of validity generalization. *Journal of Applied Psychology*, 62: 529–540.

Smith, K. G., Locke, E. A., & Barry, D. 1990. Goal setting, planning, and organizational performance: An experimental simulation. *Organizational Behavior and Human Decision Processes*, 46: 118–134.

Stedry, A. C., & Kay, E. 1966. The effects of goal difficulty on performance: A field experiment. *Behavioral Science*, 11: 459–470.

Steiner, I. D. 1972. *Group processes and productivity.* New York: Academic Press.

Stoerzinger, A., Johnston, J. M., Diser, K., & Monroe, C. 1978. Implementation and evaluation of a feedback system for employees in a salvage operation. *Journal of Organizational Behavior*, 1: 268–280.

Tubbs, M. E. 1986. Goal setting: A meta-analytic examination of the empirical evidence. *Journal of Applied Psychology*, 71: 474–483.

Wagner, J. A., & Gooding, R. Z. 1987. Shared influence and organizational behavior: A meta-analysis of situational variables expected to moderate participation-outcome relationships. *Academy of Management Journal*, 30: 524–541.

Weingart, L. R. 1992. The impact of group goals, task component complexity, effort, and planning on group performance. *Journal of Applied Psychology*, 77: 682–693.

Weingart, L. R., & Weldon, E. 1991. Processes that mediate the relationship between a group goal and group member performance. *Human Performance*, 4: 33–54.

Weldon, E., Jehn, K. A., & Pradhan, P. 1991. Processes that mediate the relationship between a group goal and improved group performance. *Journal of Personality and Social Psychology*, 61: 555–569.

Weldon, E., & Mustari, E. L. 1988. Felt dispensability in groups of coactors: The effects of share responsibility and explicit anonymity on cognitive effort. *Organizational Behavior and Human Decision Processes*, 41: 330–351.

Whitener, E. M. 1990. Confusion of confidence intervals and credibility intervals in meta-analysis. *Journal of Applied Psychology*, 75: 315–321.

Zajonc, R. B., & Taylor, J. J. 1963. The effect of two methods of varying group task difficulty on individual and group performance. *Human Relations*, 16: 359–368.

Zander, A. 1980. The origins and consequences of group goals. In L. Festinger (Ed.), *Retrospections on social psychology:* 205 –235. New York: Oxford University Press.

Yours, Mine, and Ours: Facilitating Group Productivity through the Integration of Individual and Group Goals

Deborah F. Crown
Joseph G. Rosse

The majority of studies on goal setting have been conducted at an individual level of analysis (Locke & Latham, 1990). With managers clamoring for more information on the effective management of work groups, it becomes imperative to better understand how goal setting can be used for teams. In the past few years, a significant body of research has explored the role group goals play in team environments (e.g., Klein & Mulvey, 1995; O'Leary-Kelly, Martocchio, & Frink, 1994; Weingart, 1992; Weingart & Weldon, 1991; Weldon, Jehn, & Pradhan, 1991; Weldon, Martzke & Hamilton, 1989). Although the strength of the relationship may vary, the majority of the research indicates that group goals increase group performance (see O'Leary-Kelly et al., 1994, for a comprehensive review). Yet, the role individual goals play in team performance remains elusive. Some researchers have suggested that individual goals increase group performance (Baumler, 1971; Kim & Hamner, 1976; Lawrence & Smith, 1955; Matsui, Kakuyama & Onglatco, 1987), while others have reported negative effects (Mitchell & Silver, 1990; Saavedra, Earley & Van Dyne, 1993).

One explanation for the disparity may be the nature of the task. Mitchell and Silver (1990), and Saavedra et al. (1993) proposed that the degree of interdependence in a group task is an important boundary condition on the goal setting–group performance relationship. Crown (1994) suggested that the degree of task summativity is an additional critical factor. The difference between the independent/interdependent and summative/nonsummative continuums is often confused. In its simplest terms, the independent/interdependent continuum reflects the degree to which group members must work together to accomplish a task (Mitchell & Silver, 1990), while the summative/nonsummative continuum is concerned with measurement issues. At one end of the continuum (i.e., a summative task), group performance is measured by summing the individual performances of group members; at the opposite end, task nonsummativity requires that the group product be greater than (or different from) the sum of individual outputs due to the interdependent relationships among group members (Fisher, 1974). Thus, nonsummativity requires interdependence, although interdependence does not always produce nonsummativity.

If group performance is simply the sum of individual performances as in the case of an independent or summative task, individual goals that increase individual performance will also increase group performance. This appears to be the case in some studies where individual goals were reported to have increased the performance of the group (Baumler, 1971; Kim & Hamner, 1976; Lawrence & Smith, 1955; Matsui et al., 1987). In fact, Saavedra et al. (1993) found that for pooled (i.e., summative) interdependent tasks,

From *Organizational Behavior and Human Decision Processes*, 1995, 64(2), 138–150. Reprinted with permission.

individual goals were more effective than group goals in increasing group performance. But what effect do individual goals have when the task is more than just the summation of individual performances?

Using an interdependent task Mitchell and Silver (1990) found that individual goals given alone reduced group performance. And Saavedra et al. (1993) reported that for tasks requiring greater amounts of reciprocity, group goals outperformed individual goals. Conversely, Latham and Kinne (1974) and Gowen (1985) found that both individual and group goals increased group performance. These conflicting results suggest that the nature of the task does not fully explain the effect individual goals have on group performance.

In this paper we will show that the *focus* of individual goals may be critical to groups' performance. When interdependent tasks are nonsummative, an intemperate focus on individual output may detract from group performance. The key then, for these tasks, may be in changing the individual goal from one that maximizes individual output (which we identify as an *egocentric goal*) to one where the individual goal maximizes an individual's *contribution* to the group (which we label a *groupcentric goal*). Restructuring the individual goal in this manner, and coupling it with a group goal, should result in (1) a directional goal effect toward group output, (2) a mechanism for increasing individual effort that will directly benefit the group, and (3) a reduction in the probability that members will engage in social loafing.

THEORETICAL FRAMEWORK

The theoretical basis for the efficacy of a particular combination of goals for interdependent/nonsummative tasks is derived in part from the motivational and cognitive mechanisms of goals (i.e., direction of action, strategy development, effort, and persistence; Locke, Shaw, Saari & Latham, 1981). Specifically, we propose that assigned goal structures affect group performance via their effect on performance orientation; individual and group strategy; and effort expended (see Figure 1). The first link in the model suggests that variant goal structures affect commitment to individual or group performance (i.e., performance orientation). This commitment is hypothesized to affect an individual's decision to use a cooperative or competitive strategy and represents the second link in the model. The third model link proposes that the predominant strategy choice of individuals within the group will determine the strategy the group engages in. The fourth link suggests that the group's strategy will have an effect on the performance of the group. The model also proposes that certain goal structures will stimulate member effort by increasing individuals' contribution to the group, which will

FIGURE 1   **Model of the Effects of Individual and Group Goals**

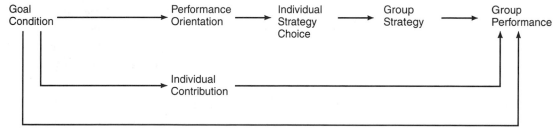

lead to subsequent increases in group performance. Ability is included in the model as a co-variate for all model links that directly affect performance.

Performance Orientation

The directive effect of goal setting is clearly seen in studies where performance on goal-directed tasks increases, but at the expense of performance on coexisting tasks (Locke & Bryan, 1969; Schmidt, Kleinbeck & Brockman, 1984; Terborg & Miller, 1978). Goals may be used to direct action toward the maximization of individual performance, group perform-ance, or both. When maximizing either individual or group output increases group perform-ance, the individual's *focus* on either individual or group performance is not an important issue. However, when maximizing individual performance does *not* directly lead to an in-crease in group performance (i.e., for nonsummative tasks), the individual's focus on indi-vidual versus group performance becomes a relevant factor.

The point where limited resources exist to maximize performance on both dimensions forces a choice of direction. A decision as to how to perform the task (i.e., strategy) may also follow. This decision about strategy has typically been assumed to result from the type or combination of goals given (i.e., goal condition). Crown (1994) suggested that an individ-ual's relative commitment to maximizing one performance dimension over the other may be a more important determinant of strategy development than goal condition. In fact, goal con-dition may increase the level of commitment to a performance dimension, which in turn may have a direct effect on strategy choice. Therefore, in group goal setting studies using inter-dependent, nonsummative tasks, an additional variable of commitment to the maximization of a performance dimension may prove important. This multilevel commitment to maximiz-ing individual and group performance will be referred to as *performance orientation*.

Performance orientation can be conceptualized on a two dimensional graph, highlighting the strength of commitment to both performance dimensions, as well as the dominance of one dimension over the other (see Figure 2). The bisecting line symbolizes an equal level of commitment to both performance dimensions, at all levels of strength. Points below this line depict individuals committed more to maximizing individual performance, with the distance from the line representative of the degree of individual performance dominance. Alternately, points above the bisection represent commitment more toward group performance, or the degree of group performance dominance.

Earlier we noted that individual and group goals stimulate performance on their level-specific performance dimension. We propose that goals also affect an individual's commit-ment to maximize a particular performance dimension. Group goal setting literature shows that group goals facilitate team productivity by directing attention toward group performance (Weingart, 1992; Weingart & Weldon, 1991; Weldon, Jehn & Pradhan, 1991). It also appears that individual goals can inhibit group productivity if they direct attention away from the group's output (Mitchell & Silver, 1990; Saavedra et al., 1993) It is logical to assume that if goals have the ability to direct attention and subsequent effort toward group or individual performance, they also have the ability to increase commitment to the dimension to which they refer. Consequently, an egocentric individual goal should increase an individual's com-mitment to maximize individual performance (i.e., Individual Performance Orientation (IPO)), while a group goal should increase commitment to maximize group performance (i.e., Group Performance Orientation (GPO)). Unfortunately, it is unclear what effect these goals would have on performance orientation when they are given in tandem.

FIGURE 2   **Performance Orientation**

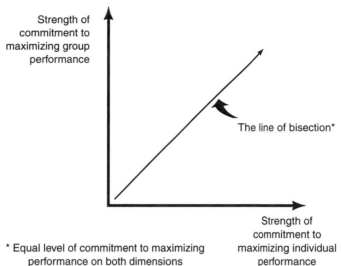

* Equal level of commitment to maximizing
performance on both dimensions

The role groupcentric individual goals play in affecting performance orientation is also ambiguous when these goals are administered without accompanying group goals. Since the groupcentric goal sets a standard for individual performance, one might expect an increase in commitment to individual performance. Yet, the focus of the goal is towards the group's output, due to the contributory nature of the goal. Therefore one would also expect commitment to group performance to increase. Consequently, it is unclear which aspect of the goal would have a stronger effect. However, when a groupcentric individual goal is coupled with a group goal, the increase in commitment to group performance should be twofold (i.e., coming from both goals), and should therefore be greater than the increase in commitment to individual performance.

The following set of hypotheses tests the first link in the model (see Figure 1).

H1.a. After subjects are assigned an egocentric individual goal given alone their commitment to individual performance (IPO) should increase.

H1.b. After subjects are assigned a group goal given alone their commitment to group performance (GPO) should increase.

H1.c. After subjects are assigned the combination of a groupcentric individual goal and group goal their performance dominance (PD) should become stronger in the direction of group performance dominance.

Strategy Development

The primary cognitive mechanism in goal setting is the stimulation of strategies (e.g., Buller & Bell, 1986; Campbell & Gingrich, 1986; Earley & Perry, 1987; Latham & Saari, 1982; Locke, Frederick, Buckner, & Bobko, 1984; Mitchell & Silver, 1990). Yet, strategy stimulation is not always beneficial to performance (Earley, Connolly & Ekegren, 1989; Huber 1985). Research shows that for complex tasks, performance is a function of *appropriate* strategy development (Earley & Perry, 1987). The appropriateness of a strategy may also be related to the nature of the task (Jewel & Reitz, 1981; Laughlin & Branch, 1972). Specifically, a nonsummative interdependent task contains an inherent level of structural conflict that may be best served by cooperative strategies (Jewel & Reitz, 1981).

The second link in the model, between individuals' performance orientation and their individual strategy choice (see Figure 1), is based on Deutsch's (1949a, 1980) theory of cooperation and competition. Deutsch contends that a situation in which the "goals" of individual members are cooperative will promote cooperative behavior, whereas a competitive social situation will promote competitive behavior. At first blush, this theory appears to support a direct link between goal condition and strategy development. However, two important factors need to be considered. First, Deutsch's theory (1949a, 1949b, 1980) concerns the "goals" shared by group members; it does not address conflicts between individual and group goals for the same person. Second, Deutsch wrote the initial piece prior to Locke's specific conceptualization of a goal. Although Deutsch never explicitly defines the term "goal," it appears to describe individuals' commitment to the maximization of either an individual or group output, not a quantified level of achievement. Therefore, based on Deutsch's research, the following hypotheses between performance orientation and individual strategy choice are presented.

H2.a. The greater the commitment to maximizing individual performance (IPO), the more likely the individual is to choose a competitive strategy.

H2.b. The greater the commitment to maximizing group performance (GPO), the more likely the individual is to choose a cooperative strategy.

Deutsch's theory also predicts that cooperative behaviors of group members will facilitate group cooperation (Deutsch, 1949a). Without looking at the process of the group, and understanding that earlier group behaviors may influence later behaviors, this contention appears almost tautological. Although we located no empirical studies that explicitly test this contention, numerous studies provide supporting information. Research on the relationship between opponents' strategies suggests that strategy selection is influenced by others' strategies (Bixenstine & Wilson, 1963; Deutsch, 1973; Esser & Komorita, 1975; Komorita & Esser, 1975; Oskamp, 1970). The work of Michelini (1971) also supports this line of reasoning. Michelini reported that a dyad's strategy was influenced by the original individual strategy of members, specifically for cooperative strategies. Based on the preceding research, as well as the overriding theoretical framework provided by Deutsch, we developed the following hypotheses about the link between individual strategy choice and the group's strategy.

H3. The more prevalent an individual cooperative strategy choice is among group members, the more likely the group is to use a cooperative strategy.

The ensuing link in the model is between the group's strategy and group performance. Deutsch (1949a) contends that cooperation within a group leads to greater productivity than intra-group competition. Hornstein's (1965) finding that competitive strategies were more likely to result in decreases in group performance supports this hypothesis. Other research also suggests a deleterious effect of competitive strategies on group outcomes (Blau, 1963; Jewell & Reitz, 1981; Sillars, Coletti, Perry, and Rogers, 1982; Steiner, 1972). Mitchell and Silver (1990) reported that groups using cooperative strategies outperformed those utilizing competitive strategies. These effects should be even more pronounced as the interdependence of the task increases.

H4. The strategy of the group will affect the group's performance.

Although Mitchell and Silver (1990) found that group strategy predicted group productivity, they were troubled because the no goal, group goal, and combined individual and group goal conditions all resulted in cooperative group strategies. Consequently, group performance was identical for all three groups. One of their conclusions was that an interdependent task will always prompt cooperative strategies. An alternate explanation may be found in the role of effort.

Effort

Goal setting is assumed to affect performance by increasing individuals' task-directed effort (Locke & Latham, 1990). We propose that this increased effort will be enhanced when group goals are complemented by groupcentric individual goals. Research on social loafing provides a basis for this proposition.

Latane, Williams, and Harkins (1979) contend that individuals working in groups often reduce their level of effort, due to reduced accountability. Williams, Nida, Bacca, and Latane (1989) found that individual effort on group activity increased when the identifiability of individual performance was high, and decreased when individual output was not identified. In a similar vein, Harkins and Szymanski (1988) suggest that effort increases when an individual can evaluate his/her own performance. Therefore, the addition of a groupcentric individual goal to a group goal may provide group members with a sense of accountability, as well as an index by which to evaluate their own *individual* performance. Conversely, if an individual goal that maximizes individual performance is given (i.e., an egocentric goal), this may become the salient index of one's own performance. Although accountability and self-evaluation directed toward individual contribution may occur when individuals are given only group goals, the likelihood should be less than when direct contribution indexes are provided (i.e., by way of a groupcentric individual goal). Therefore, when individuals can identify and evaluate themselves with reference to a part of the group's task that is "their own"—but are still contributing to the group's performance— individual effort should be maximized, resulting in an increase in group performance.

The interdependence of groupcentric individual and group goals establishes a situation whereby an increase in one dimension may facilitate an increase in the other. As group performance increases, a concomitant increase in individual contribution also occurs. Consequentially, as the group becomes more successful, individuals within the group raise their level of success in achieving their own goals. Once this dynamic has taken place, an increased level of self-efficacy may result due to the increase in inactive mastery (Bandura, 1986). This study tests the additional effects of effort by analyzing the links between (1) goal condition and individual contribution to the group, and (2) goal condition and group performance.

H5. An assigned groupcentric individual goal and group goal given in combination should result in an increase in the individual's contribution to the group over and above the contribution levels of other goal conditions.

H6. An assigned groupcentric individual goal and group goal given in combination should result in an increase in group performance over and above the performance of other goal conditions.

METHOD

Sample

Sixty preexistent groups participated in the principal study. (An additional 56 teams served as pretest groups to determine appropriate goal levels, time constraints, and task construction.) Power analysis indicated that this sample size would provide substantial statistical power (.90), assuming a medium effect size, a .05 alpha level, and equal cell size for each goal condition (Cohen & Cohen, 1983). Each group contained seven persons, producing a sample of 420 subjects.

Preexistent groups whose primary group function was the undertaking of interdependent, nonsummative production tasks were chosen for inclusion in this study. One clear example of this type of group is found among teams that participate in interdependent sports. Consequently, established sports teams were chosen to comprise the sample population. Of the 60 groups, 33 consisted of corporate intramural teams, 5 were professional sports teams, and the remaining 27 groups consisted of undergraduate- and graduate-level intramural teams. Of the 33 corporate teams, 11 also functioned as work teams.

Participants ranged from 18 to 57 years of age and were predominantly (66%) male, although the majority of groups (71%) included members of both sexes. The majority of participants (62%) held an undergraduate, masters', or doctoral degree. Teams were required to have been together for a minimum of 1 month, with the average longevity 29.7 months. Participants were also required to have been members of their team for at least 1 month, with a mean participation length of 17.6 months.

Procedure

To manipulate goal conditions, we developed a letter/word/sentence game specifically for this research. The game required individuals to use a series of 27 letters to form words while the group incorporated these words and individual letters into sentences. (Each subject in the group received a different combination of letters determined to be of equal difficulty by an independent pretest sample.) This task allowed measurement of an individual's own (egocentric) performance, an individual's contribution to the group's performance (groupcentric performance), and the group's aggregate performance.

Subjects first participated in a pretrial game with instructions to make as many three-or-more letter words as possible. Subjects were asked to place these words on their individual word lists and were also instructed to make as many group sentences as possible. At the end of the 30-minute game, the number of three-or-more letter words listed on the subject's word list was tabulated. Words did not need to be contributed to the group's sentences before being placed on the subject's word list. Therefore, words appearing on an individual's word list did not have to appear in the group's sentence. Each sentence created by the group had to contain at least one three-or-more letter word from each group member, with no upper limit to the number of words or letters each individual could contribute to the sentence.

In the second 30-minute game (i.e., the experimental trial), game conditions were identical to the first trial except subjects received different instructions depending on the goal condition they were assigned.

To leave the process of the game up to the group, no sequential task order was specified, although subjects were required to follow certain game restrictions. First, once a letter was used by an individual in a group sentence, that specific letter could not be used again. (For example, if one of three *t*'s were used in a word, that particular *t* could not be used again.) However, an individual could change the words in his/her word list in order to facilitate the group's sentence completion. Second, participants were allowed to contribute letters from their letter lists to make words with other group members, with the stipulation that the combined word did not count as either member's required word for sentence credit. In all conditions the letters contributed had to be subtracted from the individual's letter list and were not counted in the individual's final list of words.

A stratified random assignment method assigned groups to one of six goal conditions: (1) no assigned goals (i.e., "do your best"), (2) an egocentric individual goal given alone, (3) a group goal given alone, (4) an egocentric individual and group goal given in combination, (5) a groupcentric individual goal given alone, and (6) a groupcentric individual and group goal given in combination. Egocentric goals maximized individual performance (i.e., construct seven words, each consisting of three or more letters). Groupcentric individual goals maximized individual contributions to group performance (i.e., contribute 17 letters to the group's final sentences). The group goal was to construct five sentences, each with at least one three-letter word from each group member. All goals were specific and difficult; a pretest ($n = 350$) was conducted using an independent sample to determine difficult individual and group goals, which are defined by Locke to be goals that were achieved by 10% of the sample (Mitchell & Silver, 1990).

Measures

Individual Performance

Individual performance was measured by the number of three-or-more letter words listed on the subject's word list at the end of each 30-minute exercise. The difference between mean scores on the pre- and posttest measures was not significant for either the total sample ($t = .10, p > .05$), or for the group alone ($t = .18, p > .05$) (see Table 1).

Individual Contribution to the Group

Individual contribution to the group was measured by the number of letters the individual contributed to the group's sentences. Individuals were given different color pens with which to mark letters they contributed to sentences, words on their individual word lists, and words contributed to the group's sentences. The mean number of letters contributed on the experimental trial was higher than the average for the pretrial (11.09 and 9.88, respectively). However, there was no significant difference between the means of the control group ($t = 1.36, p > .05$) suggesting that practice itself did not affect individual contribution.

Group Performance

Group performance was measured by the number of sentences with at least one three-or-more letter word contributed by each group member, with no upper limit to the number of words or letters each individual could contribute. This criterion ensured the group task was

TABLE 1   **Summary Statistics for Dependent and Intervening Variables**

	Range	Mean	SD
Individual performance			
Pre	1–8	4.62	1.26
Post	1–8	4.69	1.54
Individual contribution			
Pre	0–18	9.88	4.22
Post	0–25	11.09	5.86
Group performance			
Pre	1.0–4.4	2.83	0.85
Post	0.0–6.0	3.02	1.28
Individual Performance Orientation (IPO)			
Pre	1.0–7.0	5.43	1.30
Post	1.0–7.0	5.12	1.50
Group Performance Orientation (GPO)			
Pre	1.0–7.0	5.79	1.30
Post	1.0–7.0	5.74	1.40
Performance Dominance (PD)			
Pre	1.0–6.8	3.81	1.20
Post	1.0–7.0	3.97	1.40

both nonsummative and interdependent. Pretests demonstrated that it was extremely difficult to construct a sentence with *only* seven three-or-more letter words. Therefore, this requirement increased the nonsummativity of the task by increasing the likelihood that the group product would contain more than just the sum of seven individual words (i.e., a summative task).

Completed sentences were used to form the integer, while a final incomplete sentence was scored by the percent of the sentence that was completed. Significant differences were found between the pre- and posttest for the control group, and more importantly, significant differences *between* goal conditions on the practice measures of group performance were evident ($R = .17, p < .05$). Thus, ability was included as a covariate for model links where performance was the dependent variable.

Performance Orientation

Performance orientation was measured with six seven-point Likert scale questions, and one bipolar placement scale question. The scale was initially administered after subjects participated in the first trial to obtain a baseline measure that would control for changes in performance orientation that were a function of the task itself. The second measure was taken after subjects read the instructions for their goal condition in the second trial, but prior to engaging in the task in an effort to restrict the likelihood that the strategy employed by the group would affect the individual's commitment to either performance dimension. Two items assessed the strength of Individual Performance Orientation, which represents the degree to which individuals are committed to maximizing their own individual performance ("I am committed to maximizing my individual performance in this game," "I'm not at all concerned about generating as many words as possible on my individual word list"). Two items tapped the strength of Group Performance Orientation, the degree to which an individual is committed to maximizing the performance of the group ("I am committed to maximizing the performance of my group in this game," "I'm not at all concerned about my group generating as many sentences as possible"). The three-item Performance Dominance dimension captures the performance orientation differential (i.e., Is the subject *more* committed to their own individual performance or to the performance of the group, regardless of the strength of the commitment to either?) ("I am only concerned with my individual performance in this game, I don't care how my team does," "I am only concerned with how my team does in this game, I don't care how I do individually," "Are you more committed to maximizing your personal performance or the team's performance in this game? . . ."). Negatively worded questions were reverse coded.

A factor analysis with oblique rotation was run to determine if the items assessed the three dimensions of performance orientation. Conceptually, the dimensions are not mutually exclusive, therefore delta was fixed at 0. A screen plot indicated that there were three factors, all with eigenvalues above one. The results of the factor analysis demonstrated a three-factor solution which explained 67% of the common variance. Factor 1 represents the strength of commitment to maximizing group performance (i.e., the two GPO items, with .92 and .99 factor loadings), Factor 2 represents the strength of commitment to individual performance (i.e., the two IPO items, with .65 and .99 factor loadings), and Factor 3 reflects the performance orientation differential (i.e., the three PD items, with .45, .48, and .98 factor loadings). A factor analysis was also run on the second collection of performance orientation data. The same three factors emerged with more distinct factor loadings (.87 and .88 for the two GPO items on Factor 1; .84 and .86 for the two IPO items on Factor 2; .73, .87 and .86 for three PD items on Factor 3).

Group Strategy

Group strategy was independently rated by three observers and measured via content analysis of each group session. Two raters were blind to hypotheses, with all three raters blind to condition. Utilizing the KWIC (Key-Word-In-Context, Weber, 1990) content analytic technique, relevant words, phrases, and behaviors were categorized as either cooperative or competitive, based on the works of Sillars et al. (1982) and Rahim and Buntzman (1987). (A detailed description of the categorization procedure is available from the first author.) Interrater reliability for words, behaviors and phrases being placed in the appropriate category equaled .82 for cooperative category classification, and .79 for competitive category classification. To compute the group's strategy score each of the words, phrases and behaviors of group members that were classified as either cooperative or competitive were summed, with each cooperative classification valued positive one, and each competitive classification negative one.

Individual Strategy Choice

Individual strategy choice was measured with two questions designed by Mitchell and Silver (1990). The first question asked subjects if they planned to use a strategy; the second—an open-ended question—asked what strategy they planned to use. The open-ended question was coded by two raters using the KWIC content analysis format as described above. With both raters blind to conditions and one blind to hypotheses, interrater reliability was .89.

Ability

Ability was included as a covariate of the relationship between (1) goal condition and an individual's contribution to the group, (2) group strategy and group performance, and (3) goal condition and group performance. Ability was operationalized as the scores on individual contribution and group performance for the practice trial.

RESULTS

Tests for normality were conducted by dividing the variable's skewness by the standard error of skewness. Variables that failed the assumption of normality (i.e., with Z scores greater than 2.58) were transformed using standardized or centralized scores. Bivariate scattergrams were used to test assumptions of linearity and homoscedasticity; no problems were detected. The first two hypotheses were tested at the individual level of analysis given the predictions of individual variation in these hypotheses. The remaining hypotheses utilized the group as the level of analysis.

The first set of hypotheses tested the relationship between the type of goal(s) given and individuals' performance orientation. Separate 3×2 univariate analysis of covariance (ANCOVAs) were run to test the effect of the type of individual goals (egocentric individual goals, groupcentric individual goals, no goals) and group goals (group goals, no goals) on the appropriate dimension of performance orientation (H1.a-egocentric individual goals on IPO; H1.b-group goals on GPO; H1.c-groupcentric individual and group goals on PD). The main effect for egocentric individual goals was significant ($F(1, 416) = 7.28$, $p < .007$), with IPO entered as the dependent variable and Time 1 IPO as the covariate. However, this statistic measures the effect of egocentric goals when they were given alone, as well as when they were coupled with group goals. To determine the effect of egocentric individual goals *alone* on IPO (i.e., H1.a) one-way ANCOVA was performed where the independent variable entered was egocentric individual goals given alone versus all other goal conditions. The main effect for this goal condition was even stronger, $F(1, 416) = 13.42$, $p < .000$ providing support for the hypothesis that egocentric individual goals given alone would result in increased commitment to maximizing individual performance (H1.a). The hypothesis that group goals given alone would increase commitment to maximizing group performance (i.e., H1.b) was also tested with two ANCOVAs. The 3×2 ANCOVA indicated that there was a significant main effect for group goals $F(1, 414) = 3.99$, $p < .05$) and an even stronger effect when group goals alone were contrasted with all other goal conditions, $F(1, 410) = 5.36$, $p < .02$. For both ANCOVAs the dimension of GPO was entered as the dependent variable and GPO at Time 1 the covariate. The dimension of PD was utilized to test the hypothesis that groupcentric individual and group goals given in combination would result in an increase in group performance dominance (H1.c). The full factorial model was supported, $F(6, 402 = 38.99$, $p < .000$, as was the groupcentric individual by group goal interaction, $F(2, 396) = 13.77$, $p < .000$. Inspection of the cell means suggests that the increase in group performance dominance was a function of an increase in IPO, with an even greater increase in GPO (Table 2). Although some of the other goal conditions exhibited greater increases in PD, it appears that their shifts are due in part to decreases in IPO rather than increases on both dimensions.

TABLE 2 **Changes in Performance Orientation Dimensions by Goal Type**

| | Group Goal | | | | | |
| | No Goal | | | Group Goal | | |
Individual Goal	Individual Performance Orientation	Group Performance Orientation	Performance Dominance	Individual Performance Orientation	Group Performance Orientation	Performance Dominance
No goal						
Time 1	5.54	5.60	3.99	5.27	5.65	4.01
Time 2	5.42	5.70	4.12	4.72	5.92	4.62
Change	(−.12)	(+.10)	(+.13)	(−.55)	(+.27)	(+.63)
Egocentric individual goal						
Time 1	5.44	5.66	3.62	5.43	5.81	3.59
Time 2	5.73	5.17	3.07	5.28	5.49	3.20
Change	(+.29)	(−.49)	(−.55)	(−.15)	(−.32)	(−.39)
Groupcentric individual goal						
Time 1	5.50	6.06	3.69	5.34	5.96	4.00
Time 2	4.58	6.09	4.60	5.48	6.17	4.26
Change	(−.92)	(+.03)	(+.91)	(+.14)	(+.21)	(+.26)

Discriminant function analysis was used to determine the relationship between performance orientation and individual strategy choice, the second set of hypotheses. To test the hypothesis that the greater the commitment to maximizing individual performance, the more likely the individual to choose a competitive strategy (H2.a), the IPO dimension was used as a discriminator of strategy choice (classified as cooperative or competitive). This hypothesis was supported (Wilks' Lambda = .968, $p < .003$, canonical correlation = .178), with the mean for cooperative individual strategies equaling 5.02, and 5.53 for competitive strategies. Support was also found for the hypothesis that the greater the commitment to maximizing group performance, the more likely the individual to choose a cooperative strategy (Wilks' Lambda = .98, $p < .02$, canonical correlation = .143), with the GPO mean equaling 5.98 for cooperative individual strategies, and 5.61 for competitive strategies.

A χ^2 was used to test the third hypothesis that the more prevalent individual cooperative strategy choices among group members, the more likely the group to use a cooperative strategy. The prevalence of individual strategies was determined by a composite score which was determined by adding the individual strategy classifications of group members (i.e., cooperative individual strategies were assigned a value of $+1$, no individual strategies reported were assigned a value of zero, and competitive individual strategies were assigned a value of -1). Groups were classified as competitive if their composite score was negative ($n = 21$; 35%), cooperative if their score was positive ($n = 34$; 57%), and without a dominant strategy if their composite score equaled zero ($n = 5$; 8%). The contribution of composite individual strategies for predicting group strategy (trichotomized) was significant ($\chi^2 (4, n = 60) = 13.11$, $p < .05$). In addition, percentage breakdowns revealed that groups reporting more cooperative individual strategies were more than twice as likely to use cooperative versus competitive group strategies (65% vs. 29%).

TABLE 3   **Analyses for Group Performance by Goal Condition, Controlling for Ability**

Source of Variation	Sum of Squares	DF	Mean Square	F	Significance of F
Ability covariate	.315	1	.315	.298	.588
Goal condition	38.569	5	7.714	7.286	.000
Explained	38.884	6	6.481	6.121	.000
Residual	56.115	53	1.059		
Total	94.999	59	1.610		

The fourth hypothesis predicted that the group's strategy would affect the performance of the group. The continuous scale for group strategy was used, given the continuous measurement of the dependent variable. Using multiple regression, and partialling effects for ability, group strategy was found to be a strong and significant predictor of the group's performance ($F = 37.85$, $p = .000$, $R^2 = .66$).

Hypothesis five predicted that an assigned groupcentric individual goal and group goal given in combination would result in an increase in individual contribution over and above the contribution levels of other goal conditions. The results indicate that goal condition had a direct effect on individuals' contribution to the group after controlling for ability ($F = 63.11$, $p = .000$, $R^2 = .436$). Hierarchical multiple regression, as well as one-way analysis of variance, was used to test the superiority of this goal combination versus the alternate goal conditions. This condition produced significantly higher group performance than all other goal conditions as an agglomerate (using hierarchical multiple regression, $F_{change} = 153.47$, $p = .000$, $R^2_{change} = .21$, $B = 1.25$, $SE\ B = .101$), as well as individually (utilizing both the Student–Newman–Keuls procedure and the more conservative Tukey HSD test).

Hypothesis six, that assigned groupcentric individual and group goals given in combination would increase group performance over and above the performance of alternate goal conditions, was supported. First, an ANCOVA was run to determine if there was a main effect for goal condition on group performance (see Table 3). The main effect was significant and accounted for 41 percent of the variance in group performance (after controlling for differences in ability). Student–Newman–Keuls and Tukey HSD tests indicated that subjects in the groupcentric plus group goal condition outperformed the other goal conditions both as a collection and individually (at an alpha of .05). The cell means presented in Table 4 highlight this increase in group performance. In addition, this goal condition when contrasted with all other goal conditions explained 25 percent of the variance in group performance.

DISCUSSION

A simple, yet unique goal structure for improving interdependent task group performance is apparent from these results. Although replication and refinement is necessary, the results from this study strongly suggest that groupcentric individual and group goals given in combination will increase group performance for interdependent tasks. Indeed, this combination

TABLE 4   Cell Means and Standard Deviations for Group Performance by Goal Condition

	Pre-test		Post-test	
Goal Condition	**M**	**SD**	**M**	**SD**
Control group	2.91	(1.09)	3.11	(.84)
Egocentric individual goal	3.19	(.54)	1.88	(1.20)
Group goal	2.55	(.48)	3.39	(.90)
Egocentric individual plus group goal	3.26	(.93)	2.46	(1.07)
Groupcentric individual goal	2.79	(.65)	3.01	(.96)
Groupcentric individual plus group goal	2.25	(.79)	4.30	(1.01)

of goals resulted in group performance 36% greater than that of the control group and well in excess of any other goal combination.

Perhaps the greatest advantage of combining goals in this way for interdependent tasks was found in their effect on effort. Our results suggest that not only was there a summative increase in effort expended (i.e., the effort expended for the group goal *plus* the effort expended for the individual contribution goal), there was also a multiplicative effect. It is possible that the combination of these two goals resulted in a helical effect on effort expenditure: the increase in effort expended toward group performance facilitated an increase in effort expended toward individual contribution, followed by a subsequent increase in effort expended toward group performance, and so on. Given the congruence of the goals in this condition, incremental success appears to have played a role in this process.

This combination of goals increased individuals' commitment to maximize performance on both performance dimensions. The ability to stimulate the highest level of commitment to both individual as well as group performance, coupled with a dominant group performance orientation, was important in affecting performance through the development of cooperative strategies.

Effects of Alternate Goal Conditions

As expected, effort was expended toward maximizing individual performance when an egocentric individual goal was given. However, the gain in individual performance did not translate into an automatic gain in group performance due to the nonsummativity of the task. In fact, a substantial *reduction* in group performance occurred. This result, along with findings that egocentric individual goals serve to reduce individual contribution levels to group performance and stimulate competitive strategies, further supports this goal's inappropriateness for reciprocally interdependent tasks.

Adding a group goal to an egocentric individual goal also produced the expected results: individual performance increased, while group performance decreased. However, neither the increase nor the decrease was as substantial as when an egocentric goal was administered alone. These results are consistent with the effects this combination of goals had on performance orientation, strategy choice, and individual contribution. It appears that in each relationship the group goal redirected effort and attention toward the facilitation of group performance. However, the beneficial effects from the group goal were not powerful enough to counterbalance the negative effects of the egocentric individual goal.

Although a group goal given alone produced increases in group performance, the gains were not as substantial as when group and groupcentric goals were given in combination. Failure to detect differences in individual contribution between group goal and control group conditions suggests that group goals alone, although proficient facilitators of cooperative strategies, do not stimulate vast amounts of mobilized effort toward individual contribution.

Finally, no significant difference in group performance occurred between controls and subjects given only groupcentric individual goals. Although the latter goal condition served to increase contribution, it failed to stimulate cooperative strategies. These results suggest that the stimulation of cooperative strategies in the combined goal condition was not simply the result of a "primed" strategy. Rather, the effect was stimulated by the *combination* of the goals, not by the *specific* goal fostering contribution.

The Role of Performance Orientation in Explaining Group Performance

Performance orientation was introduced in this study as an intervening variable between goal condition and strategy choice. However, to fully understand the relevance of this construct, we needed to explore the direct relationship between performance orientation and group performance. Unfortunately, this relationship was difficult to assess due to measurement problems. Performance orientation operates at an individual level; group performance, obviously, operates at the group level. Consequently, there is no error-free method of assessing the *direct* relationship between performance orientation and group performance. To correct this problem, individual contribution, which is measured at the individual level and is strongly related to group performance, was used as a proxy for a performance effect.

First, a linear relationship between how committed an individual was to maximizing group performance and individual contribution was found after controlling for ability and other performance orientation dimensions. (A similar relationship was also found when group performance served as the dependent variable.) This relationship suggests that as an individual becomes more committed to maximizing the performance of the group, there is a synchronous increase in the group's performance.

While this relationship is not surprising, the relationship between commitment to maximizing individual performance and subsequent group performance is not as intuitive. When either individual contribution or group performance was entered as the dependent variable, a curvilinear relationship in the form of an inverted U was found. This suggests that a modicum of commitment to individual performance is important to producing a high group output. Individuals overly committed to maximizing their own performance were counterproductive in producing high levels of group performance. However, this finding was only true when subjects' commitment to maximizing individual performance exceeded their commitment to maximizing group performance. Conversely, the highest levels of group performance were found among individuals who had high levels of commitment to *both* individual and group performance as well as a slightly stronger commitment to group performance (i.e., a slight group performance dominance).

These results suggest that it is more important that people are strongly committed to both dimensions of performance, rather than just *more* committed to the performance of the group. Figure 3 presents a diagram of performance orientation with the area of maximum benefit highlighted. While individuals with group performance dominance outperformed

FIGURE 3   **Performance Orientation: The Area of Maximum Benefit**

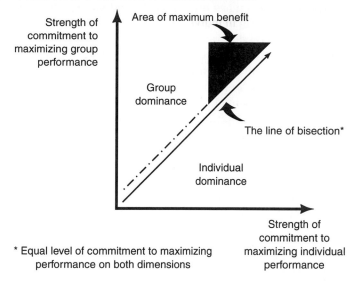

those with individual performance dominance, the closer subjects came to the area of maximum benefit, the greater their contribution to the group and the higher the group's performance. Individuals committed to the group, but also committed to maximizing their own performance may have outperformed others due to an increased level of effort that served to reduce social loafing.

Limitations and Future Research

One limitation of laboratory experiments is the problem of generalizing findings from the laboratory to an organizational setting. In an effort to offset this concern, we attempted to address other factors that serve to increase external validity. For example, several steps were taken in this study to avoid variable range restriction. First, we used a longer, more cognitively complex task designed to accommodate a wide range of possible strategies than those used in earlier studies. Second, our sample consisted of preexisting groups rather than groups created by experimenters.

External validity can also be increased by establishing a high level of internal validity. Perhaps the most significant threat to internal validity was found in tests of the hypotheses that the prevalence of a particular strategy type for individuals within the group (i.e., cooperative versus competitive strategies) would affect the nature of the group's strategy. Unfortunately, the subjectivity of the measure of individual strategy reported proved troubling. It was difficult to truly assess planned individual strategies with a subjective measure for two reasons. First, some people were reluctant to write down strategies even though they may have been formulated. Second, asking participants about strategies may have "prompted" them to design strategies when they would not have done so without provocation. (However, 50% of subjects in the control groups reported that they did not plan to use a strategy versus only 17% for subjects given goals. This suggests that even if some strategy priming was taking place the goals themselves also had an effect on strategy development.) In addition to problems with the subjective measure at the individual level, the transformation of this measure into a group-level variable was not without difficulty. The coding schema used to accomplish this relied on the equal representation (i.e., weight) of each group member's individual strategy prior to the experimental manipulation. This schema made no allowance for the interaction and evolution of individual strategies within the framework of the group. In addition, for reciprocally interdependent tasks, a single competitive individual strategy may have been more influential in affecting the group's strategy than a single negative value indicated. Consequently, additional research needs to be conducted that would allow for richer explanations of this relationship.

Power may also be an important variable in truly understanding how competitive and cooperative strategies affect group performance for interdependent tasks (Rahim & Buntzman, 1987). While a significant amount of work has focused on the role of power in dyadic conflict (Raven and Kruglanski, 1970; Stern and Gorman, 1969) as well as at the organizational level (Cobb, 1984; Krackhardt, 1990; Morris, 1991; Schein, 1977), its effect on strategy development and group performance for small groups deserves greater attention.

We should also note that there may be cultural limitations of this model. The benefits of giving dual goals, or at least the additional benefits derived from adding a groupcentric individual goal, may be further stimulated (or weakened) depending on the collectivity or individuality of the culture (Triandis, Bontempo, Villareal, Asai, & Lucca, 1988). While individualism and collectivism are typically thought of as variables at a cultural level (Triandis et al., 1988), several researchers have also measured this construct at the individual level (Erez & Earley, 1987; Hui, 1988; Triandis, Leung, Villareal, & Clack, 1985). These measures appear to reflect a trait-level construct that may moderate the performance orientation–group performance relationship. The present study demonstrated the mediating role of the state-level variable of performance orientation on the relationship between the assignment of variant goal types and subsequent group performance. What has yet to be demonstrated for group goal setting studies is the possible moderating role of the trait-level variable of collectivism (or alternatively named "allocentrism"; Triandis et al., 1985). Earley's work on the moderating effects of collectivism on social loafing (Earley, 1989, 1993) provides initial support for a similar effect in group goal setting studies. The exploration into a "fully developed construct" of collectivism and performance orientation is just beginning to emerge, and represents a fruitful area of inquiry for both group and group goal setting researchers.

Finally, it bears repeating that the domain of this model extends only to group production tasks. Therefore, before making generalizations about the superior ability of the combination of a groupcentric individual and group goal to affect task group performance, additional studies need to be conducted on both problem-solving and discussion-oriented tasks.

References

Bandura, A. (1986). *Social foundations of thought and action: A social-cognitive view.* Englewood Cliffs, NJ: Prentice Hall.

Baumler, J. V. (1971). Defined criteria of performance in organizational control. *Administrative Science Quarterly,* 16, 340–350.

Blau, P. M. (1963). *The dynamics of bureaucracy: A study of interpersonal relations in two government agencies* (Rev. ed.). Chicago: Univ. Chicago Press.

Bixenstine, V. E., & Wilson, K. V. (1963). Effects of level of cooperative choice by the other player on choices in a prisoner's dilemma game. Part II. *Journal of Abnormal and Social Psychology, 67,* 139–147.

Buller, P. F., & Bell, C. H. (1986). Effects of team building and goal setting on productivity: A field experiment. *Academy of Management Journal, 29,* 305–328.

Campbell, J. P., & Gingrich, K. F. (1986). The interactive effects of task complexity and participation on task performance: A field experiment. *Organizational Behavior and Human Decision Processes, 38,* 162–180.

Cobb, A. T. (1984). An episodic model of power: Toward an integration of theory and research. *Academy of Management Review, 9,* 482–493.

Cohen, J., & Cohen P. (1983). *Applied multiple regression/ correlation analysis for the behavioral sciences.* Hillsdale, NJ: Erlbaum.

Crown, D. F. (1994). *Facilitating group productivity through the integration of individual and group goals.* Invited address at the Society for Industrial and Organizational Psychology national meeting in recognition of the S. Rains Wallace Dissertation Award, Nashville.

Deutsch, M. (1949a). A theory of co-operation and competition upon group process. *Human Relations, 2,* 129–152.

Deutsch, M. (1949b). An experimental study of the effects of cooperation and competition upon group process. *Human Relations, 2,* 199–232.

Deutsch, M. (1973). *The resolution of conflict: Constructive and destructive processes.* New Haven, CT.

Deutsch, M. (1980) Fifty years of conflict. In L. Festinger (Eds.), *Retrospectives on Social Psychology,* New York: Oxford Univ. Press.

Earley, P. C. (1989). Social loafing and collectivism. *Administrative Science Quarterly, 34,* 565–581.

Earley, P. C. (1993). East meets west meets mideast: Further exploration of collectivistic and individualistic work groups. *Academy of Management Journal, 36(2),* 319–348.

Earley, P. C., Connolly, T., & Ekegren, G. (1989). Goals, strategy development, and task performance: Some limits on the efficacy of goal setting. *Journal of Applied Psychology, 74,* 24–33.

Earley, P. C., & Perry, B. C. (1987). Work plan availability and performance: An assessment of task strategy priming on subsequent task completion. *Organizational Behavior and Human Decision Processes, 39,* 279–302.

Erez, M., & Earley, P. C. (1987). Comparative analysis of goal setting strategies across cultures. *Journal of Applied Psychology, 72,* 658–665.

Easer, J. K., & Komorita, S. S. (1975). Reciprocity and concession making in bargaining. *Journal of Personality and Social Psychology, 31,* 864–872.

Fisher, B. A. (1974). *Small group decision making: Communication and the group process.* New York: McGraw-Hill.

Gowen, C. R. (1985). Managing work group performance by individual goals and group goals for an interdependent group task. *Journal of Organizational Behavior Management, 7(3/4),* 5–27.

Harkins, S. G., & Szymanski, K. (1988). Social loafing and self-evaluation with an objective standard. *Journal of Experimental Social Psychology, 24,* 354–365.

Hornstein, H. A. (1965). The effects of different magnitudes of threat upon interpersonal bargaining. *Journal of Experimental Social Psychology, 1,* 282–293.

Huber, V. L. (1985). Effects of task difficulty, goal setting, and strategy on performance of a heuristic task. *Journal of Applied Psychology, 70,* 492–504.

Hui, C. H. (1988). Measurement of individualism-collectivism. *Journal of Research in Personality, 22(1),* 17–36.

Jewell, L. N., & Reitz, H. J. (1981). *Group effectiveness in organizations.* Glenview, IL: Scott, Foresman.

Kim, J. S., & Hamner, W. C. (1976). Effect of performance feedback and goal setting on productivity and satisfaction in an organizational setting. *Journal of Applied Psychology, 61,* 48–57.

Klein, H. J., & Mulvey, P. W. (1995). Two investigations of the relationships among group goals, goal commitment, cohesion, and performance. *Organizational Behavior and Human Decision Processes, 61,* 44–53.

Komorita, S. S., & Esser, J. K. (1975). Frequency of reciprocated concessions in bargaining. *Journal of Personality and Social Psychology, 32,* 699–705.

Krackhardt, D. (1990). Assessing the political landscape: Structure, cognition, and power in organizations. *Administrative Science Quarterly, 35,* 342–369.

Latane, B., Williams, K., & Harkins, S. (1979). Many hands make light the work: The causes and consequences of social loafing. *Journal of Personality and Social Psychology, 37,* 822–832.

Latham, G. P., & Kinne, S. B. (1974). Improving job performance through training in goal setting. *Journal of Applied Psychology, 59,* 187–191.

Latham, G. P., & Saari, L. M. (1982). The importance of union acceptance for productivity improvement through goal setting. *Personnel Psychology, 35,* 781–787.

Laughlin, P. R., & Branch, L. G. (1972). Individual vs. tetradic performance on a complimentary task as a function of initial ability level. *Organizational Behavior and Human Performance,* 8, 210–216.

Lawrence, L. C., & Smith, P. C. (1955). Group decision and employee participation. *Journal of Applied Psychology,* 39, 334–337.

Locke, E. A., & Bryan, J. F. (1969). The directing function of goals in task performance. *Organizational Behavior and Human Performance,* 4, 35–42.

Locke, E. A., Frederick, E., Buckner, E., & Bobko, P. (1984). Effect of previously assigned goals on self-set goals and performance. *Journal of Applied Psychology,* 69, 694–699.

Locke, E. A., & Latham, G. P. (1990). *A theory of goal setting and task performance.* Englewood Cliffs, NJ: Prentice Hall.

Locke, E. A., Shaw, K. N., Saari, L. M., & Latham, G. P. (1981). Goal setting and task performance: 1969–1980. *Psychological Bulletin,* 90, 125–152.

Matsui, T., Kakuyama, T., & Onglatco, M. L. U. (1987). Effects of goals and feedback on performance in groups. *Journal of Applied Psychology,* 72, 407–415.

Michelini, R. L. (1971). Effect of prior interaction, contact, strategy and expectation of meeting on game behavior. *Journal of Conflict Resolution.* 15, 97–107.

Mitchell, T. R., & Silver, W. S. (1990). Individual and group goals when workers are interdependent: Effects on task strategies and performance. *Journal of Applied Psychology,* 75, 185–193.

Morris, A. J. (1991). *The role of political savvy in organizational politics.* Paper presented at the Annual meeting of the Academy of Management, Miami, August.

O'Leary-Kelly, A. M., Martocchio, J. J., & Frink, D. D. (1994) A review of the influence of group goals on group performances. *Academy of Management Journal,* 37(5), 1285–1301.

Oskamp, S. (1970). Effects of programmed initial strategies in a prisoner's dilemma game. *Psychonomic Science,* 19, 195–196.

Rahim, M. A., & Buntzman, G. F. (1987). *Relationships of leader power to styles of handling conflict with subordinates, compliance, and satisfaction.* Paper presented at the National Academy of Management meeting, New Orleans, August.

Raven, B. H.. & Kruglanski, A. W. (1970). Conflict and power. In P. Swingle (Ed.), *The structure of conflict.* New York: Academic Press.

Saavedra, R., Earley, P. C., & Van Dyne, L. (1993). Complex interdependence in task-performing groups. *Journal of Applied Psychology,* 78(1), 61–72.

Schein, V. E. (1977). Individual power and political behaviors in organizations: An inadequately explored reality. *Academy of Management Review,* 64–72.

Schmidt, K. H., Kleinbeck, U., & Brockman, W. (1984). Motivational control of motor performance by goal setting in a dual-task situation. *Psychological Research,* 46, 129–141.

Sillars, A. L., Coletti, S. B. F., Perry, D., & Rogers, M. A (1982). Coding verbal conflict tactics: Nonverbal and perceptual correlates of the "avoidance-distributive-integrative" distinction. *Human Communication Research,* 9, 83–95.

Steiner, I. D. (1972). *Group processes and productivity.* New York: Academic Press.

Stern, L. W., & Gorman, R. H. (1969). Conflict in distribution channels: An exploration. In L. W. Stern (Ed.), *Distribution channels: Behavioral dimensions.* Boston: Houghton Mifflin.

Terborg, J. R., & Miller, H. E. (1978). Motivation, behavior and performance: A closer examination of goal setting and monetary incentives. *Journal of Applied Psychology,* 63, 29–39.

Triandis, H. C., Bontempo, R., Villareal, M. J., Asai, M., & Lucca, N. (1988). Individualism and collectivism: Cross-cultural perspectives on self-ingroup relationships. *Journal of Personality and Social Psychology,* 54, 323–338.

Triandis, H. C., Leung, K., Villareal, M. J., & Clack, F. J. (1985). Allocentric versus idiocentric tendencies: Convergent and discriminant validation. *Journal of Research in Personality,* 19(4), 395–415.

Weber, R. P. (1990). *Basic content analysis.* Newbury Park, CA: Sage.

Weingart, L. R. (1992) Impact of group goals, task component complexity, effort, and planning on group performance. *Journal of Applied Psychology,* 77(1), 682–693.

Weingart, L. R., & Weldon, E. (1991). Processes that mediate the relationship between a group goal and group member performance. *Human Performance,* 4(1), 33–54.

Weldon, E., Jehn, K. A., & Pradhan, P. (1991). Processes that mediate the relationship between a group goal and group performance. *Journal of Personality and Social Psychology,* 61(4), 555–569.

Weldon, E., Martzke, K., & Hamilton, A. (1989). *Processes that mediate the relationship between a group goal and improved group performance.* Paper presented at the Annual Meeting of the Academy of Management, Washington, DC, August.

Williams, K. D., Nida, S. A., Bacca, L. D., & Latane, B. (1989). Social loafing and swimming: Effects of identifiability on individual and relay performance of intercollegiate swimmers. *Basic and Applied Social Psychology,* 10, 73–81.

Chapter **Five**

The Role of Affect in Motivation

Until very recently the topic of affect at work had been given little attention within the area of work motivation. Prominent theories (e.g., equity theory, expectancy theory) were built on the assumption that employees are highly rational and will exert effort only to the extent that such effort will probabilistically lead to desired outcomes. Behavior on the job was seen to stem largely from an exchange process wherein employees carefully consider how much effort to trade for organizational rewards such as pay, security, promotions, and so forth (Ashforth & Humphrey, 1995). Yet, people's perceptions and decisions can be highly influenced by their affective states (i.e., emotions and moods), individuals often act in ways that would be difficult to construe as predominantly rational, and intense task motivation exhibited by many employees appears to be grounded mainly in an emotional commitment to their jobs and an emotional immersion in their task-related experiences (Ashforth & Humphrey, 1995). Indeed, emotions seem central to the phenomenon of intrinsic motivation discussed by Ryan and Deci in Chapter 2. Clearly, an understanding of how affective experience influences work behavior seems critical to motivation research and practice.

We will reiterate here the distinction among affect, moods, and emotions described by Mitchell and Daniels in Chapter 1. Affect is a generic term that encompasses a wide variety of feelings, including emotions and moods. Emotions (e.g., anger, happiness) are intense feelings that are object specific—that is, they are directed at someone or something. Finally, moods are feelings that are not principally object specific (e.g., a blue mood) and are typically less intense than emotions.

It is also important to note that a number of typologies for emotions have been presented in social science research on the topic. For instance, a prominent scheme in the organization science literature groups emotions into six broad categories: anger, fear, sadness, disgust, surprise, and happiness (Weiss & Cropanzano, 1996). These general classes tend to consist of more specific emotional experiences. Alarm and anxiety, for example, comprise the more general emotional category of fear. While the specification of types of emotions is important for many organizational research projects, a universally accepted comprehensive typology of human emotions has yet to be developed.

Two issues relating to emotions have garnered significant recent research attention. One is the issue of managing affect at work; the other pertains to the nature and functions of emotional intelligence in organizational settings. We will briefly discuss these two issues before providing an overview of the articles included in this chapter.

MANAGING AFFECT AT WORK

Employees are usually expected to manage their emotions and moods on the job, at least to some degree. In particular, workers are expected to abide by rules and norms (often called "display rules" by researchers) requiring the expression of certain emotions and the repression of others during interactions with coworkers, customers, suppliers, and other important organizational stakeholders. "Emotional labor" is a term that has been used to refer to the effort expended in planning and controlling emotional expression so as to conform to organizational display rules (Morris & Feldman, 1996). For instance, employees at many organizations must display warmth, courtesy, and politeness toward customers while at the same time hiding any of their own frustrations, resentments, or fatigue. The degree and type of emotional labor expended in the performance of a job has important implications for employee attitudes and behaviors.

Display rules can vary across organizations. But within every organization norms exist identifying what emotions are acceptable and the degree to which they can or must be expressed. The same idea applies across cultures. That is, cultural norms exist that are relevant to the expression of emotions at work. For instance, in countries such as Japan and, to a lesser extent, the United States, cultural norms suggest it is generally inappropriate to get highly emotional in a business context. In other cultures, such as France and Italy, such displays may be more accepted or tolerated (McShane & Von Glinow, 2002). The important point is that emotional displays that are encouraged or accepted within one organizational or cultural context may be considered extremely odd or even dysfunctional in another.

EMOTIONAL INTELLIGENCE

Emotional intelligence is another fairly new topic in organization science, and it has been gaining considerable currency lately in both scholarly and practitioner literatures (see Luthans's discussion of this topic in Chapter 3). The term was initially defined as "the ability to monitor one's own and others' feelings and emotions, to discriminate among them and to use this information to guide one's thinking and actions" (Salovey & Mayer, 1990, p. 189). A more recent formulation identifies four major components of emotional intelligence as the ability to (1) perceive and express emotion, (2) assimilate emotion in thought, (3) understand and reason with emotion, and (4) regulate emotion in self and others (Mayer, Salovey, & Caruso, 2000). In general, the current research points to the importance of emotional intelligence for the effective performance of many types of jobs, especially those involving leading others.

OVERVIEW OF THE READINGS

One main function of affective states is to provide information and meaning for experience (Frijda, 1986; Lazarus, 1991). The article by Raghunathan and Pham shows how information conveyed by two different negative emotions differentially influences how people make decisions. The authors argue that sadness conveys the loss or absence of reward. Therefore, sad individuals should be motivated by an implicit goal of reward acquisition or substitution. In contrast, anxiety conveys uncertainty over an outcome and low control over a situation. Consequently, anxious individuals are expected to be more preoccupied with uncertainty reduction and risk avoidance. Consistent with their predictions, the authors found in a series of studies that sad individuals exhibit a greater preference for high-risk/high-reward decision options, while anxious people tend to prefer low-risk/low-reward options.

The second article by Venkatesh and Speier examines the relationship between positive and negative mood states during computer technology training in the workplace and trainees' subsequent intrinsic motivation and intentions to use the computer technology. They found that people in positive moods at the time of training had greater short-term intrinsic motivation and intentions to use the technology on which they were trained. However, the positive mood effect was quite transitory. Six weeks after training, intrinsic motivation and intentions to use the technology were similar to those individuals who had neutral moods at the time of training. However, the participants with negative moods at the time of training experienced not only an immediate decrease in intrinsic motivation and intention to use the technology, but also a decrease in intrinsic motivation and behavioral intentions 6 weeks after continued use of the technology. In general, the study suggests that positive and negative moods may have asymmetrical effect on intrinsic motivation and intentions to use computer technology.

References

Ashforth, B. E., & Humphrey, R. H. 1995. Emotion in the workplace. *Human Relations,* 48: 97–125.

Frijda, N. H. 1986. *The emotions.* Cambridge: Cambridge University Press.

Lazarus, R. S. 1991. *Emotion and adaptation.* New York: Oxford University Press.

McShane, S. L., & Von Glinow, M. A., 2002. *Organizational behavior,* 2nd ed. Boston: McGraw-Hill Irwin.

Mayer, J. D., Salovey, P., & Caruso, D. 2000. Models of emotional intelligence. In Sternberg, R. J. (Ed.), *Handbook of intelligence.* Cambridge: Cambridge University Press.

Morris, J. A., & Feldman, D. C. 1996. The dimensions, antecedents, and consequences of emotional labor. *Academy of Management Review,* 21: 986–1010.

Salovey, P., & Mayer, J. D. 1990. Emotional intelligence. *Imagination, Cognition, and Personality,* 9(3): 185–211.

Weiss, H. M., & Cropanzano, R. 1996. Affective events theory: A theoretical discussion of the structure, causes, and consequences of affective experience at work. In B. M. Staw and L. L. Cummings (Eds.), *Research in Organizational Behavior,* vol. 18, pp. 1–74. Greenwich, CT: JAI Press.

All Negative Moods Are Not Equal: Motivational Influences of Anxiety and Sadness on Decision Making

Rajagopal Raghunathan
Michel Tuan Pham

Common wisdom holds that one should abstain from making substantial resolutions unless one is cool and collected. Consider, however, the career moves that a recently cut-off employee has to investigate or the relocation decisions that newly divorced people often face. It is undeniable that, in spite of the common wisdom, many important decisions are made under emotionally taxing conditions. It is therefore essential to understand how people's affective states influence the way they make decisions.

Previous studies on the influence of affective states on decision processes have generally contrasted affective states of different valence, that is "positive" versus "negative" versus "neutral" (e.g., Arkes, Herren, & Isen, 1988; Conway & Giannopoulos, 1993; Isen & Geva, 1987; Wright & Bower, 1992). Implicit in these comparisons is the assumption that all positive moods, or all negative moods, are essentially equivalent.

We argue, however, that even affective states of the same valence can have distinct influences on decision making. This is because different positive affective states (e.g., price vs. cheerfulness), or different negative affective states (e.g., anger vs. sadness), may activate different implicit goals. We derive this hypothesis from recent developments on the informative value of affective states (e.g., Pham, 1998; Schwarz, 1990) combined with an analysis of the cognitive determinants of affect (e.g., Lazarus, 1991; Roseman, Spindel, & Jose, 1990).

We test this hypothesis by contrasting decision making under anxiety versus under sadness. Negative affective states provide a more powerful test of our theorizing because they are more differentiated than their positive counterparts (e.g., Averill, 1980; Ellsworth & Smith, 1988). We focus on anxiety and sadness because they are among the most widespread forms of emotional distress (Bryant & Zillman, 1984; Levi, 1967; Selye, 1956). We predicted that in decisions involving trade-offs between risk and reward, anxiety would bias preferences toward low-risk/low-reward options, whereas sadness would bias preferences toward high-risk/high-reward options. In the pages to follow, we first briefly review previous research on negative affect and decision making. We then present our theoretical framework and report three controlled experiments testing our predictions.

NEGATIVE AFFECT AS COLOR, PROCESS INTERFERENCE, AND MOOD TO BE REPAIRED

Previous research suggests that negative affective states may influence decision making in three major ways. First, negative affect may shape people's decisions by coloring the *content*

From *Organizational Behavior and Human Decision Processes,* 1999, 79(1), 56–77. Reprinted with permission.

of their thoughts. It is well established that under negative mood people's perceptions, thoughts, and judgments are often distorted toward greater negativity—an effect known as mood congruency (e.g., Carson & Adams, 1980; Cunningham, 1988; Gorn, Goldberg, & Basu, 1993; Johnson & Tversky, 1983; Mayer, Gaschke, Braverman, & Evans, 1992; Wright & Bower, 1992). The primary explanation offered for this effect is that negative affective states may cue similarly valenced materials in memory, thereby tainting people's judgments (Bower, 1981; Isen, Shalker, Clark, & Karp, 1978).

Second, negative affective states may alter the *process* through which people make decisions. It is widely held that negative affective states such as anxiety and sadness interfere with people's ability to process information (e.g., Ellis & Ashbrook, 1988; Eysenck, 1982). As a result, anxious or sad individuals are posited to process information less systematically in judgment and decision making (e.g., Conway & Giannopoulos, 1993; Sanbonmatsu & Kardes, 1988; Schwarz, Bless, & Bohner, 1991). The thesis that anxiety and sadness necessarily lead to less systematic processing has, however, been questioned (e.g., Edwards & Weary, 1993; Pham, 1996).

Third, negative affective states may influence decisions by shaping decisionmakers' *motives*. A pervasive motivational shift observed under negative affect is a heightened concern for elevating or "repairing" one's mood (e.g., Morris & Reilly, 1987; Zillmann, 1988). It was found, for instance, that sad participants having to select a partner for a problem-solving task tended to choose partners with good interpersonal skills (e.g., "friendly") over partners with task-relevant skills (e.g., "usually does well on his exams"). These sad participants apparently sought the emotional reward associated with partners with better interpersonal skills (Forgas, 1991). A motivation to repair one's mood through "feel-good" prosocial behavior may also explain the increased tendency to help that is often observed under negative affect (e.g., Schaller & Cialdini, 1990).[1]

These three major types of accounts of potential influences of negative affect on decision making share a common thread. All focus on the consequences of feeling "bad" as opposed to feeling "good" or feeling "neutral." Distinctions among negative states (e.g., anger, anxiety, sadness) are largely ignored. We discuss below a different view of negative affect—a view that recognizes potential distinctions among negative affective states.

NEGATIVE AFFECT AS INFORMATION

One primary function of affect is to provide information (e.g., Frijda, 1986; Lazarus, 1991; Schwarz, 1990). A major kind of information conveyed by affective states and feelings is one of liking versus disliking. Schwarz and Clore (1988) proposed that in order to evaluate objects, people often ask themselves, "How do I feel about it?" Negative feelings are generally interpreted as disliking or dissatisfaction, whereas positive feelings are interpreted as liking or satisfaction (e.g., Gorn et al., 1993; Martin, Ward, Achee, & Wyer, 1993; Pham, 1998; Schwarz & Clore, 1983).

---

[1]This statement does not mean that negative-mood individuals are more willing to help than positive-mood individuals. Both negative and positive moods have been found to increase helping compared to neutral moods (e.g., Manucia, Baumann, & Cialdini, 1984).

It appears, however, that the information conveyed by affective states may go beyond sheer liking or disliking. In one study (Gallagher & Clore, 1985), angry and fearful participants were asked to make judgments about the blameworthiness of a person and about the likelihood of negative life events. While angry participants reported higher assessments of blame and lower assessment of risk, fearful participants reported the reverse. In a conceptually similar study, Keltner, Ellsworth, and Edwards (1993) observed that participants modeling behavioral expressions of anger (which is typically caused by another person) were more likely to believe that future negative events would be caused by human factors, whereas participants modeling sadness (which is generally caused by circumstances) tended to believe that these events would be caused by situational factors. Both studies uncovered distinct judgmental biases even though the targets were completely unrelated to the affect-inducing stimulus. These results strongly suggest that different negative affective states may convey different types of information.

The information conveyed by a particular affective state (e.g., anxiety or sadness) can be traced back to the meaning structure underlying the typical elicitation of that affect (Schwarz, 1990). According to cognitive theories of affect (e.g., Arnold, 1960; Lazarus, 1991; Roseman et al., 1990), affective or emotional responses are mediated by a cognitive appraisal of the affect-eliciting stimulus. That is, people do not emote in response to events per se, but to their appraisal-generated mental representation of the event.[2] The same event could therefore produce different emotions depending on how it is appraised. For example, failure on a test that is attributed to oneself (e.g., "I did not study hard enough") may induce feelings of guilt or shame, whereas failure on the same test that is attributed to another person (e.g., "my roommate prevented me from studying") may result in anger (e.g., Roseman, 1991; Scherer, 1984).

To understand the effects of different affective states on decision making, it is therefore important to examine their typical underlying (appraisal-generated) meaning structures. These meaning structures determine not only the type of affect a person will experience in response to an event, but also the type of information this person is likely to infer from experiencing a given affective state. Our main thesis is that affective states such as sadness and anxiety will have distinct influences on decision making because people experiencing them will draw different inferences from their affective experiences. As a result, they will bring different implicit goals to the decision-making task. These implicit goals will influence the decision-making process even if the decision is unrelated to the event that elicited the affective state.

According to appraisal theorists, the distinctive meaning structure underlying sadnesslike emotions is the loss or absence of a reward (Lazarus, 1991; Ortony, Clore, & Collins, 1988; Roseman, 1991). Sadness-related emotions (e.g., depression, despair) are primarily experienced in response to the loss or absence of a cherished object or person (e.g., death of a family member, loss of a favorite piece of jewelry, breakup of a relationship). As a result, whenever they experience feelings of sadness, individuals should be inclined to interpret these feelings as meaning that "something (rewarding) is missing." We therefore predict that

---

[2]Note that affective states need not be based on controlled processes. Recent models of affective responses (e.g., Cohen & Areni, 1991; Leventhal, 1984) suggest that appraisal can be performed either in a controlled and elaborate mode or more automatically through the activation of affective schemata.

sad individuals should be motivated by an implicit goal of reward acquisition or substitution. This prediction is consistent with Forgas's (1991) previously mentioned finding that sad participants were primarily selecting partners based on the rewarding potential of their interpersonal skills. It is also consistent with a common tendency among consumers to buy gifts for themselves when they are feeling depressed (Mick & Demoss, 1990).

In contrast, the meaning structure underlying fearlike emotions, including anxiety, is defined by high uncertainty over an outcome and low control over a situation (e.g., Frijda, Kuipers, & ter Shure, 1989; Izard, 1977; Roseman, 1984). Anxiety is generally experienced in response to situations where the person is uncertain about an impending outcome of a personally relevant event, especially when the outcome is potentially harmful (e.g., a professor awaiting his or her tenure case decision), and feels unable to alter the course of events (e.g., investors observing the depreciation of their portfolios on the stock market). From an affect-as-information perspective (e.g., Schwarz, 1990), individuals who are experiencing anxiety are likely to interpret their feelings as signaling high uncertainty and lack of control. As a result, we predict that anxious individuals are likely to bring an implicit goal of uncertainty reduction and risk avoidance to the decision-making task. Again, we would expect this prediction to hold even if the decision target is completely unrelated to the anxiety-producing event.

In summary, building on recent work on the information value of affect (e.g., Pham, 1998; Schwarz, 1990; Schwarz & Clore, 1988) and on the cognitive structure of emotions (e.g., Lazarus, 1991; Roseman, 1991; Scherer, 1984), we argue that different negative states such as anxiety and sadness can have distinct influences on decision-making processes. This is because these affective states are likely to prompt distinct implicit goals during the decision-making process. We further propose that these distinct implicit goals may influence decision making even when the target of the decision is unrelated to the affect-eliciting event.

We tested these predictions by examining anxious and sad participants' decision in choice situations involving a trade-off between risk and reward. In each experiment, one option was associated with a higher risk and a higher reward, whereas the other option was associated with a lower risk and a lower reward. In Experiments 1 and 3, the options consisted of risky gambles; in Experiment 2 the options consisted of job profiles. Such choice situations offer a unique test of our theorizing because the trade-off between risk and reward maps directly onto the two implicit goals of uncertainty reduction and reward acquisition. It was predicted that, compared to participants in a neutral mood, sad participants would have a preference for the higher risk/higher reward option, whereas anxious participants would have a preference for the lower risk/lower reward option.

PRETEST

Given our hypothesis that anxiety and sadness can have distinct effects on decision making, it is important that we be able to manipulate these two affective states independently. Our manipulation was designed after that used by Keltner et al. (1993), which involved participants reading and projecting themselves into a hypothetical situation described in a written format. After a preliminary pretest ($n = 87$), we selected three scenarios expected to induce sadness, anxiety, or a neutral mood state.

Method

Fifty-three students at Columbia University (36 men and 17 women), who received $10 for their participation, were randomly assigned to one of three affect conditions: sad, anxious, or neutral. The study was conducted in small sessions of 7 participants per session on average. Participants were seated at least one seat apart in order to reduce distraction. The study was couched as an investigation of people's ability to empathize with hypothetical situations. Participants received a booklet, titled "Empathy Questionnaire," describing empathy as the "ability to respond with emotions similar to those of others." To increase involvement with the task, participants were told that people who score high on empathy are usually "better parents, lovers, spouses, and managers" and that they tend to be "more satisfied with their lives in general." Participants were then presented with one of three scenarios, each designed to induce a distinct affective state (anxiety, neutral, and sadness). Each scenario was one page long and structured in five paragraphs. The anxiety scenario called for participants to imagine that their doctor had called them to meet with him/her immediately because of some urgent news to divulge. The scenario hints that the person might have cancer, but does not reveal the outcome of the doctor's visit (thereby increasing the sense of uncertainty). The sadness scenario called for participants to imagine that they were returning home in response to a call regarding a serious ailment afflicting their mother. Their mother then unexpectedly died for inexplicable reasons. In the neutral-affect scenario, participants read a series of commonplace events in a day in the life of a person named Pat.[3]

Participants were asked to experience the events described in the scenario as vividly as possible and to imagine what they would feel like if they were in that situation. They were given 8–10 minutes to read the scenario, which was more time than they actually needed. After reading the one-page scenario, participants filled out several empathy-related items (e.g., "I could relate to the episode I just read," "I felt myself getting emotional as I read the passage"), which were intended to lend further credibility to the cover story.

In the next section of the questionnaire, participants were asked to "assess very carefully how you are feeling right at this time" and "be precise in expressing how you are feeling." Participants were presented with a scale consisting of 15 items each phrased in the form *I am feeling [affective term]*. Participants were asked to rate how well each item (e.g., "I am feeling angry") described their feelings on a 1 (*Described my current feelings very well*) to 7 (*Does not describe my current feelings at all*) scale. The affective terms used across items covered a broad range of affective states (e.g., anger, arousal, joy) and were selected from established scales (e.g., Mehrabian & Russell, 1974; Watson, Clark, & Tellegen, 1988). To minimize demand characteristics, the items assessing sadness and anxiety were interspersed among items assessing other affective states. A score of felt anxiety was computed by averaging (after reverse scoring) three items: nervous, anxious, and tense ($\alpha = .80$), and a similar score of felt sadness was computed from three items: sad, depressed, and empty ($\alpha = .77$).

Results and Discussion

The felt anxiety and sadness scores (see Table 1) were submitted to a 2 (type of score) $\times$ 3 (affect manipulation) mixed ANOVA, treating the type of score (felt anxiety vs. felt sadness) as a repeated factor and the affect manipulation (anxiety, sadness, or neutral mood) as a

---

[3]These affect-manipulation scenarios are available from the authors.

TABLE 1   **Pretest: Mean (and Standard Deviation) Felt Anxiety and Sadness**

	Affect Manipulation		
	Anxiety Scenario ($n = 19$)	Neutral Scenario ($n = 17$)	Sadness Scenario ($n = 16$)
Felt anxiety	4.67[a]	2.96[b]	3.35[b]
	(*SD* = 1.37)	(*SD* = 1.60)	(*SD* = 1.24)
Felt sadness	3.32[a]	3.14[a]	4.48[b]
	(*SD* = 1.36)	(*SD* = 1.49)	(*SD* = 1.21)

Note: Numbers with different superscripts in a given row are significantly different at $p < .05$.

between-subjects factor. The analysis revealed a main effect of the affect manipulation ($F(2, 49) = 4.21, p < .05, \hat{\omega}^2 = .13$) showing that the perceived intensity of both types of affect (anxiety and sadness) was higher in the sadness and anxiety scenario conditions ($M_{\text{Sadness}} = 4.02, M_{\text{Anxiety}} = 4.07$) than in the neutral scenario condition ($M = 3.10$). More importantly, this effect was qualified by an interaction with the type of affect score ($F(2, 49) = 7.55, p < .01$). Follow-up contrasts show that felt anxiety was significantly higher in the anxiety scenario condition ($M = 4.67$) than in the other two conditions, which did not differ in terms of felt anxiety ($M_{\text{Sadness}} = 3.35, M_{\text{Neutral}} = 2.96$), $F(1, 49) = 13.91, p < .001, \hat{\omega}^2 = .86$. On the other hand, felt sadness was significantly higher in the sadness scenario condition ($M = 4.48$) than in the other two conditions, which did not differ in terms of felt sadness ($M_{\text{Anxiety}} = 3.32, M_{\text{Neutral}} = 3.14$), $F(1, 49) = 9.48, p < .01, \hat{\omega}^2 = .82$. The manipulation was thus successful in inducing distinct affective states of anxiety, sadness, or neutral mood across conditions. Additional analyses showed that the manipulation did not influence ratings of anger and revengefulness, confidence and calmness, and joyfulness and cheerfulness (all p's $> .15$). This suggests that the manipulation did not inadvertently induce other affective states. The only significant effect was a lower degree of alertness in the sadness condition than in the other two conditions ($F(1, 50) = 6.18, p < .01$). As we discuss later, this difference in alertness cannot account for our results.

EXPERIMENT 1

We first tested our hypotheses in the domain of risky gambles. Anxious, sad, and neutral mood participants were asked to assess two gambles of equal expected return: (a) a higher probability–lower payoff (low-risk/low-reward) gamble and (b) a low probability–higher payoff (high-risk/high-reward) gamble. It was predicted that, compared with those in neutral moods, anxious participants would prefer the gamble with the higher probability (and lower payoff), whereas those in sad moods would prefer the one with the greater payoff (and lower probability).

Method

Eighty-three undergraduates at New York University (40 men and 43 women) participated in the study to receive course credit. They were randomly assigned to one of three affective state conditions: anxiety, sadness, and neutral. The mood-induction procedure was identical to that followed in the pretest. Under the guise of an empathy study, participants were asked to read and relate to one of the three pretested scenarios (anxiety, sadness, or neutral affect). After reading the scenarios, participants completed a seven-item "empathy scale" (which allegedly assessed how much they were able to relate to the scenarios).

Unlike in the pretest, participants' moods were not measured, because previous studies have shown that such manipulation checks can reduce the impact of the manipulated affective states on judgments (e.g., Gorn et al., 1993; Keltner et al., 1993). Instead, participants completed a "Consumer Decision Making Questionnaire," in which they were presented with two gambles: Gamble A offered a 6/10 chance of winning $5, whereas Gamble B offered a 3/10 chance of willing $10. A preliminary between-subjects pretest had shown that there were significant subjective differences between these two levels of payoffs ($F(1, 50) = 5.39, p < .05$) and two levels or probabilities ($F(1, 50) = 11.65, p < .01$). Participants first indicated their relative preference for the gambles on a 7-point scale, anchored at *I find Gamble A more attractive* and *I find Gamble B more attractive*. They then indicated which of the two gambles they would choose if they had to play. Finally, participants provided some background information.

Results

The preference ratings were converted to a 1–7 scale where higher numbers indicated a preference for Gamble B, the lower probability–higher payoff (high-risk/high-reward) option. Across conditions, preferences were skewed toward Gamble A, the higher probability–lower payoff (low-risk/low-reward) option (overall $M = 3.32$). However, as shown in Table 2, participants' relative preferences tended to differ across affect conditions. An omnibus ANOVA of these ratings yielded a marginally significant main effect of mood ($F(2, 80) = 2.56, p < 0.08, \hat{\omega}^2 = .04$). A linear trend analysis (Keppel, 1991) indicated that preference for the high-risk/high-reward option was highest in the sadness condition ($M = 3.94$) and lowest in the anxiety condition ($M = 2.84$), with the neutral affect condition in between ($M = 3.37, F(1, 80) = 5.08, p < .05, \hat{\omega}^2 = .05$). This pattern of results is consistent with the hypothesis that anxiety increases preferences for lower risk (lower reward) options, whereas sadness increases preferences for higher reward (higher risk) options.

As shown in Table 2, the affect manipulation had parallel effects on the choice probabilities. The proportion of participants who chose the high-risk/high-reward option was lowest in the anxiety condition (24%) and highest in the sadness condition (45%), with the neutral

TABLE 2   **Study 1: Mean Preference Ratings (and Standard Deviations) and Choice Probabilities**

	Affect Manipulation		
	Anxiety (*n* = 25)	Neutral (*n* = 31)	Sadness (*n* = 27)
Preference ratings	2.84[a] (SD = 1.70)	3.37[a, b] (SD = 1.91)	3.94[b] (SD = 1.78)
Choice probabilities	24%	38%	45%

Note: Higher scores imply greater preference or higher choice probability for the lower probability/higher payoff option (Gamble B). Numbers with different superscripts in a given row differ at $p < .05$.

affect condition again falling in between (38%). This linear trend approached significance (Mantel-Haenszel $\chi^2(1) = 2.58, p = .11, \phi = .18$).

Discussion

These results clearly indicate that negative affective states are not all equal in decision making. While participants in anxious moods tended to prefer the lower risk–lower payoff gamble, participants in sad moods tended to prefer the higher risk–higher payoff gamble. Neutral-mood participants' preferences fell between those of anxious and sad participants.

These results cannot be explained in terms of judgment mood congruency (e.g., Isen et al., 1978). Both anxious participants and sad participants were in a negative mood. Yet, compared to a neutral-mood condition, anxious participants' preferences tended to favor one option, whereas sad participants' preferences tended to favor the other. For the same reasons, it is difficult to explain the findings in terms of reduced processing capacity. According to previous accounts, both anxiety and sadness tend to reduce processing capacity (e.g., Conway & Giannopoulos, 1993; Ellis & Ashbrook, 1988; Eysenck, 1982; Sanbonmatsu & Kardes, 1988). However, these two affective states exhibited distinct influences on participants' preferences for the gambles. Even if the two affective states had differential effects on participants' processing capacity, a processing capacity account would not be very plausible. Processing interference effects of negative affect are primarily observed with complex tasks (e.g., Abramson, Alloy, & Rosoff, 1981; Conway & Giannopoulos, 1993; Silberman, Weingartner, & Post, 1983); the gambles used in this study were extremely simple.

It could also be argued that the findings were driven by difference in arousal across conditions. Anxiety is generally associated with high arousal, whereas sadness is generally associated with low arousal (e.g., Russell, 1980). The pretest results indeed suggest the anxiety scenario induced greater levels of alertness than did the sadness scenario. However, a difference in arousal does not appear to explain the findings. Previous research suggests that arousal should increase *risk seeking* (Mano, 1994). Yet in this experiment, anxious participants (who were presumably more aroused) were more *risk averse* than sad participants (who were presumably less aroused).

The mood-repair explanation (e.g., Schaller & Cialdini, 1990; Zillmann, 1988) may be more congenial with our theoretical explanation. That is, sad and anxious participants may have preferred one of the options because it would somehow make them "feel better." However, compared to previous accounts of mood repair, our theorizing makes more specific predictions about which type of option (low risk vs. high reward) will be preferred under different negative affective states.

A limitation of this experiment is that the observed effects were not particularly strong. Furthermore, the task of choosing between two gambles may be somewhat artificial. One is entitled to wonder whether the observed effects are reliable and generalizable to other decision problems. These issues are examined in Experiment 2.

EXPERIMENT 2

To assess the robustness and generalizability of our results, we replicated Experiment 1 in a different domain. Instead of choosing between two economically equivalent options, participants in this second experiment had to choose between two job options. One option, Job A, was described as offering a high salary with low job security, whereas the other option, Job B, was described as offering an average salary with high job security. As in Experiment 1, the decision involved a trade-off between a higher risk/higher reward option (Job A) and a lower risk/lower reward option (Job B). It was predicted that participants in an anxious mood would favor Job B, whereas participants in a sad mood would favor Job A. Participants in a neutral mood were expected to exhibit preferences between those of the other two groups.

Method

Participants were 73 students (31 men and 42 women) at Columbia University who were paid $10 for their participation. They were randomly assigned to one of three mood conditions: sadness, anxiety, or neutral. The procedure closely followed that of Experiment 1. After being induced into an anxious, sad, or neutral mood, participants were presented with the job decision. They were asked to imagine that they had to evaluate two jobs: Job A was described as "high salary with low job security," whereas Job B was described as "average salary with high job security." The participants reported their relative preferences for the two jobs on a 7-point scale anchored at *I find Job A more attractive* and *I find Job B more attractive*. They were then asked which of the two jobs they would choose. As a process check, participants were also asked to assess which characteristic of the two jobs was more important in their decision. This measure was assessed on a 7-point scale anchored at *The pay difference was more important* and *Difference in job security was more important*.

Results

As in Experiment 1, the preference ratings were converted to a 1–7 scale, where higher numbers reflected preferences for the higher risk/higher reward option (Job A). An omnibus ANOVA of these ratings revealed a significant effect of the affect manipulation, $F(2, 70) = 6.77, p < .01, \hat{\omega}^2 = .13$. As reported in Table 3, sad participants had the highest preference for Job A, the higher risk–higher reward option ($M = 5.39$), whereas anxious participants had the lowest preference for this option ($M = 3.28$). As in Experiment 1, participants in a neutral mood exhibited an intermediate level of preference for the higher risk–higher reward option ($M = 4.72$). The linear trend was highly significant, $F(1, 70) = 12.82, p < .001, \hat{\omega}^2 = .14$. The choice probabilities exhibited a similar pattern. Sad participants had the highest

TABLE 3   **Study 2: Mean Preference Ratings (and Standard Deviations) and Choice Probabilities**

	Affect Manipulation		
	Anxiety (*n* = 25)	Neutral (*n* = 25)	Sadness (*n* = 23)
Preference ratings	3.28[a]	4.72[a, b]	5.39[b]
	(*SD* = 2.21)	(*SD* = 1.90)	(*SD* = 1.99)
Choice probabilities	32%	56%	78%

Note: Higher scores imply greater preference or choice probability for the high-pay/low-job-security option (Job A). Numbers with different superscripts in a given row differ at $p < .05$.

probability of choosing Job A (78%), and anxious participants had the lowest probability (32%). (Note that the choice probabilities actually reversed across anxiety versus sadness.) The choice probabilities of participants in the neutral condition again fell between those of the other two groups (56%). The linear trend was also significant (Mantel-Haenszel $\chi^2(1) = 10.225, p = .001, \phi = .38$).

The pattern of job preferences suggests that anxious participants were primarily concerned by the differential security of the two jobs, whereas sad participants were primarily concerned by the difference in salary. We examined this interpretation further by analyzing the participants' rating of how important the difference in job security was as opposed to the pay difference in their decisions. Higher ratings indicated greater relative importance of job security and lower ratings indicated greater relative importance of pay. An ANOVA revealed that these importance ratings differed significantly across mood conditions ($F(2, 70) = 6.71$, $p < .01, \hat{\omega}^2 = 14$). Consistent with the proposed interpretation, anxious participants rated the difference in job security as relatively more important (and the difference in pay as relatively less important; $M = 5.04$), whereas sad participants rated the difference in pay as relatively more important (and the difference in job security as relatively less important; $M = 2.57$). Neutral-mood participants rated the two characteristics as equally important ($M = 3.96$). Their ratings fell between those of the other two groups. Again, the linear trend was significant ($F(1, 70) = 12.82, p < .001, \hat{\omega}^2 = .15$).

Discussion

The results of this experiment conceptually replicate those of the first experiment. While anxious participants favored the lower salary–higher security job, sad participants favored the higher salary–lower security job. It is important to note that, as in Experiment 1, neutral-mood participants exhibited intermediate-level preferences and choices. This particular pattern of results—anxiety < neutral < sadness—cannot be easily explained by previous theorizing of the effects of negative affect on decision making.

The results show that, although the effects observed in Experiment 1 were relatively small, they are reliable. It is also noteworthy that parallel results were obtained across gambling and job-selection decisions. These effects seem to be both robust and generalizable.

Although Experiments 1 and 2 provide convergent evidence of the distinct influences of anxiety and sadness on decision making, the processes underlying these effects need to be clarified. If anxious and sad individuals are pursuing different implicit goals when making decisions, is the underlying process passive and spontaneous, or more active and strategic? This question is examined in Experiment 3.

EXPERIMENT 3

One objective of this experiment was to replicate further the main result that anxiety and sadness induce distinct preferences for risky options. The main objective, however, was to examine more closely the underlying process. Two types of processes would be consistent with the explanation that anxiety and sadness prime different goals in decision making. One explanation is an overlearned attentional shift. Over time, people may have learned to attend to sources of uncertainty when experiencing anxiety and to attend to sources of reward when experiencing sadness. Because these tendencies are learned over numerous experiences, these attentional shifts would presumably be passive rather than active or strategic. Alternatively, anxiety and sadness may bias decisions through an active process of feeling-monitoring. Anxious and sad individuals may actively assess the feeling implications of their options by asking themselves, "What would I feel better about . . . ?" (see Martin, Abend, Sedikides, & Green, 1997, for a related idea). Given that different goals are presumably salient among anxious and sad individuals, the options would have different feeling implications. An option that has high (low) reward potential would feel better (worse) if the individual were sad, whereas an option that minimizes (increases) uncertainty would feel better (worse) if the individual were anxious.

Participants were presented with a choice between the two gambles used in Experiment 1. Two factors were manipulated. The first factor manipulated participants' affective states, anxiety or sadness. The second factor framed the perspective from which participants were asked to make their decisions. In the self condition, participants were instructed to evaluate the gambles from their own perspective, as in the first two experiments. That is, participants were told to examine the gambles as if they actually had to choose for themselves and face the outcome of their decisions. In the agent condition, participants were instructed to evaluate the gambles as if they were making the decision for someone else. It was emphasized that the outcome of the decision would not affect the participants personally.

The predictions were as follows. If anxiety and sadness bias decision making by prompting an overlearned (passive) attentional shift, the bias should not depend on whether participants would be personally affected by the outcome of their decisions. Compared to anxious participants, sad participants should exhibit higher preference for the high-risk/high-reward option *regardless* of whether they are making the decision for themselves or for someone else. If, on the other hand, anxiety and sadness bias decision making because individuals actively monitor the feelings associated with their decisions, the magnitude of the bias should depend on whether participants expect to experience the consequences of their decision. The bias should be more pronounced when participants (and their feelings) can be affected by the outcome of their decisions than when participants cannot be affected (see Manucia, Baumann, & Cialdini, 1984, for similar reasoning). As a result, the effects of sadness vs. anxiety on preference for the options should be stronger in the self condition than in the agent condition.

Method

Ninety-one students at Columbia University (33 men and 58 women) were recruited and paid $12 in compensation for participating in the study. They were randomly assigned to one of four conditions of a 2 (affective state: anxious vs. sad) $\times$ 2 (framing: self vs. agent) between-subjects design. The procedure closely followed that of the first two experiments, except that no neutral-mood condition was included. After being put into either an anxious or a sad state, participants were asked to evaluate the same two gambles as in Experiment 1. The framing of the decision differed across conditions. In the self condition, participants received the same instructions as in Experiment 1. They were instructed to evaluate the gambles as if they had to choose between them for themselves. In the agent condition, participants were told to make the decision on behalf of someone else. The instructions emphasized that "the decision will not affect you personally." After comparing the two options, participants first reported their relative preference on a 7-point scale, then their choice between the two gambles. Finally, participants described their feelings on a multi-item mood scale similar to that used in the pretest and completed questions assessing their attitudes toward risk.[4]

Results

As in the first study, preference ratings were converted to a 1–7 scale where higher numbers indicated a preference for Gamble B (the higher payoff, more risky option). The means are reported in Table 4. As in Experiment 1, overall preferences were skewed toward Gamble A (overall mean across conditions = 3.47). The preference ratings were submitted to a 2 (affective state) × 2 (framing) ANOVA. The analysis revealed a significant man effect of mood ($F(1, 89) = 9.36, p < 0.01, \hat{\omega}^2 = .08$), revealing that, overall, anxious participants had a relative preference for the less risky option ($M = 2.89$), whereas sad participants had a relative preference for the option with the higher payoff ($M = 4.06$). This finding replicates the first two experiments' main results.

More important, the analysis also revealed a significant mood by framing interaction ($F(1, 89) = 3.57, p < 0.06, \hat{\omega}^2 = .025$). Planned contrasts show that the simple main effect of affective states was significant in the self condition ($F(1, 89) = 11.63, p < .001, \hat{\omega}^2 = .10$) but not in the agent condition ($F < 1, ns$). The findings thus seem to support an active feeling-monitoring explanation as opposed to a more passive attentional shift.

The choice probabilities between the two gambles exhibited a directionally consistent pattern (see Table 4). A two-way (affective state by framing) log-linear analysis revealed a

TABLE 4   **Study 3: Mean Relative Preference Ratings (and Standard Deviations) and Choice Probabilities**

	Affect Manipulation	
	Anxiety (*n* = 47)	**Sadness (*n* = 46)**
Preference ratings		
Self (*n* = 49)	2.68[a]	4.63[b]
	(SD = 1.52)	(SD = 1.92)
Agent (*n* = 44)	3.08[a]	3.54[a]
	(SD = 1.82)	(SD = 2.24)
Mean	2.89[a]	4.06[b]
	(SD = 1.68)	(SD = 2.14)
Choice probabilities		
Self (*n* = 49)	27%[a]	59%[b]
Agent (*n* = 44)	20%[a]	29%[a]
Mean	23%[a]	43%[b]

Note: Higher scores imply greater preference or choice probability for the lower probability/higher payoff option (Gamble B). Numbers with different superscripts in a given row differ at $p < .05$.

[4]The purpose of these questions was to assess whether feelings of sadness and anxiety would predict participants' momentary attitudes toward pure risk activities (e.g., bungee jumping). The results (available from the authors) was inconclusive and are therefore not reported. This issue is elaborated in the General Discussion.

significant main effect of affective state ($\chi^2(1) = 3.93, p = < 0.05, \phi = .21$), showing that the probability of choosing the high-risk/high-reward option was higher among sad participants (43%) than among anxious participants (23%). This tendency was primarily driven by participants in the self condition (sad = 59%, anxious = 27%, $Z = 2.13, p < .02, \emptyset = .32$). The tendency was not significant in the agent condition (sad = 29%, anxious = 20%, $z = .76, p = .22, \phi = .11$). However, the affective state by framing interaction was not significant ($\chi^2(1) = .83, p = .36$).

Discussion

As in the previous experiments, sad participants were again found to exhibit greater preference for the high-risk/high-reward option, whereas anxious participants tended to prefer the low-risk/low-reward option. However, the pattern of preferences depended on the framing of the decision. While preferences showed the predicted affective bias in the self condition, preferences were insensitive to participants' affective states in the agent condition. This contingency appears to rule out a passive, overlearned, attentional shift. Had the process been beyond participants' control, a parallel affective bias should have been observed in the agency condition. The data appear more consistent with an active feeling-monitoring explanation. Anxious and sad individuals may be inclined to assess the feeling implications of their decisions, asking themselves, "What would I feel better about . . . ?" Sad individuals may intuit that they would feel better if they chose a high-reward option, whereas anxious individuals may intuit that they would feel better if they chose a more secure option. However, if the task is framed as an agent decision task, anxiety and sadness cease to influence people's decisions, presumably because people's feelings are less relevant when they are making decisions on behalf of someone else (see Forgas, 1991).

GENERAL DISCUSSION

All Negative Moods Are Not Equal

The pervasiveness of emotional stress in personal and organizational life underscores the importance of studying how affective states, especially negative ones, influence decision processes. Previous research on this issue has primarily focused on the contrast between positive, negative, and neutral affective states. Potential differences in decision making arising from affective states of the same valence have been largely overlooked (see Lerner & Keltner, in press, and Mano, 1992, 1994, for exceptions). This paper shows that two affective states of the same negative valence—anxiety and sadness—can have distinct influences on decision making about gambles. It was found across three experiments that sadness biases preferences toward high-risk/high-reward options, whereas anxiety biases preferences toward low-risk/low-reward options. These biases appear to arise because anxiety heightens people's preoccupation with risk and uncertainty, whereas sadness heightens people's preoccupation with reward. Despite both being negative affective states, anxiety and sadness thus seem to trigger distinct motivational inclinations. This finding echoes the recent distinction in the motivation literature between "promotion focus," which emphasizes nurturance and the search for reward, and "prevention focus," which emphasizes security and the avoidance of punishment (see Higgins, 1997). These motivational inclinations may shape decision making above and beyond previously identified effects of negative affective states, such as coloring, processing interference, and mood management. In a study contrasting the effects of anger and fear on risk perceptions, Lerner and Keltner (in press) recently observed conceptually related results.

This finding has clear substantive implications. It is noteworthy that the observed biases occurred even though the affect-inducing event (the fictitious scenarios) and the decision targets were completely unrelated. It is likely that the biases will be even more pronounced when the source of the negative affective state *is* related to the decision domain (see, e.g., Dunegan, Duchon, & Barton, 1992). For instance, a person who has been sad because of a layoff may be inordinately seduced by job options that emphasize reward characteristics (e.g., high compensation, travel opportunities) as opposed to job options that emphasize greater security. The finding also has implications for coping strategies. Lay theories of how to deal with emotional states when making decisions speak to the better established influences of affective states on decision processes. For instance, recommendations such as "look at the bright side of it" are implicitly meant to correct for the coloring effect of negative affective states (e.g., Clark & Isen, 1982). In contrast, coping strategies that address the specific biases uncovered in this research are less likely to be part of a person's repertoire.

Feelings of Risk, Feelings of Reward

The pattern of results across experiments provides some insights about the processes underlying people's decisions when sad or anxious. Had the results been obtained with gambling decisions alone, one might be tempted to conclude that the effects of anxiety and sadness on decision making are particular to expectancy-valuation processes (probability $\times$ consequence). However, the results of Experiment 2—which used stimuli that were less amenable to an expectancy-valuation process—suggest that the effects of anxiety and sadness may be independent from expectancy valuation per se.[5] The effects appear to be mediated by people's responses to the risk and reward components of the options, rather than their expectancy-valuation combination (see Aschenbrenner, 1978, for related results). We believe that these responses to risks and rewards are *feelings*.

In Experiment 3 anxious and sad participants behaved as if they were actively monitoring their feelings in response to the options. A spontaneous shift of people's attention could not account for the data. Anxious and sad individuals may consider each option and ask themselves, "What would I feel better about . . . ?" Options that are superior on the goal dimension highlighted by the affective state (low risk/high certainty versus reward) may "feel better," thereby skewing people's preferences toward these options. This process is related to the How-do-I-feel-about-it (HDIF) heuristic (Schwarz & Clore, 1988) in that feelings experienced when a person is considering a target are used as a basis for evaluating the target. However, it is important to note that the feelings that are apparently being used do not come directly from the person's affective state as in previous demonstrations of the HDIF heuristic

---

[5]Recall that participants in that experiment had to choose between a high salary with low job security and an average salary with high job security. To rely on expectancy valuation, participants would have to assess and compare expected salary streams over time. Although such a process is conceivable—and normatively sensible—it does not appear very plausible psychologically.

(e.g., Gorn et al., 1993; Schwarz & Clore, 1983). In our studies, participants' sadness or anxiety did not simply carry over to their evaluations of the two options (see Martin et al., 1997, for a similar argument). Instead, the feelings that are used appear to come from the person's affective responses to the options ("Option A/B feels better"; see Pham, 1998), which are *conditional* on the person's preexisting affective state ("I am anxious/sad"). The use of feelings in decision making may thus be more complex than previously recognized. Experiment 3's finding that anxiety and sadness influenced the decisions only when participants (in the self condition) could expect to experience the consequences of their decisions echoes recent findings suggesting that people may be flexible in choosing to use or not use feelings depending on the relevance of these feelings to the decision (Pham, 1998).

The Past and the Future

It is instructive to relate our findings with previous studies and suggest potential avenues for future research. Situational anxiety has been found to increase risk seeking in lotteries (Mano, 1992). This finding seems to conflict with the consistent risk aversion exhibited by the anxious participants in our studies. It appears, however, that it is not anxiety per se that increases risk seeking; it is the physiological arousal that often accompanies high anxiety (Mano, 1992, 1994). Heightened arousal indeed appears to be a necessary condition for increased risk taking under negative affect (Leith & Baumeister, 1996). Our scenario manipulation of anxiety may not have elevated participants' arousal as much as manipulations in other studies. It is therefore important to disentangle the effects of anxiety and arousal in studies of negative affect and decision making. While anxiety itself may produce a motivational inclination toward risk aversion, any physiological arousal that may accompany anxiety may increase risk-seeking tendencies.

Our account of the effects of sadness and anxiety in decision making combines *processing* ideas from the affect-as-information framework (e.g., Martin et al., 1997; Pham, 1998; Schwarz, 1990) with *content* ideas from cognitive theories of affect (e.g., Lazarus, 1991; Scherer, 1984). Although we believe that this account has much to offer to the study of affect and decision making, we do not regard it as a substitute for previous accounts of affect and decision making. Attempts to accommodate the wide range of affect-and-decision-making phenomena into a single, parsimonious framework may be overly ambitious. Future research should not be geared to identify which account is the most valid. It should rather be geared to formalize the conditions under which one explanation (e.g., process interference) is more likely to apply than other explanations. For instance, there is growing evidence that processing interference effects of negative affect are more likely when the processing demands of the task are high than when these demands are low (e.g., Abramson et al., 1981; Conway & Giannopoulos, 1993). We also speculate that processing-interference effects are characteristic of relatively severe affective conditions, such as depression (e.g., Abramson et al., 1981; Silberman et al., 1983), chronic dysphoria (e.g., Conway & Giannopoulos, 1993), and high physiological arousal (e.g., Pham, 1996; Sanbonmatsu & Kardes, 1988).

Under what conditions will affective states have the type of motivational influences documented by our studies? First, we offer that these influences are particular to choice situations. We suspect that the information that feelings provide consists primarily of behavioral directions ("Do A rather than B"). Unless one has a choice to make, such behavioral directions are of little use. Second, we surmise that these influences are more likely when the decision imposes a significant trade-off. Feelings are essentially heuristics (Clore, 1992; Pham, 1998; Schwarz & Clore, 1988). Their information value increases when the decision is not easily amenable to other judgment processes (Clore, Schwarz, & Conway, 1994; Strack, 1992). Decisions that involve trade-offs, such as risk versus reward, are inherently difficult to solve, especially when formal criteria, such as expected value, fail to provide a clear answer (as in Experiments 1 and 3) or are not easily applicable (as in Experiment 2). Finally, the motivational influences of affective states may be contingent on their chronicity. In chronic affective conditions, such as clinical depression, feelings may lose their perceived diagnosticity.

Aside from formalizing the conditions under which affect will have the type of motivational influences proposed in this article, three issues are clearly worthy of further investigation. First, an obvious extension of this research would be to examine how other affective states—positive (e.g., pride vs. joy) and negative (guilt vs. anger)—influence decision processes. Second, sad participants in our studies appeared to be systematically risk seeking. However, our theorizing suggests that it was not risk per se that sad participants were seeking; it was the greater reward (higher payoff or higher salary) associated with the riskier option. One way of testing this proposition would be to examine how anxious, sad, and neutral-mood individuals would respond to *pure* risk activities (e.g., thrill seeking). Third, the choice domains in our studies all revolved around potential gains rather than losses. It would be interesting—both substantively and theoretically—to investigate how anxiety and sadness influence decision processes about potential losses.

Finally, it is important to reflect on the broader theoretical implications of this research. First, the research reinforces the importance of looking at moods, feelings, and emotions as discrete entities with distinct meanings and motivational implications (see, e.g., Frijda, 1986; Roseman et al., 1990; Scherer, 1984), as opposed to continuous variations in valence and arousal (see, e.g., Russell, 1980). Second, the research suggests a different way of looking at the role of affect in decision making. As embodied by the "rational-versus-emotional" dichotomy, affect is often regarded as exerting an undesirable influence on decision making (see, e.g., Loewenstein, 1996). This view may be unduly pessimistic. It is at odds with a vast body of literature suggesting that feelings and emotions have adaptive value (Frijda, 1986; Plutchik, 1980). We would like to argue that affect often *assists* decision making (Pham, 1998). In many decisions, feelings may indeed be the most useful information people have.

References

Abramson, L. Y., Alloy, L. B., & Rosoff, R. (1981). Depression and the generation of complex hypotheses in the judgment of contingency. *Behavior Research and Therapy,* 19, 33–45.

Arkes, H. R., Herren, L. T., & Isen, A. M. (1988). The role of potential loss in the influence of affect on risk-taking behavior. *Organizational Behavior and Human Decision Processes,* 42, 181–193.

Arnold, M. B. 1960). *Emotion and personality.* New York: Columbia Univ. Press.

Aschenbrenner, K. M. (1978). Single-peaked preferences and their dependability on the gambles' presentation mode. *Journal of Experimental Psychology: Human Perception and Performance,* 4, 513–520.

Averill, J. R. (1980). On the paucity of positive emotions. In K. Blankstein, P. Pliner, & J. Polivy (Eds.), *Advances in the study of communication and affect: Vol. 6. Assessment and modification of emotional behavior* (pp. 7–45). New York: Plenum.

Bower, G. H. (1981). Mood and memory. *American Psychologist, 36*, 129–148.

Bryant, J., & Zillman, D. (1984). Using television to alleviate boredom and stress: Selective exposure as a function of induced excitational states. *Journal of Broadcasting, 28*(1), 1–21.

Carson, T. P., & Adams, H. E. (1980). Activity valence as a function of mood change. *Journal of Abnormal Psychology, 89*, 368–377.

Clark, M. S., & Isen, A. M. (1982). Toward understanding the relationship between feelings states and social behavior. In A. Hastorf & A. M. Isen (Eds.), *Cognitive social psychology* (pp. 73–108). New York: Elsevier.

Clore, G. L. (1992). Cognitive phenomenology: Feelings and the construction of judgments. In L. L. Martin & A. Tesser (Eds.), *The construction of social judgments* (pp. 133–163). Hillsdale, NJ: Erlbaum.

Clore, G. L., Schwarz, N., & Conway, M. (1994). Affective causes and consequences of social information processing. In R. S. Wyer & T. K. Srull (Eds.), *Handbook of social cognition* (2nd ed., pp. 323–417). Hillsdale, NJ: Erlbaum.

Conway, M., & Giannopoulos, C. (1993). Dysphoria and decision making: Limited information use for evaluations of multiattribute targets. *Journal of Personality and Social Psychology, 64*, 613–623.

Cunningham, M. R. (1988). What do you do when you are unhappy or blue? Mood, expectancies, and behavior. *Motivation and Emotion, 12*, 309–331.

Dunegan, K. J., Duchon, D., & Barton, S. L. (1992). Affect, risk, and decision criticality: Replication and extension in a business setting. *Organizational Behavior and Human Decision Processes, 53*, 335–351.

Edwards, J. A., & Weary, G. (1993). Depression and the impression-formation continuum: Piecemeal processing despite the availability of category information. *Journal of Personality and Social Psychology, 64*, 636–645.

Ellis, H. C., & Ashbrook, P. W. (1988). Resource allocation model of the effects of depressed mood states on memory. In K. Fiedler & J. P. Forgas (Eds.), *Affect, cognition, and social behavior* (pp. 25–43). Toronto: Hogrefe.

Ellsworth, P., & Smith, C. A. (1988). Shades of joy: Patterns of appraisal differentiating pleasing emotions. *Cognition and Emotion, 2*, 301–331.

Eysenck, M. W. (1982). *Attention and arousal, cognition and performance.* New York: Springer.

Forgas, J. P. (1991). Affective influences on partner choice: Role of mood in social decisions. *Journal of Personality and Social Psychology, 61*, 708–720.

Frijda, N. H. (1986). *The emotions.* Cambridge: Cambridge Univ. Press.

Frijda, N. H., Kuipers, P., & ter Shure, E. (1989). Relations among emotion, appraisal, and emotional action readiness. *Journal of Personality and Social Psychology, 57*, 212–228.

Gallagher, D., & Clore, G. (1985). *Effects of fear and anger on judgments of risk and evaluations of blame.* Paper presented at the meeting of the Midwestern Psychological Association, Chicago.

Gorn, G. J., Goldberg, M. E., & Basu, K. (1993). Mood, awareness, and product evaluation. *Journal of Consumer Psychology, 2*, 237–256.

Helregel, B. K., & Weaver, J. B. (1989). Mood-management during pregnancy through selective exposure to television. *Journal of Broadcasting and Electronic Media, 33*, 15–33.

Higgins, E. T. (1997). Beyond pleasure and pain. *American Psychologist, 52*, 1280–1300.

Isen, A. M., & Geva, N. (1987). The influence of positive affect on acceptable level of risk: The person with a large canoe has a large worry. *Organizational Behavior and Human Decision Processes, 39*, 145–154.

Isen, A. M., Shalker, T. E., Clark, M., & Karp, L. (1978). Affect, accessibility of material in memory, and behavior: A cognitive loop? *Journal of Personality and Social Psychology, 36*, 1–12.

Izard, C. E. (1977). *Human emotions.* New York: Plenum.

Johnson, E. J., & Tversky, A. (1983). Affect, generalization, and the perception of risk. *Journal of Personality and Social Psychology, 45*, 20–31.

Keltner, D., Ellsworth, P. C., & Edwards, K. (1993). Beyond simple pessimism: Effect of sadness and anger on social perception. *Journal of Personality and Social Psychology, 64*, 740–752.

Keppel, G. (1991). *Design and analysis: A researcher's handbook* (3rd ed.). Englewood Cliffs, NJ: Prentice Hall.

Lazarus, R. S. (1991). *Emotion and adaptation.* New York: Oxford Univ. Press.

Leith, K. P., & Baumeister, R. F. (1996). Why do bad moods increase self-defeating behavior? Emotion, risk-taking and self-regulation. *Journal of Personality and Social Psychology, 71*, 1250–1267.

Lerner, J. S., & Keltner, D. (in press). Beyond valence: Toward a model of emotion-specific influences on judgment and choice. *Cognition and Emotion.*

Levi, L. (1967). *Stress: Sources, management, and prevention.* New York: Liverright.

Loewenstein, G. (1996). Out of control: Visceral influences on behavior. *Organizational Behavior and Human Decision Processes,* 65, 272–292.

Mano, H. (1992). Judgments under distress: Assessing the role of unpleasantness and arousal in judgment formation. *Organizational Behavior and Human Decision Processes,* 52, 216–245.

Mano, H. (1994). Risk taking, framing effects, and affect. *Organizational Behavior and Human Decision Processes,* 57, 38–58.

Manucia, G. K., Baumann, D. J., & Cialdini, R. B. (1984). Mood influence on helping: Direct effects of side effects? *Journal of Personality and Social Psychology,* 46, 357–364.

Martin, L. L., Abend, T., Sedikides, C., & Green, J. D. (1997). How would I feel if . . . ? Mood as input to a role fulfillment evaluation process. *Journal of Personality and Social Psychology,* 73, 254–269.

Martin, L. L., Ward, D. W., Achee, J. W., & Wyer, R. S. (1993). Mood as input: People have to interpret the motivational implications of their moods. *Journal of Personality and Social Psychology,* 64, 317–326.

Mayer, J. D., Gaschke, Y. N., Braverman, D. L., & Evans, T. W. (1992). Mood-congruent judgment is a general effect. *Journal of Personality and Social Psychology,* 63, 119–132.

Mehrabian, A., & Russell, J. (1974). *An approach to environmental psychology.* Cambridge, MA: MIT Press.

Mick, D. G., & Demoss, M. (1990). Self-gifts: Phenomenological insights from four contexts. *Journal of Consumer Research,* 17, 322–332.

Morris, W. N., & Reilly, N. P. (1987). Toward the self-regulation of mood: Theory and research. *Motivation and Emotion,* 11, 215–249.

Ortony, A., Clore, G. L., & Collins, A. (1988). *The cognitive structure of emotions.* Cambridge: Cambridge Univ. Press.

Pham, M. T. (1996). Cue representation and selection effects of arousal on persuasion. *Journal of Consumer Research,* 22, 373–387.

Pham, M. T. (1998). Representativeness, relevance, and the use of feelings in decision-making. *Journal of Consumer Research,* 25, 144–159.

Plutchik, R. (1980). *Emotion: A psychoevolutionary synthesis.* New York: Harper & Row.

Roseman, I. J. (1984). Cognitive determinants of emotion. In P. Shaver (Ed.), *Review of personality and social psychology: Emotions, relationships, and health* (Vol. 5, pp. 11–34). Beverly Hills, CA: Sage.

Roseman, I. J. (1991). Appraisal determinants of discrete emotions. *Cognition and Emotion,* 5, 161–200.

Roseman, I. J., Spindel, M., & Jose, P. S. (1990). Appraisals of emotion-eliciting events: Testing a theory of discrete emotions. *Journal of Personality and Social Psychology,* 59, 899–915.

Russell, J. A. (1980). A circumplex model of affect. *Journal of Personality and Social Psychology,* 39, 1161–1178.

Sanbonmatsu, D. M., & Kardes, F. R. (1988). The effects of physiological arousal on information processing and persuasion. *Journal of Consumer Research,* 15, 379–385.

Schaller, M., & Cialdini, R. B. (1990). Happiness, sadness, and helping. In T. E. Higgins & R. M. Sorrentino (Eds.), *Handbook of motivation and cognition* (Vol. 2, pp. 265–296). New York: Guilford.

Scherer, K. (1984). Emotion as a multicomponent process: A model and some cross-cultural data. In P. Shaver (Ed.), *Review of personality and social psychology: Emotions, relationships, and health* (pp. 37–63). Beverly Hills, CA: Sage.

Schwarz, N. (1990). Feelings as information: Informational and motivational functions of affective states. In T. E. Higgins & R. M. Sorrentino (Eds.), *Handbook of motivation and cognition: Foundations of social behavior* (pp. 527–561). New York: Guilford.

Schwarz, N., Bless, H., & Bohner, G. (1991). Mood and persuasion: Affective states influence the processing of persuasive communications. In M. Zanna (Ed.), *Advances in experimental social psychology* (Vol. 24, pp. 161–199). San Diego, CA: Academic Press.

Schwarz, N., & Clore, G. (1983). Mood, misattribution, and judgments of well-being: Informative and directive functions of affective states. *Journal of Personality and Social Psychology,* 45, 513–523.

Schwarz, N., & Clore, G. (1988). How do I feel about it? Informative functions of affective states. In K. Fiedler & J. Forgas (Eds.), *Affect, cognition and social behavior* (pp. 44–62). Toronto: Hogrefe International.

Schwarz, N., & Clore, G. (1996). Feelings and phenomenal experiences. In T. E. Higgins & A. Kruglanski (Eds.), *Handbook of social cognition* (pp. 433–465). Hillsdale, NJ: Erlbaum.

Seyle, H. (1956). *The stress of life.* New York: McGraw-Hill.

Silberman, E. K., Weingartner, H., & Post, R. (1983). Thinking disorder in depression: Logic and strategy in an abstract reasoning task. *Archives of General Psychiatry,* 40, 775–780.

Strack, F. (1992). The different routes to social judgments: Experiential versus informational strategies. In L. L. Martin &

A. Tesser (Eds.), *The construction of social judgments* (pp. 249–275). Hillsdale, NJ: Erlbaum.

Watson, D., Clark, A. L., & Tellegen, A. (1988). Development and validation of brief measures of positive and negative affect: The PANAS scale. *Journal of Personality and Social Psychology, 54*, 1063–1070.

Wegener, D. T., & Petty, R. E. (1994). Mood management across affective states: The hedonic contingency hypothesis. *Journal of Personality and Social Psychology, 66*, 1034–1048.

Wright, W. F., & Bower, G. H. (1992). Mood effects on subjective probability assessment. *Organizational Behavior and Human Decision Processes, 52*, 276–291.

Zillmann, D. (1988). Mood management: Using entertainment to full advantage. In L. Donohew & H. E. Sypher (Eds.), *Communication, social cognition, and affect* (pp. 147–171). Hillsdale, NJ: Erlbaum.

Computer Technology Training in the Workplace: A Longitudinal Investigation of the Effect of Mood

Viswanath Venkatesh
Cheri Speier

You spent a wonderful week in Hawaii. You are upbeat. You return to work for an important executive technology training program. Alternatively, you had an argument with your spouse. Your typical 20-minute commute took over an hour due to bad traffic. You reach work and head straight for an important executive training program on a new computer software application. Will your mood, altered by either of these two highly plausible scenarios, affect your motivation and intentions related to the new technology? Further, will the positive or negative mood state at the time of training influence your long-term motivation and intentions?

One could argue that everyone is always in "some sort of mood." From a practical perspective, events in one's day-to-day activities, including those that occur in the workplace, can trigger or sway people's moods into more positive or negative mood states (Cervone, Kopp, Schaumann, & Scott, 1994; Clark & Watson, 1988; George & Jones, 1996; Isen & Levin, 1972). Even small events (e.g., finding change in a telephone booth) are sufficient to generate mood effects that influence individuals' perceptions and actions (Isen, Shalker, Clark, & Karp, 1978). Such moods typically influence an individual's behavior in a wide variety of contexts (e.g., Bower, 1991; Clark & Isen, 1982; Forgas, 1995).

From a training perspective, employees participating in a specific training session would likely be in very different moods and these moods might differentially influence training outcomes. However, the role and effects of employee mood in organizational training situations have been overlooked as have long-term effects of mood. This research addresses the gap in organization behavior literature by presenting a longitudinal investigation of how positive, negative, or neutral employee moods during technology training influence motivation to use

From *Organizational Behavior and Human Decision Processes*, 1999, 79(1), 1–28. Reprinted with permission.

that technology. This question is of critical importance given that computer technologies have become pervasive in today's workplace, and organizations spend about $20B each year on computer training (Industry Report, 1996). Unfortunately, there is growing evidence of unrealized or less than expected productivity gains due to poor user acceptance of new technologies (Keil, 1995; Swanson, 1988). Employee computer training has been identified as a necessary and essential component of individual and organizational computing success to counteract existing acceptance problems (Tannenbaum, 1990; White & Christy, 1987). While research investigating issues influencing effective computer training have begun to proliferate (Compeau & Higgins, 1995; Martocchio, 1994; Mitchell, Hopper, Daniels, George-Falvy, & James, 1994; Venkatesh, in press; Venkatesh & Davis, 1996), the effects of mood on training have yet to be fully investigated.

INFLUENCE OF MOOD ON MOTIVATION TO USE COMPUTER TECHNOLOGY

Motivation has been identified as a key determinant of behavior in a wide variety of domains (Deci & Ryan, 1985). Two broad classes of motivation—intrinsic and extrinsic—have been defined and examined across a variety of contexts and studies (Deci, 1971; Deci & Ryan, 1985; see Vallerand, 1997, for a review). Intrinsic motivation refers to the pleasure and inherent satisfaction derived from a specific activity (Deci, 1975; Vallerand, 1997), while extrinsic motivation emphasizes performing a behavior because it is perceived to be instrumental in achieving valued outcomes that are distinct from the activity such as increased pay and improved job performance (Lawler & Porter, 1967; Vroom, 1964). Such intrinsic and extrinsic motivation together influence an individual's intention to perform an activity as well as actual performance (Deci, 1975).

In the context of technology, Davis, Bagozzi, and Warshaw (1992) tested a motivational model of technology usage. Consistent with prior research investigating other behaviors, they found that extrinsic and intrinsic motivation were key drivers of an individual's intention to perform the behavior (i.e., technology usage), a construct that has been linked closely with actual behavior (see Ajzen, 1991; Sheppard, Hartwick, & Warshaw, 1988; Taylor & Todd, 1995). Davis et al. (1992) conceptualized and operationalized extrinsic motivation to use a specific technology in the workplace by relating it to performing job-related activities more productively. Individuals are often rewarded for good and productive behavior with raises, bonuses, etc. (Pfeffer, 1983; Vroom, 1964). Therefore, if a technology is perceived to be useful in facilitating the individual's productivity, she/he is likely to have extrinsic motivation to use a given technology (Davis, 1989; Davis et al., 1992; Robey, 1979). Alternatively, if a technology is not perceived as useful, it will offer the individual no advantages and possibly disadvantages in performing their work, thereby inhibiting their ability to perform their job and obtain rewards (Davis, Bagozzi, & Warshaw, 1989).

In addition to perceived productivity gains from using a technology, some individuals may have intrinsic motivation to interact with technologies. Such intrinsic motivation was conceptualized and operationalized by Davis et al. (1992) as perceived enjoyment—the extent to which using a computer is perceived to be enjoyable distinct from any performance outcomes that might be obtained (see also Carroll & Thomas, 1988; Deci, 1971; Malone,

1981a). Empirical support for enjoyment as a determinant of behavioral intentions to use a specific technology has been demonstrated for both computer games (Holbrook, Chestnut, Oliva, & Greenleaf, 1984; Malone, 1981) and for computer technology in the workplace (Davis et al., 1992).

While there is empirical support for the motivational model of technology usage (Davis et al., 1992), little is known about the underlying factors influencing extrinsic and intrinsic motivation, the key drivers of technology usage. Specifically, we examine how employee mood, a state variable, at the time of initial training on a new technology influences her/his motivation to use a new technology. Further, from the perspective of motivation and mood research, little is known about the long-term effects of motivation on technology usage behavior. To address this, the current work presents an investigation of employee mood at the time of training on long-term motivation, intention, and behavior. Thus, this research aims to further our understanding of technology usage behavior in general and the work of Davis et al. (1992) in the following three ways: (a) examining the role of an external variable (i.e., mood) in the motivational model of Davis et al. (1992), (b) studying the role of motivation as it influences technology usage in the long run, and (c) understanding potential long-term effects (on technology usage behavior) of the mood that was salient at the time of initial training on the new technology.

General Mood Research

Mood refers to how people feel when they are engaged in any number of activities (George & Jones, 1996). Mood has been examined as both a state and a trait (see George, 1989, 1991) and in this research, mood is examined as a state variable. Prior research has identified a breadth of specific moods (e.g., sadness, fear, arousal, elation) (Russell & Mehrabian, 1977; Watson & Tellegen, 1985) and a strong theoretical basis exists for categorizing these diverse mood states into either positive or negative affect (Clark & Isen, 1982; Osgood & Suci, 1955; Schwarz & Clore, 1988).

Research assessing the influence of mood on judgment, motivation, and performance has branched into two paths—research allocation (see Ellis & Ashbrook, 1988, for a review) and associative network models (Bower, 1981; Clark & Isen, 1982; Isen, 1984). The distinction between these paths relates to some extent [to] the manner in which mood interacts with cognitive processing. The resource allocation perspective suggests that moods can actually interfere with cognitive processing while the associative network model perspective suggests that mood provides a context in which cognitive processing is performed. There is empirical support for both perspectives and they may be complementary in nature (Kihlstrom, 1991). Proponents of the resource allocation path suggest that individuals have limited attentional resources and any affective state, including positive or negative moods, requires the expenditure of limited resources, decreasing the resources available for information processing (Ellis & Ashbrook, 1988; Hasher & Zacks, 1979). Although both positive and negative moods influence resource allocation, these different affective states are believed to influence resource allocation in different ways.

Individuals in positive moods expend some resources "enjoying" their mood and therefore reduce the amount of extensive information processing and engage in heuristic processing where positive information cues are particularly salient (Asuncion & Lam, 1995). With respect to negative moods, the influence on attentional resource availability is also particularly deleterious as individuals with negative moods are more likely to concentrate on their current negative mood state (Ellis & Ashbrook, 1988) and significantly limit the resources available for processing. Negative moods have resulted in reduced information recall (Ellis, Thomas, McFarland, & Lane, 1985), higher performance expectations placed upon oneself (Cervone et al., 1994), reduced task processing (Oaksford, Morris, Grainger, & Williams, 1996), and less favorable evaluations (Curren & Harich, 1994). Thus, there is mood-congruent recall of information where those in positive moods recall positive information and those in negative moods recall negative information.

An alternative perspective, the associative network model (Bower, 1981), proposes that moods are stored as nodes in memory just as information content is stored in memory nodes. When new information is learned or processed, it is associated with the nodes that are active at the time of learning, linking these content and affective state nodes together. When content that has been associated with a specific affective state is retrieved from memory, so too is the affective state, resulting in an ongoing association between the affective state and content (Bower, 1991; Curren & Harich, 1994; Forgas, 1995).

How is a positive or negative mood state during training likely to influence employee motivation to use a specific computer technology? Vallerand (1997) suggests that individual situational or social factors (i.e., "human and nonhuman factors found in our social environment . . . and variables that are present at a given point in time but not on a permanent basis") (Vallerand, 1997, p. 295) influence motivation to perform a variety of activities. Mood fits this situational role as it is a pervasive, yet nonenduring state (Swinyard, 1993). Although mood itself is not enduring, it is possible that the effects of mood on subsequent behavior may have both short- and long-term implications (Curren & Harich, 1994).

Short-Term Mood Effects

Specific to computer technology training, an individual's perception of enjoyment of technology use (i.e., intrinsic motivation) is likely to be influenced by mood. Positive moods result in more favorable assessments of one's abilities (Martin, Ward, Achee, & Wyer, 1993; Schwarz & Bohner, 1996) and enhanced perceptions of confidence (Forgas, 1991), thus potentially increasing perceptions of enjoyment and thereby intrinsic motivation. Additionally, individuals in positive moods tend to use heuristic (as opposed to analytical) processing (Worth & Mackie, 1987), resulting in increased creativity and playfulness (Isen, 1984; Schwarz & Bless, 1991), leading to greater task enjoyment (Carson & Adams, 1980) and thus greater intrinsic motivation. In general, positive moods have been shown to enhance perceptions of a given task and satisfaction (Brief, Butcher, & Roberson, 1995; Kraiger, Billings, & Isen, 1989) likely resulting in increased intrinsic motivation (George & Brief, 1996).

In contrast, individuals in a negative mood state may be less motivated to perform well in demanding tasks (Kihlstrom, 1989; Pavelcheck, Antil, & Munch, 1988; Schaller & Cialdini, 1990), in part because they must allocate some of their limited attentional resources to repairing their mood (Ellis, Ottaway, Varner, Becker, & Moore, 1997). Negative moods also result in more pessimistic assessments regarding oneself and the adequacy of existing knowledge, and other relevant aspects of the situation including external resources (Forgas, Bower, & Moylan, 1990; Schwarz & Bonner, 1996; Weary & Gannon, 1996). This negative assessment generates uncertainty and/or lack of confidence in one's ability and can result in a negative judgment towards a given situation (Weary & Gannon, 1996). Therefore:

H1(a): Individuals in positive mood states have greater intrinsic motivation to use a new computer technology than individuals in neutral moods.

H1(b): Individuals in negative mood states have less intrinsic motivation to use a new computer technology than individuals in neutral moods.

Just as mood is hypothesized to influence intrinsic motivation, mood can also influence extrinsic motivation. Specific to training, mood can influence learning and information processing as an individual in a positive mood learns and recalls positive details associated with the material more effectively and is more likely to make a more positive attribution regarding ambiguous information (Bower, 1991; Erber, 1991; Forgas, 1992, 1995). These positive attributions are likely to result in individuals recognizing greater value in using the technology specific to the technology's usefulness and increased productivity associated with their job. Additionally, individuals in positive moods apply more creativity (Schwarz & Bless, 1991) to their processing and are therefore more likely to see more subtle ways of using the technology to enhance their productivity.

In contrast, individuals in a more negative mood are more likely to make negative attributions regarding the technology's usefulness and its ability to increase their productivity and rewards. Similarly, these individuals perform more analytical, detailed-oriented processing (i.e., mood avoidance) increasing their procedural knowledge. However, their logical reasoning is characterized by limited originality, creativity, and playfulness (Schwarz & Bless, 1991). With respect to training, this is likely to result in individuals who understand how to make the technology perform specific functions, but who have limited insights into how to use the technology to improve their personal productivity (e.g., less ability to apply the acquired knowledge into domain specific requirements). Therefore:

H2(a): Individuals in positive mood states have greater extrinsic motivation to use a new computer technology than individuals in neutral moods.

H2(b): Individuals in negative mood states have less extrinsic motivation to use a new computer technology than individuals in neutral moods.

Although there is strong empirical support for the relationship between intrinsic/extrinsic motivation and intention to perform an activity (e.g., use a technology) (Davis et al., 1992; Kruglanski, Friedman, & Zeevi, 1971; Vallerand, Fortier, & Guay, 1997) and actual behavior (Deci & Ryan, 1985; Vallerand & Bissonnette, 1992; Vallerand, Fortier, & Guay, 1997), the nature of the relationship varies based on the motivational forces specific to the behavior at hand. For example, Deci (1971, 1975) indicated an interactive effect exists between extrinsic and intrinsic motivation on intention where introducing or increasing extrinsic motivation decreases intrinsic motivation for tasks that were originally purely motivated from an intrinsic perspective. However, for behaviors that are not purely intrinsic in the first place, extrinsic and intrinsic motivation play an additive role in explaining intentions and behavior (Calder & Staw, 1975; Hirst, 1988; Mossholder, 1980).

In prior technology adoption and usage research, the additive role of extrinsic and intrinsic motivation as determinants of computer usage in the workplace has been theoretically justified and empirically demonstrated by Davis et al. (1992). The earlier mood-congruent hypotheses (H1(a), H1(b), H2(a) and H2(b)) suggested that positive mood will increase while negative mood will decrease both intrinsic and extrinsic motivation to use a technology.

Given the additive role of extrinsic and intrinsic motivation for workplace computing, it follows that intention should also follow this mood-congruent pattern. Therefore:

H3(a): Individuals with positive moods will have greater intention to use a technology than individuals with neutral moods.

H3(b): Individuals with negative moods will have lower intention to use a technology than individuals with neutral moods.

In sum, in the short term, positive mood is expected to enhance both intrinsic and extrinsic motivation and the resulting intention to use the new technology. In contrast, negative mood is expected to depress both intrinsic and extrinsic motivation, thus lowering intention to use the new technology.

Long-Term Mood Effects

If mood can influence motivation at the time of training and immediate recall, are these effects sustainable? The evidence on this topic is equivocal and may be highly dependent on the specific tasks, materials, and activities (Bower, 1987; Eich, Macaulay, & Ryan, 1994; Kihlstrom, 1989). There is evidence that mood dependent effects exist only over short periods of time (Eich et al., 1994; Vallerand, 1997). However, Curren and Harich (1994) demonstrated that mood can have long-lasting effects on evaluations and judgments. Grounding their findings in the associative network model perspective, when an individual retrieves information regarding a specific activity (e.g., enjoyment or usefulness of a technology), she/he will also unconsciously retrieve information associated with her/his mood at the time this information was encoded.

Specific to negative moods, Leight and Ellis (1981) indicated that individuals in negative moods exhibited inhibited recall performance in immediate and longer term (i.e., separated by a minimum of 24 hours) assessments. Importantly, the long-term inhibited recall performance (among those who were in a negative mood at the time of initial encoding of the information) was observed despite the induction of an elated or neutral mood immediately before measurement of performance in the long term. Therefore, it would appear that the initial negative mood resulted in an inefficient or inappropriate processing strategy that became increasingly inflexible and rigid during succeeding training periods resulting in impaired long-term performance. Developing an inefficient or inflexible information processing strategy at the time of initial training is difficult to overcome, as it affects one's perceptions of intrinsic motivation regarding engaging in an activity such as computer use. Even with additional training and repeated use as seen in Leight and Ellis (1981), the initial perceptions formed may be too instantiated to overcome with direct experience.

The importance of developing effective processing during initial exposure and learning has strong corollaries to intrinsic motivation. For example, higher levels of intrinsic motivation developed during the early stages of learning lead to sustained interest and/or behavior regarding a specific activity while it is difficult to develop intrinsic motivation if it is not initially fostered during learning (Vallerand & Bissonette, 1992). Therefore, the mood at the time of stimulus and training may have a lasting effect on one's impression of that stimulus (Curren & Harich, 1994). Therefore:

H4(a): Over time, individuals who had positive moods at the time of training will have greater intrinsic motivation to use a technology than those individuals who had neutral moods.

H4(b): Over time, individuals who had negative moods at the time of training will have lower intrinsic motivation to use a technology than those individuals who had neutral moods.

It was hypothesized that mood would influence extrinsic motivation at the time of training based on an individual's positive or negative attribution regarding training information presented. While research has not investigated the potential long-term effects of mood on extrinsic motivation, there is evidence in social psychology research that suggests direct experience with the behavior in question is important in shaping/creating accurate individual attitudes toward the behavior (e.g., Doll & Ajzen, 1992; Fazio & Zanna, 1978a, 1978b, 1981; Regan & Fazio, 1977). Post-training, individuals can engage in ongoing technology use and have ample opportunity to learn from experience and share and receive opinions of the technology from their peers. It is expected that these activities create more salient perspectives on the technology's usefulness and more fully shape an individual's extrinsic motivation regarding the technology. Furthermore, these experiences and information sharing occur over a lengthy period of time after the initial mood induction, thus minimizing or possibly removing any network association of the initial mood state with current perceptions of the technology's value. Therefore:

H5: Over time, there will be no differences in extrinsic motivation between individuals who had positive, neutral, or negative moods at the time of training.[1]

The additive relationship between intrinsic and extrinsic motivation as determinants of intention to use technology in the long term is also expected to be similar to what was discussed earlier (please see H3(a) and H3(b)). It was hypothesized that a mood-congruent priming influence would affect intrinsic motivation post-training (H4(a) and H4(b)). Therefore:

H6(a): Over time, individuals who had positive moods at the time of training will have greater intentions to use a technology than those individuals who had neutral moods.

H6(b): Over time, individuals who had negative moods at the time of training will have lower intentions to use a technology than those individuals who had neutral moods.

In conclusion, the long-term effects of mood were hypothesized to be comparable to the short-term effects with the exception of extrinsic motivation.

METHOD

Setting and Participants

Three hundred eighty-eight employees of a midsize accounting firm participated in this study resulting in 316 usable responses across both waves of data collection. This firm is located in a large Midwestern city, and participants were located at three separate branches within the metropolitan area. While all the respondents had prior experience using computers, they did not have any prior knowledge about or experience with the database system or database training that occurred during the study.

---

[1]We would prefer not to use a null form of the hypothesis here. However, prior mood literature provides very little guidance when looking at long-term effects of extrinsic motivation, and other psychology research suggested that there is not likely to be a directional effect.

Of the 316 participants, 104 were women (33%) and 212 (67%) were men. The average age of the participants was 41.8, with a range from 22 to 58. On average, participants had 15.1 years of work experience, with a range of 6 months to 24 years, and 4.2 years of tenure in the specific organization, with a range from 3 months to 24 years. The participants had used computers for an average of 3.3 years, with their experience ranging from 6 months to 22 years.

Experimental Materials

Twenty-five-minute video clips were used to induce positive and negative moods in a manner consistent with prior research (Baumgardner & Arkin, 1988; Brand, Versupui, & Oving, 1997; Curren & Harich, 1993; Forgas, Bower, & Moylan, 1990). To minimize the possibility of our mood inducement being "video specific," two positive- and two negative-mood-inducing videos were used. One positive mood inducement was based on an episode of the popular NBC series "Seinfeld." The specific episode used was titled "The Soup Nazi"; Appendix 1 provides a brief description of the episode from *TV Guide*.[2] The second positive mood video, edited from the "NBA Superstar Video Series," featured the career highlights of NBA superstar Kareem Abdul-Jabbar.[3]

Similarly, two videos were used to induce negative mood. One video was an edited version of a documentary describing details from World War II. The documentary was recorded from the cable-TV channel "History." Specifically, the segment of the documentary conveyed how prisoners were treated in Hitler's concentration camps including recreations of the execution of prisoners. The second video featured a devastating injury to a college football player while playing a football game. The video presented multiple camera angles on the play causing the injury, clips from the hospital, and reactions of family and friends.

In assessing the alternatives to create a neutral mood (e.g., neutral video vs. a waiting period with no explicit manipulation), we chose to implement this manipulation by creating a 25-minute waiting period under the auspices of waiting for the training team to arrive. Although control was somewhat lost in ensuring that these participants were in a neutral mood at the start of training, manipulating the neutral condition in this manner facilitated the examination of the influence of naturally occurring moods on motivation and intentions to use technology. A manipulation check was performed assessing mood state and a post hoc analysis was performed by examining the more positive and more negative participants to understand what, if any, naturally occurring mood effects might exist.

---

[2]At the time of the development of the research plan, the authors consulted with 10 peers and 7 of them named this specific episode to be among the top-three funniest "Seinfeld" episodes, with 6 of them rating it to be the "funniest." In a brief survey of an undergraduate class, 20 of 35 rated this episode among the top three, with 14 of them rating this episode as the funniest. The chosen episode received a *TV Guide* rating of four stars (highest rating).

[3]Kareem Abdul-Jabbar was a member of the Milwaukee Bucks and Los Angeles Lakers during a career that spanned about 20 years. During this time, he was a member of six NBA championship teams, and won six "Most Valuable Player" awards. When he retired, he led the league in nine statistical categories. Recently, he was also named to the list of "The 50 Greatest Players in NBA History."

Measurement

Extrinsic motivation, intrinsic motivation, and behavioral intention were all measured using validated scales from Davis et al. (1992). Prior research assessing the influence of motivation on computer technology acceptance has measured extrinsic motivation as perceived usefulness and intrinsic motivation as perceived enjoyment (Davis et al., 1992). Perceived usefulness refers to an individual's expectation that computer usage will result in enhanced job performance/productivity (Davis, 1989; Davis et al., 1989) and was measured using a four-item scale. There has been strong and consistent empirical evidence supporting the reliability and validity of the scale (Davis, 1989; Davis et al., 1989; Mathieson, 1991; Segars & Grover, 1993; Taylor & Todd, 1995; Szajna, 1996; Venkatesh & Davis, 1996).

Similarly, intrinsic motivation has been measured in a variety of ways including an individual's perceived enjoyment (Davis et al., 1992; Wicker, Brown, Wiehe, & Simon, 1992). Specific to computer technology, enjoyment has been defined as the extent to which using a computer is perceived to be enjoyable distinct from any performance outcomes that might be obtained (Davis et al., 1992; Deci, 1971; Malone, 1981) and was measured using a three-item scale adapted from Davis et al. (1992).

Behavioral intention to use a technology was measured using a two-item scale from Davis et al. (1992) and adapted from the measures used in the Theory of Reasoned Action and the Theory of Planned Behavior (Ajzen, 1985, 1991; Ajzen & Fishbein, 1980; Fishbein & Ajzen, 1975).

To assess the effectiveness of the mood manipulation, mood was measured using the Positive Affect Scale of the Job Affect Scale (Brief, Burke, George, Robinson, & Webster, 1988). This is a 20-item scale with 10 items measuring positive affect/mood and the remaining 10 items measuring negative affect/mood at work and has been used extensively (George, 1989, 1991). The bidimensionality of the scales indicates that positive and negative moods are not opposite ends of the same continuum nor are they necessarily mutually exclusive. Prior research has suggested that the specific mood that is the most salient exerts the greatest influence on information processing (Bower, 1991; Ellis & Ashbrook, 1988).

Finally, using a validated scale from prior research (Compeau & Higgins, 1995), computer self-efficacy was measured to ensure statistical equivalence among the different groups in terms of perceptions about their ability to use computers. Two objective measures—knowledge test scores and post-training technology use—were also collected.

The longitudinal nature of this research dictated measurements at four points in time: pre-experiment (t_0), post-training (t_1), 6 weeks of continued use (t_2), and 12 weeks of continued use (t_3). The preexperimental measurement (t_0) was focused on gathering general information from participants including their mood, computer self-efficacy, demographic information, work experience, and prior computer experience. Post-training measurement (t_1) included mood, user reactions to the technology, and a knowledge test. The measurement 6 weeks after training (t_2) was the same as the post-training measurement (t_1). In addition to perceptual measures, over the first 6-week period (t_1 to t_2) and the second 6-week period (t_2 to t_3), actual usage behavior measures (number of information queries by each user) using system logs were collected to examine the predictive validity of intention. This data represented an objective measure of behavior since the system tracked and stored each employee query created using the system enabling the examination of the predictive validity of intention in this study.

Psychometric properties of the different scales were assessed. Reliability analyses indicated that all scales had acceptable reliability with Cronbach α estimates over .80 at all points of measurement. Convergent and discriminant validity was supported by factor analysis with varimax rotation where all crossloadings were less than .35. Interitem correlations also supported convergent and discriminant validity. The intercorrelations among the various constructs are provided in Table 1.

Procedure

The study was conducted on 6 days over a 2-week period with five parallel sessions each day. Training each day occurred in a different office, minimizing the opportunity for participants to share information about the training sessions. Furthermore, participants report minimal interaction with personnel in different offices ($M = 1.5$, $SD = 0.3$ on a 5-point scale where 1 was minimal and 5 was extensive).

Five teams, each team comprised of a lecturer and technical consultant, conducted each training session. Each team rotated across the treatment and control groups to minimize any effects due to a specific training team. There were no more than 20 participants in a session based on an organizational desire to provide effective training and maximize individualized attention. Participants were randomly assigned to one of five groups (four treatment and one

TABLE 1   **Means, Standard Deviations, and Correlation Matrix**

	t_0		t_1		t_2	
PM	4.0 (0.9)		4.6 (0.8)		4.2 (0.8)	
NM	4.0 (0.9)		4.7 (0.9)		4.2 (0.9)	
IM			4.6 (0.9)		4.1 (0.9)	
EM			4.8 (0.9)		4.8 (0.9)	
BI			5.0 (0.8)		4.1 (0.8)	

	PM_0	NM_0	PM_1	NM_1	IM_1	EM_1	BI_1	PM_2	NM_2	IM_2	EM_2	BI_2
PM_0												
NM_0	−.23*											
PM_1	.12	−.20*										
NM_1	.18	.08	−.23*									
IM_1	.36**	−.31**	.22*	−.27**								
EM_1	.27**	−.34**	.18*	.16	.40**							
BI_1	.31**	−.28**	.14	.15	.41**	.47**						
PM_2	.17	−.19*	.28**	−.28**	.30**	.25*	.28**					
NM_2	−.27*	.24*	−.29**	.29**	−.29*	−.14	−.27**	−.35**				
IM_2	.31**	−.28*	.32**	.08	.52**	.32**	.47**	.37**	−.37**			
EM_2	.24*	−.19	.20*	−.11	.40**	.35**	.44**	.26**	−.27**	.28**		
BI_2	.30**	−.29**	.28**	−.20*	.38**	.45**	.53**	.31**	−.25**	.48**	.55**	

Note: In the correlation matrix, 0, 1, and 2 indicate time of measurement. 0 indicates preexperimental measurement, 1 indicates post-training measurement, and 2 indicates measurement made after 6 weeks of training. PM, Positive Mood; NM, Negative Mood; IM, Intrinsic Motivation; EM, Extrinsic Motivation; BI, Behavioral Intention.

control). One hundred twelve participants provided usable responses from the positive mood intervention (54 from the "Seinfeld" intervention and 58 from the "Kareem Abdul-Jabbar" intervention), 115 usable responses were received from individuals in the negative mood intervention (59 from the "World War II" intervention and 56 from the "Player Injury" intervention), and 89 responses were received from the control group.

After arriving at the training session, all participants were told that the training team had been delayed due to traffic conditions. The treatment groups then watched the positive or negative videos to pass the "waiting period" while the control group did not experience any intervention during that time period. Participants then participated in the training program developed by the organization's "Technology Management Department." The training program took place over the course of one full work day with actual "in-class" activity lasting just over 5 hours, excluding breaks for coffee and lunch. The training program consisted of: (a) a 1-hour lecture describing the role of the new system in the organization, its basic functionality and features; (b) a 1½-hour hands-on session accompanied by a demonstration where respondents followed the lead of the lecturer; and (c) a 2-hour hands-on session where the respondents completed 14 different tasks. After a brief break following the third component, participants completed a knowledge test (maximum duration: 45 minutes) performing 24 activities facilitating the detection of any learning differences between treatments.

Analysis Procedure

Data were examined to ensure that there were no systematic differences within the positive mood and within the negative mood interventions. There were no differences between groups, and data were pooled within both positive and both negative mood interventions respectively. ANOVA was used to determine if there were significant differences between groups, and Scheffe tests were used to isolate those differences. Short-term effects were measured at t_1 while long-term effects were assessed as the mean differences between construct measures at t_1 and t_2.

RESULTS

Manipulation Checks

The results from different manipulation checks, including mood, usage behavior, and knowledge test, were examined (see Table 2). Mood measures taken before the study (t_0) were found to be statistically equivalent across the three groups: positive mood measure ($F(2, 313) = .73$, $p = ns$) and negative mood measures ($F(2, 313) = 1.01$, $p = ns$). However, mood measures assessed after the video manipulation and training indicated significant differences between interventions. Individuals in the positive mood intervention had significantly higher positive moods than those individuals in the control or negative mood interventions ($F(2, 313) = 5.27$, $p < .01$), while those individuals in the negative mood intervention had significantly higher negative moods than those individuals in the control or positive mood intervention ($F(2, 313) = 4.98$, $p < .01$). Finally, assessments of positive and negative mood measures 6 weeks after training (t_2) revealed that moods across the different groups were statistically equivalent—positive mood measure ($F(2, 313) = 1.14$, $p = ns$) and

TABLE 2 **Manipulation Check Results**

Manipulation Check Measure	Positive Mood: Manipulation		Control Group		Negative Mood: Manipulation	
	M	*(SD)*	*M*	*(SD)*	*M*	*(SD)*
Positive mood (t_0)	4.1	(.9) *(ns)*	3.9	(.9)	4.1	(.9)
Negative mood (t_0)	4.0	(.8) *(ns)*	4.0	(1.0)	4.1	(.9)
Positive mood (t_1)	5.9	(.8)**	3.8	(.8)	4.0	(.8)
Negative mood (t_1)	4.2	(1.0)**	3.9	(.9)	6.0	(.9)
Positive mood (t_2)	4.3	(.9) *(ns)*	4.2	(.8)	4.1	(.8)
Negative mood (t_2)	4.4	(.8) *(ns)*	4.0	(.9)	4.3	(.9)
Computer self-efficacy	7.3	(1.4) *(ns)*	7.1	(1.8)	7.6	(1.2)
Test score	17.2	(2.4) *(ns)*	17.9	(1.9)	17.5	(2.1)

Note: ns, not significant.
* $p < .05$.
** $p < .01$.

negative mood measure ($F(2, 313) = 1.30, p = ns$). This pattern confirms that the video-based mood interventions took effect at t_1, but the mood itself did not sustain over time consistent with prior research (George, 1991).

A preexperimental measure of computer self-efficacy indicated that there were no significant differences across interventions ($F(2, 313) = 1.41, p = ns$) and a postexperimental measure of learning using test scores indicated that learning was equivalent across the three interventions ($F(2, 313) = .53, p = ns$).

Finally, strong relationships were found between behavioral intentions at t_1 and actual usage in the 6-week period between t_1 and t_2 ($r = .57$) and between behavioral intention measured at t_2 and actual usage in the 6-week period following t_2 ($r = .59$). Further, regression analyses revealed that the effect of intrinsic and extrinsic motivation on usage was fully mediated by behavioral intention, thus providing support for the examination of behavioral intention as the key dependent variable.

Hypothesis Testing

Hpyotheses 1 through 3 examined the short-term effects of mood on motivation and intention to use the technology. Hypotheses 1(a) and 1(b) suggested that participants having positive mood states would have higher intrinsic motivation while those in negative moods would have lower intrinsic motivation immediately after training. The ANOVA suggested significant results ($F(2, 313) = 28.26, p < .001$) (see Table 3). Participants in the positive mood treatment had significantly higher intrinsic motivation ($M = 6.3$) than the control group ($M = 4.6$) ($t(200) = 2.89, p < .01$). Similarly, participants in the negative mood treatment ($M = 3.4$) exhibited significantly lower intrinsic motivation than the control group ($t(203) = 2.97, p < .01$). Therefore, H1(a) and H1(b) were supported.

Hypotheses 2(a) and 2(b) suggested that there would be a similar pattern of differences in extrinsic motivation across mood states. As indicated in Table 3, the results indicated that there were no differences ($F(2, 313) = 1.21, p = ns$) in extrinsic motivation among participants in

TABLE 3 **Short-Term Effects: Cross-Sectional Analysis of the Impact of Interventions on Constructs at t_1**

	M	*(SD)*	Significance of Difference between Intervention and Control Group
Intrinsic motivation			
Positive mood intervention	6.3	(0.8)	**
Negative mood intervention	3.4	(0.9)	**
Control group	4.6	(0.9)	
Extrinsic motivation			
Positive mood intervention	4.9	(1.0)	*ns*
Negative mood intervention	4.8	(0.8)	*ns*
Control group	4.7	(0.9)	
Behavioral intention			
Positive mood intervention	6.1	(0.9)	*
Negative mood intervention	3.9	(0.8)	*
Control group	5.0	(0.8)	

Note: ns, not significant.
* $p < .05$.
** $p < .01$.

positive ($M = 4.9$), negative ($M = 4.8$), and neutral ($M = 4.7$) mood treatments. Therefore H2(a) and H2(b) were not supported.

Hypotheses 3(a) and 3(b) suggested that there would also be mood congruent differences in participants' intention to use technology across mood states. The ANOVA suggested significant results ($F(2, 313) = 21.25, p < .001$) where participants in the positive mood treatment had significantly higher behavioral intentions to use the technology ($M = 6.1$) than the control group ($M = 5.0$) ($t(200) = 2.08, p < .05$), and participants in the negative mood treatment ($M = 3.9$) had significantly lower intention than the control group ($t(203) = 2.17, p < .05$). Therefore, H3(a) and H3(b) were supported.

Hypotheses 4 through 6 examined the sustainability of outcomes corresponding to H1 through H3. Hypotheses 4(a) and 4(b) suggested that, over time, participants having positive mood states at the time of training would have higher intrinsic motivation while those in negative moods would have lower intrinsic motivation. The ANOVA results ($F(2, 313) = 14.74, p < .001$) (see Table 4) indicated that participants in the positive mood treatment ($M = 4.9$) exhibited intrinsic motivation comparable to the control group ($t(200) = .98, p = ns$), while participants in the negative mood treatment had significantly lower intrinsic motivation ($M = 3.2$) than the control group ($M = 4.5$) ($t(203) = 2.77, p < .01$). Therefore, while H4(a) was not supported, H4(b) was supported.

Hypothesis 5 suggested that there would be no sustainable differences in extrinsic motivation across mood states over time. There were no short-term mood effects on extrinsic motivation (i.e., H2 results) and, as indicated in Table 4, there were also no long-term effects (positive mood, $M = 4.8$; negative mood, $M = 4.7$; neutral mood, $M = 4.8$) ($F(2, 313) = .97, p = ns$). Given the null hypothesis (H5), a power test was conducted (see Cohen, 1988).

TABLE 4   Long-Term Effects: Longitudinal Analysis of the Impact of Interventions on Constructs at t_2

	M	*(SD)*	Significance of Difference between Intervention and Control Group
Intrinsic motivation			
Positive mood intervention	4.9	(0.7)	*ns* (see Note)
Negative mood intervention	3.2	(0.9)	**
Control group	4.5	(1.0)	
Extrinsic motivation			
Positive mood intervention	4.8	(0.9)	*ns*
Negative mood intervention	4.7	(0.8)	*ns*
Control group	4.8	(1.0)	
Behavioral intention			
Positive mood intervention	4.9	(0.9)	*ns*
Negative mood intervention	3.7	(0.8)	**
Control group	4.9	(0.7)	

Note: Since the tests of differences supported the null hypotheses (results of power analysis reported under Results, the differences of means between measures taken at t_2 and t_1 were tested measures at t_2 were statistically significantly different from t_1, *ns*, not significant.
* $p < .05$.
** $p < .01$.

This test indicated that given the final sample size, our statistical tests were expected to detect a small effect size with a power of .80 and a medium effect size with a power of .90. While there is still a possibility that a difference that does exist may have failed detection, the lack of both short- and long-term differences preliminarily supports equivalence across mood states. Therefore, H5 was supported.

Hypotheses 6(a) and 6(b) suggested that there would be sustained effects of differences in participants' intention to use technology across mood states. The ANOVA results indicated a significant effect ($F(2, 313) = 13.87, p < .001$) (see Table 4). Participants in the positive mood treatment at the time of training did not appear to sustain their higher level of intentions at t_2 ($M = 4.9$) and were equivalent with the control group at t_2 ($t(200) = 1.19, p = ns$), while participants in the negative mood treatment at the time of training had significantly lower long-term intentions to use the technology ($M = 3.7$) than the control group ($M = 4.9$) at t_2 ($t(203) = 2.09, p < .01$). Therefore, H6(a) was not supported, but H6(b) was supported.

A graphical representation of the temporal dynamics of the effect of mood on intrinsic and extrinsic motivation to use the technology is presented in Figure 1. In sum, it suggests that while no differences are observed in extrinsic motivation, the positive mood intervention has short-term effects on intrinsic motivation and behavioral intention and the negative mood intervention has lasting effects on intrinsic motivation and behavioral intention.

Post Hoc Analysis: Control Group Data

Data from the control group was analyzed for two reasons: (a) to examine the effects of naturally occurring rather than induced moods, and (b) it is possible that individuals in the control group reacted differently to the "waiting period." Participants in the control group were

FIGURE 1
Graphical Representation of Mood Effects on (a) Intrinsic Motivation, (b) Extrinsic Motivation, and (c) Behavioral Intention

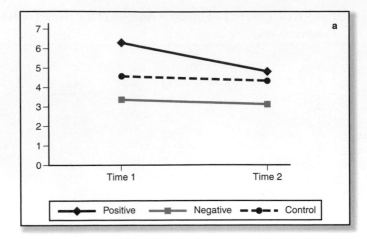

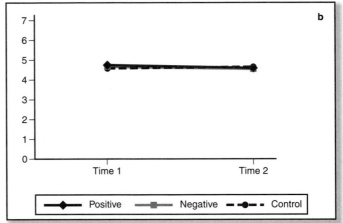

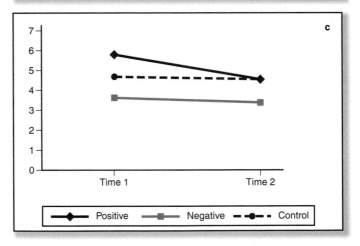

classified into positive ($n = 38$) and negative ($n = 41$) mood categories based on their naturally occurring mood as measured at t_1. Nine individuals were excluded from the analysis because their mood could not be classified as more strongly positive or negative.

Results from examining the control group were consistent with the effects in the positive and negative mood inductions. There were significant differences between more positive and more negative individuals within the control group related to short-term intrinsic motivation ($F(1, 78) = 1.66, p < .05$), short-term intentions ($F(1, 78) = 1.99, p < .05$), long-term intrinsic motivation ($F(1, 78) = 2.17, p < .05$), and long-term intentions ($F(1, 78) = 2.04, p < .05$). There were no significant effects for extrinsic motivation in either the short term ($F(1, 78) = .78, p = ns$) or long term ($F(1, 78) = .61, p = ns$).

Interestingly, the long-term effects observed among individuals in naturally occurring positive or negative mood states were also consistent with the effects observed among individuals whose moods were induced. Overall, the split control group exhibited similar characteristics to individuals in the induced mood states suggesting that the findings associated with the mood interventions appear to be generalizable to naturally occurring mood states while also minimizing the possibility that demand characteristics (e.g., the mood induction itself or the survey) influenced the outcomes.

Post Hoc Analysis: Effect of Mood as a Moderator

The stated hypotheses focused on significant differences between positive or negative mood-induced individuals and those having more neutral moods. While the hypothesized differences are by themselves important, an additional issue of interest is the overall effect of mood on the relationship between intrinsic/extrinsic motivation and an individual's intention to use a technology. Therefore, the influence of both intrinsic and extrinsic motivation on intentions over time with mood as a moderating variable was assessed.

Linear regression was performed using behavioral intention as the dependent variable and extrinsic motivation and intrinsic motivation as the independent variables in each of the three groups (two treatment and one control) at t_1 and t_2, respectively. In order to understand the short-term impact of the interventions on the decision-making process, the differences between the betas associated with each of the constructs across groups were evaluated (Pindyck & Rubenfeld, 1981, pp. 123–126). The moderation of key relationships (intrinsic motivation–behavioral intention and extrinsic motivation–behavioral intention) was tested by introducing dummy variables for the treatment/control groups and the moderation of both relationships was tested in a single regression equation. This procedure enabled an analysis of whether respondents in the different interventions placed differing emphasis on the key determinants of intention.

Results of the regression analyses indicated that the interaction terms were significant ($p < .05$) suggesting a moderating mood effect for both the intrinsic motivation–behavioral intention and extrinsic motivation–behavioral intention relationships in both the short and long terms. The relative weights of extrinsic motivation and intrinsic motivation (provided by the beta coefficients) were compared in determining behavioral intention to use the technology at t_1 (see Table 5). The beta weight of the intrinsic motivation–behavioral intention relationship of the positive mood group (.33) did not depart from the control group (.35). However, as noted in Table 6, the influence of intrinsic motivation on behavioral intention

TABLE 5   Short-Term Effects: Cross-Sectional Analysis of the Impact of Interventions on Relationships at t_1

	R^2	β	Significance of Difference between Intervention and Control Group
Positive mood intervention	0.35		
Intrinsic motivation		0.33**	ns
Extrinsic motivation		0.45**	ns
Negative mood intervention	0.36		
Intrinsic motivation		0.15*	*
Extrinsic motivation		0.59**	**
Control Group	0.35		
Intrinsic motivation		0.34**	
Extrinsic motivation		0.46**	

Note: ns, not significant.
* $p < .05$.
** $p < .01$.

TABLE 6   Long-Term Effects: Longitudinal Analysis of the Impact of Interventions on Relationships at t_2

	R^2	β	Significance of Difference between Intervention and Control Group
Positive mood intervention	0.34		
Intrinsic motivation		0.32**	ns
Extrinsic motivation		0.43**	ns
Negative mood intervention	0.37		
Intrinsic motivation		0.14*	*
Extrinsic motivation		0.61**	**
Control Group	0.36		
Intrinsic motivation		0.33**	
Extrinsic motivation		0.48**	

Note: ns, not significant.
* $p < .05$.
** $p < .01$.

was significantly lower in the negative mood intervention (.15) compared to the control group (.34). Interestingly, participants in the negative mood treatment placed a significantly higher weight on extrinsic motivation (.59) in determining behavioral intention compared to participants in the neutral (.46) and the positive mood intervention (.45). Further, as noted in Tables 5 and 6, the variance in behavioral intention explained (R^2) by intrinsic motivation and extrinsic motivation in each of the three groups was comparable, indicating a shift in the relative weighting of intrinsic motivation and extrinsic motivation in the negative mood intervention. The results at t_2 were consistent with the pattern observed at t_1.

DISCUSSION

This longitudinal field study provided interesting findings about the influence of an individual's mood on motivation to use computer technology and the sustainability of such influence. Participants in positive moods at the time of training have greater short-term intrinsic motivation and intentions to use a specific technology. However, these positive mood effects are short-lived and 6 weeks after training, intrinsic motivation and behavioral intentions are consistent with participants in neutral moods. Participants in negative moods at the time of training had immediate decreases in intrinsic motivation and intention to use technology, and these effects were persistent even 6 weeks after continued use of the system. This finding is particularly salient given that 6 weeks after training, participants were likely to have been influenced by additional exposure to and information about the technology from peers.

As established at the outset, mood has been examined using competing models—associative network and resource allocation—and it is important to reconcile our findings in light of these perspectives. On one hand, these findings are consistent with the associative network model regarding the storing of affective and content information on linked nodes. As participants in negative mood treatments assess their intrinsic motivation and behavioral intentions to use technology 6 weeks after training, the negative mood state pervasive during training emerges through the stored affective nodes. This negative affect dampens the participants' feelings of intrinsic motivation resulting in lower intentions to use the technology. Given this perspective, one would expect that the positive mood elevation of intrinsic motivation and behavioral intention would be equally sustainable—a relationship not supported by the results.

One explanation for our asymmetrical findings (positive vs. negative) relates to the differential influence of positive and negative moods on cognitive processing. From a resource allocation perspective, individuals in a positive mood are more likely to perform holistic processing (Martin, Ward, Achee, & Wyer, 1993; Murray, Surjan, Hirt, & Surjan, 1990) and may avoid extensive information processing to maintain their positive mood state (Isen, 1984, 1987). Post-training, individuals may find that using the technology requires a more thorough understanding of procedures than the holistic processing performed during training resulting in a reduction of intrinsic motivation because the user perceives the technology to be more difficult to use than originally believed. In contrast, individuals in negative moods often perform more careful processing, in part, to mitigate or attempt to change their negative mood (Asuncion & Lam, 1995). This careful processing may well result in less intrinsic motivation (e.g., following training directions carefully yet not thinking about "fun" aspects of using the technology). In other words, these individuals "learn the appropriate keys to type" but may not see the larger context in which to apply this knowledge. This rote type of learning is likely to create lower enjoyment of the technology. Furthermore, this low intrinsic motivation may well be sustainable given the difficulty of developing/increasing intrinsic motivation over time if it is not generated during initial learning (Vallerand & Bissonette, 1992). Therefore, the lowered intrinsic motivation of individuals who initially had negative moods becomes instantiated into their mindset and actual technology usage.

It is possible that taking assessments from individuals "induced" to be in a good mood actually results in artifactual inflation (e.g., halo effects; Sinclair, 1988) of technology acceptance and motivation to use it. However, a more optimistic interpretation suggests that individuals in good moods are more likely to scale the initial hurdles to technology adoption and usage. Such a favorable short-term consequence could result from a positive mood leading to more effort and time spent on a task (Csikszentmihalyli, 1975; Vallerand & Bissonnette, 1992). This is particularly plausible given both the higher levels of intrinsic motivation and greater emphasis placed on intrinsic motivation by those in good moods. Thus, creating a positive mood-oriented environment for learning will create somewhat favorable user perceptions that will potentially help overcome initial hurdles and barriers to technology adoption and usage.

Our findings are consistent with general patterns in motivation research (e.g., Vallerand & Bissonette, 1992) that developing initial intrinsic motivation during learning is critical. From a practical perspective, individuals involved with producing and/or delivering training materials should be wary of this negative mood priming effect. Results from individuals in negative mood states indicated that these moods are detrimental to intrinsic motivation and ultimately intention to use technology. Thus, developing and delivering positive mood enhancements at the beginning of training may offset the negative mood that some participants may have and also further peak the motivation of those in a neutral mood at the beginning of the training session.

The posthoc analysis indicated that the relative weights of intrinsic and extrinsic motivation were comparable between the positive mood intervention and the control group and these weights were stable over time. However, participants in the negative mood intervention placed significantly less weight on intrinsic motivation and placed much greater emphasis on extrinsic motivation in forming their intentions to use technology. Furthermore, this relationship was found to sustain over time. The strong explanatory role of extrinsic motivation and lesser role of intrinsic motivation among individuals in negative moods could potentially be the result of more systematic processing that occurs during negative moods (Clore, Schwarz, & Conway, 1994; Schwarz, 1990; Schwarz, Bless, Strack et al., 1991; Sinclair & Mark, 1992; Weary & Gannon, 1996). This systematic processing results in diminished playfulness (Schwarz & Bless, 1991) which could have contributed to: (a) greater task focus and, thus, salience and emphasis of extrinsic motivation and (b) lowered intrinsic motivation resulting in minimal emphasis on intrinsic motivation. These patterns of results are further supported by prior research that has suggested that individuals in bad moods assess costs and benefits more than those in positive or neutral moods (Schaller & Cialdini, 1990). The sustenance of the pattern observed among participants in the negative mood intervention can be explained, to a certain extent, by the minimal role of intrinsic motivation early in the learning process, thus causing it to be minimally emphasized in the long term also (Vallerand & Bissonnette, 1992).

Implications for Future Mood Research

In addition to the implications for mood effects on training, this research also makes strides in addressing theoretical and practical issues in mood research. First, this study investigates mood effects over a relatively long duration (e.g., 6 weeks). Although this is not the first research study to examine longitudinal effects (e.g., Curren & Harich (1994) examined mood effects 24 hours after inducement), it uses a significantly longer time horizon in examining the sustainability of mood effects. The significance of the negative mood induction 6 weeks after the initial training suggests that detrimental effects of mood may be far more significant and enduring than previously thought.

A second important facet of this research is the background of the participants and the manner in which mood was induced. This is perhaps the first study examining the effects of mood that has employed "real subjects" in a real-world training setting. Furthermore, prior mood research has acknowledged a concern with experimental demand characteristics of subjects "knowing" that a video, music, etc. was provided to influence their affective state and the resulting outcomes of induced versus naturally occurring moods (Kwiatkowski & Parkinson, 1994). In this research, employees did not perceive that they were participating in an experiment and therefore, the video induction was likely to be a plausible manner in which to fill time given the "traffic problems of the trainers." Therefore, the mood induction implemented is likely to be more consistent with a naturally formed mood extending the meaningfulness of the findings.

Limitations and Future Research Directions

The longitudinal nature of this research resulted in significant findings regarding the influence of mood on motivation. However, it is also plausible that the difference in effects between the short term (t_1) and the long term (t_2) may be related to factors not directly attributable to the intervention. However, our findings were quite strong and consistent across the three different offices of the participating organization, thus lending additional credence to the long-term influence of mood.

One potential limitation of the current work is that the findings are a result of demand characteristics (e.g., measurement of mood), particularly long-term mood measurement resulting in an increased salience and recall of initial reactions to the technology following training. However, given similar mood effects among control group participants, this concern is alleviated to a great extent. Other limitations of this research relate to the training and technology employed. It is possible that the corporate-designed training program somehow reinforced the mood states of the participants while other training designs might have mitigated the initial mood states. Likewise, these effects were found during training on a specific computer technology. It is possible that other technologies or training for other types of activities might further reinforce or mitigate the initial mood state of the participant. Finally, the Holocaust video negative mood intervention used in this research may have provoked some deep emotional responses that may have been greater in intensity than the positive mood manipulations. However, the use of two different negative and positive mood videos somewhat alleviates this issue.

With the caution of these limitations in mind, what future research directions appear to be most fruitful? To date, the effects of mood have been suggested to be largely short term. However, our research presents an alternative perspective that departs from accumulated knowledge in the area. Further research is warranted to examine the generalizability of our findings and also identify potential boundary conditions of these results. Understanding the generalizability and validity of these results has direct ramifications for organizations and those individuals in organizations managing training. As suggested at the outset, the importance of this issue is further amplified since organizations are spending about $20B/year on computer-related training (Industry Report, 1996). Such negative moods and [their] detrimental effects on training also offer one potential explanation for indications that only 10% of all training leads to behavior changes (Georgenson, 1982). The diminished training benefits to individuals in negative moods result in poorly spent resources and, in all likelihood, less efficient employees.

Conclusions

The longitudinal field study described in this paper sought to investigate a previously overlooked topic: the short- and long-term effects of employee mood (at the time of computer technology training) on the motivation and intention to use the specific technology. The data from our study indicated that positive moods at the time of training result in short-term increases in intrinsic motivation and intention to use the technology. However, these effects did not sustain over the long term (i.e., 6 weeks). On the other hand, employees in negative moods at the time of training exhibited decreased intrinsic motivation and intentions to use technology in the short term, and these effects were persistent 6 weeks later, even after active use of the technology. These findings have important theoretical and practical implications for employee training and at the same time contribute to the research stream assessing mood effects by examining their sustainability.

Appendix 1

Video Intervention to Foster Positive Mood: "Seinfeld" Episode Titled "The Soup Nazi"

In their quest for knee-buckling good soup, Jerry, George & Co. want to bend to the will of the abuse-ladling Soup Nazi, but their basic instincts keep getting in the way. George whines when he doesn't get free bread. ("No soup for you!" the S.N. barks.) Elaine's overly familiar tone gets her the heave-ho. When Jerry brings along his gloppily affectionate girlfriend, Sheila ("Schmoopie!"), she gets tossed, then tries to make Jerry leave too. Torn between love and bisque, Jerry finally says, "Do I know you?" Only Kramer bonds with souperman, who offers up a spare armoire when Cosmo tells him the sad tale of a friend whose antique was stolen. Little does the Soup Nazi know that the armoire is for Elaine, now his revenge-plotting enemy, or that his priceless recipes are inside. (Source: *TV Guide,* Special Edition, "Seinfeld Forever.")

References

Ajzen, I. (1985). From intentions to actions: A theory of planned behavior. In J. Kuhl & J. Beckman (Eds.), *Action control: From cognition to behavior* (pp. 11–39). New York: Springer Verlag.

Ajzen, I. (1991). The theory of planned behavior. *Organizational Behavior and Human Decision Processes,* 50, 179–211.

Ajzen, I., & Fishbein, M. (1980). *Understanding attitudes and predicting social behavior.* Englewood Cliffs, NJ: Prentice Hall.

Asuncion, A. G., & Lam, W. F. (1995). Affect and impression formation: Influence of mood on person memory. *Journal of Experimental Social Psychology,* 31, 437–464.

Baumgardner, A. H., & Arkin, R. M. (1988). Affective state mediates causal attributions for success and failure. *Motivation and Emotion,* 12, 99–111.

Bower, G. H. (1981). Mood and memory. *American Psychologist,* 36(2), 129–148.

Bower, G. H. (1987). Commentary on mood and memory. *Behavior Research and Therapy,* 25, 443–455.

Bower, G. H. (1991). Mood congruity of social judgements. In J. P. Forgas (Ed.), *Emotion and social judgments* (pp. 31–55). Elmsford, NY: Pergamon Press.

Brand, N., Verspui, L., & Oving, A. (1997). Induced mood and selective attention. *Perceptual and Motor Skills, 84,* 455–463.

Brief, A. P., Burke, M. J., George, J. M., Robinson, B., & Webster, J. (1988). Should negative affectivity remain an unmeasured variable in the study of job stress? *Journal of Applied Psychology, 73,* 193–198.

Brief, A. P., Butcher, A. H. & Roberson, L. (1995). Cookies, disposition, and job attitudes: The effects of positive mood-inducing events on job satisfaction in a field experiment. *Organizational Behavior and Human Decision Processes, 62,* 55–62.

Calder, B. J., & Staw, B. M. (1975). Self perception of intrinsic and extrinsic motivation. *Journal of Personality and Social Psychology, 31,* 599–603.

Carson, T. P., & Adams, H. E. (1980). Activity valence as a function of mood change. *Journal of Abnormal Psychology, 89,* 368–377.

Cervone, D., Kopp, D. A., Schaumann, L., & Scott, W. D. (1994). Mood, self-efficacy, and performance standards: Lower moods induce higher standards for performance. *Journal of Personality and Social Psychology, 67,* 499–512.

Clark, M. S., & Isen, A. M. (1982). Toward understanding the relationship between affect and social behavior. In A. Hastorf & A. M. Isen (Eds.), *Cognitive social psychology* (pp. 73–108). New York: Elsevier/North Holland.

Clark, L. A., & Watson, D. (1988). Mood and the mundane: Relations between daily life events and self-reported mood. *Journal of Personality and Social Psychology, 54,* 296–308.

Clore, G. L., Schwarz, N., & Conway, M. (1994). Cognitive causes and consequences of emotions. In R. S. Wyer & T. K. Srull (Eds.), *Handbook of social cognition* (2nd ed., pp. 323–417). Hillsdale, NJ: Erlbaum.

Cohen, J. (1988). *Statistical power analysis for the behavioral sciences* (2nd ed.). Hillsdale, NJ: Erlbaum.

Compeau, D. R., & Higgins, C. A. (1995). Application of social cognitive theory to training for computer skills. *Information Systems Research, 6,* 118–143.

Cook, T. D., & Campbell, D. T. (1979). *Quasi-experimentation, design, and analysis issues for field settings.* Chicago: Rand McNally.

Csikszentmihalyi, M. (1975). *Beyond boredom and anxiety.* San Francisco, CA: Jossey-Bass.

Curren, M. T., & Harich, K. R. (1993). Performance attributions: Effects of mood and involvement. *Journal of Educational Psychology, 85,* 605–609.

Curren, M. T., & Harich, K. R. (1994). Consumers' mood states: The mitigating influence of personal relevance on product evaluations. *Psychology and Marketing, 11,* 91–107.

Davis, F. D. (1989). Perceived usefulness, perceived ease of use, and user acceptance of information technology. *MIS Quarterly, 13,* 319–339.

Davis, F. D., Bagozzi, R. P., & Warshaw, P. R. (1989). User acceptance of computer technology: A comparison of two theoretical models. *Management Science, 35,* 982–1002.

Davis, F. D., Bagozzi, R. P., & Warshaw, P. R. (1992). Extrinsic and intrinsic motivation to use computers in the workplace. *Journal of Applied Social Psychology, 22,* 1111–1132.

Deci, E. L. (1971). Effects of externally mediated rewards on intrinsic motivation. *Journal of Personality and Social Psychology, 18,* 105–115.

Deci, E. L. (1975). *Intrinsic motivation.* New York: Plenum Press.

Deci, E. L., & Ryan, R. M. (1980). The empirical exploration of intrinsic motivational processes. In L. Berkowitz (Ed.), *Advances in experimental social psychology* (Vol. 13, pp. 39–80). New York: Academic Press.

Deci, E. L., & Ryan, R. M. (1985). *Intrinsic motivation and self-determination in human behavior.* New York: Plenum.

Derryberry, D., & Tucker, D. M. (1992). Neural mechanisms of emotion. *Journal of Consulting and Clinical Psychology, 60,* 329–338.

Doll, J., & Ajzen, I. (1992). Accessibility and stability of predictors in the theory of planned behavior. *Journal of Personality and Social Psychology, 63,* 754–765.

Eich, E., Macaulay, D., & Ryan, L. (1994). Mood dependent memory for events of the personal past. *Journal of Experimental Psychology: General, 123,* 201–215.

Ellis, H. C., & Ashbrook, P. W. (1988). Resource allocation model of the effects of depressed mood states on memory. In K. Fielder & J. Forgas (Eds.), *Affect, cognition and social behavior* (pp. 1–21). Toronto, Canada: Hogrefe.

Ellis, H. C., Ottaway, S. A., Varner, L. J., Becker, A. S., & Moore, B. A. (1997). Emotion, motivation, and text comprehension: The detection of contradictions in passages. *Journal of Experimental Psychology: General, 126,* 131–146.

Ellis, H. C., Thomas, R. L., McFarland, A. D., & Lane, J. W. (1985). Emotional mood states and retrieval in episodic memory: Elaborative training, semantic processing, and cognitive effort. *Journal of Experimental Psychology: Learning, Memory, and Cognition, 10,* 470–482.

Erber, R. (1991). Affective and semantic priming: Effects of mood on category accessibility and inference. *Journal of Experimental Social Psychology, 27,* 480–498.

Fazio, R. H., & Zanna, M. (1978a). Attitudinal qualities relating to the strength of the attitude-perception and attitude-behavior relationship. *Journal of Experimental Social Psychology, 14,* 398–408.

Fazio, R. H., & Zanna, M. (1978b). On the predictive validity of attitudes: The roles of direct experience and confidence. *Journal of Personality, 46,* 228–243.

Fazio, R. H., & Zanna, M. (1981). Direct experience and attitude–behavior consistency. In L. Berkowitz (Ed.), *Advances in experimental social psychology* (Vol. 14, pp. 161–202). San Diego, CA: Academic Press.

Fishbein, M., & Ajzen, I. (1975). *Belief, attitude, intentions and behavior: An introduction to theory and research.* Boston: Addison-Wesley.

Forgas, J. P. (1991). Mood effects on partner choice: Role of affect in social decisions. *Journal of Personality and Social Psychology, 61,* 708–720.

Forgas, J. P. (1992). On bad mood and peculiar people: Affect and person typicality in impression formation. *Journal of Personality and Social Psychology, 22,* 531–547.

Forgas, J. P. (1995). Mood and judgement: The affect infusion model (AIM). *Psychological Bulletin, 117,* 39–66.

Forgas, J. P., Bower, G. H., & Moylan, S. J. (1990). Praise or blame? Effective influences on attributions for achievement. *Journal of Personality and Social Psychology, 59,* 809–819.

George, J. M. (1989). Mood and absence. *Journal of Applied Psychology, 74,* 317–324.

George, J. M. (1991). State or trait: Effects of positive mood on prosocial behaviors at work. *Journal of Applied Psychology, 76,* 299–307.

George, J. M., & Brief, A. P. (1996). Motivational agendas in the workplace: The effects of feelings on focus of attention and work motivation. *Research in Organizational Behavior, 18,* 75–109.

George, J. M., & Jones, G. R. (1996). The experience of work and turnover intentions: Interactive effects of value attainment, job satisfaction, and positive mood. *Journal of Applied Psychology, 81,* 318–325.

Georgenson, D. L. (1982). The problem of transfer calls for partnership. *Training and Development Journal, 30,* 75–78.

Hasher, L., & Zacks, R. T. (1979). Automatic and effortful processes in memory. *Journal of Experimental Psychology: General, 108,* 356–388.

Heinssen, R. K., Glass, C. R., & Knight, L. A. (1987). Assessing computer anxiety: Development and validation of the computer anxiety rating scale. *Computers in Human Behavior, 3,* 49–59.

Hirst, M. K. (1988). Intrinsic motivation as influenced by task interdependence and goal setting. *Journal of Applied Psychology, 73,* 96–101.

Industry Report. (1996). *Training, 33*(10), 37–79.

Isen, A. M. (1984). Toward understanding the role of affect in cognition. In R. S. Wyer & T. K. Srul (Eds.), *Handbook of social cognition* (Vol. 3, pp. 179–236). Hillsdale, NJ: Erlbaum.

Isen, A. M. (1987). Positive affect, cognitive processes, and social behavior. In Berkowitz (Ed.), *Advances in experimental social psychology* (Vol. 20, pp. 203–253). New York: Academic Press

Isen, A. M., & Levin, A. F. (1972). Effects of feeling good on helping: Cookies and kindness. *Journal of Personality and Social Psychology, 21,* 384–388.

Isen, A. M., Shalker, T. E., Clark, M. S., & Karp, L. (1978). Affect, accessibility of material in memory, and behavior. A cognitive loop? *Journal of Personality and Social Psychology, 36,* 1–12.

Keil, M. (1995). Pulling the plug: Software project management and the problem of project escalation. *MIS Quarterly, 19,* 421–447.

Kihlstrom, J. F. (1989). On what does mood-dependent memory depend? *Journal of Social Behavior and Personality, 4,* 23–32.

Kraiger, K., Billings, R. S., & Isen, A. M. (1989). The influence of positive affective states on task perception and satisfaction. *Organizational Behavior and Human Decision Processes, 44,* 12–25.

Kruglanski, A. W., Friedman, I., & Zeevi, G. (1971). The effects of extrinsic incentive on some qualitative aspects of task performance. *Journal of Personality, 39,* 606–617.

Kwiatkowski, S. J., & Parkinson, S. R. (1994). Depression, elaboration, and mood congruence: Differences between natural and induced mood. *Memory & Cognition, 22,* 225–233.

Leight, K. A., & Ellis, H. C. (1981). Emotional mood states, strategies, and state-dependency in memory. *Journal of Verbal Learning and Verbal Behavior, 20,* 251–266.

Malone, T. W. (1981). Toward a theory of intrinsically motivating instruction. *Cognitive Sciences, 4,* 333–369.

Martin, L. L., Ward, D. W., Achee, J. W., & Wyer, R. S., Jr. (1993). Mood as input: People have to interpret the motivational implications of their moods. *Journal of Personality and Social Psychology, 64,* 317–326.

Martocchio, J. J. (1994). Effects of conceptions of ability on anxiety, self-efficacy, and learning in training. *Journal of Applied Psychology, 79,* 819–825.

Mathieson, K. (1991). Predicting user intentions: Comparing the technology acceptance model with the theory of planned behavior. *Information Systems Research, 2,* 173–191.

Mitchell, T. R., Hopper, H., Daniels, D., George-Falvy, J., & James, L. R. (1994). Predicting self-efficacy and performance during skill acquisition. *Journal of Applied Psychology, 79,* 506–517.

Mossholder, K. W. (1980). Effect of externally mediated goal setting on intrinsic motivation: A laboratory experiment. *Journal of Applied Psychology, 65,* 202–210.

Murray, N., Surjan, H., Hirt, E. R., & Surjan, M. (1990). The influence of mood on categorization: A cognitive flexibility interpretation. *Journal of Personality and Social Psychology, 59,* 411–425.

Oaksford, M., Morris, F., Grainger, B., & Williams, J. M. G. (1996). Mood, reasoning, and central executive processes. *Journal of Experimental Psychology: Learning, Memory, and Cognition, 22,* 476–492.

Osgood, C. E., & Suci, G. J. (1955). Factor analysis of meaning. *Journal of Experimental Psychology, 50,* 325–338.

Pavelchak, M. A., Antil, J. H., & Munch, J. M. (1988). The Super Bowl: An investigation into the relationships among program context, emotional experience, and ad recall. *Journal of Consumer Research, 15,* 360–367.

Pindyck, R. S., & Rubenfeld, D. L. (1981). *Econometric models and economic forecasts.* New York: McGraw-Hill.

Regan, D. T., & Fazio, R. H. (1977). On the consistency between attitudes and behavior: Look to the method of attitude formation. *Journal of Experimental Social Psychology, 13,* 38–45.

Russell, J. A., & Mehrabian, A. (1977). Evidence of a three-factor theory of emotions. *Journal of Research in Personality, 11,* 273–294.

Schaller, M., & Cialdini, R. B. (1990). Happiness, sadness, and helping: A motivational integration. In E. T. Higgins & R. M. Sorrentino (Eds.), *Handbook of motivation and cognition: Foundations of Social Behavior* (Vol. 2, pp. 265–296). New York: Guilford Press.

Schwarz, N. (1987). *Stimmung als Information: Untersuchungen zum Einflub von Stimmungen auf die Bewertung des eigenen Lebens [Mood as information].* Heidelberg: Springer-Verlag.

Schwarz, N. (1990). Feelings as information: Informational and motivational functions of affective states. In E. T. Higgins & R. M. Sorrentino (Eds.), *Handbook of social cognition: Foundations of social behavior* (Vol. 2, pp. 527–561). New York: Guilford Press.

Schwarz, N., & Bless, H. (1991). Mood congruity and social judgments. In J. P. Forgas (Ed.), *Emotion and social judgment* (pp. 55–71). Oxford: Pergamon Press.

Schwarz, N., Bless, H., Strack, F., Klumpp, P., Rittenauer-Schatka, H., & Simons, A. (1991). Ease of retrieval as information: Another look at the availability heuristic. *Journal of Personality and Social Psychology, 61,* 195–202.

Schwarz, N., & Bohner, G. (1996). Feelings and their motivational implications: Moods and the action sequence. In P. M. Gollwitzer & J. A. Bargh (Eds.), *The psychology of action: Linking cognition and motivation to behavior* (pp. 119–145). New York: Guilford Press.

Schwarz, N., & Clore, G. L. (1988). How do I feel about it? The informative function of affective states. In K. Fiedler & J. P. Forgas (Eds.), *Affect, cognition, and social behavior* (pp. 44–62). Toronto: Hogrefe.

Schaller, M., & Cialdini, R. B. (1990). Happiness, sadness and helping: A motivational integration. In E. T. Higgins & R. M. Sorrentino (Eds.), *Handbook of motivation and cognition: Foundations of social behavior* (Vol. 2, pp. 265–296). New York: Guilford Press.

Segars, A. H., & Grover, V. (1993). Re-examining perceived ease of use and usefulness: A confirmatory factor analysis. *MIS Quarterly, 18,* 517–525.

Sinclair, R. C. (1988). Mood, categorization breadth, and performance appraisal: The effects of order of information acquisition and affective state on halo, accuracy, information retrieval, and evaluation. *Organizational Behavior and Human Decision Processes, 42,* 22–46.

Sinclair, R. C., & Mark, M. M. (1992). The influence of mood state on judgment and action: Effects on persuasion, categorization, social justice, person perception, and judgmental accuracy. In L. L. Martin & A. Tesser (Eds.), *The construction of social judgments* (pp. 165–193). Hillsdale, NJ: Erlbaum.

Strack, F., Schwarz, N., & Gschneidinger, E. (1985). Happiness and reminiscing: The role of time perspective, mood, and mode of thinking. *Journal of Personality and Social Psychology, 49,* 1460–1469.

Swanson, E. B. (1988). *Information system implementation: Bridging the gap between design and utilization.* Homewood, IL: Irwin.

Swinyard, W. R. (1993). The effects of mood, involvement, and quality of store experience on shopping intentions. *Journal of Consumer Research,* 20, 271–280.

Szajna, B. (1996). Empirical evaluation of the revised technology acceptance model. *Management Science,* 42, 85–92.

Tannenbaum, S. I. (1990). Human resource information systems: User group implications. *Journal of Systems Management,* 41, 27–32.

Taylor, S., & Todd, P. A. (1995). Understanding information technology usage: A test of competing models. *Information Systems Research,* 6, 144–176.

Vallerand, R. J., & Bissonnette, R. (1992). Intrinsic, extrinsic, and amotivational styles as predictors of behavior: A prospective study. *Journal of Personality,* 60, 599–620.

Vallerand, R. J. (1997). Toward a hierarchical model of intrinsic and extrinsic motivation. *Advances in Experimental Social Psychology,* 29, 271–360.

Vallerand, R. J., Fortier, M., & Guay, F. (1997). Self-determination and persistence in a real-life setting: Toward a motivational model of high school dropout. *Journal of Personality and Social Psychology,* 72, 1161–1177.

Venkatesh, V. (in press). Creation of favorable user perceptions: Exploring the role of intrinsic motivation. *MIS Quarterly.*

Venkatesh, V., & Davis, F. D. (1996). A model of the antecedents of perceived ease of use: Development and test. *Decision Sciences,* 27, 451–481.

Watson, D., & Tellegen, A. (1985). Toward a consensual structure of mood. *Psychological Bulletin,* 98, 219–235.

Weary, G., & Gannon, K. (1996). Depression, control motivation, and person perception. In P. M. Gollwitzer & J. A. Bargh (Eds.), *The psychology of action: Linking cognition and motivation to behavior* (pp. 146–167). New York: Guilford Press.

White, C. E., Jr., & Christy, D. P. (1987). The information center concept: A normative model and a study of six installations. *MIS Quarterly,* 11, 451–458.

Wicker, R., Brown, G., Wiehe, J. A., & Shim, W. (1992). Moods, goals, and measures of intrinsic motivation. *Journal of Psychology,* 124, 75–86.

Worth, L. T., & Mackie, D. M. (1987). Cognitive mediation of positive affect in persuasion. *Social Cognition,* 5, 76–79.

Chapter **Six**

The Role of Social Influences in Motivation

Nothing much happens between or among people in work organizations unless social influence occurs. Indeed, any attempt to understand the role of motivation in affecting employee behavior in the work environment must necessarily involve attention to the process of social influence, the influence of other people in the work setting. Dating as far back as the early work of Allport (1924), Mayo (1933), and Roethlisberger and Dickson (1939), a considerable body of research data has accumulated on the effects of the social aspects of organization members' work environment on their motivation and behavior.

Social influences on employees' work motivation come primarily from three sources: (a) the immediate work group; (b) supervisors and subordinates (if any); and (c) the larger set of organizational members that transmit the organization's culture and climate (Black & Porter, 2000). We briefly look at each of these sources of social influence on motivation.

Probably the source that has received the most attention in the research literature over the years is the employee's immediate work group, which forms the most direct social context for many employees. The essential conditions necessary for an immediate work group to affect the motivation of an individual employee are (1) the existence of a group in which the individual perceives or believes he or she is a member; and (2) a strong desire on the part of the individual to continue to be part of the group and to receive its approval. When these conditions exist, the group's influence on the level of effort expended by an individual member has the potential to be very strong. The direction of this influence, however, will typically depend on the group's norms (a group's implicit or explicit standards for behavior of its members). When the norms support the goals of the larger organization, the influence will likely be to increase or at least maintain motivation. On the other hand, when a group's norms run counter to one or more of the organization's primary objectives, the influence will often be in the direction of suppressing motivation. Furthermore, as research has demonstrated over the years (e.g., Seashore, 1954; Shaw, 1981), the greater the cohesiveness of the group, the higher the likelihood of influencing the individual members' motivation levels—in either direction, depending on the group's norms.

It should be noted that the motivational influence of groups on their members can extend to aspects of work behavior other than just quality and quantity of performance. For example, a study of teenage employees working in fast-food restaurants (Krackhardt & Porter, 1985) found that, when an employee decided to leave the organization, that event's impact resulted in an increased (not decreased, as might be expected) intent on the part of close friends to continue with their jobs at the restaurant. The researchers explained this perhaps counter-intuitive finding by positing that the departed worker's friends had to reexamine or "justify" to themselves their own reasons for continuing or not continuing as an employee. This process was hypothesized to have resulted in their strengthened motivation to remain in the situation. Thus, in this case, social influence affected motivation to stay, or not stay, rather than performance.

A second strong source of social influence on an individual worker is that person's immediate supervisor and (depending on the level of the employee) subordinates. The influence of a supervisor is directly linked to the control of powerful rewards and potentially damaging punishments. Obviously, however, a given supervisor will not necessarily have the same degree or type of motivational impact on each subordinate. A supervisor can have a positive effect on some immediate subordinates and a neutral or negative effect on others (Dansereau, Graen, & Haga, 1975; Graen & Cashman, 1975). Which type of effect will occur for the several different subordinates depends considerably on the type of interpersonal relationships, and hence social influence, that have developed in given supervisor–subordinate pairs. Of course, social influence does not work only in lateral and downward directions. Subordinates can affect the motivation of those above them in the organizational structure. Although subordinates typically will not have the same total amount of power possessed by their supervisor, that does not mean they are powerless (Mechanic, 1962). In today's increasingly knowledge-based organizations, the simple act by a subordinate of withholding expertise (that the subordinate has and that the supervisor may not have) in a given situation can affect the subsequent motivation of the person (supervisor) in the ostensibly more powerful position.

The culture of the larger organization (that is, the remainder of the organization beyond the immediate work group) can also influence individuals' work motivation. This type of influence is well summarized by a management scholar who has succinctly stated: "From a management perspective, [corporate] culture in the form of shared expectations may be thought of as a social control system" (O'Reilly, 1989, p. 12). As with immediate work groups, this type of influence is exercised primarily through norms, except that in this case the norms are those of the organization (or a component of it that is larger than the immediate work group). The larger organization may have less direct social influence than that of the immediate work group, but that does not mean that such influence is inconsequential. The recent history of mergers and acquisitions in the corporate world demonstrates the potency of organizational cultures (of the merged or acquired organizations) on individuals' work motivation in newly created entities.

OVERVIEW OF THE READINGS

A general overview of how groups can influence the motivation and work effectiveness of individuals is provided in the initial reading in this chapter, by Porter, Lawler, and Hackman. The authors show how groups can affect, among other characteristics of individuals, their level of psychological arousal experienced while working and the level of effort they expend in doing their work. These two motivational factors together with individuals' performance strategies have much to do with their ultimate overall level of performance. This piece concludes with several suggested steps that organizations can take to diagnose situations and increase the positive effects of groups on the performance of their individual members.

The next article in Chapter 6 analyzes motivational causes for work-related misconduct, or what the authors, Vardi and Wiener, call "Organizational Misbehavior" (OMB), defined as "any intentional action by members of organizations that violates core organizational and/or societal norms." In other words, Vardi and Wiener focus on the motivational bases of deliberate misbehavior in work situations. The authors identify three types of such misbehavior: that intended to benefit the self (which violates organizational norms), that intended to benefit the organization but that violates societal norms, and that intended to inflict damage or be destructive (which can violate either or both organizational and societal norms). Thus, concepts of values and social norms are central to this analysis of the causes of such motivated misbehavior. The authors proceed to present a set of propositions to explain the misbehavior that can occur in organizational settings. The fundamental underlying rationale of the propositions involves either (a) normative pressures that can enhance misbehavior on behalf of the organization or one of its units, or, on the other hand, (b) organizational actions or circumstances that serve to accentuate excessive effort to engage in self-motivated instrumental behavior. It is especially interesting to note the statements the authors provide in support of the first part of the underlying rationale above regarding the normative pressures that can increase tendencies toward misbehavior on behalf of the organization: "The analyses of organizational value systems . . . suggest that organizations whose value systems are disproportionately weighted with 'elitist' values . . . are more likely to cut ethical corners, and even engage in criminal acts, than organizations whose value systems are essentially 'functional' (i.e., denote values of performance, quality, or service)." Readers might pause to think about whether there are any recent examples from the "real world" of business that might exemplify this conclusion!

The last article in this chapter, by Whyte, examines the by-now famous "groupthink" model originated by psychologist Irving Janis some three decades ago to explain disastrous decisions made by groups composed of highly competent individuals. As Janis explained (and as cited by Whyte), groupthink can be thought of as "a quick and easy way to refer to a mode of thinking that people engage in when they are deeply involved in a cohesive ingroup, when the members' striving for unanimity override their motivation to realistically appraise alternative courses of action. . . . Groupthink refers to a deterioration of mental efficiency, reality testing, and moral judgment that results from in-group pressures" (Janis, 1982, p. 9). The heart of Whyte's analysis of the groupthink phenomenon that Janis popularized is that it is a group's inflated perceptions of its own collective efficacy, rather than its cohesiveness, that is the major factor operating in instances of groupthink leading to decision fiascoes. As the author points out, and as was discussed in detail in the article by Stajkovic and Luthans in Chapter 2, self-efficacy can have many positive effects on organizational members' motivation and subsequent performance. However, Whyte's analysis emphasizes that past success can be a significant factor in the development of a group's unrealistic perceptions of collective efficacy and that "*failure to perceive the need to understand the causes of repeated success* [italics added to original text] leads to a high probability that success will soon end." Here, again, as in the case of the preceding article by Vardi and Wiener, readers when studying Whyte's article may want to consider whether recent real-world examples can be found of exaggerated collective efficacy operating in groups in organizations and whether this may have affected the motivation of individuals involved in such groups.

References

Allport, F. H. (1924). *Social psychology.* Boston: Houghton Mifflin.

Black, J. S., & Porter, L. W. (2000). *Management: Meeting new challenges.* Upper Saddle River, NJ: Prentice Hall.

Dansereau, Jr., F. E., Graen, G. B., & Haga, W. J. (1975). A vertical dyad linkage approach to leadership within formal organizations: A longitudinal investigation of the role making process. *Organizational Behavior and Human Performance, 13,* 46–78.

Graen, G. B., & Cashman, J. F. (1975). A role making model of leadership in formal organizations: A developmental approach. In J. G. Hung and L. L. Larson (Eds.), *Leadership Frontiers.* Kent, OH: Kent State University Press.

Janis, I. L. (1982). *Groupthink: Psychological studies of policy decisions and fiascoes.* Boston: Houghton Mifflin.

Krackhardt, D., & Porter, L. W. (1985). When friends leave: A structural analysis of the relationship between turnover and stayers' attitudes. *Administrative Science Quarterly, 30,* 242–261.

Mayo, E. (1933). *The human problems of industrial civilization.* New York: Macmillan.

Mechanic, D. (1962). Sources of power of lower participants in complex organizations. *Administrative Science Quarterly, 7,* 349–364.

O'Reilly, C. (1980). Corporations, culture, and commitment: Motivation and social control in organizations. *California Management Review, 31*(4), 9–25.

Roethlisberger, F. J., & Dickson, W. J. (1939). *Management and the worker.* Cambridge, MA: Harvard University Press.

Seashore, S. E. (1954). *Group cohesiveness in the industrial work group.* Ann Arbor, MI: Survey Research Center, Institute for Social Research, University of Michigan.

Shaw, M. E. (1981). *Group dynamics: The social psychology of small group behavior* (3rd ed.). New York: McGraw-Hill.

Ways Groups Influence Individual Work Effectiveness

Lyman W. Porter
Edward E. Lawler III
J. Richard Hackman

To analyze the diversity of group and social influences on individual work effectiveness, it may be useful to examine group effects separately on each of four summary classes of variables that have been shown to influence employee work behavior. These four classes of variables are:

1. The job-relevant knowledge and skills of the individual
2. The level of psychological arousal the individual experiences while working
3. The performance strategies the individual uses during his or her work
4. The level of effort the individual exerts in doing his or her work

Below, we shall examine the ways in which work groups influence each of these four major influences on individual performance.

GROUP INFLUENCES BY AFFECTING MEMBER KNOWLEDGE AND SKILLS

Performance on many tasks and jobs in organizations is strongly affected by the job-relevant knowledge and skills of the individuals who do the work. Thus, even if an employee has both high commitment toward accomplishing a particular piece of work and well-formed strategy about how to go about it, the implementation of that plan can be constrained or terminated if he or she does not know how to carry it out, or if he or she knows how but is incapable of doing so. While ability is relevant to the performance of jobs at all levels in an organization, its impact probably is somewhat reduced for lower-level jobs. The reason is that such jobs often are not demanding of high skill levels. Further, to the extent that organizational selection, placement, and promotion practices are adequate, *all* jobs should tend to be occupied by individuals who possess the skills requisite for adequate performance.

[We start with the assumption that] groups can improve the job-relevant knowledge and skills of an individual through direct instruction, feedback, and model provision. For jobs in which knowledge and skill are important determiners of performance effectiveness, then, groups can be of help. Nevertheless, the impact of groups on member performance effectiveness by improving member knowledge and skill probably is one of the lesser influences groups can have—both because employees on many jobs tend already to have many or all of

Slightly revised from L. W. Porter, E. E. Lawler, & J. R. Hackman, *Behavior in Organizations.* New York: McGraw-Hill, 1975, pp. 411–422. Used by permission.

the skills needed to perform them effectively and because there are other sources for improving skills which may be more useful and more potent than the work group, such as formal job training programs and self-study programs.

GROUP INFLUENCES BY AFFECTING MEMBER AROUSAL LEVEL

A group can substantially influence the level of psychological arousal experienced by a member—through the mere pressure of the other group members and by those others sending the individual messages which are directly arousal-enhancing or arousal-depressing. The conditions under which such group-promoted changes in arousal level will lead to increased performance effectiveness, however, very much depend upon the type of task being worked on (Zajonc, 1965).

In this case, the critical characteristics of the job have to do with whether the initially *dominant task responses* of the individual are likely to be correct or incorrect. Since the individual's output of such responses is facilitated when he is in an aroused state, arousal should improve performance effectiveness on well-learned tasks (so-called performance tasks) in which the dominant response is correct and needs merely to be executed by the performer. By the same token, arousal should impair effectiveness for new or unfamiliar tasks (learning tasks) in which the dominant response is likely to be incorrect.

It has sometimes been argued that the *mere* presence of others should heighten the arousal of individuals sufficiently for the predicted performance effects to be obtained. However, the evidence seems to indicate that the *mere* presence of others may not result in significant increases in arousal. Instead, only when the other group members are—or are seen as being—in a potentially evaluative relationship vis-à-vis the performer are the predictions confirmed (cf. Zajonc & Sales, 1966; Cottrell et al., 1968; Hency & Glass, 1968).

Groups can, of course, increase member arousal in ways other than taking an evaluative stance toward the individual. Strongly positive, encouraging statements also should increase arousal in some performance situations—for example, by helping individuals become personally highly committed to the group goal, and making sure they realize that they are a very important part of the team responsible for reaching that goal. What must be kept in mind, however, is that such devices represent a double-edged sword: While they may facilitate effective performance for well-learned tasks, they may have the opposite effect for new and unfamiliar tasks.

What, then, can be said about the effects on performance of group members when their presence (and interaction) serves to *decrease* the level of arousal of the group members—as, for example, when individuals coalesce into groups under conditions of high stress? When the other members of the group are a source of support, comfort, or acceptance to the individual (and serve to decrease his arousal level), it would be predicted that performance effectiveness would follow a pattern exactly opposite to that described above: the group would impair effectiveness for familiar or well-learned performance tasks (because arousal helps on these tasks and arousal is being lowered) and facilitate effectiveness for unfamiliar or complicated learning tasks (because in this case arousal is harmful, and it is being lowered).

The relationships predicted above are summarized in Figure 1. As the group becomes increasingly threatening, evaluative, or strongly encouraging, effectiveness should increase for

FIGURE 1   **Individual Performance Effectiveness as a Function of Type of Task and Experienced Relationship to the Group**

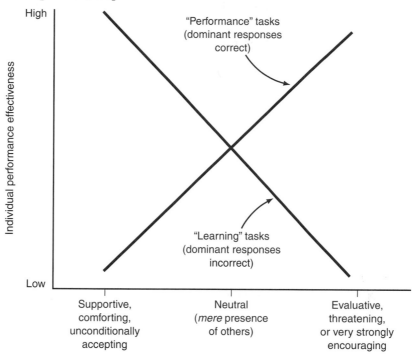

"Performance" tasks
(dominant responses
correct)

"Learning" tasks
(dominant responses
incorrect)

High

Low

Individual performance effectiveness

Supportive,
comforting,
unconditionally
accepting

Neutral
(*mere* presence
of others)

Evaluative,
threatening,
or very strongly
encouraging

Nature of the Individual's Relationship to the Group
(as experienced by the individual)

performance tasks and decrease for learning tasks. When the group is experienced as increasingly supportive, comforting, or unconditionally accepting, effectiveness should decrease for performance tasks and increase for learning tasks. And when no meaningful relationship at all is experienced by the individual between him- or herself and the group, performance should not be affected. While some of the predictions have been tested and confirmed in small group experimental settings, others await research.

Even that research which has focused on these relationships has not been designed or conducted in actual organizational settings, and the findings must be generalized with caution. It is clear, however, that individuals in organizations do use their group memberships as a means of achieving more comfortable levels of arousal. Individuals in high-pressure managerial jobs, for example, often find that they need to gather around themselves a few trusted associates who can and do provide reassurance and continuing acceptance when the going gets especially tough. This, presumably, should help reduce the manager's level of arousal and thereby increase the likelihood that he or she will be able to come up with *new and original* ways of perceiving and dealing with the immediate problem. If the theory is correct, however, this practice should not facilitate performance of the more "routine" (i.e., well-learned) parts of his or her job.

It is well known that overly routine jobs can decrease a worker's level of arousal to such an extent that his or her performance effectiveness is impaired. It seems quite possible, therefore, that the social environment of workers on such jobs can be designed so as to compensate partially for the deadening effects of the job itself and thereby lead to an increment of performance on well-learned tasks.

Finally, the supervisor probably has a more powerful effect on level of arousal of a worker than any other single individual in the immediate social environment. By close supervision (which usually results in the worker's feeling more or less constantly evaluated) supervisors can and do increase the level of arousal experienced by workers. While this may, for routine jobs, have some potential for improving performance effectiveness, it also is quite likely that the worker's negative reactions to being closely supervised ultimately will result in his or her attention being diverted from the job itself and focused instead on ways of either getting out from "under the gun" of the supervisor or somehow getting back at the supervisor to punish him or her for unwanted close supervision.

GROUP INFLUENCES BY AFFECTING LEVEL OF MEMBER EFFORT AND MEMBER PERFORMANCE STRATEGIES

The level of effort a person exerts in doing his or her work and the performance strategies he or she follows are treated together here because both variables are largely under the performer's *voluntary* control.

Direct versus Indirect Influences on Effort and Strategy

We have used a general "expectancy theory" approach to analyze those aspects of a person's behavior in organizations which are under his or her voluntary control. From this perspective a person's choices about effort and work strategy can be viewed as hinging largely upon (1) *expectations* regarding the likely consequences of choices and (2) the degree to which he or she *values* those expected consequences. Following this approach, it becomes clear that the group can have both a direct and an indirect effect on the level of effort a group member exerts at the job and on his or her choices about performance strategy.

The *direct* impact of the group on effort and strategy, of course, is simply the enforcement by the group of its own norms regarding what is an "appropriate" level of effort to expend on the job and what is the "proper" performance strategy. We previously discussed in some detail how groups use their control of discretionary stimuli to enforce group norms, and thereby affect such voluntary behaviors. Thus, if the group has established a norm about the level of member effort or the strategies members should use in going about their work, the group can control individual behavior merely by making sure that individual members realize that their receipt of valued group-controlled rewards is contingent upon their behaving in accord with the norm.

The *indirect* impact of the group on the effort and performance strategies of the individual involves the group's control of information regarding the state of the organizational environment outside the boundaries of the group. Regardless of any norms the group itself may have about effort or strategy, it also can communicate to the group member "what leads to what" in the broader organization, and thereby affect the individual's *own* choices about behavior.

For example, it may be the case in a given organization that hard work (i.e., high effort) tends to lead to quick promotions and higher pay; the group can influence the effort of the individual by helping him or her realize this objective state of affairs. Similarly, by providing individual members with information about what performance strategies are effective in the organization, the group can indirectly affect the strategy choices made by the person. Whether high quality of output or large quantities of output are more likely to lead to organizational rewards, for example, is information that the group can provide the individual with to assist him [or her] in making his or her own choices about work strategy.

Moreover, groups can affect the *personal preferences and values* of individual members—although such influences tend to occur relatively slowly and over a long period of time. When such changes do occur, the level of desire (or the valence) individuals have for various outcomes available in the organizational setting will change as well. And as the kinds of outcomes valued by the individual change, his or her behavior also will change to increase the degree to which the newly valued outcomes are obtained at work. The long-term result can be substantial revision of the choices made by the individual about the effort he or she will expend and the performance strategies he or she will use at work.

It should be noted, however, that such indirect influences on a member's effort and performance strategy will be most potent early in the individual's tenure in the organization when he or she has not yet had a chance to develop through experience his or her own personal "map" of the organization. When the individual becomes less dependent upon the group for data about "what leads to what" and "what's good" in the organization, the group may have to revert to direct norm enforcement to maintain control of the work behavior of individual members.

In summary, the group can and does have a strong impact on both the level of effort exerted by its members and the strategies members use in carrying out their work. This impact is realized both directly (i.e., by enforcement of group norms) and indirectly (i.e., by affecting the beliefs and values of the members). When the direct and indirect influences of a group are congruent—which is often the case—the potency of the group's efforts on its members can be quite strong. For example, if at the same time that a group is enforcing its *own* norm of, say, moderately low production, it also is providing a group member with data regarding the presumably *objective* negative consequences of hard work in the particular organization, the group member will experience two partially independent and mutually reinforcing influences aimed at keeping his rate of production down.

Effort, Strategy, and Performance Effectiveness

What, then, are the circumstances under which groups can improve the work *effectiveness* of their members through influences on individual choices about the level of effort and about strategy? Again, the answer depends upon the nature of the job. Unless a job is structured so that effort or performance strategy actually can make a real difference in work effectiveness, group influences on effort or strategy will be irrelevant to how well individual members perform.

Strategy: In general, groups should be able to facilitate member work effectiveness by influencing strategy choices more for complex jobs than for simple, straightforward, or routine ones. The reason is that on simple jobs, strategy choices usually cannot make much of a difference in effectiveness; instead, how well one does is determined almost entirely by how hard one works. On jobs characterized by high variety and autonomy, on the other hand, the work strategy used by the individual usually is of considerable importance in determining work effectiveness. By helping individuals develop and implement an appropriate work strategy—of where and how to put in their effort—the group should be able to substantially facilitate their effectiveness.

Effort: In the great majority of organizational settings, most jobs are structured such that the harder one works, the more effective one's performance is likely to be. Thus, group influences on the effort expended by members on their jobs are both very pervasive and very potent determiners of individual work effectiveness. There are, nevertheless, some exceptions to this generalization; the success of a complicated brain operation, for example, is less likely to depend upon effort expended than it is upon the strategies used and the job-relevant knowledge and skills of the surgeon.

When neither effort or strategy or both are in fact important in determining performance effectiveness, the individual has substantial personal control over how well he or she does in his work. In such cases, the degree to which the group facilitates (rather than hinders) individual effectiveness will depend jointly upon (1) the degree to which the group has accurate information regarding the task and organizational contingencies which are operative in that situation and makes such information available to the individual and (2) the degree to which the norms of the group are congruent with those contingencies and reinforce them.

Participation

One management practice which in theory should contribute positively to meeting both of the above conditions is the use of group participation in making decisions about work practices. Participation has been widely advocated as a management technique, both on ideological grounds and as a direct means of increasing work effectiveness. And, in fact, some studies have shown that participation can lead to higher work effectiveness (e.g., Coch & French, 1948; Lawler & Hackman, 1969). In the present framework, participation should contribute to increased work effectiveness in two different ways.

1. Participation can increase the amount and the accuracy of information workers have about work practices and the environmental contingencies associated with them. In one study (Lawler & Hackman, 1969), for example, some groups themselves designed new reward systems keyed on coming to work regularly (a task clearly affected by employee effort—i.e., trying to get to work every day). These groups responded both more quickly and more positively to the new pay plans than did groups which had technically identical plans imposed upon them by company management. One reason suggested by the authors to account for this finding was that the participative groups simply may have understood their plans better and had fewer uncertainties and worries about what the rewards were (and were not) for coming to work regularly.

2. Participation can increase the degree to which group members feel they "own" their work practices—and therefore the likelihood that the group will develop a norm of support of those practices. In the participative groups in the study cited above, for example, the nature of the work-related communication among members changed from initial "shared warnings" about management and "things management proposes" to helping members (especially new members) come to understand and believe in "our plan." In other words,

as group members come to experience the work or work practices *as under their own control or ownership,* it becomes more likely that informal group norms supportive of effective behavior vis-à-vis those practices will develop. Such norms provide a striking contrast to the "group protective" norms which often emerge when control is perceived to be exclusively and unilaterally under management control.

We can see, then, that group participative techniques can be quite facilitative of individual work effectiveness—but only under certain conditions:

1. The topic of participation must be relevant to the work itself. There is no reason to believe that participation involving task-irrelevant issues (e.g., preparing for the Red Cross Bloodmobile visit to the plant) will have facilitative effects on work productivity. While such participation may indeed help increase the cohesiveness of the work group, it clearly will not help group members gain information or develop norms which are facilitative of high work effectiveness. Indeed, such task-irrelevant participation may serve to direct the attention and motivation of group members *away from* work issues and thereby even lower productivity (cf. French, Israel, & As, 1960).

2. The objective task and environmental contingencies in the work setting must actually be supportive of more effective performance. That is, if through participation group members learn more about what leads to what in the organization, then it is increasingly important that there be real and meaningful positive outcomes which result from effective performance. If, for example, group members gain a quite complete and accurate impression through participation that "hard work around here pays off only in backaches," then increased effort as a consequence of participation is most unlikely. If, on the other hand, participation results in a new and better understanding that hard work can lead to increased pay, enhanced opportunities for advancement, and the chance to feel a sense of personal and group accomplishment, then increased effort should be the result.

3. Finally, the work must be such that increased effort (or a different and better work strategy) objectively can lead to higher work effectiveness. If it is true—as argued here—that the main benefits of group participation are (1) increased understanding of work practices and the organizational environment and (2) increased experienced "ownership" by the group of the work and work practices, then participation should increase productivity only when the *objective determinants of productivity are under the voluntary control of the worker.* There is little reason to expect, therefore, that participation should have a substantial facilitative effect on productivity when work outcomes are mainly determined by the level of skill of the worker and/or by his or her arousal level (rather than effort expended or work strategy used) or when outcomes are controlled by objective factors in the environment over which the worker can have little or no control (e.g., the rate or amount of work which is arriving at the employee's station).

IMPLICATIONS FOR DIAGNOSIS AND CHANGE

This section has focused on ways that the group can influence the performance effectiveness of individual group members. While it has been maintained throughout that the group has a substantial impact on such performance effectiveness, it has been emphasized that the nature and extent of this impact centrally depends upon the characteristics of the work being done.

To diagnose and change the direction or extent of social influences on individual performance in an organization, then, the following three steps might be taken.

1. An analysis of the task or job would be made to determine which of the four classes of variables (i.e., skills, arousal, strategies, effort) objectively affect measured performance effectiveness. This might be done by posing this analytical question: "If skills (or arousal, or effort, or strategies) were brought to bear on the work differently than is presently the case, would a corresponding difference in work effectiveness be likely to be observed as a consequence?" By scrutinizing each of the four classes of variables in this way, it usually is possible to identify which specific variables are objectively important to consider for the job. In many cases, of course, more than one class of variables will turn out to be of importance.

2. After one or more "target" classes of variables have been identified, the work group itself would be examined to unearth any ways in which the group was blocking effective individual performance. It might be determined, for example, that certain group norms were impeding the expression and use of various skills which individuals potentially could bring to bear on their work. Or it might turn out that the social environment of the worker created conditions which were excessively (or insufficiently) arousing for optimal performance on the task at hand. For effort and strategy, which are under the voluntary control of the worker, there are two major possibilities to examine: (a) that norms are enforced in the group which coerce individuals to behave in ineffective ways or (b) that the group provides information to the individual members about task and environmental contingencies in an insufficient or distorted fashion, resulting in their making choices about their work behavior which interfere with task effectiveness.

3. Finally, it would be useful to assess the group and the broader social environment to determine if there are ways that the "people resources" in the situation could be more fully utilized in the interest of increased work effectiveness. That is, rather than focusing solely on ways the group may be blocking or impeding performance effectiveness, attention should be given as well to any unrealized *potential* which resides in the group. It could turn out, for example, that some group members would be of great help to others in increasing the level of individual task-relevant skills, but these individuals have never been asked for help. Alternatively, it might be that the group could be assisted in finding new and better ways of ensuring that each group member has available accurate and current information about those tasks and environmental contingencies which determine the outcomes of various work behaviors.

The point is that the people who surround an individual at work can facilitate as well as hinder his or her performance effectiveness—and that any serious attempt to diagnose the social environment in the interest of improving work performance should explicitly address unrealized possibilities for enhancing performance as well as issues for which remedial action may be required.

What particular organizational changes will be called for on the basis of such a diagnosis—or what techniques should be used to realize these changes—will, of course, largely depend upon the particular characteristics of the organization and of the resources which are available there. The major emphasis of this section has been that there is *not* any single universally useful type of change or means of change—and that, instead, intervention should always be based on a thorough diagnosis of the existing social, organizational, and task environment. Perhaps especially intriguing in this regard is the prospect of developing techniques of social intervention which will help groups see the need for (and develop the capability of) making such interventions *on their own* in the interest of increasing the work effectiveness of the group as a whole.

References

Coch, L., & French, J. R. P., Jr. Overcoming resistance to change. *Human Relations,* 1948, 1, 512–532.

Cottrell, N. B., Wack, D. L., Sekerak, F. J., & Rittle, R. H. Social facilitation of dominant responses by the presence of an audience and the mere presence of others. *Journal of Personality and Social Psychology,* 1968, 9, 245–250.

French, J. R. P., Jr., Israel, J., & As, D. An experiment on participation in a Norwegian factory. *Human Relations,* 1960, 19, 3–19.

Hency, T., & Glass, D. C. Evaluation apprehension and the social facilitation of dominant and subordinate responses.

Journal of Personality and Social Psychology, 1968, 10, 446–454.

Lawler, E. E., & Hackman, J. R. The impact of employee participation in the development of pay incentive plans: A field experiment. *Journal of Applied Psychology,* 1969, 53, 467–471.

Zajonc, R. B. Social facilitation, *Science,* 1965, 149, 269–274.

Zajonc, R. B., & Sales, S. M. Social facilitation of dominant and subordinate responses. *Journal of Experimental Social Psychology,* 1966, 2, 160–168.

Misbehavior in Organizations: A Motivational Framework

Yoav Vardi
Yoash Wiener

INTRODUCTION

Organization scientists and practitioners are increasingly becoming more aware that patterns of work-related misconduct by members of organizations are prevalent, and that their consequences for work organizations are significant. Moreover, over the years, researchers from most social science disciplines (e.g., psychology, sociology, social psychology, criminology, management), have studied related phenomena and interpreted them from a variety of perspectives. These misbehaviors range from a mere breach or violation of psychological

From *Organization Science,* 1996, 7(2), 151–165. Reprinted with permission.

contracts (Kotter, 1973; Rousseau, 1989) to blatant acts bordering on criminal activity perpetrated against others and organizations (Henry, 1978; Hollinger, 1979). Such forms of misconduct appear to be universal. Most members of work organizations, it appears, engage in some form of misbehavior that is related to their work, albeit in varying degrees of intensity, severity and frequency. In fact, misbehavior is not restricted to certain employees; it has been recorded for both nonsupervisory and managerial members of different types of work organizations. Not surprisingly, then, both the economic and social costs of many forms of work- and organization-related misbehavior may, indeed, be quite substantial (e.g., Greenberg, 1990; Murphy, 1993).

Researchers have, in recent years, provided ample evidence for the large variety of such behaviors, and some examples may illustrate this wealth. Greenberg (1990) recently conducted a study of and reviewed the literature on employee theft, and Analoui and Kakabadse (1992) reported a longitudinal study of unconventional practices at work. Hollinger (1986) reviewed a considerable body of sociological and psychological literature on counterproductive behavior in organizations. Trevino (1986) discussed important contributions to management ethics, and Braithwaite (1985) extensively reviewed white-collar crime. In fact, the growing interest in specific events or phenomena such as whistle-blowing (Miceli & Near, 1992), professional deviant behavior (Raelin, 1986), concealing pertinent information (Reimann & Wiener, 1988a) substance abuse (Trice & Sonnenstuhl, 1988), sexual harassment at work (Gutek, 1985), or even vandalism (DeMore et al., 1988), only underscores the need to better understand this "darker" side of organizational life.

Our review of the literature seems to demonstrate that misconduct in organizations has not only been viewed as pervasive, but, for the most part, as intentional work-related behavior. It also establishes that, at the same time, we may lack a systematic approach to the understanding of such behavior. Based on these observations, we develop in this paper a conceptual framework which assumes that misbehaviors in organizations differ and vary, and that members commit such acts intentionally. We will elaborate on these fundamental arguments in further sections.

Treatment of Misbehavior in Behavioral Sciences

Several attempts to systematize the treatment of phenomena related to organizational misbehavior have been reported in the past. Hollinger (1986) observed that sociological research on employee misbehavior (defined as deviance) has centered around two foci: "Production deviance" and "Property deviance." While both constitute rule-breaking behavior, the first includes various types of behavior that are counterproductive (i.e., substandard work, slowdowns, insubordination), and the second category pertains to acts against property and assets of the organization (e.g., theft, pilferage, embezzlement, vandalism). Hollinger (1986) employed Hirschi's "social bonding" model to identify antecedents for both types of misbehavior. Based on empirical analysis he concluded that such individual acts are more likely to occur when individual attachment (e.g., commitment) to an organization is low. Other antecedents that were found to affect "productivity deviance" are mostly related to group and peer pressures (e.g., Zey-Ferrell & Ferrell, 1982), maladjustment (Raelin, 1986), increased competitive pressures (Hegarty & Sims, 1978), or disagreement with organizational goals and expectations (e.g., Gouldner, 1954). Antecedents contributing to "property deviance," such as theft, may be feelings of injustice or exploitation (Hollinger & Clark, 1982, 1983; Mars, 1974), attempts to ease personal financial pressures (Merton, 1938), moral laxity

(Merriam, 1977), available opportunities (Astor, 1972), dissatisfaction with work (Mangioni & Quinn, 1975), perceptions of pay inequity (Greenberg, 1990), and feelings of frustration (Analoui & Kakabadse, 1992). Similarly, vandalism, as property deviancy, was found to be associated with perceptions of inequity and mistreatment (DeMore et al., 1988).

Another major attempt to systematically deal with organizational misbehavior has been undertaken by Trevino (1986, 1992). Her focus is the interaction between personality and situational factors in determining ethical or unethical decisions among managers in organizations. In Trevino's model the individual level variables are the stage of moral development, ego strength, field dependence, and locus of control. The situational variables are the immediate job context, the organization culture, and characteristics of the work. Although the dependent variable (ethical/unethical behavior) is not formally defined, Trevino's work offers an extensive set of interactional propositions articulating specific predictions about unethical decisions and actions. Moreover, Trevino and Youngblood (1990) recently reported using hypothetical dilemmas in an experiment that provided partial empirical support for the multiple-influence model of managerial unethical decision making.

The present article offers a motivational framework of organizational misbehavior that is consistent with and expands Hollinger's and Trevino's contributions. However, it departs from previous work primarily in three respects. First, it offers a comprehensive definition of a new construct—Organizational MisBehavior (OMB)—which is inclusive of the various wrong-doings and counter-normative behaviors dealt with in past literature. Second, it develops a general typology of different types of OMB that allows for integration of previous notions. Third, and most importantly, it applies and expands an overall normative-instrumental model of work motivation to explain and predict different types of organizational misbehavior. This, integration, in turn, will allow predictions of both positive and negative forms of organizational behavior.

TOWARD A DEFINITION OF OMB

Definitions of behaviors that are considered as OMB may take a variety of approaches and properties depending on theoretical positions concerning (a) the criterion or yardstick against which OMB is determined, (b) the agent or agents who decide what constitutes OMB, and (c) the personal and organizational consequences of OMB. The position that our paper takes concerning these requirements is guided by one main principle: The resulting definition should be broad enough to integrate various types of misbehavior, yet capable of providing a foundation for a constructive and explanatory model of OMB. Consistent with this guideline we selected the concepts of values and norms as the criterion determining OMB, and viewed both society at large and the organization as the defining agents. Since consequences of OMB can vary in different situations (e.g., functional or dysfunctional; negative or positive; short term or long term), we did not include them in the definition itself but, rather, as a dependent variable in the overall model.

Organizational Misbehavior (OMB) is defined here as any intentional action by members of organizations that defies and violates (a) shared organizational norms and expectations, and/or (b) core societal values, mores and standards of proper conduct. Several elements of the definition require further elaboration. First, since the violation of "organizational norms and values" is the fundamental component in defining OMB, we must clarify what is meant by the construct "organization" in this context. Recognizing that most work organizations are complex social entities, often comprising multiple subunits and constituencies, the term "organization" does not convey a determinate entity. Rather, it represents the relevant unit of choice of an investigator, a manager, or a consultant interested in the phenomenon of OMB. They may, depending on their perspectives and special interests, refer to a work organization as a whole, or to any significant sector within it, such as a Strategic Business Unit. The important point is that explicit choices of the identity of the unit of interest must be made in order to identify the relevant core values against which a violation (and therefore OMB), may occur. Thus, throughout the paper, whenever the term "organization" is used, it should convey exactly this meaning.

Second, both overt action and its underlying intention are necessary to identify misbehavior; to define OMB without its underlying intention will result in including misbehavior that is unintentional or accidental. Hence, work-related actions that involve errors, mistakes, or even unconscious negligence and action-slips (e.g., a harmful mistake in a surgical procedure that is committed unintentionally) do not constitute OMB, despite their similar consequences in organizational as well as personal terms.

Third, the level of analysis is the individual rather than the group or the organization. Even though it is possible to apply the concept of OMB to misbehavior by groups (e.g., see Trice & Beyer, 1993, on deviant organizational subcultures) or by organizations (e.g., see Baucus & Near, 1991, on illegal corporate behavior), we focus here on individuals who are intentionally, actually and directly involved in some form of misbehavior. This is principally because the present model proposes the role of *individual motivation* as a source of OMB. Fourth, values and norms pertain to both formal (laws, rules and regulations, standard operating procedures, etc.) and informal social expectations. Last, and significantly, the definition acknowledges the importance of both internal (intraorganizational) and external (societal) value systems in determining OMB.

Values and Norms: A General View

Because the concept of values is a central component in the analysis of OMB, a definition of the concept itself is necessary. In the social literature there are serious inconsistencies in the definition of value and in the distinctions between value and related constructs such as attitude, belief, and norm. Nevertheless, certain formulations that allow operational definitions and measurement have gained a fair degree of acceptance (see, for example, discussions by Brown, 1976; Fallding, 1965; Meglino et al., 1986). One such definition by Rokeach (1973, p. 5) states that "a value is an enduring belief that a specific mode of conduct or end-state of existence is personally or socially preferable to an opposite or converse mode of conduct or end state of existence." In this definition values are viewed as forms of beliefs, and a major source of these values may be social expectations, particularly when they are shared. Thus, social values may indeed be viewed as normative beliefs complementing instrumental beliefs as antecedents of behavior (Fishbein & Ajzen, 1975). Further, values can be construed as internalized normative beliefs; once established, they may act as built-in normative guides for behavior, independent from the effect of rewards and punishments that are consequences of actions (Wiener, 1982).

Rokeach's definition suggests that values shared by group members, particularly values concerning modes of conduct, become similar to norms guiding members toward uniformity in behavior. Others (e.g., Kilmann, 1985), however, distinguish between norms as more specific and often more explicit behavioral expectations, and values that are broader in scope than norms. (For thorough discussions on organizational value systems consult Wiener, 1988, and on societal level values consult Rokeach, 1973.) The above analysis of the concepts of values and norms applies to various types of social units, including the two most congruous with the definition of OMB: work organizations and society at large.

OMB: Definitional Implications

The definition of OMB, as suggested above, implies four important features or attributes that seem useful for the construction of an integrative model, the measurement of variables, and the derivation of relevant predictions. We discuss these implications in the following sections.

Broadness of Scope of OMB

A basic implication of the definition is that a behavior does not have to violate *both* societal and organizational values in order to be identified as OMB. While such behaviors are not uncommon (e.g., unauthorized use of company property), it would be theoretically too narrow and not constructive to limit OMB to just such acts. According to the proposed definition, a behavior that may be consistent with organizational expectations but violates societal values (e.g., misleading customers) would be considered OMB in our model. Such organizationally condoned misbehaviors may be detrimental in the long run. Similarly, member behavior that is consistent with societal values but violates organizational expectations would be classified as OMB as well (e.g., whistle-blowing in an organization that does not sanction such a behavior). Unaccepted behaviors such as these may, however, be beneficial to organizations in the long run. We deem this kind of definitional broadness as essential in any attempt to construct an integrative and inclusive model of organizational misbehavior. It also provides a solid basis for a meaningful typology of misbehaviors that, in and of itself, would be useful in the overall understanding and prediction of organizational outcomes.

OMB: Is It "Good" or "Bad"?

A second feature of the definition is that it does not necessarily equate norm and value violation with negative and undesirable behavior. For one thing, the definition itself does not make any references to consequences of OMB. Secondly, the desirability of any value-breaking behavior is inherently, by definition, a judgmental matter. In general, a value-violating behavior would be deemed "undesirable" by a collective of individuals holding that value, but may be seen "desirable" by another collective for which this behavior meets expectations. Thus, again, cheating customers may be evaluated as undesirable by members of society at large, but quite acceptable in a particular organizational setting. By the same token, whistle-blowing may be viewed as commendable action by members of society at large, but unacceptable in a context of a particular organization.

Results of OMB

While the proposed definition does not allow attribution of inherent, absolute value to OMB, the consequences of OMB may be evaluated as to their degree of constructiveness for any given organization. The basic premise is that an organization may not be successful, in the long run, if it expects, or even allows, members to violate values of the larger society within which it operates. Thus, using the same examples of misbehavior, cheating customers would tend, in the long run, to be detrimental to organizations that allow it, but whistle-blowing may prove constructive (Miceli & Near, 1994). Organizational Behavior that simultaneously violates both societal and organizational values, such as harassing members, sabotaging work, or vandalizing equipment, is clearly destructive in its consequences.

OMB as a Variable

Since OMB is defined in relation to a set of core values of a particular social unit, and since such core values can be measured, OMB itself can be considered a variable. Moreover, because of the complex phenomenon it may tap, OMB should be treated as a multidimensional variable. Such an approach is not only useful for improved precision of the model, but is necessary for generating significant predictions about the phenomenon. In general, then, OMB may range from a low (benign) degree of misbehavior to a high (severe) degree of misbehavior, and the measurement may take two forms: behavioral and attitudinal.

The behavioral aspect of OMB can be measured using frequency counts of acts of misbehavior with respect to a given organizational unit, or with respect to individual members. This frequency measure can also be weighted by an index of severity of the observed misbehavior. Such an index may be comprised of two facets: (a) the centrality of the violated norm or value (for proposals related to the measurement of the centrality of a core value see, for example, Wiener, 1988), and (b) the degree of premeditation, preoccupation or planning seemingly involved in displaying the misbehavior. A second measure of OMB (attitudinal) may tap the individual's strength of the intention, predisposition, or propensity to engage in work- and organization-related misconduct. Although people tend to be quite reluctant to openly express intentions to misbehave, measures might be operationally developed in questionnaire form, for example.

Such multifaceted indices (behavioral and attitudinal) are used by OB [Organizational Behavior] researchers to measure specific work behaviors about which individuals are hesitant to report as withdrawal behavior (e.g., actual incidents of turnover and intentions to leave the organization), or organizational citizenship behavior (e.g., actual altruistic deeds and pro-social attitudes). Indeed, using both actual and attitudinal observations may facilitate a more meaningful classification of the misbehavior phenomenon.

Basic Types of OMB

An examination of a broad range of instances of norm violating behaviors would suggest that all such actions can be classified into three basic types in terms of the underlying *intention* of the misbehaving individual:

(a) Misbehaviors that are intended to benefit the self (OMB Type S). These misbehaviors are mostly internal to the organization, and usually victimize the employing organization or its members. Thus, such behaviors may have three categories of internal targets: (1) the work itself (e.g., distorting data); (2) the organization's property, resources, symbols or regulations (e.g., stealing and selling manufacturing secrets); and (3) other members (e.g., harassing peers). An exception to the above is a behavior by a member that appears to benefit the organization (e.g., overcharging customers), but is, in fact, intended to eventually benefit the individual (e.g., gaining a promotion).

(b) Misbehaviors that primarily intend to benefit the member's employing organization as a whole (OMB Type O). Those misbehaviors (e.g., falsifying records in order to improve chances of obtaining a contract for the organization) are mostly external in nature, usually directed toward outside "victims" such as other organizations, social institutions, public agencies, or customers. If the intention underlying this form of behavior is not primarily to benefit the organization, but is self-serving (e.g., for career considerations), it should not be classified as OMB Type O. More likely, this would be OMB Type S.

(c) Misbehaviors that primarily intend to inflict damage and be destructive (OMB Type D). Targets of these behaviors could be as listed above, both internal and external. Whereas the intentions underlying Type S and Type O misbehaviors are to *benefit* either the individual or the organization, the intention behind OMB Type D is to *hurt* others or the organization. Such intentional misbehaviors (e.g., sabotaging company-owned equipment) may be perpetuated by members either on their own initiative (e.g., as a revenge or a response to perceived or actual mistreatment), or on behalf of "significant others" (e.g., interfering with organizational operations to comply with Union's expectations). However, the underlying intention must be to cause some type of damage whether minor or considerable, subtle or visible.

While the above classification of OMB types is based on an internal psychological state (intentions), it seems that the classifying task itself should not be highly subjective; in most cases, the proper classification should be fairly accurately derived from the overt misbehavior itself. As a rule, when more than one intention seems to underlie an act of OMB and when observations yield equivocal data, the intention considered as predominant would determine the classification. Again, we emphasize, the "intention" principle which is at the core of the OMB classification is necessary for the analysis of OMB within a motivational framework. We therefore elaborate on this requirement in the following section.

THEORETICAL FOUNDATIONS

The present conception of OMB is predicated on the role of norms and values in guiding behavior of organizational members. Willful violation of such expectations (norms and values) constitutes misbehavior. Therefore, mainstream OB paradigms that make distinctions between normative, value-based processes, and instrumental-calculative ones in determining individual behavior in organizations might be also useful as a basis for a model of individual misbehavior. One such paradigm that has been effectively used in the literature to explain determinants of individual behavior is Fishbein and Ajzen's behavioral intentions theory (Fishbein and Ajzen, 1975).

The Fishbein and Ajzen Model

This model deals primarily with the prediction and understanding of behavioral intentions. It hypothesizes that an individual's behavior is a function of the intention to perform that behavior. A person's behavioral intention, in turn, is determined by two basic factors: (a) the attitude toward performing the act, that is, person's evaluation or affect with respect to the act, and (b) the subjective norm, i.e., perception of the totality of the normative pressures concerning the behavior. The first component—the person's attitude toward performing a particular act—is a function of beliefs concerning the consequences of the act and the value of the consequences for the person. These can be referred to as instrumental-cognitive beliefs. The second component, the subjective norm, is a function of a person's beliefs about what important referents think he or she should do, weighted by motivation to comply with them. Such referents may include significant others, a particular reference group, or society at large. In addition, several researchers (e.g., Fishbein, 1967; Jaccard & Davidson, 1975; Pomazal & Jaccard, 1976; Schwartz & Tessler, 1972) have suggested that the subjective norm is determined not only by social normative beliefs (i.e., a person's beliefs of how others expect him or her to act), but also by personal normative beliefs, that is, personal moral standards concerning a behavior. Personal moral standards (e.g., Jones, 1991) concerning a particular mode of conduct are established when a person internalizes expectations of others concerning this behavior. These determinants of the subjective norm can be termed "internalized subjective beliefs." When behavioral acts are guided by such internalized pressures, they are no longer dependent on their linkage with the reinforcements and punishments on which they were initially based (Jones & Gerard, 1967). In the Fishbein and Ajzen model "attitude" and "subjective norm" are viewed as predictors, and the "behavioral intention" is the criterion. Furthermore, the two components are given empirical weights in a multiple regression equation proportional to their relative importance in the determination of behavioral intentions. Importantly, the model incorporates both cognitive and affective components because attitudes, by definition, include affective or evaluative considerations concerning ensuing acts (in our case—intentional acts of misbehavior). It is clear now how this approach may be useful in the analysis of OMB as well.

The OMB Conceptual System: Core Relationships

Figure 1 represents the overall OMB conceptual framework. The core relationships are based on the Fishbein and Ajzen model as adapted by Wiener (1982) to form a normative-instrumental framework of individual commitment, and by Wiener and Vardi (1990) to conceptually integrate organizational culture and individual motivation. However, unlike the original model, in the proposed OMB system, misbehavior is not always some function of the two predictor categories: instrumental and normative. Instead, depending on its type, OMB may be determined by either one of the two predictors, or simultaneously by both.

OMB Type S reflects intention to benefit the individual rather than the employing organization. It is determined primarily by "attitude" which, in turn, is a function of the sum of beliefs concerning the consequences of the misbehavior for the individual ("instrumental motivation" according to Wiener, 1982). The reason for this assertion is inherent in the definition of OMB Type S. Because such misbehavior intends to benefit the self, it stands to reason that it would be influenced by a person's beliefs concerning the extent to which the misbehavior is likely to result in favorable or unfavorable outcomes. For instance, the probability of misusing company resources is smaller if the person believes that punishment may readily result from such act, than when no punishment is anticipated. Thus, the motivational process underling OMB Type S is primarily calculative-instrumental. Nevertheless, while this type of misconduct is a function of instrumental processes, one key constraint that can inhibit such behavior is the strength of the organization's cohesiveness (we provide further discussion of this issue in the propositions section).

OMB Type O, which by definition reflects intentions to benefit the employing organization rather than the individual directly, would be primarily determined by "subjective norms" that are a function of the totality of internalized normative beliefs concerning organizational expectations from members (see definitions and discussion of norms and values above). Thus, as a rule, Type O misbehaviors are anchored in ideology and values, and are carried out by individuals who strongly identify with their organization, its mission and its leadership, and who often are willing to sacrifice self-interests for such causes. Breaking the law to protect

FIGURE 1   **Individual and Organizational Determinants of OMB Types:**
An Instrumental-Normative Model

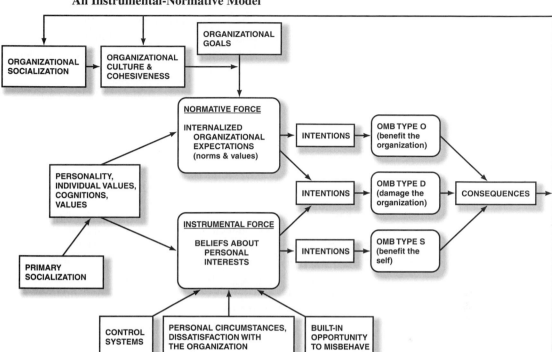

interests of the company while risking personal well-being would be a case in point. While normative pressures determine this type of OMB, one could also argue that certain instrumental factors serve as constraints (for example, when the perpetrators refrain from acting because they estimate high likelihood of being punished by external agencies). Of course, it is possible that an individual may break the law on behalf of the company for personal interests. But, as we stipulated above, this form of misbehavior should be classified as OMB Type S because the predominate motive is benefitting the self.

Unlike OMB Types S and O, OMB Type D is determined by either normative or instrumental processes, or by both simultaneously. OMB Type D reflects intentions to damage and hurt a particular organization or social unit. Underlying such intentions may be normative forces as in the case of damaging company property as a show of solidarity with striking union members. At the same time, this kind of behavior might be largely determined by instrumental factors: deriving personal satisfaction out of an act of revenge or of vandalism. This is why we contend that, in principle, both normative and instrumental forces may converge simultaneously to determine Type D misbehavior. In addition to the core relationships discussed above, Figure 1 presents the position in the model of individual and organizational factors that influence the formation of internalized organizational expectations and instrumental motivation of members. Subsequent sections will discuss additional theoretical foundations, issues that pertain to determinants of OMB, and an analysis of consequences of OMB.

Input from Decision and Social Information Theories

Misbehavior in organizations involves both calculative decision making and the processing of social information. In order to integrate such psychological processes in the OMB framework, we adapt two additional mainstream OB contributions that articulate such processes. The two models are complementary in that they describe both calculative and normative forces.

The March and Simon Model

Since in our proposed framework one major determinant of misbehavior is rational calculations of utility of behavior to self, it is important to account for the considerations that go into such a decision making process. March and Simon's (1958) seminal book on organizations offers important insights (e.g., inducement-contribution trade-offs) about causes of work-related behavior. According to their paradigm, individuals in organizations decide not only to join or leave, but also explicitly how to perform. Granted, those decisions are constrained by imperfect (bounded) rationality, yet individuals are, by and large, aware of both constraints and opportunities in their organizational environment. For instance, they use such information in their decisions to stay or leave. This rationale can be readily adapted to explain forms of misbehavior because individuals are aware (albeit imperfectly) of the opportunities, as well as the consequences of engaging in misconduct. Such knowledge, in turn, provides the sources of most instrumental or calculative considerations that, like in the case of "standard" behavior, may be limited. Thus, the paradigm provides an essential attribute of the major cognitive inputs contributing to the formation of individual interests that determine Type S misbehavior, and may contribute to OMB Type D as well.

The Salancik and Pfeffer Model

The second component determining misbehavior comprises internalized beliefs and expectations. Relevant questions that may arise are: How do members of a social unit acquire norms and values? How do members "know" when they act in defiance, and therefore when they engage in certain forms of organizational misbehavior? The Salancik and Pfeffer (1978) theory of social information may be particularly helpful. For them, the social context itself affects a person's behavior by shaping his or her perceptions and beliefs about organizational situations. Yet, one can argue, sense-making cues, transmitted through both formal and informal social interactions, pertain not only to desirable behavior, but also, and perhaps more dramatically, to misbehavior. Such cues may carry important symbolic and affective meanings, as well as instrumental ones. Thus, individual attitudes and beliefs that are formed from such perceived "socially constructed realities" may determine the intentions that lead to all three types of OMB.

CORE ANTECEDENTS OF OMB

Our definition of OMB, the proposed conceptual framework which emphasizes the distinction between normative and instrumental determinants of misbehavior, and the support from other OB paradigms, all suggest the specific antecedents that may affect the formation of the motivational components in the model. These components can be seen as intervening constructs, mediating the relationships between various antecedents, on one hand, and intentions and misbehaviors, on the other hand (see Figure 1). Generally speaking, the basic reasoning underlying the model is that antecedents contributing to the instrumental component would primarily influence Type S misbehavior, and antecedents contributing to the normative component would affect Type O misbehavior. Both forces, however, may influence OMB Type D. The purpose of this section is to identify core antecedents of OMB. Rather than providing a complete list, we selected a sample of determinants that may contribute most to the variance of the normative and instrumental components of the model, and consequently to OMB. Two major types of antecedents are proposed: individual-level and organizational-level. Specific arguments and a more detailed description of selected antecedents are further developed in the propositions section.

Individual Factors

Individuals differ in their propensity to engage in the forms of misbehavior as conceptualized in the present model, both in terms of values and attitudes, and personality traits. The model focuses on five types of individual differences as follows:

Personality

Two personality variables in particular seem to affect both motivational components and, in turn, the intention to engage in OMB. The two variables can affect both the normative process of value internalization and the "calculations" involved in forming instrumental beliefs about personal interests. First is the level of moral development of an organization member (Kohlberg, 1969). Trevino (1986) has already demonstrated the usefulness of this factor in the context of unethical behavior among managers. Second is the degree of sociopathic predisposition, that is, the state characterized by disregard for social norms and obligations without the inhibiting experience of guilt. Of course, extreme degrees of sociopathic tendencies characterize only a marginal portion of any organization's workforce.

Person-Organization Value Congruence

This antecedent refers to the degree to which personal values held by the individual are consistent with core organizational norms and values. The higher is such a congruence, the more likely is a member to identify with a referent social unit and be guided by its values and norms (Chatman, 1989; Hall & Schneider, 1972). Hence, it is reasonable to assume that this variable represents a strong contribution to the normative component of the model and, in turn, to OMB.

Generalized Value of Loyalty and Duty

This is a personal value acquired in the process of primary socialization. It represents a generalized sense of duty and obligation, namely, the belief by individuals that they have a moral obligation to exhibit loyalty in all significant social situations in which they are involved (Wiener, 1982). Regardless of their other values, individuals who rank high on Generalized Loyalty and Duty would tend to identify with their organization and behave accordingly. Therefore, this variable also represents a strong contribution to the normative component of the model.

Personal Circumstances

When an individual faces a compelling need or deprivation—material or otherwise—he or she might be more inclined to engage in misbehavior that may help them resolve such needs (e.g., Merton, 1938). Conversely, employees may be less inclined to misbehave when anticipating being at risk of losing membership. Thus, specific personal circumstances partially determine one's tendencies to engage in OMB, primarily by shaping instrumental beliefs about the value of the ensuing consequences of any given misbehavior.

Dissatisfaction of Personal Needs by the Organization

When individuals perceive being mistreated by their employing organizations, the valence of self-benefitting misbehavior may increase (e.g., Analoui & Kakabadse, 1992; Greenberg, 1990; Hollinger, 1986; Mangioni & Quinn, 1975). Indirectly, this factor may also influence the way organizational expectations are learned and internalized; it is less likely for a member to be successfully socialized by and to identify with an organization when mistreatment of self and others is perceived. Thus, dissatisfaction of needs by an organization primarily affects the instrumental component of motivation to misbehave but it can, indirectly, contribute to the normative forces as well.

Organizational Factors

Organizations differ in terms of the contextual conditions, at both the task and organization levels, that may affect the propensity of an individual member to engage in work related misbehavior. Five types of such factors are listed below:

Built-in Opportunity

Certain work organizations and jobs involve operations for which control is inherently difficult, for example, home delivery, operating cash registers, professional or food services, operations where cash transactions cannot be directly monitored by receipts, and inventory counts. In fact, most jobs may consist of some built-in opportunities to misuse or take advantage of various organizational resources (such as office equipment). The degree to which such built-in opportunities exist may enter into the instrumental calculations concerning the benefits, consequences, and risks of capitalizing on such opportunities (e.g., Astor, 1972).

Control Systems

Regardless of the inherent opportunity, control systems such as appraisal, reward and disciplinary systems, or special monitoring arrangements, in some organizations, are more effective at controlling behavior than in others. Both oppressive and lax controls may contribute to the emergence of OMB (cf. Hegarty & Sims, 1979). Thus, control systems, especially those that represent both extremes, may have a direct impact on members' instrumental considerations whether to engage in or refrain from acts of misconduct.

Organizational Culture

Organizational culture is widely regarded as a construct denoting the extent to which members share core organizational values (e.g., Wiener, 1988). Several writers (e.g., Kunda, 1992) have demonstrated the power of culture as a tool "used" by certain dominant groups (top management, for example) purposely to shape other members' values. Others (e.g., Hatch, 1993) have begun to develop a conception of cultural dynamism that looks at how elements of culture interact over time. Either way, "organizational culture" may constitute an important normative influence on the inclination of members to engage in acts of misbehavior. Trevino's (1986) model, for instance, directly relates the organizational culture variable to unethical decision behavior of managers.

Organizational Cohesiveness

Since in very cohesive social units the pressures to adhere to norms of conduct are especially high (e.g., Janis, 1982), this factor may be similar to organizational culture in its effects on misbehavior. It may, indeed, be more powerful. Accordingly, we regard this organization characteristic as a significant antecedent that may strongly contribute to the normative component in the OMB model.

Organizational Goals

By definition, organizational goals are closely associated with organizational values and expectations and, therefore, are likely to exert influence on the normative motivational component in the model. Furthermore, organizational goals may directly instigate misbehavior, particularly when they are highly demanding and unrealistic [for example, NASA's Challenger disaster (Reimann & Wiener, 1988a) and, more recently, the Hubble fiasco (Stein & Kanter, 1993)].

In the next section we begin to develop formal propositions for predicting OMB. Of the above list of antecedents, the following variables will be further discussed and the rationale behind their selection will be explained: person-organization value congruence, personal need satisfaction by the organization, level of individual moral development, and organizational cohesiveness.

PROPOSITIONS

A large number of specific propositions can be generated concerning the main and interaction effects of various antecedents on OMB. However, in this section we chose to focus on three groups of propositions that appear to most parsimoniously tap the principal relationships posited in our framework. Also, these propositions may serve as examples for the rationale and way of thinking underlying other potential hypotheses. The three groups are: (a) The effect of person-organization value congruence (POVC) on the predisposition to engage in different types of OMB, both directly and in interaction with personal need satisfaction provided by the organization (PNS); (b) The effects of levels of personal moral development on the predisposition to engage in different types of OMB; and (c) The intention to engage in OMB as a function of organizational cohesiveness. The dependent variables in all propositions are stated in terms of the strength of individual predispositions (or intentions) to engage in OMB Types S, O, and D, as articulated in the section "OMB as a variable" above. We use the predispositional rather than the behavioral measures here because they are, by definition, the immediate outcome of motivation. Moreover, for these hypotheses we do not expect any difference in predictions when applying either behavioral or intentional variables.

The basic rationale underlying the propositions is as follows: Normative pressures, when consistent with the interests of a referent social unit (i.e., an organization, or part of it), will enhance misbehavior on behalf of the unit (OMB Type O), and will suppress misbehaviors that either benefit the individual (OMB Type S) or are intended to inflict damage (OMB Type D). On the other hand, organizational actions and conditions that either frustrate instrumental interests or individual members, or lead them to believe that to engage in misconduct is self-benefitting, will tend to promote predispositions towards OMB Type S and OMB Type D.

OMB as a Function of Person-Organization Value Congruence and Personal Need Satisfaction

Person-organization value congruence (POVC), considered an essential determinant of organizational behavior (e.g., Hall & Schneider, 1972), serves as a crucial factor in predicting OMB. As an antecedent of behavior in the context of social organizations, POVC seems to be the most immediate and most potent determinant of the totality of normative pressures impinging on the individual. But POVC itself is a variable. Thus, for the purpose of developing testable hypotheses we assume three levels of congruence: *Identification:* personal values are highly consistent with those of the referent social unit; *Detachment:* personal values are unrelated or neutral vis-à-vis the referent social unit; and *Alienation:* personal values are in conflict with those of the referent social unit.

Another important antecedent variable we focus on is personal need satisfaction by the organization (PNS), postulating a dichotomy of low and high levels of satisfaction. While POVC denotes a normative antecedent, we consider this particular psychological antecedent to be a direct determinant of instrumental motivation that, in turn, influences the intention to misbehave.

First we present propositions about the expected main effects of the person-organization value congruence antecedent. These main effects are summarized in Table 1, and the predictions pertain to the anticipated strength or weakness of the intention or predisposition to engage in a particular type of misbehavior.

PROPOSITION 1. Main effect of POVC on OMB Type S. Stronger predisposition to engage in OMB Type S is expected under conditions of Detachment and Alienation, and weaker predisposition to engage in OMB Type S is expected for Identification.

PROPOSITION 2. Main effect of POVC on OMB Type O. Stronger predisposition to commit OMB Type O is expected under the Identification condition, and weaker predispositions are expected for Detachment and Alienation.

PROPOSITION 3. Main effect of POVC on OMB Type D. Stronger predisposition to engage in OMB Type D is associated with the Alienation condition, and weaker predispositions are expected under Identification and Detachment.

The next set of propositions pertains to the prediction of the predisposition to engage in OMB as a function of the interaction of the two core antecedents: person-organization value congruence (POVC) and personal need satisfaction by the organization (PNS). These variables, again, are designed to represent the normative and instrumental dimensions, respectively.

TABLE 1   The Expected Main Effects of Person-Organization Value Congruence, Moral Development, and Cohesiveness on the Predisposition to Engage in Three Types of OMB

Determinants of OMB		Types of OMB		
		Type S	Type O	Type D
Person-Organization	Identification	Low	High	Low
Value Congruence	Detachment	High	Low	Low
	Alienation	High	Low	High
Moral Development	Preconventional	High	Low	High
	Conventional	Low	High	Low
	Principled	Low	Low	Low
Organization Cohesiveness	Low Cohesion	High	Low	High
	High Cohesion	Low	High	Low

PROPOSITION 4. Interaction effects on OMB Type S. The predisposition to commit OMB Type S would be the strongest for individuals who experience dissatisfaction of their needs under POVC conditions of Detachment and Alienation. Weaker predispositions to engage in OMB Type S are expected under all other conditions.

PROPOSITION 5. Interaction effects on OMB Type O. The predispositions to commit OMB Type O would be the strongest when individuals experience satisfaction of personal needs (high PNS) under the condition of Identification. In all other conditions the predispositions to engage in OMB Type O are expected to be weaker.

PROPOSITION 6. Interaction effects on OMB Type D. The predispositions to engage in Type D misbehavior would be the strongest when individuals experience dissatisfaction of personal needs (low PNS) under the condition of Alienation. Such predispositions would be weaker under all other conditions.

Propositions 4–6 are exhibited in Table 2. The next group of propositions spell out the expected impact of moral development (as a personality factor) on the individual predisposition to engage in OMB.

Effects of Moral Development on OMB

Kohlberg (1969) classified stages of moral development into three consecutive levels which denote a progression from a lower to a higher order moral personality structure. In organizational settings individuals at the "Preconventional" level (Kohlberg's moral development stages 1 and 2) are basically obedient and instrumentally oriented towards their organizational obligations. But when faced with opportunities to misbehave they would be less hesitant to take advantage of such circumstances, especially when they do not foresee negative consequences for themselves. Organization members at the "Conventional" level of moral development (Kohlberg's stages 3 and 4), when making behavioral choices at work, are primarily guided by their acceptance of local social and organizational expectations. Because they are more strongly influenced by their social environment, such persons tend to yield to conventional normative pressures. In turn, such normative pressures may lead "conventionals" to

TABLE 2   **The Predisposition to Engage in Three Types of OMB as a Function of Person-Organization Value Congruence and Personal Need Satisfaction by the Organization**

Person-Organization Value Congruence (POVC)	Need Satisfaction by the Organization (PNS)	
	High	**Low**
Identification (Values–Congruent)	High OMB Type O	
Detachment (Values–Neutral)		High OMB Type S
Alienation (Values–Incongruent)		High OMB Type S OMB Type D

Note: Empty cells denote a low disposition to engage in any type of OMB.

violate norms which they deem irrelevant. Individuals at the "Principled" level (stages 5 and 6) are guided solely by internalized and stable universal principles that govern their judgment of right and wrong. For them these principles are absolute and, therefore, nonnegotiable. Such persons, we believe, are not inclined to misbehave under any of the hypothesized conditions. Table 1 presents a summary of the specific predictions (Propositions 7–9).

PROPOSITION 7. Effect of moral development on OMB Type S. Individuals at the Preconventional level of moral development would tend to exhibit a stronger predisposition to engage in self benefitting misbehavior at work than individuals at either the Conventional or Principled levels.

PROPOSITION 8. Effect of moral development on OMB Type O. Individuals at the Conventional level of moral development would tend to exhibit stronger predisposition to engage in organization benefitting misbehavior than individuals at either Preconventional or Principled levels.

PROPOSITION 9. Effect of moral development on OMB Type D. Individuals at the Preconventional level of moral development would tend to exhibit a stronger predisposition to engage in destructive misbehavior than would individuals at either the Conventional or Principled levels.

Effects of Organizational Cohesiveness on OMB

Cohesiveness is viewed here as the degree of attachment or attractiveness the members of a social unit (e.g., work organization) experience toward each other and toward the social unit itself. A cohesive social unit exerts strong pressures on members to learn, internalize, and adhere to its core values and norms of conduct. As a result, such pressures contribute to a relatively high degree of uniformity in actions, beliefs, and sentiments among the unit's members. Indeed, the higher the cohesiveness, the stronger the pressures toward both uniformity and conformity (Lott & Lott, 1965). Cohesiveness, then, seems to constitute a significant determinant of the normative component of our model, with the expected effects on OMB as indicated in the following propositions and in Table 1.

PROPOSITION 10. Effect of organizational cohesiveness on OMB Type S. There will be a stronger predisposition to engage in OMB Type S among members in low cohesiveness social units than among members in high cohesiveness social units.

PROPOSITION 11. Effect of organizational cohesiveness on OMB Type O. There will be a stronger predisposition to engage in OMB Type O among members in high cohesiveness social units than among members in low cohesiveness social units.

PROPOSITION 12. Effect of organizational cohesiveness on OMB Type D. There will be a stronger predisposition to engage in OMB Type D among members in low cohesiveness social units than among members in high cohesiveness social units.

The effects of high organizational cohesiveness on OMB Type O, namely the pressures to completely identify with a social unit's goals, and therefore to engage in unconventional acts on its behalf, are consistent with Janis's (1982) analysis of the "groupthink" phenomenon. In his terms, the normative pressures toward uniformity exerted on members in highly cohesive groups inevitably lead to dysfunctional decision making processes. Such dynamics, we believe, may eventually result in willful, unethical choices, as well as destructive acts.

Nevertheless, there is reason to believe that the predisposition to engage in type O misbehavior will not necessarily be strong in all high-cohesiveness social units. The analyses of organizational value-systems by Reiman and Wiener (1988b) and Wiener (1988) suggest that organizations whose value systems are disproportionately weighted with "elitist" values (i.e., those expressing superiority and uniqueness of the organization) are more likely to cut ethical corners, and even engage in criminal acts, than organizations whose value systems are essentially "functional" (i.e., denote values of performance, quality, or service). Thus, we expect the predisposition to engage in OMB Type O to be particularly strong in high cohesiveness organizational units which espouse "elitist" value systems.

CONCLUSIONS AND NEW DIRECTIONS

This paper suggests an integrative framework within which organizational misbehavior can be conceptualized from a motivational perspective. Such notions have long been due, given the prevalence of this phenomenon in organizations, the growing awareness among managers and experts, the social and financial costs of misbehaviors such as theft, estimated at over $25 billion a year in the United States (Greenberg, 1990), or substance abuse, and the relative paucity of systematic attention given to it by mainstream Organizational Behavior literature.

The present theoretical statement on OMB has several advantages. First, it brings the construct of Organizational MisBehavior to the main arena of work behavior thinking by anchoring it in widely accepted motivational principles. Second, the framework reemphasizes the role of values and normative processes in determining organizational behavior (and misbehavior). Third, the proposed model allows for research propositions that lend themselves to empirical investigation and strategic managerial implications. Fourth, the proposed typology of OMB enables integration of different categories of intentional misbehavior, such as against production, property, and people (Hollinger, 1986) with unethical behavior (Trevino, 1986), into a unified conceptual framework.

Undoubtedly, further theoretical work on the OMB phenomenon is needed to expand our understanding of both its scope and effects. The following are examples of directions for future conceptual work. First, depending on the particular type of OMB, a given act of misbehavior can be analyzed in terms of several dimensions such as: (a) origin (e.g., authorized/unauthorized), (b) sustainability (e.g., rewarded/penalized), (c) manifestation (e.g., overt/latent), (d) perpetrator (e.g., solitary/collective), and (e) intensity (e.g., severe/benign). These dimensions must be defined and refined. Second, OMB must be assessed in relation to other modes of work-related behavior, for example, in the context of performance appraisal systems (e.g., should employees receive feedback on misbehavior as well as on standard and exceptional performance?). Third, misbehavior must be better understood in terms of the choice of actual and potential targets (internal/external, other members, property, rules, symbols, etc.). For instance, how are such targets chosen and why. Fourth, more refinement is needed in order to integrate the underlying paradigms of individual choice and decision behavior (March & Simon, 1958), and of social information processing (Salancik & Pfeffer, 1978) with the proposed motivational theory of organizational misbehavior. For example, we need to know more how different types of members obtain and process relevant (personal, organizational, symbolic) information that eventually leads them to engage in the various forms of misbehavior or refrain from it. We certainly need to better understand the role of organizational cohesiveness as mitigating social information and decision processes in the context of OMB. Fifth, considerable effort must be expended on identifying outcomes and consequences of organizational misbehavior and how they affect not only the perpetrators themselves, but also their social environment (e.g., superiors, peers, subordinates), both in short and long terms. The dynamic nature of OMB in temporal perspective (How do OMB patterns change over time? What do members learn about misbehavior?), for instance, can be explored by adapting frameworks of cultural dynamics (e.g., Hatch, 1993), to account for misbehavior as well as "behavior." Finally, there is a need to more directly examine the role of acute or short-term emotional states (such as rage, mood, jealousy, hatred, vengeance) as antecedents of organizational misbehavior. While our framework emphasizes more generalized affect (values, need satisfaction) variables, it only begins to explore some of these effects, especially on the emergence of OMB Type D.

To us, OMB should become an integral part of organizational research and theory. There is no question that we must recognize the pervasive existence of misbehavior at work and use a creative approach to its research. The long-term disguised participant observation applied by Analoui and Kakabadse (1992), the anthropological design used by Mars (1982), the quasi experimental design used by Greenberg (1990), or Robinson and Bennett's (1993) recent effort to develop multidimensional scaling of workplace (destructive) deviance may represent such ingenuity. Indeed, we believe that once research designs that would overcome our apparent reluctance to study misbehavior are developed, they are bound to open fascinating avenues for investigation in organizations.

The fundamental implication of the OMB framework is that policy makers and researchers must better understand the compelling impact of instrumental and normative forces on the emergence of different forms of intentional misconduct in different kinds of organizational settings. Recognizing these differences is crucial for the design of more effective behavior control strategies. From that perspective, the exploration of organizational misbehavior promises a more insightful understanding of ways to manage the whole spectrum of behavior in organizations. We believe that the new typology and conceptual framework presented here offer an important step in that direction.

References

Analoui, F. and A. Kakabadse (1992), "Unconventional Practices at Work: Insight and Analysis Through Participant Observation," *Journal of Managerial Psychology,* 7, 1–31.

Astor, S. D. (1972), "Twenty Steps for Preventing Theft in Business," *Management Review,* 61, 34–35.

Baucus, M. S. and J. P. Near (1991), "Can Illegal Corporate Behavior be Predicted? An Event History Analysis," *Academy of Management Journal,* 34, 9–36.

Braithwaite, J. (1985), "White Collar Crime," *Annual Review of Sociology,* 11, 1–25.

Brown, M. M. (1976), "Values—A Necessary but Neglected Ingredient of Motivation on the Job," *Academy of Management Review,* 1, 15–23.

Chatman, J. A. (1989), "Improving Interactional Organizational Research: A Model of Person-organization Fit," *Academy of Management Review,* 14, 333–349.

DeMore, S. W., J. D. Fisher and R. M. Baron (1988), "The Equity-control Model as a Predictor of Vandalism among College Students," *Journal of Applied Social Psychology,* 18, 80–91.

Fallding, H. A. (1965), "A Proposal for the Empirical Study of Values," *American Sociological Review,* 30, 223–233.

Fishbein, M. (1967), "Attitude and the Prediction of Behavior," in M. Fishbein (Ed.), *Readings in Attitude Theory and Measurement,* New York: Wiley.

——and I. Ajzen (1975), *Belief, Attitude, Intention and Behavior. An Introduction to Theory Research,* Reading, MA: Addison-Wesley.

Gouldner, A. (1954), *Wildcat Strike: A Study in Worker-management Relationships,* New York: Harper and Row.

Greenberg, J. (1990), "Employee Theft as a Response to Underemployment Inequity: The Hidden Cost of Pay Cuts," *Journal of Applied Psychology,* 75, 561–568.

Gutek, B. A. (1985), *Sex in the Workplace,* San Francisco: Jossey-Bass.

Hall, D. T. and B. Schneider (1972), "Correlates of Organizational Identification," *Administrative Science Quarterly,* 17, 340–350.

Hatch, M. J. (1993), "The Dynamics of Organizational Culture," *Academy of Management Review,* 18, 657–693.

Hegarty, W. H. and H. P. Sims, Jr. (1978), "Some Determinants of Unethical Decision Behavior: An Experiment," *Journal of Applied Psychology,* 63, 451–457.

—— and —— (1979), "Organizational Philosophy, Policies and Objectives Related to Unethical Decision Behavior: A Laboratory Experiment," *Journal of Applied Psychology,* 64, 331–338.

Henry, S. (1978), *The Hidden Economy; The Cost and Control of Border-line Crime,* London: Martin Robertson.

Hollinger, R. C. (1979), *Employee Deviance: Acts against the Formal Work Organization,* Ph.D. Dissertation, University of Minnesota, Ann Arbor, MI: University Microfilm.

—— (1986), "Acts against the Workplace: Social Bonding and Employee Deviance," *Deviant Behavior,* 7, 53–75.

—— and J. P. Clark (1982), "Employee Deviance: A Response to the Perceived Quality of the Work Experience," *Work and Occupations,* 10, 97–114.

—— and —— (1983), "Deterrence in the Workplace: Perceived Certainty, Perceived Severity, and Employee Theft," *Social Forces,* 62, 398–418.

Jaccard, J. and A. R. Davidson (1975), "A Comparison of Two Models of Social Behavior: Results of a Survey Sample," *Sociometry,* 38, 497–517.

Janis, I. L. (1982), *Victims of groupthink* (revised edition), Boston: Houghton-Mifflin.

Jones, E. E. and H. B. Gerard (1967), *Foundations of Social Psychology,* New York: Wiley.

Jones, T. M. (1991), "Ethical Decision Making by Individuals in Organizations: An Issue-contingent Model," *Academy of Management Review,* 16, 366–395.

Kilmann, R. H. (1985), "Five Steps for Closing the Culture-gaps," in R. H. Kilmann, M. J. Saxton and R. Serpa (Eds.), *Gaining Control of the Corporate Culture,* San Francisco: Jossey-Bass.

Kohlberg, L. (1969), "Moral Stages and Moralization: The Cognitive-developmental Approach," in T. Lickona (Ed.), *Moral Development and Behavior, Theory, Research, and Social Issues,* New York: Holt, Rinehart & Winston.

Kotter, J. P. (1973), "The Psychological Contract: Managing the Joining-up Process," *California Management Review,* 15, 91–99.

Kunda, G. (1992), *Engineering Culture,* Philadelphia, PA: Temple University Press.

Lott, A. J. and B. E. Lott (1965), "Group Cohesiveness as Interpersonal Attraction: A Review of Relationships with Antecedent and Consequent Variables," *Psychological Bulletin,* 64, 259–309.

Mangioni, T. W. and R. P. Quinn (1975), "Job Satisfaction, Counter-productive Behavior, and Drug Use at Work," *Journal of Applied Psychology,* 11, 114–116.

March, J. G. and H. A. Simon (1958), *Organizations,* New York: John Wiley.

Mars, G. (1974), "Dock Pilferage: A Case Study in Occupational Theft," in P. Rock and M. McIntosh (Eds.), *Deviance and Social Control,* London: Tavistock Institute.

—— (1982), *Cheats at Work: An Anthropology of Workplace Crime,* Boston: G. Allen and Unwin.

Meglino, B. M., J. M. Czajka and J. C. Ullman (1986), *A Review of the Work Values Literature,* Paper presented at the Academy of Management Meeting, Chicago.

Merriam, D. (1977), "Employee Theft," *Criminal Justice Abstracts,* 9, 380–386.

Merton, R. T. (1938), "Social Structure and Anomie," *American Sociological Review,* 6, 672–682.

Miceli, M. P. and J. P. Near (1992), *Blowing the Whistle: The Organizational and Legal Implications for Companies and Employees,* New York: Lexington Books.

—— and —— (1994), "Whistleblowing: Reaping the Benefits," *Academy of Management Executive,* VIII, 65–72.

Murphy, K. R. (1993), *Honesty in the Workplace,* Belmont, CA: Brooks/Cole.

Pomazal, R. J. and J. J. Jaccard (1976), "An Informational Approach to Altruistic Behavior," *Journal of Personality and Social Psychology,* 33, 217–226.

Raelin, J. A. (1986), "An Analysis of Professional Deviance within Organizations, *Human Relations,* 39, 1103–1130.

Reimann, B. C. and Y. Wiener (1988a), "Ignorance at the Top: Why Bad News May Never Reach the Boss," *International Journal of Management,* 5, 170–179.

—— and —— (1988b), "Corporate Culture: Avoiding the Elitist Trap," *Business Horizons,* 31, 36–44.

Robinson, S. L. and R. J. Bennett (1993), *The Four P's of Destruction: A Multidimensional Scaling of Deviance in the Workplace,* Paper presented at the Academy of Management Meeting, Atlanta.

Rokeach, J. (1973), *The Nature of Human Values,* New York: Free Press.

Rousseau, D. M. (1989), "Psychological and Implied Contracts in Organizations," *Employee Responsibilities and Rights Journal,* 2, 121–139.

Salancik, G. and J. Pfeffer (1978), "A Social Information Processing Approach to Job Attitudes and Task Design," *Administrative Science Quarterly,* 23, 224–253.

Schwartz, S. and R. Tessler (1972), "A Test of a Model for Reducing Measured Attitude-behavior Discrepancies," *Journal of Personality and Social Psychology,* 24, 225–236.

Stein, B. A. and R. J. Kanter (1993), "Why Good People Do Bad Things: A Retrospective on the Hubble Fiasco," *Academy of Management Executive,* VII, 58–62.

Trevino, L. K. (1986), "Ethical Decision Making in Organizations: A Person-situation Interactionist Model," *Academy of Management Review,* 11, 601–617.

—— (1992), "The Social Effects of Punishment in Organizations: A Justice Perspective," *Academy of Management Review,* 17, 674–676.

—— and S. A. Youngblood (1990), "Bad Apples in Bad Barrels: A Causal Analysis of Ethical Decision-making Behavior," *Journal of Applied Psychology,* 75, 378–385.

Trice, H. and J. M. Beyer (1993), *The Cultures of Work Organizations,* Englewood Cliffs, NJ: Prentice Hall.

—— and W. Sonnenstuhl (1988), "Drinking Behavior and Risk Factors Related to the Workplace: Implications for Research and Prevention," *Journal of Applied Behavioral Science,* 24, 327–346.

Wiener, Y. (1982), "Commitment in Organizations: A Normative View," *Academy of Management Review,* 7, 418–428.

—— (1988), "Forms of Value Systems: A Focus on Organizational Effectiveness and Cultural Change and Maintenance," *Academy of Management Review,* 13, 534–545.

—— and Y. Vardi (1990), "Relationship between Organizational Culture and Individual Motivation: A Conceptual Integration," *Psychological Reports,* 67, 295–306.

Zey-Ferrell, M. and O. C. Ferrell (1982), "Role Set Configuration and Opportunity as Predictors of Unethical Behavior in Organizations," *Human Relations,* 32, 557–569.

Recasting Janis's Groupthink Model: The Key Role of Collective Efficacy in Decision Fiascoes

Glen Whyte

Why do talented, ethical, and experienced administrators on occasion make decisions about important matters that they knew or ought to have known were likely to end in failure? Why do groups composed of such administrators on occasion display a lack of vigilance and excessive risk taking in dealing with matters of the utmost importance? The dominant explanation for this behavior can be found in the groupthink hypothesis (Janis, 1982).

Janis (1982) used the term groupthink ". . . as a quick and easy way to refer to a mode of thinking that people engage in when they are deeply involved in a cohesive in-group, when the members' striving for unanimity override their motivation to realistically appraise alternative courses of action. . . . Groupthink refers to a deterioration of mental efficiency, reality testing, and moral judgment that results from in-group pressures" (p. 9).

Janis (1982) provides a full account of the groupthink model, which as a result will not be described in detail here. The basic model, however, is sketched in Figure 1.

The groupthink model has had enormous impact on thinking about the making of crucial decisions and is a conceptual tour de force. Growing evidence, however, suggests that the groupthink model is lacking as an explanation for episodes of decision making that result in poor decisions. This article therefore offers an alternative to the groupthink hypothesis to explain why groupthink symptoms occur, and when, and which groups will be most susceptible. The pages that follow explore the possibility that exaggerated perceptions of collective efficacy, not group cohesiveness, are the major cause of the excessive risk taking and the lack of vigilance in information processing observed in groups contaminated by groupthink.

FIGURE 1   **Janis's Groupthink Model**

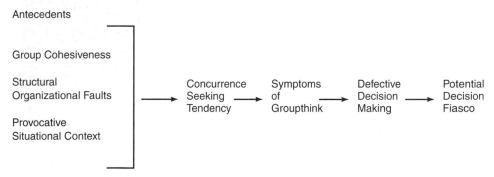

Adapted from *Organizational Behavior and Human Decision Processes,* 1998, 73(213), 185–209. Reprinted with permission.

In the section below, the results of research on the role of group cohesiveness in groupthink will be briefly examined. On the basis of that discussion, it will be suggested that cohesiveness should be deleted from the groupthink model, to be replaced by the notion of high perceived collective efficacy. The groupthink model is then recast using perceived collective efficacy as the central explanatory variable. Some evidence regarding the validity of this new model will also be advanced.

GROUPTHINK AND GROUP COHESIVENESS

Apart from groupthink, many sources of error can produce defective decisions that fail to achieve objectives, violate reasonable standards of ethical conduct, and result in ignominious failure. The unique contribution of groupthink is to suggest that, apart from the usual sources of human error, cohesive groups fall prey to a concurrence seeking tendency that may be a major source of faulty judgment. When people work closely together, share similar values, and fear a crisis, psychological pressures can arise and produce what Janis (1982) characterized as a strong desire for affiliation. It is under these conditions, as pressures for conformity mount, that groupthink is argued to occur. According to Janis (1982):

> The more amiability and esprit de corps among the members of a policy-making in-group, the greater is the danger that independent critical thinking will be replaced by groupthink, which is likely to result in irrational and dehumanizing actions directed against out-groups. (p. 245)

The primary antecedent condition of groupthink, which Janis (1982) considered to be necessary but insufficient, is group cohesiveness of a moderate to high degree. When a decision is made by a cohesive decision making group and the decision making process is highly flawed, "according to the groupthink hypothesis there is a better-than-chance likelihood that one of the causes of the defective decision was a strong concurrence-seeking tendency, which is the motivation that gives rise to all the symptoms of groupthink" (p. 10). It would thus be difficult to overstate the importance of group cohesiveness to the theory of groupthink: "When a group is moderately or highly cohesive, the more of the antecedent conditions . . . that are present, the greater the chances of defective decision making as the result of the groupthink syndrome" (Janis, 1982, p. 245). Janis therefore suggests that a highly cohesive group will not necessarily develop groupthink, but that it is likely to do so when the conditions that promote groupthink are present. Groupthink consequently may appear in some highly cohesive decision making groups but not in others.

Empirical support for the role of group cohesiveness has been discussed in two major reviews of groupthink research (Park, 1990; Aldag & Fuller, 1993). Park (1990) reviewed all 16 studies on groupthink that had been published to date and commented:

> Researchers who have studied the effects of group cohesiveness on groupthink (e.g., Flowers, 1977; Courtright, 1978) have often had methodological problems in producing cohesiveness as an antecedent condition. Janis described cohesiveness as a property of on-going groups that exists prior to decision making, but researchers have studied various *ad hoc* groups and administered posttreatment measures of cohesiveness instead. In any event, the results from these various studies (Flowers, 1977; Courtright, 1978; Foder & Smith, 1982; Callaway & Esser, 1984; Leana, 1985; Moorhead & Montanari, 1986) indicate that group cohesiveness, either alone or in interaction with other variables, does not affect groupthink in most cases. (p. 236)

Aldag and Fuller (1993) also suggest that caution should be used in drawing conclusions based on extant groupthink research. Nevertheless, on the basis of their review, they concluded that little support has been found for the view that cohesiveness plays an important or even statistically significant role in groupthink. They add (p. 539):

> Furthermore, the central variable of cohesiveness has not been found to play a consistent role. Flowers (1977) went so far as to state that "a revision of Janis's theory may be justified, one which would eliminate cohesiveness as a critical variable" (p. 895). This suggestion is diametrically opposed to Janis's (1982) view that high cohesiveness and an accompanying concurrence-seeking tendency that interferes with critical thinking are "the central features of groupthink" (p. 9).

The notion of cohesiveness as used by Janis has obviously garnered little empirical support as a central explanatory variable in groupthink. Yet Turner, Pratkanis, Probasco, and Leve (1992) had some success using a manipulation of cohesiveness that was derived from a self-categorization and social identity theory perspective. In that study, group cohesiveness was manipulated along with threat to group members' self-esteem. The results of these manipulations provided some evidence of a link between groupthink-type defective decision making and the antecedent conditions of cohesiveness and threat. These results, however, emphasized the self-categorization and social identity aspects of cohesiveness, rather than cohesiveness as mutual attraction.

In other research, Tetlock, Peterson, McGuire, Chang, and Feld (1992) used Group Dynamics QSort (GDQS) methodology to examine the groupthink model. Use of the GDQS enables investigators to achieve both richness and rigor in assessing groups. With this methodology, Tetlock and his colleagues demonstrated a considerable level of agreement between Janis and a broad consensus of historical opinion in terms of their description of the same decision making episode as reflecting either vigilant or groupthink-type decision making processes.

The Tetlock et al. (1992) findings regarding the causal structure of groupthink, however, diverged considerably from the groupthink hypothesis. Tetlock et al. examined correlations among the components of the groupthink model. Weak simple correlations were found between group cohesiveness and concurrence seeking and between provocative situational context and concurrence seeking. A structural modeling analysis revealed no causal connection between either group cohesiveness or provocative situational context and concurrence seeking. In contrast, structural and procedural faults of the organization were identified as the most critical antecedent condition, a finding that accords with research on the effects of leader directiveness and leadership style on group processes (e.g., Flowers, 1977; Fodor & Smith, 1982; Leana, 1985). On the basis of these results, Tetlock et al. suggested dropping both group cohesiveness and provocative situational context from the full groupthink model. This suggestion endorses the view of those who argue that group cohesiveness and provocative situational context are neither necessary nor sufficient causes of groupthink (e.g., Longley & Pruitt, 1980; Steiner, 1982).

If group cohesiveness along with provocative situational context were to be deleted from the groupthink model, is there another variable that could on sound theoretical and empirical grounds replace them? That is, is there another variable that characterizes the groups that Janis studied and can be linked to symptoms of groupthink? There is such a variable, and it is called perceived collective efficacy.

PERCEIVED COLLECTIVE EFFICACY

Collective efficacy as a concept is derived from the notion of self-efficacy (Bandura, 1996). Perceived self-efficacy is a key element in Bandura's (1977, 1986) social cognitive theory. Self-efficacy refers to a judgment about one's capability to perform a specific task. More precisely, self-efficacy is task-specific self-confidence. Bandura (1986) describes self-efficacy as "people's judgments of their capabilities to organize and execute courses of action required to attain designated types of performances. It is concerned not with the skills one has but with the judgments of what one can do with whatever skills one possesses" (p. 319).

Bandura (1982, 1986) has suggested that the notion of efficacy beliefs can be extended to groups and even nations. Bandura (1986) referred to the beliefs of group members that "they can solve their problems and improve their lives through concerted effort" (p. 449). More recently, Bandura (1997) defined perceived collective efficacy as "a group's belief in their conjoint capabilities to organize and execute the courses of action required to produce given levels of attainments" (p. 477). In other words, group or collective efficacy is a collective belief about the group's ability to successfully perform some task.

Self-efficacy beliefs demonstrably affect goal setting (Locke & Latham, 1990), choice of activity, amount of effort expended, analytic strategies, and persistence of coping behavior (Bandura, 1977; Wood & Bandura, 1989). The collective form of efficacy beliefs performs similar functions and operates through similar mechanisms. Bandura (1997) suggests that perceptions of collective efficacy "influence the type of future [people] seek to achieve, how they manage their resources, the plans and strategies they construct, how much effort they put into their group endeavor, their staying power when collective efforts fail to produce quick results or encounter forcible opposition, and their vulnerability to discouragement" (p. 478).

If people's beliefs in their collective efficacy affect what groups do, their effort levels, and their persistence in the face of adversity, then collective efficacy should affect and predict performance. Perceptions of collective efficacy should be positively related to group performance, just as positive perceptions of self-efficacy are generally functional for individual performance. Several studies have demonstrated a link between collective efficacy and group performance (e.g., Earley, 1993; Hodges & Caron, 1992; Little & Madigan, 1995; Prussia & Kinicki, 1996; Riggs, Warka, Babasa, Betancourt, & Hooker, 1994). Generally speaking, the more positive people's judgment of their collective efficacy, the more they accomplish.

Perceived personal and collective efficacy may normally be desirous to posses, but there are circumstances in which this assumption is questionable. Both forms of efficacy beliefs, for example, may be hazardous to hold in situations where failing courses of action have been initiated. There is a well-documented bias toward staying the course in such circumstances, even when such action may only make matters worse (Staw & Ross, 1987). There is some evidence that the tendency to escalate commitment to a losing course of action is exacerbated, at least at the individual level of analysis, by strong efficacy beliefs (Whyte, Saks, & Hook, 1997). Both forms of efficacy perceptions, however, theoretically should affect the escalation tendency because both perceived self and collective efficacy influence staying power when individual and group efforts fail to produce results.

Perceived collective efficacy may also be problematic when it becomes too high, resulting in overconfidence and ultimately poor performance. Citing an illusion of invulnerability as a groupthink symptom in which an excessive optimism induces group members to take extreme risks, Gist (1987) suggested that groupthink might reflect unrealistically high efficacy perceptions.

Lindsley, Brass, and Thomas (1995) discussed upward efficacy-performance spirals, which they described as "a pattern of consecutive increases in both perceived efficacy and performance over a minimum of three attempts" (p. 650). An upward spiral and resultant high collective efficacy might seem to be a positive development, but such conditions do not necessarily foster learning and high performance. Consistent prior success induces high self-efficacy (Bandura & Jourden, 1991), but also overconfidence, complacency, and decreased search and attention (Sitkin, 1992; Lindsley et al., 1995).

Upward spirals are potentially preventable, depending on the availability of accurate performance feedback involving cause and effect relationships. In the absence of such feedback, Lindsley et al. (1995) suggested that the development of upward spirals might be perpetuated and exacerbated through such groupthink symptoms as collective rationalizations, self-censorship, and the illusion of unanimity. Upward spirals, however, are often limited by the negative outcomes they produce. One reason for the self-correcting nature of upward spirals is the minimal learning that occurs as consecutive positive outcomes accumulate. Failure to perceive the need to understand the causes of repeated success leads to a high probability that success will soon end. Success is more likely to continue when people try to understand its causes, an act that may largely preclude self and collective efficacy from exceeding capability.

The evidence is strong (e.g., Tetlock et al., 1992) that Janis's (1982) depiction of the structure and functioning of the decision making groups he described is both accurate and consistent with that of other historical observers. The evidence is far less convincing that the groupthink model provides the best explanation, or even a good explanation, for episodes of decision making that have produced disastrous outcomes. In the following sections, an alternative explanation for the occurrence of policy fiascoes is advanced that reflects both the results of empirical research into the phenomenon (e.g., Park, 1990; Tetlock et al., 1992; Aldag & Fuller, 1993) and recent theoretical developments in related areas (e.g., Bandura, 1986, 1997; Whyte, 1989).

GROUPTHINK RECAST

The proposed new model attempts to predict the same outcomes, decision making defects, and symptoms of groupthink as predicted by the groupthink model, but relies for the most part on different explanatory mechanisms. The structure of the new model is illustrated and explained in Figure 2.

Critics of groupthink (e.g., Longley & Pruitt, 1980; Steiner, 1982) have argued that group cohesiveness and situational stressors are not sufficient nor even necessary causes of groupthink. This view of the causal structure of groupthink received support from Tetlock et al. (1992), who found structural faults of the organization to be the most important antecedent condition of groupthink.

If structural faults of the organization remain in the groupthink model, collective efficacy can be used on theoretical grounds to replace both group cohesiveness and provocative situational context as antecedent conditions of groupthink. Collective efficacy is suggested to play the same critical role in this approach to policy fiascoes as group cohesiveness does in the groupthink model. The role of collective efficacy in policy fiascoes can be described as

FIGURE 2   Groupthink Recast

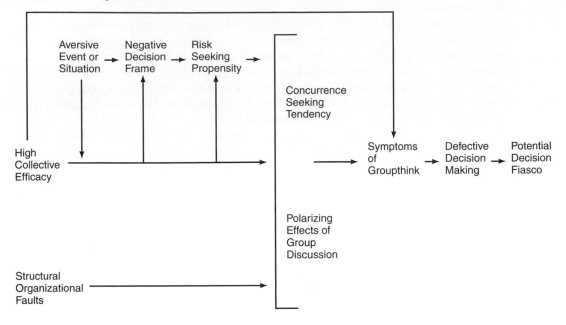

follows in Janis's (1982) own words by replacing group cohesiveness with the term collective efficacy:

> The greater the level of [collective efficacy] among the members of a leadership group, the greater the danger that independent critical thinking will be impaired by groupthink, leading to a lack of vigilance in evaluating alternative courses of action and excessively risky decision making. (p. 245)

Supplanting group cohesiveness with collective efficacy in the theory of groupthink moreover is consistent with and implies the deletion of antecedent conditions of groupthink that involve psychological stress. Janis in his model assigned these antecedent conditions of groupthink to a category that he called provocative situational context. This category is unnecessary in a groupthink model based on high collective efficacy because people's belief in their capabilities determine not only their level of motivation, but also how much stress they experience in threatening situations. Perceived self-efficacy to influence threatening events is a key determinant of anxiety arousal in social cognitive theory (Bandura, 1986). People's appraisal of threat and their affective reactions to it depend on their perceived coping capability. People display little affective arousal when faced with threats that they believe can be effectively managed. Stress only mounts in response to threats with which people doubt their ability to cope (Bandura, Reese, & Adams, 1982; Bandura, Taylor, Williams, Mefford, & Barchas, 1985; Bandura, 1989).

If those who assume that they cannot control threats become anxious as a result, whereas those who believe that they can manage difficult conditions are unperturbed by them (Lazarus & Folkman, 1984), then it is logically inconsistent for a theoretical model of groupthink that includes high collective efficacy as an antecedent condition to also include provocative situational context as an antecedent. High stress according to Janis aggravates concurrence seeking by causing group members to rely heavily on the group for social support. Given high perceived collective efficacy, however, the considerable stress that Janis concludes is caused by external threat of losses and internal threats to self-esteem should not occur.

According to this approach, collective efficacy is a necessary condition for groupthink to occur but is not alone sufficient. Administrative and structural faults of the organization, for example, remain in the model as enabling conditions of groupthink. Without these faults, groupthink may not arise for the reasons described by Janis (1982), regardless of the level of perceived collective efficacy.

It seems likely, however, that the same conditions which give rise over time to unduly high perceptions of collective efficacy may also foment over time the development of such organizational faults as directive leadership practices, insulation of the policy making group, and a lack of tradition of methodical decision making procedures. These flaws and others like them indicate few restrictions on the group from simply advocating the option preferred by the leader or the majority at the outset of discussion.

This view is based on the assumption that as collective efficacy mounts, particularly in response to repeated success, the need for impartial leadership, exposure to outside opinion, and methodical procedures will become less apparent. As leaders make decisions that become vindicated by the turn of events, they can become intolerant of opposing points of view and resentful of criticism. The capacity for frank discussion and organizational learning may thus be lost as successes mount and collective efficacy correspondingly rises (Miller, 1990).

The situation may be somewhat different when overly high collective efficacy exists at the outset of a group's existence, such as it did in the group led by President Kennedy that decided to invade Cuba at the Bay of Pigs in 1961. Structural and organizational flaws logically cannot in such a case develop in concert with high collective efficacy, which might in this case simply obscure the need for impartial leadership, objective opinion, and methodical procedures by which to make decisions. Administrative and structural faults of the organization could therefore be both partly product of collective efficacy as well as an antecedent of groupthink. . . .

COLLECTIVE EFFICACY AND GROUPTHINK SYMPTOMS

Janis posits that concurrence seeking and the various symptoms of groupthink to which it gives rise perform a valuable function in groups charged with the responsibility for making vital decisions. That function is to enable the group to maintain its capacity to perform under stress, when the consequences of failure are enormous. Viewed in this light, concurrence seeking and associated groupthink symptoms form a coherent pattern of behavior that might not seem obvious at first blush.

A different pattern, however, emerges from an attempt to link group characteristics and groupthink symptoms via collective efficacy. For example, an illusion of invulnerability and an illusion of morality are consistent with and indeed should be expected given high collective efficacy. A group high in collective efficacy will naturally believe in the reasonableness and righteousness of its decisions. Further, rationalization in the face of negative feedback and the stereotyping of opposing groups, if any, would come naturally to groups suffering from a surfeit of collective efficacy. Such behaviors would also serve to protect and maintain collective efficacy in the face of mounting evidence to the contrary.

The remaining four symptoms of groupthink are self-censorship, an illusion of unanimity, direct pressure on dissidents, and reliance upon self-appointed mind guards. These symptoms are also related on logical grounds to high collective efficacy. The stronger the perception of collective efficacy, the greater the willingness to adhere to the group's norms and the position preferred by the majority of the group or its leadership. As an individual's perception of the collective efficacy of the group rises, so too should his or her motivation to avoid criticizing fellow group members and to disagree with the emerging consensus, even if he or she has doubts. Perceptions of high collective efficacy should also increase group members' willingness to pressure those who express misgivings about the group's judgment or morality and to act as mind guards, if necessary. This behavior could protect the group from information that would surely in the member's mind have been taken into account by the group and its leadership if the information had been important. These symptoms reflect perceptions of high collective efficacy on the part of group members. In turn, the unanimity that such devices produce enable group members to preserve their sense of collective efficacy, at least until such beliefs are undeniably contradicted by subsequent events. . . .

EVIDENCE

In this section, some evidence of a causal relationship between high collective efficacy and groupthink symptoms will be examined. Four well-known cases will be discussed, including the 1961 Bay of Pigs invasion, the Cuban missile crisis, the Watergate cover-up, and the final launch of the space shuttle Challenger. Groupthink was manifest in all these cases, with the exception of the Cuban missile crisis. Collective efficacy was also very high in all these cases, with the exception of the Cuban missile crisis. In contrast, group cohesiveness was high during the Cuban missile crisis and the invasion at the Bay of Pigs, but was questionable in both the Watergate cover-up and the Challenger disaster.

Consider the decision of the Kennedy administration to invade Cuba at the Bay of Pigs in 1961. Theodore Sorensen, Counsel to President John F. Kennedy (JFK), described the plan as follows:

> With hindsight it is clear that what in fact [the President] had approved was diplomatically unwise and militarily doomed from the outset. What he thought he was approving appeared at the time to have diplomatic acceptability and little chance of outright failure. That so great a gap between concept and actuality should exist at so high a level on so dangerous a matter reflected a shocking number of errors in the whole decision making process. (Janis, 1982, p. 30)

Janis used the groupthink hypothesis to explain the Bay of Pigs fiasco, which ranks among the worst blunders ever committed by an American administration. There seems little question, however, that Kennedy's advisory group had very high collective efficacy that preceded the decision making process leading to the Bay of Pigs invasion. For example, Janis (1982) writes:

> A sense of "unlimited confidence" was widespread among the "New Frontiersmen" as soon as they took over their high government posts, according to a Justice Department confidante, with whom Robert Kennedy discussed the secret CIA plan on the day it was launched:

It seems that, with John Kennedy leading us and with all the talent he had assembled, nothing could stop us. We believed that if we faced up to the nation's problems and applied bold, new ideas with common sense and hard work we would overcome whatever challenged us. (p. 35)

These comments are also suggestive of the key determinants of collective efficacy. Presidential adviser Arthur Schlesinger indicates that Kennedy's advisers were supremely confident about his ability and his luck. One of the sources of this perception might have been the accomplishments of Kennedy himself, who overcame major obstacles and long odds to become President.

Everything had broken right for him in 1956. He had won the nomination and the election against all the odds in the book. Everyone around him thought he had the Midas touch and could not lose. (Arthur Schlesinger, quoted in Janis, 1982, p. 35)

According to Schlesinger, even Kennedy's closest advisers were "affected by the euphoria of the day." Janis (1982) comments further:

During the first three months after he took office—despite growing concerns created by the emerging crisis in Southeast Asia, the gold drain, and the Cuban exiles who were awaiting the go-ahead signal to invade Cuba—the dominant mood in the White House, according to Schlesinger, was "buoyant optimism." It was centered on the "promise of hope" held out by the President: "Euphoria reigned; we thought for a moment that the world was plastic and the future unlimited." (p. 35)

Janis (1982) also suggests that members of a cohesive group

know that no one among them is a superman, but they feel that somehow the group is a super-group, capable of surmounting all risks that stand in the way of carrying out any desired course of action: "Nothing can stop us!" Athletic teams and military combat units may often benefit from members' enthusiastic confidence in the power and luck of their group. But policymaking committees usually do not. (p. 36)

Janis described in this passage perceptions of excessively high collective efficacy. He attributes this euphoria to high group cohesiveness. As discussed, many potential sources of collective efficacy exist. There is, however, no necessary or inevitable connection between group cohesiveness and perceptions of collective efficacy, as the next example illustrates.

The quality of decision making that produced the Bay of Pigs invasion is an interesting contrast to decision making during the Cuban missile crisis. The contrast is striking, primarily because both episodes involved a cohesive group led by JFK that consisted mostly of the same membership. Groupthink, however, was absent from deliberations leading to the decision to blockade Cuba during the Cuban missile crisis (Janis, 1982; Whyte & Levi, 1994). Both Sorensen and Robert Kennedy have commented on the process leading to the making of key decisions during the crisis.

Indeed one of the remarkable aspects of those meetings was a sense of complete equality. Protocol mattered little when the nation's life was at stake. Experience mattered little in a crisis which had no precedent. Even rank mattered little when secrecy prevented staff support. We were fifteen individuals on our own, representing the President and not different departments. Assistant Secretaries differed vigorously with their Secretaries. I participated much more freely than I ever had in an NSC meeting; and the absence of the President encouraged everyone to speak his mind. (Sorensen, 1965, p. 679)

> During all these deliberations, we all spoke as equals. There was no rank, and, in fact, we did not even have a chairman. As a result, with the encouragement of McNamara, Bundy, and Ball, the conversations were completely uninhibited and unrestricted. Everyone had an equal opportunity to express himself and to be heard directly. It was a tremendously advantageous procedure that does not frequently occur within the executive branch of the government, where rank is often so important. (R. Kennedy, 1969, p. 24)

The blunder at the Bay of Pigs, committed by a cohesive group that had high collective efficacy, can be attributed to a decision process contaminated by groupthink. Decisions made during the Cuban missile crisis were also made by the same cohesive group but this time symptoms of groupthink were not apparent. One interpretation for the absence of groupthink from decision making during the Cuban missile crisis, when it was so obvious in deliberations leading up to the Bay of Pigs fiasco, can be based on the notion of collective efficacy. The Kennedy group was humbled by the Bay of Pigs invasion. As a result, its collective efficacy was precipitously reduced, illustrating the self-correcting nature of excessively high collective efficacy. No longer did this group believe that it could not lose or that JFK had the Midas touch.

Perhaps this loss of faith is not surprising given the daunting task of the Kennedy group, which was to devise a strategy for removing Soviet missiles from Cuba without causing nuclear war. That collective efficacy was low with respect to this task despite group cohesiveness is apparent from the comments of group members. For example, in the words of a member of Kennedy's inner circle:

> Not one of us believed that any of the choices before us could bring anything but either prolonged danger or fighting, very possibly leading to the deepening commitment of prestige and power from which neither side could withdraw without resorting to nuclear weapons. (Sorensen, 1965, p. 680)

According to JFK, "whatever action we took had so many disadvantages to it and each . . . raised the prospect that it might escalate the Soviet Union into a nuclear war" (Sorensen, 1965, p. 680). That Kennedy perceived the risk of failure to be high is apparent in his estimate that the probability of nuclear war as a result of the confrontation was "somewhere between one out of three and even" (Sorensen, 1965, p. 705). At every meeting of Kennedy's inner circle during the Cuban missile crisis, group members openly acknowledged that every course of action they were contemplating was fraught with risks (Janis, 1982). When Kennedy reluctantly decided to accept the group's recommended course of action to impose a naval blockade on Cuba against offensive weapons only, he stated: "There isn't any good solution. Whichever plan I choose, the ones whose plans are not taken are the lucky ones—they'll be able to say 'I told you so' in a week or two. But this one seems the least objectionable" (Janis, 1982, p. 149).

The Bay of Pigs fiasco represents an instance of groupthink arising in the context of both high cohesiveness and high collective efficacy. The Cuban missile crisis unfolded in the absence of groupthink but in the context of high cohesiveness and low collective efficacy. An additional illustration of the potential role of collective efficacy in groupthink can be found, this time in the possible absence of group cohesiveness. This example concerns the behavior of President Nixon's in-group as they responded to news about the link between one or more Republican leaders and the decision to authorize a break-in at the Watergate Hotel to plant electronic eavesdropping equipment at the National headquarters of the Democratic party.

There is clear evidence of the symptoms of groupthink in the deliberations of Nixon and his entourage as they responded to events. Whether this group was cohesive is less clear. Raven (1974) suggests that there was disharmony and a split in this group, consisting of Nixon, Haldeman, Ehrlichman, Colson, and Dean. However, Janis (1982) concludes that the core of the White House decision making group that was responsible for the Watergate cover-up, Nixon, Haldeman, and Ehrlichman, was highly cohesive. Despite this confusion, there seems little doubt that this group had high collective efficacy. As links were being drawn between the White House and the break-in, the Nixon group believed in their ability to handle any difficulties. Haldeman described his attitude as follows:

> Whatever the problems, if any, I felt I could handle them. . . . And if I somehow slipped, the most astute politician in the Nation, Richard Nixon, would step into the breach. At that point I be-lieved Nixon could accomplish anything. . . . Nothing could hurt him now. (Janis, 1982, p. 220)

T. H. White described the group's assessment of its capacity to deal with the situation as follows: "It was as if, intoxicated by the power of the White House, they truly believed that they could circumvent what it had taken 200 years of American civilization to build" (quoted in Janis, 1982, p. 220). Even John Dean, who was less confident than the others about their ability to sustain the cover-up, stated that he had "faith that the President could overcome the Watergate scandal by infinite power and wisdom" (Janis, 1982, p. 271).

The final example in this section of a possible connection between groupthink and collective efficacy is the decision to launch the space shuttle Challenger on January 28, 1986. A little more than a minute after being launched, the Challenger exploded, killing all seven crew members in the worst tragedy in the history of space flight. The space shuttle program as a result was put on hold for 32 months as the National Aeronautics and Space Administration (NASA) was restructured and its technology revamped.

There is evidence that groupthink pervaded the decision making process leading to the Challenger disaster (Esser & Lindoerfer, 1989; Moorhead, Ference, & Neck, 1991). There is also evidence that the group that made the launch decision had very high collective efficacy. The flaw that ultimately destroyed Challenger was often discussed at flight readiness meetings prior to launch. The problem was identified in 1985 by NASA as a reason not to launch, called a launch constraint in NASA terminology. This constraint was overridden in six consecutive flights leading up to the Challenger accident. Many other launch constraints were also overridden repeatedly (Vaughan, 1995).

Richard Feynman, member of the Presidential Commission on the Space Shuttle Accident, concluded that a mentality of overconfidence existed in the group. In their own minds, they could do no wrong (Moorhead et al., 1991). The source of this belief apparently was NASA's record of successful space flights. This is also known as enactive mastery, an important source of efficacy perceptions. The last time that NASA had lost an astronaut was 1967, when three perished as the result of a flash fire in the Apollo 1 space capsule. Since that time, 55 successful missions had been conducted, including 24 consecutive space shuttle flights. On the basis of this experience, in which every mission that went up came down, it is understandable that standards got lower and acceptable risk got higher (Moorhead et al., 1991). NASA had repeatedly gotten away with launching other risky missions. Beating the odds with previous missions induced the belief that NASA would beat the odds again. This evidence is also consistent with the view that the same factors which induce high collective efficacy might also contribute to the formation of structural organizational faults. . . .

References

Aldag, R. J., & Fuller, S. R. (1993). Beyond fiasco: A reappraisal of the groupthink phenomenon and a new model of group decision processes. *Psychological Bulletin,* 113, 533–552.

Bandura, A. (1977). *Social Learning Theory.* Englewood Cliffs, NJ: Prentice Hall.

Bandura, A. (1982). The self and mechanisms of agency. In J. Suls (Ed.), *Psychological perspectives on the self* (vol. 1). Hillsdale, NJ: Erlbaum.

Bandura, A. (1986). *Social foundations of thought and action: A social cognitive view.* Englewood Cliffs, NJ: Prentice Hall.

Bandura, A. (1989). Perceived self-efficacy in the exercise of personal agency. *The Psychologist: Bulletin of the British Psychological Society,* 10, 411–424.

Bandura, A. (1997). *Self-efficacy: The exercise of control.* New York: Freeman.

Bandura, A., & Jourden, F. J. (1991). Self-regulatory mechanisms governing the impact of social comparison on complex decision making. *Journal of Personality and Social Psychology,* 60, 941–951.

Bandura, A., Reese, L., & Adams, N. E. (1982). Microanalysis of action and fear arousal as a function of differential levels of perceived self-efficacy. *Journal of Personality and Social Psychology,* 43, 5–21.

Bandura, A., Taylor, C. B., Williams, S. L., Meffort, I. N., & Barchas, J. D. (1985). Catecholamine secretion as a function of perceived coping self-efficacy. *Journal of Consulting and Clinical Psychology,* 53, 406–414.

Earley, P. C. (1993). East meets west meets mideast: Further explorations of collectivistic and individualistic work groups. *Academy of Management Journal,* 36, 319–348.

Esser, J. K., & Lindoerfer, J. S. (1989). Groupthink and the space shuttle Challenger accident: Toward a quantitative case analysis. *Journal of Behavioral Decision Making,* 2, 167–177.

Flowers, M. L. (1977). A laboratory test of some implications of Janis's groupthink hypothesis. *Journal of Personality and Social Psychology,* 35, 888–896.

Fodor, E. M., & Smith, T. (1982). The power motive as an influence on group decision making. *Journal of Personality and Social Psychology,* 42, 178–185.

Gist, M. E. (1987). Self-efficacy: Implications for organizational behavior and human resource management. *Academy of Management Review,* 12, 472–485.

Hodges, L., & Caron, A. V. (1992). Collective efficacy and group performance. *International Journal of Sport Psychology,* 23, 48–59.

Janis, I. L. (1982). *Groupthink: Psychological studies of policy decisions and fiascoes.* Boston: Houghton Mifflin.

Lazarus, R. S., & Folkman, S. (1984). *Stress, appraisal and coping.* New York: Springer.

Leana, C. R. (1985). A partial test of Janis's groupthink model: Effects of group cohesiveness and leader behavior on defective decision making. *Journal of Management,* 11, 5–17.

Lindsley, D. H., Brass, D. J., & Thomas, J. B. (1995). Efficacy-performance spirals: A multi-level perspective. *Academy of Management Review,* 20, 645–678.

Little, B. L., & Madigan, R. M. (1994). *Motivation in work teams: A qualitative and quantitative exploration of the construct of collective efficacy.* Dallas, TX: Academy of Management Conference,

Locke, E. A., & Latham, G. P. (1990). *A theory of goal setting and task performance.* Englewood Cliffs, NJ: Prentice Hall.

Longley, J., & Pruitt, D. G. (1980). Groupthink: A critique of Janis's theory. In L. Wheeler (Ed.), *Review of personality and social psychology* (pp. 74–93). Beverly Hills, CA: Sage.

Miller, D., (1990). *The Icarus Paradox.* New York: Harper Business.

Moorhead, G., Ference, R., & Neck, C. P. (1991). Group decision fiascoes continue: Space Shuttle Challenger and a revised framework. *Human Relations,* 47, 929–952.

Park, W. W. (1990). A review of research on groupthink. *Journal of Behavioral Decision Making,* 3, 229–245.

Prussia, G. E., & Kinicki, A. J. (1996). A motivational investigation of group effectiveness using social–cognitive theory. *Journal of Applied Psychology,* 81, 187–198.

Raven, B. H. (1974). The Nixon group. *Journal of Social Issues,* 30, 297–320.

Riggs, M. L., Warka, J., Babasa, B., Betancourt, R., & Hooker, S. (1994). Development and validation of self-efficacy and outcome expectancy scales for job related applications. *Educational and Psychological Measurement,* 54, 793–802.

Shaw, M. (1971). *Group dynamics.* New York: McGraw-Hill.

Sitkin, S. (1992). Learning from failure: The strategy of small losses. In B. M. Staw & L. L. Cummings (Eds.), *Research in organizational behavior* (vol. 14, pp. 231–266). Greenwich, CT: JAI Press.

Sorensen, T. C. (1965). *Kennedy*. New York: Harper & Row.

Staw, B. M., & Ross, J. (1987). Behavior in escalation situations: Antecedents, prototypes, and solutions. In L. L. Cummings and B. M. Staw (Eds.), *Research in organizational behavior*. Greenwich, CT: JAI Press.

Steiner, I. D. (1982). Heuristic models of groupthink. In H. Brandstatter, J. H. Davis, & G. Stocker-Kreichgauer (Eds.), *Group decision making* (pp. 503–524). London: Academic Press.

Tetlock, P. E., Peterson, R. S., McGuire, C., Chang, S., & Feld, P. (1992). Assessing political group dynamics: A test of the groupthink model. *Journal of Personality and Social Psychology, 63,* 403–425.

Turner, M. E., Pratkanis, A. R., Probasco, P., & Leve, C. (1992). Threat, cohesion, and group effectiveness; Testing a social identity maintenance perspective on groupthink. *Journal of Personality and Social Psychology, 63,* 781–796.

Vaughan, D. (1995). *The Challenger launch decision: Risky technology, culture, and deviance at NASA*. Chicago: Univ. of Chicago Press.

Whyte, G. (1989). Groupthink reconsidered. *Academy of Management Review, 14,* 40–58.

Whyte, G., & Levi, A. (1994). The origins and function of the reference point in risky group decision making: The case of the Cuban missile crisis. *Journal of Behavioral Decision Making, 7,* 243-260.

Whyte, G., Saks, A., & Hook, S. (1997). When success breeds failure: The role of self-efficacy in escalating commitment to a losing course of action. *Journal of Organizational Behavior, 18,* 415–432.

Wood, R. E., & Bandura, A. (1989). Social cognitive theory of organizational management. *Academy of Management Review, 14,* 361–384.

Chapter Seven

The Role of Cross-Cultural Influences in Work Motivation

In an era of increasing globalization, managers from a wide variety of organizations are routinely required to interact with both colleagues and competitors from around the world. In these endeavors, an understanding of cultural differences often makes the difference between success and failure—both for organizations and careers. In view of this, the challenge of developing cultural literacy—that is, an understanding how cultural differences affect both human behavior and social interaction—has become an increasingly important goal for both organizations and their managers.

Nearly 2,500 years ago, the Chinese philosopher Confucius observed that all people are basically the same; it is only their habits that are different. Nearly four hundred years ago, the French mathematician Blaise Pascal noted that things believed to be true in one country are often believed to be false in another. And more recently, Honda Motor Company cofounder Takeo Fujisawa concluded that Japanese and American managers are 95% the same, but differ in all important respects. Confucius, Pascal, and Fujisawa, coming from very diverse cultures and different centuries, all understood what has too frequently eluded contemporary social scientists: National culture does make a difference in determining how we think and how we behave. This is equally true in our personal lives and our work lives. Unfortunately, however, in far too many cases, researchers have ignored even the most rudimentary cross-national differences while studying work and organizations. All too often, it has been assumed, incorrectly, that relationships found between variables in one culture will likely transcend other cultures.

It is simple to understand why researchers often avoid or ignore cross-cultural variables in management research. Culture is not an easy variable to define or measure. Data collection is often difficult and expensive. Translation problems complicate measurement and analysis. Personal biases, however unintentional, frequently cloud both the choice of a research topic and the interpretation of results. Causal relationships are problematic. Intercultural sensitivities often impose self-censorship on dialogue and debate. And everything requires more time than was originally planned. As a result, serious study of the relationship between culture and behavior presents researchers with a complex puzzle or enigma that is not easily understood.

Fortunately, the omission of cultural variables in the study of management has been increasingly redressed in recent years such that today there exists a reasonably solid research literature as it relates to the topic of employee motivation in organizations. As we shall see, many of our early theories of organizations and management practice, once thought to be largely universalistic, are now confirmed to be culture-bound. For example, recent studies have demonstrated that cultural variations can have a significant influence on such phenomena as work values, equity perceptions, achievement motivation, causal attributions, social loafing, and job attitudes, to name a few. This is not to say that this literature is anywhere near complete. But it is fair to say that the past decade has witnessed an increasing interest in the serious study of cross-cultural issues as they relate to managing people in work organizations.

Despite all the nettlesome complexities involved in interpreting information obtained in cross-cultural comparisons, it is important to make the effort for at least two reasons. First, such efforts help provide a useful antidote to ethnocentrism, the inherent belief in the superiority of one's own culture or group. No nation or culture has a monopoly on the best ways of doing anything. This is particularly true when it comes to understanding motivational processes in the workplace. Second, it is frequently easier to understand something through comparison than in an absolute sense. As such, our comprehension of a particular situation (e.g., motivation in American organizations) is enhanced considerably by looking at similar practices in other countries. Such is the purpose of this chapter.

OVERVIEW OF THE READINGS

The readings that follow examine several aspects of culture as it relates to motivation and work behavior. The initial reading by Geert Hofstede sets the stage by reviewing aspects of several contemporary Western theories of motivation and management to see how they apply (or fail to apply) abroad. The fundamental question addressed is the extent to which such models can be applied in various countries. For example, the concept of individual merit pay or "pay-for-performance," a common motivational tool in the United States, frequently has significantly less impact in other countries. Thus, in several Asian countries where collectivist norms stress group achievements over individual accomplishments, the positive effects of individual-based contingent pay are likely to be diminished. In fact, in Japan there is a common saying that "the nail that sticks out gets hammered down," meaning that individuals who stand out are often punished instead of rewarded.

To the extent that this is correct, we must ask what such findings say about the validity or utility of the original American theories relating to merit pay and motivation. We may also ask how these theories might be adapted to assist managers working in non-Western (or non-American) cultures. Hofstede uses metaphors as well as real-life examples from Germany, France, Holland, Japan, Russia, and China to explore this critical issue. He concludes his article by presenting an updated version of his original model for understanding how cultures can influence organizational behavior. This model is used to examine what Hofstede calls the "idiosyncrasies" of American management.

Following this, Carlos Sanchez-Runde and Richard Steers review the research literature focusing on the relationship between cultural differences and work motivation and performance. Included here are discussions about how culture affects employee behavior using need theories, reinforcement theories, and cognitive theories. In addition, the role of culture in determining social loafing and the formulation and consequences of work-related attitudes is discussed. Based on their review of available research, a process model of how cultural differences influence work motivation and job performance is presented and discussed.

Next, Michael Frese and his colleagues present some unique findings about personal initiative in a comparative study of German workers from the formerly eastern and western sectors of the country. The authors view personal initiative as synonymous with entrepreneurship and organizational spontaneity. With this in mind, they found that personal initiative was lower in the former communist eastern sector of Germany than in the more capitalistic western sector. However, in contrast to many current observers who attribute this finding to the migration of the more ambitious and highly skilled workers from the eastern to the western sector, Frese et al. found empirical evidence that such differences were in fact caused by occupational socialization conducted over a long period of time by the state government. Hence, control and complexity, not selection, were identified as the principal influences on personal initiative.

Finally, Christopher Meek introduces the concept of *ganbatte* to help explain why Japanese workers are frequently described as being more hard working, loyal, and dedicated, but less satisfied on the job than their Western counterparts. Basing his analysis on a study of Japanese culture, Meek explains how childhood and family experiences represent a significant influence on subsequent work attitudes and job performance.

Taken together, these four articles explore many of the cultural nuances that often influence job attitudes and work behavior in ways that are not always obvious to many observers. However, as the world continues to move towards the development of a truly global economy, questions arise about the extent to which cultural differences will continue to have such profound influences on work behavior for future generations.

References

Adler, N. J. (1983). Cross-cultural management research: The ostrich and the trend. *Academy of Management Review,* 8, 226–232.

Bhagat, R. S., and McQuaid, S. J. (1982). Role of subjective culture in organizations: A review and directions for future research. *Journal of Applied Psychology,* 67(5), 653–685.

Erez, M. (1997). A culture-based model of work motivation. In P. C. Earley and M. Erez (Eds.), *New Perspectives on International Industrial/Organizational Psychology* (pp. 193–242). San Francisco: Lexington.

Gannon, M., and Newman, K. (2002). *Handbook of cross-cultural management.* London: Basil Blackwell.

Roberts, K. R., and Boyacigiller, N. A. (1984). Cross-national organizational research: The grasp of the blind men. In B. Staw and L. Cummings (Eds.), *Research in Organizational Behavior.* (pp. 423–475). Greenwich, CT: JAI Press.

Steers, R., and Sanchez-Runde, C. (2002). Culture, motivation, and work behavior. In M. Gannon and K. Newman (Eds.), *Handbook of Cross-Cultural Management.* London: Basil Blackwell.

Triandis, H. C. (1995). Motivation and achievement in collectivist and individualist cultures. In M. L. Maehr and P. R. Pintrich (Eds.), *Advances in Motivation and Achievement: Culture, Motivation, and Achievement,* (Vol. 9, pp. 1–30). Greenwich, CT: JAI Press.

Cultural Constraints in Management Theories

Geert Hofstede

Management as the word is presently used is an American invention. In other parts of the world not only the practices but the entire concept of management may differ, and the theories needed to understand it may deviate considerably from what is considered normal and desirable in the USA. The reader is invited on a trip around the world, and both local management practices and theories are explained from the different contexts and histories of the places visited: Germany, Japan, France, Holland, the countries of the overseas Chinese, South-East Asia, Africa, Russia, and finally mainland China.

A model in which worldwide differences in national cultures are categorized according to five independent dimensions helps in explaining the differences in management found; although the situation in each country or region has unique characteristics that no model can account for. One practical application of the model is in demonstrating the relative position of the U.S. versus other parts of the world. In a global perspective, U.S. management theories contain a number of idiosyncrasies not necessarily shared by management elsewhere. Three such idiosyncrasies are mentioned: a stress on market processes, a stress on the individual, and a focus on managers rather than on workers. A plea is made for an internationalization not only of business, but also of management theories, as a way of enriching theories at the national level.

IN MY VIEW

Lewis Carroll's *Alice in Wonderland* contains the famous story of Alice's croquet game with the Queen of Hearts.

> Alice thought she had never seen such a curious croquet-ground in all her life; it was all ridges and furrows; the balls were live hedgehogs, and mallets live flamingoes, and the soldiers had to double themselves up and to stand on their hands and feet, to make the arches.

You probably know how the story goes: Alice's flamingo mallet turns its head whenever she wants to strike with it; her hedgehog ball runs away; and the doubled-up soldier arches walk around all the time. The only rule seems to be that the Queen of Hearts always wins.

Alice's croquet playing problems are good analogies to attempts to build culture-free theories of management. Concepts available for this purpose are themselves alive with culture, having been developed within a particular cultural context. They have a tendency to guide our thinking toward our desired conclusion.

As the same reasoning may also be applied to the arguments in this article, I better tell you my conclusion before I continue—so that the rules of my game are understood. In this article we take a trip around the world to demonstrate that there are no such things as universal management theories.

From *Academy of Management Executive*, 1993, 7(1), 81–94. Reprinted by permission.

Diversity in management *practices* as we go around the world has been recognized in U.S. management literature for more than thirty years. The term "comparative management" has been used since the 1960s. However, it has taken much longer for the U.S. academic community to accept that not only practices but also the validity of *theories* may stop at national borders, and I wonder whether even today everybody would agree with this statement.

An article I published in *Organizational Dynamics* in 1980 entitled "Do American Theories Apply Abroad?" created more controversy than I expected. The article argued, with empirical support, that generally accepted U.S. theories like those of Maslow, Herzberg, McClelland, Vroom, McGregor, Likert, Blake, and Mouton may not, or only very partly, apply outside the borders of their country of origin—assuming they do apply within those borders. Among the requests for reprints, a larger number were from Canada than from the United States.

MANAGEMENT THEORISTS ARE HUMAN

Employees and managers are human. Employees as humans was "discovered" in the 1930s, with the Human Relations school. Managers as humans was introduced in the late 40s by Herbert Simon's "bounded rationality" and elaborated in Richard Cyert and James March's *Behavioral Theory of the Firm* (1963, and recently re-published in a second edition). My argument is that management scientists, theorists, and writers are human too: they grew up in a particular society in a particular period, and their ideas cannot help but reflect the constraints of their environment.

The idea that the validity of a theory is constrained by national borders is more obvious in Europe, with all its borders, than in a huge borderless country like the U.S. Already in the sixteenth century Michel de Montaigne, a Frenchman, wrote a statement which was made famous by Blaise Pascal about a century later: *"Vérite en-deça des Pyrenées, erreur au-delà"*—There are truths on this side of the Pyrenees which are falsehoods on the other.

FROM DON ARMADO'S LOVE TO TAYLOR'S SCIENCE

According to the comprehensive ten-volume Oxford English Dictionary (1971), the words "manage," "management," and "manager" appeared in the English language in the 16th century. The oldest recorded use of the word "manager" is in Shakespeare's *Love's Labour's Lost,* dating from 1588, in which Don Adriano de Armado, "a fantastical Spaniard," exclaims (Act I, scene ii, 188):

> "Adieu, valour! rust, rapier! be still, drum! for your manager is in love; yea, he loveth."

The linguistic origin of the word is from Latin *manus,* hand, via the Italian *manegiare,* which is the training of horses in the *manege;* subsequently its meaning was extended to skillful handling in general, like of arms and musical instruments, as Don Armado illustrates. However, the word also became associated with the French *menage,* household, as an equivalent of "husbandry" in its sense of the art of running a household. The theatre of present-day management contains elements of both *manege* and *menage* and different managers and cultures may use different accents.

The founder of the science of economics, the Scot Adam Smith, in his 1776 book *The Wealth of Nations,* used "manage," "management" (even "bad management") and "manager" when dealing with the process and the persons involved in operating joint stock companies (Smith, V.i.e.). British economist John Stuart Mill (1806–1873) followed Smith in this use and clearly expressed his distrust of such hired people who were not driven by ownership. Since the 1880s the word "management" appeared occasionally in writings by American engineers, until it was canonized as a modern science by Frederick W. Taylor in *Shop Management* in 1903 and in *The Principles of Scientific Management* in 1911.

While Smith and Mill used "management" to describe a process and "managers" for the persons involved, "management" in the American sense—which has since been taken back by the British—refers not only to the process but also to the managers as a class of people. This class (1) does not own a business but sells its skills to act on behalf of the owners and (2) does not produce personally but is indispensable for making others produce, through motivation. Members of this class carry a high status and many American boys and girls aspire to the role. In the U.S., the manager is a cultural hero.

Let us now turn to other parts of the world. We will look at management in its context in other successful modern economies: Germany, Japan, France, Holland, and among the overseas Chinese. Then we will examine management in the much larger part of the world that is still poor, especially South-East Asia and Africa, and in the new political configurations of Eastern Europe, and Russia in particular. We will then return to the U.S. via mainland China.

Germany

The manager is not a cultural hero in Germany. If anybody, it is the engineer who fills the hero role. Frederick Taylor's *Scientific Management* was conceived in a society of immigrants—where large numbers of workers with diverse backgrounds and skills had to work together. In Germany this heterogeneity never existed.

Elements of the mediaeval guild system have survived in historical continuity in Germany until the present day. In particular, a very effective apprenticeship system exists both on the shop floor and in the office, which alternates practical work and classroom courses. At the end of the apprenticeship the worker receives a certificate, the *Facharbeiterbrief,* which is recognized throughout the country. About two thirds of the German worker population holds such a certificate and a corresponding occupational pride. In fact, quite a few German company presidents have worked their way up from the ranks through an apprenticeship. In comparison, two thirds of the worker population in Britain have no occupational qualification at all.

The highly skilled and responsible German workers do not necessarily need a manager, American-style, to "motivate" them. They expect their boss or *Meister* to assign their tasks and to be the expert in resolving technical problems. Comparisons of similar German, British, and French organizations show the Germans as having the highest rate of personnel in productive roles and the lowest both in leadership and staff roles.

Business schools are virtually unknown in Germany. Native German management theories concentrate on formal systems. The inapplicability of American concepts of management was quite apparent in 1973 when the U.S. consulting firm of Booz, Allen and Hamilton, commissioned by the German Ministry of Economic Affairs, wrote a study of German management from an American viewpoint. The report is highly critical and writes among other things that "Germans simply do not have a very strong concept of management." Since 1973, from my personal experience, the situation has not changed much. However, during this period the German economy has performed in a superior fashion to the U.S. in virtually all respects, so a strong concept of management might have been a liability rather than an asset.

Japan

The American type of manager is also missing in Japan. In the United States, the core of the enterprise is the managerial class. The core of the Japanese enterprise is the permanent worker group; workers who for all practical purposes are tenured and who aspire at life-long employment. They are distinct from the non-permanent employees—most women and sub-contracted teams led by gang bosses, to be laid off in slack periods. University graduates in Japan first join the permanent worker group and subsequently fill various positions, moving from line to staff as the need occurs while paid according to seniority rather than position. They take part in Japanese-style group consultation sessions for important decisions, which extend the decision-making period but guarantee fast implementation afterwards. Japanese are to a large extent controlled by their peer group rather than by their manager.

Three researchers from the East-West Center of the University of Hawaii, Joseph Tobin, David Wu, and Dana Danielson, did an observation study of typical preschools in three countries: China, Japan, and the United States. Their results have been published both as a book and as a video. In the Japanese preschool, one teacher handled twenty-eight four-year-olds. The video shows one particularly obnoxious boy, Hiroki, who fights with other children and throws teaching materials down from the balcony. When a little girl tries to alarm the teacher, the latter answers "what are you calling me for? Do something about it!" In the U.S. pre-school, there is one adult for every nine children. This class has its problem child too, Glen, who refuses to clear away his toys. One of the teachers has a long talk with him and isolates him in a corner, until he changes his mind. It doesn't take much imagination to realize that managing Hiroki thirty years later will be a different process from managing Glen.

American theories of leadership are ill-suited for the Japanese group-controlled situation. During the past two decades, the Japanese have developed their own "PM" theory of leadership, in which P stands for performance and M for maintenance. The latter is less a concern for individual employees than for maintaining social stability. In view of the amazing success of the Japanese economy in the past thirty years, many Americans have sought for the secrets of Japanese management hoping to copy them.

There are no secrets of Japanese management, however; it is even doubtful whether there is such a thing as management, in the American sense, in Japan at all. The secret is in Japanese society; and if any group in society should be singled out as carriers of the secret, it is the workers, not the managers.

France

The manager, U.S. style, does not exist in France either. In a very enlightening book, unfortunately not yet translated into English, the French researcher Philippe d'Iribarne (1989) describes the results of in-depth observation and interview studies of management methods in three subsidiary plants of the same French multinational: in France, the United States, and Holland. He relates what he finds to information about the three societies in general. Where necessary, he goes back in history to trace the roots of the strikingly different behaviors in the completion of the same tasks. He identifies three kinds of basic principles *(logiques)* of management. In the U.S.A., the principle is the *fair contract* between employer and employee, which gives the manager considerable prerogatives, but within its limits. This is really a labor *market,* in which the worker sells his or her labor for a price. In France, the principle is the *honor* of each class in a society which has always been and remains extremely stratified, in which superiors behave as superior beings and subordinates accept and expect this, conscious of their own lower level in the national hierarchy but also of the honor of their own class. The French do not think in terms of managers versus nonmanagers but in terms of *cadres* versus *non-cadres;* one becomes cadre by attending the proper schools and one remains it forever; regardless of their actual task, cadres have the privileges of a higher social class, and it is very rare for a non-cadre to cross the ranks.

The conflict between French and American theories of management became apparent in the beginning of the twentieth century, in a criticism by the great French management pioneer Henri Fayol (1841–1925) of his U.S. colleague and contemporary Frederick W. Taylor (1856–1915). The difference in career paths of the two men is striking. Fayol was a French engineer whose career as a *cadre supérieur* culminated in the position of Président-Directeur-Général of a mining company. After his retirement he formulated his experiences in a pathbreaking text on organization: *Administration industrielle et générale,* in which he focused on the sources of authority. Taylor was an American engineer who started his career in industry as a worker and attained his academic qualifications through evening studies. From chief engineer in a steel company he became one of the first management consultants. Taylor was not really concerned with the issue of authority at all; his focus was on efficiency. He proposed to split the task of the first-line boss into eight specialisms, each exercised by a different person, an idea which eventually led to the idea of a matrix organization.

Taylor's work appeared in a French translation in 1913, and Fayol read it and showed himself generally impressed but shocked by Taylor's "denial of the principle of the Unity of Command" in the case of the eight-boss-system.

Seventy years later André Laurent, another of Fayol's compatriots, found that French managers in a survey reacted very strongly against a suggestion that one employee could report to two different bosses, while U.S. managers in the same survey showed fewer misgivings. Matrix organization has never become as popular in France as it has in the United States.

Holland

In my own country, Holland, or as it is officially called, the Netherlands, the study by Philippe d'Iribarne found the management principle to be a need for *consensus* among all parties, neither predetermined by a contractual relationship nor by class distinctions, but based on an open-ended exchange of views and a balancing of interests. In terms of the different origins of the word "manager," the organization in Holland is more *menage* (household) while in the United States it is more *manege* (horse drill).

At my university, the University of Limburg at Maastricht, every semester we receive a class of American business students who take a program in European Studies. We asked both the Americans and a matched group of Dutch students to describe their ideal job after graduation, using a list of twenty-two job characteristics. The Americans attached significantly more importance than the Dutch to earnings, advancement, benefits, a good working relationship with their boss, and security of employment. The Dutch attached more importance to freedom to adopt their own approach to the job, being consulted by their boss in his or her decisions, training opportunities, contributing to the success of their organization, fully using their skills and abilities, and helping others. This list confirms d'Iribarne's findings of a contractual employment relationship in the United States, based on earnings and career opportunities, against a consensual relationship in Holland. The latter has centuries-old roots; the Netherlands were the first republic in Western Europe (1609–1810), and a model for the American republic. The country has been and still is governed by a careful balancing of interests in a multi-party system.

In terms of management theories, both motivation and leadership in Holland are different from what they are in the United States. Leadership in Holland presupposes modesty, as opposed to assertiveness in the United States. No U.S. leadership theory has room for that. Working in Holland is not a constant feast, however. There is a built-in premium on mediocrity and jealousy, as well as time-consuming ritual consultations to maintain the appearance of consensus and the pretense of modesty. There is unfortunately another side to every coin.

The Overseas Chinese

Among the champions of economic development in the past thirty years we find three countries mainly populated by Chinese living outside the Chinese mainland: Taiwan, Hong Kong, and Singapore. Moreover, overseas Chinese play a very important role in the economies of Indonesia, Malaysia, the Philippines, and Thailand, where they form an ethnic minority. If anything, the little dragons—Taiwan, Hong Kong, and Singapore—have been more economically successful than Japan, moving from rags to riches and now counted among the world's wealthy industrial countries. Yet very little attention has been paid to the way in which their enterprises have been managed. *The Spirit of Chinese Capitalism* by Gordon Redding (1990), the British dean of the Hong Kong Business School, is an excellent book about Chinese business. He bases his insights on personal acquaintance and in-depth discussions with a large number of overseas Chinese businesspeople.

Overseas Chinese American enterprises lack almost all characteristics of modern management. They tend to be small, cooperating for essential functions with other small organizations through networks based on personal relations. They are family-owned, without the separation between ownership and management typical in the West, or even in Japan and Korea. They normally focus on one product or market, with growth by opportunistic diversification; in this, they are extremely flexible. Decision making is centralized in the hands of one dominant family member, but other family members may be given new ventures to try their skills on. They are low-profile and extremely cost-conscious, applying Confucian virtues of thrift and persistence. Their size is kept small by the assumed lack of loyalty of non-family employees, who, if they are any good, will just wait and save until they can start their own family business.

Overseas Chinese prefer economic activities in which great gains can be made with little manpower, like commodity trading and real estate. They employ few professional managers, except their sons and sometimes daughters who have been sent to prestigious business schools abroad, but who upon return continue to run the family business the Chinese way.

The origin of this system, or—in the Western view—this lack of system, is found in the history of Chinese society, in which there were no formal laws, only formal networks of powerful people guided by general principles of Confucian virtue. The favors of the authorities could change daily, so nobody could be trusted except one's kinfolk—of whom, fortunately, there used to be many, in an extended family structure. The overseas Chinese way of doing business is also very well adapted to their position in the countries in which they form ethnic minorities, often envied and threatened by ethnic violence.

Overseas Chinese businesses following this unprofessional approach command a collective gross national product of some 200 to 300 billion U.S. dollars, exceeding the GNP of Australia. There is no denying that it works.

MANAGEMENT TRANSFER TO POOR COUNTRIES

Four-fifths of the world population live in countries that are not rich but poor. After World War II and decolonization, the stated purpose of the United Nations and the World Bank has been to promote the development of all the world's countries in a war on poverty. After forty years it looks very much like we are losing this war. If one thing has become clear, it is that the export of Western—mostly American—management practices *and* theories to poor countries has contributed little to nothing to their development. There has been no lack of effort and money spent for this purpose: students from poor countries have been trained in this country, and teachers and Peace Corps workers have been sent to the poor countries. If nothing else, the general lack of success in economic development of other countries should be sufficient argument to doubt the validity of Western management theories in non-Western environments.

If we examine different parts of the world, the development picture is not equally bleak, and history is often a better predictor than economic factors for what happens today. There is a broad regional pecking order with East Asia leading. The little dragons have passed into the camp of the wealthy; then follow South-East Asia (with its overseas Chinese minorities), Latin America (in spite of the debt crisis), South Asia, and Africa always trails behind. Several African countries have only become poorer since decolonization.

Regions of the world with a history of large-scale political integration and civilization generally have done better than regions in which no large-scale political and cultural infrastructure existed, even if the old civilizations had decayed or been suppressed by colonizers. It has become painfully clear that development cannot be pressure-cooked; it presumes a cultural infrastructure that takes time to grow. Local management is part of this infrastructure; it cannot be imported in package form. Assuming that with so-called modern management techniques and theories outsiders can develop a country has proven a deplorable arrogance. At best, one can hope for a dialogue between equals with the locals, in which the Western partner acts as the expert in Western technology and the local partner as the expert in local culture, habits, and feelings.

Russia and China

The crumbling of the former Eastern bloc has left us with a scattering of states and would-be states of which the political and economic future is extremely uncertain. The best predictions are those based on a knowledge of history, because historical trends have taken revenge on the arrogance of the Soviet rulers who believed they could turn them around by brute power. One obvious fact is that the former bloc is extremely heterogeneous, including countries traditionally closely linked with the West by trade and travel, like Czechia, Hungary,

Slovenia, and the Baltic states, as well as others with a Byzantine or Turkish past, some having been prosperous, others always extremely poor.

The industrialized Western world and the World Bank seem committed to helping the ex-Eastern bloc countries develop, but with the same technocratic neglect for local cultural factors that proved so unsuccessful in the development assistance to other poor countries. Free market capitalism, introduced by Western-style management, is supposed to be the answer from Albania to Russia.

Let me limit myself to the Russian republic, a huge territory with some 140 million inhabitants, mainly Russians. We know quite a bit about the Russians as their country was a world power for several hundreds of years before communism, and in the nineteenth century it has produced some of the greatest writers in world literature. If I want to understand the Russians—including how they could so long support the Soviet regime—I tend to re-read Lev Nikolayevich Tolstoy. In his most famous novel, *Anna Karenina* (1876), one of the main characters is a landowner, Levin, whom Tolstoy uses to express his own views and convictions about his people. Russian peasants used to be serfs; serfdom had been abolished in 1861, but the peasants, now tenants, remained as passive as before. Levin wanted to break this passivity by dividing the land among his peasants in exchange for a share of the crops; but the peasants only let the land deteriorate further. Here follows a quote:

> [Levin] read political economy and socialistic work . . . but, as he had expected, found nothing in them related to his undertaking. In the political economy books—in [John Stuart] Mill, for instance, whom he studied first and with great ardour, hoping every minute to find an answer to the questions that were engrossing him—he found only certain laws deduced from the state of agriculture in Europe; but he could not for the life of him see why these laws, which did not apply to Russia, should be considered universal. . . . Political economy told him that the laws by which Europe had developed and was developing her wealth were universal and absolute. Socialist teaching told him that development along those lines leads to ruin. And neither of them offered the smallest enlightenment as to what he, Levin, and all the Russian peasants and landowners were to do with their millions of hands and millions of acres, to make them as productive as possible for the common good.

In the summer of 1991, the Russian lands yielded a record harvest, but a large share of it rotted in the fields because no people were to be found for harvesting. The passivity is still there, and not only among the peasants. And the heirs of John Stuart Mill (whom we met before as one of the early analysts of "management") again present their universal recipes which simply do not apply.

Citing Tolstoy, I implicitly suggest that management theorists cannot neglect the great literature of the countries they want their ideas to apply to. The greatest novel in the Chinese literature is considered Cao Xueqin's *The Story of the Stone,* also known as *The Dream of the Red Chamber,* which appeared around 1760. It describes the rise and fall of two branches of an aristocratic family in Beijing, who live in adjacent plots in the capital. Their plots are joined by a magnificent garden with several pavilions in it, and the young, mostly female members of both families are allowed to live in them. One day the management of the garden is taken over by a young woman, Tan-Chun, who states:

> I think we ought to pick out a few experienced trust-worthy old women from among the ones who work in the Garden—women who know something about gardening already—and put the

upkeep of the Garden into their hands. We needn't ask them to pay us rent; all we need ask them for is an annual share of the produce. There would be four advantages in this arrangement. In the first place, if we have people whose sole occupation is to look after trees and flowers and so on, the condition of the Garden will improve gradually year after year and there will be no more of those long periods of neglect followed by bursts of feverish activity when things have been allowed to get out of hand. Secondly, there won't be the spoiling and wastage we get at present. Thirdly, the women themselves will gain a little extra to add to their incomes which will compensate them for the hard work they put in throughout the year. And fourthly, there's no reason why we shouldn't use the money we should otherwise have spent on nurserymen, rockery specialists, horticultural cleaners, and so on for other purposes.

As the story goes, the capitalist privatization—because that is what it is—of the Garden is carried through, and it works. When in the 1980s Deng Xiaoping allowed privatization in the Chinese villages, it also worked. It worked so well that its effects started to be felt in politics and threatened the existing political order; hence the knockdown at Tienanmen Square of June 1989. But it seems that the forces of privatization are getting the upper hand again in China. If we remember what Chinese entrepreneurs are able to do once they have become overseas Chinese, we shouldn't be too surprised. But what works in China—and worked two centuries ago—does not have to work in Russia, not in Tolstoy's days and not today. I am not offering a solution; I only protest against a naive universalism that knows only one recipe for development, the one supposed to have worked in the United States.

A THEORY OF CULTURE IN MANAGEMENT

Our trip around the world is over and we are back in the United States. What have we learned? There is something in all countries called "management," but its meaning differs to a larger or smaller extent from one country to the other, and it takes considerable historical and cultural insight into local conditions to understand its processes, philosophies, and problems. If already the word may mean so many different things, how can we expect one country's theories of management to apply abroad? One should be extremely careful in making this assumption, and test it before considering it proven. Management is not a phenomenon that can be isolated from other processes taking place in a society. During our trip around the world we saw that it interacts with what happens in the family, at school, in politics, and government. It is obviously also related to religion and to beliefs about science. Theories of management always had to be interdisciplinary, but if we cross national borders they should become more interdisciplinary than ever.

Cultural differences between nations can be, to some extent, described using first four, and now five, bipolar *dimensions.* The position of a country on these dimensions allows us to make some predictions on the way their society operates, including their management processes and the kind of theories applicable to their management.

As the word culture plays such an important role in my theory, let me give you my definition, which differs from some other very respectable definitions. Culture to me is *the collective programming of the mind which distinguishes one group or category of people from another.* In the part of my work I am referring to now, the category of people is the nation.

Culture is a *construct,* that means it is "not directly accessible to observation but inferable from verbal statements and other behaviors and useful in predicting still other observable and measurable verbal and nonverbal behavior." It should not be reified; it is an auxiliary concept that should be used as long as it proves useful but bypassed where we can predict behaviors without it.

The same applies to the *dimensions* I introduced. They are constructs too that should not be reified. They do not "exist"; they are tools for analysis which may or may not clarify a situation. In my statistical analysis of empirical data the first four dimensions together explain forty-nine percent of the variance in the data. The other fifty-one percent remain specific to individual countries.

The first four dimensions were initially detected through a comparison of the values of similar people (employees and managers) in sixty-four national subsidiaries of the IBM Corporation. People working for the same multinational, but in different countries, represent very well-matched samples from the populations of their countries, similar in all respects except nationality.

The first dimension is labelled *Power Distance,* and it can be defined as the degree of inequality among people which the population of a country considers as normal: from relatively equal (that is, small power distance) to extremely unequal (larger power distance). All societies are unequal, but some are more unequal than others.

The second dimension is labelled *Individualism,* and it is the degree to which people in a country prefer to act as individuals rather than as members of groups. The opposite of individualism can be called *Collectivism,* so collectivism is low individualism. The way I use the word it has no political connotations. In collectivist societies a child learns to respect the group to which it belongs, usually the family, and to differentiate between in-group members and out-group members (that is, all other people). When children grow up they remain members of their group, and they expect the group to protect them when they are in trouble. In return, they have to remain loyal to their group throughout life. In individualist societies, a child learns very early to think of itself as "I" instead of as part of "we." It expects one day to have to stand on its own feet and not to get protection from its group any more; and therefore it also does not feel a need for strong loyalty.

The third dimension is called *Masculinity* and its opposite pole *Femininity.* It is the degree to which tough values like assertiveness, performance, success and competition, which in nearly all societies are associated with the role of men, prevail over tender values like the quality of life, maintaining warm personal relationships, service, care for the weak, and solidarity, which in nearly all societies are more associated with women's roles. Women's roles differ from men's roles in all countries; but in tough societies, the differences are larger than in tender ones.

The fourth dimension is labeled *Uncertainty Avoidance,* and it can be defined as the degree to which people in a country prefer structured over unstructured situations. Structured situations are those in which there are clear rules as to how one should behave. These rules can be written down, but they can also be unwritten and imposed by tradition. In countries which score high on uncertainty avoidance, people tend to show more nervous energy, while in countries which score low, people are more easy-going. A (national) society with strong uncertainty avoidance can be called rigid; one with weak uncertainty avoidance, flexible. In countries where uncertainty avoidance is strong a feeling prevails of "what is different, is dangerous." In weak uncertainty avoidance societies, the feeling would rather be "what is different, is curious."

The fifth dimension was added on the basis of a study of the values of students in twenty-three countries carried out by Michael Harris Bond, a Canadian working in Hong Kong. He and I had cooperated in another study of students' values which had yielded the same four dimensions as the IBM data. However, we wondered to what extent our common findings in two studies could be the effect of a Western bias introduced by the common Western background of the researchers: remember Alice's croquet game. Michael Bond resolved this dilemma by deliberately introducing an Eastern bias. He used a questionnaire prepared at his request by his Chinese colleagues, the *Chinese Value Survey* (CVS), which was translated from Chinese into different languages and answered by fifty male and fifty female students in each of twenty-three countries in all five continents. Analysis of the CVS data produced three dimensions significantly correlated with the three IBM dimensions of power distance, individualism, and masculinity. There was also a fourth dimension, but it did not resemble uncertainty avoidance. It was composed, both on the positive and on the negative side, from items that had not been included in the IBM studies but were present in the Chinese Value Survey because they were rooted in the teachings of Confucius. I labelled this dimension: *Long-term* versus *Short-term Orientation*. On the long-term side one finds values oriented towards the future, like thrift (saving) and persistence. On the short-term side one finds values rather oriented towards the past and present, like respect for tradition and fulfilling social obligations.

Table 1 lists the scores on all five dimensions for the United States and for the other countries we just discussed. The table shows that each country has its own configuration on the four dimensions. Some of the values in the table have been estimated based on imperfect replications or personal impressions. The different dimension scores do not "explain" all the differences in management I described earlier. To understand management in a country, one should have both knowledge of and empathy with the entire local scene. However, the scores should make us aware that people in other countries may think, feel, and act very differently from us when confronted with basic problems of society.

TABLE 1 **Culture Dimension Scores for Ten Countries**

	PD	ID	MA	UA	LT
USA	40 L	91 H	62 H	46 L	29 L
Germany	35 L	67 H	66 H	65M	31 M
Japan	54 M	46 M	95 H	92 H	80 H
France	68 H	71 H	43 M	86 H	30*L
Netherlands	38 L	80 H	14 L	53 M	44 M
Hong Kong	68 H	25 L	57 H	29 L	96 H
Indonesia	78 H	14 L	46 M	48 L	25*L
West Africa	77 H	20 L	46 M	54 M	16 L
Russia	95*H	50*M	40*L	90*H	10*L
China	80*H	20*L	50*M	60*M	118 H

Key: PD=Power Distance; ID = Individualism; MA = Masculinity; UA = Uncertainty Avoidance; LT = Long Term Orientation. H = top third; M = medium third; L = bottom third (among 53 countries and regions for the first four dimensions; among 23 countries for the fifth).
  *estimated

IDIOSYNCRACIES OF AMERICAN MANAGEMENT THEORIES

In comparison to other countries, the U.S. culture profile presents itself as below average on power distance and uncertainty avoidance, highly individualistic, fairly masculine, and short-term oriented. The Germans show a stronger uncertainty avoidance and less extreme individualism; the Japanese are different on all dimensions, least on power distance; the French show larger power distance and uncertainty avoidance, but are less individualistic and somewhat feminine; the Dutch resemble the Americans on the first three dimensions, but score extremely feminine and relatively long-term oriented; Hong Kong Chinese combine large power distance with weak uncertainty avoidance, collectivism, and are very long-term oriented; and so on.

The American culture profile is reflected in American management theories. I will just mention three elements not necessarily present in other countries: the stress on market processes, the stress on the individual, and the focus on managers rather than on workers.

The Stress on Market Processes

During the 1970s and 80s it has become fashionable in the United States to look at organizations from a "transaction costs" viewpoint. Economist Oliver Williamson has opposed "hierarchies" to "markets." The reasoning is that human social life consists of economic transactions between individuals. We found the same in d'Iribarne's description of the U.S. principle of the contract between employer and employee, the labor market in which the worker sells his or her labor for a price. These individuals will form hierarchical organizations when the cost of the economic transactions (such as getting information, finding out whom to trust, etc.) is lower in a hierarchy than when all transactions would take place on a free market.

From a cultural perspective the important point is that *the "market" is the point of departure or base model,* and the organization is explained from market failure. A culture that produces such a theory is likely to prefer organizations that internally resemble markets to organizations that internally resemble more structured models, like those in Germany or France. The ideal principle of control in organizations in the market philosophy is *competition* between individuals. This philosophy fits a society that combines a not-too-large power distance with a not-too-strong uncertainty avoidance and individualism; besides the U.S.A., it will fit all other Anglo countries.

The Stress on the Individual

I find this constantly in the design of research projects and hypotheses; also in the fact that in the U.S. psychology is clearly a more respectable discipline in management circles than sociology. Culture however is a collective phenomenon. Although we may get our information about culture from individuals, we have to interpret it at the level of collectivities. There are snags here known as the "ecological fallacy" and the "reverse ecological fallacy." None of the U.S. college textbooks on methodology I know deals sufficiently with the problem of multilevel analysis.

Culture can be compared to a forest, while individuals are trees. A forest is not just a bunch of trees: it is a symbiosis of different trees, bushes, plants, insects, animals, and microorganisms, and we miss the essence of the forest if we only describe its most typical trees. In the same way, a culture cannot be satisfactorily described in terms of the characteristics of a typical individual. There is a tendency in the U.S. management literature to overlook the forest for the trees and to ascribe cultural differences to interactions among individuals.

A striking example is found in the otherwise excellent book *Organizational Culture and Leadership* by Edgar H. Schein (1985). On the basis of his consulting experience he compares two large companies, nicknamed "Action" and "Multi." He explains the differences in culture between these companies by the group dynamics in their respective boardrooms. Nowhere in the book are any conclusions drawn from the fact that the first company is an American-based computer firm, and the second a Swiss-based pharmaceutics firm. This information is not even mentioned. A stress on interactions among individuals obviously fits a culture identified as the most individualistic in the world, but it will not be so well understood by the four-fifths of the world population for whom the group prevails over the individual.

One of the conclusions of my own multilevel research has been that culture at the national level and culture at the organizational level—corporate culture—are two very different phenomena and that the use of a common term for both is confusing. If we do use the common term, we should also pay attention to the occupational and the gender level of culture. National cultures differ primarily in the fundamental, invisible values held by a majority of their members, acquired in early childhood, whereas organizational cultures are a much more superficial phenomenon residing mainly in the visible practices of the organization, acquired by socialization of the new members who join as young adults. National cultures change only very slowly if at all; organizational cultures may be consciously changed, although this isn't necessarily easy. This difference between the two types of culture is the secret of the existence of multinational corporations that employ, as I showed in the IBM case, employees with extremely different national cultural values. What keeps them together is a corporate culture based on common practices.

The Stress on Managers Rather than Workers

The core element of a work organization around the world is the people who do the work. All the rest is superstructure, and I hope to have demonstrated to you that it may take many different shapes. In the U.S. literature on work organization, however, the core element, if not explicitly then implicitly, is considered the manager. This may well be the result of the combination of extreme individualism with fairly strong masculinity, which has turned the manager into a culture hero of almost mythical proportions. For example, he—not really she—is supposed to make decisions all the time. Those of you who are or have been managers must know that this is a fable. Very few management decisions are just "made" as the myth suggests it. Managers are much more involved in maintaining networks; if anything, it is the rank-and-file worker who can really make decisions on his or her own, albeit on a relatively simple level.

An amusing effect of the U.S. focus on managers is that in at least ten American books and articles on management I have been misquoted as having studied IBM *managers* in my research, whereas the book clearly describes that the answers were from IBM *employees*. My observation may be biased, but I get the impression that compared to twenty or thirty years ago less research in this country is done among employees and more on managers. But managers derive their *raison d'être* from the people managed: culturally, they are the followers of the people they lead, and their effectiveness depends on the latter. In other parts of the world, this exclusive focus on the manager is less strong, with Japan as the supreme example.

CONCLUSION

This article started with *Alice in Wonderland.* In fact, the management theorist who ventures outside his or her own country into other parts of the world is like Alice in Wonderland. He or she will meet strange beings, customs, ways of organizing or disorganizing and theories that are clearly stupid, old fashioned or even immoral—yet they may work, or at least they may not fail more frequently than corresponding theories do at home. Then, after the first culture shock, the traveller to Wonderland will feel enlightened, and may be able to take his or her experiences home and use them advantageously. All great ideas in science, politics, and management have travelled from one country to another and been enriched by foreign influences. The roots of American management theories are mainly in Europe: with Adam Smith, John Stuart Mill, Lev Tolstoy, Max Weber, Henri Fayol, Sigmund Freud, Kurt Lewin, and many others. These theories were re-planted here and they developed and bore fruit. The same may happen again. The last thing we need is a Monroe doctrine for management ideas.

Cultural Influences on Work Motivation and Performance

Carlos J. Sanchez-Runde
Richard M. Steers

Most contemporary managers recognize that cultural differences can have a profound impact on work motivation and job attitudes. What remains elusive, however, is an understanding of *how* or *why* culture influences fundamental motivational processes. There is something about the concept of culture as it relates to organizational dynamics and management practice that makes it difficult to identify, fuzzy, complex and multifaceted, and amorphous. As anthropologist Edward T. Hall (1992, p. 210) observed: "I have come to the conclusion that the analysis of culture could be likened to the task of identifying mushrooms. Because of the nature of the mushrooms, no two experts describe them in precisely the same way, which creates a problem for the rest of us when we are trying to decide whether the specimen in our hands is edible."

Because of this, we sometimes see findings that certain actions or behaviors differ across national boundaries, but we can only speculate concerning the underlying reasons behind

This paper is adapted from an earlier chapter by Richard M. Steers and Carlos Sanchez-Runde entitled "Culture, Motivation, and Work Behavior," published in Martin J. Gannon and Karen L. Newman (Eds.), *Handbook of Cross-Cultural Management,* Blackwell, 2001. The authors wish to thank Nancy Adler, Greg Bigley, Chris Brewster, Chris Earley, Fred Luthans, Richard Mowday, Lyman W. Porter, James Terborg, and Harry Triandis for their valuable comments on an earlier draft. We also wish to express our appreciation to the U.S. Department of Education, IESE, and the University of Oregon for their support of this project.

such actions. Recognizing that managers in different countries behave differently when confronting the same challenge is important for understanding management practices, but it is only the beginning of the journey for understanding social dynamics underlying such cultural differences in the workplace. The purpose of this paper, then, is to help redress this limitation by systematically reviewing our current knowledge concerning the relationship between culture and work motivation, and then organizing these findings in such a way that improved modeling of this relationship becomes possible.

CULTURE AND WORK MOTIVATION

As a starting point for this examination, we will follow Triandis's (1972, 1995) definition of *culture* as a collectivity of people who share a common language, historical period, and geographic location, as well as possessing shared beliefs, norms, roles, values, and attitudes. With this in mind, we will examine four ways in which culture and cultural differences can influence motivation and work behavior: (1) individual needs; (2) cognitions, goals, and perceived equity; (3) incentives, rewards, and reinforcement; and (4) individual beliefs and social norms concerning levels of required effort.

Individual Needs and Work Behavior

Need theories of motivation date from the seminal works of Henry Murray (1938) and Abraham Maslow (1954). Both of these researchers argued that individuals are largely motivated by various needs that serve to guide behavior. When manifest, such needs focus individual drive toward endeavors aimed at satisfying these needs. Murray believed that people are motivated by perhaps two dozen needs (e.g., achievement, affiliation, and dominance) that become manifest or latent depending upon circumstances. By contrast, Maslow suggested that needs are pursued by individuals in a sequential or hierarchical fashion from basic deficiency needs (physiological, safety, and belongingness) to growth needs (self-esteem, and self-actualization). The original works of Murray and Maslow were later adapted to the workplace by McClelland (1961) and Alderfer (1972), respectively. McClelland (1961) focused his efforts on the three needs of achievement, affiliation, and dominance (referred to as need for power), while Alderfer's (1972) ERG theory simplified Maslow's five needs into three somewhat broader ones: existence, relatedness, and growth.

An early cross-cultural application of Maslow's need hierarchy model to the workplace was completed by Haire, Ghiselli, and Porter (1961), who found systematic differences in managerial need strengths across cultures. Later studies found the need hierarchy structure proposed by Maslow to be similar, but clearly not identical, in such countries as Peru, India, Mexico, and the Middle East. Subsequently, Hofstede (1980b) argued persuasively that Maslow's need hierarchy is not universally applicable across cultures due to variations in country values.

While Maslow's model of motivation has received some attention in other cultures, greater efforts have been directed toward applying the Murray/McClelland model, especially as it pertains to the need for achievement. The basic thesis underlying much of McClelland's work is a hypothesized relationship between aggregate levels of achievement motivation and subsequent economic growth among nations. According to this reasoning, as achievement motivation levels rise within a nation, so too does the extent of entrepreneurial behavior and economic development (McClelland & Winter, 1969). As a result, McClelland argued for the development of large-scale national training efforts in achievement motivation for underdeveloped countries.

McClelland's basic thesis, while disarmingly simple, has generated considerable controversy in the research literature as it relates to the basis of work motivation across cultures. To begin with, the projective test typically used to measure achievement is itself controversial, with a number of studies questioning its validity and reliability. Beyond this, several studies suggest that the relationship between achievement motivation and subsequent success on a national level is far more complex than first suggested. Iwawaki and Lynn (1972), for example, found national achievement motivation levels between Japan and Great Britain to be roughly identical, even though Japan's economic growth rate far exceeded Britain's. McCarthy, Puffer, and Shekshnia (1993) found similar results when comparing Russian and American entrepreneurs. However, Krus and Rysberg (1976) found that entrepreneurs from highly diverse cultures (in this case East Europeans compared to Americans) can also have significantly different levels of achievement motivation. And Salili's (1979) study of Iranian men and women suggests that gender may also influence achievement motivation. Here it was found that Iranian women had achievement motivation scores that more closely resembled their American female counterparts than their Iranian male counterparts.

Based on their comprehensive review of this subject, Bhagat and McQuaid (1982, p. 669) concluded that achievement motivation patterns will likely "arise in different cultural contexts in different forms, stimulated by different situational cues and may be channeled toward accomplishing different types of goals." Thus, DeVos (1968) found that Indians and Chinese frequently achieve considerable economic success outside their native cultures, even though their native cultures have traditionally been seen as being low in achievement motivation. And Maehr (1977) suggested that achievement should not be conceptualized or evaluated exclusively in terms of economic success. While economic or academic success may be normative indicators of achievement in the West, other variables, such as family success or success in personal relationships, may be more salient indicators elsewhere in the world. Based on a series of cross-cultural studies, Heckhausen (1971) concluded that a major limitation of McClelland's theory was its lack of differentiation between the affective orientations of fear of success and fear of failure. Both of these sentiments tend to be more prevalent in non-Western societies than Western ones.

Finally, several studies have questioned the original concept of achievement motivation as an individual effort instead of a collective one. DeVos and Mizushima (1973), for example, suggest that a major aspect of achievement motivation in Japan involves a need to belong and cooperate with others, thereby linking the need for affiliation to the need for achievement much more closely than is typically found in the West. Yu and Yang (1994) make the same argument for Korea. And, as noted elsewhere, the existence of a group achievement motive throughout much of East Asia is a preeminent driving force in many work environments, while individual achievement is neither valued nor rewarded. Indeed, it is frequently punished.

Support for this position comes from a study by Sagie, Elizur, and Yamauchi (1994). They studied managers in five countries (Holland, Hungary, Israel, Japan, and the United States) to test the universality of achievement motivation theory. Their findings led them to conclude that achievement motivation is perhaps best conceptualized as consisting of three facets (behavioral modality, type of confrontation, and time perspective) and that different cultures will excel in each of the various facets. In general, achievement motivation was found to be highest for the more individualistic American sample and lowest for the more collectivist Hungarian and Japanese samples. However, the study also concluded that a clear distinction needs to be made between individual and collective achievement motivation to reflect cultural variations.

Cognition, Motivation, and Performance

Cognitive approaches to motivation include such theories as equity theory, goal-setting theory, and expectancy/valence theory. These theories are based largely on the assumption that people tend to make reasoned choices about their behaviors and that these choices influence, and are influenced by, job-related outcomes and work attitudes. While the majority of cognitive theories, as well as much of the empirical work relating to them, derive from American efforts, a number of studies have also been conducted to test the external validity of these models outside the United States.

Equity theory focuses on the motivational consequences that result when individuals believe they are being treated either fairly or unfairly in terms of the rewards and outcomes they receive. The determination of equity is based, not on objective reality, but on the individual's perception of how his or her ratio of inputs to outcomes compares to the same ratio for a valued colleague. Accordingly, when an individual thinks that he or she is receiving less money for the same work than the referent other, the person would likely seek some remedy to return to a state of perceived equity. Remedies could include a work slowdown, filing a grievance, seeking alternative employment, etc. It is also possible for the individual to find remedy by changing his or her referent other, perhaps by rationalizing why the other person actually deserved more pay. By the same token, the theory asserts somewhat more controversially that when individuals feel overcompensated, they will likely increase their work efforts, again to achieve a balanced state compared to their referent other.

Considerable research supports the fundamental equity principle in Western work groups, particularly as it relates to conditions of underpayment. However, when the theory is applied elsewhere, results tend to be more problematic. Yuchtman (1972), for example, studied equity perceptions among managers and nonmanagers in an Israeli kibbutz production unit and found that, contrary to initial predictions, managers felt less satisfied than workers. He explained this finding by suggesting that in the egalitarian work environment managers may feel that they are being undercompensated vis-à-vis their value and effort on behalf of the organization. Results were interpreted as supporting the theory.

However, other international researchers have suggested that the equity principle may be somewhat culture bound (Hofstede, 1980b). Notably in Asia and the Middle East, examples abound concerning individuals who apparently readily accept a clearly recognizable state of inequity in order to preserve their view of societal harmony. For example, men and women frequently receive different pay for doing precisely the same work in countries like Japan and Korea. One might think that equity theory would predict that a state of inequity would result for female employees, leading to inequity resolution strategies such as those mentioned above. Yet, in many instances, no such perceived inequitable state has been found, thereby calling the theory into question. A plausible explanation here may be that women workers view other women as their referent other, not men (Steers, Bischoff, & Higgins, 1992). As a result, so long as all women are treated the same, a state of perceived equity could exist. This is not to say that such women feel "equal"; rather, compared to their female reference group they are receiving what others receive. A state of equity—if not equality—exists. Kim, Park, and Suzuki (1990) lend credence to this explanation in their study of equity perceptions in Japan, Korea, and the United States. Their results led them to conclude, "the most important general conclusion emerging from our study is that the equity norm is generalizable across countries. It appeared in all three countries" (l990, p. 195).

A second prominent cognitive theory of motivation that has received considerable attention in the West is goal-setting theory. Goal-setting models focus on how individuals respond to the existence of specific goals, as well as the manner in which such goals are determined (e.g., level of participation in goal setting, goal difficulty, goal specificity, etc.). Considerable evidence supports the conclusion that many employees perform at higher levels when given specific and challenging goals in which they had some part in setting (Locke & Latham, 1990). Despite the large number of U.S. studies on this subject, few studies have been conducted in other cultures (Erez, 1986). Most of these focused on the influence of employee participation and were conducted either at a societal level, focusing on participative and collectivistic values (Ronen & Shenkar, 1985), or on organizational level practices and their impact on job attitudes (Haire, Ghiselli, & Porter, 1966; Heller & Wilpert, 1981). Locke and Schweiger (1979) also note that participation in the determination of work goals in Europe is institutionalized by law and anchored in political systems that stress egalitarian values. Such is not the case in the United States.

However, a few studies have examined goal-setting effects at the individual level of analysis across cultures. French, Israel, and As (1960) were perhaps the first research team to compare participation in goal determination in the workplace. In contrast to previous findings among American workers, French et al. found that Norwegian workers shunned direct participation and preferred to have their union representatives work with management to determine work goals. It was argued that in Norway such individual participation would have been seen as being inconsistent with their prevailing philosophy of participation through union representatives. More recently, Earley (1986) found that, again in contrast to the United States, British workers placed more trust in their union stewards than their foremen, and therefore responded more favorably to a goal-setting program sponsored by the stewards than by management. Earley concluded that the transferability of management techniques such as participation in goal setting across cultural settings may be affected by prevailing work norms. To test this proposition, Erez and Earley (1987) studied American and Israeli subjects and found that participative strategies led to higher levels of goal acceptance and performance than the assigned strategy in both cultures. Culture did not moderate the effects of goal-setting strategies or goal acceptance, but it did appear to moderate the effects of strategy on performance for extremely difficult goals. For both samples, acceptance was significantly lower in the assigned than in the participative goal-setting conditions. However, only in the Israeli sample was acceptance highly related to performance under assigned goals.

Both the equity and goal-setting principles can be found in the integrated expectancy/valence theory of work motivation (Vroom, 1964; Porter & Lawler, 1968). This theory postulates that motivation is largely influenced by a multiplicative combination of one's belief that effort will lead to performance, that performance will lead to certain outcomes, and the value placed on these outcomes by the individual. Thus, if an employee believes that if she works hard she will succeed on a task, and that if she succeeds her boss will in fact reward her, and that if the rewards to be received are valuable to her, she will likely be motivated to perform. On the other hand, if any one of these three components is not present, her motivation level will fall precipitously. The second part of the theory uses the equity principle to examine the relationship between performance and satisfaction. This model predicts that subsequent job satisfaction is determined by employee perceptions concerning the equity or fairness of the rewards received as a result of performance. High performance followed by high rewards should lead to high satisfaction, while high performance followed by low rewards should lead to low satisfaction.

Unfortunately, while expectancy/valence theory lends itself conceptually to rich cross-cultural comparisons, it remains difficult to operationalize for purposes of empirical study. Eden (1975) applied it to a sample of workers in an Israeli kibbutz and found some support for the theory. Matsui and Terai (1979) also found expectancy/valence theory could be applied successfully in Japan. However, a key assumption of this model is that employees have considerable control over the means of performance, the outcomes they will work for, and their manager's ability to successfully identify and administer desired rewards. All three of these variables can vary significantly by culture. While Americans tend to believe they have considerable control over their environment, people in many other countries do not. Workers in Muslim cultures, for example, tend to manifest a strong external locus of control and believe that much of what happens is beyond their control. One could argue, therefore, that expectancies work best in helping to explain worker behavior in those countries that tend to emphasize an internal locus of control.

Another caution concerning the applicability of Western motivation theories in general to other cultures involves the role of attributions in the process of individual judgment. Attribution theory was largely developed in the United States based on laboratory experiments using predominantly white college undergraduates. This theory focuses on how individuals attempt to understand and interpret events that occur around them. One aspect of this theory which has been repeatedly demonstrated in American studies is the self-serving bias, which asserts that in a group situation a leader will tend to attribute group success to himself and group failure to others. Hence, a manager might conclude that his work team succeeded because of his leadership skills. Alternatively, this same manager may conclude that his team failed because of group negligence and despite his best efforts. Recent evidence by Nam (1991), however, suggests that this process may be influenced by cultural differences. In a comparison of Koreans and Americans, Nam found support for the self-serving bias among his American sample but not in his Korean sample. Following Confucian tradition, Korean leaders accepted responsibility for group failure and attributed group success to the abilities of the group members—just the opposite of the Americans. Clearly, work motivation theories, regardless of their theoretical foundations, must account for cultural variations before any assertions can be made concerning their external validity across national boundaries.

Incentives, Rewards, and Reinforcement

A third important category of work motivation research focuses on how incentives, rewards, and reinforcements influence performance and work behavior. Theoretical justification for this research can be found in both cognitive theories and reinforcement theories, including social learning theory, behavior modification, and behavioral management theory (Bandura, 1986, 1996). Critical to much of this research is the role played by self-efficacy in helping determine behavior. Bandura (1986) has argued that incentives and reinforcements can be particularly meaningful if the employees have a high self-efficacy; that is, if they genuinely believe they have the capacity to succeed. Self-efficacy is important because it helps individuals focus their attention on task, commit to challenging goals, and seek greater feedback on task effort.

Considerable research indicates that culture often plays a significant role in determining who gets rewarded and how. Huo and Steers (1993) observed that culture can influence the effectiveness of an inventive system in at least three ways: (1) what is considered important or valuable by workers; (2) how motivation and performance problems are analyzed; and (3) what possible solutions to motivational problems lie in the feasible set for managers to select from. Thus, while many American firms prefer merit-based reward systems as the best way to motivate employees, companies in less individualistic cultures like Japan, Korea, and Taiwan frequently reject such approaches as being too disruptive of the corporate culture and traditional values.

Moreover, the specific rewards that employees seek from the job can vary across cultures. As Adler (1986) points out, some cultures emphasize security, while others emphasize harmony and congenial interpersonal relationships, and still others emphasize individual status and respect. For example, a study by Sirota and Greenwood (1971) examined employees of a large multinational electrical equipment manufacturer operating in 40 countries around the world and found important similarities as well as differences in what rewards employees wanted in exchange for good performance. Interestingly, in all countries, the most important rewards that were sought involved recognition and achievement. Second in importance were improvements in the immediate work environment and employment conditions such as pay and work hours. Beyond this, however, a number of differences emerged in terms of preferred rewards. Some countries, like England and the United States, placed a low value on job security compared to workers in many nations, while French and Italian workers placed a high value on security and good fringe benefits and a low value on challenging work. Scandinavian workers deemphasized "getting ahead" and instead stressed greater concern for others on the job and for personal freedom and autonomy. Germans placed high on security, fringe benefits, and "getting ahead," while Japanese ranked low on personal advancement and high on having good working conditions and a congenial work environment.

Kanungo and Wright (1983) found similar results in their four-country study of outcome preferences among managers from Canada, France, Japan, and the United Kingdom. This study focused on the relative preferences expressed by the managers for three types of job outcomes: organizationally mediated (e.g., earnings, fringe benefits, promotion opportunities), interpersonally mediated (e.g., respect and recognition, technically competent supervision), and internally mediated (e.g., responsibility and independence, achievement). Results showed that the British managers strongly preferred internally mediated (or intrinsic) job outcomes, while their French counterparts preferred organizationally mediated (or extrinsic) outcomes. The British managers also placed a higher value on receiving respect and recognition, while the French placed more emphasis on the quality of technical supervision. Canadian managers of British heritage resembled their British counterparts in terms of outcome preferences, while Canadians of French heritage did not closely resemble their French counterparts. Finally, the Japanese were found to be more similar to the British and Canadians in their outcome preferences than to the French. Overall, the greatest cultural divergence in this study was found to be between the British and French.

Merit pay systems that are common in the United States attempt to link compensation directly to corporate financial performance, thereby stressing equity. Other cultures believe compensation should be based on group membership or group effort, thereby stressing equality. This issue requires an assessment of distributive justice across cultures, especially as it relates to individualism or collectivism. One example of this can be seen in an effort by an American multinational corporation to institute an individually based bonus system for its sales representatives in a Danish subsidiary (Schneider, Wittenberg-Cox, & Hansen, 1991). The sales force under study rejected the proposal because it favored one group over another. The Danish employees felt that all employees should receive the same amount of bonus instead of a given percent of one's salary, reflecting a strong sense of egalitarianism.

Similarly, a study of Indonesian oil workers found that individually based incentive systems created more controversy than results (Vance, McClaine, Goje, & Stage 1992). As one HR manager commented: "Indonesians manage their culture by a group process, and everybody is linked together as a team. Distributing money differently amongst the team did not go over that well; so, we've come to the conclusion that pay for performance is not suitable for Indonesia" (p. 323). Similar results were reported in studies comparing Americans with Chinese, with Russians, and with Indians. In all three cases, Americans expressed greater preference than their counterparts for rewards to be based on performance instead of equality or need.

Chen aptly (1995) points out that in studies of individualism and collectivism as they relate to issues of reward equity and distributive justice, consideration must be given to the types of rewards available to the employees. As predicted in his study of American and Chinese managers, Chen found that Americans preferred reward systems that allocated material rewards based on equity but allocated socio-emotional rewards based on equality. In contrast, Chinese managers preferred both material and socio-emotional rewards to be allocated based on equity. Chen's finding with respect to material rewards supports the earlier finding by Kim, Park, and Suzuki (1990) in Japan and Korea. Chen explained his findings by differentiating between vertical and horizontal collectivism in organizations. Evidence was found in Chen, Meindl, and Hunt (1997) to support the hypothesis that the newfound support for performance-based rewards in China may be explained by the existence of vertical collectivism. Horizontal collectivism, on the other hand, works against the equity principle. It was suggested that "collectivists are capable of adopting differential distributive logic as long as such logic is believed to be beneficial to collective survival and prosperity" (1997, p. 64). Another factor that may help explain this seemingly counterintuitive finding regarding a Chinese preference for equity over equality may lie in the nature of the Chinese sample, which consisted mainly of younger workers, with an average age 34. (The subjects in the Kim et al. study were also young.) Thus, part of this change in views towards equity-based rewards may represent a shift in employee values—especially among the young—a result of the surge in China's new quasi-market economy.

In this regard, it is interesting to note that the bases for some incentive systems have evolved over time in response to political and economic changes. China is frequently cited as an example of a country that is attempting to blend quasi-capitalistic economic reforms with a reasonably static socialist political state. On the economic front, China's economy has demonstrated considerable growth as entrepreneurs are increasingly allowed to initiate their own enterprises largely free from government control. And within existing and former state-owned enterprises, some movement can be seen toward what is called a reform model of incentives and motivation. Child (1994) makes a distinction between the traditional Chinese incentive model in which egalitarianism is stressed and rewards tend to be based on age, loyalty, and gender, and the new reform model in which merit and achievement receive greater emphasis and rewards tend to be based on qualifications, training, level of responsibility, and performance. Child and Tung both point out, however, that rhetoric in support of the reform model far surpasses actual implementation.

In Japan, meanwhile, efforts to introduce Western-style merit pay systems frequently led to an increase in overall labor costs (Sanger, 1993). Since the companies that adopted the merit-based reward system could not simultaneously reduce the pay of less productive workers for fear of causing them to lose face and disturb group harmony *(wa),* everyone's salary tended to increase. Similar results concerning the manner in which culture can influence reward systems, as well as other personnel practices, emerged from a study among banking employees in Korea (Nam, 1995). The two Korean banks were owned and operated as joint ventures with banks in other countries, one from Japan and one from the United States. In the American joint venture, U.S. personnel policies dominated management practice in the Korean bank, while in the Japanese joint venture, a blend of Japanese and Korean HRM policies prevailed. Employees in the joint venture with the Japanese bank were found to be significantly more committed to the organization than employees in the American joint venture. Moreover, the Japanese-affiliated bank also demonstrated significantly higher financial performance.

On the other hand, Welsh, Luthans, and Sommer (1993) argued that some Western incentives might work in post-communist societies. They compared three common Western incentive systems to determine their effectiveness among Russian textile factory workers: (1) tying valued extrinsic rewards to good performance; (2) administering praise and recognition for good performance; and (3) using participative techniques to involve workers in decisions affecting how their jobs were performed. Welsh et al. found that both extrinsic rewards and positive reinforcement—both considered behavioral management techniques—led to significantly enhanced job performance, while participative techniques had little impact on job behavior. The authors concluded that behavioral management techniques could represent a useful motivational tool in the post-communist culture under study. However, the researchers also suggested that the Russian employees might have been overly skeptical about the genuineness of the participatory techniques used in the study.

Cultural differences concerning uncertainty, risk, and control can also affect employee preferences for fixed versus variable compensation. As Pennings (1993) found, for example, more risk-oriented American managers were frequently prepared to convert 100% of their pay to variable compensation, while more risk-averse European managers would seldom commit to more than 10% of their pay to variable compensation. Similarly, cultural variations can influence employee preferences for financial or nonfinancial incentives. Thus, Schneider and Barsoux (1997) note that Swedes will typically prefer additional time off for superior performance instead of additional income (due in part to their high tax rates), while if given a choice Japanese workers would prefer financial incentives (with a distinct preference for group-based incentives). Japanese workers tend to take only about half of their 16-day holiday entitlement (compared to 35 days in France and Germany) because taking all the time available may show a lack of commitment to the group. Japanese workers who take their full vacations or refuse to work overtime are frequently labeled *wagamama* (selfish). As a result, *karoshi* (death by overwork) is a serious concern in Japan, while Swedes see taking time off as part of an inherent right to a healthy and happy life.

Free Riders and Social Loafing

A key concern of high performance work teams is maximizing the collective contribution of group members towards the attainment of challenging goals (Lawler, 1992). In a competitive global economy, such collective action becomes a strategic advantage that can differentiate winners from losers. As such, the tendency of select group members to restrict output in the belief that others will take up the slack represents a serious impediment to organizational effectiveness. Free riders and social loafing as social phenomena have been scrutinized in a small but important set of studies (Latane, Williams, & Harkins, 1970). In this regard, Olson (1971) notes that individuals may loaf in a group setting because they assume that the actions of others will ensure the attainment of the collective good, thereby freeing them up to redirect their individual efforts toward the attainment of additional personal gains. This perspective is consistent with agency theory of motivated behavior.

Social loafing can only be successful when individual behavior can be hidden behind group behavior. To accomplish this, group norms must support, or at least tolerate, a high level of individualism. It is therefore not surprising that such behavior tends to be more prevalent in organizations in America and Western Europe than in East Asia. Matsui, Kakuyama, and Onglatco (1987) found, for example, that Japanese workers performed better in groups than alone. Gabrenya, Latane, and Wang (1983, 1985) found similar results in a Taiwanese study. Earley (1989) specifically tested this hypothesis among Chinese and American managers and found that individualistic-collectivist beliefs moderated the tendency towards social loafing. Specifically, he found that more social loafing occurred in the individualistic American group than in the more collectivist Chinese group.

Building on these results, Earley (1993, 1997) posited that while individualists would consistently perform better when working individually rather than in a group, collectivists would perform better either when working in an in-group as opposed to in an out-group condition or working individually. Since the basis of collectivism is rooted in allegiance to the group, such individuals would only exhibit this allegiance and subsequent effort when working with members with whom they have had a long and mutually supportive relationship. Working in groups where members were relative strangers would not engender the same cohesiveness or motivational pattern. Earley (1993) tested this hypothesis using a sample of U.S., Chinese, and Israeli managers. Results supported the hypothesis. Collectivists anticipated receiving more rewards and felt more efficacious, both alone and as group members, and thus performed better, while working in an in-group situation than while working in either an out-group situation or working alone. Individualists, on the other hand, anticipated receiving more rewards and felt more efficacious, and thus performed better, when working alone than while working in either an in-group or out-group situation.

In conclusion, cultural differences have a strong influence on work motivation. Culture can influence individual need strengths, cognitive processes governing effort determination, interpretations of and responses to various forms of incentives, and output restriction mechanisms such as social loafing. What is perhaps surprising here is not so much the magnitude of this influence but its breadth. Based on available findings, cultural differences seem to permeate many aspects of both the decision to participate and the decision to produce, the two fundamental decisions facing organizational members (March & Simon, 1958). In view of these findings, it is surprising how few studies of work motivation have intentionally incorporated cultural variables into either their models or their research designs.

CULTURE AND WORK-RELATED ATTITUDES

Following the work of Allport (1939) and Triandis (1971), an *attitude* can be defined as a predisposition to respond in a favorable or unfavorable way to objects or persons in one's environment. In point of fact, attitudes represent a hypothetical construct since they are not observable and can only be inferred from self-reports and subsequent behaviors. They are generally thought to be unidimensional in nature, ranging from very favorable to very unfavorable. And they are believed to be related to subsequent behavior. Attitudes are thought to consist of three interrelated components: (1) a cognitive component, focusing on the beliefs and thoughts a person has about another person or object; (2) an affective component, focusing on a person's feelings towards a person or object; and (3) an intentional component, focusing on the behavioral intentions a person has with respect to a person or object.

The importance of job attitudes in the workplace has been the subject of intensive examination since the early work of Brayfield and Crockett (1955). These studies have generally focused on one of three attitudes: job satisfaction (Locke, 1976; Porter & Lawler, 1968), job involvement (Lodahl & Kejner, 1965), and organizational commitment (Mowday, Porter, & Steers, 1982). However, while considerable research has focused on this subject within a single-country frame of reference (most notably the United States), efforts to look at attitudes cross-culturally have been somewhat sparse. And as noted by Bhagat and McQuaid (1982), and in contrast to studies of work motivation, many of the early studies of cross-cultural influences on job attitudes were atheoretical in nature and somewhat simplistic in design. These studies examined bilateral relationships between job attitudes and specific outcome variables, such as performance or absenteeism in two different cultures. Hypotheses were frequently derived with little concern for extant theories underlying job attitudes and with little in-depth knowledge of the cultures under study.

In one study, for example, Kraut and Ronen (1975) examined various facets of job satisfaction in a large multinational corporation with locations in five countries. Results indicated that country of origin was a better predictor of job performance than any of the facets of satisfaction. While an intriguing finding, little effort was made to consider the potential role of cultural variations in influencing such findings. In another study, Slocum (1971) found that the Mexican hourly workers exhibited greater job satisfaction than their American counterparts. Culture was identified as the reason for the significant differences, although little effort was made to examine why culture should make a difference. Moreover, the study did not explore economic or work environmental factors that could also help explain the findings.

Several studies examined the relationship between locus of control and job attitudes across cultures. Runyon (1973), for example, initially suggested that the relationship between locus of control and job involvement was culture bound. However, a subsequent investigation by Reitz and Jewell (1979) questioned this finding in a study of skilled and unskilled workers in Japan, Mexico, Thailand, Turkey, Yugoslavia, and the United States. Results showed that in all six highly divergent countries workers with an internal locus of control were more involved with their jobs than those with an external locus of control. This finding, while significant for both genders, was stronger among men. Reitz and Jewell concluded that locus of control is, in fact, not culture bound. A recent study by Spector, Cooper, Sanchez, and Sparks (in press) offers the first comprehensive look at the impact of locus of control across cultures. Spector et al. found evidence of a consistent positive relationship between internal locus of control and several measures of work-related well-being, including job satisfaction, in their study of 5,000 managers in 24 nations. Locus of control was also found to be positively related to individualism, as would be predicted by theory.

In a major study of job attitudes and management practices among over 8,000 workers in 106 factories in Japan and the United States, Lincoln and Kalleberg (1990) concluded that Japanese workers were less satisfied but more committed than their American counterparts. The researchers explained this difference through an in-depth examination of both Japanese societal culture and corporate culture. For example, the age and seniority-grading system (*nenko*) prevalent in Japanese firms reinforces a familylike relationship between workers and companies; it shows concern for employee welfare. This, in turn, is reciprocated by workers in the form of stronger commitment to the organization, even if the jobs themselves are distasteful. By contrast, in the transitory culture that permeates many U.S. firms, less mutual concern exists between employers and employees. Employees frequently feel more like contract workers than members of the firm. As a result, lower commitment levels are reflected. (Whether this strong commitment exhibited by Japanese workers will continue in the face of an increasing emphasis on performance-based pay raises and promotions and more limited lifetime employment remains to be seen.) The prevalence of after-work socializing among Japanese workers (*tsukiai*) was also cited as another way for workers to reinforce their friendship ties and trust levels among themselves, thereby further solidifying their ties with the companies. Again, this contrasts sharply with the typical American practice of running for the parking lot or subway at the close of work.

In addition, Lincoln and Kalleberg argued that the differential job satisfaction levels between Japanese and American workers may occur because American culture stresses being upbeat and cheerful and putting the best possible face on events. By contrast, Japanese frequently bias their assessments in the opposite direction towards the self-critical and self-effacing. As such, using Western questionnaires to ask questions about job satisfaction may prompt workers in the two cultures to respond in opposite ways, with one group overestimating their satisfaction levels and the other underestimating them.

Aggregate work attitudes can change significantly over time as the result of structural changes in the political or economic environment. For example, Shin and Kim (1994) found that general job attitudes among Korean industrial workers declined sharply following the violent labor turmoil that erupted throughout that country in the late 1980s. Specifically, worker attitudes toward their supervisors and their companies declined (from 77% holding positive attitudes toward their supervisors and 91% holding positive attitudes toward their companies to 41% and 65%, respectively), as did their willingness to follow supervisory directions (from 94% to 59%). The rise of unionization and the ensuing labor disputes, largely sanctioned by the government, served to weaken the traditional psychological ties and obligations between workers and companies with a resulting decline in job satisfaction and commitment.

In summary, cultural differences appear to have a significant influence on attitude formation, as well as on the consequences of attitudes once formed. This conclusion supports Triandis's (1971) signal work on this topic and, again, has clear and important implications for both researchers and managers interested in how individuals and groups respond to events and actions in the workplace. Attitudes and accompanying trust levels influence the manner in which employees perceive and respond to reward systems. This, in turn, influences subsequent work motivation and performance. Thus, as suggested earlier by Porter and Lawler (1968), the consequences of job attitudes are ignored by managers at their own (and their organization's) peril.

A MODEL OF CULTURE, MOTIVATION, AND PERFORMANCE

A review of the role of culture in motivation logically raises questions concerning the manner in which key variables fit together to jointly influence work behavior. Based on the above review, we propose a model of how culture influences personal values, motivation, and work behavior as a possible guide to future research in this area (see Figure 1).

FIGURE 1   **A Model of Culture, Motivation, and Performance**

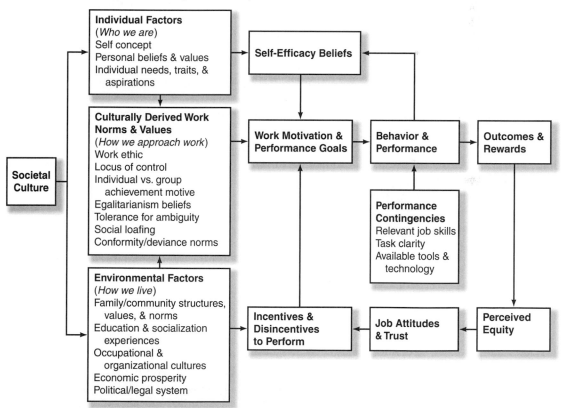

As a point of departure, our model recognizes that cultural differences represent a fundamental contextual variable that influences both individual and environmental characteristics. Culture provides the stage upon which life events transpire. *Individual factors* that can be influenced by cultural variations include the development of one's self-concept, personal values and beliefs, individual needs, traits, and aspirations. *Environmental factors* that can be influenced by culture include family and community structures, values and norms, education and socialization experiences, occupational and organizational cultures, the status of economic development, and the political and legal system. Some cultures emphasize hard work and sacrifice, while others emphasize social relationships and enjoyment. Some stress individual achievement, while others stress group achievement. Some stress communal rewards while others stress individual rewards. Culture also influences the beliefs and values of one's family and friends; younger members of a society learn what to believe in and what to strive for at least in part from older generations. Educational institutions are significantly influenced by culture, as are organizational and occupational values.

As a result of these individual and environmental characteristics, people enter the workplace already imbued with a set of *culturally derived work norms and values* about what constitutes acceptable or fair working conditions, what they wish to gain in exchange for their labor, how hard they intend to work, and how they view their career. Included in this group of culturally derived work norms and values are the general strength and quality of the employee work ethic, individual versus group achievement norms, proclivity toward egalitarianism, tolerance for ambiguity, social loafing or free rider, and norms concerning conformity and deviance from group wishes. Locus of control also seems important here in view of evidence that some societies tend to emphasize taking control of the future (internal locus), while others tend to believe that the future is beyond their control (external locus).

However, culturally based influences on work norms and values are not universal. Even in the most collectivistic societies, individual differences exist, although the magnitude of variation may differ by culture. Professionals tend to expect more from the workplace in terms of status, rewards, and freedom of action than most blue-collar workers in both Japan and the United States, for example. Moreover, some cultures attempt to minimize status and reward differences between occupational groupings (e.g., Sweden), while others tend to enhance them (e.g., Korea). Individual and group assessments of equity, or what is deemed to be fair and just, seem to underlie this process across cultures.

In addition, culture influences to some degree one's *self-efficacy beliefs* through education and socialization experiences, as well as the level of *incentives and disincentives* that are offered to employees in exchange for their labor. As we might expect, incentives and disincentives are frequently influenced by such factors as education level, occupation, corporate personnel practices, level of economic prosperity, group norms, and the political and legal system in which people work.

In turn, *work motivation and employee performance goals* are heavily influenced by three factors: (1) culturally derived work norms and values; (2) self-efficacy beliefs; and (3) rewards, incentives, and disincentives that result from performance. Work norms and values are important because they help determine the nature and quality of work effort, whether effort is to be based on the individual or group, beliefs about the equity and equality of incentives, and levels of work-related uncertainty that can be tolerated on the job. Self-efficacy is important because it determines one's confidence to put forth effort on the job. In this regard,

Erez and Earley (1993) have proposed a model that specifically addresses the relationship between culture, the self-concept, and work behavior. Finally, intrinsic and extrinsic rewards of various types are important because they provide both the incentives and disincentives to perform. Expectations concerning possible rewards represent a powerful force for employee motivation, although the magnitude and type of such incentives may vary across cultures. For example, considerable research indicates that in many Western societies pay-for-performance compensation systems can significantly help to raise productivity. In other cultures, however, merit-based systems frequently fail due to egalitarian norms.

Corporate-based incentives can also have the effect of creating disincentives to perform, largely through the intervention of group norms. Social phenomena such as social loafing and sanctions governing levels of output frequently serve to restrict the impact of incentives on performance. In some cases, employees are pressured by colleagues not to break group-determined production quotas, despite incentives to do so. In other cases, employees are legitimately concerned about working themselves out of a job if they perform at high levels.

Following from the research on cognitive theories of motivation, we would expect work motivation to strongly influence subsequent *work behavior and performance.* It is important to note here that individual, group, and organizational goal setting—particularly when these goals are specific, accepted, and moderately difficult—clearly plays a role in motivated behavior by focusing employee effort toward readily identifiable targets of performance.

However, employee motivation alone is insufficient to guarantee high performance. In addition, employees must possess several *performance contingencies.* These include having relevant personal abilities and job skills, a clear understanding of the requirements of the task, and the appropriate tools and technology to complete task assignments efficiently. To a large extent, these factors are determined by available educational opportunities, on-the-job training, supervisory competence, and the company's or country's ability to secure relevant job technology to support employee efforts. Obviously, the acquisition of some of these performance contingencies is influenced by cultural factors, although this is not shown in Figure 1 for space considerations.

As a result of subsequent job performance, employees receive a variety of *outcomes and rewards.* These can be extrinsic or intrinsic in nature. The manner in which employees interpret these consequences will largely influence their *perceived equity,* as well as the nature and quality of their resulting *job attitudes.* To the extent that employees believe that the rewards they receive are fair and just, we would expect them to develop more positive work attitudes, as well as increased confidence and trust in management to be fair. To the extent that the resulting rewards and outcomes are seen by employees as unfair or inequitable, we would expect them to develop more negative attitudes, as well as increased distrust of the future actions of management. The nature and quality of both job attitudes and employee trust then clearly feed back to influence how employees view future incentives offered by their employer, thereby influencing subsequent work motivation and performance goals. Moreover, when employee performance levels are high, we would also expect self-efficacy beliefs to be reinforced, thereby increasing or at least preserving subsequent motivational levels. We would expect the opposite impact on self-efficacy and subsequent motivation when employee performance levels are low.

In conclusion, we now have a reasonable body of evidence to suggest that cultural differences can influence work values, motivation, and job attitudes in a variety of significant ways. This conclusion necessitates a reexamination of many of our current theories of both work attitudes and behavior, as well as management theories in general, to incorporate cultural factors as a more central conceptual variable. An attempt has been made here to consider the role of culture as it specifically relates to work motivation and performance. However, more research and conceptualization along these lines would be of considerable benefit to the field. In view of the increasing globalization of markets, services, and manufacturing, ignoring cultural factors in corporate decision making and action can have significant adverse economic repercussions for companies and countries alike. It is therefore hoped that this review will stimulate future endeavors by both researchers and managers to better understand the global realities of the workplace.

References

Adler, N. J. 1986. *International Dimensions of Organizational Behavior.* Boston: PWS-Kent: 127–133.

Alderfer, C. P. 1972. *Existence, Relatedness, and Growth.* New York: Free Press.

Allport, G. W. 1937. *Personality: A Psychological Interpretation.* New York: Henry Holt.

Allport, G. W. 1939. Attitudes. In C. Murchison (Ed.), *Handbook of Social Psychology.* Worcester, Mass.: Clark University Press.

Bandura, A. 1986. *Social Foundation of Thought and Action: A Social Cognitive Theory.* Englewood Cliffs, N.J.: Prentice Hall.

Bandura, A. 1996. *Self-efficacy: The Exercise of Control.* New York: Freeman.

Bhagat, R. S., and McQuaid, S. J. 1982. Role of subjective culture in organizations: A review and directions for future research. *Journal of Applied Psychology*, 67 (5):653–685.

Brayfield, A. H., and Crockett, W. H. 1955. Employee attitudes and employee performance, *Psychological Bulletin*, 52: 396–424.

Chen, C. C. 1995. New trends in reward allocation preferences: A Sino-U.S. Comparison. *Academy of Management Journal*, 38 (2): 408–428.

Chen, C. C., Meindl, J. R., and Hunt, R. G. 1997. Testing the effects of vertical and horizontal collectivism: A study of reward allocation preferences in China. *Journal of Cross-Cultural Psychology*, 28 (1): 44–70.

Child, J. 1994. *Management in China during the Age of Reform.* Cambridge: Cambridge University Press:

DeVos, G. A. 1968. Achievement and innovation in culture and personality. In E. Norbeck, D. Price-Williams, and W. M. McCords (Eds.), *The Study of Personality:*

An Interdisciplinary Approach. New York: Holt, Rinehart, & Winston.

DeVos, G. A., and Mizushima, K. 1973. Delinquency and social change in modern Japan. In G. A. DeVos (Ed.), *Socialization for Achievement: Essays on the Cultural Psychology of the Japanese.* Berkeley: University of California Press.

Earley, P. C. 1986. Supervisors and shop stewards as sources of contextual information in goal-setting. *Journal of Applied Psychology*, 71:111–118.

Earley, P. C. 1989. Social loafing and collectivism. *Administrative Science Quarterly*, 34: 565–581.

Earley, P. C. 1993. East meets West meets Mideast: Further explorations of collectivistic and individualistic work groups. *Academy of Management Journal*, 36(2): 319–348.

Earley, P. C. 1997. *Face, Harmony and Social Structure: An Analysis of Organizational Behavior Across Cultures.* New York: Oxford University Press.

Eden, D. 1975. Intrinsic and extrinsic rewards and motives: Replication and extension with kibbutz workers. *Journal of Applied Social Psychology*, 5: 348–361.

Erez , M. 1986. The congruence of goal-setting strategies with socio-cultural values, and its effect on performance. *Journal of Management*, 12: 585–592.

Erez, M., and Earley, P. C. 1987. Comparative analysis of goal-setting strategies across cultures. *Journal of Applied Psychology*, 72 (4): 658–665.

Erez, M., and Earley, P. C. 1993. *Culture, Self-Identity, and Work.* New York: Oxford University Press.

French, J. P., Israel, J., and As, D. 1960. An experiment in a Norwegian factory: Interpersonal dimension in decision-making. *Human Relations*, 13: 3–19.

Gabrenya, W. K., Latane, B., and Wang, Y. 1983. Social loafing in cross-cultural perspective. *Journal of Cross-Cultural Psychology,* 14: 368–384.

Gabrenya, W. K., Latane, B., and Wang, Y. 1985. Social loafing on an optimizing task: Cross-cultural differences among Chinese and Americans. *Journal of Cross-Cultural Psychology,* 16: 223–242.

Haire, M., Ghiselli, E. E., and Porter, L. L. 1961. *Managerial Thinking: An International Study.* New York: Wiley.

Hall, E. T. 1992. *An Anthropology of Everyday Life: An Autobiography.* New York:Anchor.

Heckhausen, H. 1971. Trainingskurse zur Erhoehung der Leistungsmotivation und der unternehmerischen Aktivitaet in einem Entwicklungsland: Eine nachtraegliche Analyse des erzielten Motivwandels. *Zeitschrift fuer Entwicklungspsychologie und Paedagogishe Psychologie,* 3:253–268.

Heller, F. A., and Wilpert, B. 1981. *Competence and Power in Managerial Decision Making.* Chichester: Wiley.

Hofstede, G. 1980a. *Culture's Consequence: International Differences in Work-Related Values.* Beverly Hills, CA: Sage Publications.

Hofstede, G. 1980b. Motivation, leadership, and organization: Do American theories apply abroad? *Organizational Dynamics,* 9 (1): 42–63.

Huo, Y. P., and Steers, R. M. 1993. Cultural influences on the design of incentive systems: The case of East Asia. *Asia Pacific Journal of Management,* 10 (1): 71–85.

Iwawaki, S., and Lynn, R. 1972. Measuring achievement motivation in Japan and Great Britain. *Journal of Cross-Cultural Psychology,* 3: 219–220.

Kanungo, R. N., and Wright, R. W. 1983. A cross-cultural comparative study of managerial job attitudes. *Journal of International Business Studies,* Fall: 115–128.

Kim, K. I., Park, H. J., and Suzuki, N. 1990. Reward allocations in the U.S., Japan, and Korea: A comparison of individualistic and collectivistic cultures. *Academy of Management Journal,* 33(1): 188–198.

Kraut, A. I., and Ronen, S. 1975. Validity of job facet importance: A multinational, multicriteria study. *Journal of Applied Psychology,* 60: 671–677.

Krus, D. J., and Rysberg, J. A. 1976. Industrial managers and nAch: Comparable and compatible? *Journal of Cross-Cultural Psychology,* 7: 491–496.

Latane, B., Williams, K. D., and Harkins, S. G. 1979. Many hands make light the work: The causes and consequences of social loafing. *Journal of Personality and Social Psychology,* 37: 822–832.

Lawler, E. E. 1992. *The Ultimate Advantage: Creating the High Involvement Organization.* San Francisco: Jossey-Bass.

Lincoln, J. R., and Kalleberg, A. L. 1990. *Culture, Control, and Commitment: A Study of Work Organization and Work Attitudes in the United States and Japan.* Cambridge: Cambridge University Press.

Locke, E. A. 1976. The nature and causes of job satisfaction. In M. D. Dunnette (Ed.), *Handbook of Industrial and Organizational Psychology.* Chicago: Rand McNally.

Locke, E. A., and Latham, G. P. 1990. *A Theory of Goal-Setting and Task Performance.* Englewood Cliffs, N.J.: Prentice Hall.

Locke, E. A., and Schweiger, D. M. 1979. Participation in decision-making: One more look. In B. M. Staw (Ed.), *Research in Organizational Behavior, vol. 1.* Greenwich, Conn.: JAI Press.

Lodahl, T., and Kejner, M. 1965. The definition and measurement of job involvement. *Journal of Applied Psychology,* 49: 24–33.

Maehr, M. L. 1977. Sociocultural origins of achievement motivation. *International Journal of Intercultural Relations,* 1: 81–104.

Maslow, A. H. 1954. *Motivation and Personality.* New York: Harper.

Matsui, T., and Terai, I. 1979. A cross-cultural study of the validity of expectancy theory of work motivation. *Journal of Applied Psychology,* 60 (2): 263–265.

Matsui, T., Kakuyama, T., and Onglatco, M. L. 1987. Effects of goals and feedback on performance in groups. *Journal of Applied Psychology,* 72: 407–415.

McCarthy, D. J., Puffer, S. M., and Shekshnia, S. V. 1993. The resurgence of an entrepreneurial class in Russia. *Journal of Management Inquiry,* 2 (2): 125–137.

McClelland, D. C. 1961. *The Achieving Society.* Princeton, N.J.: Van Nostrand.

McClelland, D. C., and Winter, D. G. 1969. *Motivating Economic Achievement.* New York: Free Press.

Mowday, R. T., Porter, L. W., and Steers, R. M. 1982. *Employee-Organization Linkages: The Psychology of Employee Commitment, Absenteeism, and Turnover.* New York: Academic Press.

Murray, H. A. 1938. *Explorations in Personality.* New York: Oxford University Press.

Nam, S. H. 1991. *Cultural and managerial attributions for group performance.* Unpublished doctoral dissertation, Lundquist College of Business, University of Oregon.

Nam S. H. 1995. Culture, control, and commitment in international joint ventures. *International Journal of Human Resource Management,* 6: 553–567.

Olson, M. 1971. *The Logic of Collective Action.* Cambridge, Mass.: Harvard University Press.

Pennings, J. M. 1993. Executive reward systems: A cross-national comparison. *Journal of Management Studies,* 30(2): 261–180.

Porter, L. W., and Lawler, E. E. 1968. *Managerial Attitudes and Performance.* Homewood, Ill.: Irwin.

Reitz, H. J., and Jewell, L. N. 1979. Sex, locus of control, and job involvement: A six-country investigation. *Academy of Management Journal,* 22: 72–80.

Ronen, S., and Shenkar, O.1985. Clustering countries on attitudinal dimensions: A review and synthesis. *Academy of Management Review,* 3: 435–454.

Runyon, K. E. 1973. Some interactions between personality variables and management styles. *Journal of Applied Psychology,* 57: 288–294.

Sagie, A., Elizur, D., and Yamauchi, H. 1996. The structure and strength of achievement motivation: A cross-cultural comparison. *Journal of Organizational Behavior,* 17: 431–444.

Salili, F. 1979. Determinants of achievement motivation for women in developing countries. *Journal of Vocational Behavior,* 14: 297–305.

Sanger, D. E. 1993. Performance related pay in Japan. *International Herald Tribune,* October 5: 20.

Schneider, S. C., and Barsoux, J. L. 1997. *Managing Across Cultures.* London: Prentice Hall.

Schneider, S. C., Wittenberg-Cox, A., and Hansen, L. 1991. *Honeywell Europe,* INSEAD.

Sirota, D., and Greenwood, M. J. 1971. Understanding your overseas workforce. *Harvard Business Review,* 14 (1): 53–60.

Slocum, J. W. 1971. A comparative study of the satisfaction of American and Mexican operatives. *Academy of Management Journal,* 14: 89–97.

Steers, R. M., Bischoff, S. J., and Higgins, L. H. 1992. Cross-cultural management research: The fish and the fisherman. *Journal of Management Inquiry,* 1: 321–330.

Triandis, H. C. 1971. *Attitude and Attitude Change.* New York: Wiley.

Triandis, H. C. 1972. *The Analysis of Subjective Culture.* New York: Wiley.

Triandis, H. C. 1995. Motivation and achievement in collectivist and individualist cultures. In M. L. Maehr and P. R. Pintrich (Eds.), *Advances in Motivation and Achievement: Culture, Motivation, and Achievement,* vol. 9. Greenwich, Conn.: JAI Press: 1–30.

Vance, C. M., McClaine, S. R., Boje, D. M., and Stage, H. D. 1992. An examination of the transferability of traditional performance appraisal principles across cultural boundaries, *Management International Review,* 32 (4): 313–326.

Vroom, V. 1964. *Work and Motivation.* New York: Wiley

Welsh, D. H. B., Luthans, F., and Sommer, S. M. 1993. Managing Russian factory workers: The impact of U.S.-based behavioral and participative techniques. *Academy of Management Journal,* 36(1): 58–79.

Yu, A. B., and Yang, K. S. 1994. The nature of achievement motivation in collectivist societies. In U. Kim, H. C. Triandis, C. Kagitcibasi, S.C. Choi, and G. Yoon (Eds.), *Individualism and Collectivism: Theory, Method, and Application.* Thousand Oaks, Calif.: Sage: 85–119.

Yuchtman, E. 1972. Reward distribution and work-role attractiveness in the Kibbutz: Reflections on equity theory. *American Sociological Review,* 37: 581–595.

Personal Initiative at Work: Differences between East and West Germany

Michael Frese
Wolfgang Kring
Andrea Soose
Jeannette Zempel

Newspapers and anecdotal evidence have suggested that there is little personal initiative in East Germany, even since the unification of East and West.[1] Managers report that they must actively find out whether an assigned task was done at all. For example, secretaries may fail to do a task because they have the wrong telephone number, even though they could obtain the number from another person. Or blue-collar workers may wait next to broken machines until a supervisor comes by, instead of looking for him or her or for a technician who could fix the machines.

Anecdotes like these may be useful as a basis for hypothesis development, but they need to be tested empirically. A study of personal initiative in East Germany may reveal something general about initiative and also begin to illuminate psychological processes important for economic development in East Germany and in other Eastern European countries.

THE CONCEPT OF PERSONAL INITIATIVE

Recently, there has been an increasing interest in dimensions of individual performance that may influence organizational effectiveness: "intrapreneurship" (Hisrich, 1990), organizational citizenship behavior (Organ, 1988), organizational spontaneity (George & Brief, 1992; Katz, 1964), general work behavior (Hunt, Hansen, & Paajanen, 1994), and contextual performance (Borman & Motowidlo, 1993). Our study of initiative is part of this general trend.

Personal initiative is a behavior syndrome resulting in an individual's taking an active and self-starting approach to work and going beyond what is formally required in a given job. More specifically, personal initiative is characterized by the following aspects: it (1) is consistent with the organization's mission,[2] (2) has a long-term focus, (3) is goal-directed and action-oriented, (4) is persistent in the face of barriers and setbacks, and (5) is self-starting and proactive.

To explain personal initiative, we use action theory. Space limitations prevent describing the theory in detail here; Frese and Sabini (1985), Frese and Zapf (1994), and Hacker (1985) describe the theory, and Carver and Scheier (1982) take a similar approach. According to action theory, people always plan actions to a certain extent, although planning may take

From *Academy of Management Journal,* 1996, 39(1), 37–63. Reprinted with permission.
[1] Although no longer politically current, the terms East and West Germany are still prevalent in familiar speech and are used throughout this article.
[2] Obviously, employees can also develop anticompany initiative, for example, to steal effectively. This type of initiative is not considered here.

place while they are acting, and actions are guided by goals (Miller, Galanter, & Pribram, 1960). At work, tasks provide a framework from which an individual job holder develops his or her goals.

Job holders translate externally given tasks into internal tasks through a redefinition process (Hackman, 1970). For example, blue-collar workers may redefine their tasks in such a way that one of their goals is to produce a good-quality product, even though this goal was not mentioned in their contract or in the official task description. This redefinition process allows employees to define extrarole goals (cf. Staw & Boetter, 1990).

Goals may have different time frames. If a production worker is confronted with a machine breakdown, he or she may ask a repairperson to fix the machine. In this case, the worker takes a short-term approach. In contrast, the worker may use a longer time frame. He or she may recognize that the same problem is likely to reoccur and, therefore, may strive to prevent the breakdown or learn how to fix the machine on his or her own. This strategy implies thought not only about immediate problems but also about future task performance (Frese, Stewart, & Hannover, 1987). A long-term focus is an essential element of personal initiative—of overcoming problems, dealing with difficulties, and thinking of alternative ways to do a task—because it allows the person to be proactive instead of just waiting until the problem reappears.

Long-term goals have an impact only if they are translated into actions. Kuhl (1983, 1992) wrote extensively about differences in how quickly people translate intentions (goals, in our terminology) into actions. Some people may have a certain goal but do little to achieve it; Kuhl calls this "state orientation." Others quickly put goals into action, showing "action orientation." Kuhl (1983, 1992) argued that state-oriented people are more occupied with their thoughts than with their actions. Action-oriented people do not think about the problems and advantages of their goals; rather they translate these goals quickly into actions. Thus, initiative implies goal-directness and action orientation.

Employees are likely to experience problems, barriers, and setbacks in pursuing new projects and goals. A supervisor may not like a new idea, for example, or untrained actions may be poorly executed in the beginning. If an employee gives up quickly in the face of barriers, there is no initiative, which implies dealing with problems actively and persistently.

Developing goals with a long-term focus and outside role requirements, implementing these goals, and persisting in implementation allow a person to develop self-starting activities that are proactive and thus show initiative.

A number of empirical studies and theoretical analyses have suggested that personal initiative can contribute to organizational effectiveness (Borman & Motowidlo, 1993; Hunt et al., 1994; Katz, 1964; Motowidlo & Scotter, 1994; Organ, 1988). No production or service system is perfect, and unplanned events are a fact of organizational life. Thus, extrarole activities are needed in every organization, and initiative should be included as one component of a multidimensional model of nonspecific job performance.

Additionally, Hacker (1992; cf. Frese & Zapf, 1994) argued that "superworkers" (the best workers in a given department) are characterized by having a longer time perspective on their work, a better-developed mental model of their work, and a more proactive approach to work than average workers. Interestingly, the speed of working was not significantly higher in the superworkers, but their strategies were more proactive and more sophisticated. The long-term orientation and the proactive approach are also aspects of our concepts of personal initiative. The best managers are also characterized by a higher degree of initiative (Boyatzis, 1982; Klemp & McClelland, 1986).

Personal Initiative and Other Constructs

Personal initiative is related to but not identical to other constructs, such as entrepreneurship/intrapreneurship (Hisrich, 1990), organizational citizenship behavior (OCB; Munene, 1995; Organ, 1990), and organizational spontaneity (George & Brief, 1992). Entrepreneurship refers to "behaviors that include demonstrating initiative and creative thinking, organizing social and economic mechanisms to turn resources and situations to practical account and accepting risk and failure" (Hisrich, 1990: 209). Initiative is one aspect of entrepreneurship (Frese, 1995). However, initiative does not necessarily have commercial implications and is, therefore, more similar to intrapreneurship (Hisrich, 1990).

Organizational citizenship behavior refers to "organizationally beneficial behaviors and gestures that can neither be enforced on the basis of formal role obligations nor elicited by contractual guarantee of recompense" (Organ, 1990: 46). Both OCB and initiative go beyond direct role requirements, and both contribute indirectly to organizational effectiveness (Organ, 1980).

However, there are also differences. OCB involves a set of five factors, two of which—altruism and compliance (Smith, Organ, & Near, 1983)—have been the most studied. In contrast to initiative, altruism is primarily related to the social sphere. Compliance has a passive connotation, referring, for example, to conscientiousness in attendance and adherence to rules. These are not part of the concept of initiative. Moreover, OCB research often assumes a supervisor's point of view, focusing on how helpful a worker is. However, supervisors often fail to support initiative and may even punish initiative approaches; this may be particularly so in Eastern Europe (cf. Pearce, Branyciki, & Bukacsi, 1994; Schultz-Gambard & Altschuh, 1993).[3] Further, although initiative and OCB are both pro-organizational concepts, the time perspective each involves is different. Workers with high initiative contribute to long-range positive outcomes for organizations, but in the short term they may well be a nuisance to their bosses because they are constantly pushing new ideas. In contrast, OCB is more oriented toward a short-term, positive social orientation at the workplace.

The concepts of organizational spontaneity (George & Brief, 1992; Katz, 1964) and initiative both imply organizationally functional, extrarole, active behaviors. Thus, there is a large degree of overlap between these concepts. However, we prefer the term "initiative." Although "spontaneous" implies voluntary and self-controlled actions, it also implies lack of planning. Since initiative implies good planning, we do not want to stick to the term introduced by Katz.

Personal Initiative in East and West Germany

In East Germany's 40 years of bureaucratic socialism, people had little chance to express initiative at work[4] (cf. Frese, 1995). Behavior by and within companies was highly regulated

---

[3] This historical context is one reason we did not measure OCB in East Germany; we were more interested in the rebellious element of initiative that overcomes resistance against change by a supervisor.

[4] In activities outside work, however, a high degree of creativity and tenacity were necessary; individuals would search extensively to find ways to, for instance, build summer houses under conditions of scarcity.

by central planning. Middle- and low-level management and workers had little input into how things were produced. Because there was no feedback via the market, there was little pressure to change things at workplace. As there was no competition with other companies, there was little incentive to develop high-level goals. The company goal was not to reach a high productivity level but to not make mistakes. Managers in the East were by and large more conventional and risk-avoidant than managers in the West, and they showed little independent thinking or achievement orientation (Schultz-Gambard & Altschuh, 1993). For these reasons, managers were not interested in workers' initiative and even imposed negative sanctions (Ladensack, 1990; Münch, 1990; Pearce et al., 1994; Shama, 1993).

Employees in East Germany had little control at work and low complexity in their jobs. Supervision was tight, "Tayloristic," and bureaucratic (Haraszti, 1977; Münch, 1990; Wuppertaler Kreis, 1992). Although Tayloristic job design is still prevalent in West Germany as well, there have been more attempts to increase job discretion for the workforce and to enhance workers' control and responsibility for their jobs (Ulich, 1991). Thus, both workplace factors (little control over and complexity of work) and leadership factors (negative management responses to initiative) led to a lower degree of personal initiative in East than in West Germany. Moreover, the school system contributed to a low degree of initiative (Oettingen, Little, Lindenberger, & Baltes, 1994). Accordingly, we posit:

Hypothesis 1: Personal initiative is lower in East Germany than in West Germany.

Selection of Socialization Effects as Causes of Potential East-West Differences

Differences between East and West Germany in initative at work may be explained either by socialization or selection processes.

Occupational Socialization

We concentrate here on occupational socialization because it refers to change processes in the same domain as initiative at work. Control and complexity have "socializing power" because they change skills, motivation, and orientations (Frese, 1982), and they influence initiative primarily via motivational and skill development processes.

Employees must be able to make decisions with regard to their own work and working conditions (Frese, 1989). First, low *control* at work (little autonomy or job discretion) can engender a passive and helpless approach toward work (Frese, 1989; Karasek & Theorell, 1990; Seligman, 1975). Second, employee motivation to redefine work in an enlarged (extrarole) sense is increased by sufficient environmental potential for keeping up and developing an "effectance" and mastery motive (White, 1959). Third, decision-making power enhances a worker's feeling of empowerment and increases the sense of responsibility for a job (Hackman & Oldham, 1975). Fourth, lack of control may lead to more brooding than action, increasing state orientation. Fifth, if employees expect that nothing can be done because they lack control, they are unlikely to persist in the face of setbacks.

Similar arguments can be made for *complexity*. Kohn and Schooler (1983a, 1983b) showed that the complexity of work effects an active orientation to life and a higher degree of intellectual flexibility and creativity. Work complexity leads to the development and practice of a high degree of skills and knowledge. A high skill level fosters a long-term perspective and creativity. These contribute to developing ideas about how to change work processes and make them more effective. Knowledge and skills also help to overcome barriers and setbacks, should they occur. This is not a deterministic relationship; initiative is possible in low-skill jobs, but work complexity enhances the development of initiative.

Thus, work control and complexity help people to show more personal initiative at work. Since proponents of the socialization point of view argue that differences in control and complexity have led to differences in initiative, there should be East-West differences in work control and complexity.

Hypothesis 2a: East Germany and West Germany will differ in the degrees of control and complexity afforded to employees at work.

Hypothesis 2b: Work control and complexity have a socialization effect.

Selection Effects

According to a selection perspective, people high in initiative left East Germany more frequently than people low in initiative because they suffered more from the East German regime (which repressed initiative) and because they had the initiative to actually leave. The migration of more than three million East Germans to the West since 1949 (Hahn, 1994) would therefore have produced a lower level of initiative in the East.

To our knowledge, no one has examined the initiative level of migrants from socialist East Germany; thus, one cannot test this hypothesis directly any longer. Indirect tests must suffice: First, an implication of the selection hypothesis is that initiative is mainly due to stable personality traits and thus should change little over time. This idea could be tested in our longitudinal study. Second, we could also study whether people who left the East after mid-1990 (when we began our study) had been higher in initiative prior to their leaving than those who stayed. Third, since intentions are well correlated with behaviors (Fishbein & Ajzen, 1975), it was possible to compare those who would like to leave with those who did not intend to leave East Germany.

We recognize that people who left the East before 1990 (during the period of bureaucratic socialism) may well differ from those who left after 1990. Prior to 1990, migrants and refugees often lost all their belongings and risked losing their lives or suffering imprisonment. Nevertheless, the psychological processes of voluntary migration may be similar across circumstances. If initiative was an important predictor of migration during bureaucratic socialism, it should also show up in somewhat weaker form in those who left after mid-1990.

Socialization versus Selection

We find the socialization explanation of East-West differences in initiative more compelling than the selection explanation. First, personal initiative implies that a person attempts to work constructively on problems. Therefore, initiative should lead to developing active coping strategies to deal with the constraints of bureaucratic socialism (see Parker [1993] on the relationship between perceived control and constructive dissent). Second, the selection hypothesis runs counter to our concept of personal initiative as a behavior syndrome that changes slowly because of work socialization processes.

Hypothesis 3: The evidence supporting a socialization explanation for previously hypothesized differences between East and West Germany is stronger than the evidence supporting a selection explanation.

METHODS

Study Design

There are two parts to this article: In the first, we compare cross-sectional differences between East and West Germany in initiative, control, and complexity using data collected in 1991. In the second part, we test the hypotheses regarding selection and socialization with data from a longitudinal study. We restricted the longitudinal study to the East because dramatic changes occurred only there. West Germans did not feel a difference in their daily (work) lives because of unification[5] (*Der Spiegel,* 1991).

For the East German data, we were concerned with the period between July 1990 (time 1) and July 1991 (time 3), a year selected because drastic changes occurred during it. Table 1 explains the events and the timing of the study waves. The study began on July 4, 1990, four days after the introduction of the West German deutsche mark as currency in East Germany. At that time, workplaces in East Germany were still quite similar to what they had been before the Communist government was voted out of power in the spring of 1990. Management had not changed dramatically, although a few companies had already been bought by Western firms. The power structure was largely the same as before. At this time, there was practically no unemployment in East Germany. At the time of the third wave, the market system had been solidly introduced. Unemployment figures were around 10 percent; a large additional group of people did not have normal jobs anymore but were not considered unemployed as they were in auxiliary jobs or reskilling courses supported by the state unemployment agency. Western technology was noticeably more prevalent at work than it had been, and many high-level managers had been replaced.

Sample

Two representative samples were drawn from two circles. One was Dresden, a large city in the south of East Germany. It is the capital of Saxonia, houses a large technical university, and is well-off compared, for example, with cities in the north of East Germany. We sampled

TABLE 1 Events in East Germany and Data Collection

Date	Events	Data Collection
October and November 1989	Mass demonstrations start	
November 1989	Opening of the Berlin wall	
March 1990	First free election in the East	
July 1990	Economic unification	Time 1
October 1990	Political unification	
November 1990		Time 2
December 1990	First general election in all of Germany	
Throughout 1991	Serious economic crisis in East Germany	
May 1991		West German study
July 1991		Time 3

[5] This has since changed with the economic downturn in 1993.

by randomly selecting streets, then selecting every third house and in each house, every fourth apartment (in smaller houses, every third one). Native Germans between the ages of 18 and 65 with full-time employment were invited to participate (thus, we sometimes had more than one person per family). The refusal rate of 33 percent was quite low for a study of this kind. Confidentiality was assured; if an individual preferred anonymity, it was provided with the help of a personal code word. All interviewees were paid for their participation.

In wave 1, 463 people participated in Dresden. For methodological reasons,[6] we asked 202 additional people to participate at time 2. At time 3, 543 people participated. To rule out effects of experimental mortality, we compared those who dropped out between time 1 and time 3 to full participants; there were no significant differences in the initiative variables. The sample is representative of the age, social class, and gender composition of the Dresden working population.

For comparison, we chose the West German city of Mainz, which is smaller than Dresden but has similar features. It also houses a university and a state government, is relatively conservative, and contains relatively few foreigners. The selection procedure was the same as was used in the East at time 1.

Of course, any comparison between East and West German cities poses certain problems. The socioeconomic makeup of native Germans (who were the only ones asked to participate) in West German cities is different from that of those in East Germany, partly because there are more foreigners in the West, and they often occupy low-level jobs. Additionally, there was a different participation rate. West Germans, especially blue-collar workers, were less likely to participate than East Germans; the overall refusal rate was 44 percent in the West, for an *n* of 160 participants. Thus, blue-collar workers were underrepresented in the West German sample, according to statistics provided by the city of Mainz.

Analysis Strategy and Potentially Confounding Variables

Because the samples' social class makeups differed and the West German sample was not quite representative for social class, mean comparisons are based on a two-way analysis of variance in which socioeconomic status was entered first. We only sampled employed individuals in the West and therefore, only those East Germans who had full-time jobs at time 3 were included in the East-West comparisons (time 3 *n* = 450 in the East).

Finally, we used multivariate analysis of covariance (MANCOVA) to control for the following additional potential confounds: marital status, partner employment, gender, and number of children.[7]

The number of respondents varies across the analyses because data are missing and certain questions were only presented to certain people (for example, probes into questions related to continuing education). When using correlations or regression analyses, we used pairwise deletion of missing data (cf. Roth, Switzer, Campion, & Jones, 1994).

---

[6] We added new interviewees at time 2 to be able to analyze the effects of participating in a study on initiative. Initiative scores of the first-timers could be compared to those of people interviewed at both time 1 and time 2 through *t*-tests. No significant differences between the two groups emerged on the core initiative scales, education, interviewer evaluation, overcoming barriers, and active approach (data not shown).

[7] Female employment was and is much higher in East than in West Germany (*Der Spiegel,* 1991). One could argue that a partner's employment (or children at home) affect orientation toward work and the taking of initiative. Age, gender, marital status (Melamed, 1995), and number of children could also be confounds.

Interview Procedure

Structured interviews were conducted, with additional prompts used by the interviewers as necessary. The interviewers were psychology and business students from Giessen and Dresden trained during a two-day course that included role playing, particularly on how to use prompts. Interviewers were also trained in the use of coding, and examples of the end points of the scales were provided. After time 1, each newly trained interviewer conducted a first interview together with an experienced interviewer, a practice that provided additional learning.

In these interviews, three kinds of data were collected: objective facts (e.g., is the interviewee unemployed?), a judgment of behavior (rated by the interviewer on a five-point scale directly after the interview), and a narrative, which was submitted to coding at a later date. Interviewees' answers were jotted down by the interviewers in a short form, typed, and later used as the basis for numerical coding, with one of the coders being the interviewer him- or herself.[8] In the third wave of data collection, the codings were culturally cross-checked—interviews done by interviewers from East Germany were recoded by interviewers from the West, and vice versa. Interrater agreements were adequate and are presented below. The means of the coding values of both raters were used in the analyses. After an interview, the interviewee was given the questionnaire to fill out at leisure (it was usually picked up after one or two weeks).

Measurement of the Interview Variables

Table 2 presents scales, Cronbach's alphas, means, standard deviations (East and West collapsed, time 3 data), and correlations; the Appendix lists the items for the scales.

Personal Initiative

We think that there are problems in the use of direct questionnaire measures for initiative (Frese, Fay, Leng, Hiliberger, & Tag, 1996) because social desirability bias is likely to be high unless answers can be probed (as is possible in an interview). The most important issue was that of differential anchor points. Whenever questionnaire-derived mean differences are tested across different cultures, it can be argued that people simply understand the scales differently (Poortinga & Vijver, 1987). The argument has two sides: First, if respondents compared themselves only with others from the East, they might think of their own initiative as quite high, though it was in fact low relative to West Germans'. Using a questionnaire in such a case would lead to rejecting the hypothesis that there are differences between East and West, even though there are such differences. Alternatively, because East Germans know that they are low on initiative, they might describe themselves along the lines of the popular stereotypes and thereby underrate their own initiative. This would lead to an acceptance of the hypothesis in spite of true similarities between East and West. To overcome these problems, we used interview-based measures to study the core variables.

---

[8] For reasons of research economy, we did not use verbatim transcriptions of the interviews. Transcribing was not necessary because the coding system was developed beforehand and the interviewers knew which answers had to be written down to make coding possible. However, the interviewers were also trained to write down the relevant responses as word-for-word as possible: thus, the records were not just a shorthand for coding.

TABLE 2 Descriptive Statistics and Time 3 Correlations[a]

Interview Variables	1	2	3	4	5	6	7	8	9	10	Range	α	Mean	s.d.
Interview														
1. Qualitative work initiative		.61**	.18**	.27**	.10*	.15**	.03	-.02	.07	-.05	0–4	b	0.44	0.74
2. General work initiative	.67**		.26**	.41**	.25**	.31**	.19**	.20**	.20**	-.16**	1–6	.74	2.15	0.78
3. Education initiative	.29**	.37**		.52**	.33**	.40**	.18**	.29**	.08*	-.20**	0–5	b	2.13	1.63
4. Interviewer evaluation	.29**	.30**	.39**		.42**	.63**	.26**	.36**	.23**	-.32**	1–5	.93	3.75	0.85
5. Overcoming barriers	.27**	.26**	.28**	.18**		.62**	.13**	.15**	.08*	-.12**	1–6	.58(W) .70(E)	3.16(W) 2.97(E)	0.66(W) 0.74(E)
6. Active approach	.28**	.41**	.30**	.49**	.50**		.17**	.19**	.13**	-.18**	1–5	.70	3.57	0.78
Questionnaire														
7. Control at work	.22**	.30**	.14*	.22**	.14*	.25**		.50**	.29**	-.36**	1–5	.78	3.63	0.85
8. Complexity of work	.17*	.28**	.15*	.28**	.16*	.31**	.49**		.24**	-.24**	1–5	.67	3.51	0.77
9. Self-efficacy	.20**	.20**	.17*	.28**	.12	.26**	.14*	.32**		-.45**	1–5	.70	3.51	0.54
10. Control rejection	-.24**	-.28**	-.20**	-.16*	-.23**	-.23**	-.46**	-.40**	-.49**		1–5	.87	2.00	0.62

[a] Correlations above the diagonal are for East Germans; those below the diagonal are for West Germans; alphas, means, and standard deviations are for the total sample except as noted.
[b] Index measure.
* $p < .05$
** $p < .01$

Quantitative and Qualitative Initiative at Work

Direct questions on past initiative were asked. If the respondent gave an example of initiative, the interviewers probed into the nature of the problem or activity, asking whether it was the interviewee's or somebody else's idea, whether other people in his or her job would also look into these problems or do these things (to ascertain extrarole behaviors), how often it was done, and so forth. If the activity was something that only required additional energy, it was coded as an example of *quantitative initiative*. If the activity addressed new problems or included new ideas, goals, or strategies going beyond what was expected from a person in the particular job (for example, a blue-collar worker's looking into a complicated production problem or a low-level supervisor's attempting to reorganize a work structure), it was deemed to be *qualitative initiative*. Qualitative and quantitative initiative were combined to form a five-point scale *general initiative at work*. Interrater correlations were .84 in the East and .89 in the West.

In addition, we developed a special subindex on *qualitative initiative*. Here, only the extremes of qualitative initiative (ratings of 4 and above) were counted (one point was given for each coding that was 4 or higher). The coders were instructed to give a 4 or 5 if there was a high degree of qualitative initiative present. We assumed that this index would be sensitive to East-West differences because it measures the very essence of initiative. Because of the restricted variance, interrater correlations were low (East $r = .32$ and West $r = 16$).[9] The means are very low because only a few interviewees actually had more than one case in which they showed high qualitative initiative.

Education Initiative

This scale measured whether an interviewee intended to participate or participated already in some continuing education. The coding was based on what the interviewees had planned and how concrete or abstract these plans were (for example, did the person already know which course he or she would take, had he or she registered for the course, etc.). The interrater agreement was .88 in the East and .92 in the West.

Interviewer Evaluation

The interviewers were asked to fill out a semantic differential scale to rate how active, initiating, and plan- and goal-oriented the interviewees were; no rerating was done here because the scale was intended to give interviewers' impressions.

Overcoming Barriers

Overcoming barriers is central to our concept of initiative because it is a behavioral measure; it measures a person's tenacity when confronted with obstacles to the pursuit of a goal. Our measure was inspired by the situational interview (Latham & Saari, 1984). The interviewee was asked to imagine having a certain problem—or example, a colleague who always did his or her work sloppily, requiring additional effort from the interviewee. For each problem-solving response given, the interviewer would present reasons why the selected

---

[9] The low interrater reliability is due to restriction of variance. Interrater correlations for a nonrestricted version of the same items were .75 in East and .75 in West Germany.

strategy would not work, thus presenting barriers. After the third barrier (the question itself constituted the first one), the respondent was asked whether he or she could think of additional strategies. In this way, we measured how many barriers the respondent was able to overcome. Interrater agreement was .80 in the East and .86 in the West.[10]

Active Approach

Barriers can be overcome in different ways; a search for a solution can be delegated to somebody else (for example, a supervisor) or actively pursued oneself. To get at this issue, the interviewers were asked to rate how active an interviewee's propositions for overcoming barriers were. This rating was done across the four problem situations used in overcoming barriers (no rerating was done on these variables).

The initiative scales have been shown to have adequate validity (cf. Frese et al., 1996) in terms of adequate intercorrelations and significant correlations with the interviewees' life partners' (spouses, etc.) judgments of the interviewees' initiative. Moreover, people who were self-employed or who wanted to become self-employed showed more initiative in the East, and those with high initiative also had clearer career plans and executed their career plans more often than those with low initiative.

Questionnaire Variables: Auxiliary and Additional Variables

Auxiliary Variables

We have argued that initiative should not be measured by questionnaires. However, in the sense of triangulation (Webb, Campbell, Schwartz, & Sechrest, 1966), interview- and questionnaire-based measures should lead to similar results. For this reason, we also included two auxiliary measures, generalized *self-efficacy* and *control rejection,* in our analyses.

Self-efficacy and control rejection are conceptually and empirically close to personal initiative. Both are related to control at work. Self-efficacy—an expectation of mastery—is the opposite of work-related helplessness (Speier & Frese, 1996) and is a generalized expectancy. Since mastery expectations are prerequisites of initiative (Bandura, 1986), self-efficacy is closely related to initiative. It is relevant that Sandelands, Bockner, and Glynn (1988) presented evidence that self-esteem, a variable related to self-efficacy, is an antecedent of persistence.

Taking responsibility and wanting to take charge are prerequisites of initiative (Frese, Erbe-Heinbokel, Grefe, Rybowiak, & Weike, 1994). We used the scale control rejection as a variable that should be related negatively to initiative (Frese et al., 1994). A high score on this variable indicates that the individual does not want control or responsibility at work. Both self-efficacy and control rejection are trait-like measures, while personal initiative is a behavior syndrome.

---

[10] At time 3, there were two different versions of overcoming barriers. Two of the four questions asked in the West were part of the time 2 interview in the East. As we wanted to have only work-related items comparing East and West Germans, we used a mixture of two time 2 and two time 3 questions in the East to equalize the content of the scales. However, when the analyses were restricted to the East, we used the original four time 3 items, which included two non-work-related items, "losing one's apartment" and "reduction of unemployment benefits."

Additional Variables

Control at work (Semmer, 1984) assesses job discretion in terms of, for example, ability to influence working conditions and work strategies. *Complexity of work* (Semmer, 1984) describes how difficult an individual's job decisions are. Semmer showed the ratings of subjects (blue-collar workers) and observers to be highly correlated for both variables ($r = .58$ and $r = .67$ for control and complexity, respectively). There is also evidence that people report these job characteristics with little subjective bias (Zapf, 1989).

Having left East Germany was established in September 1992, when we checked what letters had been returned to us (letters were sent to interviewees prior to the time 2 and time 3 visits) against the police register to which all German citizens must report to ascertain whether subjects had moved to the West; the interviewers also asked neighbors whether people had moved, if they could not be reached at their known addresses.

An additional set of a single-item questions addressed marital status, job of partner, number of children, and age of interviewee.

RESULTS

Cross-Sectional Study: East-West Differences in Initiative

In a first step, the hypothesis that working East Germans have a lower degree of initiative than West Germans was tested with a multivariate analysis of variance (MANOVA) with all dependent (initiative plus auxiliary) variables included; for methodological reasons, socioeconomic status (SES) was included as a factor. All multivariate effects were significant (Hotelling's test). The results reveal a significant East-West multivariate effect as suggested by our hypothesis ($F_{8.379} = 4.15, p < .01$), an effect of socioeconomic status ($F_{16.756} = 4.74, p < .01$), and an interaction effect ($F_{16.760} = 2.08, p < .01$). When the potential confounds were entered into a multivariate analysis of covariance (living alone/with partner, partner employed, age, gender, and number of children), these potential confounds had a significant multivariate influence on the dependent variables ($F_{40.1.617} = 2.22, p < .01$), but they did not change the pattern of results at all [East vs. West ($F_{8.325} = 3.59, p < .01$), SES ($F_{16.648} = 4.75, p < .01$) interaction effect ($F_{16.648} = 1.76, p < .05$)]. Accordingly, no further analyses were done with these confounds added (although SES was included in all further analyses).

These data confirm our general prediction, Hypothesis 1. Since all of the effects were significant, further univariate hierarchical ANOVAs were calculated. Table 3 reports the important results regarding East-West differences.[11] Because none of the interactions were significant, they are not displayed in the table. Levels of five of the eight initiative variables were significantly higher in the West, and one additional variable was nearly significantly higher; these included the most important core variables, overcoming barriers and qualitative initiative.

Interestingly, education initiative did not differ between East and West. The reason is probably that many funds are earmarked by the government for continuing education for East Germans. Interviewer evaluation—the variable that is most likely to reflect prejudices—also

---

[11]Socioeconomic status showed significant differences in the variables in Table 5 (higher social status showing more initiative, except for self-efficacy); however, since status was entered only as a potential confound, we are not concerned with a detailed analysis of this variable.

did not differentiate between East and West. Thus, one cannot argue that the initiative differences were due to prejudices held by the interviewers and raters.

The mean differences between East and West constituted about one-fourth to two-thirds of a standard deviation. Figure 1 presents the results for overcoming barriers in a slightly different format: Here, the group of people with high performance (a score of at least one standard deviation above the mean) on the variable overcoming barriers was singled out. In the East, 13 percent were high on this measure of taking initiative, and in the West, about three times as many had high scores (35%).

TABLE 3   ANOVA Results: East-West Differences in Initiative [a]

Variables	Time 3 Standard Deviations		Time 3 Means		ANOVA *F*
	East	West	East	West	
Qualitative work initiative	0.73	0.89	0.38	0.65	7.36**
General work initiative	0.74	0.83	2.09	2.36	3.55[†]
Interviewer evaluation	0.88	0.76	3.74	3.88	n.s.
Overcoming barriers	0.62	0.66	2.82	3.17	17.31**
Active approach	0.78	0.71	3.54	3.81	4.08*
Education initiative	1.65	1.58	2.02	2.29	n.s.
Control rejection	0.61	0.58	2.08	1.72	19.87**
Self-efficacy	0.51	0.51	3.44	3.84	68.44**

[a] Hierarchical ANOVAs with socioeconomic status entered first were conducted; only employed interviewees were included in analyses. Socioeconomic status was significant for all variables except self-efficacy. All interactions were nonsignificant; ranges of *n*, 296–385 (East), 129–159 (West).
[†] $p < .10$
* $p < .05$
** $p < .01$

FIGURE 1   Percentages of People with Very High Initiative, East and West[a]

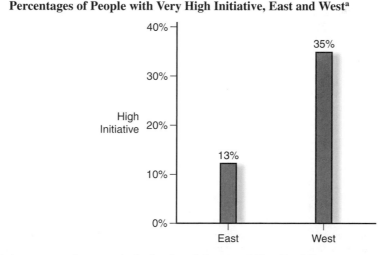

[a] Initiative was measured as overcoming barriers. One s.d. above mean 2.89 + .61 = 3.50.

Longitudinal Study: Socialization versus Selection

According to the socialization concept, control at work and work cornplexity should influence initiative. This implies that there should be significant East-West differences in control and complexity (Hypothesis 2a). In the two-way hierarchical ANOVAs (in which SES and East-West differences were factors), significant differences in control at work measured at time 3 appeared for SES ($F_{2.526} = 18.17$, $p < .01$) and for East-West differences ($\bar{x}$ [East] = 3.52, $\bar{x}$ [West] = 3.90; $F_{1.526} = 8.02$, $p < .01$). Similar results prevailed for complexity measured at time 3 (SES $F_{2.525} = 22.59$, $p < .01$) and East-West differences ($\bar{x}$ [East] = 3.43, $\bar{x}$ [West] = 3.72; $F_{1.525} = 4.53$, $p <.05$). None of the interactions were significant. Thus, Hypothesis 2a is confirmed.

Hypothesis 2b predicts that control at work and work complexity will change level of initiative, thus expressing a socialization hypothesis. We were able to test this question for those initiative variables for which we had both time 1 and time 3 data (qualitative and general work initiative measures were not used at time 1). Table 4 displays the single correlations and, more important, the squared multiple correlation coefficients, relating control and complexity with initiative in East and West (columns 3 and 6). These show that, on the average, control and complexity explain about 9 percent of the variance in initiative in the East and about 10 percent in the West.

To test whether control and complexity actually influenced changes in personal initiative, hierarchical regression analyses were calculated for the longitudinal study in the East (last column of Table 4). The time 1 initiative variables were entered first (and thereby, partialed out), and then control and complexity at time 3 were included.[12] The last column of Table 4 gives the increments in variance explained by control and complexity above and beyond the stability of the initiative variables. In all cases (except one that is nearly significant), there were significant increments. These results support the socialization hypothesis.

Hypothesis 3 states that there is more evidence for a socialization explanation of East-West differences than for a selection explanation. The selection hypothesis can be tested with two kinds of data. First, is there a change in East Germans' initiative between time 1 and time 3? There is evidence for a significant increase in two of the initiative variables (Table 5)[13] and one nearly significant increase, although education initiative and self-efficacy show a reduction, with the auxiliary variable self-efficacy being marginally significant. These results run counter to what a pure selection effect would suggest.

Second, were East Germans who wanted to leave or who had actually left higher in initiative than those who wanted to stay or stayed? Only wanting to leave the East (measured at time 1) was significantly related to self-efficacy (see Table 6).

Table 6 shows a comparison between those who had left the East to resettle in the West (we knew of 12 individuals who had done so by September 1992) and those who stayed in the East. There is one nearly significant result (from one-sided t=tests); those who left the East

[12] Control and complexity were measured at time 3 because the effects of changed jobs could be tested then.
[13] The variable overcoming barriers needs a comment. We used different kinds of situations as material to ask the interviewees to overcome barriers at time I and at time 3; this was to ensure that there would be no simple learning-from-repetition effect. However, we cannot be certain that the time 1 questions were similar in difficulty to the time 3 questions. Thus, the significant difference between time 1 and time 3 in this variable should not be taken as evidence of an increase in initiative.

TABLE 4 Correlations and Regression Analysis Results

	Cross-Sectional Study						Longitudinal Study
	East			West			
	Correlations			Correlations			
Time 3 Variables	Control	Complexity	R^{2a}	Control	Complexity	R^{2a}	ΔR^{2b}
Interviewer evaluation	.26**	.36**	.14**	.22**	.28**	.09**	.052**
Overcoming barriers	.13**	.15**	.02**	.14**	.16*	.03	.021†
Active approach	.17**	.19**	.04**	.25**	.31**	.11**	.023*
Education initiative	.18**	.29**	.08**	.14*	.15*	.03	.029**
Control rejection	−.36**	−.24**	.13**	−.46**	−.40**	.25**	.016*
Self-efficacy	.29**	.24**	.10**	.14*	.32**	.10**	.015*

[a] Work control and complexity at time 3 are cross-sectional predictors.
[b] Work control and complexity at time 1 initiative was entered in hierarchical regression analyses to test the effect of control and complexity on change in initiative.
Work control and complexity at time 3 entered after time 1 initiative.
† $p < .10$
* $p < .05$
** $p < .01$

389

TABLE 5 Changes in Initiative in the East[a]

| | Means | | |
Variables	Time 1	Time 3	t
Interviewer evaluation	3.58	3.66	−1.72[†]
Overcoming barriers	2.20	2.90	−14.52[**]
Active approach	3.06	3.45	−7.11[**]
Education initiative	2.49	2.02	5.10[**]
Control rejection	2.04	2.07	n.s.
Self-efficacy	3.47	3.43	1.86[†]

[a] The t-tests for dependent sample were to test changes for scales assessed at time 1 and time 3; for education, the comparison was between time 2 and time 3.
[†] $p < .10$
[**] $p < .01$

TABLE 6 Comparisons of Stayers and Leavers[a]

| | Wanted to Leave East, Time 1 | | | | Left vs. Stayed | | |
| | Means | | | | Means | | |
Variables	Yes	Maybe	No	F	Left East	Stayed in East	t
Qualitative work initiative, time 3	0.38	0.42	0.36	n.s.	0.13	0.38	1.97[†]
General work initiative, time 3	2.04	2.19	2.07	n.s.	1.93	2.13	n.s.
Education initiative[b]	2.13	2.19	2.00	n.s.	1.64	1.81	n.s.
Interviewer evaluation[b]	3.82	3.81	3.64	n.s.	3.36	3.45	n.s.
Overcoming barriers[b]	2.80	2.93	2.91	n.s.	2.36	2.39	n.s.
Active approach[b]	3.27	3.41	3.46	n.s.	3.27	3.18	n.s.
Control rejection[b]	2.13	1.99	2.08	n.s.	2.26	2.04	n.s.
Self-efficacy[b]	3.70	3.52	3.39	3.82[*]	3.47	3.39	n.s.
n	15	36	257		8–12	>530	

[a] By September 1992, 12 people had moved to the West; time 2 comparisons were done for leavers wherever possible; one-sided t-tests were used.
[b] When testing for differences in "wanted to leave," we used time 3 results; when testing for differences between leavers and stayers. we used time 2 data.
[†] $p < .10$
[*] $p < .05$

demonstrated somewhat *less* qualitative initiative. In addition, four of the variables showed nonsignificantly higher means for those who had stayed. Thus, the different sets of data do not provide any evidence to support a selection effect of initiative. The selection hypothesis cannot be upheld, but the socialization effect is supported by the data, confirming Hypothesis 3.

DISCUSSION

This study provides evidence that personal initiative is lower in East than in West Germany. These differences are quite robust, and they do not disappear when controls are added. As Figure 1 shows, the difference is impressive if one looks at the extremes of the distribution—representing those who matter most for organizations.

As predicted, socialization provides a better explanation of the results than does selection. Control at work and work complexity are lower in the East, and they significantly predict changes in initiative variables. The selection hypothesis was not supported by the two analyses involving people who wanted to leave and people who actually left East Germany. Although these analyses can be criticized because pre-1990 leaving may not be analogous to post-1990 migration, the selection hypothesis also assumes that initiative is a stable variable. In contrast, our results suggest that there are some slow changes.

In interpreting our results, one might argue that the interviewees either became more interested in initiative because they participated in the study or that they learned to deal with the interview questions better, showing superficial learning. However, as discussed in footnote 6, those who participated in the study twice were no different in initiative than those who participated only once.

One might also argue that the interviewers were prejudiced against East Germans. Since the initiative scales were based upon their judgments, such bias could produce differences. Three arguments speak against this interpretation. First, the auxiliary concepts that were based on the interviewees' questionnaire responses showed a pattern quite similar to that of the interview-based scales. Second, the variable interviewer evaluation, which is most strongly based on the interviewers' subjective judgment and, therefore, the most prone to be biased, did not produce significant East-West differences. Third, we had a check in the cross-cultural codings, with East German coders recording the interviews done by West Germans and vice versa.

Although only a few studies have examined psychological processes in Eastern Europe, there are some that are in line with our results. One study on self-efficacy in school children (Oettingen et al., 1994) found children in East Berlin to have lower self-efficacy and less faith in influencing their performance than those in West Berlin. Schultz-Gambard and Altschuh (1993) showed that East Germans had more conventional leadership styles and were more dependent on those above them, less self-reliant, and less achievement-oriented than West Germans. Welsh, Luthans, and Sommer (1993) evaluated different management strategies and found that participative techniques did not work in Russia.

We think that the results can probably be generalized to other Eastern European countries to a certain degree. There are similarities in upbringing, socialization, and the organization of workplaces across Eastern Europe (Frese, 1995; Haraszti, 1977; Pearce et al., 1994; Shama, 1993; Welsh et al., 1993). Additionally, all these countries have been shaken by massive changes. However, there are also differences in the transition processes. There is more interference from Westerners in East Germany than in other European countries. Thus, East Germans frequently experience a situation similar to the one that prevailed during the period of bureaucratic socialism: They are supposed to follow orders from somebody above themselves without getting any sense that their own thoughts and problem-solving approaches are important. However, this time the "somebody above" is a manager flown in from West Germany. Further, the drastic necessity to change is more salient in those Eastern European countries that receive less financial support than East Germany.

We think that this study of initiative also has general implications that go beyond Eastern Europe. First, the concept of initiative is important as one aspect of contextual performance in any society. The importance of initiative will increase with modern production systems (Womack, Jones, Roos, & Carpenter, 1990), since supervision is reduced in lean organizations and there is more reliance on shop floor employees' participating actively in organizing work, improving process and product quality, and taking care of unexpected events efficiently. None of these tasks can be put into codified form, and therefore, they rely on initiative to be done effectively.

Second, initiative may be of particular importance in change processes (Howard, 1995; Kanter, 1983). People with a high degree of initiative will also be more likely to participate in workplace changes (Frese & Plüddemann, 1993). Further, change processes cannot be programmed and prepared in such a way that nothing goes wrong. Thus, in change situations, management depends on all of an organization's employees to deal with unpredictable events and to prepare to avoid mistakes—activities that take initiative. The issue of empowerment has been important here, as is reflected in our results on control and complexity (Kanter, 1983; Wall & Jackson, 1995).

Third, the results on the influence of control and complexity on personal initiative can probably be generalized to Western countries. Although there are *mean* differences between East and West Germany, there are no *correlational* differences (the East-West correlations of the correlations displayed in Table 4 are .92 for control and .95 for complexity). Since Tayloristic production methods reduce control and complexity, this pattern implies that Tayloristic organizations run the risk of reducing their employees' initiative.

Fourth, a response of managers to employees' lack of initiative is often to "tighten the ropes" and increase supervision and outside control. Employees' degree of control at work thus declines, which can reduce initiative even further, starting a vicious cycle. Managers should be careful not to fall into this trap and should instead introduce a slow process to help increase and promote initiative.

Fifth, we assume that a certain amount of tension and conflict can develop when people from different "initiative cultures" have to work together, because their expectations of what needs to be done at work differ. This tension exists in East Germany when employees from the West do not understand why East German employees do not show initiative (Hawranek, 1990). We assume that similar problems develop when different organizational cultures collide.

In any case, one should be realistic. Certain cultures may have a lower level of initiative than others. It is fruitless to make the question of initiative a politically divisive issue to which people attach prejudices and preconceptions (as is done in Germany); rather, scientific study of initiative, its predictors, and means by which it may be increased should be pursued.

References

Bandura, A. 1986. *Social foundations of thought and action.* Englewood Cliffs, NJ: Prentice Hall.

Borman, W. C., & Motowidlo, S. J. 1993. Expanding the criterion domain to include elements of contextual performance. In N. Schmitt & W. C. Borman (Eds.), *Personnel selection in organizations:* 71–98. San Francisco: Jossey-Bass.

Boyatzis. R. E. 1982. *The competent manager: A model for effective performance.* New York: Wiley.

Carver, C. S., & Scheier, M. F. 1982. Control theory: A useful conceptual framework for personality, social, clinical, and health psychology. *Psychological Bulletin,* 92: 111–135.

Der Spiegel. 1991. Das Profil der Deutschen—Was sie vereint, was sie trennt [The profile of Germans—What unifies them and what separates them). *Spiegel-Spezial,* January.

Fishbein, M., & Ajzen, I. 1975. *Belief, attitude, intention and behavior: An introduction to theory and research.* Reading, MA: Addison-Wesley.

Frese, M. 1982. Occupational socialization and psychological development: An underemphasized research perspective in industrial psychology. *Journal of Occupational Psychology,* 55: 209–224.

Frese, M. 1989. Theoretical models of control and health. In S. L. Sauter, J. J. Hurrel, Jr., & C. L. Cooper (Eds.), *Job control and worker health:* 107–108. Chichester. U. K.: Wiley.

Frese, M. 1995. Entrepreneurship in East Europe: A general model and empirical findings. In C. L. Cooper & D. M. Rousseau (Eds.), *Trends in organizational behavior:* 65–83. Chichester, U. K.: Wiley.

Frese, M. Erbe-Heinbokel, M., Grefe, J., Rybowiak, V., & Weike, A. 1994. Mir ist es lieber, wenn ich genau gesagt bekomme, was sich tun muss: Probleme der Akzeptanz von Verantwortung und Handlungsspielraum in Ost und West [I would rather be told what I should do: Problems of acceptance of responsibility and control in East and West]. *Zeitschrift für Arbeits-und Organisationspsychologie,* 38: 22–33.

Frese, M., Fay, D., Leng, K., Hilburger, T., & Tag, A. 1996. *The concept of personal initiative: Operationalization, reliability, and validity in two German samples.* Manuscript submitted for publication.

Frese, M., & Plüddemann, K. 1993. Umstellungsbereitschaft im Osten und Westen Deutschlands [Readiness to change in East and West Germany]. *Zeitschrift fuer Sozialpsychologie,* 24: 198–210.

Frese, M., & Sabini, J. (Eds.). 1985. *Goal-directed behavior: The concept of action in psychology.* Hillsdale, NJ: Erlbaum.

Frese, M., Stewart, J., & Hannover. B. 1987. Goal orientation and planfulness: Action styles as personality concepts. *Journal of Personality and Social Psychology,* 52: 1182–1194.

Frese, M., & Zapf, D. 1994. Action as the core of work psychology: A German approach. In H. C. Triandis, M.D. Dunnette, & M. Hugh (Eds.), *Handbook of industrial and organizational psychology,* vol.4 (2nd ed.): 271–340. Palo Alto, CA: Consulting Psychologists Press.

George. J. M., & Brief, A. P. 1992. Feeling good—doing good: A conceptual analysis of the mood at work—organizational spontaneity relationship. *Psychological Bulletin,* 112: 310–329.

Hacker, W. 1985. Activity: A fruitful concept in industrial psychology. In M. Frese & J. Sabini (Eds.), *Goal directed behavior: The concept of action in psychology:* 262–284. Hillsdale, NJ: Erlbaum.

Hacker, W. 1992. *Expertenkönnen* [Expert knowledge]. Göttingen, Germany: Verlag für Angewandte Psychologie.

Hackman, J. R. 1970. Tasks and task performance in research on stress. In J. E. McGrath (Ed.), *Social and psychological factors in stress:* 202–237. New York: Holt, Rinehart & Winston.

Hackman, J. R., & Oldham, G. R. 1975. Development of a job diagnostic survey. *Journal of Applied Psychology,* 60:159–170.

Hahn, A. 1994. Geschichte und Szenarien der Übersiedlung [History and scenarios of emigration]. In R. Schwarzer & M. Jerusalem (Eds.), *Gesellschaftlicher Umbruch als kritisches Lebensereignis:* 23–48. Weinheim, Germany: Juventa.

Haraszti. M. 1977. *A worker in a worker's state.* New York: Penguin Books.

Hawranek, D. 1990. Gemeinsam ins Chaos [Together into the chaos]. *Der Spiegel,* 21: 130–133.

Hisrich, R. D. 1990. Entrepreneurship/intrapreneurship. *American Psychologist,* 45: 209–222.

Howard, A. 1995. A framework for work change. In A. Howard (Ed.), *The changing nature of work:* 3–44. San Francisco: Jossey-Bass.

Hunt, S. T., Hansen, T. L., & Paajanen, G.E. 1994. *Generic work behaviors: The components of non-job specific performance.* Paper presented at the ninth annual conference of the society of Industrial and Organizational Psychology, Nashville.

Kanter, R. M. 1983. *The change masters.* London: Routledge.

Karasek, R., & Theorell, T. 1990. *Healthy work.* New York: Basic.

Katz, D. 1964. The motivational basis of organizational behavior. *Behavioral Science,* 9: 131–146.

Klemp, G. O., & McClelland, D. C. 1986. What characterizes intelligent functioning among senior managers? In R. J. Sternberg & R. K. Wagner (Eds.), *Practical intelligence— Nature and origins of competence in the everyday world:* 31–50. Cambridge: University Press.

Kohn, M. L., & Schooler, C. 1983a. The reciriocal effects of the substantive complexity of work and intellectual flexibility: A longitudinal assessment. In M. L. Kohn & C. Schooler (Eds.), *Work and personality: An inquiry into the impact of social stratification:* 103–124. Norwood, NJ: Ablex.

Kohn, M. L., & Schooler, C. 1983b. Stratification, occupation, and orientation. In M. L. Kohn & C. Schooler (Eds.), *Work and personality: An inquiry into the impact of social stratification:* 5–33. Norwood, NJ: Ablex.

Kuhl, J. 1983. *Motivation, Konflikt und Handlungskontrolle* [Motivation, control and action control]. Berlin: Springer.

Kuhl, J. 1992. A theory of self-regulation: Action versus state orientation, self-discrimination, and some applications. *Applied Psychology: An International Review,* 41: 97–129.

Ladensack, K. 1990. Motivierung, Leiterleistungen und Leiterentwicklung—Untersucht vor der Wende in der DDR (Motivating, leader performance and leader development—

Researched before the change in the GDR). *Zeitschrift für Personalforschung,* special issue: 85–95.

Latham, G. P., & Saari, L. M. 1984. Do people do what they say: Further studies on the situational interview. *Journal of Applied Psychology,* 69: 569–573.

Melamed, T. 1995. Barriers to women's career success: Human capital, career choices, structural determinants or simply sex discrimination? *Applied Psychology: An International Review,* 44: 295–314.

Miller, G. A., Galanter, E., & Pribram, K. H. 1960. *Plans and the structure of behavior.* London: Holt.

Motowidlo, S. J., & Scotter, J. R.. van. 1994. Evidence that task performance should be distinguished from contextual performance. *Journal of Applied Psychology,* 79: 475–480.

Münch, R. 1990. Das Selbstverständnis von Personalmanagement und Mitarbeitermotivation in der DDR-Wirtschaft [The self-presentation of management and conceptualizations of motivation in the GDR-economy]. *Zeitschrift fur Personalforschung,* special issue: 103–110.

Munene, J. C. 1995. Not-on-seat: An investigation of some correlates of organizational citizenship behavior in Nigeria. *Applied Psychology: An International Review,* 44: 111–122.

Oettingen, C., Little, T. D., Lindenberger. U., & Baltes, P. B. 1992. Causality, agency, and control beliefs in East versus West Berlin children: A natural experiment on the role of context. *Journal of Personality and Social Psychology,* 66: 579–595.

Organ, D. 1988. *Organizational citizenship behavior: The good soldier syndrome,* Lexington, MA: Lexington Books.

Organ, D. 1990. The motivational basis of organizational citizenship behavior. In B. M. Staw & L. L. Cummings (Eds.), *Research in organizational behavior,* vol.12: 43–72. Greenwich, CT: JAI Press.

Parker, L. E. 1993. When to fix it and when to leave: Relationships among perceived control, self-efficacy, dissent, and exit. *Journal of Applied Psychology,* 78: 949–959.

Pearce, J., Branyciki, I., & Bukacsi, G. 1994. Person-based reward systems: A theory of organizational reward practices in reform-communist organizations. *Journal of Organizational Behavior,* 15: 261–282.

Poortinga, Y. H., & Vijver, F. I. R., van. 1987. Explaining cross-cultural differences: Bias analysis and beyond. *Journal of Cross-Cultural Psychology,* 18: 259–282.

Roth, P. S., Switzer, F. S., Campion. J. E., & Jones. S.D. 1994. *The impact of missing data in criterion-related validation research.* Paper presented at the ninth annual conference of the Society of Industrial and Organizational Psychology, Nashville.

Sandelands, L. E., Bockner, J., & Glynn, M. A. 1988. If at first you don't succeed, try, try again: Effects of persistence-performance contingencies, ego involvement, and self-esteem on task persistence. *Journal of Applied Psychology,* 73: 208–216.

Schultz-Gambard, J., & Altschuh, E. 1993. Unterschiedliche Führungsstile im geeinten Deutschland [Different leadership styles in the unified Germany]. *Zeitschrift für Sozialpsychologie,* 24 (3): 167–175.

Seligman. M. E. P. 1975. *Learned helplessness.* San Francisco: Freeman.

Semmer, N. 1984. *Stressbezogene Tätigkeitsanalyse: Psychologische Untersuchungen zur Analyse von Stress am Arbeitsplatz* [Stress-oriented activity analysis: Psychological research on the analysis of stress at work]. Weinheim, Germany: Beltz.

Shama, A. 1993. Management under fire: The transformation of managers in the Soviet Union and Eastern Europe. *Executive,* 7 (1): 22–35.

Smith, C. A., Organ, D. W., & Near, J. P. 1983. Organizational citizenship behavior: Its nature and antecedents. *Journal of Applied Psychology,* 68: 653–663.

Speier, C., & Frese, M. 1996. *Self-efficacy as a mediator between resources at work and personal initiative: A longitudinal field study in East Germany.* Manuscript submitted for publication. University of Giessen, Germany.

Staw, B. M., & Boettger, R. D. 1990. Task revision: A neglected form of work performance. *Academy of Management Journal,* 33: 534–559.

Ulich, E. 1991. *Arbeitspsychologie* [Work psychology]. Stuttgart, Germany: Poeschel.

Wall, T. D., & Jackson, P. R. 1995. New manufacturing initiatives and shopfloor job design. In A. Howard (Ed.), *The changing nature of work:* 139–174. San Francisco: Jossey-Bass.

Webb, E. J., Campbell, D. T., Schwartz, R. D., & Sechrest, L. 1966. *Unobtrusive measures: Nonreactive research in the social sciences.* Chicago: Rand McNally.

Welsh, D. H. B., Luthans, F., & Sommer, S. M. 1993. Managing Russian factory workers: The impact of U.S.-based behavioral and participative techniques. *Academy of Management Journal,* 36: 58–79.

White, R. W. 1959. Motivation reconsidered: The concept of competence. *Psychological Review,* 66: 297–333.

Womack, J. P., Jones, D. T., Roos, D., & Carpenter, D. S. 1990. *The machine that changed the world.* New York: Rawson.

Wuppertaler Kreis (Ed.). 1992. *Führungsverständnis in Ost und West* [Leadership concepts in East and West]. Köln, Germany: Deutscher Wirtschaftsdienst.

Zapf, D. 1989. *Selbst- und Fremdbeobachtung in der psychologischen Arbeitsanalyse. Methodische Probleme bei der Erfassung von Stress* am *Arbeitsplatz* [Self- and expert observations in psychological job analysis. Methodological problems in the measurement of stress at work]. Gottingen, Germany: Hogrefe.

APPENDIX

INTERVIEW MEASURES

Quantitative and Qualitative Initiative at Work

1. During the last two years, did you submit suggestions to improve work?

2. During the last two years, did you go to see the boss, because there were problems in work?

3. Can you remember a situation during the last year in which you have searched for causes for something that did not function correctly?

4. Have you changed something in your work during the last year (e.g., the sequence of activities, added other activities, etc.)? (Prompts were used like "how many," "which ones," "explain in detail," "have you done this by yourself or have others helped you," "do you typically do this in your job"; each item was coded as to whether it constituted qualitative or quantitative initiative on five-point scales: 1 = very little [quantitative/qualitative] initiative, 5 = very much initiative.)

Education Initiative

1. Does the subject intend to participate in some continuing education in the future? (yes, no)

2. Has s/he done something concrete to accomplish this? (1 = no concrete steps undertaken, 2 = few concrete steps [e.g., asked a colleague but not an official institution], 3 = some concrete steps [e.g., application], 4 = precise time is fixed, 5 = participates at the moment)

3. Has s/he actually participated in some continuing education since the last interview? (1 = did not take part, 2 = low participation [has possibly taken a small course for a few days], 3 = middle, 4 = high participation [took a longer-term qualification or longer course], 5 = very high participation [e.g., has started longer requalification training or study])

4. Was it based on his or her own decision? (1 = company or unemployment agency demanded it, 2 = there was official demand but also interest by S, 3 = middle, 4 = there was an interest by S but also company interest, 5 = it was solely achieved by S even against resistance of company)

5. Longer-range plans for occupational future? (1 = no plans, 2 = abstract plans, 3 = middle, 4 = plans with a certain degree of concreteness, 5 = plans with a high degree of concreteness [e.g., application])

An overall mean cut-off point was taken and only answers higher than the mean were counted.

Interviewer Evaluation

1. Active/inactive interview-dialogue behavior
2. Behaves actively/passively
3. Will behave actively/passively in the future
4. Goal-oriented/easily gets diverted from goal
5. Motivated to act/would rather not do anything
6. Wants to act quickly/wants to postpone
7. Internally controlled/externally controlled
8. Independent/not independent
9. Achievement-oriented/achievement is unimportant
10. Ambitious/not ambitious

Overcoming Barriers

1. Pretend for a moment that you are dismissed from your job. What will you do?
2. Pretend for a moment you want to do some further education. What will you do?
3. Pretend for a moment your work colleague always does his/her work so sloppily that you have additional work to do. What do you do?
4. Pretend for a moment that you work as a blue-collar worker on a machine and this machine breaks down. What do you do?

Coding: Overcoming a barrier was only counted when it was clearly a different response from the last one (e.g., not another supervisor when first answer was supervisor); interviewer stopped developing new barriers after 3 or when S could not give an answer.

Active Approach

The following rating was done for each item in "overcoming barriers": S/he is active/passive. Coding criteria for active: overcoming barrier by own activity, not delegating to others.

Questionnaire

All of the questionnaire-based measures had a five-point answer scale, most of the form "not true at all" (1) to "very true" (5).[a]

---

[a] Actually there is a translation problem here—the German word *zutreffren* is not easily translated into English.

Self-Efficacy

1. When I am confronted with a new task, I am often afraid of not being able to handle it (re-coded).

2. I like to make suggestions on how to improve the work process.

3. I judge my abilities to be high.

4. If I want to achieve something, I can overcome setbacks without giving up my goal.

5. When I want to reach a goal, I am usually able to succeed.

6. In case I would become unemployed, I am convinced that, because of my abilities, I will soon find a new lob.

Control Rejection

1. I do only what I am told to do. Then nobody can reproach me for anything.

2. Work is easier if I am always told how to do it.

3. You only run into trouble, if you do something on your own.

4. I would rather be told exactly what I have to do. Then I make fewer mistakes.

5. I act according to the motto: I follow orders, then nobody is going to reproach me.

6. I have to think about too many things when I have to make decisions.

7. I'd rather have routine work.

8. I prefer to have a supervisor who tells me exactly what I have to do. Then he or she is at fault if something goes wrong.

9. I want to decide more things myself (recoded).

10. Work is more interesting, if one has to make many decisions (recoded).

Complexity of Work

1. Do you receive tasks that are extraordinary and particularly difficult? (1 = never, 5 several times a week)

2. A must make very complicated decisions in his/her work, B only has to make very simple decisions. (1 exactly like A, 5 = exactly like B)

3. Can you use all your knowledge and skills in your work? (1 = very little, 5 = very much)

4. Can you learn new things in your work? (1 = very little, 5 = very much)

Control at Work

The five-point answer scale for the following items was very little, rather little, somewhat, rather much, and very much:

1. If you look at your job as a whole: How many own decisions does it allow you to make?

2. Can you determine how you do your work?

3. Can you plan and arrange your work on your own (e.g., calculate, which material/tools you need)?

4. How much can you participate in decisions of your superior (e.g., the superior asks you for your opinion and asks for suggestions)?

Ganbatte: Understanding the Japanese Employee

Christopher B. Meek

Since the early 1970s, various research findings coming from Japan on employees' work attitudes and job commitment have been contradictory. Turnover statistics, absenteeism, participation rates in company improvement programs, strike statistics, and so on all seem to suggest that Japanese employees are, overall, highly satisfied with and committed to their jobs and the companies for which they work. Certainly most of the information that has become public in the English language seems to argue that Japanese employees should be highly motivated by and satisfied with their jobs. The unique conditions provided by their management techniques and their system of lifetime employment, with its extensive corporate welfare, should virtually guarantee job satisfaction.

However, comparative research has consistently produced quite different results when using attitude survey data to compare differences in job and workplace satisfaction across national boundaries. In study after study over three decades, Japanese employees have invariably recorded the lowest levels of job satisfaction of any industrialized nation—even when compared to respondents from some of the poorest developing countries of the world.

Behavioral science researchers have been hard put to explain these contradictions. In 1955, Brayfield and Crockett pointed out quite convincingly from years of research that high levels of job satisfaction do not necessarily result in highly motivated and hard-working employees. In Japan, data have conversely shown that hard-working, dedicated employees need not also be satisfied or happy workers. Moreover, with increasing numbers of cases being reported recently of Japanese workers and managers dying from overwork (a phenomenon known as *karoshi*), further evidence suggests that the link between employee performance and job satisfaction and commitment must be somewhat more complicated—unless, of course, one presumes that the Japanese love their work and their employers so much that they literally work themselves to death. Even more recently, the problem of supervisors and coworkers bullying their subordinates and peers in the workplace, known as *ijime,* has become a major social issue. It has resulted in extensive media coverage in Japan as well as numerous lawsuits of employees against their employers in the last decade. Given the emergence of these two developments, *karoshi* and *ijime,* Japanese workplace environments

Business Horizons, 1999, January–February, 27–36. Reprinted with permission.

must be considerably more hostile than the popular image of companies as large but closely knit families or clans, promulgated for years in both the academic and popular press.

COMPARATIVE FINDINGS ON EMPLOYEE RESPONSES TO JOB SATISFACTION SURVEYS

In the early 1970s, the Japanese government conducted a survey of attitudes among young adults between the ages of 18 and 24 in 11 different countries: France, the United Kingdom, West Germany, Switzerland, Sweden, Japan, the United States, the former Yugoslavia, India, the Philippines, and Brazil. Data were collected from a representative sample of 2,000 people in each nation. Of all these groups, the Japanese respondents showed the least job satisfaction of any group among the industrialized nations. Only 59.5 percent of the Japanese respondents expressed satisfaction with their jobs, compared to 82.4 percent of the U.S. sample and 85.6 percent of the U.K. sample. Another comparative study (Cole 1979) obtained similar findings from 567 auto workers in Detroit and 459 in Yokohama. Almost three-quarters of the Detroit workers said they would advise a friend to take a job with their current employer, compared to only 44 percent of the Yokohama workers. Similarly, 54 percent of the Detroit workers said they would go into the same kind of work if they had the opportunity to pursue their careers again, compared to only 33 percent of the Yokohama group.

In a study reported in Dore (1973), workers at Hitachi, one of Japan's largest manufacturing firms, and at Babcock and Marconi, two major British companies, were asked the question: "Generally speaking, would you say [your company] is a good firm to work for?" Only 39 percent of the Japanese respondents answered an unqualified "yes" to this question, compared to 71 percent of the Marconi workers and 89 percent of the Babcock employees.

Azumi and McMillan (1975), who surveyed workers at 12 plants in Japan, Great Britain, and Sweden, found that only 39 percent of the Japanese respondents expressed satisfaction with their jobs, compared to 70 percent of the British workers and 83 percent of the Swedish employees. One of the largest studies comparing the work attitudes of Japanese and American workers was conducted between 1981 and 1983. It involved the collection of survey data from 4,567 employees at 52 manufacturing plants in the United States and from 3,735 employees at 46 plants in Japan. The findings from this study are summarized in Table 1.

More recent research conducted during the early and mid-1990s has resulted in similar findings. A 1991 Louis Harris organization study (Arthur 1992) compared the work attitudes of executives and office employees in 15 different countries and found that only 17 percent of Japanese respondents reported they were very satisfied with their jobs, compared to 43 percent in the United States, 39 percent in Canada, 36 percent in the United Kingdom, and 34 percent in Germany. Moreover, some 65 percent of European office workers and 53 percent of U.S. office workers agreed that meeting their job goals was directly related to their personal life goals, in contrast to only 31 percent of the Japanese (Steelcase 1991). The most recent published comparative studies of job and work satisfaction were conducted in 1995 and 1998 in 36 different countries by International Survey Research, Ltd. (ISR). The Japanese sample came in dead last in 1995 and second to last in 1998 in terms of the percentage of employees who responded favorably to the question, "Taking everything into account, how satisfied are you with your company as a place to work?"

TABLE 1   **Employee Responses to Job Satisfaction Questions: Japan and the United States, 1981 to 1983**

Question	United States (n = 4,567) Mean	Japan (n = 3,735) Mean
All in all, how satisfied would you say you are with your job? (0=Not at all; 4=Very)	2.95	2.12
If a good friend of yours told you he or she was interested in working at a job like yours at this company, what would you say? (0=Would advise against it; 1=Would have second thoughts; 2=Would recommend it)	1.52	0.91
Knowing what you know now, if you had to decide all over again whether to take the job you now have, what would you decide? (0=Would not take it again; 1=Would have second thoughts; 2=Would take it again)	1.61	0.84
How much does your job measure up to the kind of job you wanted when you first took it? (0=Not what I wanted; 1=Somewhat; 2=What I wanted)	1.20	0.46
Overall Index	1.54	0.96

Source: Lincoln (1989).

PROPOSED EXPLANATIONS

Why do these hard-working, loyal, and dedicated Japanese workers appear to be so unhappy and dissatisfied with their work and careers? Cole (1979) argues that lower job satisfaction in Japan is the result of the high value the Japanese place on work activities and the high expectations they have for both themselves and the organizations for which they work. As he explains:

> Because Japanese workers are so highly committed to finding fulfillment in their work, they expect a good deal more from work and are therefore likely to display greater dissatisfaction when their expectations are not met. In short, high expectations vis-à-vis work may coexist with low job satisfaction.

The 1973 study of young adults conducted by the Japanese government seems to support this argument. On the question "Why do you think man works?" some 35 percent of the Japanese respondents answered "self-fulfillment," compared to about 14 percent of those in the U.K., 15 percent of the West Germans, 14 percent of the French, 15 percent of the Swedes, 24 percent of the Swiss, and 30 percent of the Americans. Slightly more than half of the Japanese sample selected "to earn money" as the answer to this same question, considerably below the samples from other industrialized nations. Other studies have produced similar results, but the level of job commitment expressed by Japanese respondents has not been consistently higher than that expressed by respondents from other countries in cross-national

TABLE 2 **Employee Commitment to the Company Community: A Comparison of Japanese and U.S. Workers by Percentage Distribution**

Question	U.S.	Japan
I think of my company as the central concern in my life and of greater importance than my personal life.	1	9
I think of the company as a part of my life at least equal in importance to my personal life.	22	57
I think of the company as a place for me to work with management, during work hours, to accomplish mutual goals.	54	26
I think of my company as strictly a place to work and entirely separate from my personal life.	23	8

Source: Whitehill and Takezawa (1968), p. 111.

studies. On the other hand, the average Japanese scores on job satisfaction questions in these same studies have invariably been much lower than the scores of their counterparts.

Perhaps the earliest study of this topic, conducted by Whitehill and Takezawa in the 1960s, may shed the greatest light on this puzzle. The researchers did not couch their questions in terms of job commitment, satisfaction, or happiness. Rather, they set out to determine the importance of *commitment to one's employer* in each respondent's life. They specifically focused their attention on the relationship between the employee and the company rather than directly on individuals' feelings about their specific jobs, their work assignments, or even their companies. Some of the most interesting findings from this study are presented in Table 2.

Japanese employees and managers are realistic about work and the demands they are required to face in their professional lives. Although they may wish their specific work could be interesting and fulfilling, they understand that for the long-term security of both themselves and the company, fulfilling and interesting work simply may not be possible all, or even most, of the time. Japanese employees accept the fact that on many occasions, their own individual interests and desires will be sacrificed to ensure the long-term survival and success of the whole. Inevitably, individual job assignments will change, perhaps often, because the business environment is turbulent and constantly in flux. With such frequently changing assignments to meet new needs and sometimes urgent crises, employees understand that some work may be difficult, unpleasant, and demand long, stressful hours. Still, the work must be done, and employees and managers are willing to endure these conditions with exceptional effort and diligence. To do so is not merely a matter of performing one's job, or fulfilling an economic obligation; it is a matter of *on* and *giri*—a very serious *moral obligation* to one's peers, superiors, and the company itself.

Japanese employees, then, can probably be more accurately characterized as highly committed to their duties, their corporate responsibilities, and their fellow workers than to their specific personal assignment or job at any given time. It would be unrealistic for most of them, especially managers and professional employees, to expect to be assigned work they usually find personally interesting and satisfying. Indeed, given the high rate of job transfers into new functional areas that most managerial employees experience throughout their careers, they must expend a great deal of time and effort learning new skills, new products, and new markets.

The mentality required to survive and function effectively in such a demanding work environment throughout one's life can be captured by a single word: *ganbatte*. The gerund form of the Japanese verb *ganbaru,* it means to endure, to not give up, to be patient and long-suffering, to continue a difficult or stressful task as long as it may be necessary to succeed, to try one's very best to accomplish something. It means simply to put up quietly and patiently with an uncomfortable or unpleasant situation (including an obnoxious coworker, a mean boss, or a difficult customer) without complaining or becoming openly angry (so as not to cause embarrassment, create social disharmony, or disturb others' feelings).

Before administering tests, teachers will often tell their students: "*Ganbatte kudasai*"— "Don't give up, try hard, and do your best!" This phrase, used in so many different contexts and heard many times throughout the day, seems to have become the general Japanese motto or philosophy of life. Friends, coworkers, or relatives commonly say *ganbatte* to each other when parting company, as if to acknowledge that the mere act of living requires a constant effort to endure.

Such an attitude has developed over many centuries in response to the harsh and often cruel life most Japanese people have endured. Peasant farmers have maintained a meager existence through continuous and arduous labor, often working from 3:00 or 4:00 A.M. until dark raising rice and other subsistence crops. The task of surviving requires the continuous help and cooperative effort of the extended kin group as well as the periodic sharing of labor and other resources between fellow villagers. Similarly, *ganbatte* was also an essential virtue among the samurai or warrior class, who constantly faced the task of defending their lords even to the death in inter-clan rivalries and battles. Throughout the process of rapid industrialization and economic development, this same characteristic has been an essential attitude. Today, such an outlook is internalized by Japanese youth from a very early age through the severe competition they must face in preparation for entrance exams—not only for college, but even for the entry levels of preschool and kindergarten.

The quid pro quo for accepting this life of continuous hard work, study, and struggle is complete and unconditional acceptance and support, both material and emotional, from one's primary social groups: first the family, and later the corporation. In return for *ganbaru,* the family and corporation offer all-encompassing social and emotional involvement. Indeed, parents teach their children from infancy to look toward their primary group as their ultimate source of support, security, and identification. Children are encouraged to engage in highly dependent behavior, such as constantly holding on to and being carried by their mothers, receiving food and attention immediately when they cry, and sleeping and bathing with their parents, siblings, and grandparents from the earliest years of infancy and well into adolescence. Table 3 offers a statistical summary from one study that illustrates traditional co-sleeping patterns in Japan. By experiencing such socialization processes, Japanese children quite naturally seek dependence and aid from their parents and older siblings. Such behavior is described by the verb *amaeru,* which means to seek the indulgence of another.

Dependence is cultivated not only by indulgent parental behavior, but also through the use of socialization techniques and disciplinary methods. The object is to create intense fear and distrust of people outside one's primary social group, as well as an extreme fear of being separated from or rejected by one's significant others. During the solar New Year's holiday,

TABLE 3   Percentage Distribution of Sleeping Arrangements by Age for 535 Japanese Children from Primary and Secondary Nuclear Families

Sleeping Arrangements	Age of Child						
	3–4 mos. (*n*=259)	1–5 Yrs. (*n*=103)	6–10 Yrs. (*n*=28)	11–15 Yrs. (*n*=28)	16–20 Yrs. (*n*=46)	21–25 Yrs. (*n*=38)	26+ Yrs. (*n*=33)
Two Generations	90	91	79	50	17	24	18
With Parent(s)	90	79	68	46	15	24	15
With Extended Kin	—	12	11	4	2	—	3
One Generation	2	7	11	36	46	40	33
With Sibling(s)	2	7	11	36	46	37	21
With Non-Related People	—	—	—	—	—	3	12
Alone	8	2	11	14	37	37	49

* All percentages do not total 100 because of rounding error. Source: Caudill and Plath (1966).

or *shougatsu,* in the rural Japanese villages of the Tohoku region of northern Japan, local men dress as demons in strange costumes and frightening masks. These characters, or *namahage,* stop at homes where young children reside, scaring the youngsters with their appearance and threatening to take them away if they are not respectful and obedient to their parents and elders. Although the children's terror is temporary and seen as humorous by household adults, the loud and clear message is that the outside is dangerous and to be feared. Similarly, when children do misbehave, it is most common to threaten them with separation from their family, such as by abandonment or kidnapping, rather than restricting their individual freedom, as is common in the West.

A similar disciplinary tactic is to physically lock children out of the house, leaving them to scream, cry, and bang on the door after saying that their continuing to live with the family is impossible without an apology and a repentant change in behavior. Fear of ridicule by and embarrassment before individuals and groups important to the child outside the family is also employed, both to change children's behavior and to increase their dependence on the family, especially the mother. As Lebra (1976) states:

> The third person thus plays a significant role in sensitizing the child to shame and embarrassment. The mother uses the third person not only as a verbal reference but as an audience present on the scene. The child learns the difference between the dyadic situation (with only himself and his caretaker) and the triadic situation (with a third person present as audience) in terms of freedom: he feels completely free in the dyad, inhibited in the triad. . . .
>
> Appeal for empathy is used in conjunction with embarrassment. It is not so much the child himself who is said to be the victim of embarrassment. It is the mother, father, or the family as a whole who will be laughed at by neighbors because of the child's misconduct. The mother tells the child that everybody will laugh at her; that his father will lose face at his company; or that the whole family be disgraced.

Thus, as a child grows, the lesson is clear that the right to be dependent—the right to *amaeru*—is conditional on *ganbaru,* both for the purpose of maintaining the family's good name and avoiding the possibility of ridicule and shame both inside and outside the family group. Full and unconditional support, both material and emotional, under all circumstances (including disaster and any severe economic downturn) must be returned by complete and unconditional loyalty to one's primary groups. This is done through hard work, conformity to group norms and standards, and a willingness to fulfill whatever task or duty is required, regardless of how difficult, painful, or odious.

I know such patterns of encouraging both dependence and dogged persistence still prevail today because of my own personal experience during 25 years of marriage to a Japanese woman with whom I have raised a family of six children. From the time of the birth of our first child we had a separate baby crib, but seldom, if ever, did any of our infants sleep in it. Instead, I endured years of semiconsciousness at work due to loss of sleep caused by the wriggling, tossing, and turning of our children in our bed, especially during their early years. Similarly, our first and most intense marital disagreements arose over the "right way" to discipline children. This began in the late 1970s, when my wife became particularly frustrated with the uncooperative and selfish behavior of our two oldest sons. One cold winter day during a snowstorm in upstate New York, she used the classic Japanese disciplinary pattern of briefly shutting the boys out of the house until they begged forgiveness and pledged to change their behavior.

As our family grew larger, when one child would severely misbehave or talk back, my wife would encourage the rest of the family members to "just ignore him" and "pretend he isn't even there." Even when visiting and staying with in-laws in Japan, the nurturing side of these practices for encouraging dependence through close physical contact became apparent when my eight-year-old nephew repeatedly begged me to take a bath with him and then doggedly pleaded with his parents to be able to sleep with my wife and me in their guest *tatame* room.

Thus, the relationship between family and family member, as well as between employee and employer, is truly a *social contract,* an emotionally powerful *moral agreement,* bound by filial piety and absolute loyalty in return for an unbreakable pledge of support. At the family level, the nature of this relationship is especially apparent as children reach college age and then marry. Parents will spend their life savings on sending their children to the best university possible, or giving them an expensive wedding ceremony—even making a substantial down payment on an apartment for them, if not actually purchasing it outright.

Never do parents shrink from such duties; nor do they tell their grown children that they are now adults and must completely support themselves financially. Indeed, being unable to help support one's children in their studies, work, or major purchases is considered shameful and a serious misfortune. Such parents would be considered very strange and quite inhuman beings. Likewise, the best companies, who employ the most talented and well-educated professionals and workers, traditionally have been required to provide a broad range of generous financial and social support. Such a boon goes along with a system that encourages a strong sense of common identity and association with both the company and fellow employees.

Rohlen (1974) illustrates the comparability of the parent-child and employer-employee relationships, as well as the very powerful and emotional manner in which the two are linked together. He describes the *nyukoshiki,* an entrance ceremony conducted for new white collar employees, at the bank where he worked as an employee and participant-observer:

Representing the rest of the bank, [the president] expresses gratitude that such a fine group of young people are joining the organization. . . . They are now *shakaijin,* "adult members of society," he says. This means they have heavy responsibilities to serve the society and thus to repay it and their parents for the nurture and sacrifice of raising them from infancy. His tone grows more impassioned as he proceeds to outline the seriousness of working for the bank. . . .

Finally, addressing the parents, he promises to take responsibility for their children, to educate and care for them, so they may continue to grow as *shakaijin.* . . . The representative of the parents [then] expresses the parents' pleasure with the company their children are joining and offers their good wishes for its success. . . . He requests that the bank discipline and guide their offspring, who are "yet immature and naive." The parents have brought them this far, he says; it is now the bank which must continue their upbringing.

A young graduate selected from among the new recruits as their spokesperson then delivers a formal address to the employer and the parents, pledging to honor this new commitment:

We regard the bank as our life and our career. We are committed to battle with all our strength under the banner and spirit of "harmony" and "strength." We will trust and aid each other as we face the difficulties before us. We will take our responsibilities seriously, and feel joy in the bank's good name. We are young and as yet spiritually and technically underdeveloped. We ask our seniors to lead and educate us, for we know it is imperative that we become hardy and brave Uedagin men, possessing a spirit of devotion and capacity for sharp and effective action.

Such a ceremony is a clear and symbolically powerful mechanism. The parents transfer part of their duty to their children on to an employer—or, conversely, the duties of child to parent are superimposed on the employee-employer relationship—immediately after graduation from college.

Given this *social contract,* it is not surprising that the concept of lifetime employment, the *nenko* system, was adopted at top Japanese companies in the years following WWII. Similarly, it is also logical that Japanese companies have come to provide a large number of activities, programs, commemorative gifts, and special allowances to their permanent employees as a matter of standard practice. Without these support systems, it would be impossible to solicit the high level of effort and loyalty Japanese firms receive from their employees. Though they have little direct relationship to actual behavioral performance, the systems encourage a strong sense of camaraderie and moral duty among fellow workers.

Researchers who have studied the intensity and frequency of close friendships among coworkers in Japanese and U.S. manufacturing firms, according to Lincoln (1989), have found that Japanese respondents reported an average of two or more close friends at work, compared to an average of fewer than one person for the Americans. These friendships have beneficial consequences in terms of overall organizational performance. First, with more and stronger friendships at work, Japanese employees are more likely to find their coworkers willing to jump in and help when they are in need of assistance, or to cooperate with them on a project. Second, normal people feel a much stronger sense of social obligation to do their best and not disappoint their coworkers and superiors if they share close and supportive socio-emotional relationships.

On the other hand, there can also be a distinctly dark side to this mixture of strong moral duties and extreme levels of social, psychological, and economic dependence. Because of the absolute duty to *ganbaru,* the more an individual demonstrates a willingness to make personal sacrifices for the company, the greater becomes his recognized value and virtue as an employee and a person. Japanese employees, especially managers and executives, often go to great lengths to demonstrate to others how much hardship they are willing to endure in their work responsibilities. They strive to show how completely they are committed to adhering to the norm of always putting work and the company first before family and personal interests. Indeed, to fail to demonstrate one's commitment to these norms can result in grave consequences. As Okamura and Kawahito (1990) state:

> In Japanese corporations, making a contribution to the company through long working hours is one of the prerequisites for advancement. Employees who don't work overtime or who often take their allotted paid vacation days are evaluated negatively. If such negative behavior continues, it results in a slowing of one's advancement within the company as well as a large salary gap compared to [one's] peers. Some workers even find themselves being fired for refusing to work overtime.

Such an attitude has become deeply embedded in Japanese society and the Japanese psyche over many centuries. Strikingly similar observations about the link between virtue and personal sacrifice, and the excruciating demands for self-sacrifice required just to ensure survival, existed even during the feudal era. Given such conditions, and the world view they have helped produce over so many generations, Japan's corporate culture has become an atmosphere in which it is perceived to be almost shameful if one does not appear to be struggling, even suffering, under the weight of heavy work responsibilities. Dr. Misao Miyamoto, a Japanese-born but U.S.-trained psychiatrist, was shocked when he encountered such norms, even in government service, while employed as an official in the Ministry of Health:

> These days an increasing number of people are taking longer vacations, but when you look at the bureaucracy, big corporations or major banks, it is still rare to see people taking two or three weeks' vacation. . . .
>
> I was flabbergasted when I heard one of my superiors on his retirement day proudly announce that he had not taken any vacation time during his entire career. If he were to take his entire accumulated vacation time, he would have been entitled to two years off. He didn't receive any compensation for not using his vacation days. (Miyamoto 1995)

Of course, even in the West one occasionally finds people like this, but they tend to be rare. In the case of the Japanese, such a mentality is the norm. Few employees, and virtually no managers or executives, ever take even a major portion of their official allotted vacation time.

The broad impact of such a normative climate on the overall physical and emotional conditions of working in Japan is serious. First, it is possible for employees to be easily pressed into performing ever more difficult and onerous work with virtually no upper limit on what can be expected and demanded of them. Second, even when employees feel they are being pushed beyond their physical and mental limits, they really have little power to either request or demand a reduction in work load or an improvement in working conditions.

To suffer willingly for the company is seen as virtuous. But to complain and demand a reduction in one's work burden—or worse, to refuse to perform assigned work or a superior's directive—is a sign of self-centeredness and weak character. Most Japanese, faced with strenuous or demanding work requirements, choose the road of suffering in quiet resignation while they diligently, if not enthusiastically, comply with the demands placed on their shoulders.

During periods of acute economic stress, these tendencies become even more pronounced. Employees become trapped in a vicious circle, with the company steadily increasing its demands. They inevitably respond by working harder and putting in longer hours, only to find that the level of effort once recognized as making a sacrifice has now become the new standard for normal job performance. Thus, innovations such as the *kanban* system and *kaizen* are a natural extension of this mentality and situation. But their impact on individual employees is not always appreciated as working hours lengthen, vacation time is cut, and the general pace of work and level of stress escalate. A group of manufacturing engineers and workers from one of Japan's largest electronics firms told me during an informal discussion outside the factory after working hours, "If you really want to know the truth, JIT and *kaizen* are terrible. These systems can make life a living hell on earth."

IMPLICATIONS

As we can see, motivation and authority relations in Japanese society tend to function on the basis of a very different set of principles and logic than is normally the case in the West. These principles were perhaps first outlined and most clearly articulated by French sociologist Marcel Mauss in his 1926 classic analysis of social exchange in primitive and traditional societies, the *Essai sur le don (The Gift)*. Through comparative analysis of ethnographic and historical studies, Mauss found that in so-called primitive tribal societies and traditional subsistence-based agrarian societies, material and social exchanges tend to be conducted primarily on the basis of the *logic of the gift*. Hence, some social scientists and historians have since described such societies as *gift-based* or *moral economies*.

Bronislaw Malinowski vividly illustrated these societies in his early twentieth-century field studies of life among the Trobriand Islanders. In such cultures, he wrote, the most important social and economic relations on which individuals and groups depend for their survival and well-being are conducted on the basis of reciprocal giving and receiving of material goods and labor. The parties exchange these gifts instead of engaging in bargaining behavior or market exchange. Such gift-giving ranged from what Malinowski (1922) described as "the extreme case of pure gift, that is, an offering for which nothing is given in return," between extended family and kin group members, to the reciprocal and balanced exchange of gifts between neighbors and more distant kin, to the least frequent case of purely competitive cases of barter or market exchange that normally take place between strangers.

In a gift-giving society, the objectives of the parties involved, and the motivations that underlie their interactions, differ greatly from those involving barter or market exchange. As Gregory (1982) explains, superior wealth and status are not achieved in such societies through direct pursuit of profits in transactions with others, or through sharp practice. Instead, they are attained on the basis of who has given and shared their resources, material and social, with the greatest generosity to the largest number of individuals and groups. States Gregory:

> The gift transactor's motivation is precisely the *opposite* of the capitalist's: whereas the latter maximizes net incomings, the former maximizes net outgoings. The aim of the capitalist is to *accumulate profit* while the aim of the . . . gift transactor is to *acquire a large following of people* (gift-debtors) who are obligated to him. [emphasis added]

In many respects, this is precisely the logic on which traditional parent-child and employer-employee relationships have been based in Japan. Hard work, dedication, and loyalty are generated by feelings of gratitude and obligation toward the parent or employer for protection, support, and care. Parents are generous and long-suffering for their children; in return, children engage in *ganbaru* in their efforts at school, in their careers, and in family life. They do so not only because of the deep sense of gratitude they feel toward parents and employers, but also because of the severe feelings of guilt and shame they would experience if they failed to make every effort possible to live up to their parents' and employers' hopes and dreams. Behavior is not motivated by the pursuit of extrinsic rewards or love and approval. It comes from a profound feeling of indebtedness, strengthened by the extent to which the person's identity is inextricably enmeshed with the family or company. It also comes from the fear that behaving in a less than grateful and appreciative manner might ultimately lead to separation and social isolation.

This article is not intended to serve as one more among the myriad treatises already available on the "secrets" of Japanese management. Instead, it represents a sincere effort at making sense of some rather consistent yet puzzling research findings, repeated over and over again in attitude surveys spanning nearly 30 years. If my analysis is correct, we need to rethink our ideas about organization, employee attitudes, and job performance. Our Western approach to job satisfaction and motivation may be entirely appropriate in our cultural environment, where social institutions and individual attitudes are vastly different from those of Japan.

Japanese employees expect so much more from their employers, but they are also willing to settle for so much less from their individual jobs, enduring 14-hour work days and often such incredible task demands that every year many managers die from *karoshi*. Moreover, the nature of the employment relationship in Japan, and the social and moral basis for its many years of success, may be instructive far beyond the borders of the Japanese isles. The employer-employee relationship in many other late-developing nations may, when most positive and successful, also rely on a gift rather than a market economy logic to stimulate employee commitment, dedication, and motivation.

Although many aspects of the traditional Japanese "social contract" hardly seem appealing by Western work standards, in this recent era of continual corporate downsizing and restructuring it might seem much more attractive than it would have in the past. Certainly the 40,000 or so employees who only a few years ago lost their jobs in the restructuring of AT&T, as well as the additional 20,000 most recently slated for downsizing, might agree. Nevertheless, faced with a strong yen since the late 1980s until just the end of this past year, many Japanese employers have found it increasingly more difficult to remain true to the promises of lifetime employment and providing an ever-rising standard of living.

Only one major company has attempted using an "American-style layoff" to downsize the work force in an attempt to adapt to the problem of higher costs and shrinking market share. That firm was Pioneer, and it nearly lost all of its customers, suppliers, and sources of finance in Japan because it took these actions. On the other hand, many Japanese employers have recently begun to hire even new college graduates strictly on the basis of short-term, three-year contracts in the beginning.

If such practices expand and persist, the underlying logic on which perhaps the world's most loyal and hard-working industrial work force and managerial elite have been motivated to dedicate their lives to their companies will surely he undermined rapidly. Moreover, a tremendous mismatch will exist between the socialization and educational processes through which Japanese youth mature and the working environment into which they will he thrust upon graduation from high school or college.

Although the traditions and worldview of the Japanese people derive from Shinto, Buddhism, and neo-Confucianism, the Japanese economy succeeded in its formative years largely because it failed to accept Western liberal economic doctrine in its entirety. It retained instead the policies and precepts of the *moral economy* that were thrown off in Europe and the United States during the eighteenth and nineteenth centuries. Long has this strategy served the Japanese people and their nation well; now, in the 1990s, it has begun to unravel. Whether or not Japanese employees and their managers can continue following in this path—whether they can *ganbaru* and endure together as in the past—is an important question that has yet to he answered. Many Japanese managers and workers hope it will he answered in the affirmative, for they have not yet given up hope that their system can be saved and avoid breaking loose entirely from its traditional moral underpinnings.

One young manager and his colleagues strongly protested such a scenario. During an interview at a division of one of Japan's largest steel companies, I asked them if they didn't think that to stay competitive in the world market their firm would eventually have to adopt the U.S. system and just lay people off, instead of carrying the heavy economic burden of keeping them on or dispatching them to work for subcontractors with guaranteed wages and benefits until retirement. In a response that was strong, emotionally charged, and surprising in its logic, they exclaimed, "We don't believe we should have to abandon our commitment to our members who have devoted so many years of service and sacrifice to the company. As of yet we have no proof that your capitalism, American capitalism, is the true capitalism!"

References

C. Arthur, "Working Is Worse in Japan," *American Demographics,* May 1992, p. 16.

Koya Azumi and Charles J. McMillan, "Culture and Organization Structure: A Comparison of Japanese and British Organizations," *Studies of Management and Organization, 35,* 1(1975): 201–218.

Koya Azumi and Charles J. McMillan, "Worker Sentiments in the Japanese Factory: Its Organizational Determinants," in Lewis Austin (ed.), *Japan: The Paradox of Progress* (New Haven, CT: Yale University Press, 1976): 215–229.

Harumi Befu, "Gift-Giving and Social Reciprocity in Japan," *France-Asie/Asia, 21,* 2 (1967): 161–177.

Harumi Befu, "Gift Giving in Modernizing Japan," *Monumenta Nipponica, 23,* 3–4 (1968): 445–456.

Ruth Benedict, *The Chrysanthemum and the Sword* (Boston: Houghton-Mifflin, 1946).

Arthur H. Brayfield and Walter H. Crockett, "Employee Attitudes and Employee Performance," *Psychological Bulletin, 52,* 5 (1955): 396–428.

William Caudill and David Plath, "Who Sleeps by Whom? Parent-Child Involvement in Urban Japanese Families," *Psychiatry, 29,* 4 (1966): 344–366.

William Caudill and Helen Weinstein, "Maternal Care and Infant Behavior in Japan and America," *Psychiatry, 32,* 1 (1969): 12–43.

David Cheal, "Strategies of Resource Management in Household Economies: Moral Economy or Political Economy?" in Richard R. Wilk (ed.), *The Household Economy: Reconsidering the Domestic Mode of Production* (Boulder, CO: Westview Press, 1989): 11–22.

Robert E. Cole, *Japanese Blue Collar: The Changing Tradition* (Berkeley, CA: University of California Press, 1971).

Robert E. Cole, *Work, Mobility, and Participation* (Berkeley, CA: University of California Press, 1979).

George A. DeVos, *Socialization for Achievement: Essays on the Cultural Psychology of the Japanese* (Berkeley, CA: University of California Press, 1973).

Takeo Doi, *The Anatomy of Dependence* (Tokyo: Kodansha, 1973).

Ronald Dore, *British Factory-Japanese Factory* (Berkeley, CA: University of California Press, 1973).

Ronald Philip Dore, *Taking Japan Seriously A Confucian Perspective on Leading Economic Issues* (Stanford, CA: Stanford University Press, 1987).

Linda Grant, "Unhappy in Japan," *Fortune,* January 13, 1997, p.142.

C.A. Gregory, *Gifts and Commodities* (London: Academic Press, 1982).

Mikiso Hane, *Peasants, Rebels, and Outcastes: The Underside of Modern Japan* (New York: Pantheon, 1982).

ISR, *Attitudes of Japanese Employees: Some Surprises and Some Explanations* (Chicago: International Survey Research, Ltd., 1995).

ISR, 1998 correspondence with William E. Werhane, Executive Director of Global Services.

Toshio Jo, "Cries for Help from the Office Floor," *Asahi Evening News,* "Life" sect., June 6,1996, pp. 5–6.

Etsuko Hae-Jin Kang, *Diplomacy and Ideology in Japanese-Korean Relations: From the Fifteenth to the Eighteenth Century* (New York: St. Martin's Press, 1997).

Kanri Shoku Union and Nippon Rodobengodan, *Kaisha o Yameru Chichi Kara Kaisha ni Hairu Musuko-Musumetachi e* ("A Lesson from the Fathers Who Are Quitting the Company to the Sons and Daughters Who are Entering the Company") (Tokyo: Kyoiku Shiryoo Shupan Kai, 1994).

W. Dean Kinzley, *Industrial Harmony in Modern Japan: The Invention of a Tradition* (London: Routledge, 1991).

Takie Sugiyama Lebra, *Japanese Patterns of Behavior* (Honolulu, HI: University of Hawaii Press, 1976).

James R. Lincoln, "Employee Work Attitudes and Management Practices in the U.S. and Japan: Evidence from a Large Comparative Survey," *California Management Review, 32,* 1 (1989): 89–106.

James R. Lincoln and Arne L. Kalleberg, "Work Organization and Workforce Commitment: A Study of Plants and Employees in the U.S. and Japan," *American Sociological Review, 50,* 6 (1985): 738–760.

Bronislaw Malinowski, *Argonauts of the Western Pacific* (London: Routledge, Kegan Paul, 1922).

Marcel Mauss, *The Gift* (New York: W.W. Norton Co., Inc., 1967).

Masao Miyamoto, "Envy and Bullying/*Ijime:* The Core of Harmony in Japan," paper presented at the Japan Society, February 9, 1995, New York.

Chie Nakane, *Japanese Society* (Berkeley, CA: University of California Press, 1970).

Atsushi Naoi and Carmi Schooler, "Occupational Conditions and Psychological Functioning in Japan, *American Journal of Sociology, 90,* 4(1985): 729–751.

NHK (Nippon Hoso Kyokai, Japan Broadcasting Network), *"Ijime* in the Workplace," 1-hr. television documentary, June 29, 1997.

NHK, short cultural tradition segment from Shougatsu celebrations in Japan, January 1, 1998.

Kunio Odaka, *Toward Industrial Democracy: Management and Workers in Modern Japan* (Cambridge, MA: Harvard University Press, 1975).

Office of the Prime Minister of Japan, *Sekai Seinen Ishiki Chosa Hokokusho* ("Report on the World Youth Attitude Survey") (Tokyo: Youth Policy Office, 1973).

Chikanobu Okamura and Hiroshi Kawahito, *Karoshi: When the Corporate Warrior Dies* (Tokyo: Mado-Sha, 1990).

William G. Ouchi, "Markets, Bureaucracies, and Clans," *Administrative Science Quarterly 25,*1 (1980) 129–141.

Thomas P. Rohlen, *For Harmony and Strength: Japanese White-Collar Organization in Anthropological Perspective* (Berkeley, CA: University of California Press, 1974).

Thomas C. Smith, "Peasant Time and Factory Time in Japan," *Past and Present, 111* (1986): 165–197.

Social Policy Bureau, Economic Planning Agency, *Scenarios, 1990 Japan* (Tokyo: Japan Government Printing Office, 1981).

Sally Solo, "Japan's Unhappy Auto Workers," *Fortune,* October 22, 1990, pp. 10–11.

Steelcase, Inc., *World Office Environment Index Full Report: Canada* (Grand Rapids, Ml: 1991).

E. P. Thompson, *Customs in Common* (New York: New Press, 1993).

E. P. Thompson, "The Moral Economy of the English Crowd in the Eighteenth Century," *Past and Present, 50* (1971): 76–136.

Ezra F. Vogel and Suzanne H. Vogel, "Family Security, Personal Immaturity, and Emotional Health in a Japanese Sample," *Marriage and Family Living, 23,* 2 (1961): 161–166.

Arthur M. Whitehill and Shinichi Takezawa, *The Other Worker: A Comparative Study of Industrial Relations in the U.S. and Japan* (Honolulu: East-West Center Press, 1968).

Chapter **Eight**

The Role of Individual Differences in Work Motivation

On one level of analysis, the study of work motivation is also the study of individual differences. After all, individuals in the workplace can differ markedly and frequently respond in very different ways to the motivational efforts of their supervisors and coworkers. Some people readily respond to certain incentives, while others do not. For example, some people are principally motivated by money or promotion, while others are motivated by a challenging job or assignment. Still others seem largely unmoved by either of these. Some people are heavily influenced by their peers, while others seem to march to their own drum and are largely oblivious to the opinions and pressures of those around them. Some people work best in groups, while others work best alone. These individual differences make the workplace both an interesting and a frustrating place for managers.

The study of individual differences is typically divided into two areas: personality and ability. *Personality* can be defined as the relatively enduring ways in which people think, feel, believe, and behave. Personality has been shown to influence such factors as career choice, job satisfaction, stress, leadership style, and some aspects of job performance.

There are many ways to conceptualize personality. The most popular approach is to focus on what has been called the "big five" personality traits. These are thought to be the most important personality differences that affect our behavior. They include: (1) extraversion, a predisposition to experience positive emotional states—and not to be confused with extroversion; (2) neuroticism, a tendency to experience negative emotional states, feel depressed, and generally view themselves and the world around them negatively; (3) agreeableness, an ability to get along with others; (4) conscientiousness, a drive for perfection in one's activities; and (5) openness to experience, an inquisitiveness about life in general that often leads to new experiences and a willingness to take risks. Taken together, these five traits can be useful in differentiating between, and hopefully better understanding, various employees and their motives in the workplace.

In addition to the so-called "big five" personality traits, other personal characteristics can influence work behavior in important ways. These include: (1) locus of control, a belief that either an individual (internal) or external factors are the principal cause of events; (2) self-esteem, a feeling of self-worth and confidence in one's abilities; (3) self-monitoring, the manner in which people try to present themselves to others; and (4) type A personality, an intense sense of urgency and drive to achieve that often leads to stress and heart disease. Finally, we can also distinguish individuals based on certain need strengths, such as the need for achievement, affiliation, and power.

By contrast, *ability* refers to what a person is capable of doing. In the workplace, the two general types of ability are salient: cognitive abilities and physical abilities. Cognitive abilities include verbal ability, numerical ability, reasoning ability, deductive ability, perceptual ability, and spatial ability. Physical abilities include such factors as basic motor skills (that is, the ability to manipulate objects) and physical skills (such as one's fitness and strength).

OVERVIEW OF THE READINGS

The readings that follow all build on these fundamental concepts. First, Charles O'Reilly III and Jennifer Chatman examine the importance of working harder compared to working smarter in a study of the effects of motivation and ability on a sample of recently graduated MBAs. They postulate that early career performance was largely attributed to a combination of general cognitive abilities and work motivation. MBAs who were both smarter and worked harder were more successful in their job search upon graduation, earned higher salaries, received more rapid pay raises, and received more promotions during their early careers. The authors conclude that enduring individual characteristics continue to represent important factors in predicting successful managerial behavior.

Then, Anthony Pilegge and Rolf Holtz examine the effects of social identification with coworkers on self-set goals and task performance for individuals who are either high or low in self-esteem. In their study, they found that only individuals with both high self-esteem and strong social identity with a group set higher goals for themselves and achieved higher performance compared to individuals who exhibited only one of these two key traits. The authors conclude that their results emphasize the catalytic effects of social identification with coworkers on high self-esteem individuals.

References

Barrick, M. R., and Mount, M. K. (1991). The big five personality dimensions and performance: A meta-analysis. *Personnel Psychology,* 44, 1–26.

Digman, J. M. (1990). personality structure: emergence of the five-factor model. *Annual Review of Psychology,* 41, 417–440.

George, J. (1992). The role of personality in organizational life: Issues and evidence. *Journal of Management,* 18, 185–213.

Working Smarter and Harder: A Longitudinal Study of Managerial Success

Charles A. O'Reilly III
Jennifer A. Chatman

In the past several years, organizational researchers have engaged in a rather artificial debate about the extent to which individual differences or dispositions predict job outcomes such as attitudes and behaviors (e.g., Davis-Blake & Pfeffer, 1989). While the debate is provocative, a careful examination indicates that there may be less substance to this debate than it seems. By now, most organizational researchers acknowledge the fundamental importance of situational effects, the existence of stable individual differences, and their interaction as causes of behavior (Wright & Mischel, 1987; Chatman, 1989). The controversy lies in questions about the usefulness of measuring dispositions that are sometimes poorly specified and lack reliability and validity, the absence of well-developed theoretical justifications for constructs for given situations, and the frequent use of cross-sectional research designs that do not permit adequate longitudinal testing of clearly specified hypotheses (e.g., Weiss & Adler, 1984).

It is clear that poorly designed studies of dispositions exist, but some stable individual differences may predict important attitudes and behavior. Intelligence, or general cognitive ability (GCA), has a long, well-documented history of research that reliably predicts important organizational outcomes such as job performance and career success (e.g., House, Howard, and Walker, 1992). Hunter (1986, p. 340) reported a review of "hundreds of studies showing that general cognitive ability predicts job performance in all jobs." The predictive ability of GCA increases for jobs or situations that require increased information processing. This is consistent with Wright and Mischel's (1987) competency-demand hypothesis, which implies that people with more general cognitive ability are likely to perform better in cognitively demanding situations. General cognitive ability predicts performance across jobs, settings, and careers (Gottfredson, 1986; Dreher & Bretz, 1991; Schmidt, Ones, & Hunter, 1992).

Personality researchers have largely ceased to be concerned with the idea of a pure trait or dispositional approach, however, and widely agree that behavior is a function of both individual and situational factors. Kenrick and Funder (1988, p. 31) reviewed the person-situation debate and concluded that "As with most controversies, the truth finally appears to lie not in the vivid black or white of either extreme, but somewhere in the less striking gray area." Situations may affect people, while people may affect situations and maintain distinctive personal styles across situations (Schneider, 1987).

There are several problems here for organizational researchers. First, intelligence or general cognitive ability is a construct that most organizational scholars have not investigated. Instead of building on the massive evidence for the efficiency of GCA as a predictor of job-related outcomes, researchers have pursued other, less well-defined dispositional constructs (Gerhardt, 1987). This has led some experts to raise the obvious question, "If the

From *Administrative Science Quarterly,* 1999, 39, 603–627. Reprinted by permission.

predominance of the *g* [general cognitive ability] factor has been apparent to many if not most psychologists ever since mental tests were invented, why should so much time, energy, and creativity have been invested in the attempt to identify and measure more limited abilities?" (Tyler, 1986, p. 446).

Second, some of the earliest models of human performance (e.g., Heider, 1958) suggested an interactional approach, using ability and motivation, of the type called for in recent articles (e.g., Chatman, 1989). Campbell (1976, p. 64), observed that in industrial and organizational psychology, performance is a function of the interaction between ability and motivation. Pinder (1984), in his review of the motivation literature, made a similar observation and noted that it may be that high levels of one component compensate for low levels of the other. This general approach is the basis for expectancy models of motivation that conceptualize performance as the interaction between ability and effort. Motivation is a person's willingness to expend effort and persist at an activity, while ability is a person's capacity to perform certain tasks. Motivation and ability are both necessary, but neither alone may be sufficient for high levels of performance. A highly motivated person may lack critical abilities for success, while a person with ability may lack the motivation to succeed.

More recent research has refined both of these constructs. Ability, at its most global level, can be thought of as general cognitive ability or the underlying general mental abilities that are expressed in the differential performance of individuals on a class of tasks that require cognitive information processing (e.g., Carroll, 1992). This general cognitive ability, or "*g*," is common to all types of cognitive processing, such as verbal, spatial, numerical, reasoning, and musical performance and appears to be based on underlying neural processes. Motivation has often been characterized as a stable, general trait, labelled "conscientiousness," that varies across individuals (Goldberg, 1993) and reflects attributes such as dependability, attention to detail, carefulness, and responsibility. People who are highly conscientious are hardworking, persevering, organized, and achievement oriented (McCrae & Costa, 1987).

Given the evidence for the importance of general cognitive ability and motivation as stable individual differences and predictors of performance in organizations (e.g., Hunter, 1986; Barrick & Mount, 1991; Carroll, 1992) and the long tradition in industrial psychology of conceptualizing performance as the interaction of motivation and ability (e.g., Ackerman & Humphreys, 1990), it is surprising that there is so little empirical research testing this parsimonious and intuitively appealing proposition. The purpose of this study is to test the interaction of conscientiousness and general cognitive ability as predictors of early career success among a cohort of recent Masters of Business Administration (MBA) graduates.

GENERAL COGNITIVE ABILITY AND JOB PERFORMANCE

In 1986 the *Journal of Vocational Behavior* devoted an issue to a controversial topic: the "*g*" factor in employment, "*g*" referring to general mental or cognitive ability as characterized by Spearman (1927). In this issue, a number of eminent psychologists addressed a question that has been largely absent from the industrial psychological literature for the past two decades: What is the association between intelligence and job performance? Several factors make this issue both important and provocative. First, up through the 1950s, the use of intelligence or general cognitive ability tests was common in employment. Harrell (1992), for instance, reported that the military used a general mental ability test to classify over 12 million people. During the next decade, [it] fell out of favor, due to criticisms that these tests were discriminatory and invalid (Cronbach, 1975). Ironically, as Hunter (1986) and Gottfredson (1986) showed, there are hundreds of empirical studies showing that general cognitive ability (GCA) predicts performance for a wide variety of jobs. It appears that psychologists shifted their attention away from the construct of GCA for reasons other than its conceptual importance and empirical ability to predict performance.

Some argued forcefully that intelligence and aptitude tests could not predict occupational success or other important life outcomes but that "competencies" might (e.g., McClelland, 1973). But as Barrett and Depinet (1991, p. 1021) demonstrated, after a careful review of both the empirical evidence and the criticisms of the construct, ". . . McClelland and his associates have not yet been able to produce any professionally acceptable empirical evidence that their concept of competencies is related to occupational success." And Gottfredson (1986, p. 330) concluded that "'*g*' emerges as the single most useful worker attribute for predicting job performance, as a valid predictor in all types of jobs, and is an especially valid predictor of performance in more complex and higher level jobs."

The evidence linking GCA and job performance is impressive. Ree and Earles (1991a) studied over 78,000 air force enlistees across 82 jobs and concluded that a measure of general intelligence (*g*) was the best predictor of success in job training, and measures of specific abilities were not needed to increase predictive power. Nathan and Alexander (1988) showed that GCA validly predicts outcomes such as supervisory ratings and rankings, work samples, and production quality and quantity. Campbell (1990), summarizing a $25 million army study, also reported that core job performance was best predicted by general cognitive ability, with other predictors adding only small increments in validity. In a longitudinal study of over 13,000 high school graduates, Austin and Hanisch (1990, p. 83) found that after 11 years elapsed, general cognitive ability "appears to be an overriding force in determining the upper endpoint of an individual's choice of occupation. . . ." These and other studies (e.g., Howard, 1986; Schmidt, Hunter, & Outerbridge, 1986) repeatedly demonstrated the importance of GCA in predicting job performance and occupational attainment.

In examining how GCA might produce these effects, Schmidt and his colleagues (Hunter, 1986; Schmidt et al., 1988) demonstrated that higher levels of GCA enabled job incumbents to acquire important job knowledge. This increased knowledge, in turn, leads to improved performance. And, while job experience may also lead to increased job knowledge and performance, because GCA effects are independent, experience cannot compensate for GCA (Schmidt et al., 1988). When people have the same work experience, GCA differences become a critical element in determining individual differences in performance. Schmidt and Hunter (1992, p. 92) concluded that "the central determining variables in job performance may be general mental ability, job experience (i.e., opportunity to learn), and a broad trait of conscientiousness." These characteristics can lead to large and economically significant improvements in output.

GCA becomes an even more critical determinant of performance when the job demands are themselves more complex. Schmidt and Hunter (1992, p. 92), reported that "On a typical lower level job (i.e., an unskilled job), a worker at the 85th percentile in performance produces about 20% more than the average worker. . . . For professional and managerial jobs, it is about 48%." When Arvey (1986) arrayed jobs along a general cognitive ability dimension, he found that higher-level jobs, such as those held by managers, required increased cognitive abilities, including the ability to recall job-related information, identify situations quickly, and adapt and rapidly learn new procedures. Over time, this may lead to more rapid mastery of jobs and higher rates of career advancement, manifest in more promotions and higher salary levels (Rosenbaum, 1979; Howard, 1986). Thus, a large body of evidence suggests the potential importance of GCA as a predictor of job performance in general and, insofar as management jobs require complex information processing, managerial success in particular.

General Cognitive Ability: The Construct

The general notion that people might vary in intelligence or general cognitive ability was first formally proposed by Sir Francis Galton. Spearman (1927) refined the concept by specifying that intelligence comprises two kinds of mental abilities: a general ability (referred to as *g*) and specific mental abilities (referred to as *s*). General ability (*g*) is required for the performance of virtually all higher-level tasks involving complex information processing. Specific abilities (*s*) are required for the performance of specific single tasks. This theory has led to 70 years of empirical research examining both the differential aspects of mental abilities across individuals and, more recently, research into the information processing associated with variations in mental abilities (Sternberg, 1979).

But what is "*g*"? A sample of individuals will vary in how well they do on any task or pursuit that makes demands on mental effort. When results of a number of tests, all of which require cognitive ability, are aggregated, some common underlying differences in performance will emerge. The source of this variance is referred to as *g*, the general factor underlying individual differences in performance. As such, *g* cannot be described in terms of a particular type of test content, knowledge, or skill, and no actual test measures it exclusively. The most *g*-loaded tests, such as IQ tests, involve relatively complex information processing, such as abstraction, rule inference, generalization, and manipulating or transforming the content of the test item (Jensen, 1992b). In this sense, *g* is common to all tests of cognitive performance, such as tests of verbal, numerical, and spatial abilities. Studies have shown *g* to be the primary source of predictive validity for almost all cognitive tests. When the variance associated with *g* is statistically removed from tests of specific cognitive abilities, the predictive validity of the test scores is typically reduced to almost zero (Jensen, 1992a).

Because *g* is so general, it is difficult to describe in terms of a test's formal characteristics or in terms of any particular information content or skills required by specific items (Seligman, 1992); *g* is not specific to particular skills or knowledge. It is general in that it is relevant and representative of the general population. It is cognitive in that individual differences in sensory acuity or physical strength or dexterity contribute negligibly to variance in it. And it is an ability in that it refers to conscious and voluntary acts that meet some objective standard. These acts are also consciously repeatable.

While *g* is common to every type of cognitive performance, it would be a mistake to think of it as merely some kind of psychometric artifact or hypothetical construct without meaning or reality beyond the scores obtained on a test. Aside from the evidence for its strong predictive validity in job performance and occupational success (Gottfredson, 1986; Hunter, 1986; Schmidt, Ones, & Hunter, 1992), studies have shown *g* to be a highly replicable and stable construct (Gustafson, 1984; Krantzler & Jensen, 1991; Ree & Earles, 1991b).

Recently, *g* has also been reliably linked to how people apprehend, discriminate, select, encode, transform, and store information and use this information to make decisions. Studies have shown that *g* is related to reaction time on elementary cognitive tasks, capacity of short-term memory, evoked potentials, glucose metabolism in the brain, and speed of neural transmission (Vernon, 1987; Larson & Saccuzzo, 1989; Jensen, 1992b). There is a growing consensus that *g* reflects the overall capacity and efficiency of human information processing and is definitely not a measure of a particular kind of knowledge, skill, or test-taking strategy (Fagan, 1992). The content of performance on a general cognitive test is merely a vehicle for *g*. As Jensen (1992a, p. 277) observed, "As the most important factor in tests of mental ability in terms of its ubiquity and relative size among all of the factors in psychometric tests, its correlations with neuropsychiatrical variables, and with the efficiency of information processing in elementary cognitive tasks, and its relation to educationally, occupationally, and socially important criteria, the empirical reality of *g* is hardly disputable."

Criticisms of General Cognitive Ability

But criticisms of *g* remain endemic. Although the empirical evidence linking *g* to job performance is widespread, this has not convinced the skeptics (e.g., Sternberg and Wagner, 1993). Three criticisms are often raised: (1) associations between GCA and outcomes are an artifact of the association between intelligence and social origin or socioeconomic status (SES); (2) more specific aptitudes targeted at particular tasks or jobs will be better predictors of performance than general cognitive ability; and (3) measures of GCA are fundamentally biased.

Each of these criticisms reflects a concern that the findings linking GCA and performance are either spurious or disadvantageous to some groups, but investigation of these concerns typically fails to find that the biases are important. For instance, the concern that GCA-performance associations stem from differences in social origins, not veridical individual differences, is predicated on the notion that the true cause of performance comes from social advantages indexed by variables such as parents' income, education, and occupation, family structure, or region of residence, essentially that GCA is actually a function of SES. The evidence for this claim, however, is weak (e.g., Valliant, 1977; Bouchard et al., 1990). Barrett and Depinet (1991, p. 1018) reviewed this literature and concluded that "The relationship between IQ and job success is not an artifact of SES." Similarly, the argument that GCA, as a global construct, is too broad in scope and that more specific abilities may be better predictors of performance is not empirically supported (e.g., Campbell, 1990; Schmidt, Ones, & Hunter, 1992). Hunter (1986, p. 358) concluded, "A massive data base gathered by the U.S. Employment Service and even more data gathered by the U.S. Military have shown the specific aptitude hypothesis to be false." Finally, concerns about a possible cultural bias in measures of GCA have also been alleviated when tests are carefully validated and interpreted (e.g., Wightman & Leary, 1985; Hecht & Schraeder, 1986; Schmidt, Ones, & Hunter, 1992). While the full extent of this debate is beyond the scope of this paper, the preponderance of evidence suggests that GCA-performance links are not spurious or biased (Seligman, 1992). Based on the discussion thus far, we therefore hypothesize:

Hypothesis 1: Higher levels of general cognitive ability will be positively associated with career success (e.g., salary level, promotions).

THE IMPORTANCE OF MOTIVATION FOR JOB PERFORMANCE

Thus far we have argued that GCA may be an important predictor of job performance, but it is obviously not the only one. As noted previously, a number of early conceptualizations of work performance posited that both ability and motivation would jointly contribute to performance. While there is general consensus that the construct of motivation includes components of direction, amplitude, and persistence, there is much less agreement on how to measure these elements. While Campbell (1976, p. 64), observed that performance should reflect both motivation and ability, he defined motivation only broadly: "Motivation does have meaning if we take it merely as a summary label that identifies a class of independent/dependent variable relationships." When motivation isn't clearly defined, the notion that performance reflects ability and motivation begs the question of what the measure of motivation might be. This has led to numerous theoretical and empirical approaches, some emphasizing exogenous or state motivation, in which reinforcements are used to shape behavior situationally, and others focusing on endogenous or trait motivation and examining internal process (e.g., Pinder, 1984). The basic idea that motivation, whether exogenously or endogenously determined, should be linked to work performance has nevertheless been well documented (e.g., Locke & Latham, 1990), although the findings are often not as strong as expected (O'Reilly, 1991). The simple notion that those who work harder or expend more effort should, all other things being equal, perform better is generally accepted. Therefore, it is important to consider relevant motivational characteristics to understand job performance and early career success fully.

Recent research in personality shows that a trait (defined as a stable predisposition to behave in characteristic ways) labelled "conscientiousness" may represent stable individual differences in motivation (Goldberg, 1993). Importantly, conscientiousness is related to job performance (e.g., Barrick & Mount, 1991, 1993). Adjectives that characterize conscientiousness include being hardworking, careful, dependable, organized, ambitious, energetic, and persevering (McCrae & Costa, 1987; John, 1990). McCrae and Costa (1987) argued that conscientiousness represents both a will to achieve, as suggested in the classic definition of the need for achievement (McClelland et al., 1976), and the discipline and energy level that can sustain the hard work necessary for performance. At the other end of the spectrum, those who are low on conscientiousness can be characterized as undirected and lazy.

Psychological research has shown that conscientiousness correlates positively with academic achievement (Digman & Takemoto-Chock, 1981). In the organizational domain, conscientious employees are careful, dependable, organized, hardworking, and thorough. Barrick and Mount (1993), who investigated the relationships between conscientiousness and managerial success in a sample of 154 managers, found modest but statistically significant associations between conscientiousness and supervisory ratings of performance. The effects of conscientiousness were moderated by job autonomy, a situational effect. Managers who had more autonomy and who were more conscientious performed the best. Schmidt and Hunter (1992, p. 91) speculated that "conscientiousness may come to be viewed as the most important trait motivation variable in the work domain." Independent of state motivation—motives induced by incentives, goal setting, or other programs—people who are highly conscientious are likely to perform better:

Hypothesis 2: Higher levels of motivation will be positively associated with career success.

PERFORMANCE = ABILITY × MOTIVATION

The contributions of GCA and motivation to performance suggest an interaction effect of the type proposed by early industrial psychologists (Campbell, 1976). Each component by itself may not strongly predict performance and, ultimately, career attainment (Kanfer & Acker- man, 1989). A person with very high levels of cognitive ability who is highly unmotivated may find creative ways to be lazy and thus not perform well. Similarly, an industrious per- son with very low cognitive abilities may persistently demonstrate his or her ineptitude on the job, removing all doubt as to his or her poor performance. Dreher and Bretz (1991) noted that cognitive ability should account for variation in performance only when motivation is considered. Variability in motivation across individuals may dampen associations between ability and performance. Thus studies attempting to link graduate admission test scores to fu- ture compensation often report nonsignificant and sometimes negative relationships, leading to the conclusion that motivation may be an unmeasured moderator of ability (Harrell et al., 1977; Reder, 1978). Similarly, studies of motivation often fail to find strong associations with performance, leading researchers to acknowledge that ability and other situational con- straints may attenuate these relationships (Barrick & Mount, 1991, 1993). These findings suggest that Heider's (1958) original multiplicative formulation may be correct.

Some indirect support for this is provided by Anderson and Butzin (1974, p. 598), who showed that observers use judgments of both motivation and ability in estimating the per- formance of others. Although they did not specifically demonstrate that both motivation and ability lead to performance, their study did show that people use this multiplicative algebra when estimating the performance of others. Other studies have also provided some modest evidence for a multiplicative association between motivation and ability in affecting out- comes (Hollenbeck et al., 1988). While there have been numerous studies of motivation, however, there has been little consideration of the interaction of motivation and ability. Hence, while both GCA and motivation may have independent effects on performance, the strongest effect and the one we hypothesized is that it is the interaction of GCA and motiva- tion that will positively predict job performance:

> **Hypothesis 3:** The interaction of general cognitive ability and motivation will be positively associated with career success.

METHODS

Research Design and Sample

Data for this study were collected during two time periods—first, in 1986 and 1987 (with samples from both years), when respondents were enrolled in their first year of a two-year, full-time, top-20, West-Coast MBA program, and again in 1991, three and a half or four and a half years after graduating, depending on which of the two years they initially participated in the study. All first-year MBAs were informed, through announcements in their classes, of the opportunity to participate in a weekend personality and managerial assessment center. Be- cause space was not available for all the students who signed up, participants were chosen to make the sample as representative as possible of their entire MBA cohort attending this uni- versity. In general, the sample closely resembled the larger MBA cohorts (approximately 240 in each), except that fewer foreign students participated (11 percent versus an average of 15 percent of the 1986 and 1987 cohorts), and slightly more women participated (43 percent versus an average of 34 percent across the 1986 and 1987 cohorts). Most importantly, the average GMAT scores across the two years was 630, which is quite similar to the mean of 626 in our sample.

Data collection in the first period (Time 1) was done through a personality and management assessment center. The primary objective was to gather data about participants' motivation level. Participants were assessed, in groups of twelve, over a weekend from Friday night through Sunday afternoon. Eleven separate weekend assessments were conducted. The focus of the second data collection period, the follow-up, during the fall of 1991 was to gather data about participants' early career status and work outcomes, three and a half or four and a half years following graduation from the MBA program. Personality, ability, and motivation data were not collected again. Of the original 132 participants, 105 (80 percent) were successfully contacted for the 1991 follow-up. Of these 105 participants, 11 were either not employed or were employed part time and were excluded from this study. The response rate for the follow-up was, therefore, 71 percent (94 respondents).

Measures

General Cognitive Ability

Although there are differences of opinion about how to measure general cognitive ability, there is reasonable consensus that it can be measured by summing across tests of several specific aptitudes, usually verbal and quantitative. These are typically not achievement tests; they measure general knowledge rather than narrow academic curricula or technical domains. General cognitive ability tests are composed of general items, all of which are weakly correlated. A measure of general aptitude, like verbal aptitude, is developed by combining a large number of similar items. The evidence for such factor structures is impressive (e.g., Jensen, 1986; Carroll, 1992), and while some criticisms of these stable, global measures exist, critics often fail to appreciate how powerful they are at predicting general tendencies (Green, 1978; Jensen, 1986).

One frequently used measure of general cognitive ability is the Graduate Management Admissions Test (GMAT) (e.g., Hecht & Schraeder, 1986). Although the agency that develops the test does not label the GMAT as a test of intelligence, it fits the general requisites of a measure of general cognitive ability. GMAT scores were therefore used as markers of individuals' cognitive ability in this study. Respondents' GMAT scores were coded from their original graduate application materials, and most had taken the test at least ten months prior to enrolling in the MBA program. Thus, the measure of GCA used here was collected at least six or seven years prior to the outcome variables. The GMAT total score has been defined so that it ranges from 200 to 800, with an approximate mean of 500 and a standard deviation of 100. Reliability coefficients for equivalent forms exceed .90. The mean for all test takers from June 1982 through March 1985 was 478 (Hecht & Schraeder, 1986). In this sample, GMAT total scores ranged from 480 to 750 ($\bar{x} = 626$, S.D. $= 58$). As with most top-20 business schools, the study site has rigorous GMAT-score requirements for admission. A floor effect may thus constrain the possible variation in GMAT scores in this sample, making this a conservative test of the proposition and the results most generalizable to similar professionals.

Motivation

Although many definitions of motivation exist, most emphasize three common characteristics: direction, amplitude and persistence (e.g., Pinder, 1984). While some studies examined motivation as a transient state using projective tests or job-focused surveys (e.g., Miner, 1980), recent research suggests that motivation, defined as conscientiousness, can be assessed as a stable characteristic using personality inventories. According to the five-factor model of personality, five broad dimensions, "the Big Five," can be used to describe most individual differences: extraversion, agreeableness, conscientiousness, neuroticism, and openness to experience (e.g., McCrae & Costa, 1987; Goldberg, 1993). Of these, conscientiousness represents persistence or follow-through and is associated with job performance and other indicators of career success (e.g., Barrick & Mount, 1991, 1993). Conscientiousness has been assessed with selected scales from the Adjective Check List (ACL) (Gough & Heilbrun, 1980). Using factor analysis, Piedmont, McCrae, and Costa (1991) found that three ACL scales, achievement, endurance, and order, loaded most highly on the conscientiousness factor and correlated most highly with the conscientiousness factor on the NEO personality inventory, designed specifically to tap the Big Five (Costa & McCrae, 1985). These three measures of order, achievement, and endurance correspond to the motivational components of direction, amplitude, and persistence, and the measure of conscientiousness is thus conceptually similar to the general notion of motivation.

Motivation was assessed in this study by having participants complete the Adjective Check List during the assessment (Time 1). The ACL is a self-report personality inventory consisting of 300 items that fall into 37 scales. The respondent checks each item that applies to him or her and leaves blank each item that does not apply. Each scale is corrected for total endorsements to prevent artifacts that may result from subjects who merely check few or many items (e.g., Gough & Heilbrun, 1980). The three scales that are relevant to motivation (achievement, endurance, and order) consist of 77 items. Positively coded items include ambitious, energetic, industrious, initiative, reliable, and responsible; while negatively coded items include apathetic, careless, lazy, leisurely, and undependable. The mean of the three scales was used to represent participants' motivation level in this study ($\bar{x} = 51.63$, S.D. = 7.94). The interitem reliability of the composite motivation measure was .85.

While some researchers argue that self-report personality data may be subject to enhancement biases not present in observer data (e.g., John & Robins, 1994), others offer convincing arguments that self-judgments are more accurate because they include relevant and valid information not available to observers (e.g., Funder, 1989). Alternatively, some argue that differences between self- and observer ratings are due to a harshness bias by observers rather than an enhancement bias by focal individuals (Coyne and Gotlib, 1983). To check for bias, we correlated participants' self-ratings with ACL ratings by 12 trained personality assessors. These assessors observed participants continually over the course of the two-and-a-half-day assessment center's activities, which included exercises (e.g., the Leaderless Group Discussion, charades), interviews, and informal social events such as meals. At the end of the weekend assessments, the 12 assessors independently completed the ACL for each of the twelve participants (this procedure was only completed for 47 percent of our sample). These observer data were aggregated across observers and averaged across the three scales (achievement, endurance, order). The average alpha coefficient across the 12 raters for this observer's measure of motivation was .92. The correlation between the self-reported motivation measure and the observer's measure of motivation for the portion of the sample for which it was available was high ($r = .42$; $p < .001$).

A measure designed specifically to tap conscientiousness is the Big Five Index (BFI) (John & Roberts, 1993). Although we did not collect BFI measures on the subjects in our study, we do have BFI and ACL measures for another sample of 70 MBA students, assessed under similar conditions in 1991–93. Therefore we were able to correlate the BFI conscientiousness scale with our ACL composite scale for these other MBAs. The correlation between the two scales was quite high (.79; $p < .001$), providing some evidence of concurrent validity of the ACL measure of motivation for MBAs.

Early Career Success

Previous research has suggested that career success is multidimensional (e.g., Pfeffer, 1977). Early career success may be signalled as early as the initial interview process or through salary attainment or the rate of promotion (Rosenbaum, 1979; Dreher, Dougherty, & Whitely, 1985). While different researchers have examined various facets of career success, there appears to be general agreement that both promotions and salary attainment are important elements (e.g., Forbes & Piercy, 1991). Since GCA is an aggregate measure and career success is multidimensional, this study uses five indicators to assess early career success: selection success, number of job offers, current salary, salary increment, and number of promotions.

(1) *Selection ratio* and (2) *number of offers.* Respondents reported the total number of interviews they completed and the total number of offers they received during their initial job search. To ensure accurate recall, these questions were included on a brief questionnaire distributed during the spring following their graduation. Selection ratios were calculated as the number of offers divided by the number of initial interviews ($\bar{x} = .25$, S.D. $= .24$). The number of offers was simply the number of job offers respondents reported receiving ($\bar{x} = 2.44$, S.D. $= 1.33$).

(3) *Current salary* and (4) *salary increment.* As part of the 1991 follow-up survey, respondents were asked to list the compensation for all jobs they had held since graduating from the MBA program. Salary increment was calculated as their current salary divided by the salary they received from their first job after business school. One respondent, an investment banker, reported that his current salary was $450,000, which was far above the mean salary for all other respondents. In order to avoid biasing the results with this extreme outlier, data from this respondent were dropped from all analyses. Current salary for the remaining 93 respondents was simply the amount respondents reported earning in the fall of 1991 ($\bar{x} = \$63,050$, S.D. $= \$27,215$). Salary increment was $\bar{x} = 1.37$, or an average 37 percent increase (S.D. $= .40$).

(5) *Number of promotions.* On the follow-up survey, respondents also indicated which of their positions, following their initial job, represented a promotion. The total number of promotions was calculated by adding together all reported promotions ($\bar{x} = 1.03$, S.D. $= .83$).

Additional Measures

We assessed motivation and predicted career success using three additional measures. The first was a single-item, self-reported measure of *ambition.* Respondents were asked to rate themselves on a scale from 1 (extremely low) to 9 (extremely high) according to the extent to which "[They] have high aspirations for future attainments and status; strong drive for success." Ambition scores ranged from 5 to 9 ($\bar{x} = 7.44$, S.D. $= 1.05$).

The second measure was a consensus rating made by three managerial assessors of each respondent's *initiative,* defined as "[having] aptitude in initiating action, is energetic." Like the personality assessors described above, for each group of 12 participants, there were six managerial assessors, each of whom provided assessments of six participants per weekend assessment. In contrast to the personality assessors, managerial assessors confined their assessments to direct observations of participants' behaviors in one of three contexts: (1) the verbal responses in an in-depth work and professional history interview, in which participants were asked about their parents' employment, their own job history, and their future career aspirations; (2) the written responses on an individual in-basket exercise in which participants acted as a plant manager (see Staw & Barsade, 1993); and (3) demonstrated behavior in a Leaderless Group Discussion (LGD), in which participants had to negotiate with five other participants to allocate bonuses to each participant's hypothetical subordinate. At the end of all three assessment activities, managerial assessors met in groups of three (depending on the six participants they were assigned to), and each assessor presented his or her comments on the specific assessment exercise or task that he or she focused on (e.g., each assessor was randomly assigned to focus on either the LGD, in-basket, or interview for each subject; for example, assessor A focused on the LGD for participant 1 and 4, the in-basket for participant 2 and 5, and the interview for participant 3 and 6). After all information was presented on each participant, each assessor independently rated each of the six participants on each of 15 dimensions (e.g., initiative, energy, oral communication). Then the assessment teams reached consensus on the ratings for each participant by choosing the modal score of the three ratings for each of 15 managerial dimensions. According to standard procedures used in assessment center ratings (e.g., Zedeck, 1986), if any of the managerial assessor ratings differed by more than 1 point (on a 5-point scale), the assessors reexamined and rediscussed all the information about that participant until they reached consensus. The initiative scores ranged from 1 to 5 ($\bar{x} = 3.45$, S.D. $= .97$).

The third measure was respondents' self-reported number of hours they *would like* to work per week after graduation (*desired hours*). Subjects were asked this question as part of a take-home packet of materials that were filled out a few days before the weekend assessment began. Responses ranged from 30 to 60 hours ($\bar{x} = 43.13$, S.D. $= 6.50$).

Control Variables

A number of control variables were included in the regression analyses in order to rule out alternative explanations for variations in career success, since recent MBA graduates' success may be due to factors other than general cognitive ability and motivation. For instance, research has shown that gender and age may affect employment opportunities within and across organizations (Pfeffer & Langton, 1988). In addition, past work experience and the level and caliber of education may affect one's career success (Howard, 1986). Further, the specific career path one chooses may affect career outcomes (Pfeffer, 1977). For example, investment bankers are trained at a relatively low salary for the first year or two of their employment, and then their income jumps dramatically and maintains a higher level than most other MBA functional areas (e.g., cost accountant, financial analyst). Following an entrepreneurial path and running one's own business may lead to differences in career outcomes as well. Finally, national origin may also affect early career success, since countries may differ in terms of typical career paths and indicators of career success (e.g., Hofstede, 1984).

Therefore, gender (43 percent female), age ($\bar{x} = 27.7$) and citizenship (non-U.S. = 11 percent) were controlled in all equations. Further, while the initial data were collected at the same time in each respondent's MBA program, the follow-up data were collected at the same time for all respondents. This meant that the 1987 cohort had been working for a year less than the 1986 cohort at the time of the follow-up. Therefore, a dummy variable for the year the respondent graduated was also entered in all equations as a control. To address the possible idiosyncratic salary patterns generated by the investment banking and entrepreneurial paths, a dummy variable for each was entered in all equations. Race (24 percent minority, 76 percent white), college major, undergraduate grade-point average, years of previous work experience ($\bar{x} = 3.4$ years), and a dummy variable created to differentiate between those who chose a career in the public/nonprofit domain (6 percent of the sample) were initially included as controls but were subsequently dropped due to their lack of significance in affecting the career success variables.

RESULTS

Predicting Career Success

Table 1 presents the means, standard deviations, and correlations among the variables. The five dependent variables are reasonably independent, with the highest correlation existing between the number of job offers received and the selection ratio ($r = .38, p < .05$). Bivariate relationships show that investment bankers were younger and entrepreneurs were generally older, while women and foreign citizens were more likely to follow entrepreneurial career paths. General cognitive ability and motivation appear to be independent ($r = .03$, n.s.): People with higher general cognitive ability are not likely to be more or less motivated than people with lower general cognitive ability.

To examine the effects of GCA, motivation, and their interaction on managerial success, we used hierarchical regression analyses. Consistent with our conceptual discussion, we entered the control variable block first, followed by the GMAT score, the motivation score, and finally by the interaction between GMAT and motivation. Thus, when each subsequent independent variable was entered, that variable's partial correlation reflected its relationship with career success, independent of the effects of all previous control and independent variables (Cohen & Cohen, 1983, p. 122). Table 2 displays the regression results.

Selection

The equation predicting the selection ratio (offers/interviews) shows a positive effect for entrepreneurs but no significant effects for either cognitive ability or motivation or for their interaction. Investment bankers received significantly more offers, as shown in the equation predicting the absolute number of offers. Again, while no significant main effects for either GCA or motivation emerge, the interaction term significantly predicts the number of offers participants received, and in the expected positive direction. High scorers on the GMAT who were also highly motivated received significantly more job offers ($\beta = 7.64, p < .05$). Overall, neither GCA nor motivation by itself strongly predicts success in getting a job; only the interaction of the two is linked to success in the job-search process.

TABLE 1 **Means, Standard Deviations, and Correlations among Variables***

Variable	x̄	S.D.	1	2	3	4	5	6	7	8	9	10	11	12
Control variables														
1. Age	27.6	4.47	—											
2. Sex			-.14	—										
1 = female	41.9%													
2 = male	58.1%													
3. Year graduated			-.07	.04	—									
0 = 1987	44.1%													
1 = 1988	55.9%													
4. Citizenship			-.09	.23	-.11	—								
0 = U.S.	89.2%													
1 = non-U.S.	10.8%													
5. Investment banker			-.21	-.03	-.01	-.13	—							
0 = no	88.2%													
1 = yes	1.8%													
6. Entrepreneur			.23	.14	.06	.19	-.10	—						
0 = no	93.5%													
1 = yes	6.5%													
Cognitive ability														
7. GMAT total	626.2	58.2	.19	-.01	.01	-.18	-.05	-.01	—					
Motivation														
8. ACL composite	51.63	7.94	.10	.05	-.01	-.11	-.13	.15	.03	—				
Career success														
9. Number offers	2.40	1.30	.02	-.04	.04	-.15	.25	-.02	-.02	.05	—			
10. Offers/interviews	.25	.24	.07	-.02	-.13	.05	-.13	.31	-.17	.17	.38	—		
11. Current salary ($)	63K	27K	-.05	-.02	-.17	-.11	.62	-.04	.07	.04	.23	.08	—	
12. Salary increment	1.42	.40	-.17	-.03	-.21	.02	.25	.05	-.26	-.03	.14	.34	.34	—
13. Promotions	1.03	.83	-.07	-.11	-.15	-.20	-.19	-.09	-.15	.01	-.04	.13	.01	.33

*$p < .05$ for correlations greater than .20.

TABLE 2 **Hierarchical Regressions Predicting Early Career Success***

	Offers/ Interviews	Number Offers	Current Salary	Salary Increment	Promotions
1. Control variables					
Age	−.04	−.01	.07	−.18	−.17
Sex	−.06	.05	.01	−.06	−.08
Year graduated	−.13	.01	−.14	−.23	−.19
Non-U.S. citizen	.01	−.12	−.04	−.01	−.25
Investment banker	−.11	.23	.59*	.22	−.26*
Entrepreneur	.24	−.04	.01	.14	−.01
Change in R^2	.09	.08	.36	.14	.15
Adjusted R^2	.01	.01	.31	.07	.05
Change in F-ratio	.94	.96	6.75*	1.86	1.54
2. GMAT total	−.17	−.03	.08	−.23	−.19
Change in R^2	.03	.01	.01	.05	.03
Adjusted R^2	.01	.01	.30	.10	.07
Change in F-ratio	1.86	.04	.72	3.85*	2.05
3. ACL motivation	.14	.02	.11	−.01	−.04
Change in R^2	.02	.01	.01	.01	.01
Adjusted R^2	.01	.01	.31	.09	.05
Change in F-ratio	1.18	.02	1.29	.01	.09
4. Interaction	−.12	7.64*	4.54*	3.08	6.12*
Change in R^2	.01	.25	.09	.04	.16
Adjusted R^2	.01	.24	.40	.12	.23
Change in F-ratio	.01	23.49*	11.50*	3.39*	12.32*
Full equation F-ratio	.96	3.46*	6.71*	2.13*	2.91*

*$p < .05$.
*Entries represent standardized coefficients.

Salary

Investment bankers had significantly higher current salaries. Although main effects for GCA and motivation were not significant, significant variance in salary is explained by the interaction between GMAT and motivation. Together with the investment-banker dummy variable, the current salary equation explains a sizable 40 percent of the variance in MBAs' fall 1991 salaries (overall $F = 6.71, p < .05$). The equation predicting MBAs' salary increment is significant as well. As expected, those who graduated earlier experienced greater increases in their salary, with investment bankers showing slightly higher increases over the duration of the study. The only main effect for GMAT or motivation emerged in the prediction of salary increment. In contrast to expectations, GMAT scores are significant, but they are negatively related to salary increment ($\beta = -.23, p < .05$). But again, a major contribution to explained variance resides in the interaction between GMAT and motivation. Those who *both* had high GMAT scores and were more motivated (change in $R^2 = 4$ percent, overall $F = 2.13, p < .05$) experienced greater salary increases in the early years of their careers. Both overall and incremental salary are predicted by the interaction between motivation and ability.

Promotions

U.S. citizens and investment bankers were more likely to receive promotions, but significant main effects for cognitive ability and motivation did not emerge. The interaction between cognitive ability and motivation significantly predicted variance in the number of promotions respondents received (change in $R^2 = .16$, overall $F = 2.91$, $p < .05$). The results thus offer no support for either hypothesis 1 or hypothesis 2 but do provide strong support for hypothesis 3: The overall pattern of the regression results suggests that both motivation and GCA are necessary to explain early career success.

Additional Analyses

Race

One control variable that was not reported in the regression results presented in Table 2 that may be related to GCA is race. To ensure that the results were not biased by race, we re-estimated all regression equations twice: one analysis including a dummy variable that distinguished between whites and nonwhites (76.3 percent versus 23.7 percent), and a second set that used a dummy variable that distinguished between whites and Asians in one group and all other people of color in another group (85.0 percent versus 15.0 percent). Neither of these dummy variables significantly affected the career success variables. Further, only the race variable separating whites and nonwhites affected the overall amount of variance explained (adjusted R^2). Therefore, we can conclude that race failed to exert a consistent or pervasive effect on the dependent variables.

Artifacts

Because of our relatively small sample size and the paucity of main effects for GCA and motivation, the possibility exists that our interaction effects may stem from a few extreme sample points. To check for this, we examined scattergrams for each of the five interaction equations. These plots showed no salient outliers. The extremes of the plots were, in all instances, defined by a set of observations rather than a single or few data points.

Further, there were no significant gaps in the plots between interactions and the dependent variables. Taken together, these observations rule out the likelihood of artifacts causing the interaction results.

Further Evidence of the Interaction of Motivation and Ability

The additional three measures of motivation collected at time 1 (ambition, initiative, and desired hours) were each substituted for the ACL motivation measure in separate hierarchal regressions, structured identically to those described above. The pattern of results was, again, generally supportive of our prediction that the interaction between GCA and each of these measures of motivation would account for more variance in the career success outcomes than would either GCA or motivation alone. Of the 15 equations (each of five dependent variables regressed on the three motivation variables), 10 of the interaction terms were positive and significantly associated with the career success variables. Further, the interaction between GCA and motivation always explained more variance in career success than either variable alone. The amount of variance explained (adjusted R^2) by the full equation for the 10 significant equations ranged from .11 (GMAT and self-reported ambition predicting number of offers) to .53 (GMAT and self-reported ambition predicting current salary). Taken together, these results strengthen the evidence for our initial prediction, because the three motivation variables are conceptually diverse (e.g., ambition and initiative capture general personality, while desired hours captures specific behavior) and methodologically diverse (e.g., ambition and desired hours are self-reported, while initiative was generated by a consensus rating by trained observers).

We also ran the regression analyses substituting observer ratings for self-reported ACL scores. The pattern of results was comparable, although weaker than those reported above. This was clearly due, in part, to the smaller sample.

Understanding the Interaction Results

One issue that is not clarified by the regression analyses is whether greater levels of both motivation and general cognitive ability are always better or whether there is some point at which having greater motivation produces diminishing returns for those with high cognitive ability. Therefore, in addition to examining the regression coefficients for the interactions, we also analyzed their functional form. Graphing a partial derivative, or inflection point, can reveal nonmonotonic effects that are not apparent in the tabled coefficients (Schoonhoven, 1981, p. 362). Such analyses clarify the interpretation of interaction results. To plot the interactions, we assumed that the cognitive ability variable modified the effects of the motivation variables on career success. Research suggests that one's motivation level is more likely to change over time than is one's general cognitive ability (Carroll, 1992).

Following Schoonhoven (1981), we analyzed the interactions by calculating the inflection point of the interaction to determine whether the function was monotonic or nonmonotonic. All five inflection points were well below the relevant range in GMAT scores for this sample, allowing us to conclude that the interactions are monotonic. This means that any increase in motivation at increased levels of cognitive ability leads to an increase in career success.

To specify more concretely what this means in terms of the career success variables, we calculated the contribution of increases in motivation at two levels of GMAT scores— relatively low for this sample (one standard deviation below the mean GMAT score, or 568) and relatively high (one standard deviation above the mean, or 684.4), using the following equation (Schoonhoven, 1981):

$$y = b_1 x_1 + b_3 x_1 x_2$$

where b_1 = the unstandardized coefficient for motivation, x_1 = the mean motivation score (51.63), or one standard deviation above the mean (59.57), b_3 = the unstandardized coefficient for the GMAT and motivation interaction, and x_2 = the low (568) or high (684.4) score on the GMAT.

For the interaction between GMAT and motivation predicting the number of job offers received, a one standard deviation increase in motivation increased the number of offers by .93 more when the person had a high GMAT score. To understand this result, it helps to consider the difference between a one standard deviation increase in motivation when GMAT is high versus when it is low. At low levels of GMAT (568) the difference between a mean motivation score (51.63) and one standard deviation above the mean (59.57) can be compared with the same one standard deviation increase in motivation at a high GMAT score level (684.4):

Low GMAT Level:	High GMAT Level:
.01 (51.63) + .001 (51.63)(568)	.01 (51.63) + .001 (51.63)(684.4)
= 29.84	= 35.85
.01 (59.57) + .001 (59.57)(568)	.01 (59.57) + .001 (59.57)(684.4)
= 34.43	= 41.37

The important number is the difference between these two differences: (41.37 − 35.85) − (34.43 − 29.84) = 5.52 − 4.59 = .93, which represents the increase in the number of offers for a standard deviation increase in motivation for higher scorers on the GMAT relative to those with lower GMAT scores. Using the same logic, a standard deviation increase in motivation at higher GMAT levels (684.4) is worth $18,780.08 more in compensation than a standard deviation increase in motivation at lower GMAT levels (568). A standard deviation increase in motivation at high levels of GMAT is associated with a 1.85 percent greater salary increment compared with a standard deviation increase in motivation at low levels of GMAT. Finally, a standard deviation increase in motivation at high levels of GMAT is associated with .56 more promotions, compared with a standard deviation increase in motivation at low levels of GMAT.

DISCUSSION

The overall results of the study show that it is the interaction of motivation and general cognitive ability that most strongly predicts early career success for the MBA graduates studied here. Neither GCA nor trait motivation (i.e., conscientiousness) alone is a good predictor of early management success. This finding is consistent with previous studies that failed to find main effects when using graduate admission test scores to predict subsequent salary attainment among MBAs (Harrell et al., 1977; Reder, 1978). Our results suggest these earlier findings may be due to the omission of motivation as a moderator of ability. The relationship becomes clear when ability and motivation are multiplied. It is worth noting that the two individual difference constructs used here, assessed at least three and a half or four and a half years prior to the outcome variables, are statistically and practically predictive of actual job outcomes. The form of the interactions show, not surprisingly, that smart, motivated people do better than those who are either not as smart or not as motivated.

The effect of the interaction between motivation and GCA may change over time and as the MBAs move further along in their careers. For example, to the extent that upward career mobility in and across organizations is based on selecting for those high on motivation and ability, range restriction may mute interactive effects. Despite the comparatively short period of time that the subjects were followed, our findings are intuitively appealing and parsimonious: Intelligence and hard work should be associated with success. It is worth remembering that these results reflect the influence of two important, general individual difference constructs on aggregate variables assessed three and a half or four and a half years later (and longer in the case of the ability assessment). In this regard, both the independent and dependent variables are appropriate global assessments, consistent with Green's (1978, p. 666) observation that "the fact that global measures do not predict specific behaviors is not an indictment of the measures. It is a failure to appreciate the force of aggregation and the global nature of the general tendencies being measured." Explaining incremental variance on the order of 10 to 20 percent in salary attainment seems practically significant.

These findings are theoretically interesting for several reasons. First, they attest to the importance and relevance of stable individual differences as determinants of individual success in organizations. The constructs are clearly defined and measured. Both general cognitive ability and conscientiousness are well-validated constructs that have been shown to be relevant to performance in organizational contexts (e.g., Hunter, 1986; Barrick & Mount, 1993). Further, the study demonstrates the predictive validity of individual differences by using tangible outcome variables that have face validity and are not likely to be confounded by self-report and response biases. Finally, the effects of both GCA and conscientiousness on managerial performance are easy to fathom. Schmidt, Hunter, and Outerbridge (1986), for example, have explicated the mechanism through which cognitive ability may affect performance. Managers with higher levels of cognitive ability are likely to be quicker at acquiring job knowledge and assimilating new information. People who are more motivated may also accomplish more and receive higher salary increments than those who are less motivated. Although the joint effect of these two constructs [has] often been suggested, [it has] seldom been investigated (Campbell, 1976).

A second reason these results are potentially interesting is their consistency with recent theories about person-situation interactions in personality psychology. Both personality and social psychologists have recognized the interactive nature of social behavior and the limitations of focusing exclusively on either persons or situations. Wright and Mischel (1987, p. 1163), for instance, have proposed a competency-demand hypothesis that suggests that individual differences should be clearest in "psychologically demanding situations." In this sense, situations can be categorized in terms of the demands they make on people for certain competencies. People who have the relevant competencies are more likely to act in characteristic ways and to perform better than those who lack the requisite competencies. It is the configuration of situational demands and individual competencies that predicts attitudes and behaviors in a particular situation. Wright and Mischel (1988), for example, showed that children who are dispositionally more aggressive are more likely to behave this way in frustrating situations than when observed in routine circumstances. When the situation makes characteristic demands on people with predispositions to engage in situationally relevant ways, those behaviors are likely to occur. Caldwell and O'Reilly (1990) have shown, in a series of studies, that jobs or situations may be profiled in terms of the competencies they require. Individuals whose competencies match those demanded show significantly higher levels of performance and satisfaction. In the context of managerial jobs, there is good evidence that cognitive abilities and a willingness to work hard are frequently demanded (e.g., Arvey, 1986; Barrick & Mount, 1993; Chatman, Caldwell, & O'Reilly, 1994). Those who are higher on both of these dimensions can reasonably be expected to perform better, especially over extended periods of time. This is precisely what the results of this study show.

While previous research on GCA has demonstrated the importance of *g* for job performance, the results presented here suggest a somewhat different picture: It is both GCA and motivation together that lead to success. Motivation and GCA have compensatory effects such that, in this sample, being more highly motivated may compensate for less cognitive ability and vice versa. Previous studies of GCA and job performance have typically used subjects across a range of jobs with different information-processing demands (e.g., Austin & Hanisch, 1990; Ree & Earles, 1992). The impact of *g* in predicting who will be successful at jobs as disparate as cook, avionics technician, or theoretical physicist is likely to be greater than for a sample of people who are all completing a master's degree and going into management. Similarly, the motivation of people across a variety of occupations is also likely to vary more than individuals who choose to enter an MBA program. Thus, one reason we find no strong, independent results for motivation or ability may be the restricted ranges within our sample. The results of this study can thus be seen as conservative and do not rule out the independent effects of intelligence, motivation, or other individual differences. For instance, Barrick and Mount (1991) showed that extraversion may be related to performance for jobs requiring extensive public contact. It may also be the case that some strong situations can obviate individual differences or that, over time, there may be reciprocal effects of people and situations (Schneider, 1987). In this study, however, it is the interaction of motivation and ability that is associated with early career success as measured by salary and promotion.

One clear implication of the results reported here is that it may be necessary to consider motivation and GCA when investigating the effects of more specific characteristics. As amply demonstrated in previous research, the predictive validity of many tests may reflect an underlying *g* component (e.g., Hunter, 1986; Jensen, 1992a; Schmidt, Ones, & Hunter, 1992), leading to potentially spurious interpretations. This is especially likely in organizational contexts in which our outcome variables may easily reflect underlying cognitive and motivational factors. For instance, Meyer and Shack (1989) have suggested that measures of positive and negative affect may be captured by underlying personality dimensions rather than by separate constructs. Some dispositional constructs that rely on arousal or energetic components, such as negative affect (e.g., Levin & Stokes, 1989), may be surrogates for motivation. Other dispositions, such as self-esteem (Brockner, 1988), may have underlying cognitive components such that those higher in self-esteem may simply be those whose capabilities are greater, resulting in feelings of more self-efficacy. The point here is that individual difference researchers need to offer unambiguous evidence that their constructs are measuring something beyond underlying differences in levels of motivation and cognitive ability.

Practically speaking, the results of this study may have an important implication for MBA programs. If business school faculty and administrators want their graduates to be successful in the terms measured here (choice of jobs, salary attainment, and promotions), it appears that as much attention should be focused on assessing conscientiousness as GMAT scores. While it is possible that undergraduate grade-point average and essays may include a motivational component, they seem to be highly imperfect indicators of conscientiousness. It would certainly be possible to assess conscientiousness more directly through the use of specific essay questions and personal histories with validated scoring systems. Increasing the validity with which trait motivation is measured may significantly enhance the ability of MBA programs to select applicants who are likely to be successful later. Admitting students based primarily on GMAT or other graduate admissions tests does not seem as useful as considering both cognitive ability and motivational predictors.

As Arvey (1986) and others have shown, managerial and professional careers typically place high cognitive demands on incumbents (e.g., Gottfredson, 1986; Schmidt, Ones, & Hunter, 1992). It isn't surprising, then, that success in this arena may be a function of general cognitive ability and persistent effort. In this sense, the results presented here are intuitive and straightforward. What is surprising is why researchers have spent so little time considering the motivation $\times$ ability model, especially in light of continued criticism that individual difference constructs lack predictive power.

Equally remarkable is the lack of attention researchers involved in the person-situation debate have paid to basic individual differences like general cognitive ability and trait motivation. Instead of considering these fundamental individual differences, researchers focused on distal individual characteristics and devoted little attention to the competencies demanded by a particular situation. Organizational research should move beyond the lively but uninformative person-situation debate. As many researchers have already noted, dispositions need to be clearly defined and measured, and situations should be thought of in terms of the demands they place on individual competencies. In this sense, GCA and motivation appear to be broadly useful constructs for exploring person-situation interactions.

References

Ackerman, Lynne, and Lloyd G. Humphreys (1990). "Individual differences theory in industrial and organizational psychology." In M. D. Dunnette and L. M. Hough (eds.), *Handbook of Industrial and Organizational Psychology,* 2nd ed., 1: 223–282. Palo Alto, CA: Consulting Psychologists Press.

Anderson, Norman H., and Clifford A. Butzin (1974). "Performance = Motivation × Ability: An integration-theoretical analysis." *Journal of Personality and Social Psychology,* 30: 598–604.

Arvey, Richard D. (1986). "General ability in employment: A discussion." *Journal of Vocational Behavior,* 29: 415–420.

Austin, James T., and Katherine A. Hanisch (1990). "Occupational attainment as a function of abilities and interests: A longitudinal analysis using Project TALENT data." *Journal of Applied Psychology,* 75: 77–86.

Barrett, Gerald V., and Robert L. Depinet (1991). "A reconsideration of testing for competence rather than intelligence." *American Psychologist,* 46: 1012–1024.

Barrick, Murray R., and Michael K. Mount (1991). "The big five personality dimensions and job performance: A meta-analysis." *Personnel Psychology,* 44: 1–26.

Barrick, Murray R., and Michael K. Mount (1993). "Autonomy as a moderator of the relationships between the big five personality dimensions and job performance." *Journal of Applied Psychology,* 78: 111–118.

Bouchard, T. J., D. T. Lykken, M. McGue, N. L. Segal, and A. Tellegen (1990). "Sources of human psychological differences: The Minnesota Study of Twins Reared Apart." *Science,* 250: 223–228.

Brockner, Joel (1988). *Self-esteem at Work: Research, Theory, and Practice.* Lexington, MA: Lexington Books.

Caldwell, David F., and Charles A. O'Reilly (1990). "Measuring person-job fit with a profile comparison process." *Journal of Applied Psychology,* 75: 648–657.

Campbell, John P. (1976). "Motivation in industrial and organizational psychology." In Marvin D. Dunnette (ed.), *Handbook of Industrial and Organizational Psychology:* 63–130. Chicago: Rand McNally.

Campbell, John P. (1990). "An overview of the army selection and classification project (Project A)." *Personnel Psychology,* 43: 231–239.

Carroll, John B. (1992). "Cognitive abilities: The state of the art." *Psychological Science,* 5: 266–270.

Chatman, Jennifer A. (1989). "Improving interactional organizational research: A model of person-organization fit." *Academy of Management Review,* 14: 333–349.

Chatman, Jennifer A., David F. Caldwell, and Charles A. O'Reilly (1994). "Managerial personality and early career success: A profile comparison approach." Unpublished manuscript, Haas School of Business, University of California, Berkeley.

Cohen, Jacob, and Patricia Cohen (1983). *Applied Multiple Regression/Correlation Analysis for the Behavioral Sciences.* Hillsdale, NJ: Erlbaum.

Costa, Paul T., Jr., and Robert R. McCrae (1985). *The NEO Personality Inventory Manual.* Odessa, FL: Psychological Assessment Resources.

Coyne, J. C., and I. H. Gotlib (1983). "The role of cognition in depression: A critical reappraisal." *Psychological Bulletin,* 94: 472–505.

Cronbach, Lee J. (1975). "Five decades of public controversy over mental testing." *American Psychologist,* 30: 1–14.

Davis-Blake, Alison, and Jeffrey Pfeffer (1989). "Just a mirage: The search for dispositional effects in organizational research." *Academy of Management Review,* 14: 385–400.

Digman, John M., and Nancy K. Takemoto-Chock (1981). "Factors in the natural language of personality: Re-analysis, comparison, and interpretation of six major studies." *Multivariate Behavioral Research,* 16: 149–170.

Dreher, George F., and Robert D. Bretz (1991). "Cognitive ability and career attainment: Moderating effects of early career success." *Journal of Applied Psychology,* 76: 392–397.

Dreher, George F., Thomas W. Dougherty, and Bill Whitely (1985). "Generalizability of MBA degree and socioeconomic effects on business school graduates' salaries." *Journal of Applied Psychology,* 70: 769–773.

Fagan, Joseph F. (1992). "Intelligence: A theoretical viewpoint." *Current Directions in Psychological Science,* 3: 82–86.

Forbes, J. Benjamin, and J. E. Piercy (1991). *Corporate Mobility and Paths to the Top.* New York: Quorum.

Funder, David (1989). "Accuracy in personality judgment and the dancing bear." In David M. Buss and Nancy Cantor (eds.), *Personality Psychology: Recent Trends and Emerging Directions:* 210–223. New York: Springer-Verlag.

Gerhardt, Barry (1987). "How important are dispositional factors as determinants of job satisfaction? Implications for job design and other personnel programs." *Journal of Applied Psychology,* 72: 366–373.

Goldberg, Lewis R. (1993). "The structure of phenotypic personality traits." *American Psychologist,* 48: 26–34.

Gottfredson, Linda S. (1986). "Societal consequences of the *g* factor in employment." *Journal of Vocational Behavior,* 29: 379–410.

Gough, Harrison G., and Arthur Heilbrun, Jr. (1980). *The Adjective Checklist Manual.* Palo Alto, CA: Consulting Psychologists Press.

Green, Bert F. (1978). "In defense of measurement." *American Psychologist,* 33: 664–670.

Gustafson, Jan-Eric (1984). "A unifying model for the structure of intellectual abilities." *Intelligence,* 8: 179–203.

Harrell, Thomas W. (1992). "Some history of the Army General Classification Test." *Journal of Applied Psychology,* 77: 875–878.

Harrell, Margaret S., Thomas W. Harrell, Shelby H. McIntyre, and Charles B. Weinberg (1977). "Predicting compensation among MBA graduates five and ten years after graduation." *Journal of Applied Psychology,* 62: 636–640.

Hecht, Lawrence W., and William B. Schraeder (1986). "Technical report on test development and score interpretation for GMAT users." Los Angeles: Graduate Management Admissions Council, June.

Heider, Fritz (1958). *The Psychology of Interpersonal Relations.* New York: Wiley.

Hofstede, Geert (1984). *Culture's Consequences: International Differences in Work-Related Values.* Beverly Hills, CA: Sage.

Hollenbeck, John R., Arthur P. Brief, Ellen M. Whitener, and Karen E. Pauli (1988). "An empirical note on the interaction of personality and aptitude in personnel selection." *Journal of Management,* 14: 441–451.

House, Robert, Ann Howard, and Gordon Walker (1992). "The prediction of managerial success: A test of the person-situation debate." Working Paper, Wharton School of Business, University of Pennsylvania.

Howard, Ann (1986). "College experiences and managerial performance." *Journal of Applied Psychology,* 71: 530–552.

Hunter, John E. (1986). "Cognitive ability, cognitive aptitudes, job knowledge, and job performance." *Journal of Vocational Behavior,* 29: 340–362.

Jensen, Arthur R. (1986). "*G:* Artifact or reality?" *Journal of Vocational Behavior,* 29: 301–331.

Jensen, Arthur R. (1992a). "Commentary: Vehicles of *g.*" *Psychological Science,* 3: 275–278.

Jensen, Arthur R. (1992b). "Understanding *g* in terms of information processing." *Educational Psychology Review,* 4: 271–308.

John, Oliver P. (1990). "The 'big five' factor taxonomy: Dimensions of personality in the natural language and in questionnaires." In Lawrence A. Pervin (ed.), *Handbook of Personality: Theory and Research:* 66–100. New York: Guilford Press.

John, Oliver P., and Brent W. Roberts (1993). "Measuring the five-factor model on the Adjective Check List." Technical report, Institute of Personality and Social Research, University of California, Berkeley.

John, Oliver P., and Richard W. Robins (1994). "Accuracy and bias in self-perception: Individual differences in self-enhancement and the role of narcissism." *Journal of Personality and Social Psychology,* 66: 206–219.

Kanfer, Ruth, and Philip Ackerman (1989). "Dynamics of skill acquisition: Building a bridge between intelligence and motivation." In Robert J. Sternberg (ed.), *Advances in the Psychology of Human Intelligence,* 5: 83–134.

Kenrick, David, and David Funder (1988). "Profiting from controversy: Lessons from the person-situation debate." *American Psychologist,* 43: 1378–1388.

Krantzler, John H., and Arthur R. Jensen (1991). "The nature of psychometric *g:* Unitary process or a number of independent processes?" *Intelligence,* 15: 397–422.

Larson, Gerald E., and Dennis P. Saccuzzo (1989). "Cognitive correlates of general intelligence: Toward a process theory of *g.*" *Intelligence,* 13: 5–31.

Levin, Ira, and Joseph P. Stokes (1989) "Dispositional approach to job satisfaction: Role of negative affectivity." *Journal of Applied Psychology,* 74: 752–758.

Locke, Ed, and Gary Latham (1990). *A Theory of Goal-Setting and Task Performance.* Englewood Cliffs, NJ: Prentice Hall.

McClelland, David C. (1973). "Testing for competence rather than for 'intelligence'." *American Psychologist,* 28: 1–14.

McClelland, David C., John W. Atkinson, Russell A. Clark, and Edgar L. Lowell (1976). *The Achievement Motive.* New York: Appleton-Century-Crofts.

McCrae, Robert R., and Paul T. Costa (1987). "Validation of the five-factor model of personality across instruments and observers." *Journal of Personality and Social Psychology,* 57: 17–40.

Meyer, Gregory J., and John R. Shack (1989). "Structural convergence of mood and personality: Evidence for old and new directions." *Journal of Personality and Social Psychology,* 57: 691–706.

Miner, John B. (1980). "The role of managerial and professional motivation in the career success of management professors." *Academy of Management Journal,* 23: 483–508.

Nathan, Barry R., and Ralph A. Alexander (1988). "A comparison of criteria for test validation: A meta-analytic investigation." *Personnel Psychology,* 41: 290–296.

O'Reilly, Charles A. (1991). "Organizational behavior: Where we've been, where we're going." In Mark Rosenzweig and Lyman Porter (eds.), *Annual Review of Psychology,* 42: 427–458. Palo Alto, CA: Annual Reviews.

Pfeffer, Jeffrey (1977) "Effects of an MBA and socioeconomic origins on business school graduates' salaries." *Journal of Applied Psychology,* 62: 698–705.

Pfeffer, Jeffrey, and Nancy Langton (1988). "Wage inequality and the organization of work: The case of academic departments." *Administrative Science Quarterly,* 33: 588–606.

Piedmont, R. L., Robert R. McCrae, and Paul T. Costa, Jr. (1991). "Adjective Check List Scales and the Five-Factor

Model." *Journal of Personality and Social Psychology,* 60: 630–637.

Pinder, Craig (1984). *Work Motivation: Theory, Issues, and Applications.* Glenview, IL: Scott, Foresman.

Reder, M. W. (1978) "An analysis of a small, closely observed labor market: Starting salaries of University of Chicago MBAs." *Journal of Business,* 51: 263–297.

Ree, Malcolm J., and James A. Earles (1991a). "Predicting training success: Not much more than *g.*" *Personnel Psychology,* 44: 321–332.

Ree, Malcolm J., and James A. Earles (1991b). "The stability of *g* across different methods of estimation." *Intelligence,* 15: 271–278.

Ree, Malcolm J., and James A. Earles (1992). "Intelligence is the best predictor of job performance." *Current Directions in Psychological Science,* 1: 86–89.

Rosenbaum, James E. (1979). "Tournament mobility: Career patterns in a corporation." *Administrative Science Quarterly,* 24: 220–241.

Schmidt, Frank L., and John E. Hunter (1992). "Development of a causal model of process determining job performance." *Current Directions in Psychological Science,* 1: 89–92.

Schmidt, Frank L., John E. Hunter, and Alice N. Outerbridge (1986). "Impact of job experience and ability on job knowledge, work sample performance, and supervisory ratings of job performance." *Journal of Applied Psychology,* 71: 432–439.

Schmidt, Frank L., John E. Hunter, Alice N. Outerbridge, and Stephen Goff (1988). "Joint relation of experience and ability with job performance: Test of three hypotheses." *Journal of Applied Psychology,* 73: 46–57.

Schmidt, Frank L., Dennis S. Ones, and John E. Hunter (1992). "Personnel selection." In Mark Rosenzweig and Lyman Porter (eds.), *Annual Review of Psychology,* 43: 627–670. Palo Alto, CA: Annual Reviews.

Schneider, Benjamin (1987). "The people make the place." *Personnel Psychology,* 40: 437–453.

Schoonhoven, Claudia B. (1981). "Problems with contingency theory: Testing assumptions hidden within the language of contingency 'theory'." *Administrative Science Quarterly,* 26: 349–377.

Seligman, Daniel (1992). *A Question of Intelligence: The IQ Debate in America.* New York: Birch Lane Press.

Spearman, Charles (1927). *The Abilities of Man.* New York: Macmillan.

Staw, Barry M., and Sigal G. Barsade (1993). "Affect and managerial performance: A test of the sadder-but-wiser vs. happier-and-smarter hypotheses." *Administrative Science Quarterly,* 38: 304–331.

Sternberg, Robert J. (1979). "The nature of mental abilities." *American Psychologist,* 34: 214–230.

Sternberg, Robert J., and Richard K. Wagner (1993). "The g-ocentric view of intelligence and job performance is wrong." *Current Directions in Psychological Science,* 3: 1–5.

Tyler, Leona E. (1986). "Back to Spearman?" *Journal of Vocational Behavior,* 29: 445–450.

Valliant, G. E. (1977). *Adaptation to Life.* Boston: Little, Brown.

Vernon, Phillip A. (ed.) (1987). *Speed of Information Processing and Intelligence.* Norwood, NJ: Ablex.

Weiss, Howard M., and Seymour Adler (1984). "Personality and organizational behavior." In Barry M. Staw and L. L.

Cummings (eds.), *Research in Organizational Behavior,* 6: 1–50. Greenwich, CT: JAI Press.

Wright, Jack, and Walter Mischel (1987). "A conditional approach to dispositional constructs: The local predictability of social behavior. *Journal of Personality and Social Psychology,* 53: 1159–1177.

Wright, Jack, and Walter Mischel (1988). "Conditional hedges and the intuitive psychology of traits." *Journal of Personality and Social Psychology,* 55: 454–469.

Wightman, Lawrence E., and Linda F. Leary (1985). *GMAC Validity Study Service: A Three Year Summary.* Los Angeles: Graduate Management Admissions Council, May.

Zedeck, Sheldon (1986). "A process analysis of the assessment center method." In Barry M. Staw and L. L. Cummings (eds.), *Research in Organizational Behavior,* 8: 259–296. Greenwich, CT: JAI Press.

The Effects of Social Identity on the Self-Set Goals and Task Performance of High and Low Self-Esteem Individuals

Anthony J. Pilegge
Rolf Holtz

The goals we set for ourselves define our basic motivations and give purpose to our actions (Emmons & McAdams, 1991). In the context of work, commitment to specific and difficult goals produces greater effort toward goal achievement (Williams, Karau, & Bourgeois, 1993) and better performance (Locke, Shaw, Saari, & Latham, 1981).

Attempts to identify reliable worker-related predictors of self-set goals have generally not been successful (Locke & Latham, 1990). Perhaps the most surprising enigma is the influence of self-esteem on goal setting. One might expect that persons with high self-esteem, who generally feel efficacious and who act in ways to maintain their self-concept (Crocker, Blaine, & Luhtanen, 1993; Pierce, Gardner, Cummings, & Dunham, 1989; Brockner, 1988), should strive to achieve more difficult goals than their low self-esteem counterparts. Researchers have not found this, however, unless they first engaged their subjects in a task and then motivated them toward further performance with feedback about their success (Baumeister & Tice, 1985; Dossett, Latham, & Mitchell, 1979; Shrauger & Rosenberg,

From *Organizational Behavior and Human Decision Processes,* 1997 70(1), 17–26. Reprinted by permission.

1970). The purpose of the present study is to show that in specific contexts high self-esteem workers will immediately set difficult goals for themselves without managerial coaxing. A strong social identity on the part of high self-esteem persons is expected to be the critical moderator of these self-set goals.

SELF-ESTEEM AND SELF-SET GOALS

Self-esteem is defined as the favorability of an individual's characteristic self-evaluation (Brockner, 1988). Some people consistently evaluate themselves positively and report optimism about their general abilities, whereas others do not. The positive self-ratings of high self-esteem persons seem to suggest that their self-set goals should place more demands on their abilities and thus be more difficult to achieve than goals set by low self-esteem persons (Locke et al., 1981; Carrol & Tosi, 1970). In tests of the relationship between self-esteem and self-set goals, however, high and low self-esteem individuals typically set equivalent goals (Tang & Sarsfield-Baldwin, 1991; Tang, Liu, & Vermillion, 1987; Hollenbeck & Brief, 1987; Locke et al., 1981; Hall & Foster, 1977; Korman, 1970). Apparently, self-esteem is not sufficient to account for the variability of self-set goals.

Despite the lack of relationship between self-esteem and goal setting reported in the literature, specific aspects of the high self-esteem character make the search for a stable link difficult to abandon. For example, high self-esteem individuals desire to think, feel, and act in ways that enhance their self-concept, whereas low self-esteem persons engage in self-protective strategies to minimize their risk of failure (Baumeister, 1993; Crocker et al., 1993; Brockner, 1988). These quite different motivations suggest that high self-esteem persons do not respond to challenges merely to prove their basic competencies, unlike individuals with low self-esteem. Moreover, in circumstances where feedback about the success or failure of performance is ambiguous or nonexistent, high self-esteem individuals expect that they performed satisfactorily (Hewstone, 1989; Shrauger, 1972). Regardless of actual achievement, they attribute responsibility for their outcomes to internal factors like their abilities (Shrauger, 1975). In the same situation, low self-esteem persons worry about not succeeding and consequently shunt responsibility for their performance to external causes like task difficulty (Weiner, 1986).

High self-esteem persons exercise their abilities when they perceive an opportunity to gain more than they already know they possess. In the context of most goal setting studies, however, few incentives are present that would inspire high self-esteem persons to declare publicly their intention to achieve challenging goals. Generally, a statement about one's goals is made only to an experimenter, who is also the only person evaluating subsequent performance. The experimenter is usually a stranger acting in a supervisory capacity, and consequently may be distrusted. Furthermore, the experimental task is often unfamiliar and ego-uninvolving (Locke & Latham, 1990). It is perhaps ironic that high self-esteem individuals respond cautiously in situations like these. High self-esteem persons maintain their positive self-view by being selective about the tasks they undertake (Baumeister, Heatherton, & Tice, 1993; Baumeister & Tice, 1985). They are not likely to invest effort in activities that do not promise valued rewards.

Korman (1970) suggested that high self-esteem individuals perform best in an environment where their talents and abilities can be used to elicit self-affirming or self-enhancing feedback from similar others. In such a context, Tang and Reynolds (1993) studied the self-set goals of competitive dart-throwers from two dart-throwing organizations. Prior to competition, high and low self-esteem subject groups were identified using Rosenberg's (1965) measure of chronic self-esteem. Each subject also completed a short questionnaire that measured a self-set goal (i.e., the number of darts expected to be thrown in a game of "501") and then played against themselves, against a difficult competitor, and against an easy competitor in a randomized sequence. Tang and Reynolds (1993) found that when high self-esteem persons were interdependent players on a team, they set more difficult goals and performed better than low self-esteem persons. Each trial in the contest was conducted publicly. Consequently, each player was able to contribute to the team's level of success and also be recognized for that contribution.

Tang and Reynolds (1993) attributed their results to the stable and positive beliefs that high self-esteem individuals maintain about their own efficacy. The difference, however, between their outcomes and those of virtually all previous investigations suggests that the social context in which goals are set is an important moderator of the relationship between self-esteem and goal setting.

SOCIAL IDENTITY, SELF-ESTEEM, AND SELF-SET GOALS

The most striking difference between the Tang and Reynolds (1993) study and earlier studies is that real-world, competitive groups constituted the subject sample. Rather than testing subjects one-by-one (Tang & Sarsfield-Baldwin, 1991) or as an aggregate of individuals (Hall & Foster, 1977; Tang et al., 1987; Hollenbeck & Brief, 1987), Tang and Reynolds (1993) engaged teams in zero-sum competition that tested each individual's personal ability on a dimension that was central to the basis for team membership.

Intergroup competition heightens the salience of ingroup membership which can increase the value of winning beyond any objective weighting of realistic outcomes (Hogg, 1992; Hogg & Abrams, 1988). Similarly, the presence of ingroup or outgroup members, physical symbols of group membership, or even random assignment to one or another social category can direct a person's attention to specific self-defining attributes that can also be used to characterize other ingroup members (Turner, Oakes, Haslam, & McGarty, 1994; Diehl, 1990). Individuals who fail to "measure up" to these dimensions lose status within their group and often evaluate themselves negatively (Hogg, 1992). If group-relevant skills are highlighted, persons who perform poorly may threaten the integrity of their entire group. Conversely, capable members can enhance their own status and the status of their group by performing well. Matsui, Kakuyama, and Onglatco (1987) found that intergroup competition increased the difficulty of self-set goals when the needs of ingroup members were salient. Even when they are not competing, "central" group members report more pride in their group's performance and maintain higher goals for themselves than peripherally involved members (Zander, Forward, & Albert, 1969).

Individuals who become central ingroup members describe themselves, and are described by others, as representing the prototypical values and norms of their group (Hogg, Cooper-Shaw, & Holzworth, 1993). Self-ratings of prototypicality are high even among newcomers who are not yet socialized into their group (Worchel, Coutant-Sassic, & Grossman, 1992; Turner, Hogg, Oakes, Reicher, & Wetherell, 1987). Newcomers also use their own characteristics as the basis for inferring similarity between themselves and ingroup members, as well as dissimilarity to outgroup members (Holtz, 1997; Turner et al., 1994; Wilder, 1984). Accordingly, high self-esteem group members, who are certain that they possess positive attributes and abilities (Crocker et al., 1993), should readily expect those same characteristics to be manifested in the behavior of fellow ingroup members. Alternatively, low self-esteem persons may assume that members of their group share their concern for self-protection and avoiding humiliation (Baumeister, 1993). Interactions between group members who are homogeneous with regard to self-esteem are more likely to confirm these normative assumptions rather than refute them.

Thus, we tested the idea that social identification interacts with the self-esteem of ingroup members to influence their self-set goals. High and low self-esteem individuals were asked to set work goals for themselves either as part of a well-defined group or as an aggregate of individuals. We expected high self-esteem persons with a strong group identity to immediately set higher goals, and achieve more, than high self-esteem persons with a weak group identity. Strengthening the group identity of high self-esteem persons was expected to increase their perceived similarity to ingroup members thereby motivating them to strive harder on a group task (Korman, 1970). On the other hand, consistent with Tang and Reynolds (1993), social identification was not expected to influence the self-set goals of low self-esteem persons. Although a strong social identity could stabilize the self-concepts of low self-esteem persons (Festinger, 1954) and prevent them from setting extremely low goals (Baumeister et al., 1993; Brockner, 1988), increasing the perceived similarity of these self-protective individuals to other ingroup members should not facilitate counternormative, challenging goals (Turner, 1991).

The present study also provided an opportunity to measure the attributions of high and low self-esteem individuals regarding the causes of their respective performances. Consistent with their indefatigable confidence about their own efficacy, high self-esteem subjects were expected to attribute their performance to personal ability (Shrauger, 1975). In contrast, low self-esteem persons were expected to attribute their performance to the most salient self-protective attribution available to them, task difficulty (Weiner, 1986).

METHOD

Subjects and Design

Forty-two male and 78 female undergraduates participated in this study for course credit. The study constituted a 2(high vs. low self-esteem) $\times$ 2(strong vs. weak social identity) between-subjects factorial design. The proportion of males to females was approximately equal per cell.

Self-Esteem Pretest

One week prior to the experiment, Rosenberg's (1965) self-esteem scale was administered to 459 Introductory Psychology students who constituted a pool of potential participants. Test-retest reliability coefficients for this scale exceed .80 (Rosenberg, 1965), and the measure is well validated (Luhtanen & Crocker, 1992; Pierce et al., 1989). The range of our pretest scores was 15 to 40, out of a possible range of 10 to 40, with a median of 32. More than one-fourth ($n = 126$) of these pretested individuals had scores of 31 to 33. Consequently, these persons were eliminated from the pool of study-eligible students to minimize the threat of range restriction and to simultaneously increase the validity of low and high self-esteem comparisons (Kelley, 1939). Subsequent volunteers included equal numbers of high self-esteem ($n = 60$; range = 34 to 40; $M = 35.88$, $SD = 1.86$) and low self-esteem ($n = 60$; range = 15 to 30; $M = 27.92$, $SD = 3.29$) participants. These subjects correspond to high and low self-esteem samples employed by others (Crocker, Thompson, McGraw, & Ingerman, 1987).

Procedure

Six subjects, all with either high or low self-esteem, participated in each session. Preliminary instructions introduced this study as an investigation of the relationship between "perceptual judgment and divergent reasoning." Following a dot estimation task (Tajfel, 1970), each participant was randomly assigned to a three-person group.

Both groups participating in each session were randomly assigned to a strong or weak social identity condition. The procedure used to manipulate this variable was adapted from Turner, Pratkanis, Probasco, and Leve (1992). In the strong social identity condition, subjects were explicitly labeled as *Overestimators* or *Underestimators,* and each person wore a badge stating his or her group name until the end of the session. In the weak social identity condition (the "aggregate"), subjects did not receive a badge. They were told that no pattern had emerged from the dot estimation task that allowed them to be categorized systematically. They were informed that they would be working in the same room with two other individuals for the sake of convenience, and that their room assignment was made randomly. After categorization, each group moved to a different laboratory room, and no further contact occurred between the groups. The activities of each group were coordinated by either a male or a female experimenter. In the strong social identity condition, the experimenter's gender was counterbalanced with over- and underestimator categories.

All subjects were informed that their task in this phase of the study would involve "thinking of all the different possible uses for a common object." Without saying more about this task, subjects were told that participants in an earlier session generated all the possible uses for an automobile tire. Each subject then received a copy of the same list of 10 uses for a tire, which ostensibly represented a portion of one person's work from the earlier session.

This opportunity to view the task performance of a previous participant served a twofold purpose. First, the excerpt familiarized all subjects with the *type* of task they were to perform. Secondly, because the exact nature of their own upcoming task remained unspecified, subjects in the strong social identity condition could discuss the earlier work without exchanging information that might have affected their own future performance. All subjects individually evaluated the creativity of each use for a tire listed on the sheet of paper (7-point scales). These ratings did not differ reliably between social identity conditions, or self-esteem categories.[1] Subjects in the strong social identity condition also discussed each use

---

[1]Nevertheless, social identity exerted the greatest influence. Although mean ratings did not exceed the midpoint of the scale, they were somewhat lower in the strong social identity condition ($M = 4.01$, $SD = .61$) than in the weak social identity condition ($M = 4.24$, $SD = .45$), $F(1, 36) = 1.76$. $p < .20$.

for a tire with their two fellow group members to arrive at a consensual group evaluation. Thus, subjects in the strong social identity condition received an opportunity to augment their identification with ingroup members beyond that produced by social categorization alone (Ostrom & Sedikides, 1992).[2]

The author of the uses for a tire was identified to strong social identity subjects as an outgroup member to dispel uncertainty and conjecture about whether over- or underestimators originated the list (Byrne, Clore, & Smeaton, 1986). This may also have helped to polarize group identity in this condition (Wilder & Shapiro, 1984). In the weak social identity condition, the author was anonymous. Checks on the manipulation of social identity were distributed after the evaluation task. One additional item checked the validity of subjects' assignments to high and low self-esteem conditions.

Following the manipulation checks, all subjects received oral and written instructions adapted from Williams and Karau (1991):

> Now that you understand a little more about this type of task, I would like you to perform a similar type of "brainstorming" task. Your task is to come up with as many uses for a knife as you can in 10 minutes. At this time, however, I don't want you to be concerned with the quality of the uses you come up with. Rather, you should try to produce as *many* uses as you can. The uses for a knife can be ordinary or unusual. It is important, however, that you write down as many uses as you can during the 10 minute period.

In order to provide some perspective on what might be considered good performance, all subjects were told that no participant had as yet produced more than 55 uses for a knife within the 10-min interval. Furthermore, everyone was informed that individual and "room scores" would be posted after the session was over. All subjects were asked to work on the task alone.

At this point, each subject received dependent measures of goal setting, certainty, and perceived goal difficulty. When these measures were collected, subjects received a sheet of paper and were instructed to begin the task. After 10 min the uses for a knife were collected, and attribution measures and ingroup and outgroup competence measures were distributed. Finally, all subjects were debriefed.

Measures

Following their evaluation of the uses for a tire, subjects completed three items checking on the effectiveness of the social identity manipulation. Subjects indicated how successful the previous participant was at coming up with uses for a tire (1 = *Very Unsuccessful*, 7 = *Very Successful*) to determine whether this target's outgroup rubric in the strong social identity condition elicited more bias than no label in the weak identity condition. Additional measures included how similar subjects felt to other persons in their room (1 = *Very Dissimilar*, 7 = *Very*

---

[2]M. E. Turner et al. (1992), and Reese (1993) who replicated their procedure, demonstrated the difficulty of maintaining low identification between group members who interact—even when the structure of their interaction is intended to produce divisiveness, e.g., discussing interpersonal differences. In the present study, subjects in the weak social identity condition did not interact to prevent ingroup identification from developing beyond levels produced by being together in the same room. Hence, comparability between this condition and the aggregate context of earlier goal-setting research was preserved. In contrast, identity development was allowed to proceed naturally in the strong identity condition.

Similar) and how much they would like to work with the persons in their room again in the future (1 = *Not Very Much,* 7 = *Very Much*). These few questions were selected from among other potentially informative measures (e.g., group prototypicality of self, ingroup cooperativeness, and belonging) to minimize demand on subjects in the weak identity (aggregate) condition to be interconnected before they set their individual goals. At this time, subjects also rated how successful they felt they would be when thinking of their uses for an object as a check on the self-esteem assignments (1 = *Very Unsuccessful,* 7 = *Very Successful*).

After they received instructions about their own task, all subjects indicated their self-set goal (i.e., the number of uses for a knife they would generate in a 10-min interval), their certainty about achieving their self-set goal (expressed as a percentage between 0 and 100), and the perceived difficulty of achieving this goal (1 = *Very Easy,* 7 = *Very Hard*). No differences were found between experimental conditions regarding the latter measure, so it will not be discussed further. Task performance was measured by a tally of the number of uses for a knife each person listed.

Upon completion of the uses-for-a-knife task, subjects responded to four questions regarding the extent to which ability, effort, task difficulty, and luck contributed to their performance (1 = *Very Little,* 7 = *Very Much*). They also completed two additional items concerning the perceived competency of persons "in their room" and "in the other room," i.e., ingroup and outgroup members, respectively (1 = *Very Incompetent,* 7 = *Very Competent*).

RESULTS

Because subjects participated in mixed-gender groups, preliminary analyses were conducted with gender as a factor in the design. No effects were found for subjects' gender, so the data from each three-person group were averaged to control for possible nonindependence between subjects' responses. Thus, each group became the unit of analysis ($n = 40$).

Manipulation Checks and the Competency of Others

Subjects in the strong social identity condition rated the author of the uses for a tire marginally less successful at this task ($M = 4.87$, $SD =. 74$) than subjects in the weak social identity condition did ($M = 5.28$, $SD = .60$), $F(1, 36) = 3.81$, $p < .06$. On the other hand, strong identity subjects rated themselves considerably more similar to persons in their lab room ($M = 4.90$, $SD = .68$) than weak identity subjects did ($M = 3.72$, $SD = .59$), $F(1, 36) = 33.38$, $p < .0001$. Furthermore, persons in the strong identity condition expressed a greater desire to work with persons from their room in the future ($M = 5.35$, $SD = .67$) than did persons in the weak identity condition ($M = 4.43$, $SD = .62$), $F(1, 36) = 20.09$, $p < .0001$. Clearly, the social identity manipulation was successful, particularly in regard to its influence on evaluations of ingroup members. No effects of self-esteem were found on these measures.

When asked about their own likelihood of successfully generating uses for an object, high self-esteem persons expected to be more successful ($M = 4.72$, $SD = .60$) than low self-esteem persons ($M = 4.25$, $SD = .58$), $F(1, 36) = 6.03$, $p < .02$. This finding upholds the validity of the high and low self-esteem subject assignments. Social identity had no effect on this measure, which shows that subjects' expectations for successful task performance were not affected by the procedure for manipulating social identity.

Social identity also exerted no influence in a 2(social identity) × 2(self-esteem) × 2(target of evaluation) mixed-model ANOVA conducted on the ratings of ingroup and outgroup competence. Apparently, the marginal intergroup bias that existed before goals were set abated by the time the uses-for-a-knife task was completed. Furthermore, no effects for self-esteem or target of evaluation were found (overall target ratings: ingroup, $M = 5.03$, $SD = .73$; outgroup, $M = 4.87$, $SD = .69$). Nevertheless, ratings of ingroup and outgroup competence were highly correlated, $r(38) = .78$, $p < .0001$. The absence of self-esteem effects was likely due to antipodal correlations between self-ratings on the Rosenberg self-esteem measure and judgments of competence rendered by high and low self-esteem persons. Among high self-esteem individuals, self-ratings on the Rosenberg scale correlated positively with perceived ingroup competence, $r(18) = .39$, $p < .05$, and marginally with estimates of outgroup competence, $r(18) = .33$, $p < .08$. For low self-esteem persons, self-ratings correlated negatively with perceived outgroup competence, $r(18) = -.46$, $p < .02$, and marginally in the same direction with ratings of ingroup competence, $r(18) = -.35$, $p < .07$. Generally, high self-esteem individuals expected others to be as competent as they knew themselves to be. On the other hand, increments in the self-esteem scores of low self-esteem persons predicted relatively negative ratings of others' competence, especially outgroup members.

Self-Set Goals

The primary dependent measure of goal setting was analyzed using a 2(self-esteem) × 2(social identity) between-subjects ANOVA. The results indicated that high self-esteem persons set more difficult goals than persons with low self-esteem, $F(1, 36) = 8.56$, $p < .006$; and strong social identity subjects set higher goals than weak identity subjects, $F(1, 36) = 8.11$, $p < .007$. Both of these main effects were qualified by an interaction showing that the only group who truly set higher goals for themselves were the high self-esteem subjects in the strong social identity condition, $F(1, 36) = 8.20$, $p < .007$. These means and standard deviations are presented in Table 1.

A multiple regression ANOVA that tested self-esteem as a continuous variable (which does not require that every score be represented) corroborated the findings of the median split ANOVA. Main effects were found for social identity, $F(1, 36) = 7.68$, $p < .01$, and self-esteem, $F(1, 36) = 6.89$, $p < .025$; and the interaction between these variables was significant, $F(1, 36) = 7.06$, $p < .025$.

As expected, among high self-esteem persons, goal setting correlated with perceived similarity to coworkers, $r(18) = .48$, $p < .02$. This relationship was not found among low self-esteem persons, $r(18) = -.0002$, ns., and correlations with the other manipulation checks were nonsignificant. Thus, individuals with high self-esteem set higher goals for themselves as their perceived similarity to coworkers increased, and perceived similarity increased as their group identity developed.[3]

---

[3]It is noteworthy that the self-set goals of low self-esteem subjects in the weak social identity condition were negatively correlated with perceived similarity to coworkers, $r(8) = -.59$, $p < .04$, and with liking, $r(8) = -.69$, $p < .01$. Apparently, greater interpersonal attraction to coworkers was associated with less achievement striving. This relationship was not found among low self-esteem subjects in the strong identity condition.

TABLE 1 Effects of Social Identity and Self-Esteem on Self-Set Goals

Self-Esteem	Social Identity		
	Strong	Weak	Pooled
High			
M	28.27$_a$	16.13$_b$	22.20
SD	8.29	5.03	9.12
Low			
M	15.97$_b$	16.00$_b$	15.98
SD	6.84	6.31	6.41
Pooled			
M	22.12	16.07	
SD	9.72	5.56	

Note: High scores indicate more difficult self-set goals. Means with different subscripts differ from each other. $p < .001$.

Task Performance

Subjects with high self-esteem generated more uses for a knife than their low self-esteem counterparts, $F(1, 36) = 4.46, p < .04$. Moreover, persons with a strong social identity produced more uses for a knife than persons with a weak social identity, $F(1, 36) = 4.12, p < .05$. To test the form of the interaction between self-esteem and social identity that was predicted at the outset of this study and that characterized the pattern of goals subjects set, orthogonal weights were applied to the mean uses for a knife in each experimental condition. As expected, more uses for a knife were listed by high self-esteem subjects in the strong identity condition than in any of the other three experimental conditions, $F(1, 36) = 8.76, p < .01$. These means and standard deviations are presented in Table 2.

Across all conditions, the number of listed uses for a knife correlated with the goals subjects set for themselves, $r(38) = .63, p < .0001$. Furthermore, like the goals high self-esteem subjects set, the actual number of uses they generated correlated with their perceived similarity to coworkers, $r(18) = .38, p < .05$. This relationship was nonsignificant for low self-esteem subjects, $r(18) = -.009$.

Certainty

Consistent with Tang et al. (1991, 1993), high self-esteem subjects were more certain ($M = 78.85, SD = 10.38$) than low self-esteem subjects ($M = 69.45, SD = 11.80$) that they would achieve their goals, $F(1, 36) = 7.23, p < .02$. For low self-esteem subjects, certainty about goal attainment correlated with expected success, $r(18) = .38, p < .05$, their self-set goals, $r(18) = .42, p < .04$, and actual task performance, $r(18) = .44, p < .03$. For high self-esteem subjects, certainty was not correlated with their expected success, $r(18) = .15$, goals, $r(18) = .14$, or performance, $r(18) = .07$. No other effects were found on this measure.

Attributions for Task Performance

As expected, performance on the uses for a knife task was attributed more to personal ability by high self-esteem subjects ($M = 5.02, SD = .96$) than by low self-esteem subjects ($M = $

TABLE 2   **Effects of Social Identity and Self-Esteem on Task Performance**

Self-Esteem	Social Identity		
	Strong	Weak	Pooled
High			
M	26.20$_a$	20.23$_b$	23.22
SD	6.82	6.83	7.32
Low			
M	20.07$_b$	17.80$_b$	18.93
SD	7.15	4.50	5.93
Pooled			
M	23.13	19.02	
SD	7.50	5.76	

Note: High scores indicate greater performance. Means with different subscripts differ from each other. $p < .01$.

4.28, $SD = .65$), $F(1, 36) = 7.73$, $p < .01$. No effects involving social identity were found on this measure. For high self-esteem persons, performance and ability attributions were correlated, $r(18) = .42$, $p < .04$. This correlation was not found for low self-esteem persons, $r(18) = .27$, ns.

The attribution we expected to be most salient to low self-esteem subjects to account for their performance involved their task. Indeed, the fewer uses for a knife that low self-esteem individuals listed, the more they blamed the cause of their performance on task difficulty, $r(18) = -.41$, $p < .04$. The same was not true of high self-esteem individuals, $r(18) = -.08$, ns.

A 2(self-esteem) × 2(social identity) ANOVA conducted on attributions of task difficulty revealed only an interaction between these factors, $F(1, 36) = 10.95$, $p < .002$. As anticipated, performance was attributed to task difficulty more by low self-esteem persons with a weak social identity ($M = 4.97$, $SD = .67$) than by high self-esteem persons with a weak identity ($M = 3.87$, $SD = .80$), $t(36) = 3.93$, $p < .001$. However, low esteem/weak identity subjects also blamed their performance on task difficulty more than low esteem/strong identity subjects did ($M = 4.13$, $SD = .93$), $t(36) = 3.00$, $p < .01$. This may indicate that low esteem/strong identity subjects had another external attribution available to them—their fellow ingroup members (Brockner, 1988). On the other hand, attributions of task difficulty made by low esteem/weak identity individuals matched attributions made by high esteem/strong identity individuals ($M = 4.90$, $SD = 1.10$), $t(36) < 1$. In the latter condition, subjects set more difficult goals for themselves and, therefore, did face a more difficult task. This explanation is suggested by a positive correlation between self-set goals and attributions of task difficulty found only among high self-esteem subjects, $r(18) = .42$, $p < .04$.

Finally, the effort high self-esteem subjects reported investing in their task was correlated only with their attributions about their ability, $r(18) = .39$, $p < .05$. For low self-esteem subjects, effort correlated only with perceived task difficulty, $r(18) = .42$, $p < .04$. No other effects were found regarding effort, nor were any effects found concerning luck.

DISCUSSION

This study is important because it demonstrates the catalytic effect of identification with co-workers on high self-esteem persons. As expected, high self-esteem individuals who strongly identified with their group set higher goals and achieved more than high self-esteem persons with a weak social identity, or low self-esteem esteem persons irrespective of the strength of their social identity. Individuals who strongly identify with their group define themselves by attributes that all ingroup members are assumed to share (Turner et al., 1987, 1994). In the present study, both high and low self-esteem persons perceived greater similarity between themselves and ingroup members in the strong identity condition than in the weak identity condition. Increasing perceived similarity to coworkers, however, only predicted higher self-set goals and better task performance for individuals with high self-esteem.

Whether perceived similarity to coworkers augments self-set goals and performance depends upon the specific attributes that individuals believe they share with other members of their group. In the present study, persons with high self-esteem judged the competence of ingroup members positively commensurate with their own pretest self-esteem score. Working with competent coworkers requires extraordinary effort, particularly when task success is defined by how well one's work compares to the work of others. High self-esteem persons need to perceive those ingroup members with whom they compare themselves as similarly capable people (Korman, 1970). Otherwise, their comparative successes have no utility for enhancing their confidence about their abilities or their pride in accomplishment (Crocker et al., 1993; Festinger, 1954). We demonstrated that high self-esteem persons do not need a strong social identity to expect to be successful or to attribute apparently successful performance to their abilities. These are chronic cognitions of high self-esteem personalities that likely stem from self-knowledge about earlier achievements (Shrauger, 1972, 1975). The level of aspiration that serves as the criterion of their success, however, is influenced by the productivity norm that these individuals perceive is prototypical of their group (Hogg, 1992; Turner, 1991; Festinger, 1942). Thus, although it is often futile to exhort high self-esteem individuals to action (Brockner, 1988), we showed that they can be inspired to achieve high goals when they identify with coworkers whom they judge to be competent.

Unlike the self-set goals and performance of high self-esteem persons, the goals and performance of individuals with low self-esteem were linked to their certainty about what they could accomplish. Regardless of social identity strength, persons with low self-esteem were less certain about achieving their goals than high self-esteem individuals were, and they expected to be less successful. Furthermore, their readiness to attribute the cause of their performance to external constraints such as task difficulty is additional evidence that low self-esteem persons were concerned about their possibility of failing (Baumeister, 1993; Crocker et al., 1993; Shrauger, 1972). Like high self-esteem individuals, persons with low self-esteem rated their similarity to coworkers greatest in the strong social identity condition. Competence, however, was not a characteristic they reported sharing with other members of their group. Increments in their pretest self-esteem scores (within the low self-esteem category) predicted negative ratings of others' competency—especially outgroup members.

By differentiating themselves from others on the dimension of competence, low self-esteem individuals may have protected or even enhanced their personal self-concept.

Downward comparison to outgroup members can help low self-esteem subjects sustain at least a middling positive self-view (Baumeister, 1993; Baumgardner, Kaufman, & Levy, 1989). Evidence showing that ingroup members were also the target of downward social comparison suggests that low self-esteem persons may experience difficulty developing and maintaining intragroup cohesion, particularly when failure on a group task is expected (Crocker et al., 1993; Lott & Lott, 1965). Group cohesion is at risk if members habitually distort their perceptions of each other to fortify their own self-concepts.

Future research can clarify the range of dimensions on which low (and high) self-esteem persons actually acknowledge their similarity to ingroup members. If any of these attributes contribute to a negative group identity, then follow-up work can assess the influence of such an identity on group commitment and productivity (Moreland, Levine, & Cini, 1993; Hogg, 1992). In both low and high self-esteem persons, egoism and associated self-regulation failure (cf. Baumeister, Heatherton, & Tice, 1993) might be mitigated if subjects remain alert to their continuing interdependence and common fate with other ingroup members.

The self-set goals and performance of low self-esteem subjects do not indicate any attempt to compensate for the failings of coworkers, real or imagined (Williams & Karau, 1991). Likewise, social compensation cannot explain the goals and performance of high self-esteem persons because they expected ingroup members to be competent. High self-esteem persons were most likely trying to establish themselves as valuable members of their new work group. Hence, they may have competed with ingroup members to determine who was most prototypically competent (Codol, 1975). This situation can account for why the goals and performance of high self-esteem persons correlated only with ingroup similarity and not with liking to work together in the future. Interestingly, low self-esteem individuals probably also desired positive status in their group, but apparently adopted negative attitudes toward others to achieve this mien—in lieu of actually achieving uncertain goals.

Notwithstanding the link between low self-esteem scores and outgroup competence ratings, social identification had a relatively weak effect on evaluations of the outgroup author of the uses for a tire, and no effect on the mean intergroup ratings of competence. Furthermore, intergroup bias was not influenced by levels of self-esteem, nor did the opportunity to engage in intergroup discrimination affect subjects' perceived likelihood of success, i.e., one component of self-esteem (cf. Hogg & Abrams, 1990, 1993; Hogg & Sunderland, 1991; Abrams & Hogg, 1988). Only subjects in the strong social identity condition might have been expected to rely on intergroup differentiation as a method of self-evaluation (Turner, 1975). Even here, however, goals were set independently by each group member, and personal accomplishment was a more salient basis for reward than group accomplishments. If social comparison had followed goal-setting, other ingroup members were more relevant and accessible targets than outgroup members (Ruscher, Fiske, Miki, & Van Manen, 1991). In minimal group studies (Diehl, 1990), no opportunity to engage in intragroup comparison exists. When such an opportunity is available, high self-esteem group members are more likely than low self-esteem members to realistically assess each others' goals and performances before turning their attention to intergroup comparisons (Crocker et al., 1993).

Early in group development, social projection processes may make actual ingroup heterogeneity on dimensions related to self-esteem immaterial to social identification (Holtz, 1997). As interactions multiply, however, social comparison between high and low self-esteem persons can alter individual self-concepts and the strength of members' identification with their group (Pelham & Wachsmuth, 1995; van Knippenberg & Ellemers, 1993; Festinger, 1954). Our findings suggest that managerial concern for the social identity of workers who remain low in self-esteem will augur little change in their productivity. On the other hand, allowing the social identity of high self-esteem workers to enervate unchecked heralds decreases in their productivity and diminished organizational returns.

References

Abrams, D., & Hogg, M. A. (1988). Comments on the motivational status of self-esteem in social identity and intergroup discrimination. *European Journal of Social Psychology, 18,* 317–338.

Baumeister, R. F. (1993). *Self-esteem: The puzzle of low self-regard.* New York: Plenum Press.

Baumeister, R. F., Heatherton, T. F., & Tice, D. M. (1993). When ego threats lead to self-regulation failure: Negative consequences of high self-esteem. *Journal of Personality and Social Psychology, 64,* 141–156.

Baumeister, R. F., & Tice, D. M. (1985). Self-esteem and responses to success and failure: Subsequent performance and intrinsic motivation. *Journal of Personality, 53,* 450–467.

Baumgardner, A. H., Kaufman, C. M., & Levy, P. E. (1989). Regulating affect interpersonally: When low self-esteem leads to greater enhancement. *Journal of Personality and Social Psychology, 56,* 907–921.

Brockner, J. (1988). *Self-esteem at work: Research, theory, and practice.* Lexington, MA: Lexington Books.

Byrne, D., Clore, G. L., & Smeaton, G. (1986). The attraction hypothesis: Do similar attitudes affect anything? *Journal of Personality and Social Psychology, 51,* 1167–1170.

Carroll, S. J., & Tosi, H. L. (1970). Goal characteristics and personality factors in a management by objectives program. *Administrative Science Quarterly, 15,* 295–305.

Codol, J. P. (1975). On the so-called "superior conformity of the self" behavior: 20 experimental investigations. *European Journal of Social Psychology, 5,* 457–501.

Crocker, J., Blaine, B., & Luhtanen, R. (1993) Prejudice, intergroup behaviour and self-esteem: Enhancement and protection motives. In M. A. Hogg & D. Abrams (Eds.), *Group motivation: Social psychological perspectives* (pp. 52–67). Hemel Hempstead: Harvester Wheatsheaf, and New York: Prentice Hall.

Crocker, J., Thompson, L. L., McGraw, K. M., & Ingerman, C. (1987). Downward comparison, prejudice, and evaluations of others: Effects of self-esteem and threat. *Journal of Personality and Social Psychology, 52,* 907–916.

Diehl, M. (1990). The minimal group paradigm: Theoretical explanations and empirical findings. *European Review of Social Psychology, 1,* 263–292.

Dossett, D. L., Latham, G. P., & Mitchell, T. R. (1979). Effects of assigned vs. participatively set goals, knowledge of results, and individual differences on employee behavior when goal difficulty is held constant. *Journal of Applied Psychology, 64,* 291–298.

Emmons, R. A., & McAdams, D. P. (1991). Personal strivings and motive dispositions: Exploring the links. *Personality and Social Psychology Bulletin, 17,* 648–654.

Festinger, L. (1954). A theory of social comparison processes. *Human Relations, 7,* 117–140.

Festinger, L. (1942). Wish, expectation, and group standards as factors influencing level of aspiration. *Journal of Abnormal and Social Psychology, 37,* 184–200.

Hall, D. T., & Foster, L. W. (1977). A psychological success cycle and goal setting: Goals, performance, and attitudes. *Academy of Management Journal, 20,* 282–290.

Hewstone, M. (1989). *Causal attribution: From cognitive processes to collective beliefs.* Oxford: Blackwell.

Hogg, M. A. (1992). *The social psychology of group cohesiveness: From attraction to social identity.* London: Harvester Wheatsheaf, and New York: New York University Press.

Hogg, M. A., & Abrams D. (1988). *Social identification: A social psychology of intergroup relations and group processes.* London: Routledge and Kegan Paul.

Hogg, M. A., & Abrams, D. (1990). Social motivation, self-esteem and social identity. In D. Abrams & M. A. Hogg (Eds.), *Social identity theory: Constructive and Critical advances* (pp. 28–47). Hemel Hempstead: Harvester Wheatsheaf, and New York: Springer-Verlag.

Hogg, M. A., & Abrams, D. (1993). Towards a single-process uncertainty-reduction model of social motivation in groups. In M. A. Hogg & D. Abrams (Eds.), *Group motivation: Social psychological perspectives* (pp. 173–190). Hemel Hempstead: Harvester Wheatsheaf, and New York: Prentice Hall.

Hogg, M. A., Cooper-Shaw, L., & Holzworth, D. W. (1993). Group prototypicality and depersonalized attraction in small interactive groups. *Personality and Social Psychology Bulletin,* 19, 452–465.

Hogg, M. A., & Sunderland, J. (1991). Self-esteem and intergroup discrimination in the minimal group paradigm. *British Journal of Social Psychology.* 30, 51–62.

Hollenbeck, J. R., & Brief, A. P. (1987). The effects of individual differences and goal origin on goal setting and performance. *Organizational Behavior and Human Decision Processes,* 40, 392–414.

Holtz, R. (1997). Length of group membership, assumed similarity, and opinion certainty: The dividend for veteran members. *Journal of Applied Social Psychology,* 27, 539–555.

Kelley, T. L. (1939). The selection of upper and lower groups for the validation of test items. *Journal of Educational Psychology,* 30, 17–24.

Korman, A. K. (1970). Toward a hypothesis of work behavior. *Journal of Applied Psychology,* 54, 31–41.

Locke, E. A., & Latham, G. P. (1990). *A theory of goal setting and task performance.* Englewood Cliffs, NJ: Prentice Hall.

Locke, E. A., Shaw, K. N., Saari, L. M., & Latham, G. P. (1981). Goal setting and task performance: 1969–1980. *Psychological Bulletin,* 90, 125–152.

Lott, A. J., & Lott, B. E. (1965). Group cohesiveness as interpersonal attraction. *Psychological Bulletin,* 64, 259–309.

Luhtanen, R., & Crocker, J. (1992). A collective self-esteem scale: Self-evaluation of one's social identity. *Personality and Social Psychology Bulletin,* 18, 302–318.

Matsui, T., Kakuyama, T., & Onglatco, M. L. U. (1987). Effects of goals and feedback on performance in groups. *Journal of Applied Psychology,* 72, 407–415.

Moreland, R., Levine, J., & Cini, M. (1993). Group socialization: The role of commitment. In M. A. Hogg & D. Abrams (Eds.), *Group motivation: Social psychological perspectives* (pp. 105–129). Hemel Hempstead: Harvester Wheatsheaf, and New York: Prentice Hall.

Ostrom, T. M., & Sedikides, C. (1992). Out-group homogeneity effects in natural and minimal groups. *Psychological Bulletin,* 112, 536–552.

Pelham, B. W., & Wachsmutt, J. O. (1995). The waxing and waning of the social self: Assimilation and contrast in social comparison. *Journal of Personality and Social Psychology,* 69, 825–838.

Pierce, J. L., Gardner, D. G., Cummings, L. L., & Dunham, R. B. (1989). Organization-based self-esteem: Construct definition, measurement, and validation. *Academy of Management Journal,* 32, 622–648.

Reese, C. L. (1993). *Social support, Projected attitude similarity, and opinion certainty.* Unpublished master's thesis, Lamar University, Beaumont, TX.

Rosenberg, M. (1965). *Society and the adolescent self-image.* Princeton, NJ: Princeton University Press.

Ruscher, J. B., Fiske, S. T., Miki, H., & Van Manen, S. (1991). Individuating processes in competition: Interpersonal versus intergroup. *Personality and Social Psychology Bulletin,* 17, 595–605.

Shrauger, J. S. (1972). Self-esteem and reactions to being observed by others. *Journal of Personality and Social Psychology,* 72, 192–200.

Shrauger, J. S. (1975). Responses to evaluation as a function of initial self-perceptions. *Psychological Bulletin,* 82, 581–596.

Shrauger, J. S., & Rosenberg, S. E. (1970). Self-esteem and the effects of success and failure feedback on performance. *Journal of Personality* 38, 404–417.

Tajfel, H. (1970). Experiments in intergroup discrimination. *Scientific American,* 223, 96–102.

Tang, T. L. P., & Sarsfield-Baldwin, L. (1991). The effect of self-esteem, task label, and performance feedback on goal setting, certainty and attributions. *Journal of Psychology,* 125, 413–418.

Tang, T. L. P., Liu, H., & Vermillion, W. H. (1987). Effects of self-esteem and task labels (difficult vs. easy) on intrinsic motivation, goal setting, and task performance. *Journal of General Psychology,* 114, 249–262.

Tang, L. P. T., & Reynolds, D. B. (1993). Effects of self-esteem and perceived goal difficulty on goal setting, certainty, task performance, and attributions. *Human Resource Development Quarterly,* 4, 153–170.

Turner, J. C. (1975). Social comparison and social identity: Some prospects for intergroup behavior. *European Journal of Social Psychology,* 5, 5–34.

Turner, J. C. (1991) *Social influence.* Pacific Grove, CA: Brooks/Cole.

Turner, J. C., Hogg, M. A., Oakes, P. J., Reicher, S. D., & Wetherell, M. S. (1987). *Rediscovering the social group: A self-categorization theory.* Oxford: Basil Blackwell.

Turner, J. C., Oakes, P. J., Haslam, S. A., & McGarty, C. (1994). Self and collective: Cognition and social context. *Personality and Social Psychology Bulletin, 20,* 454–463.

Turner, M. E., Pratkanis, A. R., Probasco, P., & Leve, C. (1992). Threat, cohesion, and group effectiveness: Testing a social identity maintenance perspective on groupthink. *Journal of Personality and Social Psychology, 63,* 781–796.

van Knippenberg, A., & Ellemers, N. (1993). Strategies in intergroup relations. In M. A. Hogg & D. Abrams (Eds.), *Group motivation: Social psychological perspectives* (pp. 17–32). Hemel Hempstead: Harvester Wheatsheaf, and New York: Prentice Hall.

Weiner, B. (1986). *An attributional theory of achievement motivation and emotion.* New York: Springer-Verlag.

Wilder, D. A. (1984). Predictions of belief homogeneity and similarity following social categorization. *British Journal of Social Psychology, 23,* 323–333.

Wilder, D. A., & Shapiro, P. N. (1984). Role of outgroup cues in determining social identity. *Journal of Personality and Social Psychology, 47,* 342–348.

Williams, K. D., & Karau, S. J. (1991). Social loafing and social compensation: The effects of expectations of co-worker performance. *Journal of Personality and Social Psychology, 61,* 570–581.

Williams, K. D., Karau, S., & Bourgeois, M. (1993). Working on collective tasks: Social loafing and social compensation. In M. A. Hogg & D. Abrams (Eds.), *Group motivation: Social psychological perspectives* (pp. 130–148). Hemel Hempstead: Harvester Wheatsheaf, and New York: Prentice Hall.

Worchel, S., Coutant-Sassic, D., & Grossman, M. (1992). A developmental approach to group dynamics: A model and illustrative research. In S. Worchel, W. Wood, & J. A. Simpson (Eds.), *Group process and productivity* (pp. 181–202). Newbury Park: Sage.

Zander, A., Forward, J., & Albert, R. (1969). Adaptation of board members to repeated failure or success by their organization. *Organizational Behavior and Human Performance, 4,* 56–76.

Chapter **Nine**

Rewards

One of the central issues—if not *the* central issue—in considering motivation in work situations concerns the types of rewards and reward systems used in and by organizations. Applying the concept of reward in its broadest sense as something given in return for "good received," we can see that rewards are part of an exchange relationship between employers and employees. Organizations, or those individuals functioning in their behalf (e.g., managers and supervisors), provide rewards to employees in return for "good received," such as membership, attendance, and performance. The types of rewards and the ways in which they are distributed at work have considerable impact on employee motivation.

While reward systems are a cornerstone of organizational performance, experience has shown that they can be quite difficult to design and implement in ways that both employers and employees will view as mutually beneficial and satisfactory. Therefore, a basic understanding of the nature and function of rewards and reward systems is essential to managerial effectiveness. Before providing an overview of the articles included in this chapter, we distinguish between major types of rewards, describe the general sorts of employee behaviors organizational rewards are designed to motivate, and identify several difficulties associated with the implementation of reward systems at work.

TYPES OF REWARDS

There is a wide array of types of rewards that can be obtained by organizational members, ranging from obvious ones such as pay, fringe benefits, and promotion, to praise, autonomy in decision making, and feelings of accomplishment and competency. These different kinds of rewards can be classified along two major dimensions: intrinsic versus extrinsic and systemwide versus individual (as depicted in Exhibit 9.1). Intrinsic rewards are those that the individual provides himself or herself (e.g., feelings of accomplishment) as a result of performing some task. Tasks that motivate intrinsically are inherently satisfying, interesting, and enjoyable. In contrast, extrinsic rewards are those that are provided *to* the individual by someone else. Task performance that is extrinsically motivated is carried out to acquire independent material or social payoffs, such as pay or promotion. Ryan and Deci provide a review and assessment of the research on intrinsic versus extrinsic motivation in Chapter 2 of this volume. We will not reproduce their discussion here. We will, however, highlight several of their points that have implications *for* rewards and reward systems in organizations.

First, rewards that foster a sense of task competence, autonomy (the belief that behavior on tasks is self-determined or volitional rather than compliant), and relatedness (feelings of belongingness or connectedness with others) facilitate intrinsic motivation, as discussed by Ryan and Deci in Chapter 2. While the potential for intrinsic motivation exists only insofar as an activity or task holds some sort of inherent interest for a person, the extent to which that person's competence, autonomy, and relatedness needs are met influences whether intrinsic motivation is enhanced or frustrated. In addition, providing extrinsic rewards for a previously intrinsically motivated task can lead to a shift from an internal locus of causality (i.e., a sense of autonomy) to an external locus of causality, thereby potentially reducing intrinsic motivation. As Deci (1972, pp. 224–225) states:

> [T]he effects of intrinsic motivation and extrinsic motivation are not additive. While extrinsic rewards such as money can certainly motivate behavior, they appear to be doing so at the expense of intrinsic motivation; as a result, contingent pay systems do not appear to be compatible with participative management systems.

It should be noted, however, the extant empirical evidence regarding the hypothesis that providing extrinsic rewards reduces the impact of intrinsic rewards is mixed, and the issue is still hotly debated.

Several of the readings in this chapter will focus primarily on extrinsic rewards, those provided by the organization or some designated official (e.g., supervisor) *to* the individual. In considering extrinsic versus intrinsic rewards, however, the reader should be aware that in the literature on motivation at work these terms sometimes take on other meanings. Guzzo (1979) has made the point that any particular reward has multiple attributes (self-generated or not, immediate or delayed, of long or short duration, etc.). Thus, it is important to keep in mind that there are many variations of types of rewards within the two broad categories of extrinsic and intrinsic. As just one example among many that could be provided, consider that while a simple pat on the back from a supervisor and a promotion to a higher-status job with a significant increase in pay are both extrinsic rewards, their effects on the individual's performance may be quite different.

EXHIBIT 9.1   **Types of Rewards**

	Systemwide	Individual
Extrinsic	Example: Insurance benefits	Example: Large merit increase
Intrinsic	Example: Pride in being a part of a "winning" organization	Example: Feeling of self-fulfillment from the completion of a particular task

The other major dimension that can be used to classify types of rewards in organizational settings is the distinction emphasized by Katz (1964): systemwide rewards versus individual rewards. These different types of rewards may have distinct effects on work behavior. Systemwide rewards are those provided by the organization to everyone in a broad category of employees. Examples would be certain fringe benefits (e.g., medical insurance) that everyone in the organization receives simply by being an employee, or the dining room facilities provided to all managers above a certain level. In contrast, individual rewards are provided to particular persons but not to all people of a particular category of employees. Examples of individual rewards would be bonuses and merit increases.

If we combine the two dimensions, intrinsic versus extrinsic and systemwide versus individual, we have a convenient way of categorizing any particular type of reward, as shown in Exhibit 9.1. It is useful to keep this classification system in mind when considering the intended functions of reward systems discussed in the next section and in the readings contained in this chapter. A particular type of reward will often be very effective for one function, but very ineffective for another.

FUNCTIONS OF REWARDS AND REWARD SYSTEMS

Organizations provide rewards for many reasons. These are summarized in Exhibit 9.2 (based on categorization schemes suggested by March & Simon, 1958, and Katz, 1964). Rewards can motivate two broad categories of behavior: participation in the organization and performance in the organization.

The first of these categories, participation, can in turn be divided into membership and attendance. Membership refers to the act of joining the organization and the decision to remain with it. The other participation category is attendance (or the avoidance of absenteeism). Absenteeism can represent a major expense for organizations and, therefore, is a type of behavior that organizations would likely want to minimize. Most organizations devote considerable effort to designing reward systems to induce individuals to become members in the first place, and, having once joined, to instill in them a strong desire to remain with the organization and show up at work (both physically and psychologically).

The second major category of behavior that reward systems are designed to facilitate is job performance (or the "decision to produce" in March & Simon's terminology). Here, again, there are two distinct subcategories: "normal" or expected role (job) performance, and

EXHIBIT 9.2   **Types of Rewards**

> A. Participation
> 　　　1. Membership
> 　　　　　a. Joining
> 　　　　　b. Remaining
> 　　　2. Attendance (i.e., avoidance of absenteeism)
> B. Performance
> 　　　1. "Normal" or "Expected" role (job) performance
> 　　　2. "Extrarole behavior" (e.g., going well beyond duty to help a coworker)

what is called "extrarole behavior." The former refers to performance that meets the basic standards that the organization has set for someone in a particular job. When the standards are met, the organization would consider that the employee's part of the reciprocal deal has been fulfilled. The employee has, in effect, exchanged at least adequate job performance for an agreed-upon level of compensation.

Extrarole behavior, on the other hand, goes "above and beyond" what is normally expected by the organization for a particular job. It is behavior that is spontaneous and, perhaps, quite innovative (Katz, 1964). Many examples could be offered, of course, such as the clerk who goes out of the way to placate a dissatisfied customer, or the manager who voluntarily stays overtime to solve some particular production problem. Most organizations probably would not function very well if the only type of behavior exhibited by employees was the routine job performance mentioned previously. Hence, organizations need to find ways to motivate extrarole behavior from at least some of their employees.

The problem, from the organization's point of view at least, is that rewards effective in generating role-specific performance (such as merit pay) may not be very useful in motivating extrarole behavior. Thus, to the extent that such extraordinary behavior is needed, the organization is presented with a considerable challenge in the design and application of reward systems.

IMPLEMENTATION OF REWARD SYSTEMS

The best-designed reward systems can often go awry in producing their intended results because of the manner in which they are implemented. Several of the articles in this chapter deal directly with reward allocation and implementation problems. As one reviews the detailed discussions in these articles, it is useful to keep in mind several of the broad issues involved.

One important issue in implementing reward systems, and perhaps the most basic issue of all, concerns the evaluation or appraisal of performance—a point also stressed by Komaki in Chapter 2. If rewards are to be distributed in such a way that they have a positive impact on employee motivation to perform, it is crucial that the organization have effective means for assessing the quality and quantity of performance. If the appraisal systems that organizations use are unreliable or lack reasonable validity, it can hardly be expected that rewards distributed on the basis of such systems can have much effect on motivation, at least in the desired direction.

A second issue involves the questions of how and whether rewards are, in fact, related to performance. While it might seem obvious, at first glance, that rewards should be distributed directly in relation to performance differences, there are many reasons organizations do not do so. One reason was discussed already—the problem of accurately appraising performance. Another reason is the possibility that rewarding a particular aspect of job performance will focus attention away from other desirable performance dimensions, such as extrarole behavior. In addition, rewarding certain individuals or groups for high performance could have a negative effect on other individuals or groups. Also, many organizations believe they are relating rewards directly to performance when, in fact, the relationship is not seen or believed by those receiving the rewards. This, of course, reduces the motivational impact of the rewards.

The message here is threefold: First, it is not an easy matter to set up reward systems that relate rewards closely to performance. Second, it may not always be desirable to do so, at least from the organization's perspective. Third, even when organizations are both willing and able to tie rewards closely to particular aspects of employee task performances, the link may not be perceived by the intended reward recipients.

Another issue in reward systems implementation is the question of how well the systems in a particular organization relate to the general management style that characterizes an organization (Porter, Lawler, & Hackman, 1975). For example, organization theorists often distinguish between two broad categories of management style, an open/participative style versus a more traditional/authoritarian one. (Of course, many organizations, if not most, represent a blend of these two styles.) To the extent that a particular firm or agency is managed in accordance with one or the other of these styles, the more likely it is that a reward system will be ineffective if it is implemented in a way that is inconsistent with the particular management style. For example, a participative appraisal system coupled with a highly participative approach in the decisions regarding reward distribution is not likely to work well in an organization that is otherwise run in a very hierarchical, authoritarian manner. Likewise, attempting to have a rigid reward system based only on highly quantified and objective measures of performance is unlikely to have positive effects in an organization that prides itself on its open and participative way of operating.

A final implementation issue revolves around the question of whether there should be relative openness or secrecy regarding various aspects of monetary compensation. This issue is particularly acute in the management ranks of organizations, where typically there are fairly wide variations in pay for individuals at roughly the same level of the organization. Organizations vary considerably in how "open" the information provided is. Some provide extensive information about how rates of pay are determined but not very much information, if any, about the amount. Other organizations provide relatively little information about either. A minority of organizations (mostly in the public sector) provide open information both about methods of determining pay and about amounts. The issue, then, for most organizations (particularly in the private sector) is not so much whether to be open or secret, but rather the degree of openness.

OVERVIEW OF THE READINGS

The first reading in this chapter provides insight about how effective reward systems in organizations can, in fact, be designed and implemented. Lawler argues for the necessity of taking a strategic approach to compensation and the criticality of tying rewards to the achievement of corporate strategic objectives. He makes the important point that organization design and management policies must be compatible with, and supportive of, a reward system if it is to be organizationally effective.

In the next reading, Kerr makes the critical observation that reward systems can become quite "fouled up," so that unwanted behaviors are actually rewarded while desirable behavior goes completely uncompensated. In this widely cited article, the author illustrates his points with numerous examples from both work organizations and society. He concludes with suggestions about how organizations and managers can increase the likelihood that rewards will produce their hoped-for effects.

The next two readings provide additional cautionary signs about the not well thought-out use of pay at work. Pearce looks specifically at the issue of merit pay and considers why it often fails to achieve its intended objectives. She points out that contingent pay plans attempt to mimic marketplace contracts in how they motivate employee performance. However, the uncertainty, complexity, and dependence associated with the work carried out in most organizations tend to undermine the usefulness of contingent pay plans in organizations. Pearce emphasizes that pay plans must take into account the organizational contexts within which they are implemented.

Pfeffer takes a broader perspective on compensation and identifies six erroneous assumptions that managers tend to make about pay that lead them to adopt reward systems that are much less effective than they otherwise could be. Two examples of such assumptions are that labor costs constitute a significant portion of total costs and that people work for money. He discusses the origins of these assumptions and the evidence of their mistakenness. Pfeffer concludes with advice about implementing pay systems that work.

Finally, Duncan highlights some potential benefits of using stock ownership to motivate employees throughout the organization. He discusses the motivational effects of stock ownership from agency, equity, and reinforcement theory perspectives. He also explicates a number of dangers associated with using stock ownership, especially in the form of incentive stock options, to motivate employees. For instance, the value of stock options can decline and stock options can be expensive to exercise. Duncan ends with a summary of the benefits of using ownership to motivate employees, such as the ideas that "Ownership adds the promise of extraordinary personal wealth creation to otherwise modest compensation programs" and "Ownership makes it attractive for talented and mobile employees to stay with the company rather than bouncing from one job to another for higher base pay."

References

Deci, E. L. (1972). The effects of contingent and non-contingent rewards and controls on intrinsic motivation. *Organizational Behavior and Human Performance,* 8, 217–229.

Deci, E. L. (1975). *Intrinsic Motivation.* New York: Plenum.

Guzzo, R. A. (1979). Types of rewards, cognitions, and work motivation. *Academy of Management Review,* 4, 75–86.

Katz, D. (1964). The motivational basis of organizational behavior. *Behavioral Science,* 9, 131–146.

March, J. G., & Simon, H. A. (1958). *Organizations.* New York: Wiley.

Porter, L. W., Lawler, E. E., III, & Hackman, J. R. (1975). *Behavior in Organizations.* New York: McGraw-Hill.

The Design of Effective Reward Systems

Edward E. Lawler III

Reward systems are one of the most prominent and frequently discussed features of organizations. Indeed, the organizational behavior and personnel-management literature is replete with examples of their functional and dysfunctional roles (see, for example, Whyte, 1955). Too seldom, however, do writers examine thoroughly the potential impact of reward systems on organizational effectiveness and how they relate to the strategic objectives of the organization.

This chapter will focus on the strategic design choices that are involved in managing a reward system, and their relationship to organizational effectiveness, rather than on specific pay-system technologies. The details of pay-system design and management have been described in numerous books (e.g., Henderson, 1979; Patten, 1977; and Ellig, 1982). The underlying assumption in this [reading] is that a properly designed reward system can be a key contributor to organizational effectiveness. But careful analysis is required of the role reward systems should play in the strategic plan of the organization.

OBJECTIVES OF REWARD SYSTEMS

Reward systems in organizations have six kinds of impact that can influence organizational effectiveness: attraction and retention of employees, motivation of performance, motivation of skill development, cultural effects, reinforcement of structure, and cost.

Attraction and Retention

Research on job choice, career choice, and turnover clearly shows that the rewards an organization offers influences who is attracted to work for it and who will continue to work for it (see, for example, Lawler, 1973; Mobley, 1982). Overall, organizations that give the greatest rewards tend to attract and retain the most people. High reward levels apparently lead to high satisfaction, which in turn leads to lower turnover. Individuals who are currently satisfied with their jobs expect to remain so, and thus want to stay with the same organization.

The relationship between turnover and organizational effectiveness is not simple. It is often assumed that the lower the turnover rate, the more effective the organization is likely to be. Turnover is expensive. Replacing an employee can cost at least five times his or her monthly salary (Macy & Mirvis, 1976). However, not all turnover is harmful to organizational effectiveness. Organizations may actually profit from losing poor performers. In addition, if replacement costs are low, as they may be in unskilled jobs, it can be more cost effective to keep wages low and accept high turnover. Thus, the effect of turnover depends on its rate, the employees affected, and their replacement cost.

The objective should be to design a reward system that is very effective at retaining the most valuable employees. To do this, the system must distribute rewards in a way that will lead the more valuable employees to feel satisfied when they compare their rewards with those received by individuals performing similar jobs in other organizations. The emphasis here is on *external* comparisons, for it is the prospect of a better situation elsewhere that induces an employee to leave. One way to accomplish this is to reward everyone at a level above that prevailing in other organizations. This strategy can be very costly, however. Moreover, it can cause feelings of intraorganizational inequity. The better performers are likely to feel unfairly treated if they are rewarded at the same level as poor performers in the same organization, even though they fare better than their counterparts elsewhere. They may not quit, but they are likely to be dissatisfied, complain, look for internal transfers, and mistrust the organization.

The best solution is to have competitive reward levels and to base rewards on performance. This should satisfy the better performers and encourage them to stay with the organization. It should also attract achievement-oriented individuals, because they like environments in which their performance is rewarded. However, it is important that the better performers receive *significantly more* rewards than poor performers. Rewarding them only slightly more may simply make the better and poorer performers *equally* dissatisfied.

In summary, managing turnover means managing anticipated satisfaction. Ideally, rewards will be effectively related to performances. When this difficult task cannot be accomplished, an organization can try to reward individuals at an above-average level. If turnover is costly, this should be cost-effective strategy, even if it involves giving out expensive rewards.

Research has shown that absenteeism and satisfaction are related, although not as strongly as satisfaction and turnover. When the workplace is pleasant and satisfying, individuals come to work regularly; when it isn't, they don't.

One way to reduce absenteeism is to administer pay in ways that maximize satisfaction. Several studies have also shown that absenteeism can be reduced by tying pay bonuses and other rewards to attendance (Lawler, 1981). This approach is costly, but sometimes less costly than absenteeism. In many ways such a system is easier to administer than a performance-based one, because attendance is more readily measured. It is a particularly useful strategy in situations where both the work content and the working conditions are poor and do not lend themselves to meaningful improvements. If such improvements are possible, they are often the most effective and cost-efficient way to deal with absenteeism.

Motivation of Performance

Under certain conditions, reward systems have been shown to motivate performance (Lawler, 1971; Vroom, 1964). Employees must perceive that important rewards are tied in a timely fashion to effective performance. Individuals are inherently neither motivated nor unmotivated to perform effectively. Rather, they each use their own mental maps of what the world is like to choose behaviors that lead to outcomes that satisfy their needs. Thus, organizations get the kind of behavior that leads to the rewards their employees value. Performance motivation depends on the situation, how it is perceived, and the needs of people.

The most useful approach to understanding how people develop and act on their mental maps is called "expectancy theory" (Lawler, 1973). Three concepts serve as the key building blocks of the theory.

Performance-Outcome Expectancy Each individual mentally associates every behavior with certain outcomes (rewards or punishments). In other words, people believe that if they behave in a certain way, they will get certain things. Individuals may expect, for example, that if they produce ten units, they will receive their normal hourly pay rate, while if they produce fifteen units, they will also receive a bonus. Similarly, they may believe that certain levels of performance will lead to approval or disapproval from members of their work group or their supervisor. Each performance level can be seen as leading to a number of different kinds of outcomes.

Attractiveness Each outcome has a certain attractiveness for each individual. Valuations reflect individual needs and perceptions, which differ from one person to another. For example, some workers may value an opportunity for promotion because of their needs for achievement or power, while others may not want to leave their current work group because of needs for affiliation with others. Similarly, a pension plan may have much greater value for older workers than for young employees on their first job.

Effort-Performance Expectancy Individuals also attach a certain probability of success to behavior. This expectancy represents the individual's perception of how hard it will be for him or her to achieve such behavior. For example, employees may have a strong expectancy (e.g., 90 percent) that if they put forth the effort, they can produce ten units an hour, but may feel that they have only a 50-50 chance of producing fifteen units an hour if they try.

Together, these concepts provide a basis for generalizing about motivation. An individual's motivation to behave in a certain way is greatest when he or she believes that the behavior will lead to certain outcomes (performance–outcome expectancy), feels that these outcomes are attractive, and believes that performance at a desired level is possible (effort–performance expectancy).

Given a number of alternative levels of behavior (ten, fifteen, or twenty units of production per hour, for example), a person will choose the level of performance with which the greatest motivational force is associated, as indicated by a combination of the relevant expectancies, outcomes, and values. In other words, he or she considers questions such as Can I perform at that level if I try? If I perform at that level, what will happen? and How do I feel about those things that will happen? The individual then decides to behave in a way that seems to have the best chance of producing positive, desired outcomes.

On the basis of these concepts, it is possible to construct a general model of behavior in organizational settings (see Figure 1). Motivation is seen as a force impelling an individual to expend effort. Performance depends on both the level of the effort put forth *and* the individual's ability—which in turn reflects his or her skills, training, information, and talents. Effort thus combines with ability to produce a given level of performance. As a result of performance, the individual attains certain outcomes (rewards). The model indicates this relationship in a dotted line, reflecting the fact that people sometimes are not rewarded although they have performed. As this process of performance reward occurs repeatedly, the actual events provide information that influences an individual's perception (particularly expectancies) and thus influences motivation in the future. This is shown in the model by the line connecting the performance-outcome link with motivation.

Rewards can be both external and internal. When individuals perform at a given level, they can receive positive or negative outcomes from supervisors, coworkers, the organization's

FIGURE 1 The Expectancy-Theory Model

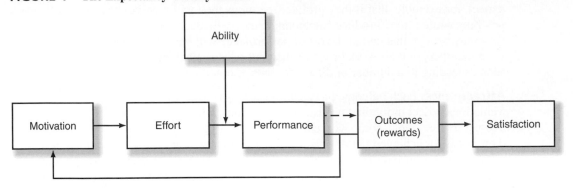

A person's motivation is a function of:
1 Effort-to-performance expectancies
2 Performance-to-outcome expectancies
3 Perceived attractiveness of outcomes

reward system, or other environmental sources. A second type of reward comes from the performance of the task itself (e.g., feelings of accomplishment, personal worth, achievement). In a sense individuals give these rewards to themselves when they feel they are deserved. The environment cannot give them or take them away directly; it can only make them possible.

The model also suggests that satisfaction is best thought of as a result of performance rather than as a cause of it. Strictly speaking, satisfaction does influence motivation in some ways. For instance, when it is perceived to come about as a result of performance, it can increase motivation because it strengthens people's beliefs about the consequences of performance. Also, satisfaction can lead to a decrease in the importance of certain outcomes (a satisfied need is no longer a motivation), and as a result, it can decrease motivation.

The expectancy model is a deceptively simple statement of the conditions that must exist if rewards are to motivate performance. It suggests that all an organization has to do is relate pay and other frequently valued rewards to obtainable levels of performance. But if the reward system is to be an effective motivator, the connection between performance and rewards must be visible, and a climate of trust and credibility must exist in the organization. The belief that performance will lead to rewards is essentially a prediction about the future. Individuals cannot make this kind of prediction unless they trust the system that is promising them the rewards. Unfortunately, it is not always clear how a climate of trust in the reward system can be established. However, as will be discussed later, research suggests that a high level of openness and the use of participation can contribute to trust in the pay system.

Skill Development

Just as reward systems can motivate performance, they can motivate skill development. They can do this by tying rewards to skill development. To a limited degree most pay-for-performance systems do this indirectly by rewarding the performance that results from the skill. Pay systems that pay the holders of higher-level, more complex jobs also reward skill development when and if it leads to obtaining a higher-level job.

Technical ladders, which are often used in research and development settings, are intended to reward skill development more directly. As will be discussed later, some skill-based pay plans have recently been installed in some settings. They give individuals more pay as they develop specific skills. Like merit pay systems these systems are often difficult to manage because skill acquisition can be hard to measure. When they are well designed and administered, however, there is little question that they can motivate skill development (Lawler, 1981).

The relationship between skill development and organizational effectiveness is not always a direct one. The nature of the technology an organization deals with or the availability of skilled labor may make this a low priority for an organization. Thus, although the reward system may be used to motivate skill development, in some instances this may not have a positive impact on organizational effectiveness.

Culture

Reward systems contribute to the overall culture or climate of an organization. Depending upon how they are developed, administered, and managed, reward systems can help create and maintain a human-resources-oriented, entrepreneurial, innovative, competence-based, bureaucratic, or participative culture.

Reward systems can shape culture precisely because of their important influence on motivation, satisfaction, and membership. The behaviors they evoke become the dominant patterns of behavior in the organization and lead to perceptions about what it stands for, believes in, and values.

Perhaps the most obvious connection between reward systems and culture concerns the practice of performance-based pay. A policy of linking—or not linking—pay and performance can have a dramatic impact on the culture because it so clearly communicates what the norms of performance are in the organization. Many other features of the reward system also influence culture. For example, relatively high pay levels can produce a culture in which people feel they are an elite group working for a top-flight company, while innovative pay practices such as flexible benefits can produce a culture of innovativeness. Finally, having employees participate in pay decisions can produce a participative culture in which employees are generally involved in business decisions and as a result are committed to the organization and its success.

Reinforcement and Definition of Structure

The reward system can reinforce and define the organization's structure (Lawler, 1981). Because this effect is often not fully considered in the design of reward systems, their structural impact may be unintended. This does not mean it is insignificant. Indeed, the reward system can help define the status hierarchy, the degree to which people in technical positions can influence people in line-management positions, and the kind of decision structure used. As will be discussed later, the key issues here seem to be the degree to which the reward system is hierarchical and the degree to which it allocates rewards on the basis of movements up the hierarchy.

Cost

Reward systems are often a significant cost factor. Indeed, the pay system alone may represent over 50 percent of the organization's operating cost. Thus, it is important in strategically designing the reward system to focus on how high these costs should be and how they will vary as a function of the organization's ability to pay. For example, a well-designed pay system might lead to higher costs when the organization has the money to spend and lower costs when it does not. An additional objective might be to lower overall reward-system costs [below] business competitors.

In summary, reward systems in organizations should be assessed from a cost-benefit perspective. The cost can be managed and controlled and the benefits planned for. The key is to identify the outcomes needed for the organization to be successful and then to design the reward system in such a way that these outcomes will be realized.

RELATIONSHIP TO STRATEGIC PLANNING

Figure 2 presents a way of viewing the relationship between strategic planning and reward systems. It suggests that once the strategic plan is developed, the organization needs to focus on the kinds of human resources, climate, and behavior that are needed to make it effective. The next step is to design reward systems that will motivate the right kind of performance, attract the right kind of people, and create a supportive climate and structure.

Figure 3 suggests another way in which the reward system needs to be taken into consideration in strategic planning. Before the strategic plan is developed, it is important to assess a variety of factors, including the current reward system, and to determine what kind of behavior, climate, and structure they foster. This step is needed to ensure that the strategic plan is based on a realistic assessment of the organization's current condition and the changes likely to be needed to implement the new strategic plan. This point is particularly pertinent to organizations that are considering going into new lines of business, developing new strategic plans, and acquiring new divisions.

Often, new lines of business require a different behavior and therefore a different reward system. Simply putting the old reward system in place can actually lead to failure in the new business. On the other hand, developing a new reward system for the new business can cause problems in the old business because of the comparisons that will be made between different parts of the same organization. The need for reward system changes must be carefully assessed before an organization enters into new business sectors.

DESIGN OPTIONS

Organizational reward systems can be designed and managed in virtually an infinite number of ways. A host of rewards can be distributed in a large number of ways. The rest of this chapter focuses on the visible extrinsic rewards that an organization can allocate to its members on a targeted basis: promotion, status symbols, and perquisites. Little attention will be given to such intrinsic rewards as feelings of responsibility, competence, and personal growth and development.

All organizational systems have a content or structural dimension as well as a process dimension. In a reward system, the content is the formal mechanisms, procedures, and practices (e.g., the salary structures, the performance-appraisal forms)—in short, the nuts and bolts of the system. Its communication and decision processes are also important. Key issues

FIGURE 2   Goals and Reward-System Design

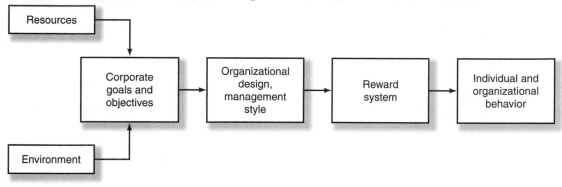

FIGURE 3   Determinants of Strategic Plan

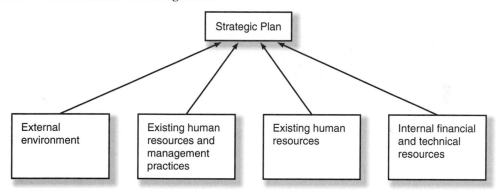

here are how much is revealed about how the reward system operates and how people are rewarded, and how much participation is allowed in the design and administration of the system. Many organizations administer rewards in a top-down, secretive way. Often this practice does not reflect a conscious choice. As discussed subsequently, organizations may wish to consider other ways that rewards can be administered.

Reward systems play important roles in organizational change efforts. They can aid or inhibit efforts to increase effectiveness. Ordinarily, major changes in other important organizational systems require a modification of the reward systems to ensure that all systems work well together. A key design decision then concerns the coordination of reward-system changes with other changes (for example, should they lead or lag?).

To begin the discussion of design choices, we will look at some key structural choices and then some key process choices. Finally the issue of pay and organizational change will be considered.

STRUCTURAL DECISIONS

Bases for Rewards

Job Based

Traditionally in organizations such rewards as pay and perquisites have been based on the type of job a person does. Indeed, with the exception of bonuses and merit salary increases, the standard policy in most organizations is to evaluate the job, not the person, and then to set the reward level. This approach is based on the assumption that job worth can be determined and that the person doing the job is worth only as much to the organization as the job itself is worth. This assumption is in many respects valid, because such techniques as job-evaluation programs make it possible to determine what other organizations are paying people to do the same or similar jobs. A job-based reward system assures an organization that its compensation costs are not dramatically out of line with those of its competitors, and it gives a somewhat objective basis to compensation practices.

Skill Based

An alternative to job-based pay that has recently been tried by a number of organizations is to pay individuals for their skills. In many cases this approach will not lead to pay rates very different from those of a job-based system. After all, people's skills are usually matched reasonably well with their jobs. A skill approach can, however, produce some different results in several respects. Often people have more skills than the job uses, in which case they would be paid more than under a job-based system. In other cases, newly appointed job-holders do not initially have all the skills associated with the position; they would have to earn the right to be paid whatever it is the job-related skills are worth.

Perhaps the most important changes introduced with skill-based or competence-based pay are in organizational climate and motivation. Instead of being rewarded for moving up the hierarchy, people are rewarded for increasing their skills and developing themselves. This policy can create a climate of concern for personal growth and development and produce a highly talented work force. It also can decrease the attractiveness of upward mobility and the traditional type of career progression. In factories where this system has been used, many people learn to perform multiple tasks, so that the work force becomes highly knowledgeable and flexible.

Skill-based pay tends to produce an interesting mix of positive and negative features as far as the organization is concerned (Lawler, 1981). It typically produces somewhat higher pay levels for individuals, but this higher cost is usually offset by greater work-force flexibility. Lower staffing levels are also possible, there are fewer problems when absenteeism or turnover occur, and indeed absenteeism and turnover may be reduced, because people like the opportunity to utilize and be paid for a wide range of skills. On the other hand, skill-based pay can be rather challenging to administer. There is no easy way of determining how much a skill is worth, and skill assessment can often be difficult. Several systems have been developed for evaluating jobs and comparing them to the marketplace, but there are no analogous systems for workers' skills.

There are no well-established rules to determine which organizational situations best fit job-based pay and which best fit skill- or competence-based pay. In general, skill-based pay seems best suited to organizations that want to have a flexible, relatively permanent work force that is oriented toward learning, growth, and development. It also seems to fit particularly well with new plant start-ups and other situations in which the greatest need is for skill development. Despite its newness and the potential operational problems, skill-based pay seems to be a system that more and more organizations will be using.

Performance Based

Perhaps the key strategic decision made in the design of any reward system is whether or not it will be based on performance. Once this decision is made, other features of the system tend to fall into place. The major alternative to basing pay on performance is to tie it to seniority. Many government organizations, for example, base their rates on the job the person does and then on how long he or she has been in that job. In Japan, individual pay is often based on seniority, although individuals may receive bonuses based on corporate performance.

Most business organizations in the United States say that they reward individual performance and describe their pay system and their promotion system as merit-based. A true merit pay or promotion system is often more easily aspired to than done, however. It has been observed that many organizations would be better off if they did not try to relate pay and promotion to performance, but relied on other bases for motivating performance (Kerr, 1975; Goldberg, 1977; Hills, 1979). It is difficult to specify what kind of performance is desired and often equally difficult to determine whether that performance has been demonstrated. There is ample evidence that a poorly designed and administered reward system can do more harm than good (see, for example, Whyte, 1955; Lawler, 1971). On the other hand, when pay is effectively related to the desired performance, it clearly helps to motivate, attract, and retain outstanding performers. Thus, when it is feasible, it is usually desirable to relate pay to performance.

How to relate pay to performance is often the most important strategic decision an organization makes. The options are numerous. The kind of pay reward that is given can vary widely, and many include such things as stock and cash. In addition, the interval between rewards can range from a few minutes to many years. Performance can be measured at various levels. Each individual may get a reward based on his or her own performance. In addition, rewards based on the performance of a particular group can be given to each of its members. Or everyone in the organization can be given an award based on the performance of the total organization. Finally, many different kinds of performance can be rewarded. For example, managers can be rewarded for sales increases, productivity volumes, their ability to develop their subordinates, their cost-reduction ideas, and so on.

Rewarding some behaviors and not others has clear implications for performance. Thus decisions about what is to be rewarded need to be made carefully and with attention to the overall strategic plan of the business (see, for example, Galbraith & Nathanson, 1978; Salscheider, 1981). Consideration needs to be given to such issues as short- versus long-term performance, risk taking versus risk aversion, division performance versus total corporate performance, ROI (return on investment) maximization versus sales growth, and so on. Once key performance objectives have been defined for the strategic plan, the reward system needs to be designed to motivate the appropriate performance. Decisions about such issues as the use of stock options (a long-term incentive), for example, should be made only after careful consideration of whether they will encourage the kind of behavior that is desired (see, for example,

Crystal, 1978; Ellig, 1982). In large organizations, it is quite likely that the managers of different divisions should be rewarded for different kinds of performance. Growth businesses call for different reward systems from those of "cash cows," because the managers are expected to produce different results (see Stata & Maidique, 1980, for an example).

A detailed discussion of the many approaches to relating pay and performance is beyond the scope of this [reading]. Table 1 gives an idea of some of the design features that are possible in a reward system, and some of the advantages and disadvantages of each.

The first column in the table rates each plan in terms of its effectiveness in creating the perception that pay is tied to performance. In general, this indicates the degree to which the approach leads employees to believe that higher pay will follow good performance. Second, each plan is evaluated in terms of whether it produced the negative side effects often associated with performance-based pay plans (such as social ostracism of good performers, defensive behavior, and giving false data about performance). Third, each plan is rated as to its ability to encourage cooperation among employees. Finally, employee acceptance of the plan is indicated. The ratings were developed on the basis of a review of the literature and my experience with the different types of plans (see, for example, Lawler, 1971).

Several patterns appear in the ratings. Pay to performance are seen as most closely linked in the individual plans; group plans are rated next; and organizational plans are rated lowest. In organizational plans, and to a lesser extent in group plans, an individual's pay is not directly a function of his or her behavior, but depends on the behavior of many others. In addition, when some types of performance measures (e.g., profits) are used, pay is influenced by external conditions that employees cannot control.

Bonus plans are generally seen as more closely tied to performance than pay-raise and salary-increase plans. The use of bonuses permits substantial variation in an individual's pay from one time period to another. With salary-increase plans, in contrast, such flexibility is very difficult because past raises tend not to be rescinded.

Approaches that use objective measures of performance are rated higher than those that rely on subjective measures. In general, objective measures enjoy higher credibility; that is, employees will often accept the validity of an objective measure, such as sales volume or units produced, when they will not accept a superior's evaluation of their performance. When pay is tied to objective measures, therefore, it is usually clear to employees that it is determined by performance. Objective measures are also often publicly measurable. Thus the relationship between performance and pay is much more visible than when it is tied to a subjective, nonverifiable measure, such as a supervisor's rating. Overall, the data suggest that individually based bonus plans that rely on objective measures produce the strongest perceived connection between pay and performance.

The ratings indicate that most plans have little tendency to produce negative side effects. The notable exceptions here are individual bonus and incentive plans below the management level. These plans often lead to situations in which good performance leads to social rejection and ostracism, so that employees present false performance data and restrict their production. These side effects are particularly likely to appear where trust is low and subjective productivity standards are used.

In terms of the third criterion—encouraging cooperation—the ratings are generally higher for group and organizational plans than for individual plans. Under group and organizational plans, it is generally to everyone's advantage that an individual work effectively, because all

TABLE 1 Ratings of Various Pay-Incentive Plans

		Tie pay to Performance	Negative Side Effect	Encourage Cooperation	Employee Acceptance
Salary Reward					
Individual plan	Productivity	4	1	1	4
	Cost effectiveness	3	1	1	4
	Superiors' rating	3	1	1	3
Group plan	Productivity	3	1	2	4
	Cost effectiveness	3	1	2	4
	Superiors' rating	2	1	2	3
Organizational plan	Productivity	2	1	3	4
	Cost effectiveness	2	1	2	4
Bonus					
Individual plan	Productivity	5	3	1	2
	Cost effectiveness	4	2	1	2
	Superiors' rating	4	2	1	2
Group plan	Productivity	4	1	3	3
	Cost effectiveness	3	1	3	3
	Superiors' rating	3	1	3	3
Organizational plan	Productivity	3	1	1	4
	Cost effectiveness	3	1	3	4
	Profit	2	1	2	4

Note: On a scale of 1 to 5, 1 = low and 5 = high.

share in the financial fruits of higher performance. This is not true under an individual plan. As a result, good performance is much more likely to be supported and encouraged by others when group and organizational plans are used.

Most performance-based pay plans achieve only moderate employee acceptance. The ratings show individual bonus plans to be least acceptable, particularly among nonmanagement employees, presumably because of their tendency to encourage competitive relationships between employees and the difficulty of administering such plans fairly.

No one performance-based pay plan represents a panacea, and it is unlikely that any organization will ever be completely satisfied with the approach it chooses. Furthermore, some of the plans that make the greatest contributions to organizational effectiveness do not make the greatest contributions to quality of work life, and vice versa. Still, the situation is not completely hopeless. When all factors are taken into account, group and organizational bonus plans that are based on objective data receive high ratings, as do individual-level salary-increase plans.

Many organizations employ multiple or combination reward systems. For example, they may use a salary-increase system that rewards workers for their individual performance while at the same time giving everybody in the division or plant a bonus based on divisional performance. Some plans measure group or company performance, calculate the bonus based on divisional performance. Some plans measure group or company performance, calculate the bonus pool generated by the performance of a group, and then divide it among group members on the basis of individual performance. By rewarding workers for both individual and group performance, the organization tries to motivate individuals to perform all needed behaviors (see, for example, Lincoln, 1951; Fox, 1979).

A common error in the design of many pay-for-performance systems is the tendency to focus on measurable short-term operating results because they are quantifiable and regularly obtained in any case. In particular, many organizations reward their top managers on the basis of quarterly or annual profitability (Fox, 1979). Such a scheme can make managers very short-sighted in their behavior and encourage them to ignore strategic objectives important to the long-term profitability of the organization. A similar error is the tendency to depend on completely subjective performance appraisals for the allocation of pay rewards. There is considerable evidence that these performance appraisals are often biased and invalid, and instead of contributing to positive motivation and a good work climate that improves superior-subordinate relationships, they do just the opposite (see, for example, DeVries et al., 1981; Latham & Wexley, 1981). Other common errors include the giving of too small rewards, failure to explain systems clearly, and poor administrative practices.

In summary, the decision of whether to relate pay to performance is a crucial one in any organization. It can be a serious error to assume automatically that they should be related. A sound linkage can contribute greatly to organizational effectiveness. But a poor job can be harmful. Specifically, if performance is difficult to measure and/or rewards are difficult to distribute on the basis of performance, a pay-for-performance system can motivate counterproductive behaviors, invite lawsuits charging discrimination, and create a climate of mistrust, low credibility, and managerial incompetence. On the other hand, to declare that pay is unrelated to performance would be to give up a potentially important motivational tool and perhaps condemn the organization to a lower level of performance. The ideal, of course, is to foster conditions in which pay can be effectively related to performance and as a result contribute to the effectiveness of the organization.

Promotion, training opportunities, fringe benefits, and status symbols are important extrinsic rewards that, like pay, can be linked to performance. When they are linked to pay and are important, they, like pay, can motivate performance. The issues involved in relating them to performance are very similar to those involved in relating pay to performance, thus they will not be discussed in detail. As a general rule they are not usually tied to performance in organizations to the degree that pay is. They also are less flexible than is pay. That is, they are harder to give in varying amounts and to take away once they have been given.

Market Position

The reward structure of an organization influences behavior partially as a function of how the size of its rewards compares to what other organizations give. Organizations frequently have well-developed policies about how their pay levels should compare with the pay levels in other companies. For example, some companies (e.g., IBM) feel it is important to be a leader and consciously pay more than any of the companies with which they compete. Other companies are content to set their pay levels at or below the market for the people they hire. This structural issue in the design of reward systems is a critical one because it can strongly influence the kind of people that are attracted and retained by an organization as well as the turnover rate and the number of job applicants. Simply stated, organizations that pay above market end up attracting and retaining more people. From a business point of view this policy may pay off for them, particularly if turnover is a costly factor in the organization and if the business strategy requires a stable, highly talented staff.

On the other hand, if many of the jobs in the organization are low skilled and people are readily available in the labor market to do them, then a corporate strategy of high pay may not be effective. It can increase labor costs without offsetting benefits. Of course, organizations need not pay above market for all their jobs. Indeed, some organizations identify certain key skills that they need and pay generously for them, while offering average or below-average pay for other skills. This approach has some obvious business advantages, because it allows the organization to attract critically needed skills and at the same time to control costs.

Although it is not often recognized, the market position that a company adopts with respect to its reward systems can also affect organization climate. For example, a policy of paying above market can make people feel that they are members of an elite organization that employs only competent people and that they are indeed fortunate to be there. A policy that awards extra pay to certain skilled employees but leaves the rest of the organization at a lower pay level can cause divisive social pressures within the organization.

Finally, some organizations try to offer more noncash compensation than the average as a way of competing for the talent they need. They talk in terms of producing an above-average quality of work life, and stress not only hygiene factors but interesting and challenging work. This stance potentially can be a very effective one and could give the organization a competitive edge, at least in attracting people who value these things. Still other organizations stress such noncash rewards as status symbols and perquisites. This approach also can be effective in attracting certain kinds of people.

In summary, the market position and mix of an organization's total reward package has a critical effect on both the behavior of members and the climate of the organization. This decision needs to be carefully related to the general business strategy of the organization, in particular, to the kind of human resources needed and the organization climate desired.

Internal/External-Pay-Comparison Oriented

Organizations differ in the degree to which they strive toward internal equity in their pay and reward systems. An internal-equity-oriented company tries to see that individuals doing similar work will be paid the same even though they are in very different parts of the country and/or in different businesses. Some corporations (e.g., IBM) base their national pay structure on the highest pay that a job receives anywhere in the country. Organizations that do not stress internal equity typically focus on the external labor market as the key determinant of what somebody should be paid. Although this approach does not necessarily produce different pay for people doing the same job, it may. For example, two industries—say, electronics and automobiles—may differ significantly in what they pay for the same job.

The internal-equity approach has both advantages and disadvantages. It can facilitate the transfer of people from one location to another, because there will be no pay difference to contend with. Similarly, it avoids the problems of rivalry and dissatisfaction that can develop within the organization if one location or division pays more than another. In addition, it can produce an organizational climate of homogeneity and the feeling that all work for the same company and all are treated fairly.

On the other hand, a focus on internal equity can be very expensive, particularly if pay rates across a diversified corporation are set at the highest level that the market demands anywhere in the corporation (Salscheider, 1981). If it pays much more than is necessary to attract and retain good people, the organization may become noncompetitive in certain businesses and find that it has to limit itself to businesses in which its pay structures permit competitive labor costs. Overly high labor costs have, for example, often made it difficult for auto and oil and gas companies to compete in new business areas.

In summary, the difference between focusing on external equity and internal equity is a crucial one in the design of pay systems. It can influence the organization's cost structure as well as its climate and behavior. The general rule is that highly diversified companies are pulled more strongly toward an external market orientation, while organizations that are based on a single industry or single technology typically find themselves more comfortable with an internal-equity emphasis.

Centralized/Decentralized Reward Strategy

Closely related to the issue of internal versus external equity is the question of centralization. Organizations that adopt a centralized-reward-system strategy typically make the corporate staff responsible for seeing that such things as pay practices are similar throughout the organization. They ordinarily develop standard pay grades and pay ranges, standardized job-evaluation systems, and perhaps standardized promotion systems. In decentralized organizations, decisions about pay, promotion, and other rewards are left to local option. Sometimes the corporations suggest broad guidelines or principles to follow, but the day-to-day administration and design of the system is left up to the local entity.

The advantages of a centralized structure rest primarily in the expertise that can be accumulated at the central level and the homogeneity that is produced in the organization. This homogeneity can lead to a clear image of the corporate climate, feelings of internal equity, and the belief that the organization stands for something. It also eases the job of communicating and understanding what is going on in different parts of the organization. The decentralized strategy allows for local innovation and for closely fitting reward practices to the particular business.

There is no one right choice between the centralized and decentralized approaches to reward system design and administration. Overall, the decentralized system tends to make the most sense when the organization is involved in businesses that face different markets and perhaps are at different points in their life cycles (Greiner, 1972; Galbraith & Nathanson, 1978). It allows variation in practices that can give a competitive advantage to one part of the business but may prove to be a real hindrance in another. For example, such perquisites as cars are often standard operating procedure in one business but not in another. Similarly, extensive bonuses may be needed to attract one group of people, for example, oil-exploration engineers, but not others, for example, research scientists. Overall, then, an organization needs to look carefully at its mix of businesses and the degree to which it wants a single set of principles or policies to prevail across all its operating divisions, and then decide whether a centralized or decentralized reward strategy is likely to be more effective.

Degree of Hierarchy

Closely related to the issue of job-based versus competence-based pay is the strategic decision concerning the hierarchical nature of the organization's reward systems. Often no formal decision is ever made to have a relatively hierarchical or relatively egalitarian approach to rewards. A hierarchical approach simply happens because it is so consistent with the general way organizations are run. Hierarchical systems usually pay people more money and give them greater perquisites and symbols of office as they move higher up the organization ladder. This approach strongly reinforces the traditional hierarchical power relationships in the organization and fosters a climate of different status and power levels. In some cases, a hierarchical reward system may include more levels than the formal organization chart, creating additional status differences in the organization.

The alternative to a hierarchical system is one that downplays differences in rewards and perquisites based only on hierarchical level. For example, in large corporations that adopt an egalitarian stance to rewards (e.g., Digital Equipment Corporation), such privileges as private parking spaces, executive restrooms, and special entrances are eliminated. People from all levels in the organization eat together, work together, and travel together. Further, high levels of pay are not restricted to managers but can be earned by those who have worked their way up a technical ladder. This approach to rewards produces a distinctive climate in an organization, encouraging decision making by expertise rather than by hierarchy position, and minimizing status differentials in the organization.

In general, a steeply hierarchical system makes the most sense when an organization needs relatively rigid bureaucratic behavior, strong top-down authority, and a strong motivation for people to move up the organizational hierarchy. A more egalitarian approach fits with a more participative management style and the desire to retain technical specialists and experts in nonmanagement or lower-level-management roles. It is not surprising, therefore, that many of the organizations that emphasize egalitarian perquisites are in high-technology and knowledge-based industries.

Reward Mix

The kind of rewards that organizations give to individuals can vary widely. Monetary rewards, for example, can take many forms, from stock to medical insurance. When cash rewards are translated into fringe benefits, perquisites, or other trappings of office, they may lose their value for some people and as a result may be a poor investment for the employer (see, for example, Nealy, 1963; Lawler, 1971). On the other hand, certain benefits can best be obtained through mass purchase, and therefore many individuals want the organization to provide them. In addition, certain status symbols or perquisites may be valued by some individuals beyond their actual dollar cost to the organization and thus represent good buys. Finally, as was mentioned earlier there often are some climate and organizational structure reasons for paying people in the form of perquisites and status symbols.

One interesting development in the area of compensation is the flexible or cafeteria-style benefit program (Fragner, 1975; Lawler, 1981). The theory is that if individuals are allowed to tailor their own reward packages to fit their particular needs, the organization will get the best value for its money, because it will give people only those things that they desire. Such an approach also has the advantage of treating individuals as mature adults rather than as dependent people who need their welfare looked after in a structured way. While flexible benefit programs have not yet been widely implemented, the results of experiments to date have been favorable, and there is reason to believe that other organizations may adopt this approach in the near future, because it can offer a strategic cost-benefit advantage in attracting and retaining certain types of employees.

Overall, the forms in which the organization rewards its members should be consistent with the climate it hopes to foster. For example, a flexible compensation package is highly congruent with a participative open organization climate that treats individuals as mature adults and wants to attract talented mature people. A highly status-symbol-oriented approach, on the other hand, may appeal to people who value position power and need a high level of visible reinforcement for their position. This would seem to fit best in a relatively bureaucratic organization that relies on position power and authority to carry out its actions.

PROCESS ISSUES AND REWARD ADMINISTRATION

Reward system design and administration raise numerous process issues. Indeed, process issues are confronted more frequently than structure and content issues, because organizations must constantly make reward-system management, implementation, and communication decisions while structures tend to be relatively firmly fixed in place. Rather than discussing specific process issues here, the focus will be on broad process themes that can be used to characterize the way reward systems are designed and administered.

Communication Policy

Organizations differ widely in how much information they communicate about their reward systems. At one extreme, some organizations are extremely secretive, particularly in the area of pay. They forbid people to talk about their individual rewards, give minimal information to individuals about how rewards are decided upon and allocated, and have no publicly disseminated policies about such things as market position, the approach to gathering market data, and potential increases and rewards for individuals. At the other extreme, some organizations are so open that everyone's pay is a matter of public record, as is the overall organization pay philosophy (many new high-involvement plants operate this way; see, for example, Lawler, 1978; Walton, 1980). In addition, all promotions are subject to open job postings, and in some instances peer groups discuss the individual's eligibility for promotion.

The difference between an open and a closed communication policy in the area of rewards is enormous. There is no clear right or wrong approach. The issue is rather to choose a position on the continuum from open to secretive that is supportive of the overall climate and types of behavior needed for organizational effectiveness. An open system tends to encourage people to ask questions, share data, and ultimately be involved in decisions. A secretive system tends to put people in a more dependent position, to keep power concentrated at the top, and to allow an organization to keep its options open with respect to commitments to individuals. Secrecy can lead to considerable distortion in people's beliefs about the rewards given to other organization members, and can create a low-trust environment in which the relationship between pay and performance is not clear (see, for example, Lawler, 1971; Steele, 1975). Thus, a structurally sound pay system may end up being rather ineffective because its strong secrecy policies open it to misperceptions.

Open systems put considerable pressure on organizations to do an effective job of administering rewards. Thus, if such difficult-to-defend policies as merit pay are to be implemented, considerable time and effort needs to be invested in pay administration. If such policies are poorly administered, strong pressures usually develop to eliminate discrimination and pay everyone the same (see, for example, Burroughs, 1982). Ironically, therefore, if an organization wants to spend little time administering rewards but still wants to base pay on merit, secrecy may be the best policy, although secrecy in turn may limit the effectiveness of the merit pay plan.

Decision-Making Practices

Closely related to the issue of communication is the matter of how decisions about compensation are to be made. If individuals are to be actively involved in decisions concerning reward systems, they need to have information about policy and actual practice. Open communication makes it possible to involve a wide range of people in the decision-making process. Secrecy by its very nature limits the number of people who can be involved in pay decisions.

It is important to distinguish between decisions concerning the design and ongoing administration of reward systems. Traditionally, of course, organizations have made both design and administration decisions in a top-down manner. But it is possible to adopt a different decision-making style for each type of decision.

Systems typically have been designed by top management with the aid of staff support and administered by strict reliance on the chain of command. The assumption has been that this approach provides the proper checks and balances in the system and locates decision making where the expertise rests. In many cases this is a valid assumption and certainly fits well with an organizational management style that emphasizes hierarchy, bureaucracy, and control through the use of extrinsic rewards. It does not fit, however, with an organization that believes in more open communication, higher levels of employee involvement, and control through individual commitment to policies. Nor does it fit when expertise is broadly spread throughout the organization, as is often true in companies that rely heavily on knowledge workers or spend a great deal of effort training their people to become expert in technical functions.

Some organizations have experimented with involving employees in the design of pay systems (Lawler, 1981). Favorable results have generally been achieved when employees help design their own bonus system. They tend to raise important issues and provide expertise not normally available to the designers of the system. And perhaps more importantly, once the system is designed, it is well accepted and understood. Employee involvement often makes possible a rapid start-up of the system and creates a commitment to see it survive long-term. In other cases systems have been designed by line managers, because they are the ones that need to maintain it. Unless they have had an opportunity for design input, it often is unrealistic to expect line people to have the same level of commitment to the pay system as the staff people have.

Some organizations have also experimented with having peer groups and low-level supervisory people handling the day-to-day decision making about who should receive pay increases and how jobs should be evaluated and placed in pay structures. The best examples are the new participative plants that use skill-based pay (see, for example, Walton, 1980). In these plants, the work group typically reviews an individual's performance and decides whether he or she has acquired the new skills. This approach appears to work well. Peers often have the best information about performance and thus are in a good position to make a performance assessment. In traditional organizations their expertise is of no use, because they lack the motivation to give valid feedback and to respond responsibly. In more participative open systems, this motivational problem seems to be less severe, and as a result involvement in decision making is more effective.

In a few cases, executives have been asked to assess each other in a peer-group reward system (e.g., in Graphic Controls Corporation). Again, this approach can apparently work well in an organization that has a history of open and effective communication. Deciding on rewards is clearly not an easy task, and thus should not be assigned to a group unless members have good confrontation skills and can talk openly and directly about each other's performance.

Overall, there is evidence that some participative approaches to reward systems can be effective because of their congruence with the overall style and because the skills and norms needed to make them work are already in place. In more traditional organizations, the typical top-down approach to reward-system design and administration probably remains the best. From a strategic point of view, then, the decision about how much participation is desirable in reward-system design and administration depends on whether a participative, high-involvement type of organization is best suited to accomplish the strategic objectives of the business. If so, then participation in pay decisions and reward-system decisions should be considered.

REWARD SYSTEMS AND ORGANIZATIONAL CHANGE

In many major organizational changes, it is difficult to alter all the relevant systems in the organization simultaneously. Typically one change leads to another. Modification of the reward systems may either lead or lag in the overall change process.

Reward as a Lead

Perhaps the most widely discussed example of pay as a lead change is the use of a gain-sharing plan to improve plant productivity (Moore & Ross, 1978; Lawler, 1981). In these situations the initial change effort is the installation of a system of bonuses based on improvements in productivity. In the case of the Scanlon Plan, attempts are also made to build participative problem-solving groups into the organization, but the clear emphasis is on the gain-sharing formula and the financial benefits of improved productivity. The participative management structure is intended to facilitate productivity improvement, which in turn will result in gains to be shared. Not surprisingly, once gain-sharing starts and factors inhibiting productivity are identified, other changes follow. Typical of these are improvements in the organization structures, the design of jobs and work, and additional training programs. The gain-sharing plan itself provides a strong motivation to swiftly and effectively deal with those issues.

Other reward system changes can also lead to broader organizational change efforts. For example, the introduction of skill-based pay can potentially prompt a broad movement to participation because it gives people the skills and knowledge they need to participate. The movement to a more flexible fringe-benefit program can change organizational climate by creating one of innovation in the area of human-resource management.

In a somewhat different vein, a dramatic change in the pay-for-performance system can be very effective in shaping an organization's strategic directions. For example, installing bonus systems that reward previously neglected performance indicators can dramatically shift the directions of an organization. Similarly, a long-term bonus plan for executives can lead them to change their time horizons and their decision-making practices in important ways.

Rewards as a Lag

In most major organization change efforts, pay is a lag factor. As an organization moves toward participative management, for example, the initial thrust often comes in such areas as team building, job redesign, and quality circles. It is only after these practices have been in place for some time that the organization makes the associated changes in the reward system. Often, the organization does not originally anticipate a need to revise the reward system. But because all organizational systems are interconnected, it is almost inevitable that major changes in strategic direction or management style and practices will require that changes be made in the reward system as well.

New participative plants represent an interesting example of the simultaneous installation of participative reward systems and other participative practices (Lawler, 1981). The success of these plants is probably due in part to the fact that all their systems have operated in a participative manner from the outset.

Rewards as a Motivator of Change

Major strategic changes are often difficult to accomplish even though they don't involve a change in management style. The forces of equilibrium have the effect of canceling out many changes. To the extent that changing one component of an organizational system reduces its congruence with other components, energy will develop to limit, encapsulate, or reverse the change. In addition, attention may be diverted from other important tasks by the need to direct a change, deal with resistance, and cope with the problems created by change.

Management is therefore faced with two key tasks if change is to be brought about. The first is *motivating change*—overcoming natural resistance and encouraging individuals to behave in ways that are consistent with both the immediate change goals and long-range corporate strategy. The second major task is *managing change.*

It is useful to think of organizational changes in terms of transitions (Beckhard & Harris, 1977). The organization exists in a current state (C). An image has been developed of a future state of the organization (F). The period between C and F can be thought of as the transition period (T). The question is how to manage the transition. Too often, however, managers overlook the transition state, assuming that all that is needed is to design that best possible future. They think of change as simply a mechanical or procedural detail.

In most situations, the management systems and structures developed to manage either C or F are simply not appropriate for the management of T. They are steady-state management systems, designed to run organizations already in place rather than transitional management systems. During the transition period, different systems, and specifically different reward systems, may be needed temporarily. Many change efforts are resisted because organization members see them as a threat to their pay level. Particularly when the present system is highly standardized and tied to objective measures, such as the number of subordinates, people may resist a reorganization or other type of change whose impact on their pay is unclear but potentially negative. There is no magic formula for overcoming this resistance, but two approaches can help.

First, a floor should be put under individual pay rates throughout the transition period. That is, no one should have to fear losing pay during the change process. This point is critical in the case of a major reorganization, which may require some people to give up some subordinates and responsibilities, and to accept a lower salary if their jobs were reevaluated. If this problem is likely to be severe, the organization may want to assure individuals that their pay will not be cut, even after the change is in place.

A second important step is to appoint a group of high-level managers to develop an approach to compensation that will fit the new organization: This group should articulate a corporate rewards philosophy that includes the following:

1. The goals of the pay system

2. How the pay system will fit the new organizational structure

3. The fit between the management style of the organization and the process used to administer the pay system

4. How the pay system will be managed once it is developed

There are several reasons for developing a compensation system in this way. First, a philosophical base is needed for an effective pay system. More and more evidence is accumulating that, unless supported by some sort of widely accepted philosophy, corporate pay administration ends up being haphazard and a source of internal conflict. A philosophy cannot answer all the problems associated with rewards, but it can at least provide a touchstone against which new practices, policies, and decisions can be tested.

A second advantage of the group approach is that it will give key individuals a chance to influence how they will be paid in the future. A big unknown in the new organization thus becomes something under their control, rather than a potentially threatening factor about the reorganized structure. Moreover, by seriously considering how the pay system will have to change to fit other changes, the group can prevent "surprise" pay-system problems from occurring once the other changes have been implemented. Finally, as discussed further below, by assuring that an acceptable supporting pay system will exist, the group can promote institutionalization of the new organization structure.

Putting a floor under existing salaries helps reduce resistance, but it does nothing to encourage good implementation of change. It is possible, however, to use the reward system to support implementation of the reorganization. First of all, the organization needs to make it clear that the jobs and associated rewards given to managers after the transition will depend on their contribution to an effective transition process. One-time bonuses and payments may also ease the transition. In most cases, it makes sense to award these one-time financial payments on a group basis rather than on an individual basis.

It is important that transition goals specify, as precisely as possible, both the rate at which change is introduced and the process used to introduce it. One-time bonuses should be tied to meeting these goals, which can be a critical ingredient in the effective motivation of change. The organization should specify target dates for particular implementation events, such as having a new unit operating or completing the relocation of personnel. In addition, measures should be defined for the process used to implement change; examples might include people's understanding of the new system, the degree to which it was explained to them, the level of turnover among people that the organization wished to retain, signs of stress among people involved in the transition, and the willingness of managers to give up people to other parts of the organization where they can make a greater contribution.

Rewards, goals, and performance measures are critical tools in managing the transition process. They can help to assure that the change strategy is implemented rapidly and in a way that minimizes the dysfunctional consequences for both the organization and the people who work in it.

REWARD SYSTEM CONGRUENCE

For simplicity, we have so far treated each reward-system design feature as an independent factor. Overall system congruence is an important consideration, however. There is considerable evidence that reward-system design features affect each other and thus should be supportive of the same types of behavior, the same business strategy, and reflect the same overall managerial philosophy.

Table 2 illustrates one effort to define congruent sets of reward-system practices (Lawler, 1977). The two management philosophies portrayed here are the traditional bureaucratic management style and a participative employee-involvement strategy. Their reward-system practices are different in every respect. The practices associated with traditional bureaucratic models tend to be more secretive, top-down, and oriented toward producing regularity in behavior. The participative practices, in contrast, encourage self-development, openness, employee involvement in reward-system allocation decisions, and ultimately more innovation and commitment to the organization.

TABLE 2   Appropriate Reward-System Practices

Reward System	Traditional or Theory X	Participative or Theory Y
Fringe benefits	Vary according to organizational level	Cafeteria—same for all levels
Promotion	All decisions made by top management	Open posting for all jobs; peer-group involvement in decision process
Status symbols	A great many carefully allocated on the basis of job position	Few present, low emphasis on organization level
Pay		
Type of system	Hourly and salary	All salary
Base rate	Based on job performed; high enough to attract job applicants	Based on skills; high enough to provide security and attract applicants
Incentive plan	Piece rate	Group and organization-wide bonus; lump sum increase
Communication policy	Very restricted distribution of information	Individual rates, salary-survey data, and all other information made public
Decision-making locus	Top management	Close to location of person whose pay is being set

Greiner (1972) and Galbraith and Nathanson (1978) have pointed out that reward-system practices need to be congruent with the maturity of the organization and the market in which the business operates. For example, rapidly developing businesses need to stress skill development, attraction, high-potential individuals, and incentives tied to business growth, while declining businesses need to reward expense reduction and to have a formalized job-evaluation system that closely tracks the market.

The reward system also needs to fit other features of the organization to ensure congruence in the total human-resource-management system. The reward system should be consistent with the way jobs are designed, the leadership style of the supervisors, and the types of career tracks available in the organization, to mention just a few examples. Unless this kind of fit exists, the organization will be riddled with conflicts, and the reward system practices may be canceled out by practices in other areas. For example, even the best performance-appraisal system will be ineffective unless accompanied by interpersonally competent supervisory behavior and jobs designed to allow for good performance measure (see DeVries et al., 1981).

CONCLUSION

An effective reward system should be designed to fit well with the other design features of the organization as well as with its business strategy. Thus there is no one best set of reward practices; indeed, it is impossible to design an effective reward system without knowing how other features of the organization are arrayed. Decisions about the reward system should be made in an interactive fashion: shaped by the business strategy, tentative reward-system design choices would then be tested against how other features of the organization are being designed. The ultimate goal is to develop an integrated human-resource-management strategy that is consistent in the ways it encourages people to behave, attracts the kind of people that can support the business strategy, and encourages them to behave appropriately.

References

Beckhard, R., and R. Harris. 1977. *Organizational Transitions: Managing Complex Change.* Reading, Mass.: Addison-Wesley.

Burroughs, J. D. 1982. "Pay Secrecy and Performance: The Psychological Research." *Compensation Review* 14, no. 3:44–54.

Crystal, G. S. 1978. *Executive Compensation.* 2d ed. New York: AMACOM.

DeVries, D. L., A. M. Morrison, S. L. Shullman, and M. L. Gerlach. 1981. *Performance Appraisal on the Line.* New York: Wiley, Interscience.

Ellig, B. R. 1982. *Executive Compensation—A Total Pay Perspective.* New York: McGraw-Hill.

Fox, H. 1979. *Top Executive Bonus Plans.* New York: Conference Board.

Fragner, B. N. 1975. "Employees' 'Cafeteria' Offers Insurance Options." *Harvard Business Review* 53: 2–4.

Galbraith, J. R., and D. A. Nathanson. 1978. *Strategy Implementation: The Role of Structure and Process.* St. Paul, Minn.: West.

Greiner, L. 1972. "Evolution and Revolution as Organizations Grow." *Harvard Business Review* 50, no. 4:37–46.

Goldberg, M. H. 1977. "Another Look at Merit Pay Programs." *Compensation Review* 3:20–28.

Henderson, R. I. 1979. *Compensation Management: Rewarding Performance.* 2d ed. Reston, Va.: Reston.

Hills, F. S. 1979. "The Pay-for-Performance Dilemma." *Personnel,* no. 5:23–31.

Kerr, S. 1975. "On the Folly of Rewarding A, While Hoping for B." *Academy of Management Journal* 18:769–783.

Latham, G. P., and K. N. Wexley. 1981. *Increasing Productivity Through Performance Appraisal.* Reading, Mass.: Addison-Wesley.

Lawler, E. E. 1971. *Pay and Organizational Effectiveness: A Psychological View.* New York: McGraw-Hill.

———. 1973. *Motivation in Work Organizations.* Monterey, Calif.: Brooks/Cole.

———. "Reward Systems." In *Improving Life at Work,* ed. J. R. Hackman and J. L. Suttle, pp. 163–226. Santa Monica, Calif.: Goodyear.

———. 1978. "The New Plant Revolution." *Organizational Dynamics* 6, no. 3:2–12.

———. 1981. *Pay and Organization Development.* Reading, Mass.: Addison-Wesley.

Lincoln, J. F. 1951. *Incentive Management.* Lincoln Electric Co., Cleveland, Ohio.

Macy, B. A., and P. H. Mirvis. 1976. "A Methodology for Assessment of Quality of Work Life and Organizational Effectiveness in Behavior-Economic Terms." *Administrative Service Quarterly* 21:217–26.

Mobley, W. H. 1982. *Employee Turnover: Causes, Consequences, and Control.* Reading, Mass.: Addison-Wesley.

Moore, B. E., and T. L. Ross. 1978. *The Scanlon Way to Improved Productivity.* New York: Wiley, Interscience.

Nealy, S. 1963. "Pay and Benefit Preferences." *Industrial Relations* 3: 17–28.

Patten, T. H. 1977. "Pay: Employee Compensation and Incentive Plans." New York: Free Press.

Salscheider, J. 1981. "Devising Pay Strategies for Diversified Companies." *Compensation Review* 58, no. 6:15–24.

Stata, R., and M. A. Maidique. 1980. "Bonus System for Balanced Strategy." *Harvard Business Review* 58, no. 6:156–63.

Steele, F. 1975. *The Open Organization.* Reading, Mass.: Addison-Wesley.

Vroom, V. H. 1964. *Work and Motivation.* New York: Wiley.

Walton, R. E. 1980. "Establishing and Maintaining High Commitment Work Systems." In *The Organization Life Cycle,* ed. J. R. Kimberly, R. N. Miles, and associates. San Francisco: Jossey-Bass.

Whyte, W. F., ed. 1955. *Money and Motivation: An Analysis of Incentives in Industry.* New York: Harper.

On the Folly of Rewarding A, While Hoping for B[1]

Steven Kerr

Whether dealing with monkeys, rats, or human beings, it is hardly controversial to state that most organisms seek information concerning what activities are rewarded, and then seek to do (or at least pretend to do) those things, often to the virtual exclusion of activities not rewarded. The extent to which this occurs of course will depend on the perceived attractiveness of the rewards offered, but neither operant nor expectancy theorists would quarrel with the essence of this notion.

Nevertheless, numerous examples exist of reward systems that are fouled up in that the types of behavior rewarded are those which the rewarder is trying to discourage, while the behavior desired is not being rewarded at all.

From *Academy of Management Executive,* 1995, 9(1), 7–14. Reprinted by permission.

FOULED-UP SYSTEMS

In Politics

Official goals are "purposely vague and general and do not indicate . . . the host of decisions that must be made among alternative ways of achieving official goals and the priority of multiple goals. . . ."[2] They usually may be relied on to offend absolutely no one, and in this sense can be considered high acceptance, low quality goals. An example might be "All Americans are entitled to health care." Operative goals are higher in quality but lower in acceptance, since they specify where the money will come from, and what alternative goals will be ignored.

The American citizenry supposedly wants its candidates for public office to set forth operative goals, making their proposed programs clear, and specifying sources and uses of funds. However, since operative goals are lower in acceptance, and since aspirants to public office need acceptance (from at least 50.1 percent of the people), most politicians prefer to speak only of official goals, at least until after the election. They of course would agree to speak at the operative level if "punished" for not doing so. The electorate could do this by refusing to support candidates who do not speak at the operative level. Instead, however, the American voter typically punishes (withholds support from) candidates who frankly discuss where the money will come from, rewards politicians who speak only of official goals, but hopes that candidates (despite the reward system) will discuss the issues operatively.

In War

If some oversimplification may be permitted, let it be assumed that the primary goal of the organization (Pentagon, Luftwaffe, or whatever) is to win. Let it be assumed further that the primary goal of most individuals on the front lines is to get home alive. Then there appears to be an important conflict in goals—personally rational behavior by those at the bottom will endanger goal attainment by those at the top.

But not necessarily! It depends on how the reward system is set up. The Vietnam war was indeed a study of disobedience and rebellion, with terms such as "fragging" (killing one's own commanding officer) and "search and evade" becoming part of the military vocabulary. The difference in subordinates' acceptance of authority between World War II and Vietnam is reported to be considerable, and veterans of the Second World War were often quoted as being outraged at the mutinous actions of many American soldiers in Vietnam.

Consider, however, some critical differences in the reward system in use during the two conflicts. What did the GI in World War II want? To go home. And when did he get to go home? When the war was won! If he disobeyed the orders to clean out the trenches and take the hills, the war would not be won and he would not go home. Furthermore, what were his chances of attaining his goal (getting home alive) if he obeyed the orders compared to his chances if he did not? What is being suggested is that the rational soldier in World War II, whether patriotic or not, probably found it expedient to obey.

Consider the reward system in use in Vietnam. What did the soldier at the bottom want? To go home. And when did he get to go home? When his tour of duty was over! This was the case whether or not the war was won. Furthermore, concerning the relative chance of getting home alive by obeying orders compared to the chance if they were disobeyed, it is worth noting that a mutineer in Vietnam was far more likely to be assigned rest and rehabilitation (on the assumption that fatigue was the cause) than he was to suffer any negative consequence.

In his description of the "zone of indifference," Barnard stated that "a person can and will accept a communication as authoritative only when . . . at the time of his decision, he believes it to be compatible with his personal interests as a whole."[3] In light of the reward system used in Vietnam, wouldn't it have been personally irrational for some orders to have been obeyed? Was not the military implementing a system which rewarded disobedience, while hoping that soldiers (despite the reward system) would obey orders?

In Medicine

Theoretically, physicians can make either of two types of error, and intuitively one seems as bad as the other. Doctors can pronounce patients sick when they are actually well (a type 1 error), thus causing them needless anxiety and expense, curtailment of enjoyable foods and activities, and even physical danger by subjecting them to needless medication and surgery. Alternately, a doctor can label a sick person well (a type 2 error), and thus avoid treating what may be a serious, even fatal ailment. It might be natural to conclude that physicians seek to minimize both types of error.

Such a conclusion would be wrong. It has been estimated that numerous Americans have been afflicted with iatrogenic (physician *caused*) illnesses.[4] This occurs when the doctor is approached by someone complaining of a few stray symptoms. The doctor classifies and organizes these symptoms, gives them a name, and obligingly tells the patient what further symptoms may be expected. This information often acts as a self-fulfilling prophecy, with the result that from that day on the patient for all practical purposes is sick.

Why does this happen? Why are physicians so reluctant to sustain a type 2 error (pronouncing a sick person well) that they will tolerate many type 1 errors? Again, a look at the reward system is needed. The punishments for a type 2 error are real: guilt, embarrassment, and the threat of a malpractice suit. On the other hand, a type 1 error (labeling a well person sick) is a much safer and conservative approach to medicine in today's litigious society. Type 1 errors also are likely to generate increased income and a stream of steady customers who, being well in a limited physiological sense, will not embarrass the doctor by dying abruptly. Fellow physicians and the general public therefore are really *rewarding* type 1 errors while *hoping* fervently that doctors will try not to make them.

A current example of rewarding type 1 errors is provided by Broward County, Florida, where an elderly or disabled person facing a competency hearing is evaluated by three court-appointed experts who get paid much more *for the same examination* if the person is ruled to be incompetent. For example, psychiatrists are paid $325 if they judge someone to be incapacitated, but earn only $125 if the person is judged competent. Court-appointed attorneys in Broward also earn more—$325 as opposed to $175—if their clients lose than if they win. Are you surprised to learn that, of 598 incapacity proceedings initiated and completed in the county in 1993, 570 ended with a verdict of incapacitation?[5]

In Universities

Society hopes that professors will not neglect their teaching responsibilities but *rewards* them almost entirely for research and publications. This is most true at the large and prestigious universities. Clichés such as "good research and good teaching go together" notwithstanding, professors often find that they must choose between teaching and research-oriented activities when allocating their time. Rewards for good teaching are usually limited to outstanding teacher awards, which are given to only a small percentage of good teachers and usually bestow little money and fleeting prestige. Punishments for poor teaching are also rare.

Rewards for research and publications, on the other hand, and punishments for failure to accomplish these, are common. Furthermore, publication-oriented résumés usually will be well-received at other universities, whereas teaching credentials, harder to document and quantify, are much less transferable. Consequently it is rational for university professors to concentrate on research, even to the detriment of teaching and at the expense of their students.

By the same token, it is rational for students to act based upon the goal displacement[6] which has occurred within universities concerning what they are rewarded for. If it is assumed that a primary goal of a university is to transfer knowledge from teacher to student, then grades become identifiable as a means toward that goal, serving as motivational, control, and feedback devices to expedite the knowledge transfer. Instead, however, the grades themselves have become much more important for entrance to graduate school, successful employment, tuition refunds, and parental respect, than the knowledge or lack of knowledge they are supposed to signify.

It therefore should come as no surprise that we find fraternity files for examinations, term paper writing services, and plagiarism. Such activities constitute a personally rational response to a reward system which pays off for grades rather than knowledge. These days, reward systems—specifically, the growing threat of lawsuits—encourage teachers to award students high grades, even if they aren't earned. For example:

> When Andy Hansen brought home a report card with a disappointing C in math, his parents . . . sued his teacher. . . . After a year and six different appeals within the school district, another year's worth of court proceedings, $4000 in legal fees paid by the Hansens, and another $8500 by the district . . . the C stands. Now the student's father, auto dealer Mike Hansen, says he plans to take the case to the State Court of Appeals. . . . "We went in and tried to make a deal: They wanted a C, we wanted an A, so why not compromise on a B?" Mike Hansen said. "But they dug in their heels, and here we are."[7]

In Consulting

It is axiomatic that those who care about a firm's well-being should insist that the organization get fair value for its expenditures. Yet it is commonly known that firms seldom bother to evaluate a new TQM, employee empowerment program, or whatever, to see if the company is getting its money's worth. Why? Certainly it is not because people have not pointed out that this situation exists; numerous practitioner-oriented articles are written each year on just this point.

One major reason is that the individuals (in human resources, or organization development) who would normally be responsible for conducting such evaluations are the same ones often charged with introducing the change effort in the first place. Having convinced top management to spend money, say, on outside consultants, they usually are quite animated afterwards in collecting rigorous vignettes and anecdotes about how successful the program was. The last thing many desire is a formal, revealing evaluation. Although members of top management may actually *hope* for such systematic evaluation, their reward systems continue to *reward* ignorance in this area. And if the HR department abdicates its responsibility, who is to step into the breach? The consultants themselves? Hardly! They are likely to be too busy collecting anecdotal "evidence" of their own, for use on their next client.

In Sports

Most coaches disdain to discuss individual accomplishments, preferring to speak of teamwork, proper attitude, and one-for-all spirit. Usually, however, rewards are distributed according to individual performance. The college basketball player who passes the ball to teammates instead of shooting will not compile impressive scoring statistics and is less likely to be drafted by the pros. The ballplayer who hits to right field to advance the runners will win neither the batting nor home run titles, and will be offered smaller raises. It therefore is rational for players to think of themselves first, and the team second.

In Government

Consider the cost-plus contract or its next of kin, the allocation of next year's budget as a direct function of this year's expenditures—a clear-cut example of a fouled-up reward system. It probably is conceivable that those who award such budgets and contracts really hope for economy and prudence in spending. It is obvious, however, that adopting the proverb "to those who spend shall more be given" rewards not economy, but spending itself.

In Business

The past reward practices of a group health claims division of a large eastern insurance company provides another rich illustration. Attempting to measure and reward accuracy in paying surgical claims, the firm systematically kept track of the number of returned checks and letters of complaint received from policyholders. However, underpayments were likely to provoke cries of outrage from the insured, while overpayments often were accepted in courteous silence. Since it was often impossible to tell from the physician's statement which of two surgical procedures, with different allowable benefits, was performed, and since writing for clarifications would have interfered with other standards used by the firm concerning percentage of claims paid within two days of receipt, the new hire in more than one claims section was soon acquainted with the informal norm: "When in doubt, pay it out!"

This situation was made even worse by the firm's reward system. The reward system called for annual merit increases to be given to all employees, in one of the following three amounts:

1. If the worker was "outstanding" (a select category, into which no more than two employees per section could be placed): 5 percent.

2. If the worker was "above average" (normally all workers not "outstanding" were so rated): 4 percent.

3. If the worker committed gross acts of negligence and irresponsibility for which he or she might be discharged in many other companies: 3 percent.

Now, since the difference between the five percent theoretically attainable through hard work and the four percent attainable merely by living until the review date is small, many employees were rather indifferent to the possibility of obtaining the extra one percent reward. In addition, since the penalty for error was a loss of only one percent, employees tended to ignore the norm concerning indiscriminant payments.

However, most employees were not indifferent to a rule which stated that, should absences or latenesses total three or more in any six-month period, the entire four or five percent due at the next merit review must be forfeited. In this sense, the firm was *hoping* for performance, while *rewarding* attendance. What it got, of course, was attendance. (If the absence/lateness rule appears to the reader to be stringent, it really wasn't. The company counted "times" rather than "days" absent, and a ten-day absence therefore counted the same as one lasting two days. A worker in danger of accumulating a third absence within six months merely had to remain ill—away from work—during a second absence until the first absence was more than six months old. The limiting factor was that at some point salary ceases, and sickness benefits take over. This was usually sufficient to get the younger workers to return, but for those with 20 or more years' service, the company provided sickness benefits of 90 percent of normal salary, tax-free! Therefore. . . .)

Thanks to the U.S. government, even the reporting of wrongdoing has been corrupted by an incredibly incompetent reward system that calls for whistleblowing employees to collect up to thirty percent *of the amount of a fraud without* a stated limit. Thus prospective whistleblowers are encouraged to delay reporting a fraud, even to actively participate in its continuance, in order to run up the total and, thus, their percentage of the take.

I'm quite sure that by now the reader has thought of numerous examples in his or her own experience which qualify as "folly." However, just in case, Table 1 presents some additional examples well worth pondering.

CAUSES

Extremely diverse instances of systems which reward behavior A although the rewarder apparently hopes for behavior B have been given. These are useful to illustrate the breadth and magnitude of the phenomenon, but the diversity increases the difficulty of determining commonalities and establishing causes. However, the following four general factors may be pertinent to an explanation of why fouled-up reward systems seem to be so prevalent.

TABLE 1 **Common Management Reward Follies**

We Hope for...	But We Often Reward...
• long-term growth; environmental responsibility	• quarterly earnings
• teamwork	• individual effort
• setting challenging "stretch" objectives	• achieving goals; "making the numbers"
• downsizing; rightsizing; delayering; restructuring	• adding staff; adding budget; adding Hay points
• commitment to total quality	• shipping on schedule, even with defects
• candor; surfacing bad news early	• reporting good news, whether it's true or not; agreeing with the boss, whether or not (s)he's right

1. **Fascination with an "Objective" Criterion**

Many managers seek to establish simple, quantifiable standards against which to measure and reward performance. Such efforts may be successful in highly predictable areas within an organization, but are likely to cause goal displacement when applied anywhere else.

2. **Overemphasis on Highly Visible Behaviors**

Difficulties often stem from the fact that some parts of the task are highly visible while other parts are not. For example, publications are easier to demonstrate than teaching, and scoring baskets and hitting home runs are more readily observable than feeding teammates and advancing base runners. Similarly, the adverse consequences of pronouncing a sick person well are more visible than those sustained by labeling a well person sick. Team-building and creativity are other examples of behaviors which may not be rewarded simply because they are hard to observe.

3. **Hypocrisy**

In some of the instances described the rewarder may have been getting the desired behavior, notwithstanding claims that the behavior was not desired. For example, in many jurisdictions within the U.S., judges' campaigns are funded largely by defense attorneys, while prosecutors are legally barred from making contributions. This doesn't do a whole lot to help judges to be "tough on crime" though, ironically, that's what their campaigns inevitably promise.

4. **Emphasis on Morality or Equity Rather than Efficiency**

Sometimes consideration of other factors prevents the establishment of a system which rewards behavior desired by the rewarder. The felt obligation of many Americans to vote for one candidate or another, for example, may impair their ability to discuss the issues. Similarly, the concern for spreading the risks and costs of wartime military service may outweigh the advantage to be obtained by committing personnel to combat until the war is over. The 1994 Clinton health plan, the Americans with Disabilities Act, and many other instances of proposed or recent governmental intervention provide outstanding examples of systems that reward efficiency, presumably in support of some higher objective.

ALTERING THE REWARD SYSTEM

Managers who complain about lack of motivation in their workers might do well to consider the possibility that the reward systems they have installed are paying off for behavior other than what they are seeking. This, in part, is what happened in Vietnam, and this is what regularly frustrates societal efforts to bring about honest politicians and civic-minded managers.

A first step for such managers might be to explore what types of behavior are currently being rewarded. Chances are excellent that these managers will be surprised by what they find—that their firms are not rewarding what they assume they are. In fact, such undesirable behavior by organizational members as they have observed may be explained largely by the reward systems in use.

This is not to say that all organizational behavior is determined by formal rewards and punishments. Certainly it is true that in the absence of formal reinforcement some soldiers will be patriotic, some players will be team oriented, and some employees will care about doing their job well. The point, however, is that in such cases the rewarder is not *causing* the behavior desired but is only a fortunate bystander. For an organization to *act* upon its members, the formal reward system should positively reinforce desired behavior, not constitute an obstacle to be overcome.

POSTSCRIPT

An irony about this article's being designated a management classic is that numerous people claim to have read and enjoyed it, but I wonder whether there was much in it that they didn't know. I believe that most readers already knew, and act on in their nonwork lives, the principles that underlie this article. For example, when we tell our daughter (who is about to cut her birthday cake) that her brother will select the first piece, or inform our friends *before* a meal that separate checks will be brought at the end, or tell the neighbor's boy that he will be paid five dollars for cutting the lawn *after* we inspect the lawn, we are making use of prospective rewards and punishments to cause other people to care about our own objectives. Organizational life may seem to be more complex, but the principles are the same.

Another irony attached to this "classic" is that it almost didn't see the light of day. It was rejected for presentation at the Eastern Academy of Management and was only published in *The Academy of Management Journal* because Jack Miner, its editor at the time, broke a tie between two reviewers. Nobody denied the relevance of the content, but reviewers were quite disturbed by the tone of the manuscript, and therefore its appropriateness for an academic audience. A compromise was reached whereby I added a bit of the great academic cure-all, data (Table 1 in the original article, condensed and summarized in this update), and a copy editor strangled some of the life from my writing style. In this respect, I would like to acknowledge the extremely competent editorial work performed on this update by John Veiga and his editorial staff. I am grateful to have had the opportunity to revisit the article, and hope the reader has enjoyed it also.

Endnotes

1. Originally published in 1975, *Academy of Management Journal*, 18, 769–783.
2. Charles Perrow, "The Analysis of Goals in Complex Organizations," in A. Etzioni (ed.), *Readings on Modern Organizations* (Englewood Cliffs, NJ: Prentice Hall, 1969), 66.
3. Chester I. Barnard, *The Functions of the Executive* (Cambridge, MA: Harvard University Press, 1964), 165.
4. L. H. Garland, "Studies of the Accuracy of Diagnostic Procedures," *American Journal Roentgenological, Radium Therapy Nuclear Medicine,* Vol. 82, 1959, 25–38; and Thomas J. Scheff, "Decision Rules, Types of Error, and Their Consequences in Medical Diagnosis," in F. Massarik and P. Ratoosh (eds.), *Mathematical Explorations in Behavioral Science* (Homewood, IL: Irwin, 1965).

5. *Miami Herald,* May 8, 1994, 1a, 10a.
6. Goal displacement results when means become ends in themselves and displace the original goals. See Peter M. Blau and W. Richard Scott, *Formal Organizations* (San Francisco, CA: Chandler, 1962).

7. *San Francisco Examiner,* reported in *Fortune,* February 7, 1994, 161.

Why Merit Pay Doesn't Work: Implications from Organizational Theory

Jone L. Pearce

Compensation plans that base pay on an individual's recent performance, such as merit pay, enjoy prominence in both the professional compensation literature and in the popular imagination. Such plans have the attraction of clear communication of performance expectations and give employees the opportunity to increase their incomes through their own efforts. That these plans have become synonymous with "fairness" is reflected in the widespread support for President Reagan's call for merit pay for schoolteachers. Compensation textbooks and journals reflect the general belief in these plans through their devotion of substantial space to discussions of the design and implementation of such programs, despite the fact that individual performance-contingent pay makes up a very small portion of most employees' total compensation.

In practice, however, we know that such pay programs are fraught with problems (see Winstanley, 1982; Pearce & Perry, 1983; Pearce, Stevenson, & Perry, 1985). Edward Morse from Hay put it bluntly as 1986 drew to an end: "Our traditional reward systems have failed. The decline in U.S. productivity growth during the past 20 years signals loudly that our current [pay-for-performance] system is no longer meeting our needs" (p. 85). Although the limitations of these plans have been known for decades (see Sayles, 1952; Whyte, 1955; Meyer, 1975), it is a rare author who does not end the list of "merit pay problems" with upbeat suggestions for the successful implementation of such programs (e.g., Hamner, 1975).

Here it will be suggested that advice concerning the improvement of the implementation of such plans has not substantially improved their success. Real organizations are messy, indeterminate places, and a compensation idea that is not feasible except in pristine laboratory environments needs to be reexamined. Further, it will be proposed that the failure of individual merit pay plans should not reflexively be blamed on the practitioners struggling to put these programs in place. Rather, it will be suggested that these failures are the result of a flawed theoretical assumption behind individually contingent pay. Practicing managers are aware of the deficiencies of their own organizations' performance-contingent pay systems, but they have an incomplete rationale to explain these inadequacies. The result is frustration. Individually contingent pay, as an idea, needs to be analyzed in its organizational context. Therefore in this paper, the implications of "organizational theory" for individually based pay are developed.

From D. B. Balkin & L. R. Gomez-Mejia (Eds.), *New Perspectives on Compensation* (pp. 169–178). Englewood Cliffs, NJ: Prentice Hall, 1987. Reprinted by permission.

It is important to emphasize at the outset that the present argument is concerned only with the problems of merit pay based on *individual* performance, not on group or organizational performance-based merit pay or bonuses. Advocates of individual performance-based programs suggest that to be effective, performance expectations need to be clearly stated in advance. These true pay-for-performance systems (rather than the ones based mostly on retrospective subjective judgments) are the focus of the present discussion.

These pay programs are based on the assumption that overall organizational performance is the simple additive combination of individual employees' separate contributions. Alternatively, it will be proposed that the greater the uncertainty, interdependence, and complexity of organizational work, the greater the cooperation among employees required for successful organizational performance, and that individual performance-based pay can provide powerful disincentives for cooperation. This is not the traditional suggestion that money is not a powerful motivator (Deci, 1975). Quite to the contrary, individually contingent pay programs can be pernicious because they so effectively direct and sustain individuals' motivation; but such plans can direct motivation away from the actions that are most functional for organizations.

The idea itself seems to hold such power that these programs are usually explained as failures of implementation or intention that, at best, suggest additions to the list of moderating or limiting conditions. Most often managers are blamed for not implementing such programs properly. For example, Hamner (1975) states that "it is not the merit pay theory that is defective. Rather, the history of the actual implementation of the theory is at fault" (p. 220).

This is not to suggest that individually based incentive pay programs are always correctly implemented but that too often evidence of "failure" receives reflexive condemnation rather than thoughtful analysis. This unexamined belief in the idea of pay for individual performance has led to a straining for explanations. The dazzle of high individual motivation has deflected theoretical attention away from a focus on what actions are being motivated. The following arguments and testable propositions derived from them are more fully developed in Pearce (1985).

ORGANIZATION THEORY AND MERIT PAY

Individual performance-contingent pay derives from an assumption that the organization's effectiveness is the simple additive combination of individuals' separate performances. Such pay programs are based on the development of "compensation contracts" in which pay is linked to the employee's performance in an explicit agreement. The clarity, "fairness," and motivating potential of these compensation contracts distract us from the fact that the employee-employer relationship has not been based on such "fixed contracts" for the simple reason that this is a less productive relationship for the kinds of uncertain, interdependent, and complex work organizations undertake.

Uncertainty in Organizations

The authority relationship between supervisors and subordinates has been a long-standing interest of organization and management theorists. Simon's (1957) definition of authority bears repeating: Subordinates accept authority whenever they permit their behavior to be guided by the decision of a supervisor, *without independently examining the merits of that decision.* When exercising authority, the supervisor does not seek to convince subordinates, only to obtain acquiescence. Organization theorists have argued that the authority of supervisors is accepted by employees in exchange for wages. It is important to recognize that this "employment contract" is an open-ended one. In exchange for pay, employees offer not specific services but their undifferentiated time and effort, which can be directed by the supervisors as they see fit. This is because, as Simon notes, from the viewpoint of the organization, there is no point in offering inducements to employees unless their actions could be brought into the coordinated system of organizational actions through their acceptance of its authority. Simon argues that open-ended employment contracts allow organizations the flexibility to respond to future uncertainty.

If performance requirements are indeed uncertain, the writing of a fixed-compensation contract restricts the ability of managers to respond to these changes. Pay for individual performance attempts to modify these traditional employment contracts so that they are less open-ended and more like the closed-ended (behaviors specified in advance) contracts of the marketplace. Simon (1957) implies that under circumstances of uncertainty, closed-ended performance contracts would be difficult to write. If conditions are genuinely uncertain, how can these contracts be detailed in advance?

In practice, these pay programs are frequently adapted to uncertainty by combining "subjective judgment" with objective measures (Lawler, 1981). Such adaptations certainly help to retain open-ended authority relationships, but they have side effects of their own. For example, Carroll and Schneier (1982) note that the more subjective the rating criterion, the more rater judgment is required, not only regarding the degree to which the ratee meets the criterion but also regarding what the measure actually means. Therefore, as Lawler (1981) notes, subjectively based judgments require high levels of trust. Thus attempts to retain the authority relationship by using subjective supervisory judgments remove the clarity and fairness advantages of fixed contracts.

Recognition of the importance of uncertainty in organizational life helps us to understand otherwise inexplicable research findings. For example, researchers have found only a slight positive correlation between merit raises and performance ratings. Others usually interpret these data as missed opportunities to use a valued reward to increase motivation (e.g., Lawler, 1971). Alternatively, supervisors may not tie such a salient reward to individually measured performance because they recognize not only that good performance is not completely represented in performance appraisals but also that these closed-ended contracts reduce their own ability to respond to unanticipated events. Supervisors face myriad uncertainties, requiring levels of flexibility that cannot be captured in individual performance contracts. Such supervisors use the discretion that merit raises afford to reward critical accomplishments, to cope with such concerns as inflation and salary compression, and to compensate for a particularly unattractive assignment or absence of an expected promotion. Pay does, in fact, serve a multitude of purposes in organizations, and mandating that it be dominated by an individual's measured performance in the most recent performance period impedes the ability of managers to manage.

Interdependence in Organizations

In describing the ways in which individually contingent pay interferes with the dependence of individuals on their organizations, it is useful to draw on Thompson's (1967) three-part categorization of dependence relations in organizations. First, individuals are most interdependent when they must work together, interacting during task performance, in order to complete their work. Individually contingent pay would rarely be advocated in the case of this "reciprocal interdependence," since credit and blame are virtually impossible to assign to individuals. However, Thompson's two other kinds of interdependence—sequential and pooled—are not readily seen as prohibiting individually contingent pay.

Sequentially dependent employees rely on others for either their inputs, for the disposal of their outputs, or for both. It is for this kind of interdependence that we have the most vivid descriptions of contingent pay dysfunctions (e.g., Whyte, 1955; Babchuk & Goode, 1951). Since the problems resulting from the use of individually contingent pay for sequentially dependent employees have been well documented, this discussion focuses on pooled interdependence.

Pooled interdependence is the collective dependence of employees on the continued success of the organization. Thompson argues that employees may not be directly independent with others for their task performance but are still jointly dependent with all other participants on their organization's ability to provide employment and other resources.

Individually contingent compensation contracts distract employees' attention from this more abstract dependence relationship and interfere with members' commitment to their colleagues and employer. By treating them as labor contractors, employees are encouraged to work only on activities represented in their contracts. Drawing on Kerr (1975), we might hope that they will cooperate with their colleagues and supervisors, but we are rewarding them for fulfilling the terms of a fixed contract.

Thus employees are seen by the organization and come to view themselves as "contractors," with a written "track record" provided by the compensation system that can be marketed to another employer. It can be speculated that it is this growing use of performance-based compensation contracts for professionals and managers, rather than massive changes in personal values, that has led to the popularly perceived shift among American managers and professionals from "organization men" (Whyte, 1956) to "job-hopping professional managers" ("The Money Chase," 1981). Therefore, it should be no surprise to find that recent advocates of Japanese-style concern with fostering employee loyalty advocate abandoning individually contingent pay in favor of organizationwide bonuses (Ouchi, 1981).

It is further suggested that pay for individual performance, since it provides incentives that run counter to the pooled interdependence among organization members, can actually undermine the quality of employer-employee relationships. Numerous scholars have attempted to articulate the positive attitude that frequently emerges among employees in their relationship with their employing organization (e.g., Pearce & Peters, 1985). For example, Barnard (1938) describes the importance of "cooperation," and recently there has been a renewed interest in "organizational commitment" (Mowday, Porter, & Steers, 1982; Wiener, 1982).

These pay plans can damage organizational commitment, since they treat the employee as a labor contractor. Such contracts communicate that the employer is only concerned with the employee's performance as it is reflected in the "contract measures" and is, in effect, indifferent to past contributions and experience (since the employer pays only for the recent performance period), to the employee's potential for other kinds of work, and to any extenuating circumstances that may have influenced the recent performance measures. There is recent evidence that merit pay programs do have significant and long-lasting (fifteen months) negative effects on organizational commitment (Pearce & Porter, 1985).

Complexity in Organizations

The work of Williamson (1975) illustrates the complexity of organizational work and helps to clarify why the fixed contracts of individually contingent pay can be dysfunctional for overall organizational effectiveness. This economist has sought to understand the conditions under which economic activity takes place either in markets—in which transactions involve exchange between autonomous economic entities—or in organizations. He suggests that organizations are more efficient than marketplace contracting under conditions of future uncertainty, complex transactions, and dependence on individuals willing to exploit their advantage.

Under these circumstances, employment contracts in organizational settings have certain advantages over labor market contracting that makes employment more efficient. Particularly relevant to the present discussion, Williamson argues that organizations are better able to encourage cooperation among opportunistic specialists (employees). Thus organizations are the more efficient forms under certain circumstances because they can more easily compensate individuals for cooperation.

Williamson's work has important implications for the design of pay systems. It suggests that despite its advantages of clarity and apparent fairness, market contracting is not suited to all types of economic exchange. Employment relationships dominate the labor market today because work has become more complex, more dependent on particular individuals, and must be conducted under conditions of future uncertainty. If such conditions are not present, Williamson suggests that it is more efficient to use marketplace contracting for services rather than employment.

Therefore, individually contingent pay, by tying an employee's pay to his or her performance during a specific time period, is an attempt to reformulate the employer-employee relationships into a pseudocontract between buyer and seller. Under conditions of uncertainty, interdependence, and complexity, such pseudocontracts cannot be completely specified. They can, at best, cover only a portion of the desired actions and become a forced and artificial representation of the kind of performance that would be most effective for the organization (a familiar problem for those who have had experience with merit pay programs). Further, since pay can be such a powerful motivator, all the problems in the use of pseudocontracting in organizations are made worse when pay is attached to fulfilling the terms of the contract.

Pay-for-individual-performance systems, despite their motivating power, would not, then, be expected to result in enhanced organizational effectiveness. Such systems build in disincentives for the management of uncertainty, interdependence, and complexity and so discourage the kinds of cooperative actions that lead the organizational form to be more efficient than labor contracting. If the organization does, in fact, have individual tasks that are predictable, simple, and independent, this analysis suggests that it would be more efficient to hire contractors than employees. Pay for individual performance is neither a labor contract (since the authority relationship remains) nor a conventional employment relationship (with rewards allocated based on *post hoc* judgments of overall employee historical and potential contributions). Thus organizations that use such forms of compensation would be expected to have less effective performance than those not using such systems, since their compensation system is working against the advantages of the organizational form. We certainly could not expect the greater overall organizational effectiveness implied by pay-for-performance advocates.

This suggests a reinterpretation of the research reporting that executives' pay is uncorrelated (Redling, 1981; Perham, 1971) or, at best, weakly associated (Patton, 1961; Gomez-Mejia, Tosi, & Hinkin, 1984) with their organizations' financial performance. Instead of deploring this evidence as representing a lack of "the will to pay for performance" (Redling, 1981), it may more accurately reflect attempts to pay for performance that simply have no influence on corporate performance. Booz-Allen and Hamilton (1983) reported that while the "shareholder value" of Standard and Poor's 400 corporations declined 10.5 percent from 1970 to 1982, the use of performance-based bonuses for these firms' chief executive officers nearly doubled (from 23 percent of total compensation in 1971 to 41 percent in 1981). This appears to reflect an increasing effort to tie a larger proportion of executive pay to measures of performance. These compensation committees were apparently trying to pay for individual performance, despite the fact that organizational performance was declining during this period. This certainly doesn't prove that individually contingent pay caused the decline in firm performance, but it does suggest that the absence of a strong positive relationship between executive pay and firm performance does not necessarily reflect a lack of "the will to pay for performance." Rather, perhaps, corporate compensation committees have been using the wrong model of the ways in which individuals' performances contribute to overall organizational performance.

IMPLICATIONS

The argument developed here has implications for both research and practice. Research hypotheses derived from these arguments need to be tested empirically; a discussion of possible tests appears in Pearce (1985).

Regarding compensation practice, this article was intended to help explain the gap between the popular belief in the power of merit pay and the actual track record of these programs by examining one of the relatively neglected assumptions behind individually contingent pay. At this point one could reasonably ask: Since virtually no compensation system is actually dominated by individual performance-contingent compensation, what practical difference does it make if an important assumption is flawed?

Such a large discrepancy between compensation practice and popular theory is demoralizing to practitioners and can lead to poor practice. Professional compensation specialists are led to feel uncomfortable that their own organization's actual system deviates so far from "accepted advice," and they have no way to explain coherently *why* true pay for performance plays such a limited role in their employees' overall compensation. This discussion is intended to confirm that there is no need to feel guilty about the small role of merit pay.

Virtually all compensation textbooks note that pay is intended to attract and retain employees as well as motivate greater individual performance (Nash & Carroll, 1975; Ellig, 1982; Wallace & Fay, 1983). Wallace and Fay argue that compensation systems must meet employees' expectations for equity or fairness and that individual job performance is only one of many factors—including prevailing labor market wages, the responsibility of the position, and skill and knowledge requirements—that contribute to perceived compensation fairness. Pay systems are already burdened by spiraling labor market demand, pay compression, demands for comparable worth, inflation, and the like, and advocating that they also be harnessed as the primary short-term performance-contingent incentive is not realistic.

In conclusion, individually contingent pay plans are based on a false assumption. These plans attempt to mimic marketplace contracts under conditions of uncertainty, complexity, and dependence for which they are not appropriate. Pay can be a powerful incentive, but compensation specialists need to ensure that the dazzle of high performance motivation doesn't distract from a concern with *what* performance is being motivated. Paying people on the basis of their recent measured individual performance simply does not build on the relative advantages of the organizational form. Most kinds of organizations succeed because of cooperation among their members, not because of members' discrete, independent performance. Such cooperation is particularly critical among employees with either valuable expertise (which may be the basis for the organization's competitive advantage) or the discretion to commit the organization's resources (i.e., managers). It is simply not in the organization's interest to encourage short-term single-transaction expectations among such important employees. Pay is important, and the ways in which organizations dispense it tell us a lot about the actions they expect from their employees. Compensation theory could reflect organizational realities better if it had as great a concern for the organizational context in which employees must work as it does for their levels of individual effort.

References

Babchuk, N., and W. J. Goode (1951), "Work Incentives in a Self-determined Group," *American Sociological Review* 16, 679–687.

Barnard, C. I. (1938), *The Functions of the Executive.* Cambridge, Mass.: Harvard University Press.

Booz-Allen, and Hamilton Inc. (1983), *Creating Shareholder Value: A New Mission for Executive Compensation.* New York: New York.

Carroll, S. J., and C. E. Schneier (1982), *Performance Appraisal and Review Systems: The Identification, Measurement, and Development of Performance in Organizations.* Glenview, Ill.: Scott, Foresman.

Deci, E. L. (1975), *Intrinsic Motivation.* New York: Plenum.

Ellig, B. R. (1982), *Executive Compensation: A Total Pay Perspective.* New York: McGraw-Hill.

Gomez-Mejia, L. R., H. Tosi, and T. Hinkin (1984, August), *Organizational Determinants of Chief Executive Compensation.* Paper presented at the meeting of the Academy of Management, Boston.

Hamner, W. C. (1975), "How to Ruin Motivation with Pay," *Compensation Review* 7, no. 3, 17–27.

Kerr, S. (1975), "On the Folly of Rewarding A while Hoping for B," *Academy of Management Journal* 18, 769–783.

Lawler, E. E. (1971), *Pay and Organizational Effectiveness: A Psychological View.* New York: McGraw-Hill.

—— (1981), *Pay and Organization Development.* Reading, Mass.: Addison-Wesley.

Morse, E. (Fall 1986), "Productivity Rewards for Non-Management Employees," in *Topics in Total Compensation,* ed. R. C. Ochsner. Greenvale, New York: A Panel Publication.

Meyer, H. H. (1975), "The Pay-for-Performance Dilemma," *Organizational Dynamics* 3, no. 3, 39–50.

"The Money Chase: Business School Solutions May Be Part of the U.S. Problem," *Time,* May 4, 1981, p. 20.

Mowday, R. T., L. W. Porter, and R. M. Steers (1982), *Employee-Organization Linkages: The Psychology of Commitment, Absenteeism, and Turnover.* New York: Academic Press.

Nash, A. N., and S. J. Carroll (1975), *The Management of Compensation.* Belmont, Calif.: Wadsworth.

Ouchi, W. G. (1981), *Theory Z.* Reading, Mass.: Addison-Wesley.

Patton, A. (1961), *Men, Money, and Motivation.* New York: McGraw-Hill.

Pearce, J. L. (1985), *An Organization Is Not the Sum of Its Employees: An Unexamined Assumption of Performance-contingent Compensation.* Working paper, Graduate School of Management, University of California, Irvine.

————, and J. L. Perry (1983), "Federal Merit Pay: A Longitudinal Analysis," *Public Administration Review* 43, 315–325.

————, and R. H. Peters (1985), "A Contradictory Norms View of Employer-Employee Exchange," *Journal of Management* 11, 19–30.

————, and L. W. Porter (1985), *Employee Responses to Formal Performance Appraisal Feedback.* Working paper, Graduate School of Management, University of California, Irvine.

————, W. B. Stevenson, and J. L. Perry (1985), "Managerial Compensation Based on Organizational Performance: A Time-Series Analysis of the Impact of Merit Pay," *Academy of Management Journal* 28, 261–279.

Perham, J. (1971), "What's Wrong with Bonuses?" *Dun's Review and Modern Industry* 98, 40–44.

Redling, E. T. (1981), "Myth vs. Reality: The Relationship Between Top Executive Pay and Corporate Performance," *Compensation Review* 13, no. 4, 16–24.

Sayles, L. R. (1952), "The Impact of Incentives on Inter-group Work Relations: A Management and Union Problem," *Personnel* 28, 483–490.

Simon, H. A. (1957), *Administrative Behavior,* 2nd ed. New York: Free Press.

Thompson, J. D. (1967), *Organizations in Action.* New York: McGraw-Hill.

Wallace, M. J., and C. H. Fay (1983), *Compensation Theory and Practice.* Boston: Kent.

Whyte, W. F. (1955), *Money and Motivation.* New York: Harper & Row.

———— (1956), *The Organization Man.* New York: Simon & Schuster.

Wiener, Y. (1982), "Commitment and Organizations: A Normative View," *Academy of Management Review* 7, 418–428.

Williamson, O. E. (1975), *Markets and Hierarchies: Analysis and Antitrust Implications.* New York: Free Press.

Winstanley, N. B. (1982), "Are Merit Increases Really Effective?" *Personnel Administrator* 4, 37–41.

Six Dangerous Myths about Pay

Jeffrey Pfeffer

Consider two groups of steel minimills. One group pays an average hourly wage of $18.07. The second pays an average of $21.52 an hour. Assuming that other direct-employment costs, such as benefits, are the same for the two groups, which group has the higher labor costs?

An airline is seeking to compete in the low-cost, low-frills segment of the U.S. market where, for obvious reasons, labor productivity and efficiency are crucial for competitive success. The company pays virtually no one on the basis of individual merit or performance. Does it stand a chance of success?

A company that operates in an intensely competitive segment of the software industry does not pay its sales force on commission. Nor does it pay individual bonuses or offer stock options or phantom stock, common incentives in an industry heavily dependent on attracting and retaining scarce programming talent. Would you invest in this company?

From *Harvard Business Review,* 1998, May–June, 109–119. Reprinted by permission.

Every day, organizational leaders confront decisions about pay. Should they adjust the company's compensation system to encourage some set of behaviors? Should they retain consultants to help them implement a performance-based pay system? How large a raise should they authorize?

In general terms, these kinds of questions come down to four decisions about compensation:

- how much to pay employees;

- how much emphasis to place on financial compensation as a part of the total reward system;

- how much emphasis to place on attempting to hold down the rate of pay; and

- whether to implement a system of individual incentives to reward differences in performance and productivity and, if so, how much emphasis to place on these incentives.

For leaders, there can be no delegation of these matters. Everyone knows decisions about pay are important. For one thing, they help establish a company's culture by rewarding the business activities, behaviors, and values that senior managers hold dear. Senior management at Quantum, the disk drive manufacturer in Milpitas, California, for example, demonstrates its commitment to teamwork by placing all employees, from the CEO to hourly workers, on the same bonus plan, tracking everyone by the same measure—in this case, return on total capital.

Compensation is also a concept and practice very much in flux. Compensation is becoming more variable as companies base a greater proportion of it on stock options and bonuses and a smaller proportion on base salary, not only for executives but also for people further and further down the hierarchy. As managers make organization-defining decisions about pay systems, they do so in a shifting landscape while being bombarded with advice about the best routes to stable ground.

Unfortunately, much of that advice is wrong. Indeed, much of the conventional wisdom and public discussion about pay today is misleading, incorrect, or sometimes both at the same time. The result is that businesspeople end up adopting wrongheaded notions about how to pay people and why. They believe in six dangerous myths about pay—fictions about compensation that have somehow come to be seen as the truth.

Do you think you have managed to avoid these myths? Let's see how you answered the three questions that open this article. If you said the second set of steel minimills had higher labor costs, you fell into the common trap of confusing labor *rates* with labor *costs*. That is Myth #1: that labor rates and labor costs are the same thing. But how different they really are. The second set of minimills paid its workers at a rate of $3.45 an hour more than the first. But according to data collected by Fairfield University Professor Jeffrey Arthur, its labor costs were much lower because the productivity of the mills was higher. The second set of mills actually required 34% fewer labor hours to produce a ton of steel than the first set and also generated 63% less scrap. The second set of mills could have raised workers' pay rate by 19% and still had lower labor costs.

Connected to the first myth are three more myths that draw on the same logic. When managers believe that labor costs and labor rates are the same thing, they also tend to believe that they can cut labor costs by cutting labor rates. That's Myth #2. Again, this leaves out the important matter of productivity. I may replace my $2,000-a-week engineers with ones that earn $500 a week, but my costs may skyrocket because the new, lower-paid employees are inexperienced, slow, and less capable. In that case, I would have increased my costs by cutting my rates.

Managers who mix up labor rates and labor costs also tend to accept Myth #3: that labor costs are a significant portion of total costs. Sometimes, that's true. It is, for example, at accounting and consulting firms. But the ratio of labor costs to total costs varies widely in different industries and companies. And even where it is true, it's not as important as many managers believe. Those who swallow Myth #4—that low labor costs are a potent competitive strategy—may neglect other, more effective ways of competing, such as through quality, service, delivery, and innovation. In reality, low labor costs are a slippery way to compete and perhaps the least sustainable competitive advantage there is.

Those of you who believed that the airline trying to compete in the low-cost, low-frills segment of the U.S. market would not succeed without using individual incentives succumbed to Myth #5: that the most effective way to motivate people to work productively is through individual incentive compensation. But Southwest Airlines has never used such a system, and it is the cost *and* productivity leader in its industry. Southwest is not alone, but still it takes smart, informed managers to buck the trend of offering individual rewards.

Would you have invested in the computer software company that didn't offer its people bonuses, stock options, or other financial incentives that could make them millionaires? You should have because it has succeeded mightily, growing over the past 21 years at a compound annual rate of more than 25%. The company is the SAS Institute of Cary, North Carolina. Today it is the largest privately held company in the software industry, with 1997 revenues of some $750 million.

Rather than emphasize pay, SAS has achieved an unbelievably low turnover rate below 4%—in an industry where the norm is closer to 20%—by offering intellectually engaging work; a family-friendly environment that features exceptional benefits; and the opportunity to work with fun, interesting people using state-of-the-art equipment.

In short, SAS has escaped Myth #6: that people work primarily for money. SAS, operating under the opposite assumption, demonstrates otherwise. In the last three years, the company has lost *none* of its 20 North American district sales managers. How many software companies do you know could make that statement, even about the last three months?

Every day, I see managers harming their organizations by believing in these myths about pay. What I want to do in these following pages is explore some factors that help account for why the myths are so pervasive, present some evidence to disprove their underlying assumptions, and suggest how leaders might think more productively and usefully about the important issue of pay practices in their organizations.

WHY THE MYTHS EXIST

On October 10, 1997, the *Wall Street Journal* published an article expressing surprise that a "contrarian Motorola" had chosen to build a plant in Germany to make cellular phones despite the notoriously high "cost" of German labor. The *Journal* is not alone in framing

Truth and Consequences: The Six Dangerous Myths about Compensation

Myth	Reality
1. Labor rates and labor costs are the same thing.	1. They are not, and confusing them leads to a host of managerial missteps. For the record, labor rates are straight wages divided by time—a Wal-Mart cashier earns $5.15 an hour, a Wall Street attorney $2,000 a day. Labor costs are a calculation of how much a company pays its people and how much they produce. Thus German factory workers may be paid at a rate of $30 an hour and Indonesians $3, but the workers' relative costs will reflect how many widgets are produced in the same period of time.
2. You can lower your labor costs by cutting labor rates.	2. When managers buy into the myth that labor rates and labor costs are the same thing, they usually fall for this myth as well. Once again, then, labor costs are a function of labor rates and productivity. To lower labor costs, you need to address *both*. Indeed, sometimes lowering labor rates increases labor costs.
3. Labor costs constitute a significant proportion of total costs.	3. This is true—but only sometimes. Labor costs as a proportion of total costs vary widely by industry and company. Yet many executives assume labor costs are the biggest expense on their income statement. In fact, labor costs are only the most immediately malleable expense.
4. Low labor costs are a potent and sustainable competitive weapon.	4. In fact, labor costs are perhaps the most slippery and least sustainable way to compete. Better to achieve competitive advantage through quality; through customer service; through product, process, or service innovation; or through technology leadership. It is much more difficult to imitate these sources of competitive advantage than to merely cut costs.
5. Individual incentive pay improves performance.	5. Individual incentive pay, in reality, undermines performance—of both the individual and the organization. Many studies strongly suggest that this form of reward undermines teamwork, encourages a short-term focus, and leads people to believe that pay is not related to performance at all but to having the "right" relationships and an ingratiating personality.
6. People work for money.	6. People do work for money—but they work even more for meaning in their lives. In fact, they work to have fun. Companies that ignore this fact are essentially bribing their employees and will pay the price in a lack of loyalty and commitment.

business decisions about pay in this way. The *Economist* has also written articles about high German labor "costs," citing as evidence labor rates (including fringe benefits) of more than $30 per hour.

The semantic confusion of labor rates with labor costs, endemic in business journalism and everyday discussion, leads managers to see the two as equivalent. And when the two seem equivalent, the associated myths about labor costs seem to make sense, too. But, of course, labor rates and labor costs simply aren't the same thing. A labor rate is total salary divided by time worked. But labor costs take productivity into account. That's how the second set of minimills managed to have lower labor costs than the mills with the lower wages. They made more steel, and they made it faster and better.

Another reason why the confusion over costs and rates persists is that labor rates are a convenient target for managers who want to make an impact. Labor rates are highly visible, and it's easy to compare the rates you pay with those paid by your competitors or with those paid in other parts of the world. In addition, labor rates often appear to be a company's most malleable financial variable. It seems a lot quicker and easier to cut wages than to control costs in other ways, like reconfiguring manufacturing processes, changing corporate culture, or altering product design. Because labor costs appear to be the lever closest at hand, managers mistakenly assume it is the one that has the most leverage.

For the myths that individual incentive pay drives creativity and productivity, and that people are primarily motivated by money, we have economic theory to blame. More specifically, we can blame the economic model of human behavior widely taught in business schools and held to be true in the popular press. This model presumes that behavior is rational—driven by the best information available at the time and designed to maximize the individual's self-interest. According to this model, people take jobs and decide how much effort to expend in those jobs based on their expected financial return. If pay is not contingent on performance, the theory goes, individuals will not devote sufficient attention and energy to their jobs.

Additional problems arise from such popular economic concepts as agency theory (which contends that there are differences in preference and perspective between owners and those who work for them) and transaction-cost economics (which tries to identify which transactions are best organized by markets and which by hierarchies). Embedded in both concepts is the idea that individuals not only pursue self-interest but do so on occasion with guile and opportunism. Thus agency theory suggests that employees have different objectives than their employers and, moreover, have opportunities to misrepresent information and divert resources to their personal use. Transaction-cost theory suggests that people will make false or empty threats and promises to get better deals from one another.

All of these economic models portray work as hard and aversive—implying that the only way people can be induced to work is through some combination of rewards and sanctions. As professor James N. Baron of Stanford Business School has written, "The image of workers in these models is somewhat akin to Newton's first law of motion: employees remain in a state of rest unless compelled to change that state by a stronger force impressed upon them—namely, an optimal labor contract."

Similarly, the language of economics is filled with terms such as *shirking* and *free riding*. Language is powerful, and as Robert Frank, himself an economist, has noted, theories of human behavior become self-fulfilling. We act on the basis of these theories, and through our own actions produce in others the behavior we expect. If we believe people will work hard only if specifically rewarded for doing so, we will provide contingent rewards and thereby condition people to work only when they are rewarded. If we expect people to be untrustworthy, we will closely monitor and control them and by doing so will signal that they can't be trusted—an expectation that they will most likely confirm for us.

So self-reinforcing are these ideas that you almost have to avoid mainstream business to get away from them. Perhaps that's why several companies known to be strongly committed to managing through trust, mutual respect, and true decentralization—such as AES Corporation, Lincoln Electric, the Men's Wearhouse, the SAS Institute, ServiceMaster, Southwest Airlines, and Whole Foods Market—tend to avoid recruiting at conventional business schools.

There's one last factor that helps perpetuate all these myths: the compensation-consulting industry. Unfortunately, that industry has a number of perverse incentives to keep these myths alive.

First, although some of these consulting firms have recently broadened their practices, compensation remains their bread and butter. Suggesting that an organization's performance can be improved in some way other than by tinkering with the pay system may be empirically correct but is probably too selfless a behavior to expect from these firms.

Second, if it's simpler for managers to tinker with the compensation system than to change an organization's culture, the way work is organized, and the level of trust and respect the system displays, it's even easier for consultants. Thus both the compensation consultants and their clients are tempted by the apparent speed and ease with which reward-system solutions can be implemented.

Third, to the extent that changes in pay systems bring their own new predicaments, the consultants will continue to have work solving the problems that the tinkering has caused in the first place.

FROM MYTH TO REALITY: A LOOK AT THE EVIDENCE

The media are filled with accounts of companies attempting to reduce their labor costs by laying off people, moving production to places where labor rates are lower, freezing wages, or some combination of the above. In the early 1990s, for instance, Ford decided not to award merit raises to its white-collar workers as part of a new cost-cutting program. And in 1997, General Motors endured a series of highly publicized strikes over the issue of outsourcing. GM wanted to move more of its work to nonunion, presumably lower-wage, suppliers to reduce its labor costs and become more profitable.

Ford's and GM's decisions were driven by the myths that labor rates and labor costs are the same thing, and that labor costs constitute a significant portion of total costs. Yet hard evidence to support those contentions is slim. New United Motor Manufacturing, the joint venture between Toyota and General Motors based in Fremont, California, paid the highest wage in the automobile industry when it began operations in the mid-1980s, and it also offered a guarantee of secure employment. With productivity some 50% higher than at comparable GM plants, the venture could afford to pay 10% more and still come out ahead.

Yet General Motors apparently did not learn the lesson that what matters is not pay rate but productivity. In May 1996, as GM was preparing to confront the union over the issue of outsourcing, the "Harbour Report," the automobile industry's bible of comparative efficiency, published some interesting data suggesting that General Motors' problems had little to do with labor rates. As reported in the *Wall Street Journal* at the time, the report showed that it took General Motors some 46 hours to assemble a car, while it took Ford just 37.92 hours, Toyota 29.44, and Nissan only 27.36. As a way of attacking cost problems, officials at General Motors should have asked why they needed 21% more hours than Ford to accomplish the same thing or why GM was some 68% less efficient than Nissan.

For more evidence of how reality really looks, consider the machine tool industry. Many of its senior managers have been particularly concerned with low-cost foreign competition, believing that the cost advantage has come from the lower labor rates available offshore. But for machine tool companies that stop fixating on labor rates and focus instead on their overall management system and manufacturing processes, there are great potential returns. Cincinnati Milacron, a company that had virtually surrendered the market for low-end machine tools to Asian competitors by the mid-1980s, overhauled its assembly process, abolished its stockroom, and reduced job categories from seven to one. Without any capital investment, those changes in the production *process* reduced labor hours by 50%, and the company's productivity is now higher than its competitors' in Taiwan.

Even U.S. apparel manufacturers lend support to the argument that labor costs are not the be-all and end-all of profitability. Companies in this industry are generally obsessed with finding places where hourly wages are low. But the cost of direct labor needed to manufacture a pair of jeans is actually only about 15% of total costs, and even the direct labor involved in producing a man's suit is only about $12.50.[1]

Compelling evidence also exists to dispute the myth that competing on labor costs will create any sustainable advantage. Let's start close to home. One day, I arrived at a large discount store with a shopping list. Having the good fortune to actually find a sales associate, I asked him where I could locate the first item on my list. "I don't know," he replied. He gave a similar reply when queried about the second item. A glance at the long list I was holding brought the confession that because of high employee turnover, the young man had been in the store only a few hours himself. What is that employee worth to the store? Not only can't he sell the merchandise, he can't even find it! Needless to say, I wasn't able to purchase everything on my list because I got tired of looking and gave up. And I haven't returned since. Companies that compete on cost alone eventually bump into consumers like me. It's no accident that Wal-Mart combines its low-price strategy with friendly staff members greeting people at the door and works assiduously to keep turnover low.

Another example of a company that understands the limits of competing solely on labor costs is the Men's Wearhouse, the enormously successful off-price retailer of tailored men's clothing. The company operates in a fiercely competitive industry in which growth is possible primarily by taking sales from competitors, and price wars are intense. Still, less than 15% of the company's staff is part-time, wages are higher than the industry average, and the company engages in extensive training. All these policies defy conventional wisdom for the retailing industry. But the issue isn't what the Men's Wearhouse's employees cost, it's what they can do: sell very effectively because of their product knowledge and sales skills. Moreover, by keeping inventory losses and employee turnover low, the company saves money on shrinkage and hiring. Companies that miss this point—that costs, particularly labor costs, aren't everything—often overlook ways of succeeding that competitors can't readily copy.

Evidence also exists that challenges the myth about the effectiveness of individual incentives. This evidence, however, has done little to stem the tide of individual merit pay. A survey of the pay practices of the *Fortune* 1,000 reported that between 1987 and 1993, the proportion of companies using individual incentives for at least 20% of their workforce increased from 38% to 50% while the proportion of companies using profit sharing—a more collective reward—decreased from 45% to 43%. Between 1981 and 1990, the proportion of retail salespeople that were paid solely on straight salary, with no commission, declined from 21% to 7%. And this trend toward individual incentive compensation is not confined to the United States. A study of pay practices at plants in the United Kingdom reported that the proportion using some form of merit pay had increased every year since 1986 such that by 1990 it had reached 50%.[2]

Despite the evident popularity of this practice, the problems with individual merit pay are numerous and well documented. It has been shown to undermine teamwork, encourage employees to focus on the short term, and lead people to link compensation to political skills and ingratiating personalities rather than to performance. Indeed, those are among the reasons why W. Edwards Deming and other quality experts have argued strongly against using such schemes. Consider the results of several studies. One carefully designed study of a performance-contingent pay plan at 20 Social Security Administration offices found that merit pay had no effect on office performance. Even though the merit pay plan was contingent on a number of objective indicators, such as the time taken to settle claims and the accuracy of claims processing, employees exhibited no difference in performance after the merit pay plan was introduced as part of a reform of civil service pay practices. Contrast that study with another that examined the elimination of a piecework system and its replacement by a more group-oriented compensation system at a manufacturer of exhaust system components. There, grievances decreased, product quality increased almost tenfold, and perceptions of teamwork and concern for performance all improved.[3]

Surveys conducted by various consulting companies that specialize in management and compensation also reveal the problems and dissatisfaction with individual merit pay. For instance, a study by the consulting firm William M. Mercer reported that 73% of the responding companies had made major changes to their performance-management plans in the preceding two years, as they experimented with different ways to tie pay to individual performance. But 47% reported that their employees found the systems neither fair nor sensible, and 51% of the employees said that the performance-management system provided little value to the company. No wonder Mercer concluded that most individual merit or performance-based pay plans share two attributes: they absorb vast amounts of management time and resources, and they make everybody unhappy.

One concern about paying on a more group-oriented basis is the so-called free-rider problem, the worry that people will not work hard because they know that if rewards are based on collective performance and their colleagues make the effort, they will share in those rewards regardless of the level of their individual efforts. But there are two reasons why organizations should not be reluctant to design such collective pay systems.

First, much to the surprise of people who have spent too much time reading economics, empirical evidence from numerous studies indicates that the extent of free riding is quite modest. For instance, one comprehensive review reported that "under the conditions described by the theory as leading to free riding, people often cooperate instead."[4]

Second, individuals do not make decisions about how much effort to expend in a social vacuum; they are influenced by peer pressure and the social relations they have with their workmates. This social influence is potent, and although it may be somewhat stronger in smaller groups, it can be a force mitigating against free riding even in large organizations. As one might expect, then, there is evidence that organizations paying on a more collective basis, such as through profit sharing or gain sharing, outperform those that don't.

Sometimes, individual pay schemes go so far as to affect customers. Sears was forced to eliminate a commission system at its automobile repair stores in California when officials found widespread evidence of consumer fraud. Employees, anxious to meet quotas and earn commissions on repair sales, were selling unneeded services to unsuspecting customers. Similarly, in 1992, the *Wall Street Journal* reported that Highland Superstores, an electronics and appliance retailer, eliminated commissions because they had encouraged such aggressive behavior on the part of salespeople that customers were alienated.

Enchantment with individual merit pay reflects not only the belief that people won't work effectively if they are not rewarded for their individual efforts but also the related view that the road to solving organizational problems is largely paved with adjustments to pay and measurement practices. Consider again the data from the Mercer survey: nearly three-quarters of all the companies surveyed had made *major* changes to their pay plans in just the past two years. That's tinkering on a grand scale. Or take the case of Air Products and Chemicals of Allentown, Pennsylvania. When on October 23, 1996, the company reported mediocre sales and profits, the stock price declined from the low $60s to the high $50s. Eight days later, the company announced a new set of management-compensation and stock-ownership initiatives designed to reassure Wall Street that management cared about its shareholders and was demonstrating that concern by changing compensation arrangements. The results were dramatic. On the day of the announcement, the stock price went up 1¼ points, and the next day it rose an additional 4¾ points. By November 29, Air Products' stock had gone up more than 15%. According to Value Line, this rise was an enthusiastic reaction by investors to the new compensation system. No wonder managers are so tempted to tamper with pay practices!

But as Bill Strusz, director of corporate industrial relations at Xerox in Rochester, New York, has said, if managers seeking to improve performance or solve organizational problems use compensation as the only lever, they will get two results: nothing will happen, and they will spend a lot of money. That's because people want more out of their jobs than just money. Numerous surveys—even of second-year M.B.A. students, who frequently graduate with large amounts of debt—indicate that money is far from the most important factor in choosing a job or remaining in one.

Why has the SAS Institute had such low turnover in the software industry despite its tight labor market? When asked this question, employees said they were motivated by SAS's unique perks—plentiful opportunities to work with the latest and most up-to-date equipment and the ease with which they could move back and forth between being a manager and being an individual contributor. They also cited how much variety there was in the projects they worked on, how intelligent and nice the people they worked with were, and how much the organization cared for and appreciated them. Of course, SAS pays competitive salaries, but in an industry in which people have the opportunity to become millionaires through stock options by moving to a competitor, the key to retention is SAS's culture, not its monetary rewards.

People seek, in a phrase, an enjoyable work environment. That's what AES, the Men's Wearhouse, SAS, and Southwest have in common. One of the core values at each company is *fun.* When a colleague and I wrote a business school case on Southwest, we asked some of the employees, a number of whom had been offered much more money to work elsewhere, why they stayed. The answer we heard repeatedly was that they knew what the other environments were like, and they would rather be at a place, as one employee put it, where *work* is not a four-letter word. This doesn't mean work has to be easy. As an AES employee noted, fun means working in a place where people can use their gifts and skills and can work with others in an atmosphere of mutual respect.

There is a great body of literature on the effect of large external rewards on individuals' intrinsic motivation. The literature argues that extrinsic rewards diminish intrinsic motivation and, moreover, that large extrinsic rewards can actually decrease performance in tasks that require creativity and innovation. I would not necessarily go so far as to say that external rewards backfire, but they certainly create their own problems. First, people receiving such rewards can reduce their own motivation through a trick of self-perception, figuring, "I must not like the job if I have to be paid so much to do it" or "I make so much, I must be doing it for the money." Second, they undermine their own loyalty or performance by reacting against a sense of being controlled, thinking something like, "I will show the company that I can't be controlled just through money."

But most important, to my mind, is the logic in the idea that any organization believing it can solve its attraction, retention, and motivation problems solely by its compensation system is probably not spending as much time and effort as it should on the work environment—on defining its jobs, on creating its culture, and on making work fun and meaningful. It is a question of time and attention, of scarce managerial resources. The time and attention spent managing the reward system are not available to devote to other aspects of the work environment that in the end may be much more critical to success.

SOME ADVICE ABOUT PAY

Since I have traipsed you through a discussion of what's wrong with the way most companies approach compensation, let me now offer some advice about how to get it right.

The first, and perhaps most obvious, suggestion is that managers would do well to keep the difference between labor rates and labor costs straight. In doing so, remember that only labor costs—and not labor rates—are the basis for competition, and that labor costs may not be a major component of total costs. In any event, managers should remember that the issue is not just what you pay people, but also what they produce.

To combat the myth about the effectiveness of individual performance pay, managers should see what happens when they include a large dose of collective rewards in their employees' compensation package. The more aggregated the unit used to measure performance, the more reliably performance can be assessed. One can tell pretty accurately how well an organization, or even a subunit, has done with respect to sales, profits, quality, productivity, and the like. Trying to parcel out who, specifically, was responsible for exactly how much of that productivity, quality, or sales is frequently much more difficult or even impossible. As Herbert Simon, the Nobel-prize-winning economist, has recognized, people in organizations are interdependent, and therefore organizational results are the consequence of collective behavior and performance. If you could reliably and easily measure and reward individual contributions, you probably would not need an organization at all as everyone would enter markets solely as individuals.

In the typical individual-based merit pay system, the boss works with a raise budget that's some percentage of the total salary budget for the unit. It's inherently a zero-sum process: the more I get in my raise, the less is left for my colleagues. So the worse my workmates perform, the happier I am because I know I will look better by comparison. A similar dynamic can occur across organizational units in which competition for a fixed bonus pool discourages people from sharing best practices and learning from employees in other parts of the organization. In November 1995, for example, *Fortune* magazine reported that at Lantech, a manufacturer of packaging machinery in Louisville, Kentucky, individual incentives caused such intense rivalry that the chairman of the company, Pat Lancaster, said, "I was spending 95% of my time on conflict resolution instead of on how to serve our customers."

Managers can fight the myth that people are primarily motivated by money by de-emphasizing pay and not portraying it as the main thing you get from working at a particular company. How? Consider the example of Tandem Computer which, in the years before it was acquired by Compaq, would not even tell you your salary before expecting you to accept a job. If you asked, you would be told that Tandem paid good, competitive salaries. The company had a simple philosophy—if you came for money, you would leave for money, and Tandem wanted employees who were there because they liked the work, the culture, and the people, not something—money—that every company could offer. Emphasizing pay as the primary reward encourages people to come and to stay for the wrong reasons. AES, a global independent power producer in Arlington, Virginia, has a relatively short vesting period for retirement-plan contributions and tries not to pay the highest salaries for jobs in its local labor market. By so doing, it seeks to ensure that people are not locked into working at a place where they don't want to be simply for the money.

Managers must also recognize that pay has substantive and symbolic components. In signaling what and who in the organization is valued, pay both reflects and helps determine the organization's culture. Therefore, managers must make sure that the messages sent by pay practices are intended. Talking about teamwork and cooperation and then not having a group-based component to the pay system matters because paying solely on an individual basis signals what the organization believes is actually important—individual behavior and performance. Talking about the importance of *all* people in the organization and then paying some disproportionately more than others belies that message. One need not go to the extreme of Whole Foods Market, which pays no one more than eight times the average company salary (the result being close to $1 billion in sales at a company where the CEO makes less than $200,000 a year). But paying large executive bonuses while laying off people and asking for wage freezes, as General Motors did in the 1980s, may not send the right message, either. When Southwest Airlines asked its pilots for a five-year wage freeze, CEO Herb Kelleher voluntarily asked the compensation committee to freeze his salary for at least four years as well. The message of shared, common fate is powerful in an organization truly seeking to build a culture of teamwork.

Making pay practices public also sends a powerful symbolic message. Some organizations reveal pay distributions by position or level. A few organizations, such as Whole Foods Market, actually make data on individual pay available to all members who are interested. Other organizations try to maintain a high level of secrecy about pay. What message do those organizations send? Keeping salaries secret suggests that the organization has something to hide or that it doesn't trust its people with the information. Moreover, keeping things secret just encourages people to uncover the secrets—if something is worth hiding, it must be important and interesting enough to expend effort discovering. Pay systems that are more open and transparent send a positive message about the equity of the system and the trust that the company places in its people.

Managers should also consider using other methods besides pay to signal company values and focus behavior. The head of North American sales and operations for the SAS Institute has a useful perspective on this issue. He didn't think he was smart enough to design an incentive system that couldn't be gamed. Instead of using the pay system to signal what was important, he and other SAS managers simply told people what was important for the company and why. That resulted in much more nuanced and rapid changes in behavior because the company didn't have to change the compensation system every time business priorities altered a little. What a novel idea—actually talking to people about what is important and why, rather than trying to send some subtle signals through the compensation system!

Perhaps most important, leaders must come to see pay for what it is: just one element in a set of management practices that can either build or reduce commitment, teamwork, and performance. Thus my final piece of advice about pay is to make sure that pay practices are congruent with other management practices and reinforce rather than oppose their effects.

BREAKING WITH CONVENTION TO BREAK THE MYTHS

Many organizations devote enormous amounts of time and energy to their pay systems, but people, from senior managers to hourly workers, remain unhappy with them. Organizations are trapped in unproductive ways of approaching pay, which they find difficult to escape. The reason, I would suggest, is that people are afraid to challenge the myths about compensation. It's easier and less controversial to see what everyone else is doing and then to do the same. In fact, when I talk to executives at companies about installing pay systems that actually work, I usually hear, "But that's different from what most other companies are saying and doing."

It must certainly be the case that a company cannot earn "abnormal" returns by following the crowd. That's true about marketplace strategies, and it's true about compensation. Companies that are truly exceptional are not trapped by convention but instead see and pursue a better business model.

Companies that have successfully transcended the myths about pay know that pay cannot substitute for a working environment high on trust, fun, and meaningful work. They also know that it is more important to worry about what people do than what they cost, and that zero-sum pay plans can set off internal competition that makes learning from others, teamwork, and cross-functional cooperation a dream rather than the way the place works on an everyday basis.

There is an interesting paradox in achieving high organizational performance through innovative pay practices—if it were easy to do, it wouldn't provide as much competitive leverage as it actually does. So while I can review the logic and evidence and offer some alternative ways of thinking about pay, it is the job of leaders to exercise both the judgment and the courage necessary to break with common practice. Those who do will develop organizations in which pay practices actually contribute rather than detract from building high-performance management systems. Those who are stuck in the past are probably doomed to endless tinkering with pay; at the end of the day, they won't have accomplished much, but they will have expended a lot of time and money doing it.

Endnotes

1. John T. Dunlop and David Weil, "Diffusion and Performance of Modular Production in the U.S. Apparel Industry," *Industrial Relations,* July 1996, p. 337.

2. For the survey of the pay practices of *Fortune* 1,000 companies, see Gerald E. Ledford, Jr., Edward E. Lawler III, and Susan A. Mohrman, "Reward Innovations in *Fortune* 1,000 Companies," *Compensation and Benefits Review,* April 1995, p. 76; for the salary and commission data, see Gregory A. Patterson, "Distressed Shoppers, Disaffected Workers Prompt Stores to Alter Sales Commissions," the *Wall Street Journal,* July 1, 1992, p. B1; for the study of U.K. pay practices, see Stephen Wood, "High Commitment Management and Payment Systems," *Journal of Management Studies,* January 1996, p. 53.

3. For the Social Security Administration study, see Jone L. Pearce, William B. Stevenson, and James L. Perry, "Managerial Compensation Based on Organizational Performance: A Time Series Analysis of the Effects of Merit Pay," *Academy of Management Journal,* June 1985, p. 261; for the study of group-oriented compensation, see Larry Hatcher and Timothy L. Ross, "From Individual Incentives to an Organization-Wide Gainsharing Plan: Effects on Teamwork and Product Quality," *Journal of Organizational Behavior,* May 1991, p. 169.

4. Gerald Marwell, "Altruism and the Problem of Collective Action," in V. J. Derlega and J. Grzelak, eds., *Cooperation and Helping Behavior: Theories and Research* (New York: Academic Press, 1982), p. 208.

Stock Ownership and Work Motivation

W. Jack Duncan

What motivates people to work and be more productive has been an ongoing concern of leadership and management. Writers in the early days of scientific management viewed work as the means whereby "workers" acquired their daily bread. The equation was simple. To get more money, you do more work. Human-relations advocates viewed work in a broader social context, and nonmonetary rewards became part of a more complex motivational equation. Contemporary behavioral scientists have suggested the importance of meaningful work, clear and concise goals, a sense of achievement, positive reinforcement, and numerous other factors as keys to higher levels of individual and organizational performance.

OWNERSHIP AND MOTIVATION

Note that motivation theory and research applied to work settings have always focused on how "employees" are motivated. Employees may be managers or rank-and-file workers, but they are most definitely employees. It has simply been assumed that owners were not in need of motivation—the act of ownership assures the motivation to work. Has anyone ever read an article or book about "how to motivate owners"? There are, of course, exceptions. We can all relate accounts of sons or daughters of the founder of a successful company who valued consuming the wealth acquired by previous generations more than building additional wealth and adding to the family's fortune. Far more familiar, however, is the son or daughter who works without ceasing to perpetuate and build the family business.

Ownership creates such a strong commitment to work that it is difficult to understand why the subject has not received more attention in the theory, practice, and research of leadership

From *Organizational Dynamics,* 2001, 30(1), 1–11. Reprinted by permission.

and management. Although it has not received the attention it deserves, in fairness, it has not been completely ignored. Especially in recent years, when the stock markets were booming, more attention was given to the manner in which ownership can build incredible wealth for some particularly fortunate people.

If you were lucky enough to be one of the favored software engineers or key executives who were given stock options when Microsoft Corp. went public in 1986, you would be a millionaire today. Just six years after its initial public offering, 20% of Microsoft's employees were millionaires because of their ownership in the company. The same was true of many employees at Oracle Corp., Dell Computer Corp., and other high tech firms. Ownership, however, should not be associated exclusively with high tech firms. For example, today the typical technology company puts aside almost 20% of its outstanding stock for employee incentives, but some large financial companies such as Lehman Brothers Holdings Inc. and Merrill Lynch & Co. put aside over 50%.

The idea of making employees owners of company stock is not new. Henry Sturgis Dennison and the manner in which he shared ownership to preserve the Dennison Manufacturing Company as a family business for more than a century may best exemplify an appreciation for the motivational power of ownership.

MOST INTERESTING BUSINESSMAN OF HIS TIME

In his autobiography, John Kenneth Galbraith stated that Henry Dennison was "arguably the most interesting businessman at the time." Galbraith met Dennison in 1936. At the time they met, Dennison had successfully led the Dennison Manufacturing Company for almost 20 years. He created a personnel department, a system of unemployment insurance for employees, a company clinic, library, savings bank, and an employee representation plan for improving work practices and handling grievances. Most important for our purposes, Dennison had invented an alternative corporate form of organization that relied less on absentee investors and more on employee owners.

Dennison's father and uncle founded the Dennison Manufacturing Company in 1843. In 1878, the company incorporated and distributed stock to the owner-managers. By 1910, substantial blocks of the company's stock were held by outsiders. Dennison worried that absentee investors would exercise too much influence on operations. He sought a means to ensure that those who knew the business best and had the greatest impact on firm performance held voting control. The company survived until it merged with the National Blank Book Company in 1967 and later became a subsidiary of Avery-Dennison, Inc.

The financial structure of the company was revised so that investors—who in Dennison's judgment performed only one act of importance to the company by entrusting their funds to the firm—were issued cumulative, nonvoting, preferred stock. Managers and employees held all the common stock and all the voting rights. Dennison was convinced, using the experiences of workers in Great Britain, that once employees achieved a subsistence level the distribution of profits became an important determinant of their productivity. He believed that despite the possibility of increased earnings, employees would reduce their effort if they thought their productivity increases also increased the returns to absentee investors. There was a perceived inequity when beneficial results accrued to people who had not contributed to profitability. The only way workers could reduce that perception was to reduce their effort. Rather than take such a risk, Dennison made managers and employees owners.

Different Ways to Become an Owner

Fortunately, working for the most interesting businessman of [the] time is not the only way employees become owners. Employees become owners by participating in 401(k) plans when the proceeds are invested in company stock, through broad-based stock option programs, or by becoming beneficiaries of an employee stock ownership plan (ESOP). When discounts and matching grants for stock purchases are offered, employees are given an opportunity to accelerate their ownership. Of course, the motives of existing owners in offering employees a piece of the company sometimes have more to do with estate planning, the desire to perpetuate the business in a particular form, or the need for financial liquidity than shared ownership. The effect, however, is the same regardless of the motive.

For example, the Post Register, a family owned newspaper in Idaho Falls, Idaho, made employees part owners of the business to avoid selling out to a newspaper chain or communication conglomerate. The president and his brother own 55% of the company, and employees own the remaining 45%. The principals of T Juniors, Inc., transferred half of the company's stock to employees to "perpetuate the business" and ensure a retirement income for the owners. They sold half of their stock to an ownership trust, thereby ensuring a comfortable retirement, while making employees owners of the business through the sale of stock from the trust. Employee stock ownership ensured the existence of the business beyond the active careers of the founders.

Does Ownership Make a Difference?

A North American Employee Ownership Association survey indicated that the number of U.S. companies with employee stock ownership plans increased from 200 in 1974 to 10,000 in 1998. It was estimated that 10% of the American workforce is employed by companies with ESOPs. A study of a sample of these companies indicated that 75% experienced increases in sales, profits, and stock price when employees became owners. One half of the companies experienced improvements in customer satisfaction.

From 1992 to 1998, the American Capital Strategies' Employee Index outperformed the Dow by almost 20% and has outperformed the Standard & Poor's 500 by 80% over the past five years. A study by Hewitt Associates and Northwestern University's Kellogg Graduate School of Management indicated that companies with employee stock ownership plans had total shareholder returns almost 7% greater than firms where employees did not have an opportunity for ownership. Average return on assets was about 3% higher when employees owned stock in the company.

WHY OWNERSHIP WORKS

Dennison observed that employees produce less when absentee investors reap the benefit of their labor. This observation provided the basis for his restructuring even though he did not have the benefit, as we do, of more than three-quarters of a century of motivation research.

Although there are many possible explanations, there are three theories of work motivation that help explain the powerful impact of ownership on worker performance. These are agency theory, equity theory, and reinforcement theory.

Owners Not Agents

Agency theory assumes that the organizational form with the lowest agency cost is one where employees (including managers) own 100% of the firm. When employees are not owners they are agents, and agents and owners frequently pursue different goals. The customary way corporations, where ownership, managers, and employees are separate by definition, have attempted to mitigate the agency problem is by sharing ownership. When employees become owners, the agency problem diminishes and they begin to think and behave differently. Research suggests, as noted previously, that resulting performance increases can have extraordinary impact on the bottom line. The managing director of Pearl Meyer & Partners, an executive compensation consulting firm, stated in *Investor Relations Business,* "The belief is that placing stock in the hands of management and employees ties their interests with those of stockholders."

Among the nation's largest corporations, stock options account for more than half of the total compensation of chief executive officers (CEOs) and about 30% of senior operating managers' pay. In 1999, Jack Welch's unexercised options in General Electric Co. were valued at more than $260 million. Over the past 15 years, the total value of stock options has increased 10-fold. It is estimated that workers now own about 8% of all corporations through stock options, 401(k) plans, profit sharing, and ESOPs. Two-thirds of technology companies offer stock to all employees. One study found that long-term stock incentives account for 54% of the total compensation of CEOs, 49% for chief operating officers and chief financial officers, and 21% for middle managers. For lower-level exempt employees, these incentives are as much as 14% of annual compensation.

Question of Fairness

Stock ownership is a useful way of addressing the agency problem but it often contributes to an equity problem when only executives and key employees are eligible to participate. Equity theory was initially proposed as a way of describing how employees react to situations in which they are treated less favorably than other employees. When we perceive we are treated inequitably (e.g., the boss is given stock options but we are not, and we believe we are doing equally important work) we try to reduce the tension caused by the perceived inequity by either reducing our effort or finding another job.

Much of the current debate about executive compensation results from this perceived inequity. Consider the following:

- The average American worker who earned $23,000 per year in 1990 earned a little less than $30,000 in 1999. The average worker's pay increased a little over 25%, or about 3% per year.

- The average compensation package of the top two executives in the nation's 365 largest public companies rose from $1.8 million in 1990 to $10.6 million in 1998. This represented an increase of more than 480% or about 60% per year.

- In 1978, the average chief executive officer's pay was 28.5 times that of the average worker. Today it is 115 times the average worker's pay.

- In 1978, Americans in the top 20% of the income distribution made 7.7 times more than those in the bottom 20%. Today, the gap has grown to more than 11 times.

- According to the Federal Reserve Board, in 1997 the middle 20% of American households held less than $7,800 in all forms of stocks, including mutual funds and defined contribution pension plans. Of the 30 million people who participate in 401(k) plans, the average balance is less than $40,000.

- The wealthiest 1% of households, on the other hand, owned about $2.5 million in stocks, while the holdings of the next 9% averaged about $275,000.

Despite the fact that more people are making more money, the equity of the "spread" between top executive and rank-and-file employee pay continues to be a source of controversy. The trend, however, is changing. According to a survey by Pearl Meyer and Partners, the 200 largest U.S. corporations set aside almost 14% of their equity for employee stock incentive plans last year. This percentage has doubled over the past decade.

Reinforcing Outstanding Performance

The final motivation theory relates to how ownership is acquired, and is applicable to only certain types of ownership. Reinforcement theory, in its most general form, relates to what happens when one employee performs at a higher level than others, and the manner in which rewards are received. When a person receives a weekly salary regardless of level of productivity, performance is likely to peak at a consistently acceptable level, but the worker is not provided an incentive for exceptionally high performance. Reinforcement theory suggests that certain schedules of reinforcement, which provide rewards after a certain number of behaviors or at unpredictable times, create a greater incentive for high performance.

Although stock purchase through 401(k) and ESOPs provide ownership, they do not address the motivational issue that is central to reinforcement theory. Discounts and matching grants for purchase of company stock take place at predictable intervals and according to precise formulas. Incentive stock options (ISOs), on the other hand, provide the additional incentive of being obtainable only when specified levels of performance or other conditions are achieved. Incentive stock options reduce agency costs by making employees owners. When they are broad-based and allow the participation of all employees, the equity problem is addressed—as rank-and-file employees have the opportunity to build significant wealth as the company's fortunes increase. Moreover, incentive stock options provide an added incentive because they are contingent on high levels of performance.

SHARING RISKS AND REWARDS: OPTIONS FOR EVERYONE

In a practical sense, company ownership through 401(k) plans and ESOPs has more to do with retirement planning than work motivation. Broad-based stock option plans, on the other hand, go more directly to the motivation issue.

- A survey of 133 public and private companies by KPMG's Compensation Consulting Practice found that 100% of the executives, 72% of the middle managers, 35% of exempt employees, and 12% of nonexempt employees received long-term stock incentive awards. 78% of the executives received nonqualified stock options (receipt not contingent on any set of conditions) and the remainder received incentive stock options. Exempt employees below middle management and nonexempt employees eligible for long-term incentives most often received nonqualified stock options.

- A 1999 survey of 350 large American corporations by William M. Mercer found that 17% granted options to 50% or more of their employees, which was up from only 6% in 1993. Companies such as Procter & Gamble Co., Gap Inc., AT&T Corp., General Electric Co., and Bank of America Corp. award stock options to employees at all levels.

- According to the National Center for Employee Ownership, in 1998 the average value of stock options to professional and technical employees was $37,000 and $41,000 respectively. Even administrative personnel received an average of $12,500 in options that could result in a 10 to 12% increase in compensation when the options are exercised.

Expanding the Base

At Starbucks Corp., CEO Howard Schultz decided to offer stock options to all employees working 20 hours a week or more. Almost 40% of the eligible employees participate in this "bean stock program." One of the positive outcomes of participation is an employee turnover rate that is only one-third the industry average.

Broadcom Corporation went public in 1998, and at one point it was estimated that 75% of the company's 800 employees were millionaires (at least on paper) because of stock options. The ownership has not only made employees rich, the stock price increased by 600%. The company is described as a "stimulating place to work, employees feel a sense of ownership, and senior management is smart enough to create ongoing stock incentives to keep people working for the Company."

GTE Corporation (now merged with Bell Atlantic to form Verizon Communications) allotted almost 10 million shares to its Partnership Shares program and provided options to more than 80,000 employees. GTE's CEO stated, "By making all our employees owners of GTE, we allow them to share in the success that their hard work and dedication has brought the Company." In 1996 Chevron Corp. granted eligible employees an option for 150 shares of stock with vesting contingent on two performance conditions. The conditions were met and vesting occurred in June 1997. All unexercised options expired at the end of March 1999. Employees own approximately 11% of Chevron under various stock ownership plans. NCR Corp.'s WorldShare Plan, Monsanto Company's Shared Success Stock Option Plan, and PepsiCo's SharePower Stock Option Plan all represent broad-based plans that are becoming increasingly popular means of extending ownership to large numbers of employees.

Every Employee an Owner

There has never been much disagreement about the importance of ownership. The controversy has surrounded the means by which employees become owners. Some of the more compelling reasons for making employees owners are apparent.

- Owners are more committed to the success of the enterprise because business success is transferred directly into personal wealth. If the company's stock goes up above the option price, financial gain results from exercised options. Stock price is related to earnings, financial performance, and a number of other factors that employees can directly influence. Bean stock at Starbucks caused people to treat the organization's money like it was their own. That is the point, it is!

- Owners are committed to improving the business in every way possible, because in doing so they reap the financial rewards associated with improved performance. The *Atlanta Journal* reported that the technology accelerator unit at Red Hot Law Group has developed an innovative way of giving all employees, from receptionists to attorneys, a stake in the success of their clients. The firm represents a number of high-tech companies and collects 5% of the client's stock as part of its legal fees. Red Hot then distributes 15% of the acquired stock to its own employees as stock options. A smashing success on the part of a client can mean a lot of money to employees of the law firm.

- Ownership opportunities assist in recruiting and retaining the best candidates in the labor market. Enterprising employees who receive stock options are allowed to participate in the success of the organization. Leaving the firm before vesting results in forfeiture of a potentially significant amount of personal wealth. At a time when the unemployment rate has dropped below 4%, and the labor market for skilled and experienced employees is as tight as anyone can remember, making employees owners is a valuable recruitment and retention tool. Stock options, project completion bonuses, and other forms of gain sharing are the common currency in the Silicon Valley and are spreading to all areas of the economy. The value of stock options often amounts to several times a rank-and-file employee's annual salary.

- Corporations can offer significant value to employees through stock options and receive extremely favorable treatment from the Internal Revenue Service. Stock Options do not cost the company anything (except dilution of ownership when exercised) because they have no cash value. Moreover, when the options are exercised the tax code allows companies to deduct the gain as an expense even though no money has been spent. Employers can give increases in pay that do not cost them anything.

BEWARE OF THE DANGERS

Ownership is a two-way street. When owners receive large returns on their investment, it is because they take great financial risks. Employees customarily receive fixed but predictable paychecks because they take little risk, thereby avoiding significant losses or significant gains. Microsoft shared stock with key employees before its initial public offering (IPO). Broadcom's stock increased dramatically, as did the number of millionaires on its payroll. But there is no guarantee of riches. Risk involves a downside as well as an upside potential for gain.

Not Everyone Wins

Economic boom times and well-publicized success stories often lure careless opportunists. Returns are always received in proportion to the risk taken and owning a piece of the company is not a guarantee of riches. If you listen to business news, you may conclude that going public is the automatic high road to riches. Do not be deceived. Most IPOs do not perform as well as "typical" stocks. One study of more than 1,200 IPOs found that while 12% provided a first day return of 30% or more, twice as many traded below the offering price on the first day. The typical 1993 IPO provided only one-third the return of the S&P 500 by mid-October, 1998. Of the companies that went public during the past five years, more than half are trading below their offer price—one in three by more than 50%.

What about the conventional kinds of risks assumed when employees become owners? Obviously, the types of risk result from the particular equity ownership program developed. ISOs, while offering some of the greatest opportunities for building wealth, possess some of the greatest risks.

Stock options, because they are designed to encourage long-term retention of valuable employees, require recipients to remain in the employment of the company for a period of time before the options can be exercised. Incentive stock options (ISO) vest over a specified period, and the recipient has a limited time to exercise the options. Since ISOs have conditions attached they may not be granted at all. For example, Chevron announced an employee stock option program whereby options would ordinarily vest in two years; however, they could vest in one year if the company had the highest total stockholder return among its competitor group. The condition was not met, so the options did not vest for two years. Even unqualified stock options are not always winners. Xerox Corp. awarded options to 48,000 of its 52,000 employees in January 1999. After Xerox's stock peaked at almost $64 per share, it dropped when lower than expected earnings were announced. The stock fell to the low $20s. At that price all the options were underwater or could not be exercised, because the option price was significantly above the current market price.

Repricing is the normal remedy for underwater options. One survey discovered that one-third of the responding companies repriced their options to restore the employee incentives. However, frequent repricing destroys, to a great extent, the performance incentive—even though it may be good for morale. Even if employees understand the risks, how likely are they to go the extra mile when their options are underwater? Absentee investors at least can sell their stock and take their losses. Employees have to take the losses and go back to work in a company where the financial future and their own jobs are in question.

Exercising Options Is Expensive

Even if stock prices increase, employees may have difficulty exercising the options. The old saying that you "have to have money to make money" is certainly true with regard to stock options. To illustrate, assume you have 500 nonqualified options that have vested, and that you were granted the options at a price of $10 per share. Your company has experienced outstanding performance over the past three years and the stock price is now $55 per share. Your options are worth $27,500. However, you must have $5,000 ($10 × 500 shares) to exercise the options. Moreover, the Internal Revenue Service (IRS) regards the difference between the market value of the nonqualified options when exercised and what you paid for the stock ($27,500 − $5,000 = $22,500) ordinary income, if you do not hold it long enough to qualify for a capital gains rate. If you need the money immediately and are in the 30% tax bracket, you owe Uncle Sam another $6,750. The state where you live will want some of your profit as well. You have options on stock worth $27,500, but it will cost you at least $11,750 to exercise them.

The tax implications of ISOs are even more complicated. Although you owe taxes under the regular system only when the stock is actually sold, when the options are exercised the difference in the value of the stock and what it cost you to exercise the options is subject to the alternative minimum tax (AMT). The AMT is designed to ensure that some tax is paid even if it is less than might be required under the regular tax system. Moreover, the IRS applies the PICA liability to the income received from the exercise of the ISOs. Capital gains rates may reduce the payment but taxes will certainly account for a significant amount of any profit an employee receives from stock options.

Possible Paradox

There is another possibility that must be considered. Is there any reason to believe that employees will behave differently from absentee investors when they become owners? An overweighting of equity pay could cause employees to pursue the same bizarre behaviors that are designed to increase stock price in the short-run, and develop attitudes similar to the venture capitalists, absentee stockholders, and institutional investors. There is, of course, no guarantee this will not occur. However, since the percentage of equity pay for most rank-and-file employees who enjoy the benefit of a stock option is significantly less than their base pay, the fatal short-term perspective is not likely to persist even if it does emerge.

The hope is that long-term employees/owners think and behave differently from absentee stockholders. They should, since their incentives are different. However, when employees are no longer agents, who knows how they/we will behave. One study found a disturbing possibility. According to this analysis, as option pay increased, companies tended to engage more in merger and acquisition activities and spend less on internal investments such as research and development. Maybe employee/owners do become more like venture capitalists and absentee stockholders after all.

Full Disclosure

Finally, companies have not always done an effective job of communicating the benefits and risks of stock option to employees. Few have clearly disclosed the tax implications of options when they are exercised, and virtually none make recipients aware of the danger of downside risk. Imagine the devastating impact on morale that might have resulted if Maytag Corp. had a broad-based stock option plan in September 1999—when the company warned investors that it would not meet analysts' earnings estimates. The company's stock dropped 25% in two days. Within two weeks, the stock was down almost 50% from its July 1999 high. If employees had held large numbers of underwater stock options the adverse motivational impact could have been significant. Operations and strategies were sound, employees and executives were doing their jobs, but many stock options would be worthless. Ownership involves risks, and risks have downside as well as upside potential. You cannot have it both ways.

A survey sponsored by the Oppenheimer Fund found that employees viewed stock options as important factors in selecting a job, but only 34% knew much about them and how they worked. Frequently, employees did not know what kind of options they had (nonqualified or ISOs), 11% allowed profitable options to expire without exercising them, and almost three-fourths knew nothing about the alternative minimum tax and how it might affect their tax liability when incentive stock options were exercised.

DeVry, Inc., found that an elaborate communication strategy was an essential part of its broad-based options grant program. For large corporations, communicating the benefits and risks of equity ownership plans can be expensive and one is never sure of how well the word gets out. For example, Knight-Ridder Inc. introduced a stock program primarily as an employee benefit, but only 20% of the employees enrolled in the plan—even though a 15% discount on company stock was available. One study found that 90% of shares received from exercising stock options were sold on the same day, underscoring the likelihood that recipients understood little about how to maximize the benefits of the options.

There is one more complication. Not all companies are publicly traded and, therefore, cannot effectively utilize stock options to increase employee ownership. Fortunately, that is not entirely true. Recent changes by the Securities and Exchange Commission make it easier for private companies to implement stock option plans. Each year under SEC Rule 701, private companies are allowed to issue shares equal to either 15% of total assets or 15% of outstanding shares, whichever dollar value is higher. If the shares amount to more than $5 million, the company must file all the documents any public company is required to file with the SEC. In 1999, the $5 million ceiling was removed, even though the 15% rule remains. Between 1988 and 1993, the SEC estimated that an average of 214 private companies sold stock to employees. With the new change, it is expected that the number will increase to 300 companies. One illustrative company, Forte Systems, Inc., an information-technology consulting firm, allows its 435 employees to buy stock in the company. Even though Forte reserves the option of going public in the future, the liberalization of Rule 701 will allow more employees to have a larger equity stake in the company if and when there is an initial pubic offering.

OWNERSHIP AND EMPLOYEE INCENTIVES: WHAT ALL THIS MEANS

More than a decade of economic prosperity has changed the landscape of American business. Despite our insistence to the contrary, most of the action today is financial. Initial public offerings, acquisitions, mergers, and strategic alliances occupy much more of our attention than supply chains, manufacturing infrastructure, and workforce development. The implications are significant, particularly for those who earn their livelihood making products and delivering services. Increasingly, the core services of the business and those who perform them appear less important than the imagination of financial deal-makers.

For many years motivation theorists have suggested that one of the most effective ways, perhaps the most effective way, to energize employees and managers is to "make everyone an owner" of the enterprise. Nonqualified and incentive stock options have been used to successfully "incentivize" managers and retain valued executives. Why should they not be used to incentivize and retain valued rank-and-file employees as well?

The problems of employee incentives have some important implications for management decision makers. The following are a few of the more important.

- *Ownership adds the promise of extraordinary personal wealth creation to otherwise modest compensation programs.* The data are clear—routine salary increases alone will not significantly increase the real earnings of rank-and-file employees. During one of the longest periods of prosperity in our recent history, workers have averaged only about 3%

per year increases in pay. Incentive stock options that merely reflected broad stock averages could have netted 20% or more in the late 1990s. Ownership effectively reduces the perceived inequity problem.

- *ISOs add an element of excitement to otherwise boring compensation programs.* Pay for performance could go a long way toward restoring some excitement to the typical workday. Tracking the company stock everyday keeps the importance of personal contributions to corporate performance on the mind of everyone who has a stake in the stock price. Moreover, when performance targets are attained, the award of the ISO is immediate. This recognizes the importance of contingency rewards and reinforcement.

- *Ownership makes it attractive for talented and mobile employees to stay with the company rather than bouncing from one job to another for higher base pay.* As retirement funds become more portable, vesting schedules will become increasingly important as a means of retaining valuable employees and executives. The agency problem is reduced.

- *Ownership, particularly in the form of ISOs, is an economically attractive way of rewarding employees for high performance.* If targets are not attained, no options are granted. If tax laws remain unchanged and targets are attained, the company prospers and, except for dilution effects, employees are rewarded with options that cost nothing. Moreover, when the options are exercised, the company can deduct the gain on the options as an expense—even though there is no monetary outlay.

- *Ownership works only when employees understand the risks.* Communication of the risks should be a part of any stock option program. Performance targets may not be met; if not, the extra earnings will not be forthcoming. Industry factors may affect the market so that even if performance targets are attained or exceeded, the options may have little or no value when they vest. Issues relating to perceived inequity may be increased unless employees understand the risks as well as the rewards of ownership. Moreover, stock options create unique, complex, and frequently adverse tax affects. Companies should at the very least alert recipients to obtain competent tax advice on how to account for the value of the options received.

The bottom line is simple. Is it worth a try to recognize the contributions all employees make to organizational success? Would it not be good to have a workforce composed of millionaires in the plant and sales office as well as the executive suite? Perhaps it is time to offer long-term, nonexecutive employees the same opportunity for wealth creation that is afforded to those at the very top of today's corporations? The costs are not so great. Only the will is lacking.

Selected Bibliography

For details on Henry Sturgis Dennison and his ideas about corporate restructuring, see Gorton James, *Profit Sharing and Stock Ownership for Employees* (New York: Harper & Brothers, 1926), 259–268; and Henry S. Dennison, "The Principles of Industrial Efficiency Applied to the Corporate Form of Organization" in *Annals of the American Academy of Political and Social Sciences,* 1915, 61 (September), 183–186. See also John Kenneth Galbraith, *A Life in Our Times: Memoirs* (Boston: Hougton Mifflin, 1981).

Information on stock ownership can be found in Brian J. Hall, "What You Need to Know about Stock Options," *Harvard Business Review* 2000, 78(2), 121–129; and Laurie Krigman, Wayne H. Shaw, and Kent L. Womack, "The Persistence of IPO Mispricing and the Predictive Power of Flipping," *Journal of Finance,* 1999, 54(3), 1015–1044. See also M. L. Stein, "ESOPs Fables: Idaho Daily Shares Ownership with Employees," *Editor & Publisher,* 1998, 131(48), 14; Jules Abend, "T Juniors: Puts Stock in Sharing with Employees," *Bobbin,* 1998, 39(8), 34–38; and "Companies Boost Equity-Based Pay but Stock-Based Incentives Will Slow if Market Volatility Increases," *Investor Relations Business,* 2000, 11 (September), 1.

For sources on the selected motivation theories and research see Maureen L. Ambrose and Carol T. Kulik, "Old Friends, New Faces: Motivation Research in the 1990s," *Journal of Management,* 1999, 25(3), 231–292; Theresa M. Welbourne and Linda A. Cry, "Using Ownership as an Incentive," *Group & Organization Management,* 1999, 24(4), 438–460; and Todd R. Zenger and C. R. Marshall "Determinants of Incentive Intensity in Group-Based Rewards," *Academy of Management Journal,* 2000, 43(2), 149–163.

For some evidence on the benefits of employee ownership, see J. Stephen Heinen and Edward S. Bancroft, "Performance Ownership: A Roadmap to a Compelling Employment Brand," *Compensation & Benefits Review,* 2000, 32(1), 65–71; and Joseph E. Godfrey, "Does Employee Ownership Really Make a Difference?" *The CPA Journal,* 2000, 70(1), 13–16.

Information on broad-based stock option plans can be found in the following sources: Fay Hansen, "More Companies Are Offering Stock Options," *Compensation & Benefits Review,* 1998, 30(3), 7–8; Jeff Staiman and Kerry Thompson, "Designing and Implementing a Broad-Based Stock Option Plan," *Compensation & Benefits Review,* 1998, 30(4), 23–35; and Thomas B. Wilson, *Rewards That Drive High Performance* (New York: AMACOM Books, 1999).

Information on new SEC rules for private company stock program may be found in Michael Alcamo, "SEC Allows Expanded Stock Incentive Plans," *International Financial Review,* 1999, 18(9), 24–26; and Rule 701-Exempt Offerings Payment to Compensatory Arrangements, Securities and Exchange Commission, 17 CFR Part 230, July 1999.

Chapter **Ten**

Punishment

Punishment is a technique for shaping employee behavior that is often used by managers. Along with reinforcement (discussed by Komaki in Chapter 2 of this volume), it is a method of operant conditioning that involves the administration of a negative event or the removal of a positive one following a particular behavior, the effect of which is to decrease the probability of that behavior occurring in the future (Arvey & Jones, 1985). Examples of more common forms of punishments used by managers in organizations include reprimands (verbal and written), reductions in pay, removal of privileges, transfers to less desirable tasks, and suspension. It is important to keep in mind that the simple dispensation of displeasing events does not constitute punishment, at least according to the definition we employ here. Negative events occurring in organizations that are not related to particular employee behaviors or do not have the consequence of reducing the probability of the occurrence of the behavior would not be considered punishment from the perspective we take.

It is also worth noting here that punishment is frequently confused with another form of operant conditioning—negative reinforcement. However, punishment and negative reinforcement differ in important respects. Negative reinforcement (like positive reinforcement) increases the probability of a particular response, whereas punishment decreases its probability. In addition, negative reinforcement involves removing an aversive consequence when desired behavior occurs. In contrast, punishment entails administering an aversive consequence or removing a pleasurable one following undesired behavior.

Research suggests that the extent to which punishment is generally effective depends on several features of its administration (e.g., Arvey & Ivancevich, 1980). For instance, punishment is likely to be most effective when it immediately and consistently follows the undesirable behavior, when it is impersonal and adequately severe from the perspective of the recipient, and when the punisher clearly explains the reason for the sanctions and what the contingencies for punishment will be in the future. In addition, punishment is more likely to be effective when alternatives to the punished behavior are positively reinforced and the punisher (e.g., supervisor) has a relatively good relationship with the one punished.

However, there are a number of reasons why it is often difficult for managers to devise punishments for their employees that exhibit the features mentioned above. For instance, the extent to which an event is considered aversive is frequently person-dependent. For example, one individual may find a reduction in job responsibility to be repugnant, whereas another person may find such a job change to be quite welcome. Supervisors may not always know whether a chosen consequence is indeed a punishment for the person in question.

Furthermore, it is often difficult to implement a punishment immediately in an organization. For example, the administration of some punishments (e.g., withholding a raise) may be tied to the performance review process, which may be conducted on an annual basis. For another example, the meting out of some types of punishments, such as demotions or suspensions, may be subject to a lengthy appeals process by the intended recipient of the punishment.

Consistency can be another problem in the administration of punishments within an organizational context. For example, an employee can be subjected to punishment from different superiors who may have discrepant ideas regarding the type and amount of punishment appropriate for a certain undesirable behavior. Also, managers generally tend to punish highly valued employees less severely than employees who are considered less valuable to the organization. Additionally, consistency may be influenced by the mood of the punisher, and punishment may be more severe when the punisher is aware of the negative consequences of the misbehavior than when the punisher is not aware of the outcomes.

For these reasons and others, it can be difficult for managers to implement punishment policies and procedures. Moreover, punishment may have some unexpected or unintended side effects (perhaps due to the difficulties associated with its administration). For instance, it may create so much resentment and negative feeling on the part of the punished person that he or she may seek revenge on the punisher through physical and other types of aggression—thereby engaging in even more undesirable behavior. In addition, punishment may threaten employees' self-esteem, and the punished person may withdraw from work. The administrative difficulties and unintended side effects of punishment seem to suggest that managers should use it with a degree of caution.

Finally, initial research on punishment in organizations took the perspective of the recipients and investigated the behavioral and attitudinal effects of punishment on them. More recent studies, however, have widened the original focus. In work settings, employees frequently witness firsthand, or otherwise become aware of, punishment delivered to other organizational members. In fact, individuals receiving punishment may ardently attempt to persuade coworkers of its injustice, thereby generating undesirable effects on other employees, at least from management's perspective. Therefore, employees other than those subjected to sanctions learn something about the rules and about the consequences of rule violation. As a result, research has begun to examine how punishment may function to uphold (or undermine) social norms, deter misconduct, and create perceptions of supervisory or organizational fairness (e.g., Trevino, 1992). Research has also identified a number of factors that may influence observer assessments regarding the fairness or legitimacy of an act of punishment, including knowledge or opinions concerning the recipient's prior disciplinary history, the recipient's apparent culpability for the infraction, whether the punishment seems to fit the crime, and whether other people had committed similar offenses and had gone unpunished (Avery & Jones, 1985).

OVERVIEW OF THE READINGS

The readings in this chapter describe two other ways in which the research focus on punishment in organizations has been widened. In the first reading, George investigates the effects of punishments (contingent and noncontingent) and rewards (contingent and noncontingent) on the phenomenon of social loafing in groups. Intuitively, one might think that the effects of punishments and rewards have symmetrical effects on the occurrence of social loafing. That is, contingent punishments for social loafing and contingent rewards for performance should both decrease social loafing incidents. Likewise, one would think that rewards unrelated to performance and punishments not associated with social loafing would both have no effect on the occurrence of social loafing. However, George proposes and finds that the effects of punishments and rewards are actually asymmetrical. Contingent rewards appear to reduce the likelihood of social loafing, but contingent punishments have no effect on the phenomenon. Noncontingent rewards seem to be unrelated to social loafing, but noncontingent punishments actually appear to increase its occurrence. George provides further evidence that the relationship between types of conditioning techniques (rewards versus punishments) and employee behavior in organizations is much more complex than it might first appear. Her work is also important because it focuses on teamwork—a context becoming increasingly prevalent in modern complex organizations.

As mentioned previously, most of the existing research on punishment focuses on the recipient's perspective. Recent investigations have started to expand beyond these subordinate-centered studies. The reading by Butterfield, Trevino, and Ball represents work along these lines. Their approach is interesting in that it takes the viewpoint of managers. In particular, the authors identify a number of factors that come to bear on managers' decisions to punish employees and the wide range of perceived outcomes of punishment acts.

References

Arvey, R. D., & Ivancevich, J. M. (1980). Punishment in organizations: A review, propositions, and research suggestions. *Academy of Management Review,* 5: 123–132.

Arvey, R. D., & Jones, A. P. (1985). The use of discipline in organizational settings: A framework for future research. In B. M. Staw & L. L. Cummings (Eds.), *Research in Organizational Behavior,* vol. 7: 367–408. Greenwich, CT: JAI Press.

Trevino, L. K. (1992). The social effects of punishment in organizations: A justice perspective. *Academy of Management Review,* 17: 647–676.

Asymmetrical Effects of Rewards and Punishments: The Case of Social Loafing

Jennifer M. George

Actual group productivity often falls short of potential productivity (Steiner, 1972). One explanation for this is that individuals exert less effort when they work in groups as opposed to working individually. This phenomenon was studied over 100 years ago by a French agricultural engineer named Ringelmann (Kravitz & Martin, 1986) and has since been called social loafing (Latané, Williams, & Harkins, 1979). Latané et al. (1979, p. 823) define social loafing as "a decrease in individual effort due to the social presence of other persons." Social loafing has been demonstrated to occur on a wide variety of tasks in laboratory settings (e.g. Brickner, Harkins, & Ostrom, 1986; Earley, 1989; Jackson & Williams, 1985; Kerr & Bruun, 1981; Petty, Harkins, & Williams, 1980; Zaccaro; 1984). Recently, George (1992) demonstrated that some of the results of laboratory studies of social loafing appear to generalize to workers in ongoing groups in organizational settings.

One cause of social loafing is the fact that individual effort or contributions are often perceived to be unidentifiable when work is performed in groups. When individuals in a group think that their efforts or contributions will be identifiable to others and there is the potential for evaluation of these efforts, social loafing is effectively eliminated (e.g. Harkins & Jackson, 1985; Kerr & Bruun, 1981; Williams, Harkins, & Latané, 1981).

Why should identifiability be a deterrent to social loafing? The principal explanation for this finding is that when individual contributions are unidentifiable, the perceived linkage between individual effort and rewards and punishments is low, resulting in decreased motivation (Jones, 1984). Conversely, when individual effort is perceived to be identifiable, individuals are accountable for their own behaviour and hence can expect resultant positive or negative consequences. As Latané et al. (1979, p. 830) indicate, "since individual scores are unidentifiable when groups perform together, people can receive neither precise credit nor appropriate blame for their performance. . . . Individuals could 'hide in the crowd' (Davis, 1969) and avoid the negative consequences of slacking off, or they may have felt 'lost in the crowd' and unable to obtain their fair share of the positive consequences for working hard." Hence, one reason individuals engage in social loafing is because they think that their individual efforts will go unrewarded and/or a lack of effort will not be punished (Jones, 1984; Latané et al., 1979). A key question which has heretofore not been addressed is whether contingent rewards and punishments have parallel effects on social loafing. In this regard, converging evidence from several areas in psychology and organizational behaviour suggests that rewards and punishments do not have symmetrical effects on individuals and their behaviours. This suggests that contingent rewards and contingent punishments may not be equally efficacious in curtailing the occurrence of social loafing in organizations.

This [reading] reviews work in several areas of psychology and organizational behaviour which suggests that rewards and punishments have asymmetrical effects on individuals and

From *Journal of Occupational and Organizational Psychology,* 1995, 68, 327–338. Reprinted by permission.

their behaviour. Based upon this review, hypotheses are developed concerning the relationship between contingent rewards and contingent punishments and social loafing. Additionally, the effects of non-contingent rewards and punishments on social loafing also are explored.

ASYMMETRICAL EFFECTS OF REWARDS AND PUNISHMENTS

Evidence suggesting that rewards and punishments have asymmetrical effects can be found in a variety of areas in psychology and organizational behaviour. Below, theory and research from three such areas is briefly reviewed.

Perhaps the most basic argument in support of the asymmetrical effects of rewards and punishments comes from work on brain structure. For example, Gray's theory of personality and emotion (Gray, 1971, 1981, 1987) links rewards and punishments to different types of brain activity or neuronal systems. More specifically, Gray (1981) posits that the behavioural inhibition system influences responses when signals of punishments are present and the behavioural activation system regulates responses when signals of rewards are present (Larsen & Katelaar, 1991). These two physiological systems are independent of each other (Gray, 1981). Gray's theory and research in support of it, therefore, suggest that signals of reward and punishment are processed in different systems in the brain. Hence, rewards and punishment have differential effects on behaviours, in part, because they are responded to by different physiological systems.

Any discussion of rewards and punishments brings to mind the operant conditioning paradigm, a second topical area dealing with the asymmetrical effects of rewards and punishments. From this perspective, rewards are seen as increasing the probability of a behaviour and punishments are viewed as decreasing the probability of a behaviour. However, it has long been recognized that the effects of punishment are distinct from the effects of rewards in that they do not have parallel (or opposite) influences on behaviour. For example, Skinner (1953, p. 183) noted that "in the long run, punishment, unlike reinforcement, works to the disadvantage of both the punished organism and the punishing agency. The aversive stimuli which are needed generate emotions, including predispositions to escape or retaliate, and disabling anxieties . . . the suspicion has also arisen that punishment does not in fact do what it is supposed to do." Skinner goes on to discuss a variety of unintended negative consequences of punishment. This point also has been acknowledged in the organizational literature on operant conditioning. For example, Fedor & Ferris (1981) discuss several problems with the use of punishment in organizations including the potential for retaliatory behaviours. More generally, organizational behaviour modification discourages the use of punishment (Fedor & Ferris, 1981).

Finally, research on the effects of leader reward and punishment behaviour suggests that rewards and punishments do not have symmetrical effects on behaviour. For example, Podsakoff, Todor, Grover, and Huber (1984) review results which suggest that contingent rewards consistently have positive effects on performance whereas the effects of contingent punishment are much less clear cut (e.g. Cherrington, Reitz, & Scott, 1971; Greene, 1973, 1979; Podsakoff, Todor, & Skov, 1982; Sims, 1977; Sims & Szilagyi, 1975). Consistent with this reasoning, Sims (1980, p. 134) concluded in his review that "the relationship between reward behavior and subordinate performance is much stronger than the relationship between punitive behavior and performance." More recently, Podsakoff et al. (1984) found that leader contingent reward behaviour was positively associated with subordinate performance while contingent punishment behaviour was found to be unrelated to performance. Additionally, Podsakoff et al. (1984) found that non-contingent reward behaviour was unrelated to performance whereas leader non-contingent punishment behaviour was negatively associated with subordinate performance.

In summary, theory and research from several areas of psychology and organizational behaviour suggest that rewards and punishments do not have symmetrical effects on individuals and their behaviours. Hence, it stands to reason that contingent rewards and punishments would not be equally efficacious in terms of reducing social loafing in organizations, contrary to a common assumption in this literature (e.g. Latané et al., 1979).

EFFECTS OF CONTINGENT REWARDS AND CONTINGENT PUNISHMENTS ON SOCIAL LOAFING

When a supervisor or leader contingently rewards a subordinate, he or she conveys several pieces of information to that subordinate. Principal among these is the fact that the subordinate's behaviour or actions have been noticed by the supervisor and are considered to be important or valued. Contingent rewards also give subordinates information or feedback concerning their competence and effectiveness. Hence, when supervisors contingently reward subordinates, even if work is performed in groups, subordinates are likely to perceive that their own efforts are identifiable (i.e. they would have to be to be contingently rewarded for them) and that they will receive rewards for them. Social loafing should be less likely under these circumstances since individuals will be more confident that their efforts will be appropriately rewarded (Shepperd, 1993). Both the operant conditioning paradigm and the social loafing literature are supportive of this expectation (e.g. Latané et al., 1979). Thus:

Hypothesis 1: The extent to which supervisors contingently reward subordinates based upon individual performance is negatively associated with social loafing.

What about the effects of contingent punishment on social loafing? While intuitively we might expect them to be similar in that when a supervisor contingently punishes a subordinate for substandard performance, social loafing should be less prevalent, we know from the literature discussed above that punishment appears to have phenomenologically distinct effects from rewards. For example, the research reviewed above on brain structure, operant conditioning and leader behaviour all suggest that rewards and punishments have asymmetrical effects.

Deci's cognitive evaluation theory (e.g. Deci, 1971; Deci, Connell, & Ryan, 1989; Deci & Ryan, 1980) provides a useful framework from which to explore these effects in the case of social loafing. Two premises of this theory, which are also echoed in other psychological approaches to human nature, are that people have a need for self-determination or like to believe that they have control over their own actions, and that people also like to feel that they are competent. Contingent punishment is used precisely when one party has control or power over the other (Skinner, 1953) and, in the case of the supervisor–subordinate relationship, is likely to drive home to the subordinate the fact that his or her supervisor has control. In the case of social loafing, this puts the subordinate in a bit of a quandary. On the one hand, contingent punishment sends the signal that social loafing will be noticed and negative consequences may ensue. On the other hand, the subordinate's needs for self-determination may be thwarted if he or she succumbs to the control of the supervisor's punishing behaviour. For example, in response to such a situation, one way to assert one's self-determination would be to engage in social loafing. Consistent with this reasoning is Miles & Greenberg's (1993) unexpected finding in their study of social loafing that higher levels of punishment threats lead to lower levels of individual performance among swimmers. Miles & Greenberg posit that such threats may be seen as challenges to individual freedom and one way to re-establish such freedom is through lower performance (p. 260).

The idea that contingent punishment generates competing motives for and against social loafing is also somewhat consistent with Shepperd's (1993) recent motivational analysis of social loafing. Building from Shepperd's (1993) approach, contingent punishment may discourage social loafing to the extent that it increases the value of individual effort expenditure (e.g. as a means to avoid punishment). On the other hand, contingent punishment may encourage social loafing to the extent that it increases the cost of effort expenditure (e.g. it is unpleasant to work hard for someone who has recently punished you). Given these conflicting tendencies towards and against social loafing engendered by contingent punishment and the fact that the supervisor can not realistically punish every single instance of social loafing (Skinner, 1953), it is likely that contingent punishment will show no appreciable relationship to social loafing in a positive or negative direction. In particular, contingent punishment behaviour is unlikely to reduce social loafing, contrary to an assumption in the social loafing literature (e.g. Latané et al., 1979). Thus:

Hypothesis 2: The extent to which supervisors contingently punish subordinates based upon individual performance is unrelated to social loafing.

At this point, it should be noted that contingent reward behaviour is not expected to threaten workers' feelings of self-determination (as in the case of contingent punishment described above) due to the fact that the contingent rewards investigated served an informational function and provided workers with feedback on their actions and capabilities (Deci & Ryan, 1980). In providing information concerning one's effectiveness and/or capabilities, rewards do not threaten self-determination and may enhance feelings of competence leading to increased motivation (Deci & Ryan, 1980). As Deci and Ryan (1980, p. 63) indicate, "positive competence feedback should always increase intrinsic motivation." While one could argue that contingent punishment also provides subordinates with information, the fact that this information is very likely to be negative will not enhance feelings of competence. Moreover, the controlling nature of the punishment is likely to be most salient.

EFFECTS OF NON-CONTINGENT REWARDS AND NON-CONTINGENT PUNISHMENTS ON SOCIAL LOAFING

Podsakoff et al. (1984) emphasized the need to consider the effects of non-contingent reward and punishment behaviour on subordinate responses in addition to the effects of contingent reward and punishment behaviour. In the case of non-contingent reward behaviour, since rewards are administered irrespective of performance levels, social loafing should be unaffected. Alternatively, it could be argued that non-contingent reward behaviour may actually encourage social loafing since workers may perceive that they will receive rewards regardless of their efforts and thus can get away with social loafing. Workers also may feel that their efforts are unnecessary when they are non-contingently rewarded, encouraging social loafing (Shepperd, 1993).

However, a countervailing force is likely to offset the incentive to engage in social loafing under conditions of non-contingent reward. That is, theories of social exchange suggest that people seek to reciprocate with others from whom they receive benefits or rewards (Blau, 1964). Hence, in the case of social loafing, whereas non-contingent reward behaviour may encourage social loafing to the extent that it signals that one can get away with it, it also may discourage social loafing to the extent that workers feel the need to reciprocate with their benefactors (i.e. their rewarding supervisors), one of the most readily available means of reciprocating being effort on the job. Thus, while from a strict operant conditioning paradigm non-contingent reward should have no effect on social loafing since it is, by definition, not conditional upon individual contributions, any incentive to social loafing engendered by such reward is likely to be offset by desires for reciprocity in social exchange (Blau, 1964). Thus:

> *Hypothesis 3:* The extent to which supervisors non-contingently reward individual subordinates is unrelated to social loafing.

Non-contingent punishment behaviour occurs when a supervisor punishes a subordinate for no apparent reason. While such behaviour is likely to engender negative emotional reactions on the part of the subordinate, it also is likely to have behavioural implications (e.g. Podsakoff et al., 1984). For example, receiving non-contingent punishment may cause workers to desire to retaliate against the supervisor or the organization. From an equity theory perspective, receiving non-contingent punishment is likely to result in perceptions of unfairness and the resultant desire to restore equity (Adams, 1963). In such a situation, one way to restore equity would be to lower one's efforts by engaging in social loafing. Thus:

> *Hypothesis 4:* The extent to which supervisors non-contingently punish individual subordinates is positively associated with social loafing.

The results of a study designed to test these hypotheses are described and discussed below.

METHOD

Data for this study came from a larger study conducted in eight branches of a major retailer in the United States. The data used in this study have not been previously published in any form. The sample consisted of salespeople who worked in primary work-groups ranging in size from four to 10 members. A primary work-group was defined as a group of salespeople who worked together, shared group responsibilities, worked together towards the attainment of group goals, and whose members and management at the retailer were viewed as being in the same work-group. The salespeople always worked in their primary work-groups. The human resources department, in conjunction with branch management, identified each of the groups and their members who were included in the study. All primary work-groups in the eight branches for which there were no ambiguities regarding group membership were included in the study.

The salespeople were given questionnaires at work with a postage-paid return envelope to return their completed questionnaires directly to the researcher. The questionnaires included measures of the extent to which a salesperson's supervisor engaged in contingent reward behaviour, contingent punishment behaviour, non-contingent reward behaviour and non-contingent punishment behaviour with regard to the salesperson's own on-the-job behaviours. Participation was voluntary and complete confidentiality was guaranteed. A total of 579 questionnaires were distributed and 448 completed questionnaires were returned for a 77 percent response rate. Approximately 85 percent of the respondents were female. The average age of the respondents was 41 years and 53 percent of the sample reported having attended a college or technical school.

While the salespeople worked in primary work-groups, discussions with top, middle and lower level management at the retailer and the supervisors themselves indicated that the supervisors of the salespeople were aware of individual effort and performance levels. Indeed, part of the supervisors' responsibilities was the evaluation of the contributions of individual salespersons to the group and organization. Discussions with the supervisors indicated that social loafing was a very real phenomenon in the groups they managed and confirmed that they had ample opportunity to observe it. The supervisors of the salespeople received a rating form for each of their subordinates who was included in the study. The rating forms included a measure of the extent to which each of the salespersons engaged in social loafing. The supervisors were given the rating forms at work with a postage-paid envelope to return the completed forms directly to the researcher. Participation was voluntary and respondents were guaranteed complete confidentiality. Sixty-four supervisors received rating forms and 53 returned completed forms for a response rate of 83 percent. Because of missing data (e.g. receipt of a subordinate's questionnaire but no corresponding rating form from the subordinate's supervisor and vice versa), the sample size for analyses ranged from 345 to 448.

Measures

Contingent Reward Behaviour, Contingent Punishment Behaviour, Non-Contingent Reward Behaviour and Non-Contingent Punishment Behaviour

The extent to which the supervisors of the salespeople engaged in these behaviours was measured with scales described by Podsakoff et al. (1984). The Contingent Reward Behaviour scale contained 10 items, the Contingent Punishment Behaviour scale contained five items, and the Non-contingent Reward and Punishment scales each contained four items. Information on the development and psychometric properties of these scales is provided by Podsakoff et al. (1984). Sample items from the Contingent Reward Behaviour scale are: "My supervisor commends me when I do a better than average job," and "My supervisor gives me special recognition when my work performance is especially good." Responses were made on a seven-point scale ranging from "strongly disagree" to "strongly agree."

Social Loafing

Social loafing was measured by the supervisors of the salespeople with the 10-item Social Loafing scale developed by George (1992). This scale measures the extent to which a worker puts forth low effort on the job when others are present to do the work. Information on the development and psychometric properties of the Social Loafing scale is provided by George

(1992). A sample item is: "Puts forth less effort on the job when other salespeople are around to do the work." The supervisors were instructed to rate how characteristic of the salesperson being evaluated each of the items was on a five-point scale ranging from "not at all characteristic" to "very characteristic." The complete Social Loafing scale is provided in the Appendix.

RESULTS

Means, standard deviations, internal consistency reliabilities and intercorrelations among the study variables are presented in Table 1. All of the internal consistency reliabilities for the scales used were acceptable (Nunnally, 1978). Hypotheses 1 and 2 concerned the relationships between contingent reward behaviour and contingent punishment behaviour and social loafing. In support of hypothesis 1, contingent reward behaviour was significantly and negatively associated with social loafing ($r = -.26$; $p \le .001$). Consistent with hypothesis 2, contingent punishment behaviour showed no appreciable relationship to social loafing ($r = -.07$; n.s.).

Hypotheses 3 and 4 pertained to the associations between non-contingent reward behaviour and non-contingent punishment behaviour and social loafing. Consistent with hypothesis 3, non-contingent reward behaviour was found to be unrelated to social loafing ($r = .02$; n.s.). In support of hypothesis 4 non-contingent punishment behaviour was significantly and positively related to social loafing ($r = .25$; $p \le .001$).

Hypotheses 1 through 4 can also be tested using multiple regression. Table 2 contains the results of regressing social loafing simultaneously on contingent reward behaviour, contingent punishment behaviour, non-contingent reward behaviour, and non-contingent punishment behaviour. In support of hypotheses 1 and 4, the beta weights for contingent reward behaviour (beta $= -.15$; $p \le .05$) and non-contingent punishment behaviour (beta $= .18$; $p \le .01$) were each statistically significant and in the expected directions. Consistent with hypotheses 2 and 3, contingent punishment behaviour and non-contingent reward behaviour showed no appreciable relationship to social loafing.

Finally, results highly consistent with those reported in Table 2 were found controlling for branch. That is, in a regression equation in which branch membership was represented by seven dummy-coded variables (Cohen & Cohen, 1983), the beta weights for contingent reward behaviour (beta $= -.16$; $p \le .01$) and non-contingent punishment behaviour (beta $= .18$; $p \le .01$) were each statistically significant and in the hypothesized direction while the betas for contingent punishment behaviour and non-contingent reward behaviour were non-significant. This supplemental analysis was performed in case there was some difference across branches which was, in fact, partially responsible for the results obtained. Such a difference was not expected and the results were consistent with this expectation. Once again, these results support hypotheses 1–4.

DISCUSSION

Consistent with a dominant assumption in the social loafing literature (e.g. Jones, 1984; Latané et al., 1979), a supervisor's contingent reward behaviour was found to be negatively associated with social loafing in ongoing groups. Hence, a supervisor who positively

TABLE 1   Summary Statistics

Variables	Means	SD	Correlations[a]				
			1	2	3	4	5
1. Contingent reward behaviour	44.33	13.75	(.95)	.15***	.14***	−.54***	−.26***
2. Contingent punishment behaviour	25.38	5.35		(.86)	−.29***	.12**	−.07
3. Non-contingent reward behaviour	10.83	4.47			(.77)	.02	.02
4. Non-contingent punishment behaviour	10.19	5.01				(.88)	.25***
5. Social loafing	17.34	7.83					(.93)

*$p \leq .05$; **$p \leq .01$; ***$p \leq .001$.
[a]Coefficient alphas are in parentheses on the diagonal.

TABLE 2   Results of Regressing Social Loafing on Leader Behaviours

Independent Variables	Beta
Contingent reward behaviour	−.15*
Contingent punishment behaviour	−.07
Non-contingent reward behaviour	.01
Non-contingent punishment behaviour	.18**
$R = .30$***	
$R^2 = .09$***	

*$p \leq .05$; **$p \leq .01$; ***$p \leq .001$.

reinforces desirable behaviour appears to help curtail the occurrence of social loafing in groups. Importantly, for supervisor contingent reward behaviour to be effective, it is necessary that workers perceive that rewards are, in fact, contingently administered.

Since social loafing is an undesirable behaviour, intuitively one might expect that contingent punishment would help to curtail social loafing. Indeed, the social loafing literature assumes that contingent rewards and punishments will have symmetrical effects on social loafing (e.g. Harkins, Latané, & Williams, 1980; Latané et al., 1979). However, the effects of punishment are not necessarily simple or straightforward as suggested by the literature reviewed earlier. Rewards and punishments do not have symmetrical effects on behaviours and punishment appears to engender unintended negative consequences. In the case of social loafing, a supervisor's contingent punishment behaviour does not appear to be a deterrent, as hypothesized. Hence, while a supervisor's first reaction to substandard performance may be to reprimand a worker, in the long run such behaviours are not likely to be as effective as noticing and reinforcing desirable behaviours.

In this study, while the work was performed in groups, supervisors were aware of individual effort and contributions. However, in other contexts it is likely that supervisors may not be able to determine individual effort or contributions to group performance. This may be the case, for example, when a group of workers is physically separated from the supervisor or when the nature of the group work necessitates a high degree of reciprocal interdependence among group members (Jones, 1984; Thompson, 1967). Under those circumstances, supervisors cannot engage in contingent reward behaviour at the level of the individual worker since individual contributions cannot be isolated. While supervisors can certainly administer group-based rewards contingent upon group performance, social loafing may still be a problem since rewards are administered to the group as a whole and not to individuals (Jones, 1984). At the individual level, supervisors may be tempted to use non-contingent rewards; however, the results of this study suggest that this may have no appreciable effect on social loafing. Finally, a supervisor's non-contingent punishment behaviour may increase the incidence of social loafing.

Additionally, it should be noted that on some kinds of jobs workers receive direct feedback in the course of performing work tasks, On these kinds of jobs, the informational value of rewards from supervisors is lessened because workers already know how they are doing. Under these conditions, contingent rewards may have somewhat different effects on the incidence of social loafing.

Given what seems to be an increasing reliance on groups and teams in organizations (or at least the espousing of the benefits of group work), it is surprising that very little research has been conducted on social loafing in ongoing groups. In fact, with few exceptions (e.g. George, 1992; Hardy & Latané, 1988; Williams, Nida, Baca, & Latané, 1989), social loafing has been studied exclusively in laboratory settings. Moreover, studies of social loafing in ongoing groups have not tended to focus on work-groups *per se* (e.g. Hardy & Latané, 1988; Williams et al., 1989). If group work is becoming more popular, then social loafing is an important issue organizations will have to face. As mentioned earlier, the ubiquity of social loafing has been demonstrated for many different types of tasks in laboratory settings (e.g. Earley, 1989; Harkins et al., 1980). Further research is needed which focuses on the occurrence of social loafing in groups in organizations and ways to reduce it.

Social loafing is not just a problem in terms of the lost productivity of the individuals who engage in social loafing. Rather, if some group members engage in social loafing, others may reduce their own effort levels so as not to be "suckers" (Kerr, 1983). For example, research conducted by Jackson and Harkins (1985) indicates that when group members expect others to engage in social loafing they may reduce their own efforts to approximate the effort levels of the social loafers. Hence, social loafing by one or a few members of a group may cause others to lower their own efforts as well.

Once again, while results of the current study suggest that supervisor contingent reward behaviour is an effective means of reducing social loafing, when individual contributions cannot be identified, this is not an option. Future research is needed to uncover other ways to help reduce the occurrence of social loafing under these circumstances. For example, if group members themselves are able to assess individual contributions, then group-administered contingent rewards (to individuals based upon their individual contributions) may be one option to consider. A precondition necessary for such an option to result in outcomes consistent with organizational goals is that group goals are congruent with the organization's goals. The efficacy of this and other ways to help reduce the occurrence of social loafing in such contexts is an empirical question in need of future research.

This study is not without limitations. For example, due to the non-experimental nature of the data, the direction of causality cannot be determined unambiguously. For example, rather than supervisor reward and punishment behaviour having an effect on the incidence of social loafing, it may be that social loafing is influencing supervisor behaviour. However, an examination of the pattern of correlations observed partially mitigates this concern. That is, if social loafing was determining supervisor behaviour, then one would expect to find a positive association between social loafing and contingent punishment behaviour such that when individuals engaged in social loafing their supervisors were more likely to punish them contingently. However, consistent with hypothesis 2 and the theoretical reasoning behind it, contingent punishment was found to be unrelated to social loafing. Another limitation of the study is the fact that two of the hypotheses (hypotheses 2 and 3) are null hypotheses or predict the absence of a significant relationship. These and other potential limitations notwithstanding, it is hoped that this study prompts other theorists and researchers to explore social loafing in ongoing work-groups and ways to eliminate it or at least reduce its occurrence.

References

Adams, J. S. (1963). Toward an understanding of inequity. *Journal of Abnormal and Social Psychology,* 67, 422–436.

Blau, P. M. (1964). *Exchange and Power in Social Life.* New York: Wiley.

Brickner, M. A., Harkins, S. G., & Ostrom, T. M. (1986). Effects of personal involvement: Thought-provoking implications for social loafing. *Journal of Personality and Social Psychology,* 51, 763–769.

Cherrington, D. J., Reitz, H. J., & Scott, W. E. (1971). Effects of contingent and noncontingent rewards on the relationship between satisfaction and performance. *Journal of Applied Psychology,* 55, 531–536.

Cohen, J., & Cohen, P. (1983). *Applied Multiple Regression/correlation Analysis for the Behavioral Sciences.* Hillsdale, NJ: Erlbaum.

Davis, J. H. (1969). *Group Performance.* Reading, MA: Addison-Wesley.

Deci, E. L. (1971). Effects of externally mediated rewards on intrinsic motivation. *Journal of Applied Psychology,* 18, 105–115.

Deci, E. L., Connell, J. P., & Ryan, R. M. (1989). Self-determination in a work organization. *Journal of Applied Psychology,* 74, 580–590.

Deci, E. L., & Ryan, R. M. (1980). The empirical exploration of intrinsic motivational processes. *Advances in Experimental Social Psychology,* 13, 39–80.

Earley, P. C. (1989). Social loafing and collectivism: A comparison of the United States and the People's Republic of China. *Administrative Science Quarterly,* 34, 565–581.

Fedor, D. B., & Ferris, G. R. (1981). Integrating OB MOD with cognitive approaches to motivation. *Academy of Management Review,* 6, 115–125.

George, J. M. (1992). Extrinsic and intrinsic origins of perceived social loafing in organizations. *Academy of Management Journal,* 35, 191–202.

Gray, J. A. (1971). The psychophysiological basis of introversion–extraversion. *Behaviour Research and Therapy,* 8, 249–266.

Gray, J. A. (1981). A critique of Eysenck's theory of personality. In H. J. Eysenck (Ed.), *A Model for Personality,* pp. 246–276. New York: Springer.

Gray, J. A. (1987). Perspectives on anxiety and impulsivity: A commentary. *Journal of Research in Personality,* 21, 493–509.

Greene, C. N. (1973). Causal connections among managers' merit pay, job satisfaction, and performance. *Journal of Applied Psychology,* 58, 95–100.

Greene, C. N. (1979). Questions of causation in the path–goal theory of leadership. *Academy of Management Journal,* 22, 22–41.

Hardy, C. J., & Latané, B. (1988). Social loafing in cheerleaders: Effects of team membership and competition. *Journal of Sport & Exercise Psychology,* 10, 109–114.

Harkins, S., & Jackson, J. (1985). The role of evaluation in eliminating social loafing. *Personality and Social Psychology Bulletin,* 11, 457–465.

Harkins, S. G., Latané, B. S., & Williams, K. (1980). Social loafing: Allocating effort or taking it easy. *Journal of Experimental Social Psychology,* 16, 457–465.

Jackson, J. M., & Harkins, S. G. (1985). Equity in effort: An explanation of the social loafing effect. *Journal of Personality and Social Psychology,* 49, 1199–1206.

Jackson, J. M., & Williams, K. D. (1985). Social loafing on difficult tasks: Working collectively can improve performance. *Journal of Personality and Social Psychology,* 49, 937–942.

Jones, G. R. (1984). Task visibility, free riding and shirking: Explaining the effect of structure and technology on employee behavior. *Academy of Management Review,* 9, 684–695.

Kerr, N. L. (1983). Motivation losses in small groups: A social dilemma analysis. *Journal of Personality and Social Psychology,* 45, 819–828.

Kerr, N. L., & Bruun, S. E. (1981). Ringelmann revisited: Alternative explanations for the social loafing effect. *Personality and Social Psychology Bulletin,* 7, 224–231.

Kravitz, D. A., & Martin, B. (1986). Ringelmann rediscovered: The original article. *Journal of Personality and Social Psychology,* 50, 936–941.

Larsen, R. J., & Katelaar, T. (1991). Personality and susceptibility to positive and negative emotional states. *Journal of Personality and Social Psychology,* 61, 132–140.

Latané, B., Williams, K. D., & Harkins, S. (1979). Many hands make light the work: The causes and consequences of social loafing. *Journal of Personality and Social Psychology,* 37, 822–832.

Miles, J. A., & Greenberg, J. (1993). Using punishment threats to attenuate social loafing effects among swimmers. *Organizational Behavior and Human Decision Processes,* 56, 246–265.

Nunnally, J. C. (1978). *Psychometric Theory.* New York: McGraw-Hill.

Petty, R. E., Harkins, S. G., & Williams, K. D. (1980). The effects of group diffusion of cognitive effort on attitudes: An information processing view. *Journal of Personality and Social Psychology.* 3, 579–582.

Podsakoff, P. M., Todor, W. D., Grover, R. A., & Huber, V. L. (1984). Situational moderators of leader reward and punishment behaviors: Fact or fiction? *Organizational Behavior and Human Performance,* 34, 21–63.

Podsakoff, P. M., Todor, W. D., & Skov, R. (1982). Effects of leader contingent and noncontingent reward and punishment behaviors on subordinate performance and satisfaction. *Academy of Management Journal,* 25, 810–821.

Shepperd, J. A. (1993). Productivity loss in performance groups: A motivational analysis. *Psychological Bulletin,* 113, 67–81.

Sims, H. P. Jr. (1977). The leader as a manager of reinforcement contingencies: An empirical example and a model. In J. G. Hunt & L. L. Larson (Eds.), *Leadership: The Cutting Edge.* Carbondale, IL: Southern Illinois University Press.

Sims, H. P. Jr. (1980). Further thoughts on punishment in organizations. *Academy of Management Review,* 5, 133–138.

Sims, H. P., & Szilagyi, A. D. (1975). Leader reward behavior and subordinate satisfaction and performance. *Organizational Behavior and Human Performance,* 14, 426–438.

Skinner, B. F. (1953). *Science and Human Behavior.* New York: Macmillan.

Steiner, I. (1972). *Group Processes and Productivity.* San Diego, CA: Academic Press.

Thompson, J. D. (1967). *Organizations in Action.* New York: McGraw-Hill.

Williams, K., Harkins, S., & Latané, B. (1981). Identifiability as a deterrent to social loafing: Two cheering experiments. *Journal of Personality and Social Psychology,* 40, 303–311.

Williams, K. D., Nida, S. A., Baca, L. D., & Latané, B. (1989). Social loafing and swimming: Effects of identifiability of individual and relay performance of intercollegiate swimmers. *Basic and Applied Social Psychology,* 10, 73–81.

Zaccaro, S. J. (1984). Social loafing: The role of task attractiveness. *Personality and Social Psychology Bulletin,* 10, 99–106.

Appendix
The Social Loafing Scale

1. Defers responsibilities he or she should assume to other salespeople.
2. Puts forth less effort on the job when other salespeople are around to do the work.
3. Does not do his or her share of the work.
4. Spends less time helping customers if other salespeople are present to serve customers.
5. Puts forth less effort than other members of his or her work-group.
6. Avoids performing housekeeping tasks as much as possible.
7. Leaves work for the next shift which he or she should really complete.
8. Is less likely to approach a customer if another salesperson is available to do this.
9. Takes it easy if other salespeople are around to do the work.
10. Defers customer service activities to other salespeople if they are present.

Supervisors are instructed to indicate how characteristic each of the items are of the salesperson they are rating on the following five-point scale:

1	2	3	4	5
Not at all characteristic	Slightly characteristic	Somewhat characteristic	Characteristic	Very characteristic

Responses to the 10 items are summed for an overall score.

Source: George (1992).

Punishment from the Manager's Perspective: A Grounded Investigation and Inductive Model

Kenneth D. Butterfield
Linda Klebe Trevino
Gail A. Ball

Despite scholarly advice to avoid punishment, virtually all managers find themselves delivering oral reprimands to subordinates and occasionally having to suspend or even fire an employee. Yet, except for a small amount of research regarding how managers perceive these highly charged events (e.g., Ball & Sims, 1991; Ball & Trevino, 1990; Fandt, Labig, & Urich, 1990; Mitchell, Green, & Wood, 1981), little is known about what managers actually think and feel about punishing their subordinates. In the research described here, we used qualitative methods to probe how managers actually think and feel about real punishment episodes.

Adapted from *Academy of Management Journal,* 1996, 39(6), 1479–1512. Reprinted by permission.

THEORETICAL BACKGROUND

Punishment has been defined as a superior's application of a negative consequence or the removal of a positive consequence following a subordinate's undesirable behavior, with the intention of decreasing the frequency of that behavior. Organizational punishment research has generally been guided by this definition, reflecting the prevailing view that the goal of punishing is to modify the subordinate's undesirable behaviors. Thus, previous organizational punishment literature (as reviewed in Arvey and Ivancevich [1980] and Arvey and Jones [1985]) has been subordinate-centered, focusing primarily on the effects of punishment on specific subordinate behaviors, such as theft, absenteeism, and performance, or on procedures (e.g., timing, privacy) that influence punishment's effectiveness. This literature indicated that although punishment may provide short-term benefits, such as temporary subordinate compliance, it can foster negative behaviors and attitudes, including resentment, hostility, and even sabotage, over the long run. Accordingly, the subordinate-centered literature has suggested that truly effective punishment may not be possible and that managers should therefore try to avoid punishing their subordinates (e.g., Sims, 1980). Management textbooks reflect this view. Some barely address punishment or discipline at all (e.g., Daft, 1994; Griffin, 1993), indirectly suggesting that discipline is not an essential part of the managerial role. Others acknowledge that punishment is sometimes necessary and provide advice about what to do to reduce undesirable side effects (e.g., follow company policies, be consistent and moderate, be timely, punish in private), but they fail to address what the punishment process is like for managers and what their reactions to it might be (e.g., Bartol & Martin, 1994).

Researchers have begun to expand the scope of this literature in several ways. First, investigators have suggested expanding the focus beyond the punished subordinate to include other organizational members. Arvey and Jones (1985) proposed that researchers should consider punishment's indirect and social learning effects. Trevino (1992) provided a conceptual framework for studying these social effects. She argued that observers (organizational members beyond the manager-subordinate dyad who are aware of a particular punishment event) may experience a broad range of reactions. These include emotional reactions, such as feelings of pleasure when justice has been served or anger when justice has not been served and cognitive reactions, including justice evaluations and attitudinal responses like commitment, loyalty, satisfaction, and trust. The nature of observers' reactions depends upon their understanding, expectations, attributions, and evaluations of an incident. Trevino further suggested that managers should consider observers' reactions important—perhaps even more important than the punished subordinate's reaction to the discipline. Some empirical research has investigated observers' reactions to punishment (O'Reilly & Puffer, 1989; Schnake, 1986, 1987). However, researchers know little about whether managers are aware of these reactions and whether they take them into account in disciplinary situations.

Another extension has involved moving beyond content research to an emphasis on underlying psychological and social psychological processes, including attributions (e.g., Gioia & Sims, 1986; Mitchell et al., 1981), justice evaluations and punishment expectancies (Ball, Trevino, & Sims, 1994; Trevino, 1992), and cognitive and affective mechanisms (e.g., Ball & Sims, 1991). Ball and Sims (1991) used a schematic information-processing perspective to emphasize the role of emotion in punishment situations, arguing that explicit consideration of their own and others' emotions can help managers punish more effectively. Much of this work on psychological and social psychological processes has focused on punished subordinates, observers, or both. Further empirical work is needed to understand managers' cognitive and affective processes in punishment situations and the effects of those situations on managers.

A third stream of research has more directly considered managers in relation to punishment. Theoretical work within this manager-centered stream includes Podsakoff's (1982) treatment of the variables that can affect managers' use of rewards and punishments. According to Podsakoff, these can be divided into three categories: contextual variables (e.g., task structure, organizational policy), subordinate characteristics (e.g., performance, likableness), and supervisor characteristics (e.g., personality, attributions). Yet few empirical manager-centered studies have been conducted. Three exceptions bear mention. First, Mitchell and coauthors (1981) offered and tested an attributional model of how managers respond to subordinates who are performing poorly, suggesting that at least two factors (a subordinate's work history and the seriousness of the subordinate's performance failure) influence managers' attributions and punitive responses. Second, Fairhurst, Green, and Snavely's (1985) qualitative study indicated that when subordinate performance declines to a sufficiently low level, "breakpoints" in the ongoing manager-subordinate relationship are likely to occur, points at which managers intervene and take corrective actions (if a problem can be corrected). Fairhurst and colleagues' research also suggested that managers' disciplinary actions are outcomes of an active, complex "sense-making" process that allows managers to cope with and understand changes and discrepancies in subordinate performance. Third, Fandt and colleagues' (1990) laboratory experiment suggested that managers may differentially punish subordinates depending on the amount of available evidence and the degree to which the managers like the subordinates.

In sum, theorists have begun to broaden their focus and to consider the perspective of manager as well as those of observers and punished subordinates. A small number of empirical studies have extended understanding of punishment from a managerial perspective. However, these studies have focused primarily on when and why managers punish subordinates rather than on broader questions of how managers think and feel about punishment situations. Thus, the manager's perspective on punishment remains a largely uncharted territory. We hoped to contribute to knowledge about this important and inevitable aspect of the managerial role through systematic analysis of qualitative interview data grounded in managers' punishment experiences.

In this research, we had several broad goals. In general, we wanted to gain insight into what managers think and how they feel about their punishment experiences. We wanted to know whether they can easily talk about punishment incidents, whether they can differentiate between effective and ineffective incidents, and if so, how they distinguish between them.

METHODS

We employed a qualitative interview approach to gathering and analyzing managers' retrospective accounts regarding two incidents in which they had punished subordinates. Each manager identified one incident as having been effective—as having led to the results the manager desired—and the other as ineffective: as not having yielded the desired results. From these data, grounded in managers' actual experiences, new insights emerged regarding punishment from a manager's point of view.

Sample and Data Collection

This study employed a convenience sample of 77 managers, each representing a different work organization. The organizations ranged from small ones, such as a local movie theater, to large ones, such as the United States Army. The average age of managers was 38.7 years (range: 22 to 63); individuals had an average of 17.3 years of work experience (range: 2 to 40) and an average of 12.4 years of managerial experience (range: 0.5 to 29), and they currently supervised 25.2 subordinates (range: 2 to 141). . . . [Additional details of the methodology are included in the original article.]

FINDINGS AND CONTRIBUTIONS

How Managers Think and Feel about Punishment: Themes and Categories

The key question driving this research was, How do managers think and feel about punishment? Analysis of the interviews yielded 48 categories that we organized into seven major themes: (1) instrumental nature of punishment, (2) impression management, (3) attributions, (4) awareness of and concern for other employees, (5) awareness of and concern for the subordinates, (6) fairness concerns, and (7) emotions. Our discussion of the themes and categories is designed to highlight major findings, support for existing theory, and, most important, contributions that go beyond existing theory and research.

Table 1 includes theme names, category names, frequencies (the number of times each category appeared in the data), and examples of each category. Although many of the emergent categories are consistent with previous theoretical or empirical research, many were unanticipated. Thus, this research contributes to a manager-centered perspective on punishment in two ways: the anticipated categories provide empirical support (often the first such support) for previous theorizing, whereas the unanticipated categories uncover new knowledge regarding how managers think and feel about punishment. Table 1 illustrates the extent to which the data either support existing theory and research or make new contributions. The reader is encouraged to use Table 1 as a guide to the discussion that follows.

The Instrumental Nature of Punishment

The instrumental theme contains the highest frequency of responses overall, suggesting that managers think about punishment quite instrumentally. We define instrumental as "serving as a means to some end." These managers were concerned about whether the punishment worked or did not work and about positive or negative effects on themselves, the employees involved, and their work groups and organizations.

The first set of instrumental categories (categories 1–5) support a traditional view of punishment—as instrumental for changing a subordinate's attitudes and behavior. Statements demonstrating this theme include the following

> A great improvement in his attendance record. . . .
> It turned out well. She was later promoted into a more responsible position.
> His sales have shot up considerably because of discipline.

However, at least three unanticipated categories (categories 6–8) suggest that managers view punishment incidents as instrumental in ways that extend beyond modifying punished

TABLE 1 Themes and Categories Derived from Interviews

Theme and Category[a]	Example	Research Supported/New Contribution
Instrumental nature of punishment		
1. Positive outcomes/punishment worked (202)	From my perspective, it turned out to be a positive experience . . . As a result, I feel that I have a better employee than I had before.	Support: Categories 1–5 confirm previous research suggesting punishment can be instrumental in improving subordinates' behavior and attitudes (e.g., Arvey & Jones, 1985; Arvey & Ivancevich, 1980).
2. General positive outcomes (128)	Through discipline [he] turned out to be an excellent employee.	
3. Negative outcomes/punishment didn't work (48)	She did not respond to the reprimand. Even after pointing out that [the undesirable behavior] affected her job performance and interrupted the office, the tardiness still continued.	
4. General negative outcomes (105)	She was spiteful, insubordinate . . . so this definitely had a negative outcome to it.	
5. Mixed outcomes (positive and negative) (39)	Although we hate to lose people, it was a gain for us.	
6. Manager's desire for respect from subordinate/others (32)	I think they probably gained a new ounce of respect for me, I guess, as their leader. [The subordinate] gained a lot of respect for me . . . from that disciplinary action.	Contribution: Categories 6–8 suggest that managers also view punishment as instrumental in maintaining respect and promoting organizational and vicarious learning.
7. Manager's concern for/recognition of vicarious effects on co-workers (139)	People know they can't get away with anything like that in the future. If he was not fired, the employees would see that the management was [lackadaisical].	
8. Positive outcomes for manager/organization (20)	I think it was a good learning experience for myself and all the managers.	

continues

TABLE 1 Continued

Theme and Category[a]	Example	Research Supported/New Contribution
Impression management		Support: Greenberg (1990) and Tedeschi suggested that managers are likely to engage in impression management tactics when punishing subordinates. Categories 9–14 correspond to these tactics: justifications, excuses, entitlings, enhancements.
9. Manager's implicit theories/advice regarding management/punishment (67)	Positive reinforcement is probably more important than negative.	
10. Manager did his/her part, employee didn't respond/do his/her part (117)	The associate had every opportunity to correct her problem. She received several warnings and unfortunately she didn't heed any of the warnings.	
11. Manager justifications for/reasons for punishing (79)	We decided to proceed with disciplining for a number of reasons. First of all, it was an offense by the individual. We do not want to condone anything like that in the office or the workplace. Second of all, it's the law.	
12. Manager's role responsibility (67)	I did not want to do what I had to do, but I did my job.	
13. Manager searched for more information (24)	I tried to find out if there were any extenuating circumstances that might have been involved.	
14. Manager/management made no mistake/handled situation properly (68)	I think that it was handled exactly the way it should have been handled.	Contribution: Categories 15 and 16 extend Greenberg's (1990) thesis. These categories suggest that managers are willing to acknowledge their past mistakes and desire to learn from these mistakes.
15. Manager/organization made a mistake (81)	I feel that I could have been a lot harder than I was, but I think, you know, no one is perfect, we all make mistakes.	
16. Situation should never have happened/could have been avoided (34)	We called her into the office . . . drew up a document and had her sign it. This was ridiculous. It never should have happened in the first place.	

continues

TABLE 1 Continued

Theme and Category[a]	Example	Research Supported/New Contribution
Attributions		
17. Manager's understanding based upon internal attributions (174)	She's just that type of person. She's against authority. She has a problem with authority figures and she has a problem with anybody telling her what to do. So, it's more of a personal problem she has.	Partial Support/Contribution: Mitchell et al. (1981) demonstrated that managers form attributions regarding their subordinates' poor performance. Categories 17 and 18 extend this research to punishment contexts, indicating that managers frequently make such attributions in justifying their use of punishment and most frequently make internal attributions.
18. Manager's understanding based upon external attributions (39)	She was in the middle of a divorce with a child in a day center. She couldn't do all those things and be at work on time.	
Awareness of/concern for subordinate		
19. Miscellaneous subordinate reactions (121)	This person actually came back the next day and apologized for not doing his job.	Support: Previous research (e.g., Arvey & Ivancevich, 1980; Mitchell et al., 1981; Greenberg, 1987; Ball & Trevino, 1990) has suggested that, when punishing subordinates, managers may consider the subordinates' reactions (e.g., justice reactions) and their past relationships with the subordinates. Categories 19–21 support this claim.
20. Knowledge of subordinate's justice/injustice reactions (23)	At that time, he felt that he had really been treated unfairly.	
21. Positive history (47)	I had no idea what was happening because this gentleman had up to that time been a very reliable employee.	
22. Subordinate expected punishment (27)	When I approached him and told him what was going on, he said he knew it was coming.	Contribution: Categories 22–24 show that managers consider more than previous research suggests. Managers also consider the subordinates' expectations, whether or not the subordinates accepted responsibility for their behavior, and whether or not the subordinates accepted the discipline.
23. Subordinate accepted responsibility for wrongdoing (41)	After the confrontation, he realized that the problem was him, not the system . . . he said that he would correct it himself.	
24. Subordinate did not accept discipline/responsibility (38)	The individual felt that this was totally wrong because he didn't feel that it was his responsibility.	
25. Manager's interest in/concern for person/family/livelihood (58)	You are concerned and you always keep in the back of your mind that this is his livelihood.	Categories 25 and 26 indicate that managers seek to avoid punishment whenever possible, and that managers are generally concerned about subordinates and their livelihoods and families.
26. Manager's reluctance to punish (63)	Nobody really likes to discipline anybody. It's the most difficult thing to do.	

continues

TABLE 1 Continued

Theme and Category[a]	Example	Research Supported/New Contribution
Awareness of/concern for co-workers/others		
27. Co-workers'/others' nonemotional reactions to punishment (44)	The co-workers and the other union people felt the company was correct in taking the action.	Support: Trevino (1992) argued that managers should be aware of others' cognitive expectations, cognitive reactions (e.g., justice evaluations), and emotional reactions. Categories 7 and 27–30 provide empirical support for this theory.
28. Co-workers'/others' knowledge of/reaction to misconduct (51)	A lot of people felt that he should have been fired immediately.	
29. Co-workers/others' knowledge of/expectations of punishment (25)	As far as what other people thought . . . I think they probably thought I would really chew him out good.	
30. Knowledge of others/co-workers' justice/injustice reactions (40)	The others felt that it was a fair decision and that their well-being was looked out for.	
31. Manager's concern for organization (finance, morale, customers, etc.) (92)	It is important to think about the repercussions like the morale of the employees.	Contribution: Category 31 suggests that, in addition to having an awareness of observers, managers also have larger concerns regarding the entire organization (e.g., morale) and outside interests (e.g., customers).
Fairness concerns		
32. Concern for punishment contingency (71)	I put it in writing . . . if she kept up this attitude, if she kept doing the things that she'd been doing wrong, she was going to be terminated.	Support: Previous subordinate-centered research suggests that managers should punish contingently, constructively, with appropriate severity, privately, consistently, and in a timely fashion. Categories 32–37 confirm that managers do consider these factors, although some categories (e.g., contingency) clearly were more prevalent than others (e.g., equity, timeliness).
33. Concern for constructiveness (65)	I have spent time with him, showing him how he can do his job better with less aggravation.	
34. Concern about punishment severity (31)	I believe the oral reprimand was correct based on the severity of the offense. Some people, you can merely counsel them and they will see the error of their ways. Others, you have to use more harsh punishment to get their attention.	

continues

TABLE 1 Continued

Theme and Category[a]	Example	Research Supported/New Contribution
35. Concern for privacy (61)	I handled it privately. I did not feel that it was something that needed (to be) broadcast to the other employees.	Contribution: Category 38 (along with categories 32–37) suggests that managers are significantly more concerned about procedural justice issues (e.g., using standard procedures) than distributive justice issues (equity, severity) when considering their punishment incidents. Category 39 suggests that managers also consider flexibility important when punishing their subordinates.
36. Concern for equity/consistency (13)	It was fair. The other employees would get the same discipline.	
37. Concern for timing/timeliness (7)	The disciplinary action was taken immediately after the incident happened, which is very important.	
38. Concern about punishment procedures (199)	According to the union, they have to have a union representative with me when I discipline, whether it be verbal or other.	
39. Punishment should be flexible (39)	They don't deserve the same punishment, even if they did the same crime.	
Emotions		
40. Manager's negative emotions (203)	I was very fidgety and very nervous and scared for her and embarrassed for her because I know that that is probably the worst conversation anyone can have with you.	Support: Categories 40–44 support previous work (e.g., Ball & Sims, 1991; Ball & Trevino, 1990; Trevino, 1992) which has suggested that the manager, the subordinate, and observers are likely to experience a variety of (primarily negative) emotions when punishing their subordinates.
41. Manager's positive and/or nonnegative affect (41)	I did not feel guilty anymore. When it was done. I felt terrific.	
42. Manager's general or mixed emotions (24)	I had mixed emotions. I was pleased and I was displeased at the same time.	

continues

541

TABLE 1 Continued

Theme and Category[a]	Example	Research Supported/New Contribution
43. Others'/co-workers' emotional reactions (71)	The other people in the class were initially very shocked.	Contribution: Categories 45 and 46 suggest that managers perceive that their punished subordinates experience positive as well as negative emotions. Category 47 indicates that managers believe that certain punishment situations require that they conceal their emotions. Category 48 suggests that managers perceive that punishment situations create an inherently emotional "atmosphere."
44. Subordinate's negative emotional reactions (98)	Since the employee was denying the charges . . . it made it very difficult, very embarrassing, and very unpleasant for the employee.	
45. Subordinate's positive and/or nonnegative affect (32)	He was pretty understanding. He did not have any hard feelings.	
46. Subordinate's mixed feelings/general feelings (8)	He was upset at first, but now he realizes that it was good. It has helped him.	
47. Manager's lack of feelings (20)	I approached it in that manner without any real emotions one way or the other. I was very hot, but did not let it show.	
48. Punishment atmosphere as emotional/tense (23)	It was a very emotional issue and touched a lot of people. There's always emotion when you discipline someone.	

[a]Figures in parentheses are frequencies, the total number of times a category appeared in the data.

subordinates' attitudes and behavior. In fact, their thoughts reach far beyond the subordinates to the instrumental impact on the managers (respect earned), other workers (vicarious learning accomplished), and the organization as a whole (organizational learning accomplished).

The largest of these categories was "manager's concern for/recognition of vicarious effects on co-workers," for which there were 139 representative statements. Many managers view punishment as an opportunity to promote vicarious learning (Bandura, 1977) by delivering a message to all of their subordinates that certain types of misconduct will not be tolerated. These vicarious effects of punishment incidents were recognized as important whether the managers decided to discipline or not. In the words of one interviewee, when discipline was imposed, other workers learned that "they can't get away with anything like that in the future" (category 6). Alternately, another manager said "If he was not fired, the employees would see that the management was lackadaisical" (category 7). Statements of both types show that managers are quite aware of the indirect learning effects of their punishment decisions.

Second, managers made statements regarding maintaining or increasing respect from subordinates and other employees (category 6). Punishment served to enhance perceptions of the managers as good and competent and improved working relations. As one manager said,

> This was one of the few, if only, incidents that I ever knew about where somebody was let go and I was the one to do it. . . . I think I gained the respect of a lot of people a lot more quickly than I would have just showing how good a manager I [am] in other ways. So I think it was good, I had other people responding . . . in time they knew I did the right thing . . . and I think they respected me and worked with me better afterwards.

Finally, managers said that they, their organizations, or both learned from the incidents (category 8): "I think it was a good learning experience for myself and all the managers." This finding represents an important subtheme embedded in the more general instrumental theme. This subtheme relates to the impact of punishment incidents on learning for the focal managers and subordinates, other subordinates, and the organizations. When something goes wrong (e.g., a rule is broken, a standard is not met) a manager has an opportunity to respond. Whether the response involves punishment or not, a number of people can learn from the incident, including the manager. Given the recent emphasis in the management literature on organizational learning, researchers may want to consider the role of discipline in the organizational learning process. It is important to note that this learning subtheme extends well beyond the narrow type of learning discussed in the conventional organizational behavior modification literature (e.g., Luthans & Kreitner, 1985).

In sum, these findings suggest that managers view punishment incidents as instrumental in achieving a broader set of objectives—respect, vicarious learning, and personal learning—than previous research has suggested. Although it is unclear whether managers intended to obtain these outcomes in advance or perceived them as post hoc benefits, managers clearly view punishment as instrumental in obtaining a variety of desirable outcomes beyond changing an individual subordinate's attitudes or behaviors.

Impression Management

Schlenker defined impression management as "the conscious or unconscious attempt to control images that are projected in social interactions" (1980, p. 6). We have labeled the second theme "impression management" because the categories under this theme represent managers' attempts to present a positive image to the interviewers—to demonstrate that they were doing what had to be done, knew what they were doing, and were justified in doing it. According to Leary and Kowalski's (1990) summary (for additional reviews, see Baumeister [1982], Schlenker [1980], and Tedeschi [1981]), impression management theorists maintain that organization members are "intuitive politicians" (Tetlock, 1985, p. 204), attempting to create an impression for both themselves and others that their intentions, decisions, and actions are fair, consistent, reasonable and legitimate (e.g., Greenberg, 1990). Researchers have yet to examine impression management as it relates to organizational punishment, despite the fact that punishment events provide fertile ground for the use of impression management tactics. This research provides the first empirical evidence in this area.

Schlenker and Weigold (1992) explored how people attempt to explain or account for events that challenge their desired social identities. When confronted by such a challenge, people often deal with it by constructing self-serving explanations (e.g., Tedeschi & Reiss, 1981), such as making excuses, offering justifications, and offering apologies (Schlenker & Wiegold, 1992). In addition, theorists have suggested a variety of tactics that managers use to manage impression of fairness, including excuses, justifications, apologies, attempts to take responsibility for positive events and their consequences, and attempts to augment the positive implications of their actions (e.g., Greenberg, 1990; Tedeschi & Melburg, 1984; Tedeschi & Norman, 1985).

The impression management tactics interviewees used generally corresponded to those discussed in the literature. For instance, managers offered a variety of justifications and explanations for why punishment was required (category 11). Most of the justifications pertained to subordinate rule breaking, unsatisfactory performance, or undesirable attitudes, such as lack of commitment or dedication. Examples of these justifications include the following:

> I felt my authority was being directly challenged.
> There were many things that led up to this person being an undesirable employee as far as work habits, attendance. . . .
> Her attitude was so bad and she was very insubordinate that night.

The largest impression management category (category 10) represented the managers' attempts to blame the employees for not doing their parts, despite the managers' attempts to do what was right. For example:

> We were very pleasant to him . . . but it was his own personal thing. He just was very lax and couldn't be motivated.
> I had really gone out of my way to help . . . and to have them come back and lie to me. . . .
> He was told that if it happened again, it would result in termination. . . . He really created his own destiny in that situation.

This last category suggests that managers see punishment as embedded in a reciprocal social process. Both manager and subordinate have to do their parts to maintain the job relationship. If a subordinate doesn't live up to his or her part of this implied agreement, but the manager has done so, the manager's punishment action becomes more justifiable.

Other managers justified their actions in terms of its ultimately benefiting the organization or the subordinate. For instance, after firing an employee, one manager remarked of him,

He wasn't happy here. He'd be happier in a place where there are direct customer relations.

Many managers also commented on their role responsibilities as representatives of their organizations (category 12). These comments struck a note of obligation. Examples include these statements:

> It is your job and something you have to do.
> It was just part of my job to find out his problems and find out if it was our fault. If it was or not, we needed to deal with it.
> I wasn't happy about doing it, that's for sure. But, I knew it had to be done. In business there's some hard decisions you have to make and there are many of them you don't like. And you do them anyway.

It is also interesting to note that managers often admitted making errors or admitted that situations could have been avoided (categories 15 and 16). This finding supports our general subtheme of learning; many managers recognized that they had made mistakes and suggested that they learned from the experience.

Consistent with Arvey and Ivancevich's (1980) research, these findings suggest that managers use a variety of impression management strategies to communicate their competence, both to themselves and to others. These managers provided a variety of reasons why the punishments were necessary and the subordinates were to blame. They also felt pressure to punish stemming from managerial role responsibilities and generally claimed that they did their best. When they made mistakes in the process, they learned from them.

Attributions

The attribution process refers to individuals' attempts to understand the causes of events, in this case the causes of the attitude or behavior problem that precipitated the punishment event. The presence of the attributions theme supports previous research (Mitchell et al., 1981), which demonstrated that managers form attributions regarding their subordinates' poor performance (categories 17 and 18). As in research on the actor-observer bias (Jones & Nisbett, 1972), in our findings the managers' attributions were much more frequently internal (frequency = 174) than external (frequency = 39). These internal (to the subordinates) causes of poor performance included age, attitudes, moods, irresponsibility, motivation, carelessness, laziness, physical or emotional problems, substance abuse, lack of ability, lack of knowledge, and lack of skills. For example:

> She was an alcoholic, and this precipitated the lost time, the lack of responsibility on her part, the tardiness, the whole issue.

External attributions included problems at home, peer pressure, role overload, differences in background or culture, and the specific circumstances preceding the incident. For example:

> I thought maybe [the infraction] was some kind of reaction to the loss of his wife.

As noted, most of the attributions were internal. The overwhelming internal focus of the attributions allowed managers to deflect responsibility for the problem away from themselves and convince the listener (and perhaps themselves) that they acted appropriately. Thus, these findings can be considered an extension of the previous impression management theme.

Awareness of and Concern for Subordinates

This theme contains two closely related subthemes: managers' awareness of the punished subordinates (their expectations, reactions, and so forth) and managers' concern for the punished subordinates' well-being. Previous literature suggests that when punishing a subordinate, a manager often considers factors that pertain to the subordinate's specific situation. These considerations include the subordinate's work history, the previous manager-subordinate relationship (Ball & Trevino, 1990; Fandt et al., 1990), and the seriousness of the subordinate's performance failure (Fairhurst et al., 1985; Mitchell et al., 1981). Our findings were generally consistent with this previous research, providing evidence that managers acknowledge subordinates and take them into account both in deciding whether to punish and in interpreting the punishment event. More specifically, these managers stated that they took subordinates' reactions—such as justice reactions (category 20)—and past work histories and past relationships with subordinates (category 21) into account when deciding whether (and to what degree) to punish them.

However, the findings indicated that managers consider a greater number of factors than previous research would suggest. Managers' statements suggested that subordinates sometimes accepted responsibility for their misconduct (category 23). For example, one manager said, "he realized that the problem was him, not the system." Further, some employees expected to be disciplined (category 22): "He said he knew it was coming." Finally, categories 25 and 26 suggested that managers are quite reluctant to punish their subordinates and are concerned about the subordinates as people with families and lives that will be affected. Statements representing this theme are:

> You are concerned and you always keep in the back of your mind that this is his livelihood.
> It was definitely a negative situation in the eyes of the employee that was terminated and it was one that I don't feel proud of, as far as putting somebody out on the street, somebody with a family and responsibilities just like the rest of us.

These results extend previous research in several ways that provide further evidence of managers' broad perspective on punishment situations. First, managers saw their subordinates as thinking human beings who sometimes expected punishment and took responsibility for their misconduct. This is far from the conventional behaviorist portrayal of subordinates as automatically having negative responses to punishment. Managers also portrayed their subordinates as feeling beings with families and responsibilities. These managers were clearly concerned with more than just the subordinates' performance, behaviors, and job attitudes; they were also concerned with their futures and livelihoods and the impact of the discipline on others close to them. This theme suggests that, for managers, the context surrounding punishment is wider than the workplace and that they view subordinates as much more than punishment targets. Managers came across as reluctant disciplinarians who were often sympathetic to the subordinates' family situations—aware that punishment can have far-reaching effects. Future researchers may wish to consider whether a subordinate's family status influences decisions about matters like the severity of a punishment and whether subordinates with families are given more opportunities to improve before being suspended or fired.

Awareness of and Concern for Co-Workers and Work Groups

In this theme, the focus of attention and concern shifts to other employees, particularly those in the immediate work group of a focal subordinate. The presence of this theme suggested that managers are well aware of others' (especially their other subordinates') reactions to punishment events. Managers believe that their other employees expect them to punish wrongdoing and see doing so as fair (categories 27–30). Exemplary statements included "A lot of people felt that he should have been fired immediately" and "The others felt that it was a fair decision and that their well-being was looked out for."

Trevino (1992) argued that organizational punishment should be viewed as a social phenomenon that typically also involves "third-party observers." These observers make sense of what they observe and its implications for themselves and their group. The data supported these contentions. It was clear that managers were aware that their other subordinates knew about the punishment situations and had opinions about and reactions to them.

One category was not explicitly addressed by previous work. Managers were also aware that, beyond their other workers, their entire organization could be affected by a problem employee who was not dealt with appropriately. Negative effects on morale, finances, and customers were mentioned (category 31). This category suggests that, from the manager's perspective, researchers should broaden their view of punishment even more, stretching beyond punished subordinates and other subordinates to the effect of misconduct and its handling on organizations and even customers.

Fairness Concerns

For the most part, past research drove our placement of categories within this theme. The organizational justice literature suggests that people evaluate fairness from two perspectives: distributive and procedural justice (e.g., Greenberg, 1987). Distributive justice concerns the fairness of outcome distributions (e.g., Adams, 1965). For example, to be distributively fair, punishment outcomes should be administered consistently across subordinates, situations, and time, and they should be clearly tied to (contingent on) the misconduct and administered at a level appropriate to it (Ball, Trevino, & Sims, 1994).

Procedural justice concerns the fairness of the decision-making process (e.g., Leventhal, Karuza, & Fry, 1980; Lind & Tyler, 1988; Thibaut & Walker, 1975). The punishment and procedural justice literatures have also suggested several procedural factors. For example, "constructive" punishment refers to managers' attempts to correct and improve undesirable subordinate behavior through techniques such as teaching, counseling, and constructive criticism (Baron, 1988). Writers on punishment have also long proposed that punishment should be carried out in private and in a timely manner (e.g., Arvey & Ivancevich, 1980; Arvey & Jones, 1985; Sims, 1980). Finally, research has shown that reactions to bad news are more positive when causal accounts (i.e., clear explanations) are given (e.g., Bies, Shapiro, & Cummings, 1988).

Our results were generally consistent with this literature. Managers did discuss topics that could be classified in terms of distributive and procedural fairness. For example, they talked about punishment contingency (category 32), equity (category 36), and severity (category 34), all notions reflecting distributive fairness. Touching on procedural fairness, they discussed constructiveness (category 33), privacy (category 35), and timing (category 37).

Two additional procedural categories seemed uniquely manager-centered. First, several managers expressed the need to be flexible when selecting punishment procedures. They felt that they should use judgment to consider individual circumstances and that they needed to make exceptions at times (category 39). Examples were,

> What if a good soldier made a mistake? What if a dud is continually making mistakes? . . . They don't deserve the same punishment even if they did the same crime.

> Some people you can counsel them and they will see the errors of their ways. Others you have to use more harsh punishment to get their attention.

Second, by far the largest fairness category (category 38) pertained to a general concern for following punishment procedures that either a union contract or a personnel department prescribed; such procedures include involving the personnel department, providing evidence and documentation, issuing warnings, and providing explanations. For instance, one interviewee said,

> I had the industrial relations people and my immediate supervisor put on notice that [the incident] was going on. We officially had the files adjusted to show that he was on probation. And, after the three months [probationary period]. . .we met again.

These results suggest that managers' concerns about fairness in punishment situations focus more on the procedural aspects than on distributive concerns. This conclusion is particularly interesting when compared to the work of Ball, Trevino, and Sims (1994), which suggested that punished subordinates are influenced more by distributive aspects of a disciplinary event—such as its severity and consistency—than by procedural issues.

Although previous research has linked punishment and fairness, it has not done so from a managerial perspective. The results of this research suggest that managers are clearly concerned about fairness. However, because organizational due process systems emphasize procedures (warnings, documentation, etc.), managers seem to be focusing more on those than on the distributive issues that may be most important to their subordinates. Thus, a mismatch may exist between managers' and punished subordinates' perceptions of punishment fairness. Future research should investigate this potential disparity and its consequences.

Punishment as an Emotional Experience

Finally, nine categories (40–48) provide the first empirical evidence of the highly charged emotional nature of punishment for managers, employees, and observers. The evidence suggests that managers perceived the atmosphere surrounding punishment episodes to be highly emotional (category 48), with most of the emotions being negative. However, managers did admit to having mixed emotions themselves (category 42) and acknowledged that punished subordinates sometimes experienced mixed or even positive emotions (categories 45 and 46) as a result of being disciplined.

Our data generally support previous conceptual work, in particular, Ball and Sims's (1991) suggestion that punishment is a complex cognitive and emotional process for managers as well as subordinates, and that the emotions involved are most likely negative. In these interviews, managers talked about their own feelings, and the feelings they expressed were overwhelmingly negative (132 statements regarding managers' negative affect compared to only 26 statements regarding positive or nonnegative affect). The following are some of the negative words and phrases managers used to describe how they felt:

> I was completely frustrated.
> I guess later I felt sorry for him.
> It made me angry.
> I must have been partially to blame . . . I was embarrassed.
> It's a bad feeling . . . You watch this person, you try to give your energy, your input . . . it's kind of like a failure on your part.

Several managers also talked about the punished subordinates' emotional reactions. Again, most of the discussion focused on the negative emotions generated by the punishment. Managers perceived the punished subordinates as experiencing a wide variety of emotions, including defensiveness, fear, discomfort, embarrassment, resentment, frustration, guilt, dissatisfaction, bitterness, disappointment, hostility, shock, fury, unhappiness, awkwardness, and anger.

Managers also made a large number of statements about the wide variety of emotions expressed by their other subordinates. Although usually negative, these emotions were not always so; positive emotions on the part of other subordinates, such as relief, pleasure, happiness, sympathy, surprise, and satisfaction, were also mentioned.

Finally, managers displayed an awareness of what might be termed the overall affective atmosphere surrounding the punishment incidents. These statements reflected employee moods that prevailed within an office at the time of the discipline as well as general, depersonalized statements regarding the "mood" of the incident.

Overall, these findings suggest that managers report primarily negative emotions surrounding the incidents but that managers, the punished subordinates, and other organizational members also occasionally experienced nonnegative (and even positive) emotions. This is the first study to document the highly charged emotions managers feel in punishment situations. The findings suggest that supervisory training should incorporate this knowledge to help managers deal more effectively with their own feelings and the feelings of others.

Differentiating between Effective and Ineffective Punishment Incidents

Our final goal was to find out how managers distinguished between effective and ineffective incidents. The overwhelming finding here is that most of the categories did not allow significant differentiation between effective and ineffective incidents, suggesting that managers think about the two in similar ways—they think about the instrumental outcomes, they feel the need to justify their behavior, they try to understand the causes of performance problems (attributions), they think about fairness and feelings and are concerned about the punished subordinates and what others will think and how they will react.

However, a few of the categories do offer differentiation between effective and ineffective incidents and are noteworthy. First, managers were more likely to discuss positive outcomes and the fact that the punishment worked in effective incidents (categories 1 and 2). Similarly, they were more likely to discuss negative outcomes and the fact that the punishment didn't work in ineffective incidents (categories 3 and 4). These findings clearly support the traditional instrumental view of punishment effectiveness.

Five additional categories (6, 9, 27, 32, and 39) represented types of statements managers were significantly more likely to make in disciplinary situations they identified as effective: They were more likely to discuss the respect gained from subordinates, to provide advice and to share their own theories of punishment effectiveness, and to acknowledge their other workers' reactions (e.g., co-workers' awareness of the misconduct and their desire to see something done about it). Managers also were more likely to use "if/then" contingency statements when discussing effective incidents, expressing a clear relationship between the misconduct and the punishment outcome. Finally, managers were more likely to talk about the need for flexibility in effective incidents. Thus, managers connect effective incidents with an awareness of work group expectations, concerns about disciplinary process issues such as flexibility, and instrumental relationships with a number of positive outcomes, including subordinate respect.

Only one additional category represented statements managers were significantly more likely to make in ineffective incidents. This was category 20, referring to knowledge of subordinates' reactions concerning justice or injustice. Most of the statements in that category referred to a subordinate's perception that she or he had been treated unfairly in the punishment incident. It appears managers connect ineffective punishment incidents with subordinates' injustice claims.

For each category, Table 2 displays (1) the number of managers who made more statements representing that category when discussing effective incidents than ineffective incidents, (2) the number of managers who made more statements representing that category when discussing ineffective incidents than effective incidents, and (3) the results of the McNemar test.

IMPLICATIONS FOR RESEARCH AND PRACTICE

Our further study and analysis of the findings contributed to the development of an inductive model of punishment from a managerial perspective that brings together variables addressed in previous research and variables that emerged from this study. Figure 1 graphically depicts the model. The "manager as disciplinarian" stands at its center. The model highlights the key relationships, influential variables, processes, and outcomes that are important to understanding punishment from a manager's perspective. It also suggests research and management implications beyond those already addressed.

In the more conventional subordinate-centered perspective on punishment, subordinates were the focus of decision-making concern, the key relationship was that between subordinate and supervisor, and the important outcomes were the subordinates' attitude and behavior changes and potential negative side effects. The manager-centered perspective suggests that managers view punishment in a broader and more complex manner than past work has suggested. As disciplinarians, managers experience cognitive and emotional complexity and participate in a set of important relationships; they are both influencing and being influenced by their organizations, work groups, subordinates, and selves.

Multiple Influences on Managers' Punishment Decisions

Managers making decisions about whether and how to punish are central to this model. The arrow pointing in the direction of the manager represents the various pressures placed on a person in this role regarding these decisions. Past research has suggested that managers' punishment decisions are influenced by variables that have to do with themselves (e.g., attributions), the subordinates involved (e.g., work history, performance failure, evidence of misconduct), and the relationship between the two parties (Fairhurst et al., 1985; Fandt et al., 1990; Mitchell et al., 1981). The model that emerged from this research expands the influences on managers' decision making considerably by incorporating influences of work group and organization and additional influences of the managers themselves.

TABLE 2   Comparison of Effective and Ineffective Incidents[a]

Category	Number of Managers Who Made More Such Statements about Effective Incidents	Number of Managers Who Made More Such Statements about Ineffective Incidents	χ^2
Instrumental nature of punishment			
1. Positive outcomes/punishment worked	53	5	39.72*
2. General positive outcomes	27	13	4.90*
3. Negative outcomes/punishment didn't work	2	19	13.76*
4. General negative outcomes	6	35	20.51*
5. Mixed outcomes (positive and negative)	9	14	1.09
6. Manager's desire for respect/integrity from subordinate and others	9	2	4.45*
7. Manager's concern for/recognition of vicarious effects on co-workers	18	19	0.03
8. Positive outcomes for manager/organization	2	6	2.00
Impression management			
9. Manager's implicit theories/advice regarding management/punishment	19	4	9.78*
10. Manager did his/her part, employee didn't respond/do his/her part	15	25	2.50
11. Manager justifications for/reasons for punishing	12	20	2.00
12. Manager's role responsibility	16	13	0.31
13. Manager searched for more information	8	5	0.69
14. Manager/management made no mistake/handled situation properly	13	12	0.04
15. Manager/organization made a mistake	11	10	0.05
16. Situation should never have happened/could have been avoided	8	9	0.06
Attributions			
17. Manager's understanding based upon internal attributions	19	22	0.22
18. Manager's understanding based upon external attributions	10	11	0.05
Awareness of and concern for subordinate			
19. Miscellaneous subordinate reactions	27	18	1.80
20. Knowledge of subordinate's justice/injustice reactions	3	11	4.57*
21. Positive history	11	9	0.20
22. Subordinate expected punishment	6	8	0.29
23. Subordinate accepted responsibility for wrongdoing	12	7	1.32

continues

TABLE 2   Continued

Category	Number of Managers Who Made More Such Statements about Effective Incidents	Number of Managers Who Made More Such Statements about Ineffective Incidents	χ^2
24. Subordinate did not accept discipline/responsibility	9	9	0.00
25. Manager's interest in/concern for person/ family/livelihood	16	10	1.38
26. Manager's reluctance to punish	20	12	2.00
Awareness of and concern for co-workers/others			
27. Co-workers'/others' nonemotional reactions to punishment	15	6	3.86*
28. Co-workers'/others' knowledge of/reaction to misconduct	8	16	2.67
29. Co-workers'/others' knowledge of/expectations of punishment	7	7	0.00
30. Knowledge of others'/co-workers' justice/injustice reactions	10	7	0.53
31. Manager's concern for organization	20	12	2.00
Fairness concerns			
32. Concern for punishment contingency	19	7	5.54*
33. Concern for constructiveness	11	12	0.04
34. Concern about punishment severity	8	6	0.29
35. Concern for privacy	15	13	0.14
36. Concern for equity/consistency	3	2	0.20
37. Concern for timing/timeliness	3	1	1.00
38. Concern about punishment procedures	30	26	0.29
39. Punishment should be flexible	16	4	7.20*
Emotions			
40. Manager's negative emotions	26	20	0.78
41. Manager's positive and/or nonnegative affect	13	7	1.80
42. Manager's general or mixed emotions	7	4	0.82
43. Others'/co-workers' emotional reactions	10	18	2.29
44. Subordinate's negative emotional reactions	18	22	0.40
45. Subordinate's positive and/or nonnegative affect	9	7	0.25
46. Subordinate's mixed feelings/general feelings	3	2	0.20
47. Manager's lack of feelings (e.g., no emotion, calm)	4	7	0.82
48. Punishment atmosphere as emotional/tense	5	6	0.09

[a]$N = 76$. The chi-square results are based on the McNemar test (Daniel, 1990).
*$p < .05$

FIGURE 1 **An Inductive Model of Punishment from the Manager's Perspective**

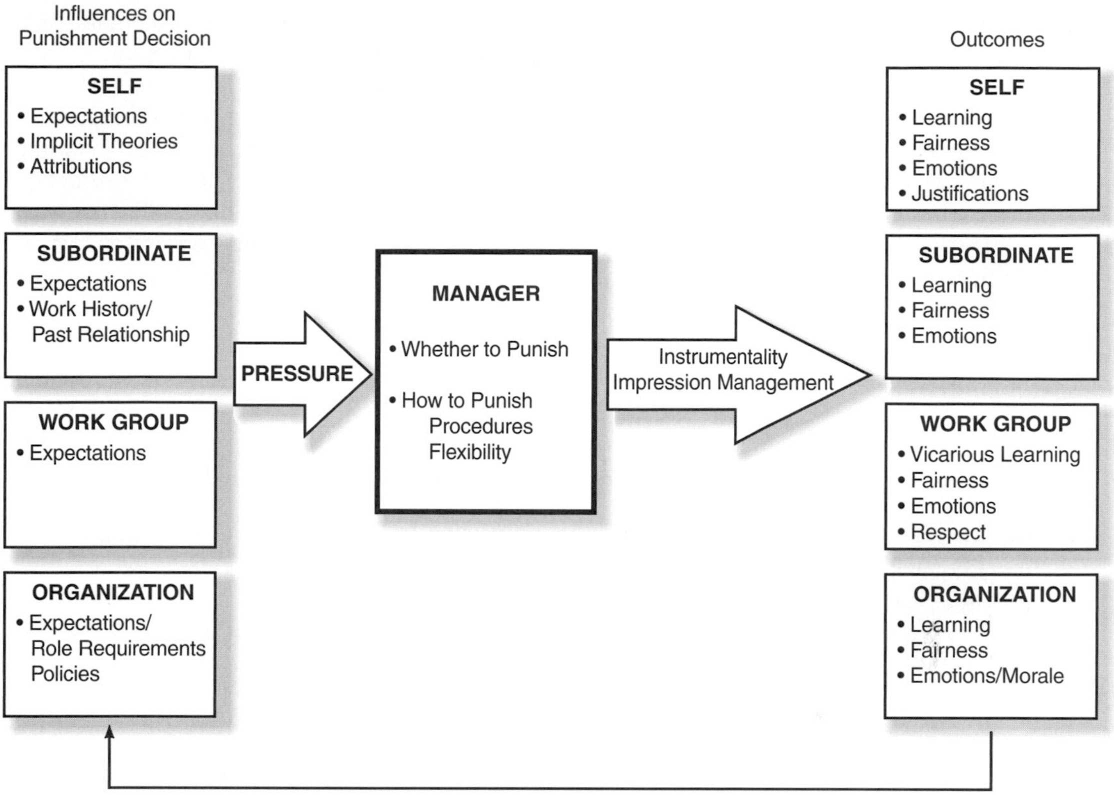

Influences on
Punishment Decision

Outcomes

SELF
• Expectations
• Implicit Theories
• Attributions

SUBORDINATE
• Expectations
• Work History/
  Past Relationship

PRESSURE

MANAGER

• Whether to Punish

• How to Punish
  Procedures
  Flexibility

WORK GROUP
• Expectations

Instrumentality
Impression Management

ORGANIZATION
• Expectations/
  Role Requirements
  Policies

SELF
• Learning
• Fairness
• Emotions
• Justifications

SUBORDINATE
• Learning
• Fairness
• Emotions

WORK GROUP
• Vicarious Learning
• Fairness
• Emotions
• Respect

ORGANIZATION
• Learning
• Fairness
• Emotions/Morale

A common influential variable, operating at multiple levels, is expectations, many of which push managers in the direction of punishing. A manager's own expectations are derived from implicit theories of good management and disciplinary practice that can affect the decision to punish or not to punish as well as the punishment process. These expectations, combined with overwhelmingly internal attributions, generally push the manager to punish. In addition, subordinates have expectations that are based upon their histories and relationships with their supervisors. Somewhat surprisingly, subordinates sometimes expect to be punished. Work group members also expect that rule violators will be punished and that managers will fulfill the disciplinary part of their role, and managers are very aware of these expectations. Finally, organizations create and impose managerial role requirements as well as disciplinary policies and procedures that managers feel compelled to carry out. Therefore, managers see themselves as pressured by expectations from multiple sources and levels, many of which seem to be pushing them toward punishing.

Decisions about how to punish are also influenced by these expectations, particularly by managers' concerns with following organizational policy and procedures at the same time they are trying to be flexible and to consider their subordinates' specific circumstances. In making these decisions, managers are aware that their other subordinates, the punished subordinate, and the organization will all evaluate their actions.

An Array of Punishment Outcomes

In Figure 1, the arrow pointing from the manager to outcomes represents instrumentality and impression management, two prominent mechanisms by which managers' punishment decisions affect themselves, punished subordinates, work groups, and organizations. Previous approaches to punishment represented a narrow instrumental view, focusing on the effects of punishment on a subordinate's subsequent attitudes and behaviors, in particular on avoiding negative side effects. This research suggests that managers see punishment as instrumental in accomplishing a wider variety of goals related to multiple constituencies. The view of managers goes beyond the obvious instrumentality of punishment's effects on subsequent attitudes and behaviors; managers see punishment incidents as highly charged cognitive and emotional events with far-ranging implications for a variety of outcomes, including—but not limited to—learning, fairness perceptions, emotions, respect, and employee morale.

Learning is a common instrumental outcome that emerged across multiple levels. First, as did previous researchers, we found that managers believed that punished subordinates could benefit from punishment experiences and were likely to have improved work performance. Second, managers were concerned about the messages they were sending to the rest of their subordinates by their actions. Perhaps most important is managers' awareness of the vicarious learning that took place as a result of their decisions to either punish or not to punish. Finally, managers considered their own potential to learn from the events as well as the potential for organizational learning.

Managers were also aware of and concerned about fairness issues at multiple levels. In contrast to subordinates' tendency to focus on issues of distributive justice, managers' own fairness concerns tended to focus on procedural issues, such as whether organizational policies and procedures were followed. Managers were also frequently aware of and concerned about the fairness perceptions of punished subordinates, their work groups, and their larger organizations.

Evidently, managers are aware that punishment is a highly salient issue and that their actions can influence the impressions they make on all of their workers. As a result, punishment situations offer more to managers than a means for achieving desired outcomes; punishment situations also present opportunities for impression management.

Finally, managers are also aware of and concerned about emotional reactions (which they perceive as mostly negative) to highly charged punishment events. These reactions range from their own reactions through those of the punished subordinates and their work groups to morale in general. All of these outcomes—learning, fairness perceptions, emotions—then feed back into ongoing expectations and punishment decision-making processes.

Implications for Future Research and Management Practice

This research, grounded in managers' punishment experiences, has contributed to knowledge about organizational punishment by supporting previous theory and research and by providing a broader and deeper understanding of punishment from a manager's perspective. Numerous insights emerged from the data, several of which offer potential avenues for future research.

One way to draw implications from the model is to consider what these managers did not discuss. For example, it was interesting to note that the managers interviewed for this study talked little about the negative side effects of punishment that are so much a focus of the previous literature. Admittedly, the impression management category suggests that managers were trying to put a positive face on an unpleasant task. However, the managers discussed an equal number of effective and ineffective incidents. Therefore, it remains somewhat surprising that there was little discussion of problems such as sabotage or workplace violence resulting from punishment. Discussion of subordinates' negative emotional reactions comes closest to capturing this conventional concern. However, managers were almost as concerned with their other workers' emotional reactions as they were with those of the punished subordinates.

Also, managers did not talk about their peers or their superiors. The data suggest that managers don't discuss disciplinary problems or practices with other managers. And, although they often referred to their organizations (their expectations, policies, and learning outcomes), the managers' superiors were surprisingly absent from the discussion, suggesting that disciplinary practices may not be an important part of their superiors' evaluations of them. In general, these managers came across as isolated decision makers who reluctantly made tough disciplinary decisions without seeking or receiving guidance or input from their peers or superiors.

In addition, because managers in this study talked about situations in which they decided to punish, the data don't address situations in which they decided to ignore a problem situation or to take some action other than punishment. Therefore, for an even broader understanding, future research should consider the restraining factors that keep managers from punishing. Asking managers to talk about performance problems and how they dealt with them might provide insight into alternatives to or substitutes for punishment that managers may use when struggling with disciplinary problems.

We can also draw a number of implications by examining what managers did discuss. First, future research should reflect the expanded perspective offered by this model. For example, attempts to predict a manager's decision to punish should include multilevel influences from organizational punishment procedures, work group expectations and concerns about vicarious learning, and the more typical variables such as attributions and subordinates' characteristics and past work performance. Studies of punishment outcomes (justice perceptions, emotions, impressions) should take into account work group reactions and organizational outcomes as well as subordinate reactions. Also, a more complete multiperspective understanding of punishment incidents will require that data be collected from multiple parties involved in a disciplinary event (Ball et al., 1994).

Future studies may also wish to explore in more depth managers' implicit theories of what constitutes good disciplinary practice and what managers think they can do to make a good impression on others. Ferris, Russ, and Fandt (1989) suggested that impression management is more likely to occur when few constraints prevent it, when there is uncertainty and ambiguity, and when actors are self-conscious. Therefore, these interview situations represented nearly ideal circumstances for impression management. However, it would be particularly interesting for future investigations to consider the impression management tactics managers might use with different audiences with an interest in a punishment event.

Explanations and justifications for punishment are an additional avenue for future research. These managers provided a variety of explanations and justifications to the interviewers. But the data did not capture the explanations and justifications provided to punished subordinates and to work groups. The procedural justice literature suggests that explanations can improve reactions to bad news or negative outcomes (e.g., Bies et al., 1988), but the organizational punishment literature has just begun to explore this effect (Ball et al., 1994). Future investigations may wish to consider the types of explanations and justifications managers are likely to provide in different punishment situations and the effects of these on outcomes for different constituencies.

We see this study as providing input to management training that has taken a rather narrow view of punishment in the past. Managers have been provided with a list of dos and don'ts that focus on finding alternatives to punishment if at all possible and on avoiding negative side effects stemming from actions of punished subordinates if punishment becomes necessary. This research suggests that managers should be educated to view punishment in a much more complex manner, taking into account work group and organizational expectations, as well as those of punished subordinates. Further, it may help managers to understand the wide variety of potential outcomes of a punishment event, including the potential for learning at all levels.

References

Adams. J. S. 1965. Inequity in social exchange. In L. Berkowitz (Ed.), *Advances in experimental social psychology*, vol. 2: 267–299. New York: Free Press.

Arvey, R. D., & Ivancevich, J. M. 1980. Punishment in organizations: A review, propositions, and research suggestions. *Academy of Management Review*, 5: 123–132.

Arvey, R. D., & Jones, A. P. 1985. The use of discipline in organizational settings: A framework for future research. In B. M. Staw & L. L. Cummings (Eds.), *Research in organizational behavior*, vol. 7: 367–408. Greenwich, CT: JAI Press.

Ball, G. A., & Sims, H. P. 1991. A conceptual analysis of cognition and affect in organizational punishment. *Human Resource Management Review*, 1: 227–243.

Ball, G. A., & Trevino, L. K. 1990. *Leader reactions to punishing subordinates: Justice evaluations and emotional responses*. Paper presented at the annual meeting of the Academy of Management, San Francisco.

Ball, G. A., Trevino, L. K., & Sims, H. P. 1994. Just and unjust punishment: Influences on subordinate performance and citizenship. *Academy of Management Journal*, 37: 299–322.

Bandura, A. 1977. *Social learning theory*. Englewood Cliffs, NJ: Prentice Hall.

Baron, R. A. 1988. Negative effects of destructive criticism: Impact on conflict, self-efficacy, and task performance. *Journal of Applied Psychology*, 73: 199–207.

Bartol, K. M., & Martin, D. C. 1994. *Management* (2nd ed.). New York: McGraw-Hill.

Baumeister, R. F. 1982. A self-presentation view of social phenomena. *Psychological Bulletin*, 91: 3–26.

Bies, R. J., Shapiro, D. L., & Cummings, L. L. 1988. Causal accounts and managing organizational conflict. *Communication Research*, 15: 381–399.

Daft, R. L. 1994. *Management* (3rd ed.). Fort Worth, TX: Dryden Press.

Fairhurst, G. T., Gelen, S. G., & Snavely, B. K. 1985. Managerial control and discipline: Whips and chains. In M. McLaughlin (Ed.), *Communication yearbook*: 558–593. Beverly Hills, CA: Sage.

Fandt, P. M., Labig, C. E., & Urich, A. L. 1990. Evidence and the liking bias: Effects on managers' disciplinary actions. *Employee Responsibilities and Rights Journal*, 3(4): 253–265.

Ferris, G. R., Russ, G. S., & Fandt, P. M. 1989. Politics in organizations. In R. A. Giacalone & P. Rosenfeld (Eds.), *Impression management in the organization*: 143–170. Hillsdale, NJ: Erlbaum.

Greenberg, J. 1987. A taxonomy of organizational justice theories. *Academy of Management Review*, 12: 9–22.

Greenberg, J. 1990. Looking fair vs. being fair: Managing impressions of organizational justice. In B. M. Staw & L. L. Cummings (Eds.), *Research in organizational behavior*, vol. 12: 111–157, Greenwich, CT: JAI Press.

Griffin, R. W. 1993. *Management* (4th ed.). Boston: Houghton Mifflin.

Jones, E. E., & Nisbett, R. E. 1972. The actor and the observer: Divergent perceptions of the causes of behavior. In E. E. Jones, D. E. Kanouse, H. H. Kelley, R. E. Nisbett, S. Valins, & B. Weiner (Eds.), *Attribution: Perceiving the causes of behavior:* 79–94. Morristown, NJ: General Learning Press.

Leary, M. R., & Kowalski, R. M. 1990. Impression management: A literature review and two-component model. *Psychological Bulletin,* 107: 34–47.

Leventhal, G. S., Karuza, J., & Fry, W. R. 1980. Beyond fairness: A theory of allocation preferences. In G. Mikula (Ed.), *Justice and social interactions:* 167–218. New York: Springer-Verlag.

Lind, E. A., & Tyler, T. R. 1988. *The social psychology of procedural justice.* New York: Plenum.

Luthans, F., & Kreitner, R. 1985. *Organizational behavior modification and beyond.* Glenview, IL: Scott, Foresman.

Mitchell, T. R., Green, S. G., & Wood, R. E. 1981. An attributional model of leadership and the poor performing subordinate: Development and validation. In B. M. Staw & L. L. Cummings (Eds.), *Research in organizational behavior,* vol. 3: 197–234. Greenwich, CT: JAI Press.

O'Reilly, C. A., III, & Puffer, S. 1989. The impact of rewards and punishments in a social context: A laboratory and field experiment. *Journal of Occupational Psychology,* 62: 41–53.

Podsakoff, P. M. 1982. Determinants of a supervisor's use of rewards and punishments: A literature review and suggestions for further research. *Organizational Behavior and Human Performance,* 29: 58–83.

Schlenker, B. R. 1980. *Impression management: The self-concept, social identity, and interpersonal relations.* Monterey, CA: Brooks/Cole.

Schlenker, B. R., & Weigold, M. F. 1992. Interpersonal processes involving impression regulation and management. In

M. R. Rosenzweig & L. W. Porter (Eds.), *Annual review of psychology,* vol. 43: 131–168. Palo Alto, CA: Annual Reviews.

Schnake, M. E. 1986. Vicarious punishment in a work setting. *Journal of Applied Psychology,* 71: 343–345.

Schnake, M. E. 1987. Vicarious punishment in a work setting: A failure to replicate. *Psychological Reports,* 71: 379–386.

Sims, H. P. 1980. Further thoughts on punishment in organizations. *Academy of Management Review,* 5: 133–138.

Tedeschi, J. T. 1981. *Impression management theory and social psychological research.* New York: Academic Press.

Tedeschi, J. T., & Melburg, V. 1984. Impression management and influence in the organization. In S. B. Bachrach & E. J. Lawler (Eds.), *Research in the sociology of organizations,* vol. 3: 31–58. Greenwich, CT: JAI Press.

Tedeschi, J. T., & Norman, N. 1985. Social power, self-presentation, and the self. In B. R. Schlenker (Ed.), *The self and social life:* 293–322. New York: McGraw-Hill.

Tedeschi, J. T., & Reiss, M. 1981. Verbal strategies in impression management. In C. Antaki (Ed.), *The psychology of ordinary explanations of social behavior:* 271–309. London: Academic.

Tetlock, P. E. 1985. Toward an intuitive politician model of attribution processes. In B. R. Schlenker (Ed.), *The self and social life:* 203–234. New York: McGraw-Hill.

Thibaut, J., & Walker, J. 1975. *Procedural justice: A psychological analysis.* Hillsdale, NJ: Erlbaum.

Trevino, L. K. 1992. The social effects of punishment in organizations: A justice perspective. *Academy of Management Review,* 17: 647–676.

Appendix

Interview Protocol

(1) Incident background. Tell me in your own words the background of the incident. In other words, how did this incident come about? What led up to it? (If the following questions are not answered, ask:)

Who was involved?
What were their relationships?
What led up to the incident?

What was the person being disciplined for?
What was the infraction?
Was it a formal rule or a more informal norm that was broken?
Was it a first or repeat offense?

(2) The incident. Now, thinking about the same disciplinary incident, tell me what happened. In other words, how was the discipline carried out? (If the following questions are not answered, ask:)

What did the discipliner say or do?
What did the disciplinee say or do?
Who knew about it? How did they find out?
Were other people involved? How?
What form did the discipline take (verbal reprimand, suspension, demotion, termination, etc.)?

(3) Emotions. Continuing to think about the same incident, please describe the emotions and feelings that surround the incident. How did you feel about it? Why? How did others feel about it? Why? (be sure to get at the *whys*)

Was it fair, just, appropriate? Why?
Would some other disciplinary action have been more appropriate? Why?
Were you pleased, happy? Why?
How did the person being disciplined feel? Why?
How did others feel? Why?

(4) Outcomes. What was (were) the outcomes of this disciplinary incident? Why do you think it turned out the way it did?

What were the positive outcomes? Why were they positive?
What were the negative outcomes, if any? Why were they negative?
Did the discipline have the intended effect? Why?
Did the person's behavior improve? Why?
Did the discipline help to clarify the person's job?
Did the discipline help to clarify what is appropriate/inappropriate behavior?

Chapter **Eleven**

Motivating Creativity and Innovation

Today's competitive organizations are increasingly characterized by employees at all levels who bring new ideas and solutions to the challenges of the workplace. These ideas could be for a new product or technology, a new manufacturing process, a refinement on an existing product, an improved service, or a new way to retain valued employees. Without this creativity and innovation, many organizations would cease to exist in an increasingly turbulent environment. As a result, efforts to motivate employees to be more creative or innovative on the job emerge as a critical managerial responsibility.

Creativity is the process by which individuals or groups develop unique ideas or novel solutions to emerging problems. Creativity involves developing new ways of thinking or acting on both existing and emerging challenges. Innovation, by contrast, focuses on the successful implementation of creative or new ideas. Creativity and innovation work together to help facilitate organizational effectiveness by enhancing an organization's return on investment in its human resources.

The creative process can be described in several ways. One approach describes creativity as beginning with the recognition of a problem or opportunity. Once the issue has been identified, efforts are made to gather relevant information that can help resolve the issue. This, in turn, leads to the identification or generation of possible creative solutions. A decision is then made among the possible alternatives about which potential solution best fits the problem. Finally, efforts are made to implement the new idea.

A second approach to understanding creativity involves a four-step process beginning with *preparation,* including problem identification and data gathering; *incubation,* or reflection on the problem and its underlying causes; *insight,* or the identification of possible solutions; and *verification,* or confirmation that the new solution actually works. Both models essentially describe the same general process.

In reality, however, the creative process is not so simple or straightforward as is suggested by these models. Creativity is much more of an intuitive and interactive process than a rational and linear one. Sometimes, no solutions emerge to solve the problem. Other times, potential solutions lead to dead ends or prove to be infeasible. This often leads to frustrations and conflicts and questions concerning the desirability of staying the course. Ironically, it is this frustration that often leads to the final and most suitable solution to a problem. Hence, the challenge for employees and managers alike is how to keep people motivated or on track to seek the best new ideas.

The research literature on creativity has consistently demonstrated that creative behavior tends to result from a combination of individual difference characteristics and situational characteristics. Some individuals are naturally predisposed to be more creative than others. At the same time, some work environments tend to stimulate and reward greater creativity than others. The goal for the manager is to understand both of these sets of factors and to merge them in ways that maximize the chances for success. This is clearly not an easy task. This interplay between individuals and situations forms the basis for the readings that follow.

OVERVIEW OF THE READINGS

In the first reading, Teresa Amabile builds on research focusing on intrinsic motivation to develop a componential theory of both individual and organizational innovation based on three key factors: expertise, creative thinking, and intrinsic task motivation. It is argued that these factors create the most conducive work environments for creative activities, and that managers play a crucial role in developing and sustaining such environments.

This is followed by a second reading by Anne Cummings and Greg Oldham that likewise focuses on the interplay between individuals and work environments in the creative endeavor. Cummings and Oldham identify variations in employee problem-solving styles as well as personality types that either help or hinder the creative process. Next, the authors examine the motivational potential of various work contexts. Important factors in this regard include the extent of job complexity, supportive supervision, and stimulating team members. Two studies examine how this model can apply and what managers can do to improve creativity processes in their own organizations.

References

Amable, T. M. (1988). A model of creativity and innovation in organizations. In B. M. Staw and L. L. Cummings (Eds.), *Research in Organizational Behavior.* Greenwich, CT: JAI Press, 123–167.

Baron, F. B., and Harrington, D. M. (1981). Creativity, intelligence, and personality. *Annual Review of Psychology, 32,* 439–479.

Kabanoff, B., and Rossiter, J. R. (1994). Recent developments in applied creativity. *International Review of Industrial and Organizational Psychology, 9,* 283–324.

Parv, V. (1998). The idea toolbox: Techniques for being a more creative writer. *Writer's Digest, 78,* 18.

Woodman, R. W., Sawyer, J. E., and Griffin, R. W. (1993). Toward a theory of organizational creativity. *Academy of Management Review, 18,* 293–321.

Woodman, R. W., and Schoenfeldt, L. F. (1989). Individual differences in creativity: An interactionist perspective. In J.A. Glover, R. R. Ronning, and C. R. Reynolds (Eds.), *Handbook of Creativity.* New York: Plenum Press, 77–92.

Motivating Creativity in Organizations: On Doing What You Love and Loving What You Do

Teresa M. Amabile

Arthur Schawlow, winner of the Nobel prize in physics in 1981, was once asked what, in his opinion, made the difference between highly creative and less creative scientists. He replied, "The labor of love aspect is important. The most successful scientists often are not the most talented. But they are the ones who are impelled by curiosity. They've got to know what the answer is."[1] Schawlow's insights about scientific creativity highlight the importance of *intrinsic motivation:* the motivation to work on something because it is interesting, involving, exciting, satisfying, or personally challenging. There is abundant evidence that people will be most creative when they are primarily intrinsically motivated, rather than extrinsically motivated by expected evaluation, surveillance, competition with peers, dictates from superiors, or the promise of rewards.[2]

Interestingly, this Intrinsic Motivation Principle of Creativity applies not only to scientific creativity, but to business creativity as well. Often, financial success is closely tied to a passion for the work itself. Michael Jordan, who by the mid-1990s was the most financially successful basketball player in history, insisted on a "love of the game" clause in his contract—securing for him the right to play in "pick-up" games whenever he wished. Robert Carr, a primary developer of the first pen computer, was captivated by the opportunity to do something spectacular that had never been done before. When entrepreneur Jerry Kaplan described the idea to him, Carr reacted with intense excitement: "Jerry, it's not a question of *whether* I want to do this. I *have* to do this. This is important. This is profound. . . . It's not very often that opportunities like this come along—something really big, a chance to really make a difference. Maybe once a decade or so. I think you've got one here."[3]

When Steve Wozniak invented the micro-computer, he demonstrated creativity in new product development; for all intents and purposes, such a thing had not existed before. When Walt Disney created Disneyland, he demonstrated creativity in new service development; he essentially invented a new form of entertainment. Although most people think of creativity in business as limited to the creation of something new to sell, there are other forms as well. When Fred Smith developed the concept for Federal Express, he certainly was not inventing a new service or a new product; humans had been delivering messages and packages to each other for thousands of years. In this instance, the creativity resided in the system for delivery: a hub system, where all packages were flown to Memphis on the same day, sorted, and distributed for air delivery the next day. Creativity exists in less famous, more humble, examples as well: the ad campaign that revitalizes a dying brand, or the product line extension that captures additional market share.

At its heart, creativity is simply the production of novel, appropriate ideas in *any* realm of human activity, from science, to the arts, to education, to business, to everyday life. The ideas must be novel—different from what's been done before—but they can't be simply

From *California Management Review,* 1997, 40(1), 39–58. Reprinted by permission.

bizarre; they must be appropriate to the problem or opportunity presented. Creativity is the first step in innovation, which is the successful implementation of those novel, appropriate ideas. And innovation is absolutely vital for long-term corporate success. Because the business world is seldom static, and because the pace of change appears to be rapidly accelerating, no firm that continues to deliver the same products and services in the same way can long survive. By contrast, firms that prepare for the future by implementing new ideas oriented toward this changing world are likely to thrive.[4]

INDIVIDUAL CREATIVITY

To some extent, intrinsic motivation resides in a person's own personality.[5] Some people are more strongly driven than others by the enjoyment and sense of challenge in their work. For example, Pablo Casals was driven by passion for the cello from the day he first heard the instrument played: "I had never heard such a beautiful sound before. A radiance filled me. I said, 'Father, that is the most wonderful instrument I have ever heard. That is what I want to play.'"[6] The novelist John Irving, in explaining his motivation to write for up to 14 hours in a single day, said, "The unspoken factor is love. The reason I can work so hard at my writing is that it's not work for me."[7]

Although part of intrinsic motivation depends on personality, my students, colleagues, and I have discovered in 20 years of research that a person's social environment can have a significant effect on that person's level of intrinsic motivation at any point in time; the level of intrinsic motivation can, in turn, have a significant effect on that person's creativity. Einstein described the dampening effect of a militaristic classroom environment on his own intrinsic motivation when he said, "This coercion had such a deterring effect upon me that, after I had passed the final examination, I found the consideration of any scientific problems distasteful for an entire year."[8] He later concluded, "It is a very grave mistake to think that the enjoyment of seeing and searching can be promoted by means of coercion and a sense of duty."[9]

Much of the evidence on this connection between the social environment, intrinsic motivation, and creativity comes from controlled laboratory experiments.[10] In one such study, for example, college students were presented with a simple artistic creativity task—making a paper collage with a standard set of materials.[11] Half of the students were randomly assigned to a condition where they were offered a reward (money) for making the collage, and half were simply given the collage activity to do. In addition, half within each group were given a choice; they were asked whether they would agree to make the collage in order to get the money (in the choice/reward condition), or they were simply asked whether they wanted to make the collage (in the choice/non-reward condition). Students in the no-choice condition were not offered any choice in the matter; those in the no-choice/reward condition were simply presented with the reward as a bonus, and those in the no-choice/non-reward condition were simply given the collage task.

The results were quite clear and striking. The students who had essentially made a contract to do the activity in order to get the reward (choice/reward condition) exhibited strikingly lower levels of creativity in their collages than the other three groups. The "means-end" work environment—"Do this task as a means to the end of getting this reward"—appears to have undermined their creativity. In contrast, however, those students who received the reward as a bonus showed no diminishment in creativity. In fact, their creativity was *higher* than those of the other groups. And, in keeping with the Intrinsic Motivation Principle of Creativity, students' creativity was correlated with their reported interest in the collage activity; the more interested they were, the more creative their collages were judged by art experts. Thus, it was not the *fact* of reward, but the *perception* of reward (resulting from the way in which it was presented) that made the difference.

Another experiment addressed the Intrinsic Motivation hypothesis even more directly. In this study, young creative writers were asked to fill out a short questionnaire before writing a poem.[12] The questionnaire was designed to have them focus on either their intrinsic reasons for being a writer (such as getting a lot of pleasure out of something good that you have written) or their extrinsic reasons for being a writer (such as getting rich and famous). (Participants in a control condition filled out an unrelated, non-motivational questionnaire.) They then wrote poems, which were later judged by experts in creative writing. The writers in the intrinsic condition and the control condition wrote poems that were judged as quite creative, on average. However, those who had focused for just a few minutes on the extrinsic motivations for their work wrote poems that were significantly less creative.

THE COMPONENTIAL THEORY OF INDIVIDUAL CREATIVITY

According to conventional wisdom, creativity is something done by creative people. Even creativity researchers, for several decades, seemed to guide their work by this principle, focusing predominantly on individual differences: What are creative people like, and how are they different from most people in the world? Although this person-centered approach yielded some important findings about the backgrounds, personality traits, and work styles of outstandingly creative people,[13] it was both limited and limiting. It offered little to practitioners concerned with helping people to become more creative in their work, and it virtually ignored the role of the social environment in creativity and innovation. In contrast to the traditional approach, the Componential Theory of Creativity assumes that all humans with normal capacities are able to produce at least moderately creative work in some domain, some of the time—and that the social environment (the work environment) can influence both the level and the frequency of creative behavior.

The theory includes three major components of individual (or small team) creativity, each of which is necessary for creativity in any given domain: expertise, creative-thinking skill, and intrinsic task motivation (see Figure 1).[14] The componential theory suggests that creativity is most likely to occur when people's skills overlap with their strongest intrinsic interests—their deepest passions—and that creativity will be higher, the higher the level of each of the three components. This is the "creativity intersection" depicted in Figure 1.

Expertise

Expertise is the foundation for all creative work. It can be viewed as the set of cognitive pathways that may be followed for solving a given problem or doing a given task—the problem solver's "network of possible wanderings."[15] The expertise component includes memory for factual knowledge, technical proficiency, and special talents in the target work domain—such as expertise in gene splicing, or in computer simulation, or in strategic management. For example, a high-tech engineer's expertise includes his innate talent for imagining and thinking about complex engineering problems, as well as focusing in on the

FIGURE 1   **3 Component Model of Creativity**

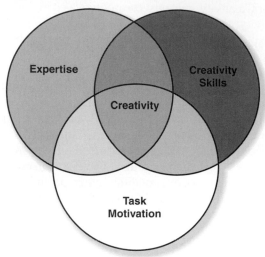

important aspects of those problems; his factual knowledge about electronics; his familiarity with past work and current developments in high-tech engineering; and the technical skills he has acquired in designing, carrying out, and interpreting research.

Creative Thinking

This component provides that "something extra" of creative performance.[16] Assuming that a person has some incentive to perform an activity, performance will be "technically good" or "adequate" or "acceptable" if the requisite expertise is in place. However, even with expertise at an extraordinarily high level, the person will not produce creative work if creative thinking skills are lacking. These skills include a cognitive style favorable to taking new perspectives on problems, an application of techniques (or "heuristics") for the exploration of new cognitive pathways, and a working style conducive to persistent, energetic pursuit of one's work.

Creative thinking depends to some extent on personality characteristics related to independence, self-discipline, orientation toward risk-taking, tolerance for ambiguity, perseverance in the face of frustration, and a relative lack of concern for social approval.[17] However, creativity skills can be increased by the learning and practice of techniques to improve cognitive flexibility and intellectual independence.

An engineer's arsenal of creativity skills might include his ability to break out of a preconceived perception or expectation when examining testing results, his tolerance for ambiguity in the process of deciding on the appropriate interpretation for puzzling data, his ability to suspend judgment as he considers different approaches, and his ability to break out of strict algorithms for attacking a problem. He might also have learned to employ some of the creativity heuristics described by theorists: "When all else fails, try something counterintuitive;"[18] or "Make the familiar strange."[19] Finally, if he is productively creative, his work style is probably marked by an ability to concentrate effort for long periods of time[20] and an ability to abandon unproductive strategies, temporarily putting aside stubborn problems.[21]

Intrinsic Task Motivation

Although the two skill components determine what a person is capable of doing in a given domain, it is the task motivation component that determines what that person actually will do. Motivation can be either intrinsic (driven by deep interest and involvement in the work, by curiosity, enjoyment, or a personal sense of challenge) or extrinsic (driven by the desire to attain some goal that is apart from the work itself—such as achieving a promised reward or meeting a deadline or winning a competition). Although combinations of intrinsic and extrinsic motivation are common, one is likely to be primary for a given person doing a given task. A number of studies have shown that a primarily intrinsic motivation will be more conducive to creativity than a primarily extrinsic motivation.

Task motivation makes the difference between what an engineer can do and what he will do. The former depends on his levels of expertise and creative thinking skills. But it is his task motivation that determines the extent to which he will fully engage his expertise and creative thinking skills in the service of creative performance. To some extent, a high degree of intrinsic motivation can even make up for a deficiency of expertise or creative thinking skills. A highly intrinsically motivated person is likely to draw skills from other domains, or apply great effort to acquiring necessary skills in the target domain.[22]

Although a person's development of expertise and practice of creative thinking skills can be influenced to some extent by the social environment, the strongest and most direct influence of the environment is probably on motivation. Certainly, a person starts out with a level of intrinsic motivation that depends on his or her basic enjoyment of the work. But experiments like those described earlier have shown how a person's basic motivational orientation for a task, and resulting creativity on that task, can be influenced by even momentary alterations in the work environment. For example, an engineer may be highly intrinsically motivated to undertake a new project of his own design, but he may be singularly uninterested in a project handed to him by the director of the lab.

Motivational Synergy

The prevailing psychological model of the interaction between intrinsic and extrinsic motivation suggests an antagonism: as extrinsic motivation for an activity increases, intrinsic motivation must decrease.[23] But there is considerable evidence from field research that, under certain conditions, certain forms of extrinsic motivation may combine synergistically with intrinsic motivation, enhancing (or at least not undermining) the positive effects of intrinsic motivation on creativity.[24] For example, research in business organizations has uncovered several extrinsic motivators operating as *supports* to creativity: reward and recognition for creative ideas, clearly defined overall project goals, and frequent constructive feedback on the work.[25]

What determines whether extrinsic motivation will combine positively with intrinsic motivation, or detract from it, in influencing creativity? There are three important determinants: the person's initial motivational state, the type of extrinsic motivator used, and the timing of the extrinsic motivation.

First, the initial level of intrinsic motivation may play a crucial role. It may be that, if a person is deeply involved in the work because it is interesting or personally challenging, that degree of intrinsic motivation may be relatively impervious to the undermining effects of extrinsic motivators. Research has shown that a person's attitudes and motives will be most subject to external influences when those attitudes and motives are vague or ambiguous.[26] So, we might expect additive effects of intrinsic and extrinsic motivation when intrinsic motivation toward the work is already strong and salient. On the other hand, we might expect negative effects when intrinsic motivation is relatively weak. Thus, if an engineer is passionately interested in the development of the products he is working on, he may be relatively immune to negative effects of extrinsic motivators on his intrinsic motivation and creativity.

Second, the type of extrinsic motivation may make a difference. "Synergistic extrinsic motivators," including certain types of reward, recognition, and feedback, do not necessarily undermine intrinsic motivation; indeed, they may actually enhance some aspects of performance. These outcomes can result from reward, recognition, and feedback that either confirm competence or provide important information on how to improve performance; these are called *informational extrinsic motivators.*[27] Positive outcomes can also result from reward, recognition, and feedback that directly increase the person's involvement in the work itself; these are called *enabling extrinsic motivators.* For example, if a high tech firm recognizes outstanding performance by approving the allocation of additional technical resources to its engineers, the effects on intrinsic motivation are likely to be positive. On the other hand, constraint on how work can be done, as well as other types of reward, recognition, and feedback, will be detrimental to intrinsic motivation and performance. These "nonsynergistic extrinsic motivators," which are *controlling extrinsic motivators,* may never combine positively with intrinsic motivation, because they undermine a person's sense of self-determination.[28] The engineer who works under stringent controls on how to approach a project, or for whom rewards signify attempts to control his behavior, will likely evidence decreased intrinsic motivation and creativity.

Third, the timing of extrinsic motivation may be important. Recall that creative ideas are marked by both novelty and appropriateness. While some stages of the creative process are most important in determining the novelty of an idea, other stages are more important in determining appropriateness. Synergistic extrinsic motivators may be most useful at those stages of the creative process where high degrees of novelty do not come into play—such as the gathering of background information or the validation of a chosen solution. Here, some level of outward focus, engendered by extrinsic motivation, may cue the problem-solver to the appropriateness of certain kinds of information or the workability of final solutions. However, it may be optimal to reduce all types of extrinsic motivators at those stages requiring the greatest novelty—such as the initial problem formulation or the generation of ideas.

The Intrinsic Motivation Principle

All of this research on motivation leads to the Intrinsic Motivation Principle of Creativity, which can be formally stated as follows: *Intrinsic motivation is conducive to creativity. Controlling extrinsic motivation is detrimental to creativity, but informational or enabling extrinsic motivation can be conducive, particularly if initial levels of intrinsic motivation are high.*

THE WORK ENVIRONMENT FOR CREATIVITY

Although the experimental research is important in establishing causal connections between the social environment, motivation, and creativity, the most directly relevant information comes from interview and survey studies within corporations. It is through these studies that we began to understand the social environment in organizations and how it might impact creativity.

Recently, with my colleagues Regina Conti, Heather Coon, Jeffrey Lazenby, and Michael Herron, I studied the work environments surrounding project teams in a large company that we call High Tech Electronics International.[29] Our purpose was to determine whether and how the work environments of highly creative projects differed from the work environments of less creative projects. The primary research tool was an instrument called *KEYS: Assessing the Climate for Creativity.*[30] It consists of 78 items that constitute eight scales addressing different aspects of the work environment, plus two scales assessing the work outcomes of creativity and productivity.[31] Of the eight environment scales, six focus on Environmental Stimulants to Creativity—factors that should be positively related to creative work outcomes—including freedom, positive challenge, supervisory encouragement, work group supports, organizational encouragement, and sufficient resources. Two scales focus on Environmental Obstacles to Creativity—factors that should be negatively related to creative work outcome—including organizational impediments and excessive workload pressure. (See Table 1 for scale descriptions.) Data on *KEYS* gathered over a 12-year period, with over 12,000 individual employees from 26 different companies, have established the reliability and validity of this instrument.[32]

High Tech is a United States company of over 30,000 employees providing diversified electronics products to international markets. The company has several divisions, with a large number of research and development projects going on within each division at any point in time. We conducted this study in three phases, across four divisions and a large number of projects. In Phase 1, we asked both technical and non-technical middle-level managers individually to nominate both the highest-creativity and the lowest-creativity project with which they had been involved during the previous three years in the company. For both projects, we asked them to select only from that set of projects in which creativity was both possible and desirable. This eliminated any low creativity projects that simply involved carrying out a routine task, and it allowed us to focus on differences between successful and unsuccessful attempts at creative project work. Instructions to the nominating managers defined creativity as "the production of novel and useful ideas by individuals or teams of individuals." These managers briefly described each nominated project (using a standard questionnaire) and completed a *KEYS* work environment assessment on each nominated project.

Phase 2 of the study was conducted to validate the creativity nominations of Phase 1, by allowing independent expert assessments of the level of creativity in the projects nominated in Phase 1. A group of experts from each of the four target divisions was asked to independently rate the projects nominated from that division on creativity and several other dimensions. These experts were unaware of the initial nomination status of the projects, and high- and low-creativity projects were randomly intermixed in the experts' rating questionnaires. (They were asked to skip the ratings for any projects with which they were not familiar.)

TABLE 1 **Summary of Results from Study of High-Creativity and Low-Creativity Projects at High Tech Electronics International**

KEYS Scale Name	*KEYS* Scale Description	Direction of Difference	Magnitude of Difference in Phase 1[a]	Magnitude of Difference in Phase 3
CREATIVITY STIMULANT SCALES				
Organizational Encouragement	An organizational culture that encourages creativity through the fair, constructive judgment of ideas, reward and recognition for creative work, mechanisms for developing new ideas, an active flow of ideas, and a shared vision of what the organization is trying to do.	High-Creativity higher	Strong[b]	Strong[b]
Supervisory Encouragement	A supervisor who serves as a good work model, sets goals appropriately, supports the work group, values individual contributions, and shows confidence in the work group.	High-Creativity higher	Strong[b]	Moderate[b]
Work Group Supports	A diversely skilled work group in which people communicate well, are open to new ideas, constructively challenge each other's work, trust and help each other, and feel committed to the work they are doing.	High-Creativity higher	Strong[b]	Strong[b]
Sufficient Resources	Access to appropriate resources, including funds, materials, facilities, and information.	High-Creativity higher	Moderate[b]	None
Challenging Work	A sense of having to work hard on challenging tasks and important projects.	High-Creativity higher	Strong[b]	Strong[b]
Freedom	Freedom in deciding what work to do or how to do it; a sense of control over one's work.	High-Creativity higher	Strong[b]	Moderate[c]
CREATIVITY OBSTACLE SCALES				
Organizational Impediments	An organizational culture that impedes creativity through internal political problems, harsh criticism of new ideas, destructive internal competition, an avoidance of risk, and an overemphasis on the status quo.	Low-Creativity higher	Strong[b]	Moderate[c]
Workload Pressure	Extreme time pressures, unrealistic expectations for productivity, and distractions from creative work.	Low-Creativity higher	Weak[b]	None
CRITERION SCALES				
Creativity	A creative organization or unit, where a great deal of creativity is called for and where people believe they actually produce creative work.	High-Creativity higher	Strong[b]	Strong[b]
Productivity	An efficient, effective, and productive organization or unit.	High-Creativity higher	Strong[b]	Moderate[b]

Notes:
a. "Strong" designates effect sizes (partial eta-squared) of .21–.54. "Moderate" designates effect sizes of .10–.20. "Weak" designates effect sizes of .05–.09. "None" designates effect sizes of less than .05.
b. Statistically significant.
c. Marginal ($.06 < p < .15$)

Phase 3 was conducted to validate any work environment differences between the high- and low-creativity projects discovered in Phase 1. We selected a sub-set of the projects from Phase 1, those that had been most strongly and reliably rated by the expert judges as either high in creativity or low in creativity. We then asked each member of those project teams to complete a key survey to describe the work environment of his or her particular project. These respondents did not know that the study concerned creativity, or that their projects had been chosen for any particular reason. In fact, people were eliminated from participation in Phase 3 if they had participated in Phase 1. Furthermore, each respondent in Phase 3 focused on only one project, rather than the two contrasting projects for Phase 1 respondents. In this way, we attempted to eliminate any biases that might have arisen when the Phase 1 respondents explicitly contrasted the work environment of a project that they considered highly creative with one that they considered quite uncreative.

In Phase 1, the nominated high-creativity projects were significantly higher than the nominated low-creativity projects on all six work environment stimulant scales, and significantly lower on the two work environment obstacle scales. (See Table 1.) In addition, the high-creativity projects were higher on the two outcome scales assessing creativity and productivity.

In Phase 2, the expert ratings confirmed the initial nominations made in Phase 1: the previously-nominated high-creativity projects were indeed rated significantly higher on creativity than the previously-nominated low-creativity projects.

Phase 3 confirmed most of the findings from Phase 1 (see Table 1). Analyses of the responses from project-team members showed that the high-creativity projects were significantly higher than the low-creativity projects on four of the six work environment stimulant scales, and marginally higher on a fifth work environment stimulant scale. In addition, the high-creativity projects were marginally lower on one of the two work environment obstacle scales. Finally, as in Phase 1, the high-creativity projects were higher on the two outcome scales assessing creativity and productivity.

Table 1 summarizes the work environment findings from Phases 1 and 3 of this study at High Tech Electronics International. Clearly, although all aspects of the work environment may exert influence, some appear to carry more weight in the differentiation between high- and low-creativity projects. Somewhat surprisingly, three dimensions seem to play a relatively less prominent role in organizational creativity: resources, workload pressure, and freedom. However, the differences between high- and low-creativity projects on five dimensions were striking. In particular, positive challenge in the work, organizational encouragement, work group supports, supervisory encouragement, and organizational impediments may play an important role in influencing creative behavior in organizations. Thus, this study clearly indicates that the work environment within which people work relates significantly to the creativity of the work that they produce.

Other researchers have also discovered aspects of work environments that appear to affect creativity and innovation. Our tentative finding of the positive impact of freedom or autonomy echoes a result obtained in a study of 200 R&D managers in eight semi-conductor companies, where independence among R&D personnel was identified as a key determinant of success.[33] Various organizational supports have likewise appeared in other findings. In a survey of 77 strategic business units, the presence of innovation norms emerged as the single most important predictor of the effectiveness of entrepreneurial strategy.[34] Using a critical incidents methodology, another study examined the treatment of new ideas in high-technology and health-services organizations by gathering data from several hundred managers.[35] Several features of successful innovations were identified, including: the earmarking of special funds for highly experimental research and development; the formal consideration of innovators' ideas, followed by feasibility studies; consideration of marketing issues in the early stages of decision-making about an idea; substantial modification of most original ideas prior to final adoption; adequate funding and consistent monitoring of such projects; and initial small-scale implementation of the new idea.

HOW THE WORK ENVIRONMENT FOR CREATIVITY CHANGES DURING SIGNIFICANT ORGANIZATIONAL EVENTS

In another recent study, Regina Conti and I set out to determine how the environment for creativity and innovation might change in an organization that is undergoing rapid transition.[36] Several months after our earlier study at High Tech Electronics International, the company's management announced a major (15–30%) downsizing. We returned and proceeded to collect *KEYS* data at three additional points in time: half-way through the downsizing, just as the downsizing had ended, and four months after the end of the downsizing. In addition, we conducted interviews with surviving employees at each of these three time periods. The results showed a striking pattern. All of the Environmental Stimulants to Creativity declined during the downsizing, but appeared to rebound as the downsizing came to an end. The most dramatic declines were seen in challenge, work group supports, and organizational encouragement—three of the dimensions which, according to the previous study, carry the most weight in differentiating between high and low creativity. Moreover, these same three dimensions showed the weakest rebound by four months after the downsizing ended. Although workload pressure remained unchanged during the downsizing, the Environmental Obstacle of organizational impediments increased significantly; however, this factor declined as the downsizing ended. Importantly, both creativity and productivity (as assessed by *KEYS*) declined during the downsizing; only productivity had rebounded to a significant degree by four months after the downsizing. In addition, potentially longer-term effects on creativity were suggested by a decline in the per-capita invention disclosures logged by the company's engineers during the downsizing. Invention disclosures are the first step in patent applications and, in a company like High Tech Electronics, patents are the lifeblood of its future innovative product streams.

Additional questionnaire and interview data collected as part of the downsizing study allow some insight into mechanisms by which these negative effects might have occurred. Surprisingly, the degree of actual downsizing that people experienced in their own department did not relate strongly to their perceptions of the work environment or to reported work behaviors. However, regardless of how much downsizing had gone on in their own department, people were less creative and reported poorer work environments when the stability of their own work-group had been disrupted. Moreover, the degree of *anticipated* downsizing strongly related to a large number of perceptions and behaviors. The more downsizing that people expected in the coming months, the poorer the work environment in the department, the lower the morale, and the less creative their approach to their work. However, even in those departments anticipating considerable downsizing, people responded more positively on all of these dimensions when they felt that their own management was trustworthy, communicated honestly with them, and listened to their concerns.

The downsizing study suggests that, given the potentially devastating effects on surviving employees' motivation and creativity, managers should attempt to avoid downsizing if possible. If that is not possible, they would do well to carry it out in a timely fashion (thus reducing the negative effects of anticipated downsizing), with good, clear, all-directional communication about the reasons behind the action and the processes being used. Moreover, attention should be paid to the stability of groups where a high level of creative productivity is desired. If those groups are disrupted by the downsizing, the new teams might be helped by team-building interventions.

RESEARCH SUMMARY

On the basis of our two studies at High Tech Electronics International, we now know that the work environment within an organization—which is strongly influenced by management at all levels—can make the difference between the production of new, useful ideas for innovative business growth and the continuance of old, progressively less useful routines. We also know that management actions that result in significant changes within the organization, such as downsizing, can have dramatic and potentially long-lasting effects on creativity.

These results, as well as the results of many other studies, have led to a comprehensive Componential Theory of Creativity and Innovation in Organizations.[37] The aim of this theory is to adequately capture all of the major elements influencing creativity and innovation within organizations. The organizational theory is built on the foundation of the Componential Theory of Individual Creativity and incorporates that theory.

THE COMPONENTIAL THEORY OF ORGANIZATIONAL CREATIVITY AND INNOVATION

Figure 2 presents a simplified schematic diagram depicting the major elements of the componential theory, integrating individual creativity with the organizational work environment.[38] The three upper circles in the figure depict the organizational components (features of the work environment) that are considered necessary for innovation. The three lower circles in the figure depict the components of individual creativity.

The central prediction of the theory is that elements of the work environment will impact individuals' creativity (depicted by the solid arrow). The theory also proposes that the creativity produced by individuals and teams of individuals serves as a primary source for innovation within the organization (depicted by the dotted arrow). The most important feature of the theory is the assertion that the social environment (the work environment) influences creativity by influencing the individual components. Although the environment can have an impact on any of the components, the impact on task motivation appears to be the most immediate and direct. The three components of the organizational work environment include all aspects investigated in the study of high- and low-creativity projects at High Tech Electronics International, combined into conceptually coherent categories.

FIGURE 2 **Impact of the Organizational Environment on Creativity**

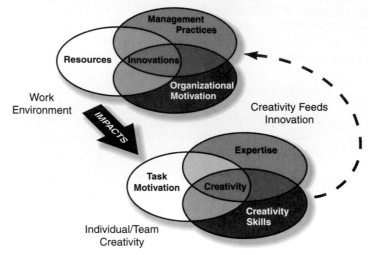

Organizational Motivation to Innovate

This component is made up of the basic orientation of the organization toward innovation, as well as supports for creativity and innovation throughout the organization. The orientation toward innovation must come, primarily, from the highest levels of management, but lower levels can also be important in communicating and interpreting that vision. In the studies at High Tech, this component was manifested in differences on Organizational Encouragement and (in the negative direction) Organizational Impediments. On the basis of these studies and work by other researchers, it appears that the most important elements of the innovation orientation are: a value placed on creativity and innovation in general, an orientation toward risk (versus an orientation toward maintaining the status quo), a sense of pride in the organization's members and enthusiasm about what they are capable of doing, and an offensive strategy of taking the lead toward the future (versus a defensive strategy of simply wanting to protect the organization's past position).[39] The primary organization-wide supports for innovation appear to be mechanisms for developing new ideas; open, active communication of information and ideas; reward and recognition for creative work; and fair evaluation of work—including work that might be perceived as a "failure."[40] Notably, the organizational motivation toward innovation includes the absence of several elements that can undermine creativity: political problems and "turf battles," destructive criticism and competition within the organization, strict control by upper management, and an excess of formal structures and procedures.[41]

Resources

This component includes everything that the organization has available to aid work in the domain targeted for innovation. In the studies at High Tech, it was manifested in differences on the Sufficient Resources scale and (in the negative direction) the Workload Pressure scale. These resources include a wide array of elements: sufficient time for producing novel work in the domain, people with necessary expertise, funds allocated to this work domain, material resources, systems and processes for work in the domain, relevant information, and the availability of training.[42]

Management Practices

This component includes management at all levels, but most especially the level of individual departments and projects.[43] In the High Tech studies, this component was represented by the Challenging Work, Work Group Supports, Supervisory Encouragement, and Freedom scales. Several earlier researchers and theorists have suggested that creativity and innovation are fostered by allowing a considerable degree of freedom or autonomy in the conduct of one's work[44] although, as noted, the high-low creativity study at High Tech did not provide strong support for this assertion. Some earlier work has suggested the importance of appropriately matching individuals to work assignments, on the basis of both skills and interests, to maximize a sense of positive challenge in the work.[45] Several aspects of project supervision appear to be important, starting with an ability to clearly set overall project goals while allowing procedural autonomy.[46] In addition, project supervision is likely to foster creativity when it is marked by clear planning and feedback, good communication between the supervisor and the work group, and enthusiastic support for the work of individuals as well as the entire group.[47] Finally, management practices for creativity include the ability to constitute effective work groups that represent a diversity of skills, and are made up of individuals who trust and communicate well with each other, challenge each other's ideas in constructive ways, are mutually supportive, and are committed to the work they are doing.[48]

IMPLICATIONS FOR MANAGEMENT

The Componential Theory of Creativity, and the research that underlies it, suggest a number of management implications concerning the motivation for creativity in business and the effect of the work environment on that motivation.

- Because human motivation is so complex and so important, the successful management of creativity for the next century must include management education about the types of motivation, their sources, their effects on performance, and their susceptibility to various work environment influences.

- We cannot hope to create a highly and appropriately creative workforce simply by "loading up" the intrinsic and the extrinsic motivators in the work environment, without paying attention to the *type* of extrinsic motivators and the context in which they are presented.

- Because a positive sense of challenge in the work is one of the most important predictors of creativity, it is imperative to match people to work that utilizes their skills, stretches their skills, and is clearly valued by the organization. As much as possible, all work should be designed to maximize intrinsically motivating aspects.

- Organizations must demonstrate a strong orientation toward innovation, which is clearly communicated and enacted, from the highest levels of management, throughout the organization.

- Organizations should orient themselves toward the generation, communication, careful consideration, and development of new ideas. This includes fair, constructive judgment of ideas, non-controlling reward and recognition for creative work, mechanisms for developing new ideas, and an active flow of ideas. It excludes turf battles, conservatism, and excessively negative criticism of new ideas.

- Work groups should be constituted of diversely skilled individuals with a shared intrinsic motivation for their work and a willingness to both share and constructively criticize each other's ideas. These groups should be led by supervisors who clearly set overall goals for projects but allow operational autonomy in achieving those goals. Performance feedback should be highly informational and work-focused.

- People should be given at least adequate resources to carry out their work, and at least minimally sufficient time to consider alternative approaches.

Organizational leaders and managers must begin to think of human motivation at work as a complex system where it is possible to achieve synergy between persons and their work environments, and between the different types of motivation. The system is complex, but it is not unknowable. We already know much about how to nurture the motivation for creativity, and we are learning more every day.

SUMMARY

Maintaining your own creativity in your work depends on maintaining your intrinsic motivation. This means two things. You should do what you love, and you should love what you do. The first is a matter of finding work that matches well with your expertise, your creative thinking skills, and your strongest intrinsic motivations. The second is a matter of finding a work environment that will allow you to retain that intrinsic motivational focus, while supporting your exploration of new ideas.

Managers who learn these lessons will recruit for people who already have that spark of passion for their work (as well as the requisite skills and experience), but they will also nurture that spark by creating a work environment that downplays the obstacles and fosters the stimulants to creativity. Only then will their organizations be poised to lead through innovation.

Notes

1. "Going for the Gaps," interview in *The Stanford Magazine* (Fall 1982), p. 42.
2. T. M. Amabile, *The Social Psychology of Creativity* (New York, NY: Springer Verlag, 1983); T. M. Amabile, *Creativity in Context: Update to the Social Psychology of Creativity* (Boulder, CO: Westview Press, 1996).
3. J. Kaplan, *Startup* (New York, NY: Penguin Books, 1994), p. 30.
4. Importantly, it has been found that innovation within organizations has additional benefits aside from the creation of new products, services, and processes. In a study of 288 bank employees, the degree of innovation within a group was a significant negative predictor of turn-over among employees in the group. M. McFadden and E. Demetriou, "The Role of Immediate Work Environment Factors in the Turnover Process: A Systemic Intervention," *Applied Psychology: An International Review,* 42 (1993): 97–115. In a similar study of 314 nurses, job satisfaction was significantly predicted by innovation. S. E. Robinson, S. L. Roth, and L. L. Brown, "Morale

and Job Satisfaction among Nurses: What Can Hospitals Do?" *Journal of Applied Social Psychology,* 23 (1993): 244–251.

5. T. M. Amabile, K. G. Hill, B. A. Hennessey, and E. Tighe, "The Work Preference Inventory: Assessing Intrinsic and Extrinsic Motivational Orientations," *Journal of Personality and Social Psychology,* 66 (1994): 950–967.

6. A. E. Kahn, *Joys and Sorrows: Reflections by Pablo Casals* (New York, NY: Simon and Schuster, 1970), p. 35.

7. T. M. Amabile, *Growing Up Creative* (New York, NY: Crown, 1989), p. 56.

8. A. Einstein, "Autobiography," in P. Schilpp, *Albert Einstein: Philosopher-Scientist* (Evanston, IL: Library of Living Philosophers, 1949), p. 18.

9. Ibid., p. 19.

10. See Amabile (1996), op. cit.

11. T. M. Amabile, B. A. Hennessey, and B. S. Grossman, "Social Influences on Creativity: The Effects of Contracted-For Reward," *Journal of Personality and Social Psychology,* 50 (1986): 14–23.

12. T. M. Amabile, "Motivation and Creativity: Effects of Motivational Orientation on Creative Writers," *Journal of Personality and Social Psychology,* 48 (1985): 393–399.

13. For example, F. Barron, "The Disposition toward Originality," *Journal of Abnormal and Social Psychology,* 51 (1955): 478–485; F. Barron, *Creativity and Personal Freedom* (New York, NY: Van Nostrand, 1968); D. W. MacKinnon, "The Nature and Nurture of Creative Talent," *American Psychologist,* 17 (1962): 484–495; D. W. MacKinnon, "Personality and the Realization of Creative Potential," *American Psychologist,* 20 (1965): 273–281.

14. T. Amabile, "The Social Psychology of Creativity: A Componential Conceptualization," *Journal of Personality and Social Psychology,* 45 (1983b): 357–377; Amabile (1983) op. cit.

15. A. Newell and H. Simon, *Human Problem Solving* (Englewood Cliffs, NJ: Prentice Hall, 1972), p. 82.

16. Termed "creativity-relevant skills" in Amabile (1983), op. cit., and "creativity-relevant processes" in Amabile (1996), op. cit.

17. Barron (1955), op. cit.; D. Feldman, *Beyond Universals in Cognitive Development* (Norwood, NJ: Ablex, 1980); S. E. Golann, "Psychological Study of Creativity," *Psychological Bulletin,* 60 (1963): 548–565; R. Hogarth, *Judgement and Choice* (Chichester: Wiley, 1980); MacKinnon (1962), op. cit.; M. I. Stein, *Stimulating Creativity,* Vol. 1 (New York, NY: Academic Press, 1974).

18. A. Newell, J. Shaw, and H. Simon, "The Processes of Creative Thinking," in H. Gruber, G. Terrell, and M. Wertheimer, eds., *Contemporary Approaches to Creative Thinking* (New York, NY: Atherton Press 1962).

19. W. W. Gordon, *Synectics: The Development of Creative Capacity* (New York, NY: Harper & Row, 1961).

20. D. Campbell, "Blind Variation and Selective Retention in Creative Thought as in Other Knowledge Processes," *Psychological Review,* 67 (1960) 380–400; Hogarth, op. cit.

21. H. Simon, "Scientific Discovery and the Psychology of Problem Solving." in *Mind and Cosmos: Essays in Contemporary Science and Philosophy* (Pittsburgh, PA: University of Pittsburgh Press, 1966).

22. See, for example, the work of S. Harter ["Effectance Motivation Reconsidered: Toward a Developmental Model," *Human Development,* 21 (1978) 34–64] and C. Dweck ["Motivational Processes Affecting Learning," *American Psychologist,* 41 (1986): 1040–1048].

23. See, for example, E. L. Deci, "Effects of Externally Mediated Rewards on Intrinsic Motivation," *Journal of Personality and Social Psychology,* 18 (1971): 105–115; M. R. Lepper, D. Greene, and R. Nisbett, "Undermining Children's Intrinsic Interest with Extrinsic Rewards: A Case of the 'Overjustification' Hypothesis," *Journal of Personality and Social Psychology,* 28 (1973): 129–137; M. R. Lepper and D. Greene, *The Hidden Costs of Reward* (Hillsdale, NJ: Lawrence Erlbaum Associates, 1978); E. L. Deci and R. M. Ryan, *Intrinsic Motivation and Self-Determination in Human Behavior* (New York, NY: Plenum, 1985).

24. T. M. Amabile, "Motivational Synergy: Toward New Conceptualizations of Intrinsic and Extrinsic Motivation in the Workplace," *Human Resource Management Review,* 3 (1993): 185–201.

25. T. M. Amabile, R. Conti, H. Coon, J. Lazenby, and M. Herron, "Assessing the Work Environment for Creativity," *Academy of Management Journal,* 39 (1996) 1154–1184; T. M. Amabile and S. S. Gryskiewicz, *Creativity in the R&D Laboratory,* Technical Report Number 30 (Greensboro, NC: Center for Creative Leadership, 1987); T. M. Amabile and N. Gryskiewicz, "The Creative Environment Scales: The Work Environment Inventory," *Creativity Research Journal,* 2 (1989): 231–254.

26. D. Bem, "Self-Perception Theory," in L. Berkowitz, ed., *Advances in Experimental Social Psychology,* Vol. 6 (New York, NY: Academic Press, 1972).

27. Deci and Ryan (1985) op. cit.

28. Ibid.

29. Amabile et al. (1996), op. cit.

30. T. M. Amabile, *KEYS: Assessing the Climate for Creativity* (Greensboro, NC: Center for Creative Leadership, 1995).

31. *KEYS* was developed on the basis of several earlier studies of the work environment for creativity, in particular a critical-incidents study of 120 R&D scientists. Amabile and Gryskiewicz, op. cit.

32. Amabile et al. (1996) op. cit.

33. A. Abbey and J. W. Dickson, "R&D Work Climate and Innovation in Semiconductors," *Academy of Management Journal,* 26 (1983): 362–368.

34. R. D. Russell and C. J. Russell, "An Examination of the Effects of Organizational Norms, Organizational Structure, and Environmental Uncertainty on Entrepreneurial Strategy," *Journal of Management,* 18 (1992): 839–856.

35. A. L. Delbecq and P. K. Mills, "Managerial Practices That Enhance Innovation," *Organizational Dynamics,* 14 (1985) 24–34.

36. T. M. Amabile and R. Conti, "What Downsizing Does to Creativity," *Issues and Observations* 15 (1995): 1–6 (Greensboro, NC: Center for Creative Leadership).

37. T. M. Amabile, "A Model of Creativity and Innovation in Organizations," in B. Staw and L. L. Cummings, eds., *Research in Organizational Behavior,* Vol. 10 (Greenwich, CT: JAI Press, 1988).

38. Ibid.

39. Amabile and Gryskiewicz, op. cit.; L. L. Cummings, "Organizational Climates for Creativity," *Journal of the Academy of Management,* 3 (1965): 220–227; J. Hage and R. Dewar, "Elite Values Versus Organizational Structure in Predicting Innovation," *Administrative Science,* 18 (1973): 279–290; R. G. Havelock, *Planning for Innovation* (Ann Arbor, MI: Center for Research on Utilization of Scientific Knowledge, University of Michigan, 1970); R. M. Kanter, *The Change Masters* (New York, NY: Simon and Schuster, 1983); J. R. Kimberly, "Managerial Innovation," in P. C. Nystrom and W. H. Starbuck, eds., *Handbook of Organizational Design* (Oxford: Oxford University Press, 1981); C. Orpen, "Measuring Support for Organizational Innovation: A Validity Study," *Psychological Reports,* 67 (1990): 417–418; S. M. Siegel and W. F. Kaemmerer, "Measuring the Perceived Support for Innovation in Organizations," *Journal of Applied Psychology,* 63 (1978): 553–562.

40. Amabile and Gryskiewicz, op. cit.; S. J. Ashford and L. L. Cummings, "Proactive Feedback Seeking: The Instrumental Use of the Information Environment," *Journal of Occupational Psychology,* 58 (1985): 67–80; Cummings, op. cit.; J. E. Ettlie, "Organizational Policy and Innovation among Suppliers to the Food Processing Sector," *Academy of Management Journal,* 26 (1993): 27–44; Kanter, op. cit.; P. R. Monge, M. D. Cozzens, and N. S. Contractor, "Communication and Motivational Predictors of the Dynamics of Organizational Innovation," *Organizational Science,* 3 (1992): 250–274; J. G. Paolillo and W. B. Brown, "How Organizational Factors Affect R&D Innovation," *Research Management,* 21 (1978): 12–15.

41. Amabile and Gryskiewicz, op. cit.

42. Ibid.

43. This component was termed "skills in innovation management" in the original presentation of the model. Amabile (1988), op. cit.

44. Amabile and Gryskiewicz, op. cit.; F. M. Andrews and G. F. Farris, "Supervisory Practices and Innovation in Scientific Teams," *Personnel Psychology* (1967); G. Ekvall, *Climate, Structure, and Innovativeness of Organizations: A Theoretical Framework and an Experiment,* Report 1, The Swedish Council for Management and Organizational Behaviour, 1983; N. King and M. A. West, "Experiences of Innovation at Work," SAPU Memo No. 772, University of Sheffield, Sheffield, England, 1985; D. C. Pelz and F. M. Andrews, *Scientists in Organizations* (New York, NY: Wiley, 1966); Paolillo and Brown, op. cit.; Siegel and Kaemmerer, op. cit.; M. A. West, *Role Innovation in the World of Work,* Memo no. 670, MRC/ESRC Social and Applied Psychology Unit, University of Sheffield, Sheffield, England, 1986.

45. Amabile and Gryskiewicz, op. cit.

46. L. Bailyn, "Autonomy in the Industrial R&D Laboratory," *Human Resource Management,* 24 (1985): 129–146.

47. Amabile and Gryskiewicz, op. cit.

48. T. L. Albrecht and D. T. Hall, "Facilitating Talk about New Ideas: The Role of Personal Relationships in Organizational Innovation," *Communication Monographs,* 58 (1991): 273–288; Amabile and Gryskiewicz, op. cit.; Ekvall, op. cit.; Monge et al., op. cit.

Enhancing Creativity: Managing Work Contexts for the High Potential Employee

Anne Cummings
Greg R. Oldham

To survive and succeed, firms must innovate. Intensified global competition and an emphasis on rapidly changing technologies have only reinforced this long-held notion. To remain competitive, firms must develop and introduce new products or services to external markets. But they must also innovate within their organizational boundaries—focusing internally to improve the efficiency of the ways in which inputs become outputs, value is created, and work gets done.

A key source of external and internal innovation for all firms is the creativity of the people they employ. Employees may exhibit creativity by developing new knowledge, advancing technologies, or making process improvements that change or improve a firm's products or services. However, this creativity does not happen automatically. Firms and their managers must ensure that their employees will make creative contributions. They must first hire people with the potential for creativity, and then they must structure their employees' environment in order to bring out this creative potential. Only by fostering the right people in the right place can creativity in organizations be maximized.[1]

Employees exhibit creativity when they generate a product, service, or process that is both *novel and useful* with respect to the firm. Contributions are *novel* when they offer something original or unique relative to what is already available within the firm's repertoire of products, services, or practices. However, this contribution also needs to be useful. It must be directly relevant to the goals of the organization and it must be something from which the firm can reasonably expect to extract some value in either the short term or in the longer run.

Employees may make creative contributions individually or as members of teams. An individual may suggest, for example, manufacturing process improvements via a suggestion program by speaking with or writing a memo to his supervisor. Alternatively this employee may develop the same suggestion while working with colleagues and then collectively submit the recommendation as part of a special task force or work group. Similarly, a design engineer may write a patent disclosure proposal for her supervisor's review as a result of her individual work or as part of a multi-functional project team.

Further, these creative employee contributions may reflect a significant recombination of existing materials or an introduction of completely new materials. Pursuing the above examples, the manufacturing suggestion might involve reorganizing the order in which various steps in the manufacturing process are conducted, or it might involve introducing an entirely new step into the same process. Similarly, the patent disclosure proposal might involve the introduction of a new adhesive compound, or it might suggest a new application from recombining existing compounds. Each of these novel and useful contributions is an example of employee creativity.

From *California Management Review,* 1997, 40(1), 22–38. Reprinted by permission.

Scholars often draw a distinction between the terms "innovation" and "employee creativity."[2] While innovation refers to the successful implementation of new outcomes by a firm, implementation need not be complete for us to consider an employee to have made a creative contribution. Instead, "employee creativity" refers to individuals' generation of novel and useful products, ideas, and procedures that are the raw material for innovation. By developing and implementing these creative outcomes, firms innovate. So, while a firm's innovation might be the introduction of an adhesive product to a new market, the earlier patent disclosure proposal reflected the employee's creativity. Or, whereas the manufacturing employee's recommendation for re-engineering part of his production line is an example of his creativity, the changes in product efficiency or quality resulting from implementation of his suggestions represent an innovation for the firm.

When employees generate a novel and useful product, or when they formulate new procedures or ideas, they are essentially providing the firm with options. Creative inputs enable a firm to choose from a broader array of products, ideas, or procedures for development and later implementation. This variety provides the firm with flexibility with which it can respond to external demands and opportunities. Thus, creative inputs by employees can determine how much raw material exists for a firm to innovate—to identify a new market niche, to re-engineer a complicated work procedure, or to generate new technical knowledge.

Given the importance of these creative contributions by employees, what do we know about enhancing them? Psychologists and some educators have long held that some individuals possess personal characteristics that are more creative than others.[3] Thus, some employees have greater potential for, or derive greater satisfaction from, producing creative outcomes at work than others. But beyond these differences in individuals' potential, other research has shown that where employees work, how they are treated by supervisors and colleagues, and what work they are asked to perform affects their creativity in important ways.[4] Employees are more creative when their contexts support their efforts at novelty because their work situations offer them complexity, stimulation, and sufficient support. Finally, these work contexts need to "fit" the creative potential that employees bring to work. Employing people with lots of creative potential will only have an impact on creative outcomes if the context is set up to nurture and encourage that creative potential. This article presents two studies that suggest how to place and support high potential employees in order to maximize their creative contributions.

TYPES OF EMPLOYEES

"Types" of employees refers to a set of stable and enduring personal characteristics that can relatively consistently distinguish some individuals from others. Psychologists have long attempted to identify personal characteristics that separated more creative people from less creative individuals. In particular, they have examined such characteristics as IQ, sex, and educational background and have attempted to show that people with certain profiles produce more creative work than others. However, most of these efforts have been disappointing since they do not typically show large differences in creative output for people with different profiles. Nevertheless, a few personal characteristics have been somewhat successful in consistently predicting creative behavior; these are differences in individuals' problem-solving styles and differences in individuals' personalities. These two types of differences respectively address the questions, "With what kind of style does this employee typically approach a problem at work?" and "Is this employee generally a creative person?"

Employee Problem-Solving Style

One important difference between types of employees is the style with which they characteristically approach decisions or problems. While assessment of personal styles has long been of interest to managers and human resource professionals (e.g., the widespread use of the Myers-Briggs Type Indicator), of particular relevance to employee creativity is how individuals' styles differ on an adaptive-innovative dimension. Michael Kirton and his colleagues argue that different problem-solving styles lead employees to go about being creative in different ways.[5] People with *adaptive* styles work incrementally on problems, within established rules and frameworks, to generate new and useful outcomes that generally reinforce the given paradigm of the problem. So, a manufacturing employee with an adaptive style might suggest improving product quality by further reducing errors in each manufacturing step.

Employees with *innovative* styles, however, are more likely to ignore established frameworks, reframe the problem itself, and therefore to generate more frame-breaking outcomes in their problem-solving efforts. A manufacturing employee with an innovative style might approach the same quality improvement problem by suggesting complete reorganization of the steps in the manufacturing process or the introduction of a new step.

Michael Kirton has developed a reliable, copyrighted instrument to assess these differences in problem-solving style—the Kirton Adaption-Innovation Inventory, or KAI.[6] This paper and pencil test provides individuals with 32 descriptive statements and asks them how easy or hard it is for them to be a person with those certain characteristics. Examples of characteristics that adaptors find easy are: "a person who likes bosses and work patterns which are consistent," "a person who enjoys the detailed work," and "a person who holds back ideas until they are obviously needed." Innovators, on the other hand, find it difficult to hold these characteristics and instead find it easy to "vary set routines at a moment's notice," to be "alone in disagreeing with a group," and to "sooner create something than improve it." They are less likely to be wedded to rules and the status quo, and they are more likely to approach problems with a broader frame of reference. Several characteristics of employees with innovative problem-solving styles appear in Box 1.

Studies using the KAI suggest that it is a reasonably good predictor of employees' creativity at work—innovators produce more creative outcomes than adaptors.[7] Because employees with innovative problem-solving styles exhibit less fear of or respect for traditional boundaries, they may well take risks with their solutions and extend outcomes in ways that are more novel and more useful for the firm.

Employee Personality

Another difference between employees is a more general one—their overall personality profiles. Studies of creative people in a variety of settings (e.g., Nobel prize winners, engineers, managers, and students) indicate that these people share a particular group of personality descriptors.[8] For example, highly creative people are generally self-confident, attracted to complexity, tolerant of ambiguity, and intuitive. As a result of some of these studies, a variety of tools exist for measuring these characteristics.[9] One of the most widely used and respected

BOX 1 **Some Characteristics of an Innovative Problem-Solving Style**

An employee with an innovative problem-solving style . . .
would sooner create than improve
has fresh perspectives on old problems
copes with several new ideas at the same time
is not methodical and systematic
does not impose strict order on matters within own control
does not like the protection of precise instructions
seeks to bend or break the rules
often risks doing things differently
can stand out in disagreement against group
acts without proper authority

Note: These descriptions come from Kirton's Adaption-Innovation Inventory, or the KAI; for more detail on this instrument see note #6.

of these measures is Gough's Creative Personality Scale, or CPS. This test was derived from studies of architects, mathematicians, research scientists, students in psychology and engineering, Air Force officers, and other individuals from the general population.[10] It is a paper and pencil test that includes 30 adjectives, and respondents check those adjectives that describe them. Several validity studies provide moderate support for the notion that those individuals with the highest creative performance on a variety of indicators typically check one core set of adjectives, such as "self-confident" and "interests wide," whereas individuals with lower creative performance check another set of adjectives, such as "conventional" and "interests narrow." Several of the core set of adjectives describing individuals with generally creative personalities appear in Box 2.

Employees with generally creative personalities may therefore approach their work settings with broad interests that encourage them to seek out resources from varied constituencies and enable them to recognize divergent information and opinions. They also likely possess the self-confidence and tolerance for ambiguity to be patient with potentially competing views, and to persist in developing novel ideas into concrete suggestions and beyond. All other conditions being equal, these employees are likely to produce a higher number of creative outcomes—and to make contributions that are more creative—than employees whose general personalities more strongly reflect other characteristics.

WORK CONTEXTS

Does it make sense for managers to focus only on types of employees and thereby implement a strategy consisting largely of identifying and selecting people with innovative problem-solving styles and creative personalities to be employees in their firms? Probably not in isolation. As noted earlier, most employee behavior is a function of both the person *and* the place.[11] Furthermore, while innovative problem-solving styles and generally creative personalities have modestly predicted high levels of creative accomplishment, *they have not been uniformly good predictors.* Indeed, one reason for this may be that these employees

BOX 2 **Some Adjectives Describing a Creative Personality**

An employee with a generally creative personality is . . .
clever
humorous
informal
insightful
inventive
original
reflective
resourceful
self-confident
sexy
snobbish
unconventional

Note: These adjectives come from the Creative Personality Scale, or CPS; for more detail on this instrument see note #10.

worked in a variety of different contexts—some contexts allowed employees to use their high creative potential, whereas others did not.

This suggests that to achieve the highest levels of creative performance, firms need to surround individuals that have high creative potential—i.e., those with high KAI and CPS scores—with a work context that nurtures this potential and provides it with the opportunity to emerge and develop. Three key features of the work context facilitate the creativity of individuals with high creative potential: job complexity; supportive and non-controlling supervision; and stimulating co-workers.

Job Complexity

Managerial practice has long recognized that the way in which work is organized affects employees' performance. When their jobs are complex rather than simple, employees are more motivated, more satisfied, and often more productive.[12] More complex jobs should, however, also encourage employees to be more creative. Highly complex jobs allow employees to see the significance of and exercise responsibility for an entire piece of work; have the autonomy to exercise choices about how and when the work gets done using a variety of skills; and receive enough feedback from the work itself to monitor their progress. These characteristics (which appear in Box 3) are important because they provide employees with the information and freedom to recognize divergent needs and pursue novel ideas in useful ways. Because employees with creative personal characteristics are attracted to complexity and frequently take frame-breaking approaches to situations, jobs that are complex and challenging provide them room and support for their potential to develop. Such jobs allow them the freedom to focus simultaneously on multiple dimensions of their work, permit them to conduct their activities without extensive external controls or constraints, and may also enhance their interest in persisting with their novel approaches and completing creative activities. Simple or routine jobs, in contrast, may inhibit such focus and excitement, and thereby thwart the creative potential of these employees.

BOX 3 **Characteristics of Complex Jobs**

> **A complex job . . .**
> requires a variety of skills and talents to complete the work
> allows an employee to complete a whole, identifiable piece of work from beginning to end
> provides an employee with freedom and discretion to determine work procedures and scheduling
> provides direct information (via the work itself) to an employee about performance effectiveness
> has a substantial impact on the lives of other people, inside or outside of the firm

Note: For more detail, see note #12.

Supportive, Non-Controlling Supervision

Managerial practice has also long recognized the importance of supervisory style on employees' behavior.[13] However, maximizing employees' creative potential may require a special focus on being supportive and non-controlling. When supervisors are supportive, they show concern for employees' feelings and needs, encourage them to voice their own concerns, provide positive and informational feedback, and facilitate skill development among employees. These actions promote employees' feelings of self-determination and personal initiative at work, allowing employees to consider, develop, and ultimately contribute more creative outcomes. At the same time, supervisors should not be controlling; they should not closely monitor employee behavior, not make decisions without employee involvement, and generally not pressure employees to think, feel, or behave in certain ways. These controlling supervisory behaviors shift an employee's focus of attention away from his or her own ideas and toward external concerns. Because employees with high creative potential are self-confident, intuitive, tolerant of ambiguity, and tend to solve problems by thinking outside of established paradigms, it is particularly important that supervisors not thwart their creative potential by overly controlling, pressuring, or even monitoring these employees. And by also providing concern for those employees' opinions, needs, and skill development, supervisors may in fact enhance the creativity of those with high potential. These characteristics of supervisory style appear in Box 4.

Stimulating Co-Workers

Lastly, employees with creative personal characteristics need to be surrounded by colleagues who help excite them about their work but don't distract them from it. With increasing emphases on employees working in teams,[14] the nature of co-worker interaction is increasingly important for firms to address. To nurture and support the creative potential of employees with generally creative personalities and with innovative problem-solving styles, managers should ensure that these employees' interactions with their co-workers do not inhibit their ability to integrate divergent information, to pursue frame-breaking ideas, or to focus on their work. In addition, some co-worker interaction may actually provide important further motivation to these employees, by stimulating wider interests, adding complexity, or introducing some competitive pressure to enhance the novelty, usefulness, or number of their contributions relative to their co-workers.

BOX 4 **Some Characteristics of Supportive, Non-Controlling Supervisors**

Supportive & non-controlling supervisors . . .

keep informed about how employees think and feel about things, also allowing employees to make decisions about work on their own

encourage employees to participate in important decisions, to speak up when they disagree; they also explain their actions to employees

help employees solve work-related problems, and encourage them to develop new skills

praise good work and reward good performance, but refrain from always checking on employees' work

Note: For a fuller description of these supervisory styles see note #17.

Thus, employees' high creative potential will be maximized when this potential is stimulated and motivated by the work context. Only when individuals with creative personalities and innovative problem-solving styles are excited by their work and free of external constraints[15] can they make full "use" of their divergent interests, tolerance of ambiguity, attention to complexity, self-confidence, and frame-breaking approaches. And it is under these conditions that firms will benefit from the most creative contributions from employees.

STUDY 1

To examine the roles of employee personality, two aspects of the work context (jobs and supervisory styles), and how people with different personalities respond to these work contexts, we studied two manufacturing facilities. We first visited the firms to observe when and how employees were contributing to both product and process innovations. Then, based on our observations, we developed a survey to assess various aspects of the employees' work contexts. In particular, this survey included several questions measuring the complexity of employees' jobs using the dimensions presented earlier in Box 3. For example, we asked about the amount of autonomy, variety, significance, and feedback that each employee's job offered. In addition, the survey included questions about how supportive and non-controlling each employee's supervision was, using the characteristics presented [above] in Box 4. For example, we asked the degree to which supervisors encouraged participation, refrained from checking on employees' work, explained their actions, and praised good work. Finally, this survey also used the CPS (Box 2) to measure how generally creative each employee's personality was.

Of the approximately 200 employees we asked, 171 people completed the survey. These employees held a variety of positions within the firms, including design engineer, manufacturing engineer, design drafter, technician, toolmaker, and production line specialist. We then averaged each employee's responses to the questions assessing creative personality characteristics and each dimension of the context to create a CPS score, a job complexity score, and a degree of supportive and non-controlling supervision score for each employee. We kept all employee responses and scores completely confidential.

Next, we assessed the creativity of these employees. First, we asked each employee's direct supervisor to rate several dimensions of that employee's work. We asked them: to what degree the employee developed ideas, methods, or products that were both novel and useful to the firm; to what degree the employee used existing information or materials to develop these ideas, methods, or products; and to what degree the work was creative. We then averaged the supervisor's confidential responses to these three questions to form a measure of rated creativity that reflected how creative, in general, that employee's work was.

To get a second measure of each employee's creativity, we also examined the contributions he or she made to the firm's formal suggestion program. In this program, employees could contribute ideas either individually or as part of a team. These suggestions usually involved ideas about procedural or process changes in work methods, such as changes in quality inspections, new material use, or waste disposal. Employees submitted their written suggestions to a multi-functional committee of middle-level managers. This committee regularly reviewed all submitted recommendations and only accepted for implementation those that were both novel and useful. The second measure of creativity, then, assessed how many of the individual's ideas were accepted (considered creative) by the multi-functional committee.[16]

Our findings from Study 1 show that individuals with more creative personalities (high scores on the CPS) did not necessarily produce more creative work than those employees with less creative personalities. Indeed, employees with high CPS scores produced highly creative outcomes *only* when they were surrounded by a context that facilitated their creativity. As shown in Figures 1 and 2, employees with creative personalities (represented by the shaded bars) produced more creative work than those with low CPS scores (represented by the white bars) *when* they held complex jobs and had supportive, non-controlling

FIGURE 1 **Suggestions Produced by Creative Personalities in Complex Jobs**

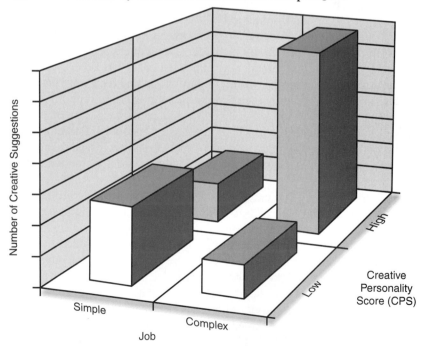

supervisors.[17] Specifically, when employees with high CPS scores held complex jobs (Figure 1), they produced more creative suggestions than anyone else. In addition, when these employees worked on a complex job and for a supervisor who was supportive and non-controlling (Figure 2), their work was rated as the most creative.

These results suggest that in order for firms to reap benefits from employing individuals with generally creative personalities, these employees must be placed in complex jobs and under supportive, yet non-controlling, supervisors. These conditions seem to allow employees with generally creative personalities the freedom to focus simultaneously on multiple dimensions of their work, by providing them opportunities to voice concerns and receive plenty of positive, constructive feedback and to work without too many external controls or constraints. These employees can thereby take advantage of their creative potential. In contrast, when employees with generally creative personalities work under conditions that lack one of these contextual features, their creativity is reduced. Simple jobs and controlling, non-supportive supervisors seem to inhibit the expression of their attraction to complexity, tolerance of ambiguity, intuition, and their self-confidence.

FIGURE 2   **Creativity of Work by Creative Personalities in Complex Jobs with Supportive, Non-Controlling Supervisors**

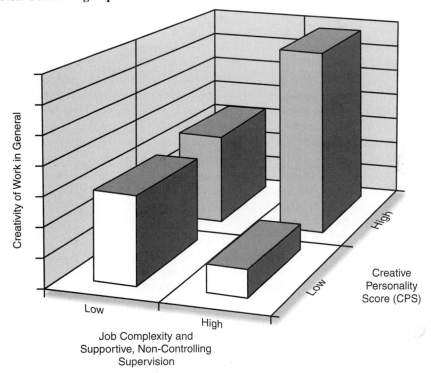

STUDY 2

To further explore how the type of employee and the work context matter, we revisited 118 of the employees in one of the two firms from Study 1. Here, we explored how employee creativity was related to the third feature of the work context—stimulating co-workers. In particular, we were interested in how *competition* among employees was related to the creativity of their work. Competition is interesting because it can work in either of two conflicting ways. On the one hand, competition may enhance employees' creativity because competing with co-workers for resources or to see who will do the best job further stimulates and excites employees to pursue novel and useful ideas. This may be particularly true for employees with innovative styles and creative personalities—the stimulation may enhance their already considerable focus and persistence. On the other hand, competition may constrain employees' creativity because competing for resources or comparing their performance with that of co-workers encourages them to focus on relationships external to the work itself and thereby distracts them from making thoughtful, novel, and useful contributions. Following this argument, competition may be particularly detrimental for employees with less creative potential. That is, it may especially hamper the creativity of employees who have little self-confidence and who typically emphasize established rules and frameworks.

We examined the influence of co-worker competition on the creativity of employees with both kinds of creative potential—innovative problem-solving styles and generally creative personalities. To assess problem-solving styles, we administered the KAI (Box 1). Employees with high scores on this measure have innovative problem-solving styles; employees with lower KAI scores have adaptive problem-solving styles.

To assess the level of competition, we asked each employee to indicate the degree to which their co-workers engage in three types of competition—competition over who can do the best job, competition for resources, and general competition.[18] We then averaged each employee's responses to these questions to create a level of competition score for that employee. To assess employees' creativity, we used the same two measures as in Study 1—how creative their supervisors considered their work in general and the number of creative recommendations accepted for implementation by the suggestion program's multi-functional evaluation committee.

The results of Study 2 show that, as in Study 1, different types of employees responded differently to their work contexts. In Study 2, employees with generally creative personalities and innovative problem-solving styles reacted positively to high amounts of competition among co-workers, but those with less creative personalities or with adaptive problem-solving styles did not.[19] Figure 3 shows that while competing with co-workers had little effect on the number of creative suggestions most employees made (the white bars), competition had a pronounced positive effect on employees with both creative personalities and innovative styles (the shaded bars in the figure). Under conditions of high competition, these employees produced the highest number of creative suggestions. But when competition among co-workers was low, these employees produced fewer creative suggestions than other employees. Figure 4 shows that competition also had a positive effect on how creative their work was. While competing with co-workers did not apparently affect the creativity of most employees' work (white bars in Figure 4), it did enhance the creativity of those employees with creative personalities *and* innovative styles (the shaded bars).

FIGURE 3 **Suggestions Produced by Employees with Both Personal Characteristics, under High Competition**

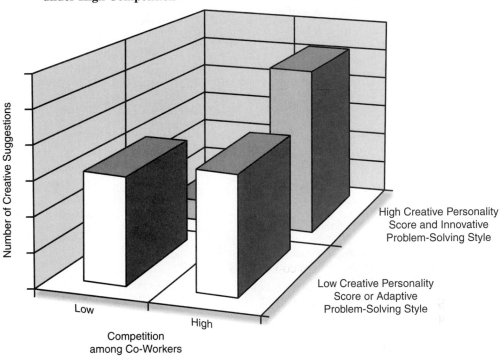

These results suggest that competition can help maximize the creativity of employees. While competition among co-workers does not appear to have a detrimental effect on the creativity of any employees, encouraging it among employees with innovative problem-solving styles and generally creative personalities has a substantial positive impact. Indeed, competition may stimulate their broad interests and frame-breaking styles or it may help convert these interests into novel and useful outcomes for the firms. Moreover, these competitive conditions did not appear to distract employees from the nature of the work itself. Instead, when co-workers were highly competitive, employees with high creative potential produced markedly more creative suggestions and their work was rated as more creative. Future research needs to replicate this finding before strong recommendations about competition are appropriate, but this study does suggest that firms may want to consider incentive programs that encourage co-workers to compete for "best job" honors, or for resources.

CONCLUSIONS AND IMPLICATIONS

Most firms today value innovation and the competitive advantage it provides; and most managers realize that employees' contributions of novel and useful products, ideas, and procedures are critical to any organization's successful innovation efforts. In order to maximize both the number of creative contributions employees make and the overall creativity of those

FIGURE 4   **Creativity of Work by Employees with Both Personal Characteristics, under High Competition**

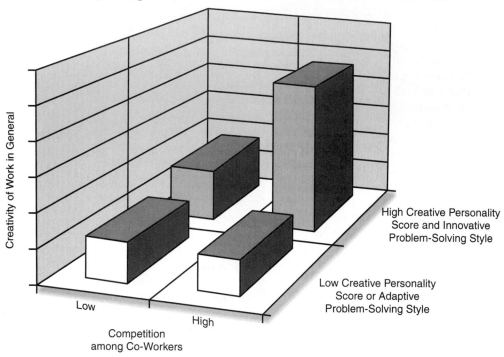

contributions, managers need to endorse a two-factor approach. First, managers need to consider the "type" of employee—specifically, the personal characteristics related to creativity. But identifying people with high creative potential only offers a firm the possibility for innovation, not its realization. To take advantage of this potential, managers must also address a second factor—employees need to be surrounded by a context that nurtures their creative potential.

This two-factor approach has several implications for managerial practice. With regard to employee hiring, managers may wish to consider giving selection priority, when appropriate, to those applicants with high creative potential. In particular, our research suggests that managers should consider two personal characteristics of potential employees—their problem-solving styles and how generally creative their personalities are. By assessing these personal characteristics using reliable and valid instruments (such as the CPS and KAI), managers may evaluate the creative potential of each applicant. And by giving priority to potential employees with high scores on these instruments, firms can enhance the overall level of creative potential available to them.

Following selection, managers must place employees with high creative potential in a creativity-nurturing context. That is, managers need to assign these new employees to complex jobs, to supervisors who display supportive, non-controlling styles, and to situations with stimulating, competitive co-workers. Obviously, this also requires the careful assessment of the current contextual conditions before differentially assigning new employees to jobs, supervisors, and work teams.

It is worth noting that many firms may, very understandably, find it inappropriate to use creative potential as a hiring criterion. In these cases, managers might still consider individual creative potential in placement decisions about employees who were hired based upon other characteristics or criteria. That is, using the same reliable instruments described above, managers can assess the creative potential of all their existing employees, and then transfer those with high potential to contexts that ensure high job complexity, supportive supervision, and stimulating co-workers.

If a manager cannot easily move, re-assign, or intermittently transfer employees, he or she may work to change the context surrounding particular employees. That is, after assessing the creative potential of their employees, managers may seek to make the specific context surrounding those employees with high potential more nurturing. These managerial efforts can include restructuring a high potential employee's job so that it provides the employee more freedom and autonomy at work, requires more variety in the skills required to complete the job, provides the employee with additional reliable feedback about performance effectiveness, and ensures that the employee completes a whole and identifiable piece of work.[20] Adjusting the context also can include training individual supervisors to be supportive and non-controlling. People can change their supervisory styles—they can learn to explain their actions to employees, to allow employees to participate in important decisions, to give constructive feedback, and to limit their monitoring activities. Establishing training programs to help supervisors change their behavior in this fashion, and then rewarding them for implementing these behaviors, is an effective way to nurture the creative potential of employees. Finally, adjusting the context for high potential employees also can involve boosting the level of competition among co-workers. Managers can establish idea generation contests that offer rewards for useful ideas that are also frame-breaking; award competitive internal grants for further development of ideas judged as creative; or conduct between-team competitions for product development bonuses based upon improvement suggestions that most substantially reduce production costs.

Generating and maintaining a good fit between employees' creative potential and their work context requires on-going attention. Over time, employees with high creative potential may actually *adapt* to the challenge and complexity present in their jobs, to the management styles of their supervisors, and to the degree of competition among their co-workers. Therefore, firms may need to provide increasing levels of these contextual conditions to maintain a nurturing environment. Given this possibility, managers should regularly evaluate the degree of employees' adaptation to each of these conditions and re-assign employees or further adjust their work contexts by restructuring jobs, training supervisors, or revising competition incentives as needed.

In addition, employees' preferences, priorities, and problem-solving styles may actually change over time. This, too, would require adjustments to ensure the proper fit between employees' creative potential and their work contexts. While personal characteristics related to creativity are reasonably stable, they are not unalterable traits. An interesting possibility is that the work context itself might exert long-term influence on the personality and problem-solving styles of the employee.[21] For example, it is possible that an employee's problem-solving approach may become *more* frame-breaking if she is repeatedly confronted with the challenges of a complex job. Or, an employee may express fewer creative personality characteristics over time if he seldom has to deal with the stimulation present in a competitive work team. All of this suggests that managers should assess employees' creative potential on an on-going basis and periodically adjust their work contexts to fit this potential. Only by considering the dynamic nature of both types of people and types of work contexts can a firm ensure it is maximizing its innovation potential via the creativity of its employees.

Notes

1. The notion of the right people in the right place is more generally developed elsewhere. See B. Schneider, "Interactional Psychology and Organizational Behavior," in L. L. Cummings and B. M. Staw, eds., *Research in Organizational Behavior,* 5 (1983): 1–31.

2. See, for example B. M. Staw, "An Evolutionary Approach to Creativity and Innovation," in M. A. West and J. L. Farr, eds., *Innovation and Creativity at Work* (Chichester, U.K.: Wiley, 1990), pp. 287–308.

3. See M. Csikszentmihalyi, *Creativity: Flow and the Psychology of Discovery and Invention* (New York, NY: HarperCollins, 1996); F. B. Barron and D. M. Harrington, "Creativity, Intelligence, and Personality," *Annual Review of Psychology,* 32 (1981): 439–476.

4. See, for example, D. C. Pelz and F. M. Andrews, *Scientists in Organizations: Productive Climates for Research and Development,* 2nd Edition (New York, NY: Wiley, 1976); S. G. Scott and R. A. Bruce, "Determinants of Innovative Behavior: A Path Model of Individual Innovation in the Workplace," *Academy of Management Journal,* 37 (1994): 580–607.

5. For a complete discussion, see M. J. Kirton, *Adaptors and Innovators* (London: Routledge, 1989).

6. Details of the instrument can be obtained from M. J. Kirton, Occupational Research Center, Highlands, Gravel Path, Berkhamsted, Herts, U.K. HP4 2PQ or in M. J. Kirton, "Adaptors and Innovators: A Description and Measure," *Journal of Applied Psychology,* 61/5 (October 1976): 622–629.

7. See R. T. Keller, "Predictors of the Performance of Project Groups in R&D Organizations," *Academy of Management Journal,* 29 (1986): 715–726: R. T. Keller and W. E. Holland, "A Cross Validation Study of The Kirton Adaption-Innovation Inventory in Three Research and Development Organizations," *Applied Psychological Measurement,* 2 (1978): 563–570.

8. See works cited in Note 3, plus C. Martindale, "Personality, Situation, and Creativity," in J. A. Glover, R. R. Ronning, and C. R. Reynolds, eds., *Handbook of Creativity* (New York, NY: Plenum, 1989), pp. 211–232.

9. For a comprehensive review of these tools, see G. A. Davis, "Testing for Creative Potential," *Contemporary Educational Psychology,* 14 (1989): 257–274.

10. The CPS was empirically derived from a broader, 300-item personality test, called the Adjective Check List. This broader instrument is the work of H. G. Gough and A. B. Heilbrun and details are available in *The Adjective Check List Manual* (Palo Alto, CA: Consulting Psychologists Press, 1965). Details of the 30-item CPS can be found in H. G. Gough, "A Creative Personality Scale for the Adjective Check List," *Journal of Personality and Social Psychology,* 37/8 (August 1979): 1398–1405.

11. See, for example, J. R. Terborg, "Interactional Psychology and Research on Human Behavior in Organizations," *Academy of Management Review,* 6/4 (October 1981): 569–576.

12. See J. R. Hackman, G. Oldham, R. Janson, and K. Purdy, "A New Strategy for Job Enrichment," *California Management Review,* 17/4 (Summer 1975): 57–71.

13. See, for example, D. McGregor, *The Human Side of Enterprise* (New York, NY: McGraw-Hill, 1960).

14. B. Dumaine, "The Trouble with Teams," *Fortune,* September 5, 1994, pp. 86–92.

15. This argument derives largely from Teresa Amabile and her colleagues, who argue that people will be creative when they are intrinsically motivated by the work itself, rather than extrinsically motivated by external factors such as rewards. See T. M. Amabile, *The Social Psychology of Creativity* (New York, NY: Springer-Verlag, 1983).

16. Accepted suggestions were scheduled for implementation. Once these suggestions were implemented, a senior executive of the firm attached a monetary value to them. By the end of the study period, the value of each employee's implemented suggestions ranged from $217 to $374,899.

17. These results display statistical interactions previously reported in G. R. Oldham and A. Cummings, "Employee Creativity: Personal and Contextual Factors at Work," *Academy of Management Journal,* 39/3 (June 1996): 607–634. Figure 1 illustrates the CPS × job complexity two-way interaction and Figure 2 shows the CPS × job

complexity × supportive supervision × non-controlling supervision four-way interaction.

18. For a detailed list of these measures of competition, please contact one of the authors.

19. Figures 3 and 4 display three-way statistical interactions between scores on the CPS, scores on the KAI and the amount of co-worker competition present. These interactions were determined using hierarchical Ordinary Least Squares Regression and were plotted by dividing employ-ees into groups based on above-median versus below-median scores on the CPS and the KAI. The number of creative suggestions shown in Figure 3 reflects a log-linear scale.

20. For more detail, see Hackman et al., op. cit.

21. For evidence supporting this general notion, see M. L. Kohn and C. Schooler, "Job Conditions and Personality: A Longitudinal Assessment of Their Reciprocal Effects," *American Journal of Sociology,* 87 (1973): 1257–1286.

Cases

Raymond Hargrove

Craig Johnson was debating whether he should simply fire Raymond Hargrove, assign him to a new sales area, or have another talk with him. Unfortunately, none of the alternatives had much appeal.

After six years in the Navy, where he had achieved the rank of lieutenant, Raymond became a salesman for the fertilizer division of Northwest Industries about four years ago and had reported to Craig Johnson, the district sales manager, from the beginning. Raymond's father, a wealthy businessman who had passed away while he was in the Navy, was a close friend of the CEO and founder of Northwest Industries, Mr. Gerold Simon. After Raymond got out of the Navy, his mother mentioned her son to Mr. Simon, who then arranged for Raymond to be interviewed for the job.

Raymond was a tall, handsome, and well-dressed man of 31. After completing the company training he was given a sales area in Oregon. The sales area was large and required his being away from home two or three nights per week. The person who had the area before Raymond had done well enough to be promoted to district manager of another but related division.

Raymond enjoyed his home in Oregon and spent many hours taking care of his lawn and garden. He also had made several additions and modifications to his home. His wife and young sons also enjoyed the area and liked living in the country. In particular, Raymond liked the different geological formations that could be found in the area, and he often spent weekends either fishing or just exploring the area.

At first, Raymond's performance was about average with an occasional period in which he would rise into the top 20 percent of salesmen for the division. However, over the last two years his performance had gradually declined.

When Craig first approached Raymond about his declining performance, Raymond simply responded that he must be getting lazy but that he would try harder in the future. However, he failed to properly fill out the sales reports unless specifically directed to do so. About the only project in which Raymond exceeded what was required of him was a marketing research study that Craig had not had time to complete.

About a year before Raymond's sales reached the bottom, he had written a report in which he described an accident in which he had been involved. On his way back from a sales call, a little boy had suddenly run out from behind a bush right in front of Raymond's car. Because the accident occurred out in the country, he had rushed the boy and his mother to the nearest hospital. The boy was not seriously hurt and had only minor cuts and bruises. When

Reprinted with permission from Richard M. Steers and Stewart J. Black, *Organizational Behavior.* New York: HarperCollins, 1996, pp. 159–161.

Craig talked with Raymond on the phone about the accident, it was one of the few times Raymond had seemed unsettled.

About three months after the accident, Raymond and his family went to San Francisco to spend the holidays with his mother and the family's "downtown" home on Nob Hill. After the vacation, Craig noticed a significant drop in Raymond's performance. Before long he was the bottom salesperson in Craig's district. Craig estimated that while the performance bonus for the top salesperson in his district would be roughly 10 percent of base salary, Raymond was unlikely to make any bonus at all. At the monthly sales meeting, some of the other salespeople joked about Raymond being from money so there was no need for him to work hard.

In an effort to think of some reason for Raymond's poor performance, Craig took advantage of a lunch with the CEO to ask him about Raymond's background and see if Mr. Simon had any advice. Mr. Simon said that he was sure Raymond would eventually come around and that he was not to be disciplined without Mr. Simon's review of the case. He also told Craig that Raymond's mother had asked him to see if he could get Raymond to write to her more frequently, and asked Craig to pass the message to Raymond.

Raymond had invited Craig to go on one of their frequent fishing trips next week, and Craig was determined to take advantage of the situation. But he still wasn't sure what he should do.

QUESTIONS FOR DISCUSSION

1. Using the concepts of need for achievement, affiliation, autonomy, and power, how would you describe Raymond Hargrove?

2. How would you explain Raymond's behavior and performance?

3. What course of action would you take if you were Craig Johnson?

Pamela Jones

Pamela Jones enjoyed banking. She had taken a battery of personal aptitude and interest tests that suggested that she might like and do well in either banking or librarianship. Since the job market for librarians was poor, she applied for employment with a large chartered bank, the Bank of Winnipeg, and was quickly accepted.

Her early experiences in banking were almost always challenging and rewarding. She was enrolled in the bank's management development program because of her education (a B.A. in languages and some postgraduate training in business administration), her previous job experience, and her obvious intelligence and drive.

During her first year in the training program, Pamela attended classes on banking procedures and policies, and worked her way through a series of low-level positions in her branch. She was repeatedly told by her manager that her work was above average. Similarly, the

C. C. Pinder, *Work Motivation: Theory, Issues, and Applications* (Glenview, IL: Scott, Foresman and Company, 1984), pp. 311–318, Reprinted by permission of Scott, Foresman and Company.

training officer who worked out of the main office and coordinated the development of junior officers in the program frequently told Pamela that she was "among the best three" of her cohort of twenty trainees.

Although she worked hard and frequently encountered discrimination from senior bank personnel (as well as customers) because of her sex, Pamela developed a deep-seated attachment to banking in general, and to her bank and branch, in particular. She was proud to be a banker and proud to be a member of the Bank of Winnipeg. After one year in the management development program, however, Pamela found she was not learning anything new about banking or her employer. She was shuffled from one job to another at her own branch, cycling back over many positions several times to help meet temporary problems caused by absences, overloads, and turnover. Turnover—a rampant problem in banking—amazed Pamela. She couldn't understand, for many months, why so many people started careers "in the service" of banking, only to leave after one or two years.

After her first year, the repeated promises of moving into her own position at another branch started to sound hollow to Pamela. The training officer claimed that there were no openings suitable for her at other branches. On two occasions when openings did occur, the manager of each of the branches in question rejected Pamela, sight unseen, presumably because she hadn't been in banking long enough.

Pamela was not the only unhappy person at her branch. Her immediate supervisor, George Burns, complained that because of the bank's economy drive, vacated customer service positions were left unfilled. As branch accountant, Burns was responsible for day-to-day customer service. As a result, he was unable to perform the duties of his own job. The manager told Burns several times that customer service was critical, but that Burns would have to improve his performance on his own job. Eventually, George Burns left the bank to work for a trust company, earning seventy dollars a month more for work similar to that he had been performing. This left Pamela in the position of having to supervise the same tellers who had trained her only a few months earlier. Pamela was amazed at all the mistakes the tellers made but found it difficult to do much to correct their poor work habits. All disciplinary procedures had to be administered with the approval of Head Office.

After several calls to her training officer, Pamela was finally transferred to her first "real" position in her own branch. Still keen and dedicated, Pamela was soon to lose her enthusiasm.

At her new branch, Pamela was made "assistant accountant." Her duties included the supervision of the seven tellers, some customer service, and a great deal of paperwork. The same economy drive that she had witnessed at her training branch resulted in the failure to replace customer service personnel. Pamela was expected to "pick up the slack" at the front desk, neglecting her own work. Her tellers seldom balanced their own cash, so Pamela stayed late almost every night to find their errors. To save on overtime, the manager sent the tellers home while Pamela stayed late, first to correct the tellers' imbalances, then to finish her own paperwork. He told Pamela that as an officer of the bank, she was expected to stay until the work of her subordinates, and her own work, were satisfactorily completed. Pamela realized that most of her counterparts in other B. of W. branches were willing to give this sort of dedication; therefore, so should she. This situation lasted six months with little sign of change in sight.

One day, Pamela learned from a phone conversation with a friend at another branch that she would be transferred to Hope, British Columbia, to fill an opening that had arisen. Pamela's husband was a professional, employed by a large corporation in Vancouver. His company did not have an office in Hope; moreover, his training was very specialized, and he could probably find employment only in large cities anyway.

Accepting transfers was expected of junior officers who wanted to get ahead. Pamela inquired at Head Office and learned that the rumor was true. Her training officer told her, however, that Pamela could decline the transfer if she wished, but he couldn't say how soon her next promotion opportunity would come about. Depressed, annoyed, disappointed, and frustrated, Pamela quit the bank.

QUESTIONS FOR DISCUSSION

1. First, let us try to understand what is happening. Use a relevant motivational theory to explain Pamela's behavior at the bank.

2. From a motivational perspective, what concrete steps could be taken to ensure that people like Pamela do not leave their positions?

Leo Henkelman

Despite his bearlike stature, Leo Henkelman was invisible to his employer. To Sandstrom Products, he was nothing more than a strong-backed laborer, a paint mixer who attended to the mill for over a decade. The plant was full of such employees, who came to work each day, did their job, complained about the college-educated lab technicians, and collected their paychecks. The money was good and the work was steady, but still Henkelman could not help thinking, "This ain't living." Things would have to change, not only at work but in his personal life.

Henkelman's first job out of high school had been in the slaughterhouse where his father was the foreman. Five days a week, on a shift that began at 3:00 A.M., his task was to stand in the production line and hammer purple USDA stamps onto the sides of every carcass of beef that passed by. The work was extremely boring, but the pay was decent. He might have stayed at the job longer had he not had a fight with another employee, who landed in the hospital. It was his father who fired him.

After a short stint in construction, Henkelman landed a job at Sandstrom Products, a $5.5 million maker of paints, coating, and lubricants. He started as a paint runner, the bottom job at the plant, and spent his days putting paint into cans and putting the cans into boxes. After a year, he was promoted to a mill operator and began mixing paints in a blender, following the formulas supplied by the labs. Henkelman's work environment was the plant floor—dark, noisy, and reeking of strong fumes. Adjacent to the plant was the lab, filled with college-educated professionals who wore white shirts and carried business cards. In his work, Henkelman was forced to interact with the lab, particularly if a formula did not work.

Republished with permission of *Inc.* magazine, Goldhirsh Group, Inc., 38 Commercial Wharf, Boston, MA 02110. "Before and After," David Whitford, June 1995. Reproduced by permission of the publisher via Copyright Clearance Center, Inc.

Time after time, he would suggest solutions to the problem, and the lab basically rejected his ideas. Extremely frustrated, Henkelman realized that the company was not interested in his brain but in his brawn.

To solve the problems with paint mixing, Henkelman learned to rely less on the formulas supplied by the labs and more on his own experience. Although the mill operators helped each other, the lab mandated that they were to follow the formulas or else. Henkelman admitted that "we did a lot of things under the cover of 'Don't tell nobody that we did this, but we're gonna check this out to see whether it works, because we don't believe the guys in the lab.'" The ongoing feud between the blue-collar plant and the white-collar lab was not only costly and inefficient to the company, but demeaning to all parties involved. As the product quality suffered, customers began to drop off, and Sandstrom saw its profits eroding.

Finding little at work to challenge him, Henkelman sought solace in spending time with friends at bars after work. On many days, he would show up for work with a hangover, only to turn around and return home sick. On other days, he drove around with friends and lost track of time, forgetting to show up for work at all. Once, he was arrested and lost his driver's license. Realizing that he needed to straighten out his life, Henkelman sought help and slowly began to change his life. Then he underwent back surgery, which caused him to miss three months of work, and his wife threw him out of the house. For a while, he lived on the edge of despair, wondering if his life would ever change.

In the meantime, Sandstrom's future was severely threatened. For the past five years, the company's net income had been negative. Jim Sandstrom and Rick Hartsock, the company's top executives, knew that they had to make radical changes. Employees were not solving problems as they should, and morale at work was at a record low. Ironically, Rick Hartsock realized that to save the company from failure, he would have to hand the reins to the employees to solve their own problems. It was then that the company decided to experiment with a motivation technique it called "open book management."

Like many of his colleagues, Leo Henkelman was skeptical. "Just another fad," he thought. What did appeal to him, however, was the focus on results and not on process. Under open book management, the top brass would provide the objectives and allow employees to figure out how to achieve them through creative problem solving, teamwork, and individual initiative. Hungry for the trust and respect that were offered to him, Henkelman signed up for three teams right away: plant equipment, process control, and merit pay.

The first task for the plant equipment team was a proposal to buy a new $18,000 forklift. The old forklift was over 20 years old and, according to its driver, unreliable and unsafe. The team completed a cost and productivity analysis and presented it to the corporate heads. But management argued that, while it was not a bad idea to buy a new forklift, funds were limited and could be used for something more worthwhile. Henkelman could not help but feel let down and began to feel skeptical again. Same old story, he thought. However, a few days later, Henkelman and his team were surprised to learn that the forklift expenditure was approved. Spirits boosted, Henkelman said, "It gave me the idea that we *can* make a difference. It made me feel that we weren't doing all this work for nothing."

As Sandstrom transformed into a company managed by its employees, Henkelman saw the barriers to information begin to fade away. Where the lab had always ruled over the technical manuals, Henkelman and the other plant workers were now allowed to consult them if they wanted to resolve an issue. He eventually even received a password that gave him access to the formulas on the computer, an event unheard of in prior times. No longer paralyzed in a specific job role, he could update the formulas so the process flowed more smoothly. His attitude began to change in his work.

Henkelman's life began to turn around at the same time. He stopped drinking and got an apartment, where he lived alone. With so much spare time, he went into the office and explored the computer, teaching himself about the business. He filled his empty hours, but more importantly, he filled himself with knowledge, with confidence, and with hope. As a virtual new "owner" in the company, he thought it was his duty to understand every aspect of the business. In the old days, he had only learned what he needed to know to do his narrow job well. Now he wanted to understand the entire process, to help grow the business.

Henkelman and the members of the merit pay team took on the challenge of redesigning an entirely new compensation system. Plant managers had previously used a mixture of seniority and favoritism to compensate their employees, and the subordinates had always been unhappy about this. The workers believed that pay should more closely reflect performance: how useful a worker was on the job, how much a worker knew, and how well tasks were done. These beliefs were not altogether contradictory to that of management; both wanted a highly skilled and effective workforce.

The first proposal drawn by the team offered plant workers incentives to cross-train in their jobs. However, when management and the team fully analyzed the numbers, they both concluded that the proposal was unrealistic. Rather than dismiss the issue, however, management asked for a proposal that made fiscal sense to almost everyone. Deep in the middle of the analysis, Henkelman came to the realization that he was beginning to think like an owner, not like an hourly employee. The new proposal found a way to pay for the added costs of training but at the expense of some paychecks. Some members of the team quit, but Henkelman was determined to stick it out. After months of hard work—meeting formally, debating with coworkers, striking a balance between paying incentives and maintaining equality among workers—the team came up with an innovative compensation system, which was eventually adopted by the company.

This was a critical turnaround in Henkelman's career. Despite the demands that management made on the team's process, Henkelman felt needed and alive for the first time in his working career. He noted, "Because of that I felt and still feel today that I have control of my destiny."

His attitude completely overhauled, Henkelman sought other responsibilities within the company to tap into his strengths. Taking a major promotion, Henkelman was put in charge of scheduling production and even became plant manager for a while. What he found was that neither job suited him. Always a doer, he found it difficult to delegate tasks to others. In a few months, a technician job opened up in the lab. Generally, technicians had college degrees in chemistry, and Henkelman had not even taken chemistry in high school. But Bob Sireno, the lab's technical director, wanted Henkelman for the job. He eventually got it.

Henkelman put away his blue-collar shirt and moved into the lab. He would still do what he had always done—make paint—but instead of following orders, he would guide the process from the beginning to the end. His new job allowed him to work with customers, to develop new formulas, and to use his hands-on experience to solve problems where other less-experienced chemists had failed. Bob Sireno admitted that in a year's time Henkelman had developed skills that had taken college graduates five years to develop. When a complex problem appeared, it was Henkelman who was chosen to solve the problem—shirt sleeves rolled up and mind determined to make it work.

With a new identity and a new attitude about work, Henkelman remains a valuable team member to Sandstrom Products. Instead of dreading the feuding and the tedium of mixing paint, he now looks forward to each new day, wondering what challenges he will overcome.

QUESTIONS FOR DISCUSSION

1. Identify the basic needs that Leo Henkelman was attempting to fulfill. How did these needs manifest themselves? How were these needs eventually satisfied?

2. Assess the variables that affected Leo Henkelman's motivation—characteristics of the individual, of the job, and of the work situation.

3. Analyze Leo Henkelman's motivation: (a) as a worker on the plant floor prior to the introduction of "open book management;" and (b) as a technician in the laboratory.

4. The company's open book management approach was designed to get all employees to focus on helping the business make money. What do you think of "open book management" as a tool for motivating employees? In what kind of organizational circumstances would it work best? In what kind of circumstances might it be ineffective?

Jim Preston

Ever since the Atlas Electrical Supply Co. was bought out by Carey and Co., Jim Preston had been in a sales slump. A leading salesman for Atlas for the past twenty-eight years, Preston had enjoyed handsome monthly bonuses, thanks to the company's incentive pay system. He had always been proud of the extra money, both as a symbol of his value to the company and for the practical uses to which he had applied it. He often boasted that the bonuses had helped him complete his mortgage several years early as well as finance his daughter's education at the University of Toronto. In the four months since the new management had taken over, however, Jim's sales had fallen off sharply, along with his enthusiasm and company spirit, even though the bonus system was still being used. In fact, he had not collected a bonus in months. Sarah Powell, Jim's new supervisor since the takeover, was concerned. She held a series of informal discussions with Jim and several other sales personnel to try to get to the bottom of Jim's problems.

Mrs. Powell learned from her meetings that Jim resented being supervised by a woman who was younger than his own daughter—now a college graduate. He blew up at her during one of their meetings, yelling, "All of you new brass are the same—always trying to squeeze more out of the little guy. You think you know everything about selling! I was selling electrical parts and supplies before you or any of the other Carey supervisors were old

C. C. Pinder, *Work Motivation: Theory, Issues, and Applications* (Glenview, IL: Scott, Foresman and Company, 1984). Reprinted by permission of Scott, Foresman and Company.

enough to know what they are. Now you're telling me how to do my job. Why don't you get off my back? It's my business if I don't earn any bonuses!"

Sarah was startled by Preston's outburst and concerned by his apparent resentment and hostility toward her. She learned that several of Preston's fellow salesmen, who were mostly younger than he, also resented his resistance to the recent attempt to unionize the office staff. Several of them claimed that he was "a real company man," even though his sales figures didn't reflect it. She also learned that Jim was periodically receiving sales directives from Stan Campbell, Jim's former boss who had been moved laterally at the time of the takeover. Jim claimed he was never told clearly who his new supervisor was, now that the companies had merged.

Also attending a luncheon meeting on job redesign, Sarah tried to "motivate" higher sales from Jim by adding to the product lines he carried, giving him a larger district to cover, and letting him move upstairs into a slightly larger office. She hoped that the changes would arouse new energy in Preston, who, to her added frustration, seemed increasingly more preoccupied with his imminent retirement to a country town. Finally, Sarah asked Jim if he would like to retire early. He declined the offer, but Sarah recommended to her boss that they give old Jim "the golden handshake." Nothing else had worked. Assume you are Sarah Powell.

QUESTIONS FOR DISCUSSION

1. On the basis of the materials presented in this book, how would you explain Jim Preston's behavior?

2. What course of action would you take to turn Preston around into a more motivated employee if your boss declined your suggestion to fire him?

North American Shipping

North American Shipping is currently riding the crest of an industry boom. Before the year is out, analysts expect the company to post record earnings and revenues. But Sherry Summers, a middle manager at corporate headquarters in Chicago, offers a different perspective. Her story follows:

When I first came here fifteen years ago, I never paid attention to titles. I worked for an executive. We disagreed a lot, but we respected each other and could discuss problems or disagreements. Everything went fine until mid-1995, when we moved to Chicago from Los Angeles and my boss retired. All of a sudden, our department fell apart. We had no leadership. Other officers and our consultants recommended me as a replacement for my former boss, but instead we got a new guy from outside. Then came what I call the "Mafia," because he brought all these guys with him. I found myself explaining really elementary stuff to them. They didn't know what they were doing.

This case was prepared by Richard M. Steers. It is based on actual events, although the names and some of the circumstances have been modified.

When the new executive arrived, I told him, "Here are the problems." But instead of listening to me, he spent more time complaining about the past administration than cleaning up the problems we faced. From day one, he insisted upon a complete divorce from the past—and of course I was a part of that past. It happens to a lot of middle managers. They go only so far, particularly where you have a change of administration.

We had another executive who also retired. He had an assistant who had helped run the department. He got passed over, and all of a sudden he retired. There was nothing left for him. The company replaced him with an insider who seemed incompetent to me. He was trained for six months and then all of a sudden they decided no, they wouldn't give him the job, either. Now they're looking outside. They've passed over five or six good people.

If it weren't for my particular expertise, I'd probably be fired. I would take early retirement if I could live off of it. You just realize there is nothing in the future. I feel like I've just hit a wall. I uprooted my family for the move, and I really don't want to change locations again. And I'm old enough so that a move would be very difficult. Sometimes I think I am obsolete, I'm at a dead end. There's no way up. No way down. And no way out.

The company gives us a rose on our birthdays. I just threw it away. We get a bonus in a good year. And last year I got the biggest bonus I've ever gotten, and the money was nice. But it didn't make me feel good. Nothing I did affected my bonus because it's based on overall corporate earnings. There is a mathematical formula that I couldn't describe to anybody, and they made a great to-do of it. As long as the fifty-first floor is prepared to give me $60,000, I'll take it. Did I work any harder, or less hard? No. The industry just went up. We just happen to be here at the right time.

Our benefits have been cut back. They changed the retirement plan. The old formula was not the best, but not too bad. Do you know what they replace it with? I figured it out for myself, and my retirement income turned into a significant drop. Our VP for employee relations two years ago wanted to count Labor Day as vacation time if you take the day off. He got his ears burned off.

Despite cutbacks, we're still not lean, either. We have more make-work executive and middle management–type jobs than we need. We've got a lot more junior executives than we know what to do with. They just sit around reading the *Wall Street Journal.* I think we've created a lot of jobs that aren't really jobs. And how do you bring managers up when they aren't doing anything? Now, we've got great plant management, real dedicated people. It's the secret of the company. But when you get down to it, we just aren't lean and mean.

QUESTIONS FOR DISCUSSION

1. In your view, what is really wrong at North American Shipping?

2. What factors are influencing Sherry Summers's view of the situation?

3. If you were in charge of HRM, what course of action would you take to remedy the present situation?

4. What roadblocks would you expect if you tried to implement your plan?

5. Who in the organization would need to support your actions for you to be successful?

TCA Microelectronics

Stephanie Wilson is the general manager of TCA Microelectronics, a small nonunion Massachusetts-based electronics assembly company that is part of a larger conglomerate. Reporting directly to Ms. Wilson are several key department managers, the office manager, the HR and safety manager, and the production manager. The various assembly units have unit supervisors, who report directly to the production manager.

Within each assembly group, employees have clear expectations concerning their responsibilities, as well as their rights and privileges. Some rights and privileges are obvious, whereas others are rather subtle. One of the more widely held values on the part of the employees is the importance of team autonomy. Employees know they have a job to do and they expect management to leave them alone to do it. Work groups believe their main obligation to the company is to produce high-quality output in a timely fashion. Supervisors are expected to focus their attention on coordination, productivity, and quality control. Hostility often results when managers use discipline as means of asserting the will of management. By the same token, employees appreciate management when they are given certain privileges or when flexibility is shown in discipline.

A second traditional benefit at TCA is job bidding for vacant jobs. This can be prompted by a desire for either a job with higher status or a means of escaping an unpleasant foreman. Employees often use this as a way to circumvent formal supervisory authority. The supervisors resent this practice, because they feel that they should have the prerogative of choosing their own subordinates.

A third long-standing benefit of working at TCA is the right to use company material for home repairs. Employees expect that they should have access to company equipment for use in making home repairs.

Recently, Ms. Wilson received word from the home office that she could expect about $15 million worth of new equipment to be added to his plant's assembly facility. Along with the equipment, the home office notified Wilson that they were transferring Ralph Moxon from the home office to replace TCA's retiring production manager. Moxon had served as an officer in the U.S. Marines and had an outstanding industrial record following his service. The board of directors hoped that the change in leadership and the addition of equipment would add to TCA's productivity and profit margin.

Upon his arrival, Moxon quickly established a routine of making the rounds of the plant every hour or so to check on the progress of the workflow. During the course of his first four months, he instituted several technical changes designed to speed up production and reduce labor costs. During this period, however, tensions with the employees mounted. Dissatisfaction over the installment of new machinery became a focal point of the disruption. If the

This case was prepared by Richard M. Steers. It is based on actual events, although the names and some of the circumstances have been modified.

company could afford to spend so much for machinery, employees complained, why couldn't it afford higher wages?

After six months on the job, Moxon received a notice from the home office inviting him to attend a month-long management training seminar in New York. Ms. Wilson decided to leave Moxon's position vacant in his absence and to ask each shift supervisor to be responsible for his or her particular shift with no further supervision. Shortly after Moxon left, Wilson learned from a supervisor that the employees wanted the lunchroom painted; it had been years since it was last painted, and it looked dismal. Without hesitation, Wilson instructed the maintenance crew to go to work on the job. In addition, she told the supervisors to feel free to handle minor grievances and requests on their own authority until Moxon returned.

During the following week, another complaint emerged from the employees. This time the problem concerned the company's policy of requiring mandatory overtime to get production out. Wilson considered the complaint and proposed that if production reached 3,000 units per day (a 500-unit increase), she could eliminate mandatory overtime. Within a few days production reached the targeted level. Unfortunately, this action backfired, because the head of the office then demanded that production be increased again to meet a new backlog of orders. Wilson went back to her employees and asked that they return to the overtime schedule until the back orders were filled. Although there was some grumbling, most of the employees continued to perform effectively. Within a week, the press for more production was reduced so that it was possible to drop the overtime requirement again.

A third problem the employees brought up concerned the plant whistle. This whistle traditionally blew at the beginning and end of the shift. It was also used to regulate breaks and lunch periods. One of the employees suggested that the company use the public address system instead. At first, some employees ridiculed the new system, but in a few days they took announcements as a matter of course. In one instance, when the announcement was not made, the employees returned from lunch at the appropriate time anyway. Later on in the month, announcements were dropped, yet the employees continued to start and stop work on time.

A month after Moxon had left for New York, Ms. Wilson surveyed the production record for the plant and discovered that it had actually increased by 15 percent. She couldn't understand what had happened. Production had increased significantly without the presence of the production manager.

QUESTIONS FOR DISCUSSION

1. Why do you think production was up by 15 percent, despite the absence of the production manager?

2. What role do social processes play in understanding this case?

3. How do you think Wilson's actions affected employee goal setting and intentions?

4. Do you think Stephanie Wilson handled the situation correctly?

5. What would you do now if you were Wilson?

Software Research, Inc.

Late on a Friday afternoon, 24-year-old software specialist David Grant entered Jim Rogers's office. "Jim, you're going to have to do something about Sellers, or my people are going to walk out on the Micro-Tech project. He knows nothing about what we're doing, and he's upsetting my team with his constant interference. Either he goes, or our project will fall apart!"

Rogers, principal stockholder and CEO of Software Research, Inc. (SRI), knew that Grant was right. As he leaned back in his chair, he wondered how he might confront his longtime friend and minority partner Steven Sellers about the crisis that was now brought to a head. He knew also that Sellers was having marital problems and that one of his children had just dropped out of college. The timing was not good. Even so, Rogers felt he had to confront the issue head-on. If Grant's warning was to be taken seriously, the stakes were high, and a confrontation could not be postponed. Now was probably as good a time as any. The Micro-Tech software program had fallen five months behind schedule. If the company couldn't get the project back on schedule and out to the market, they risked being surpassed by their competitors and the company itself might falter.

Walking toward Sellers's office, Rogers began to outline his alternatives. He could buy up Sellers's 17 percent equity and put an end to the immediate crisis. On the other hand, he needed Sellers. Though worried about Sellers's addiction to work, Rogers knew that it was Sellers's single-minded commitment to his job and the firm that had contributed so much to SRI's success. Was Sellers now at the breaking point, he wondered? During the past seven years, they had worked as a team, pulling together a group of bright programmers by buying up several small and innovative software houses that needed capital injections. Only recently had Sellers begun to make irrational moves and develop an edgy personal style that seemed to annoy those around him. In fact, his workaholism had all the marks of real psychological dependence, not unlike alcoholism.

It was the first time Sellers's behavior had become a liability. Until now, the two had made a good team. The introspective and analytical Sellers drew on his vast contacts in the software industry to identify acquisitions, and the outgoing Rogers negotiated the deals. It was a partnership that brought them both fun and profit. Working behind the scenes, performing best under pressure, Sellers acted as the engine, merging new companies into SRI and imposing his will on others to facilitate a solid integration with SRI before moving on to the next acquisition. Though he ruffled feathers, he never stayed long enough with the new units to cause any permanent damage. In fact, Sellers had been invaluable in SRI's acquisition strategy. Now, however, with the acquisition of Micro-Tech, a start-up company founded by Grant, things were really starting to go awry.

Sellers understood applications software, but he knew within days of taking over the Micro-Tech project that he was out of his league technically. Grant held the upper hand in this one. Moreover, as the project dragged on, it became clear to everyone else that Sellers was not coping well. He lacked the interpersonal skills needed to lead a longer-term team effort. Distraught with the thought of failure, Sellers began to closely monitor progress and set unrealistic development targets. When the targets were not met, he began pushing Grant's

This case was prepared by Richard M. Steers. It is based on actual events, although the names and some of the circumstances have been modified.

programmers to match his round-the-clock efforts, provoking incidents such as Grant's outburst in Rogers's office.

Rogers slowly walked down the half-darkened corridors and found the lights still on in Sellers's office. "Hey Steve, what the problem with Grant?" Rogers asked as casually as he could.

A strained and tense Sellers looked up from his screen and replied, "I've taken the Micro-Tech team off flex time."

"What?" Rogers asked in stunned disbelief. "That's part of our ethos. Most of these guys are hackers. They spend as much time working on their computer as they do in the office."

"Maybe so," Sellers replied. "But they're not pulling the lab hours we need to get the project done. I am putting in my hours, and there is no reason to let them cruise in and out as they please."

"Steve, these guys are self-starters. Putting them on a 9 to 5 regime will demotivate them. Are you sure you are doing the right thing here? Maybe you need a holiday," Roger finally said.

"That's just an excuse to take me off the project," Sellers shot back belligerently, jumping up and grabbing his jacket. His face had turned red, and his voice quaked.

"Steve you are killing yourself with work. What am I going to do with you?" Rogers pleaded.

"I don't know. You tell me," Sellers said, stalking out the door.

QUESTIONS FOR DISCUSSION

1. What in your view is the fundamental motivational issue at Software Research?

2. Suppose that you are in Jim Rogers's place. Both Sellers and Grant—and the Micro-Tech project—are important to the organization. How would you resolve this dilemma?

3. What problems might you expect as a result of your plan of action?

Granville Diagnostics

Granville Diagnostics is a small manufacturing company located in Brooklyn, New York, that manufactures clinical analyzers and other health care products for hospitals, clinical laboratories, and physicians. A little over a year ago, Granville instituted a pay-for-performance merit compensation system. Each division was asked to establish specific performance objectives and reward employees on the basis of their performance against these goals.

You are the division manager for the assembly plant for the clinical analyzers. You oversee six production supervisors, each of whom is responsible for one work team. As part of the new system, you have established three performance goals for the supervisors in your division: (1) reduce raw material waste rates by 12%; (2) increase overall production by

This case was prepared by Richard M. Steers. It is based on actual events, although the names and some of the circumstances have been modified.

10%; and (3) decrease the number of quality rejects by 15%. You have made it clear to your supervisors that meeting or exceeding these performance objectives will be a major determinant of their merit pay increase for the year.

All six supervisors manage similar production lines. Each production line is about the same size, and the skill levels of the average workers in each group are similar. In fact, the various production teams often see themselves as being in competition with each other to achieve their production goals. A profile of each supervisor is as follows:

- Terry O'Leary: age 25, married with no children. O'Leary has been with Granville for a little over a year since graduating from Syracuse University. This is his first full-time job since graduation. O'Leary is a physical fitness enthusiast and is well liked by all employees. He has exhibited a high level of enthusiasm for his work.

- Susan Mitchell: age 28, single. Mitchell has been with the company for three years since receiving her degree from the University of Delaware. She recently received a job offer from another company for a similar position that would provide her with a 15 percent pay raise over her current salary. Granville does not want to lose her because her overall performance has been excellent. The job offer would require her to move to another state, which she views unfavorably. Thus, Granville could probably retain her if it could come close to matching her salary offer.

- Kareem Jackson: age 32, married with three children. Jackson has been with Granville for over four years since his graduation from high school. Born in poverty, he started community college but dropped out after a year and a half to support his family. He is a reliable supervisor and spends his outside time counseling poor inner-city kids. However, his subordinates are known to be unfriendly and sometimes uncooperative with both him and other employees.

- Alexander Wilenski: age 33, married with four children. Wilenski has a high school equivalent education and one year with the company. He immigrated to this country seven years ago from Poland and has recently become a U.S. citizen. He is a steady worker and is well liked by his co-workers, but has had difficulty mastering English. As a result, certain problems of communication within his group and with other groups have developed.

- Inge Swensen: age 27, divorced with two children. Swensen has been with the company for two years and received a technical associate arts degree (a two-year college degree) in her native Sweden before coming to the United States. Since her divorce two years ago, her performance has begun to improve. Prior to that, her performance had been erratic, with frequent absences. She is the sole provider for her two children.

- Angelo Scarpelli: age 29, single. Scarpelli has been with Granville for over two years and graduated from New York University. Scarpelli is one of the best liked employees at the company, but he has shown a lack of initiative and ambition on the job. He often appears to be preoccupied with his social life. However, no one at the company has ever complained to him about this preoccupation on the job.

Either individually or in small groups, your assignment is to assume you are the division manager responsible for the allocation of pay raises to the six supervisors. Exhibit 1 summarizes the performance data for each supervisor's team for the past year. This table also

EXHIBIT 1 Supervisory Salaries, Previous Performance Ratings, and Goal Performance

Supervisor	Current Salary	Annual Performance Review					Goal Performance*		
		Job Effort	Knowledge of Job	Attitude & Cooperation	Human Relations Skills		Waste Rates	Quality Rejects	Overall Production
Terry O'Leary	$38,000	Outstanding	Good	Outstanding	Good		10%	16%	12%
Susan Mitchell	$39,000	Outstanding	Outstanding	Outstanding	Outstanding		12%	12%	14%
Kareem Jackson	$39,000	Good	Good	Outstanding	Good		6%	4%	3%
Alexander Wilenski	$37,000	Outstanding	Average	Good	Average		4%	12%	5%
Inge Swensen	$34,000	Average	Good	Average	Average		12%	8%	10%
Angelo Scarpelli	$41,000	Average	Average	Average	Average		7%	4%	10%

*Goal performance was calculated as the percent reduction in waste rates and in quality rejects and the percent increase in overall productivity.

shows their current salaries, as well as their most recent performance appraisal. The budget for the upcoming year provides for an average 7 percent pay raise for employees; this amounts to $16,000 across the six supervisors. Top management has indicated that at least some of the salary increase money should be given across the board as a cost-of-living raise and that part should be given on the basis of merit. The actual percentage of raises given is completely up to you. However, in making the merit pay increase decisions, you should keep the following points in mind:

- Your salary decisions will likely set a precedent for future salary and merit increase considerations.

- No salary increases should be excessive but should be representative of the supervisor's performance during the past year. It is hoped that the supervisors develop a clear perception that performance will lead to monetary rewards and that this will serve to motivate them to even better performance.

- Your decisions should be concerned with equity; that is, they ought to be consistent with one another.

- Granville does not want to lose any of these experienced supervisors to other firms. The top management of this company not only wants the supervisors to be satisfied with their salary increases but also wants to further develop the feeling that Granville is a good company for advancement, growth, and career development.

With these constraints in mind, you (or your group) should do the following:

1. Identify the criteria you will use to allocate the pay raises.

2. Based on these criteria, allocate the $16,000 to the six supervisors.

3. Identify any negative consequences associated with your allocation decisions. What might you do to soften these negative repercussions?

Name Index

Subject Index